A detailed history of

BRITISH RAILWAYS STANDARD STEAM LOCOMOTIVES

Volume Four – The 9F 2-10-0 Class

JOHN WALFORD

PAUL HARRISON

THE RAILWAY CORRESPONDENCE AND TRAVEL SOCIETY
2008

Cover photo: 92220 *Evening Star*, allocated to Cardiff Canton, is in pristine condition as it awaits its next turn of duty at Old Oak Common shed, just two weeks old on 2nd April 1960. *(R.C. Riley)*

A Section of Colour Illustrations Is Presented On Pages xv - xxii

www.rcts.org.uk
ISBN 090 1115 95 9

Published by the Railway Correspondence and Travel Society
70 Heathfields, Downend, Bristol, BS16 6HS, England

Cover Design By John Holroyd
Printed by The Amadeus Press, Cleckheaton, BD19 4TQ
Typesetting by Highlight Type Bureau Ltd, Bradford BD8 7BY

92097 leaves South Pelaw with a Tyne Dock-Consett ore train in the 1963/4 period. Later, the engine visited Consett with the RCTS North East Rail Tour No. 2 of 10th April 1965 when it was observed in immaculate condition.

(J. W. Armstrong Trust)

CONTENTS

LIST OF TABLES

LIST OF APPENDICES

LIST OF DIAGRAMS

LIST OF FIGURES (ALPHABETIC)

PREFACE

This volume in the British Railways Standard Steam Locomotives series covers the short but interesting history of Britain's powerful Class 9F 2-10-0s. Intended as freight engines, they soon put in some sterling work hauling passenger trains, some of which are described in this book. Their short lives, however, were the result of British Railways modernisation plan in 1955 to replace steam engines as soon as possible with diesel and electric traction.

A fifth volume will appear in due course which will include additional information that has come to light after Volumes 1 - 3 were produced, together with a few corrections and amplifications. In addition to these topics, there will be sections covering Motive Power organisation between 1948 and 1968, including the considerable changes of shed codes particularly in the later years. There will also be a comprehensive index covering the entire series which has been asked for by several of our readers.

Contrary to what was written in the preface to Volume 1, the War Department 'Austerity' 2-8-0 and 2-10-0 locomotive classes will be covered in an independent volume. This will now not be under the heading of British Railways Standard Steam Locomotives.

R. K. Taylor,
(Hon. Editor, British Railways Standard Steam Locomotives Series)
'The Meadows'
Bardon Mill,
Hexham
Northumberland
NE47 7AA

BR Standard 9F 2-10-0 Class Summary of Construction

Built	Crewe	Swindon	Totals
1954	32	-	32
1955	38	-	38
1956	39	6	45
1957	47	10	57
1958	42	19	61
1959	-	15	15
1960	-	3	3
Totals	198	53	251

BRITISH RAILWAYS STANDARD CLASS 9F 2-10-0s 92000-92250: SUMMARY OF YEAR END TOTALS

Year	1954	1955	1956	1957	1958	1959	1960	1961	1962	1963	1964	1965	1966	1967	1968
Delivered during year	32	38	45	57	61	15	3	-	-	-	-	-	-	-	-
Withdrawn during year	-	-	-	-	-	-	-	-	-	-	16	64	46	107	18
Total Stock at Year End	32	70	115	172	233	248	251	251	251	251	235	171	125	18	-

Delivered to Traffic

1954 (32) 92000-19, 92030-41

1955 (38) 92020-29, 92042-69

1956 (45) 92070-92, 92097-99
92100-18

1957 (57) 92093-96, 92119-62
92168-70, 92178-83

1958 (61) 92163-67, 92171-77
92184-99, 92200-02
92221-50

1959 (15) 92203-17

1960 (3) 92218-20

Withdrawn from Service

1964 (16) 92034/6, 92169/70/1/5/6/7/96/8/9, 92207/10/29/32/45

1965 (64) 92000/3/5/7/33/7-42/4/57/66
92140-4/7/8/9/68/74/8-81/4-95/7
92200/2/9/14/6/9-22/5/6/30/5-8/40/1/2/4/6/8/50

1966 (46) 92010/3/28/35/43/53/9-64/7/8/72/5/81/5/92/5/7/8/9
92115/6/24/30/4/6/45/6/55/8/61/4/72/3/82/3
92201/13/7/31/9/43/7

1967 (107) 92001/2/6/8/11/2/4-27/9-32/45-52/5/6/8/65/70/1/3/4/6/8/9/80/2/3/4/6/7/9/90/3/6
92100-14/7/9-23/5-9/31/2/3/5/7/8/9/50/1/2/4/6/7/9/62/3/6
92203-6/8/11/5/24/7/8/34

1968 (18) 92004/9/54/69/77/88/91/4
92118/53/60/5/7
92212/8/23/33/49

Note: 1963 was the only full year when all 251 class members were active.
The last Crosti conversion (92022) was not completed until June 1962, the engine having been in store since May 1959.

ABBREVIATIONS USED IN THIS BOOK

Companies and Organisations

ARLE	Association of Railway Locomotive Engineers
BMC	British Motor Corporation
BR	British Railways
	British Rail (from January 1965)
BRB	British Railways Board
CR	Caledonian Railway
CLC	Cheshire Lines Committee
DB	Deutsche Bundesbahn
	German Federal Railways
ELR	East Lancashire Railway
ER	Eastern Region
FA	Football Association
FS	Ferrovie dello Stato
	Italian State Railways
GC/GCR	Great Central Railway
GE	Great Eastern Railway
GN/GNR	Great Northern Railway
G&SWR	Glasgow and South Western Railway
GWR	Great Western Railway
ICI	Imperial Chemical Industries
LCGB	Locomotive Club of Great Britain
LMA	Locomotive Manufacturers Association
LMR	London Midland Region
LMS	London Midland and Scottish Railway
LNER	London and North Eastern Railway
LNWR	London and North Western Railway
LTSR	London Tilbury and Southend Railway
LYR/ L&YR	Lancashire and Yorkshire Railway
MoD	Ministry of Defence
MoS	Ministry of Supply
MR	Midland Railway
NBR	North British Railway
NCB	National Coal Board
NER	North Eastern Region
NYMR	North Yorkshire Moors Railway
OBB	Oesterreiches Bundesbahn
	Austrian State Railways
ORC	Other Railway Companies
ROD	Railway Operating Division (Royal Engineers)
RR	Railroad (USA)
ScR	Scottish Region
S&D/ S&DJR	Somerset and Dorset Joint Railway
SMJ/S&MJ	Stratford upon Avon and Midland Junction Railway
SR	Southern Railway (pre-1948)
	Southern Region (from 1st January 1948)
UK	United Kingdom
USA	United States of America
WD	War Department
WR	Western Region

Other Abbreviations

ATC	Automatic Train Control
AWS	Automatic Warning System
Bo	Four-wheeled bogie
BthU	British Thermal Units
Cl.	Class
CME	Chief Mechanical Engineer
CMEE	Chief Mechanical and Electrical Engineer
cu.	cubic
DBHP	Drawbar Horsepower
ECML	East Coast Main Line
ecs	empty coaching stock
e.g.	for example
EHC	Engine History Card
ERC	Engine Record Card
f.o.b.	free on board
FSX	Fridays and Saturdays Excepted
ft	feet (measurement)
GBP	Great Britain Pound (Sterling currency)
H.P.	High Pressure (cylinders)
hr.	hour
i.e.	that is
IHP	Indicated Horsepower
in	inch (es)
Ing.	Engineer (continental European title)
lb	pounds weight
L.P.	Low Pressure (cylinders)
min	minute(s)
MML	Midland Main Line
MO	Mondays Only
MX	Mondays Excepted
M-F	Mondays to Fridays
MPD	Motive Power Depot
mph	miles per hour
psi	pounds per square inch
RA	Route Availability (Route Authorisation)
ROI	Return On Investment
SO	Saturdays Only
SPM	St. Philips Marsh MPD (Bristol)
sq	square
swg	standard wire gauge
SX	Saturdays Excepted
Th.	Thursday
TIA	Traitement Intégral Armand (French water treatment system)
Tu.	Tuesday
USD	United States Dollar
VAT	Value Added Tax
Vol.	Volume
WCML	West Coast Main Line
WW	World War

Note

Although not devised until well after the withdrawal of steam traction from British Railways, the widely recognised TOPS (Total Operations Processing System) classification is used in this book as a simplified means for the identification of non-steam locomotive classes

92220 *Evening Star* approaches Ribblehead on the northbound "Cumbrian Mountain Express" on 21st April 1984. *(Rodney Lissenden)*

92067 (Annesley) emerges from Catesby tunnel on the GCR main line with a freight bound for Banbury in October 1963. *(R. C. Riley)*

92017 (Carlisle Kingmoor) approaches Winnick Junction, north of Warrington with a down fitted freight on 28th August 1965.
(Hugh Ballantyne)

92007 (Bristol Barrow Road) passes Kingham between Honeybourne Junction and Oxford with empty Esso oil tanks from Bromford Bridge to Fawley Refinery on 29th September 1962.
(Hugh Ballantyne)

Celebrating the occasion of the 75th anniversary of the founding of the Foster Yeoman Company at Merehead on 27th June 1998, 92212 and 92203 haul a demonstration freight consisting of 16 loaded hopper wagons weighing more than 1,700tons. *(Hugh Ballantyne)*

92067 (Annesley) heads a Class 'H' freight bound for Banbury at Culworth Junction, south of Woodford, on 12th October 1963. *(R. C. Riley)*

92001 (Tyseley) leaves Basingstoke on Saturday 7th August 1965 with the 11.10am Bournemouth-Newcastle via the GCR route.
(C. R. Berridge)

92159 (Kirkby-in-Ashfield) plods through Kibworth on the MML between Wigston and Market Harborough with coal for Brent on 12th May 1964.
(R. C. Riley)

92118 (Saltley) trundles through Birmingham Snow Hill on 14th May 1964 with iron ore empties for the Banbury area. *(C. R. Berridge)*

92054 (Wellingborough) heads south on a ballast working near Sundon, north of Luton on 8th September 1962. *(Rodney Lissenden)*

92245 has just transferred to Bath Green Park shed from Cardiff Canton for the summer timetable. The engine is seen here leaving Bath with the 9.03am Bristol-Bournemouth West on 5th June 1962. *(Hugh Ballantyne)*

92220 *Evening Star* (Bath Green Park) is piloted by Standard Class 4 2-6-0 76015 (Bournemouth) as it leaves Shepton Mallet on a down passenger train on 1st September 1962. *(R. C. Riley)*

92017 (Carlisle Kingmoor) passes Settle Junction with a Long Meg-Widnes anhydrite train on 2nd September 1967. *(C. R. Berridge)*

92193 (Doncaster) passes Wood Green with a fast fitted freight on 13th September 1958. *(R. C. Riley)*

92108 (Birkenhead) blasts through Altrincham station towards Northwich and Chester with loaded ICI hoppers from Tunstead in July 1967. *(Alan Porter)*

92041 (Colwick) climbs steadily up from Grantham to Great Ponton with a Class 'H' freight on 3rd September 1963. *(C. R. Berridge)*

1. Introduction

Freight Engine Development in Great Britain

The background to the production of the British Railways Standard Classes of steam locomotives was dealt with in Volume One of this series. The last but one of the twelve classes to appear was the Class 9F 2-10-0 in January 1954, although as will be seen, there was very little in the design which could be regarded as 'standard' with the other eleven classes.

Like any other infant, the 9F had two parents. These can be regarded as:

(a) the process of standardisation and

(b) the development of previous heavy goods locomotives, via the WD 2-8-0 and 2-10-0 designs of 1943.

The process of standardisation was summarised in Volume One of this series. In his review, Dr P. T. Gilbert cited the progress made before the 1923 Railway Grouping by such varied companies as the Midland, Lancashire and Yorkshire, London and North Western and Great Western Railways. It was therefore no coincidence that after 1923, the greatest progress in this field was made by their successors, the London Midland and Scottish and the Great Western Railways. The LMS influence extended to the British Railways Standard steam locomotive designs through the triumvirate of three former LMS engineers, R. A. Riddles, Member of the Railway Executive (formed at Nationalisation) in charge of mechanical and electrical matters, R. C. Bond, Chief Officer for locomotive construction and maintenance, and E. S. Cox, Executive Officer responsible for design.

The more specific line of descent in the development of the heavy goods engine follows the realisation at the turn of the nineteenth century (with the notable exception of the Midland Railway) that the traditional 0-6-0 classes could not meet the growing need for more powerful locomotives to convey longer and heavier freight trains, especially for coal traffic. At this stage, the need for higher speeds made possible by partially or fully braked freight trains had not yet arisen.

While the logical development of the 0-6-0 for heavy haulage could be considered to be the 0-8-0 locomotive, the Great Western Railway went straight for the 2-8-0 wheel arrangement in the shape of G. J. Churchward's 28XX class. A total of 167 of the latter was built over the period 1903-42 including a batch of 83 incorporating detail alterations from 1938. The design was very successful, so much so that, as will be noted in Section 1.2, the Western Region (WR) put up a case for even more of the class to be built in preference to receiving further allocations of 9Fs in the 1950s. Similarly, after building some 89 0-8-0s to class 8A (LNER class Q4) from 1902 to 1911, the Great Central Railway also plumped for the 2-8-0 in large numbers; these emerged as J. G. Robinson's Class 8K (LNER Class O4).

The Robinson Class 8K design appeared in 1911, the original 126 for the GCR's use being followed by another 521 ordered for the Ministry of Munitions for use during the Great War (World War I) although three of the latter were in fact immediately purchased by the GCR. After the war, batches of twenties and thirties were purchased by individual railways, the GWR eventually receiving twenty of the class to work alongside the Churchward 28XXs to be followed later by another 80. These engines known on the GWR as the ROD (Railway Operating Department) class continued working on into BR days, the last examples being withdrawn by early October 1958. Although the GCR operated a number of the Class 8K on loan from the government after WWI, these were returned in 1921 as an agreement on purchase price could not be reached. Later, after Grouping in 1923, some 273 examples went into LNER stock (at a much more favourable price for the railway company). Almost all of these, some of which had been subject to modification, survived into BR stock on Nationalisation. Thus the longevity of both the GWR and GCR 2-8-0 designs provided ample evidence of their success.

In an article in *British Railways Journal* No. 60, John Marshall describes how George Hughes, Chief Mechanical Engineer of the Lancashire and Yorkshire Railway, was impressed by the 2-10-0 heavy freight engine designed by M. Jean Baptiste Flamme of the Belgian Railways. In 1913, J. A. F. Aspinall, General Manager to the LYR, himself a former CME of the company, asked Hughes to examine the comparative haulage costs of single-headed and double-headed goods trains, the heavy export coal traffic to Goole Docks being uppermost in his mind. He expressed his concern at 'the policy of hauling a few extra wagons by means of two six-coupled engines or one eight-coupled and one six-wheeled [engine]'.

In September 1913, Hughes spelled out his views on the desirability of producing a four-cylinder 2-10-0 which would be capable of hauling 1,090 tons at 36mph on level track. The Horwich Drawing Office duly produced an outline drawing dated 18th June 1914 of a 2-10-0 with 4 ft 10 in driving wheels and four 19 in x 28 in cylinders. At least two other designs were considered by the LYR at this time, a four-cylinder simple 2-8-2 and a four-cylinder compound 2-8-0. However, within two months, the Great War had broken out and no further development took place. Cecil J. Allen also refers to this locomotive in an article in the 1955 *Trains Annual* (Ian Allan) stating that while Hughes was subsequently in charge of locomotive affairs on the LMS some ten years later, the design was again seriously considered together with a proposed 2-8-2 compound designed by Sir Henry Fowler, the successor to Hughes on the LMS. The 2-8-2s would have been used on Midland Line coal trains between Toton and Brent (Cricklewood), but were eventually ruled out on account of both height and weight restrictions; after due deliberation, the LMS opted for a batch of 33 2-6-0 + 0-6-2T Beyer Garratts for this traffic.

Other pre-World War I heavy freight designs were proposed by the GCR. The Gorton Drawing Office Register listed a diagram for a proposed superheated 2-10-0 for the GCR as early as July 1910; a 2-8-2 design was also listed but the celebrated Robinson 1911 2-8-0 design referred to earlier was selected for production in preference. In 1914, a 2-10-2 design was produced by the Baldwin Works in the USA at the request of the GCR principally for their burgeoning Immingham export coal traffic whilst Robinson came up with a similar slightly more powerful Gorton design, again for a 2-10-2 in the same year. It is of interest to note that the Gorton 2-10-2 scheme appeared within a few days of the LYR 2-10-0 proposal. Again both the GCR- initiated designs

Table 1.1
BR Standard Class 9F 2-10-0s
Comparison of Leading Dimensions of Some Heavy Freight Steam Locomotive Classes

Class	Year	Cylinders[1] Diameter x Stroke	Coupled Wheel Diameter ft. in.	Boiler Pressure p.s.i	Total Heating Surfaces sq. ft.	Super-heater sq. ft.	Grate Area sq. ft.	Tractive Effort at 85% boiler pressure lb.	Engine Weight in Working Order tons	Adhesion Weight tons	Factor of Adhesion	Diagram Reference
BR Standard Designs												
BR 9F 2-10-0 Standard	1954	20" x 28"	5' 0"	250	2,015	535	40.2	39,667	86.70	77.50	4.38	A1 - A4
BR 9F 2-10-0 Crosti boiler	1955	20" x 28"	5' 0"	250	2,510 [2]	411	40.2	39,667	90.20	79.45	4.48	B
BR 9F 2-10-0 Crosti after conversion	1959	20" x 28"	5' 0"	250	1,432	411	40.2	39,667	83.60	74.90	4.23	C
BR 9F 2-10-0 Mechanical Stoker-fitted	1958	20" x 28"	5' 0"	250	2,015	535	40.2	39,667	88.50	80.30	4.56	D
BR Proposed Designs												
BR 8F 2-10-0	1951	20" x 28"	5' 0"	250	2,030	718	42.0	39,667	89.20	79.40	4.48	E
BR 9F 2-10-0 Crosti boiler	1951	20" x 28"	5' 0"	250	2,502 [2]	425	40.2	39,667	89.20	79.40	4.48	F
BR 8F 2-8-2	1948	19½" x 28"	5' 3"	225	[3]	[3]	36.0	32,321	[3]	66.00	4.57	G
BR 8F 2-8-2	1951	19½" x 28"	5' 3"	250	2,474	718	42.0	35,912	94.60	67.60	4.22	H
BR 8F 2-8-0 BR HQ design	1953	19" x 28"	5' 0"	250	1,650	369	28.7	35,799	[3]	[3]	[3]	I
BR 8F 2-8-0 Derby Development Office design	1953	A 18¾" x 28"	5' 0"	250	[3]	[3]	41.2	34,863	80.90	70.00	4.50	J
		B 19¾" x 28"	5' 0"	225	[3]	[3]	41.2	38,813	80.90	70.00	4.05	J
		C 20" x 28"	5' 0"	225	[3]	[3]	41.2	35,700	80.90	70.00	3.95	J
Earlier Designs												
LNER 8F O1 2-8-0	1944	20" x 26"	5' 6"	225	1,676 [4]	344	27.9	35,518	73.30	65.85	4.15	K
WD 8F 2-10-0	1943	19" x 28"	4' 8½"	225	1,951	423	40.0	34,215	78.30	67.15	4.40	L
WD 8F 2-8-0	1943	19" x 28"	4' 8½"	225	1,680	310	28.6	34,215	70.25	61.25	4.01	M
USA 'S160' 2-8-0	1943[5]	19" x 26"	4' 9"	225	1,773	480	41.0	31,490	72.50	62.90	4.47	N
LMS 8F 2-8-0	1935	18½" x 28"	4' 8½"	225	1,650	248 [6]	28.7	32,438	72.10	63.10	4.28	O
LMS Garratt 2-6-0+0-6-2T	1930	4 x 18½" x 26"	5' 3"	190	2,137	500	44.5	45,620	155.50	122.10	6.00	P
LNER P1 2-8-2	1925	3 x 20" x 26"	5' 2"	180	2,930	525	41.3	38,500 [7]	99.95	71.45	4.16	Q
GWR 8F 28XX 2-8-0 [8]	1903	18½" x 30"	4' 7½"	225	1,841	253	27.1	35,380	75.50	67.50	4.27	R
Earlier Proposed Designs												
GWR Collett 2-10-2T	1938	19" x 30"	4' 7½"	250	2,522	290	30.3	41,465	109.60	87.50	4.73	S
LMS Fowler 2-8-2	1925	[9]	5' 3"	240	2,578	631	43.5	44,400 (80%)	99.00	72.00	3.63	T
CR Pickersgill 2-10-2	1918	28" x 30"	4' 9"	200	5,065	400	54.0	60,000	144.00	114.00	4.25	U
L&YR Hughes 2-10-0	1914	4 x 19" x 28"	4' 10"	180	2,345	758	27.5	53,328	90.00	80.00	3.36	V
GCR Baldwin 2-10-2	1914	4 x 18" x 30"	4' 8"	190	4,475	820	57.0	56,100	121.00	100.00	3.99	W
GCR Robinson 2-10-2	1914	26" x 30"	4' 8"	200	3,428	690	[3]	61,715	135.00	110.00	3.99	X
Powell 7P8F 'Heavy' 2-8-2	1977	20" x 28"	5' 6"	250	3,164	677	42.0	36,106	95.50	68.00	4.22	Y
Powell 6P7F 'Light' 2-8-2	1977	19⅝" x 26"	5' 3"	225	2,678	592	36.0	30,398	88.70	62.20	4.58	Z

KEY
1 Two cylinders except where stated; 2 Includes preheater (1021 sq. ft.) & exhaust steam jacket (57 sq. ft.); 3 Information not traced;
4 From 11.45, total heating surfaces were 1661 sq.ft; 5 Date of introduction into Great Britain;
6 From 8012 onwards variations occurred in this figure ranging from 215 sq. ft. to 248 sq. ft. dependent on changes to superheater element diameter and thickness;
7 With booster, increases to 47,000 lb; 8 As modified with Superheater; 9 4-cyl Compound: 2 x H.P. cyls. (16¾" x 26"), 2 x L.P. cyls. (23⅝" x 26")

Figure 1
92014 passes the closed station of Charwelton with one of the down Annesley 'windcutter' coal empties on 19th September 1964. By this time, the 'windcutters' had less than a year to run, GC line freights being withdrawn in June 1965. The redundant 92014 then joined the procession of LMR 9Fs to Merseyside and the north west. *(Hugh Ballantyne)*

were rejected, due mainly to height restrictions but not before Sir Sam Fay, General Manager of the GCR, had considered a project to demolish the Conisborough tunnel, the only significant height restriction on the line from the Yorkshire coalfields to the Humber.

Towards the end of the war in 1918, the Caledonian Railway Drawing Office at St. Rollox (Glasgow) worked on a scheme for a 2-10-2 freight engine with enormous 28 in x 30 in cylinders. This was perhaps prompted by the CR's contribution to the hauling of huge volumes of coal (the celebrated 'Jellicoe Specials') towards Grangemouth and Scapa Flow from South Wales for the Grand Fleet during the previous four years; it is worth noting however that the CR does not appear to have employed its heaviest freight engines, the McIntosh Class 600 0-8-0s on the 'Jellicoes'. The design was similar in dimensions to the two GCR schemes but apparently was not seriously considered by the Board's Locomotive Sub-Committee. Designs for 2-8-2s and large 2-8-0s were also listed at St. Rollox at the same time but this may have been more to do with developing the Association of Railway Locomotive Engineers (ARLE) standard locomotive schemes of that period.

H. N. Gresley (later Sir Nigel) CME of the GNR also examined the possibility of building a 2-10-2 in 1922 during the last few months before Grouping but the company opted instead to remain with its trusty 2-8-0s. Later, in 1925, Gresley produced the P1 2-8-2 design for the LNER, to which two engines were built and used for the New England-Ferme Park coal traffic, the service on which some thirty years later, an allocation of 9Fs was deployed; Gresley also introduced 2-8-2s of the P2 class for passenger work on the Edinburgh-Aberdeen road in 1934. The only other 2-8-2 design seriously considered was by Bulleid for the SR in 1938 also intended mainly for passenger work; two locomotives to this design were authorised but not built. In the event, Bulleid's attention turned to developing what eventually resulted in the Merchant Navy Pacific class.

One other proposed and fully worked out scheme was a 2-10-2 tank engine for the GWR, developed in 1937/8. This design would have been the heaviest, most powerful tank engine in Britain, excluding the Beyer Garratt types. It was intended for the Ebbw Vale iron ore traffic, the service which later saw the original WR allocation of BR 9F 2-10-0s 92000-7 employed from 1954.

Apart from these developments, nothing seriously challenged the superiority of the 2-8-0 for heavy freight work in the 1920s and 1930s. A comparison of the leading dimensions of the above schemes together with other heavy freight designs including the BR Standard designs is given in Table 1.1.

For four years during W. A. Stanier's reign as Chief Mechanical Engineer on the LMS, R. A. Riddles held the post of Principal Assistant to the CME. Then, after a short spell as Mechanical and Electrical Engineer, Scotland, and a visit with the "Coronation Scot" to the USA, he moved to the Ministry of Supply at the start of World War II. Here, Riddles' main role as Director of Transportation Equipment was the provision of such facilities for the Royal Engineers during their service overseas. After considering the alternatives, the LMS Class 8F 2-8-0, designed by Stanier and introduced in 1935, was selected as the most suitable motive power from the point of view of ease of maintenance and route availability. Some 208 engines were constructed to this design by the North British Locomotive Co. in Glasgow and Beyer Peacock in Manchester whilst 51 LMS locomotives were also requisitioned by the War Department. In all, 852 of these locomotives were built by private builders and the workshops of all four British railway companies for use at home and overseas.

While the Stanier 2-8-0 was undoubtedly the best choice of the designs available at the time for the immediate needs of Great Britain's railway companies, it became apparent that these engines could not be built in sufficient numbers in time to meet the anticipated requirements for the planned Allied invasion of continental Europe. There was, therefore, a need for a simpler locomotive in terms of construction time and use of scarce materials.

By this time, Riddles had been appointed Deputy Director-General, Royal Engineer Equipment, and obtained on loan the services of F. G. Carrier from the LMS Drawing Office at Derby. The task was to design a completely new locomotive which would have the minimum attachments, the maximum accessibility for ease of maintenance and repair and be easy to prepare for traffic. The firm chosen to work with Riddles' team on this project was the North British Locomotive Company.

In these days of prototypes, pilot schemes and procrastination, it is difficult to visualise a situation in which such a large number of engines would have been ordered straight off the drawing board. What emerged was a much simplified version of the Stanier 8F 2-8-0 incorporating a round-top parallel boiler, replacement of steel castings, forgings and wheel centres by fabricated plate structures or cast iron, simplified lubrication arrangements, 'Laird-type' crosshead with twin bars above the piston rod, simplified cab and footplate arrangements and a large eight-wheeled tender.

The first of the class was handed over on 16th January 1943, a mere five months from the placing of the order. Eventually 935 locomotives were built to this design, second only in quantity to the 943 Class DX 0-6-0s built for the LNWR and LYR between 1858 and 1874. The success of the design prompted a request for a similar locomotive but with a reduced axle load of around 13.5 tons, compared with the 2-8-0's 15.5 tons, for operating over the many examples of substandard track inevitably encountered in theatres of war. The specification was met with a 2-10-0 wheel arrangement which also included the provision of a wide firebox. Grate area was correspondingly increased from 28.6 to 40.0 square feet enabling low grade fuel to be burnt more easily. A total of 150 of the 2-10-0s was built between 1943 and 1945 and at the end of hostilities, 25 passed into service on BR along with some 733 of the Riddles 2-8-0 design.

For the record it is worth noting that the first 2-10-0 was built in the USA in 1867 by the Lehigh Valley RR and the last in Turkey in 1961. Particularly large numbers were built to German designs in Europe, almost half during World War II. Standard gauge 2-10-0s constituted the last new main line steam locomotives to be built in several eastern European countries; Poland and Czechoslovakia (1958), Romania and East Germany (1960) and Turkey (1961).

In Great Britain the development of the Riddles 2-8-0 and 2-10-0 so-called Austerity locomotives was regarded with suspicion by the CMEs of the British railway companies as 'engines on the cheap' and hence of potentially dubious reliability. They nevertheless proved to be an immediate success with the operating staff when on loan to those companies before despatch for service abroad. The engines of both classes were in use well into BR days working alongside the last few Stanier 8F 2-8-0s, surviving almost to the end of steam in 1968.

In retrospect, it is fair to trace the Stanier 8F's parentage specifically to Churchward's 28XX Class 2-8-0 introduced in 1903 by the GWR. In his book, **Riddles and the 9Fs,** Col. H. C. B. Rogers tells of a letter from R. F. Hanks, later to be Chairman of the Western Area Board of the British Transport Commission, to Sir William Stanier congratulating him on the performance of one of his Class 8F 2-8-0s on emergency express passenger duty (shades of the future 9Fs!). Stanier is said to have replied 'Give the credit to G. J. Churchward and the Great Western!' This could only have referred to Stanier's belief that his Class 8F was simply a development of the GWR's 28XX design.

BR Freight Business in the 1950s and 1960s

In an effort to counter the increasing loss of freight traffic to road competition during the 1950s, British Railways adopted several initiatives; these included improved infrastructure such as new or updated marshalling yards and freight terminals. Coupled with rapid moves towards dieselisation and electrification of the network BR also placed great hopes in a policy to concentrate certain types of traffic into train loads or 'block' workings.

Experience in the delivery of coal to power stations and iron ore to steel plants using early versions of the 'merry-go-round' system had indicated that, given speedy turnarounds during loading and discharging, bulk traffic could be moved very economically at a cost of around half a new penny (or one 'old' penny) per ton mile, a figure which the alternatives of either road or water haulage could not approach.

Two other sources of goods for bulk haulage were in industries not normally regarded as natural bedfellows for the railway industry, i.e. oil companies and motor vehicle manufacturers. As a result, during the 1960s several distribution contracts with these industries were successfully negotiated. Rail carriage from coastal refineries to inland distribution centres in the case of the oil industry was competitive in the early 1960s compared with the alternative of transfer by pipeline; in any case the latter were not yet in place. Since then, massive increases in the volumes to be moved have decisively favoured the economics of the pipeline option. Refineries at that time were being located for strategic and national security reasons in several different parts of the country, the major locations being Milford Haven and Llandarcy in South Wales, Fawley on the Solent and several locations on the Thames estuary; in the north facilities were located on Merseyside, Humberside, Heysham in Lancashire and Grangemouth in Scotland. BR took advantage of these opportunities and was able to sign long term contracts with oil

Figure 2
92042 (Langwith Junction) drifts through Shirebrook Junction with a train of mineral empties on 5th August 1965. The engine was fitted with AWS in July 1960 while still allocated to New England; 92042 saw only a few more months of service before withdrawal at the end of 1965.
(Rodney Lissenden)

companies which built fleets of large oil tanker wagons with a projected 25 years life span to cater for the loads envisaged. Similarly, train load movements of finished motor vehicles and manufacturing components for the motor industry were also a significant revenue source for BR; the majority of this traffic was between the Midlands, Merseyside and Scotland.

The wisdom of these moves by BR was confirmed in the mid-1960s by the figures given in the appendix to the government White Paper *'Railway Policy'* published in 1967. This document envisioned a dramatic change in the pattern of freight traffic for the rest of the century. Estimates were given for the volume and revenue of BR freight traffic in 1975 compared with 1966. In particular, the demand for coal over this period was expected to reduce by some 33% as shown:

	Millions of Tons	
	1966	1975
Power Stations	68	65
Gas Industry	17	-
Coke Ovens	24	22
Domestic Users	22	10
Industry	22	10
Others	25	13
Total	178	120

Although BR could be expected to retain a large portion of this traffic, effect on revenues would be disproportionately severe because of the projected reduction in haulage distances which would result; hence by 1975 revenue from this traffic was forecast to reduce by almost 50% from £100m to £53m per annum.

For the iron and steel traffic, overall transport demand for raw materials and output was expected to show an increase as follows:

	Millions of Tons	
	1966	1975
Crude Steel	24	31
Castings	4	5
Home Produced Ore	14	8
Imported Ore	17	24
Scrap	10	12
Limestone	5	6
Total	74	86

The decline in domestic production of ore would again have a disproportionate effect on BR because, assuming ore quality was not a significant factor, the long-haul traffic from ore-fields would be the first to be curtailed for economic reasons. Moreover, the projected increase in volumes of imported ore would not necessarily compensate BR if the material were handled at ports on the doorsteps of the steel production plants. So again, reduction in BR revenues would result. Alternatively, if the concept of designating a strategically located single fully equipped port facility set up to handle very large ore carriers were accepted, a significant opportunity for BR would develop in the form of trainload movements in specially designed high capacity wagons. A further possibility was the option that the then National Steel Corporation would rationalise its stock holding arrangements which would again increase the scope for block train working.

Analysis of 1966 block train tonnages for individual traffics compared with projected values for 1975 are shown below:

	Millions of Tons	
	1966	1975
Iron and Steel		
- Raw Materials	14.7	19.0
- Products & Scrap	2.7	7.0
Oil & Petrol	7.9	16.2
Chemicals & Fertiliser	1.1	3.8
Vehicles	0.6	1.1
Earth & Stone	4.6	8.3
Other	3.4	4.6
Total	35.0	60.0

Compared with 1966, a transition from wagonload to block working was projected to continue and perhaps accelerate although the amount of wagonload business was still expected to be significant in 1975. The method of handling this traffic had been under review for some years and it was not readily apparent how this could be profitably dealt with by BR. One option was to abandon the business altogether and in many cases, this is effectively what occurred if only by default. Projected freightliner business was not expected to be one of great growth potential once the 1975 level had been achieved. Although existing wagonload business would be one source of such traffic, freightliners would only be economically attractive for distances of at least 100 and preferably 200 miles; the volume of wagonload traffic falling into this category was small. Figures for 1966 BR volume movements in coal, minerals and merchandise categories compared with those projected for 1975 are as follows:

	1966		1975	
	Vol. moved by BR m. tons	% of total BR freight traffic	Vol. moved by BR m.tons	% of total BR freight traffic
Coal				
- Block trains	55	42	75	78
- Wagonload	75	58	21	22
Total	130	100	96	100
Minerals & Merchandise				
- Block trains	35	43	60	52
- Wagonload	47	57	24	21
- Freightliner	-	-	32	27
Total	82	100	116	100

In the early days of block goods traffic development, the 9Fs made a significant contribution. With the breakneck pace of dieselisation of passenger services, the provision of diesel units capable of matching the power of the 9Fs was not a priority and it was not until well into the 1960s that such units became widely available for heavy freight working. This may have been a factor in the decision to continue building more 9Fs for some five years after the appearance of the first BR Modernisation Plan. Although the 1955 plan originally envisaged a careful evaluation of diesel power and did not rule out further steam power being authorised, it was reported that the 1958 batch of 9Fs was ordered for the WR in September 1956 'with reluctance', after establishing that there were no economical diesel alternatives available. Despite these reservations, the 9F heavy freight design proved to be a relatively cheap and reliable stopgap until the advent of suitable diesel power for heavy freight services.

Figure 3
This view dated 13th March 1957 shows 92102 (Toton) heading an empty mineral train through Trent station. The record indicates the engine visited Crewe Works in the same month for rectification of collision damage.
(J. P. Wilson)

1.1 Purpose

It was during the closing months of 1947 that R. A. Riddles was appointed as Member of the Railway Executive for Mechanical and Electrical Engineering. It was not surprising that he selected former LMS colleagues R. C. Bond and E. S. Cox for the senior posts of Chief Officer (Locomotive Construction and Maintenance) and Executive Officer (Design) respectively and the triumvirate formally started work for the Railway Executive on 1st January 1948.

To establish the steam locomotive requirements for the newly nationalised organisation, three projects were given priority. The first was a series of Interchange Trials to compare the performance and efficiency of the four previous companies' principal types of locomotive. In the Heavy Freight category, the GWR Class 28XX, LMS Class 8F, LNER Class O1 and the WD Class 2-8-0s were compared with the WD 2-10-0 on workings between New England (Peterborough) and Ferme Park, Toton and Brent (Cricklewood), Acton and Severn Tunnel Junction, Eastleigh and Bristol; the 28XX was not tested between Toton and Brent for clearance reasons. The operating vagaries inherent in freight train working meant that these tests showed a wider spread of results than with the passenger locomotives. E. S. Cox wrote that "... there was little to choose between them other than a tendency for the WD 2-8-0 to come out bottom in any relative assessment".

The second task was to set up a Locomotive Standards Committee to consider the possibility of selecting a limited range of existing classes for construction in the short term until new standard designs were developed. The third project was to identify the areas where new designs were needed and initiate detailed work for their development.

In the heavy freight category the aim was to provide suitable power in connection with the medium term objective of converting much of BR's freight operation from unbraked, loose-coupled trains to continuously braked stock operated at higher speeds and E. S. Cox regarded the 2-8-2 design as the optimum for this role. The development of the project attracted a lower priority than the other eleven designs in the proposal however as the considerable resources required for the huge task of upgrading the wagon stock to incorporate continuous braking were not yet available. In addition, BR's freight services had benefited from a large number of WD 2-8-0s recently repatriated from continental Europe following the end of World War II, so the appearance of a new freight design was not critical at this juncture.

Heavy Freight Design: 2-8-2 versus 2-10-0

On 14th June 1948, E. S. Cox completed his 'Report on Proposed Standard Steam Locomotives' recommending twelve types of locomotive to cover the major traffic requirements of British Railways. Among his suggested 'Entirely New Designs' was the Class 8 2-8-2 (Mikado) freight locomotive; the classification '8' referred to the LMS power rating which was subsequently altered to '9' in the new British Railways organisation. This was to be a two-cylinder locomotive with double blastpipe and chimney, an axle load of 16.5 tons on 5 ft 3 in coupled wheels, wide firebox, bar frames and standard outside bearing carrying wheels on engine and tender (see Diagram G). At this stage, it was intended that the new 2-8-2 should have the same boiler, cylinders, motion and trailing truck as the proposed class 5 Pacific (which later became a 4-6-0). The proposed new design was intended to replace the GWR 28XX, LMS 8F, LNER O1 2-8-0s and presumably in due course (although not stated specifically by Cox) the WD 2-8-0s and 2-10-0s.

R. A. Riddles apparently did not endorse the view that a 2-8-2 was the best configuration for BR's new heavy freight design. His doubts were based on the observation that freight engines relied to a large extent for their effectiveness on their adhesion properties. In a 2-8-2, he argued, some of the adhesive weight would be lost on starting a heavy train since a portion of the weight would inevitably be 'set back' on to the trailing truck as the engine began to move its train. In practice therefore, it would add little or no extra adhesion to that of the existing 2-8-0s despite the increase in power. Similarly, the stopping power of a 2-8-2 was thought to be insufficient, there being only eight coupled wheels to provide braking compared with ten for the 2-10-0. Design work was done to see whether the 2-8-2 hind truck could be braked but the idea was rejected despite the common usage of such devices in other countries. Further, Riddles had been impressed by the performance of his 1943 Austerity 2-10-0 as an eminently suitable and robust heavy freight design and the 25 units BR had purchased from the MoD after World War II were now operating satisfactorily on the Scottish Region.

The key point for Riddles was locomotive adhesion however and it is worth summarising the main factors which must be taken into account when considering the adhesion characteristics or 'slipping' propensities of locomotives. The tractive effort which can be transmitted to a pair of wheels is directly proportional to the adhesion weight imposed on those wheels. Whether or not a pair of wheels slips is solely dependent on the torque applied to them (torque is defined as any force which can cause rotation).

Weight transfer can occur as a result of the drawbar pull. On an engine with coupled wheels at the rear end, e.g. a 4-6-0 or a 2-10-0, the weight transfer should give a positive increase in adhesion. Curvature of the track and the design of bogies and trucks can also have an effect on propensity to slip. In some designs, the tendency is to lift the engine on a curve so reducing the adhesion weight on the coupled wheels. Stiffness and internal friction of the springs also affects adhesion weight.

Once the wheels do begin to slip, the coefficient of friction between wheels and the rails reduces immediately to a value much lower than that which obtained before slipping commenced. In the absence of restraint, e.g. the application of sand to increase the coefficient of friction artificially, or the closing of the regulator or reduction of cut-off to reduce the applied torque, the slip will continue to build up until the torque is balanced by the increased internal friction of the engine. This build-up of slip is rapid in comparison with the time needed for the driver to react and take remedial action.

Each of the pairs of coupled wheels should carry an identical or at least a very similar portion of the engine weight. Otherwise it is possible that one pair of coupled wheels may instantaneously begin to slip which the other pairs, when the additional load is transmitted to them by the coupling rods, are then powerless to stop; the result is that all the coupled wheels then begin to slip. Care must be exercised during assembly of the engine when built and during works visits, since erecting inaccuracies and clearances in axlebox journals and guides, coupling rod bushes and joint pins could result in the same effect.

In view of the rapid build-up of slipping speed on modern

Figure 4
A southbound mineral train is headed through Wellingborough Midland Road by 92085 (Kettering) on 13th May 1961. Three months later, 92085 would enter Crewe Works for a Heavy General overhaul with boiler change after completing 142,000 miles on similar MML duties since delivery in May 1956. *(L. Hanson)*

Figure 5
Before the arrival of the M6 motorway, an unidentified 9F hurries a southbound fitted freight through the Lune Gorge near Tebay on 15th July 1967. The 9Fs based at Carlisle Kingmoor and other WCML depots such as Warrington were regulars on this type of traffic in the mid-1960s. *(Courtney Haydon)*

Figure 6
92017 (Carlisle Kingmoor) nears Winwick Junction, north of Warrington, with a WCML down Class 'D' fitted goods on 12th August 1967. The engine, one of the first 9Fs to be allocated to the LMR Central Division, Newton Heath in 1958, had been withdrawn by the end of 1967.
(Hugh Ballantyne)

engines in which steam pipes are designed to pass large quantities of steam without impedance, the quantity of steam that can be held in the main steam pipe between the regulator and the valve chests becomes of paramount importance, since it is difficult to arrest the slipping until most of this steam has been exhausted. This facet clearly shows the advantage (as in the case of the Standard Pacifics but not the 9F) of fitting a multiple valve regulator on the superheater side of the header rather than in the dome, for then the only steam remaining in the main steam pipe after the regulator is closed is that in the cylinder steam pipes and valve chests. Regulator valves may be insufficiently sensitive, as a result of the port opening being too large in the early stages of movement. Regulator stiffness may also be a factor and it may be necessary to make design modifications in the light of operating experience as in the case of the 9Fs (see Section 9.1).

It seems clear that both R. C. Bond and E. S. Cox were still very much in favour of the 2-8-2 concept however and in August 1950, the latter penned a memo citing no fewer than ten good reasons why the 2-8-2 was to be preferred to the 2-10-0 for the fast freight role envisaged; a summary of his argument is as follows:

(1) a 2-10-0 would most probably be limited by the British loading gauge to a coupled wheel diameter of no more than 4 ft 10 in. At 50mph, approximately 18% less tractive effort would be available for haulage compared with a 2-8-2 having, say, 5 ft 6 in diameter coupled wheels. *(It should be noted here that the original calculations to support this assertion were later 'revised and corrected' to the extent that no disadvantage accrued to the 2-10-0 design).*

(2) the greater tractive effort at speed required for the new fast freight concept clearly favours the 2-8-2. *(Again, no longer supportable given the recalculations noted above).*

(3) a 2-10-0 boiler would necessarily be restricted in size due to the need to carry the firebox above the final coupled wheels.

(4) the free gas area of the 2-10-0 (for the design then visualised) would be a very low 11.4% of grate area compared with the 16.2% value obtainable with the 2-8-2; experience indicated that to ensure the tube bank could absorb the maximum heat the grate was able to produce, a minimum figure of 15% was desirable. *(Relatively low values for this figure did not always result in poor performance however. Table 1.2 compares a number of designs for both passenger and freight classes. Although the 15% figure appears to be about the norm, the Pacifics of the LMR Princess Royal, LMR Duchess, SR Merchant Navy, ER A1 and BR Duke of Gloucester classes all had similar or lower values of 'Free Gas Area' as % of grate area compared with the Standard 9F Class 2-10-0 as built).*

Table 1.2
BR Standard Class 9F 2-10-0s
Total Free Gas Area as Percentage of Grate Area
Comparison of 9Fs with Other Classes

Class	Total Free Gas Area (square feet)	Grate Area (square feet)	Total Free Gas Area as % of Grate Area
BR 9F 2-10-0 Standard	5.49	40.2	13.7
BR 9F 2-10-0 Crosti Total	6.59	40.2	16.4
Boiler	4.59	40.2	11.4
Preheater	2.00	40.2	5.0
MOS WD 2-10-0	4.64	40.0	11.6
LNWR G2 0-8-0	3.96	23.6	16.8
S&DJR 2-8-0	4.16	28.4	14.7
LMS 7F 0-8-0 Standard	3.89	23.6	16.5
LMS Beyer Garratt	6.40	44.5	14.4
LMS 8F 2-8-0	4.36	28.65	15.2
MOS WD 2-8-0	4.83	28.65	16.9
ER O1 2-8-0	4.45	27.9	16.0
GWR 28XX 2-8-0	4.26	27.07	15.7
BR 8 4-6-2 *Duke of Gloucester*	6.79	48.6	14.0
BR 7 4-6-2 Britannia	6.79	42.0	16.2
BR 6 4-6-2 Clan	5.73	36.0	15.9
BR 5 4-6-0	4.50	28.7	15.9
BR 4 4-6-0	3.78	26.7	14.2
BR 4 2-6-4T	3.78	26.7	14.2
BR 3 2-6-2T	3.054	20.35	15.0
ER A1 4-6-2	6.28	50.0	12.6
ER A3 4-6-2	6.28	41.25	15.2
ER A4 4-6-2	6.28	41.25	15.2
ER V2 2-6-2	6.28	41.25	15.2
ER B1 4-6-0	4.44	27.9	15.9
LMR Princess Royal 4-6-2	5.49	45.0	12.2
LMR Duchess 4-6-2	6.89	50.0	13.8
LMR Royal Scot 4-6-0			
Unrebuilt †	5.31	31.2	17.0
Rebuilt	4.86	31.25	15.6
LMR Patriot 4-6-0 (unrebuilt)†*	4.70	30.5	15.4
LMR Jubilee 4-6-0 (final version of 3A boiler)*	4.33	31.0	14.0
LMR 5 4-6-0	4.54	28.65	15.9
SR Merchant Navy 4-6-2	6.28	48.5	13.0
SR WC/BB Light 4-6-2	6.28	38.25	16.4
WR King 4-6-0 (low superheat)	5.24	34.3	15.3
WR Castle 4-6-0 (medium superheat)	4.86	29.36	16.6
WR County 4-6-0	4.46	28.84	15.5
WR Hall 4-6-0 (medium superheat)	4.39	27.07	16.2

Key
† Parallel boiler
* For Rebuilt versions, see Royal Scot 4-6-0 data
Data source: NRM, York

Figure 7
Severn Tunnel Junction shed is host to Banbury's 92218 on 20th June 1965; the engine has probably arrived on an ore train from the south Midlands. Later photographs show 92218 paired with a BR1C tender which it may have acquired at Crewe during overhaul in May 1966. 92218 lasted almost until the end of steam, being withdrawn from Speke Junction shed in May 1968. *(Courtney Haydon)*

(5) firebox volume, an important factor when burning some types of inferior quality coal would be only 202 cu ft for the 2-10-0 compared with 273 cu ft for the 2-8-2.

(6) the ashpan volume for the 2-10-0 would be restricted to 38 cu ft whilst with the 2-8-2, a figure of 49 cu ft would be achieved. This, together with the fact that the portion of the pan situated over the rear wheels would necessarily be very shallow on the 2-10-0, was likely to result in a significant build-up of ash over a long non-stop run thus reducing the effective grate area.

(7) a 2-10-0 design with five axles loaded at around 13½ tons does not give better adhesion and braking features compared with a 2-8-2 having axle loads of approx. 17½ tons; the adhesion weight of the 2-10-0 is restricted as much by the limited size of boiler it is possible to fit as by any axle weight limitation.

(8) a 2-10-0 has a higher internal resistance than a 2-8-2 and would thus reduce the amount of power available for haulage; roller bearings would reduce this problem but would be much more expensive to fit compared with plain bearings. *(In practice, a full valve gear arrangement drawing was made for the 2-8-2 in the Development Office which was not listed in the production drawing run).*

(9) a 2-8-2 design is capable of being built up with many of the same components envisaged for the proposed Class 7 Pacific (Britannia) design; the same flanging blocks could also be used for boiler construction.

(10) it is worth noting that overseas practice in, for example, the USA, Germany, France, India and Australia favours the 2-8-2 concept for the fast freight role and has been very successful.

Over the next few months a considerable amount of design work was authorised on the development of the 2-8-2 and a fresh design appeared in early 1951 very similar in appearance to the 9F subsequently built (see Diagram H). R. A. Riddles was still convinced however that a suitably designed 2-10-0 would show advantages over the Mikado wheel arrangement; this resulted in a scheme for a 2-10-0 produced by F. G. Carrier of the Derby Drawing Office in June 1951. The design ingeniously remedied some of E. S. Cox's objections to the 2-10-0 in his ten-point pro-Mikado 2-8-2 memo of the previous year, a key feature being the ability to accommodate an increase in the coupled wheel diameter from 4 ft 8 in to 5 ft.

Despite this development, R. C. Bond still favoured the 2-8-2 concept as he felt the future lay with continuous brakes on all freight trains with the emphasis on higher speeds and thus on boiler capacity rather than on starting tractive effort and adhesive weight. Many years later, he went on to say "As events turned out, I might well have been wrong. There are still [1975] many thousands of wagons running about without power brakes and it seems as though there will be for some years yet. The 2-10-0s were perhaps the most successful of them all [the new Standard classes]".

For many such projects, the 'goal posts' had indeed been changed as R. C. Bond had observed. In this case less emphasis was now being placed on the fast fitted-freight concept originally put forward and more on providing power for the heavy and slower-moving 1,000 ton mineral trains of yore. Perhaps R. A. Riddles, with his considerable experience during World War II of Government 'processes', had already become convinced that available resources for the plan to fit all freight wagons with continuous brakes could be a long time coming (if indeed they were ever to be made available) and that the proportion of the time the new class would spend on such work even in the medium term would be very much less than previously anticipated. Meanwhile there was the general limit, then applying, of a 40mph maximum speed for unfitted mineral trains. Thus the need now was for a more powerful locomotive with the ability to reduce transit times by climbing banks faster, rather than achieving the higher running speeds originally envisaged for the fast freight services.

At any rate, the new 2-10-0 design tipped the balance of the argument in its favour. Recognising this, E. S. Cox produced another memo in June 1951, (the same month that F. G. Carrier had produced the 2-10-0 scheme) in which he endorsed the 2-10-0 as the better design for the duties now envisaged. The main points of Cox's conclusions are summarised below:

"The 2-10-0 design is to be preferred for the following reasons:

(1) more tractive effort at all speeds.
(2) better adhesion and more economical use of available weight.
(3) lower first cost due to lower weight.
(4) with modern valve events and the fitting of roller bearings, the 3 in lower coupled wheel diameter compared with the 2-8-2 design would be no detriment.
(5) the smaller boiler will supply all steam necessary for the anticipated freight haulage conditions. (The total free gas area to grate area ratio had been improved to 13.7% and was now on a par with the 13.8% figure for the LMR Duchess Pacific design).
(6) the long wheel base will still allow curves of 4½ chains (99 yards) radius to be negotiated with the provision of flangeless tyres where appropriate and increased side-play on the leading and trailing coupled wheels.
(7) although the ashpan arrangement is not ideal, the capacity is at least as great as that for the 2-8-2 and the arrangement of its sloping sides somewhat better, for example, than that on the LMS Duchess Pacifics.
(8) the anticipated advantage at higher speeds for the 2-8-2 due to its larger coupled wheel diameter does not materialise because the greater adhesion weight of the 2-10-0 permits it to carry a 20 x 28 in cylinder as opposed to the maximum 19½ x 28 in value for the 2-8-2.

E. S. Cox concluded his memo by noting that although the starting tractive effort of the 2-10-0 was only marginally higher than that of the existing regional 2-8-0s, the performance at higher speeds would be greater due to the increased steam producing capacity of the boiler. Also, the ability to maintain uphill speeds of nearer 20mph than 10mph would represent a much greater saving in journey time than running downhill at 50mph rather than 40mph.

Thus the Standard heavy freight engine for BR was constructed to a 2-10-0 design. As noted earlier, R. C. Bond still retained doubts about the wisdom of the decision believing that the 2-8-2 would have been the better choice. Similarly A. J. Powell, an engineer with considerable experience in positions at CME headquarters in Derby and also at the Railway Executive was of the opinion that a 2-8-2 could have fulfilled a valuable role in handling fast fitted freight traffic on a number of busy or difficult main lines. He even went to the extent of producing diagrams for two 2-8-2 types, a 7P8F and a 6P7F published in his book, **Living with London Midland Locomotives** (Ian Allan, 1977) reproduced here as Diagrams Y and Z. Despite these reflections however, there is no doubting the great success of the Standard Class 9F 2-10-0 as designed and built and that is probably the most convincing argument of all.

Ironically during a visit to the 71000 *Duke of Gloucester* Steam Locomotive Trust at the Great Central Railway at Loughborough in September 1980, Riddles then well into his eighties reportedly confirmed during a conversation (*Steam Railway*, Issue No. 9, November-December 1980, p.49) that his "....ideal locomotive would have been a 2-8-2 with two large cylinders, Caprotti valve gear and driving wheels about 5 ft 6 in in diameter...it would have handled anything at a high average [speed]". And so, given different circumstances, the BR heavy freight design might well have appeared as a 2-8-2 after all.

1.2 Design Development
Standard Boiler Engines: 92000-92019, 92030-92250

The 9F 2-10-0, the last but one of the dozen BR Standard designs to appear, was regarded as one of the two most successful, the other being the Britannia Pacific on which the original 2-8-2 Standard heavy freight type was to have been based. However, the decision to adopt the 2-10-0 wheel arrangement meant that it would not be possible to include more than a few component parts utilised in the Britannia design; these were confined to the connecting rods, some valve gear components and the cab and tender fittings common to the other Standard classes. Such was the amount of new design work required, that the 2-10-0 was viewed at the outset as being only distantly related to the other Standard types.

The 9Fs incorporated from new a number of modifications derived from the operating experience with the other Standard classes. These included the inherently stronger plain section coupling rods as replacements for the I-section type originally adopted for all the Standard designs and the restoration of the hinged fall plate on the tender to reduce footplate draughts. Similarly the bearings on the coupled wheels were of the plain type, the provision of expensive roller bearings having been deemed unnecessary following successful earlier modifications to certain members of the Britannia class. The short life of the 9Fs well vindicated this decision as the longer lasting, lower maintenance cost advantages of the roller bearings would not have been realised. In any event, no problems were reported with the axleboxes of the 9Fs and their riding qualities were reported as very smooth and steady, equivalent according to some accounts to that obtainable on the best Pacific express passenger designs. As with the other Standard designs however, roller bearings were used on the tender wheels. The other significant difference between the 9F and the Britannia Pacific was the replacement of the expensive and weighty smokebox-mounted Melesco regulator by a horizontal grid type regulator located in the dome.

Apart from the Crosti boiler engines, 92020-92029, covered in the following Section 1.3, four other variations on the basic 9F design were developed as listed below:

- double blastpipe and chimney:
  from new, 92165-7/78/83-250
  retro-fitted, 92000/1/2/5/6
- Westinghouse air pumps: 92060-6/97-9
- Mechanical Stoker: 92165-7
- Giesl Oblong Ejector: 92250.

Design details of all six varieties of the 9F are covered later in this section.

The problem of the post-World War II national steel shortage in Great Britain had not been resolved by the early 1950s and delays in the construction of the Standard classes soon developed into a substantial backlog of uncompleted orders. In late 1950, the Locomotive Manufacturers' Association (LMA) representing the still considerable capacity in Great Britain for steam engine construction had approached British Railways for permission to quote for some of the new business. This initiative was at first discouraged by BR as their

Figure 8
92062 (Tyne Dock) passes South Pelaw Junction with empty ore hoppers returning from Consett to Tyne Dock about 1965. Track and signal maintenance is underway at this busy junction.
(J. W. Armstrong Trust)

workshops were operating at well below capacity (partly because of the lack of steel). Belatedly it was realised that one option for dealing with the order backlog was to explore the possibility of inviting bids from LMA members, thus accessing a portion of their steel quotas otherwise unavailable to BR.

As a result, quotations were sought for some 70 Class 9Fs (along with 50 Class 5 4-6-0s) for the provisional 1955 building programme. The Vulcan Foundry at Newton-le-Willows and the North British Locomotive Company of Glasgow each quoted for 35 9Fs at £31,268 and £30,058 respectively for each locomotive. These figures compared with the contemporary Crewe Works First Cost Estimate of £24,691 per engine and probably as a direct result only twenty 9Fs were eventually sanctioned from the private contractors. In the event, the 1955 programme was revoked to allow for the completion of orders from the previous programmes. By this time, interest in the private sector was becoming increasingly focused on diesel and electrical power and the steam engine initiative was dropped by BR in favour of preparatory work for its imminent modernisation plan based on these alternative technologies.

Two Western Region Initiatives

Even before the first 9Fs arrived on the Western Region (WR) in early 1954, attempts had been made by the WR management to redirect them to other Regions. After the early brake and regulator problems with its first batch of 9Fs, (see Section 9), the region believed its worst fears were confirmed and became deeply unimpressed with the class. Efforts were redoubled to halt the delivery of the remaining engines nominally destined for WR allocation.

The first move was a request to the Railway Executive for permission to build a further batch of 48 engines to the basic 1903 (Cl. 8F) 28XX Churchward design as later modified by the addition of superheating (presumably to be numbered in the 38XX and 98XX series). This request was met with a degree of incredulity at BR Headquarters but was backed up by a memo from K. W. C. Grand, the WR's Chief Regional Officer, on 20th January 1953 pointing out the economic advantages of such a move. In it the cost of manufacture of the proposed 28XXs was put at £14,150 each as opposed to £23,500 for each of the 9Fs; relative annual running costs as displayed in Table 1.3 were also shown to favour the 28XXs. The matter was duly dealt with in the memo dated 30th July 1953 to R. A. Riddles from R. C. Bond and is reproduced below.

R. C. Bond wrote:

Locomotive Building Programme, Western Region

Ref: memo from K. W. C. Grand, 20.01.53.

"In calculating the annual charges for the BR 2-10-0s, I have deducted £2,000 from the estimated first cost of the engine as representing the cost of the flanging blocks, jigs etc. so as to make the comparison (with the 28XX) valid, having regard to the fact that it is unlikely that anything is included for these items in the WR cost of the 28XX or WD 2-8-0s. In the

Table 1.3
Heavy Freight Engine Operation on WR
Estimated Relative Annual Charges (£ of 1953)

Freight Class	WD 2-10-0	WD 2-8-0	GW 28XX	BR 2-10-0
Coal	Control	+ 44	+ 44	= Control
Maintenance	Control	- 39	- 48	+ 57
Annual Charges	Control	- 39	- 69	+ 284
Total	Control	- 34	- 73	+ 341

Figure 9
92077 (Newton Heath) and Ivatt Class 4 2-6-0 43025 (Workington) drift down from Shap summit towards Tebay on 28th June 1964. Unusually, for an LMR-based 9F at this time, 92077 has retained the original lamp bracket configuration.
(Rodney Lissenden)

Figure 10
On 29th April 1967, 92058 (Warrington) ambles through the Cheshire countryside with an RCTS rail tour special, the Wrexham, Mold and Connah's Quay Centenary Tour. This started at Crewe and ran via Sandbach, Northwich, Mouldsworth Junction, Hooton, Chester, Mold Junction, Rhydymwyn, Hope Junction, Wrexham Croes Newydd, Brymbo, Wrexham Central, Ruabon, Llangollen, Neston, Bidston, New Brighton, Chester, Northwich, Sandbach and back to Crewe. 92058 shared the trip with Stanier Class 8F 2-8-0 48697 and Stanier 2-cylinder 2-6-4 tank engines 42616 and 42647.
(Courtney Haydon)

attached table (Table 1.3) the WD 2-10-0 is taken as the basis case.

Basis

Coal: in a memo dated 14.11.52, from the Locomotive Testing Committee, the coal consumption for the 28XX can be taken as equivalent to that of the WD 2-8-0 whilst that for the BR 2-10-0 would be the same as for the WD 2-10-0.

Maintenance: in the individual costing returns for the 28XX for 1950, the 0.61d (0.254p) per mile per light weight ton is uplifted by 14.5% to reach 1953 price levels and is equal to 0.698d (0.291p) per mile per light weight ton. The annual mileage for all types of freight locomotive is set at 27,000 (as per the Testing Committee memo of 14.11.52).

Annual Charges: the standard 45-year life span is assumed for all types; similarly interest charges of 4.0% on gross replacement costs and 0.826% on net replacement costs are assumed.

From the above, it will be seen that if engaged in hauling trains of the same weight, the BR 2-10-0 will be approximately £414 per annum more expensive to run than the WR 28XX. The comparison is, of course, open to modification if we are able to show the WR cost for building 28XX locomotives is not correct. The situation will also be

Figure 11
On 14th February 1954 92002 calls in at Swindon Works for examination and the commissioning of WR ATC apparatus; the engine was en route to its first shed, Newport Ebbw Junction during delivery from Crewe Works where the ATC was installed. Fitted with a double chimney in November 1960, 92002 was one of the last of the class to be reported on passenger work (GC route, August 1966, see Table 7.3)
(E. W. Fry)

different if, as I understand is likely, Sir Michael Barrington-Ward (Operating Member, Railway Executive) does not accept the views expressed by Mr. Grand that the greater tractive effort of the 2-10-0s, whether measured in terms of load or increased speed cannot be turned to good account on the WR. If however, it has to be accepted that the greater power capacity of the 2-10-0s cannot be utilised effectively on the WR, we could not argue (against the fact that) they would be more expensive to run than a 2-8-0 although their long-term advantage in enabling inferior coal to be effectively used must not be overlooked. If, however, it is considered that this advantage does not at present justify the increased annual cost of running 2-10-0s on the WR, the right course would seem to be to send the 2-10-0s which will be built, to the London Midland or Eastern Regions who will no doubt be very glad of them and they should transfer an equal or greater number of 2-8-0s to the WR. If Mr. Grand is unwilling to have Austerities (WD 2-8-0s) transferred to his region, LMS 2-8-0s would be available and although their tractive effort is slightly less than the WR 28XX, they are in the same power class and should be able to meet the WR requirements".

As a final paragraph in his memo, R. C. Bond concluded: "The above should be considered as interim notes on the matter pending receipt of Sir Michael Barrington-Ward's views on the operating questions involved and also the report of the Accountant's Mechanical Engineering Sub-Committee which may enable us to to probe further into the building costs of the WR 28XX locomotives".

The final outcome of the debate was exactly that suggested in the above memo, i.e. the LMR eagerly accepted a larger number of the 9F 2-10-0s releasing an equivalent number of (Swindon-built) Stanier Class 8F 2-8-0s displaced as the new engines arrived on the Midland Division.

Before this however, the WR made a second initiative. This was the proposal for a new Standard Class 8F 2-8-0 design for their region, with the suggestion that it should be adopted for the whole BR network as older 2-8-0s became life-expired. Two 2-8-0 schemes, initial diagrams rather than drawings, were proposed in November 1953, one being an updated version of the Stanier 8F and the other a pruned-down form of the 9F 2-10-0 but still retaining the wide firebox; initial drawings are depicted in Diagrams I and J. The proposal was to include five engines in the 1956 building programme, with a possible 48 more examples, eighteen for the 1957 and 30 for the 1958 programmes; the class was expected to be numbered in the 93000-52 series. In the event, the designs were not progressed beyond the initial diagram stage and the units in the 1956-58 programmes were turned out as 9F 2-10-0s.

Table 1.5 displays the five Annual Building Programmes for the class, summarising the lot numbers, delivery dates and initial region of allocation. The lion's share of the construction was at Crewe which built 198 examples with 53 engines emerging from Swindon. The last of the Crewe builds, 92221-50, was completed in December 1958, four months before the first of the final Swindon-built batch, 92203-20 was delivered to traffic.

It was reported that the North Eastern Region (NER) put in a bid for more 9Fs around 1955 but this proposal was not pursued. In the same year, the Associated Locomotive Equipment Co. Ltd. submitted quotations for Caprotti valve gear for batches of 30, 60 and 90 9Fs. It is unclear whether this was unsolicited but around 1955-56, consideration was given to fitting several other classes with Caprotti gear; these included WR King and County 4-6-0s and SR rebuilt Merchant Navy Pacifics. Further batches of 9Fs, possibly incorporating Caprotti gear, were tentatively considered by the London Midland Region (LMR) for the 1958/60 building programmes; this would have resulted in a class total of some 308 engines. In the event, these additional 9Fs were not sanctioned, resources by then being concentrated on bringing forward proposed diesel and electric construction schemes.

1.3 Design Development
Crosti Boiler Engines: 92020-92029

In 1947, the year of the Nationalisation of the coal industry in Great Britain, the newly formed National Coal Board (NCB) continued with the established programme of modernisation aimed at increasing safety and productivity in the coal mines. In October 1950, the Board published proposals for a national 'Plan For Coal'. With UK coal consumption in 1950 of 201.7

Figure 12
92074 (Annesley) hustles a southbound GC line coal train up the seven mile, 1 in 176 Ashby bank between Leicester and Lutterworth on a fine and frosty 8th February 1964. On withdrawal of the GC line freights in June 1965, 92074 was transferred successively to Banbury, Saltley and Croes Newydd before ending its days at Carlisle Kingmoor in April 1967.
(M. Mitchell)

million tons (see Appendix 10) and a forecast for the years 1961-65 put at between 230 and 250 million tons per annum, the plan envisaged an investment of some £520 million (at mid-1949 prices) to have any chance of achieving the target. The capital would be used to improve the productivity of existing mines and to seek out new sources of production as the older seams were worked out.

A key component of this exercise involved the increasing use of higher-speed mechanised coal cutters at the coal face as a substitute for less efficient cutters or the uneconomic and rapidly disappearing traditional practice of hewing coal by hand. The physical form of the mineral produced by high speed cutting tended to be much smaller than the standard 'large' form produced by previous methods. Thus the proportion of 'large' coal produced by the NCB was forecast to diminish, leading to possible availability problems in the two main markets, domestic home heating (around 32.5 million tons per year) and fuel for the British Railways steam fleet (14.5 million tons per year).

Coal Quality and Source

Years of experience on Britain's railways had confirmed that the 'medium-large' form displayed by far the best characteristics for steam raising on locomotives. The use of 'small' and inferior quality coal was highly likely to result in the thickening of the firebed through accumulation of ash and clinker which inevitably had a deleterious effect on the ability to raise steam efficiently; on the other hand, too large a size of lump tended to result in the development of an uneven firebed which was similarly inefficient.

Apart from imported coal, open cast and patent fuels, there were some 1,000 types and sizes of coal offered for locomotive use post-World War II; in practice, some 90% of the tonnage used was covered by only around 250 sorts and sizes. Experience indicated that the ideal size for use on a hand fired locomotive was a 4 in cube although 3 in to 6 in cubes were readily usable.

At the time the Standard locomotives were coming into service in the early 1950s, two sizes of coal were regarded as the optimum for hand firing, 5 in x 3 in and 6 in x 3 in. The first dimension in these descriptions was the size of the screen mesh which the coal passed through whilst the second was the screen size over which the fuel passed without falling through the mesh.

The grading of coal used by British Railways at the time is given in Table 1.4. Many of the types were described by names which referred to the colliery of their origin e.g. Blidworth Top Hard (Grade 2B when supplied as 'small cobbles', 5 in x 3 in), Bestwood High Main Screened Large

Table 1.4
BR Grading of Steam Locomotive Coal

Grade		Description
1A	–	for through runs of up to 300 miles.
	–	good size; little 'fines' or dust.
	–	typical calorific value 13,500 B.Th.U./lb.
1B	–	not so good as 1A but an acceptable substitute.
2A	–	for through runs of up to 150 miles.
	–	good size; low level of 'fines' dust.
	–	typical calorific value 12,500 B.Th.U./lb.
2B	–	not so good as 2A but an acceptable substitute.
3A	–	for shunting and trip working.
	–	much 'fines' and small coal present.
	–	relatively high moisture levels.
	–	typical calorific value 11,000 B.Th.U./lb. or less
3B	–	not as good as 3A but usable if nothing better available.
U	–	unwanted coal; sometimes used 'as a last resort'.

Table 1.5
BR Standard Class 9F 2-10-0s: Annual Building Programme

Programme Year (Authorisation Date)	Works	Lot Numbers	Engine Numbers	Total	Delivery Date	Initial Allocated Region
1953 (11.51)	Crewe	E487	92000-07	8	01.54-02.54	Western
			92008-09	2	03.54	London Midland
			92010-14	5	04.54-05.54	Eastern
	Crewe	E491	92015-19	5	09.54-10.54	London Midland
	Crewe	E488	92020-29	10	05.55-07.55	London Midland
1954 (12.52)	Crewe	E489	92030-44	15	11.54-01.55	Eastern
			92045-49	5	02.55-03.55	London Midland
	Crewe	E490	92050-59	10	08.55-10.55	London Midland
			92060-66	7	11.55-12.55	North Eastern
			92067-76	10	12.55-03.56	Eastern
			92077-86	10	03.56-06.56	London Midland
	Swindon	421*	92087-96	10	08.56-04.57	Eastern
1956 (02.55)	Crewe	E493	92097-99	3	06.56-07.56	North Eastern
			92100-34	35	07.56-05.57	London Midland
	Crewe	E494	92135-39	5	06.57	London Midland
			92140-49	10	07.57-10.57	Eastern
			92150-64	15	10.57-04.58	London Midland
			92165-67	3	04.58-05.58	London Midland
			92168-77	10	12.57-03.58	Eastern
	Swindon	422	92178-99	22	09.57-10.58	Eastern
			92200-02	3	11.58-12.58	Eastern
1957 (12.55)	Swindon	429	92203-20	18	04.59-03.60	Western
1958 (09.56)	Crewe	E497	92221-50	30	05.58-12.58	Western

* Order transferred from Crewe, February 1954

Figure 13
LMR-based 92129 (Saltley) is depicted on shed at Eastleigh on 28th July 1962 in company with 92206 (Eastleigh) paired with a different tender type; the line includes WR 28XX 2-8-0 2852 (Swindon), representing a freight design introduced around half a century earlier. Worthy of note is the size and bulk of the 9F design compared with that of the 28XX. A serious proposal was put forward by the WR in 1954 for the building of more of the 28XX class rather than receiving further 9Fs from the Standard programme. *(Courtney Haydon)*

(Grade 3B when supplied as pieces exceeding 6 in) or Markham Main Washed Cubes (Grade 2B as 6 in. x 3 in. cubes). Mixtures of coal sizes were often used by British Railways but unlike on some continental European systems, blends of different types were not supplied to BR as there were apparently no facilities to prepare such mixes on the scale required.

At times of shortage in the post-World War II years, coal had to be imported into the UK. The most serious instance was at the end of 1950 when the country's total coal reserves had reached the alarmingly low level of 12.5 million tons, i.e. just over three weeks stock at the prevailing consumption rate (see Appendix 11); there was also a shortage of coal in the continental European markets experiencing a similar mismatch of supply and demand. The only other available source was the USA from where some 1.2 million tons were purchased by the NCB on the open market during December at a price for 'large coal' of about 10 USD per ton (f.o.b. US East Coast Port). With a USD : GBP exchange rate of 2.8 : 1 and a freight rate of over £3 per ton, the UK landed cost of such material was not far short of £7 per ton compared with the NCB pithead average price of £2 7s 10d (£2.39).

In anticipation of problems, UK export coal business (mainly to Scandinavia and continental Europe) had been delayed or curtailed from the late summer where contract arrangements had allowed; shipments by December 1950 were running at around 600,000 tons, just under half the level of those for the previous January. Similarly to assist further in the conserving of stocks, restrictions were placed on the filling of the bunkers of foreign ships calling at UK ports.

Under these circumstances, there was a clear incentive to use domestic coal as efficiently as possible and so it was that late in 1950, a Government directive required BR to reduce its consumption of 'large' coal by approximately 3.3% amounting to around 9,000 tons per week; in practice, this was achieved, somewhat lamely, by reducing the number of timetabled passenger services on offer.

It was against this background that in early 1951, having decided to go ahead with its new heavy freight class, the 9F 2-10-0, BR began to examine options for increasing the efficiency of the design as a contribution to reducing overall coal demand for its fleet. The potential advantages of the Franco-Crosti boiler system which had been developed in Italy from the mid-1930s were obvious. This system claimed to have achieved significant fuel economies with existing FS (Ferrovie dello Stato) designs after their conversion to the Crosti format.

The Crosti system, described fully in Section 2, was designed to obtain useful work from the large amount of heat inevitably lost through the chimney of an engine equipped with a conventional boiler system. For the 9F this 'unused' energy amounted to a staggering 82% of that nominally available from the burnt fuel as indicated by tests carried out on a new engine in 1954. In the Franco-Crosti system, the hot gases from combustion, before expulsion to the atmosphere, were passed through preheaters to raise boiler feed water temperature almost to boiling point under pressure; the heated water injected into the main boiler thus allowed for a more efficient steam production than if the water entered at ambient temperatures straight from the tender.

The first such boiler design by Ing. Attilio Franco appeared in 1914 but it was not until 1932 that an engine incorporating his system appeared; this was built by the Syndicat Belge des Locomotives at the Tubize Works of the Atèliers Mètallurgique in Belgium. The engine had two main boilers and two preheaters carried on a wheel arrangement of 0-6-2 + 2-4-2-4-2 + 2-6-0; the preheater units were located on separate articulated units; this was known as the Franco boiler arrangement. It would seem that this was essentially an experimental design as it was clearly much too large and

Figure 14
Crosti boiler 92021 heads a southbound coal train towards Sharnbrook summit on the MML on 26th September 1955. On this occasion the smoke from the side chimney is being thrown well clear of the cab without the need for the smoke deflector later installed on all the Crosti 9Fs. *(H. Whitby)*

Figure 15
Crosti boiler 92020 is seen along with another of the class at Crewe Works in May 1955 before delivery to Wellingborough shed. The engine was back at Crewe six months later for the fitting of a smoke deflector to the side chimney in an attempt (partially successful) to reduce the incidence of smoke swirling into the cab under certain weather conditions. *(G. Wheeler)*

Figure 16
92064 (Tyne Dock) enjoys banking assistance as it leaves Consett Low Yard with an afternoon freight for Tyne Yard in 1964.
(P. J. Robinson)

Figure 17
Tyne Dock 9Fs meet at South Pelaw Junction; 92098 returning from Consett to Tyne Dock with a train of empty ore hoppers sails past 92065 plodding in the opposite direction with a load of iron ore for Consett in the summer of 1959.
(A. Burn)

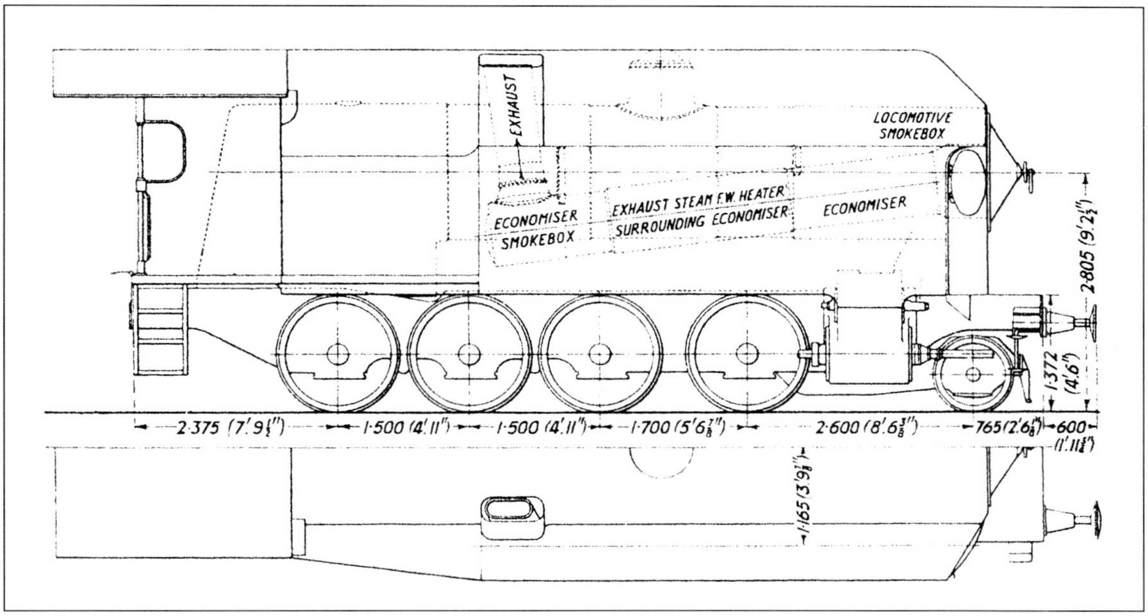

Figure 18
This is a half-plan and elevation of an FS Class 740 2-8-0 as modified to the Franco Crosti system, streamlined and subsequently renumbered into Class 743. (First published in Railway Gazette, 2nd August 1940, p. 116).

powerful to be of practical value on any European railway system. In addition, the need for two firemen absorbed any financial savings accruing from the use of the new boiler system. The engine was reported out of use by 1935.

The next attempt to utilise the concept was the rebuilding of an example of the FS 670 Class 4-6-0 in 1935. This class, originally introduced in 1900 by the Rete Adriatica (RA) railway as the 3701, (later the 500) Class was of a novel 'cab-forward' design (in Italian *'alla rovescia'* or 'back-to-front'). Coal was accessed from relatively small bunkers, (capacity four metric tonnes), situated parallel to the boiler whilst water was carried in the form of a large trailing tank coupled next to the chimney. Some 43 of these engines were built and attracted the sobriquet *'Mucca'* ('Cow') due it was said to the stately motion of the coupled wheels and valve gear at the maximum speed of around 70mph; this unusual design was exhibited at the 'Universal Exposition' in Paris in 1900 and caused considerable comment.

Engine no. 670.030 of the class was rebuilt as with the Belgian locomotive, using the Franco system (preheater located on the trailing unit which also carried the final chimney) and given a streamlined casing; the engine was renumbered as FS Class 672.001. Proving trials accompanied by technical modifications were carried out in comparison with another of the *'Mucca'* class, itself now modified with a Schmidt superheater and renumbered FS 671.026. Compared with the latter, the road tests on the Bologna-Ancona and Bologna-Piacenza routes demonstrated coal economy for the Franco-boilered 672.001 of around 14.5% when working express trains, increasing to 20% when operating on semi-fasts; it was deduced that the streamlining contributed very little to fuel economy below speeds of about 80mph; 672.001 was scrapped in 1948.

After the untimely death of Ing. Franco in 1936 in Persia when working on a railway building assignment, Dott. Ing. Piero Crosti took up the development of the concept. Ing. Crosti had wide experience in the engineering field, initially engaged in the building of dams for hydro-electric schemes in the Alps and later being involved in aircraft engine maintenance and the design of engines for midget submarines.

To reduce the complication of having the preheater located on a trailing unit, Ing Crosti designed the new conversions such that each had two drums mounted on each side of the main boiler; both had smokebox and chimney at the rear end in front of the cab; this arrangement was known as the Franco Crosti system. Five each of the FS 685 Class 2-6-2s (actually 686 Class, as they had acquired Caprotti valve gear) and the 740 Class 2-8-0s were modified becoming 683 Class (1940) and 743 Class (1941) respectively. Both classes were fitted with streamline casings and gave many years' service on local and secondary pasenger services on the Udine-Venezia-Milano routes.

Further conversions occurred during the 1950s. The FS 740 2-8-0 Class, which with 470 units represented the most numerous class on the FS, was again chosen for treatment. Over the period 1942-53, some 94 Class 740s were given Franco Crosti boilers with the twin preheater arrangement parallel to the main boiler; these were renumbered into the 743 Class. Later, from 1954 to 1960, a further 81 Class 740s were also converted but with one single preheater situated centrally under the main boiler and projected forward into the smokebox; these engines were renumbered into a new group, the 741 Class. This new arrangement was known as the Crosti boiler system and was the configuration subsequently adopted for the BR 9Fs which were thus officially referred to as the Crosti boiler engines. It is worth noting that none of the only 2-10-0s operating on the FS system, the 18 units of the 480 Class, built in 1922 mainly for the tourist traffic and heavy freight work on the Bolzano-Brennero Pass route into Austria, was considered for conversion.

The last group of FS engines to be modified were 35 2-6-0s of the FS 625 Class which became the 623 Class. Work was carried out between 1952 and 1954 and reverted to the Franco-Crosti configuration of twin preheaters situated parallel to the main boiler, resulting in an appearance of surpassing ugliness. These engines were not regarded as an unqualified success, the remaining examples in the summer of 1968 being used on local services on the Ravenna-Rimini route. Later, in January 1970, the last two 623s were in store prior to withdrawal. On the same date some 75 FS 741s remained, 19 of which were in store whilst 43 of the remaining 56 FS 743 Class were working. Several engines of

Figure 19
FS Class 623.432 Crosti boiler 2-6-0 pictured at Udine (Friuli-Venezia) is an example of the Franco Crosti principle applied by the Italian State Railways (Ferrovie dello Stato) *(P. Ransome Wallis)*

Figure 20
DB (Deutsche Bundesbahn) Crosti boiler 2-10-0 Series 50. 4019 was equipped with a single preheater centrally below the boiler and a single chimney containing four blast nozzles similar to the the BR Crosti 9F arrangement. *(P. Ransome-Wallis)*

Figure 21
92106 (Kettering) is ready at its home shed for the next turn of duty on 17th August 1957. The engine survived for almost another decade, being withdrawn from Birkenhead in July 1967. 92106 had no less than three visits to Gorton Works for attention in the early 1960s. *(RCTS Collection)*

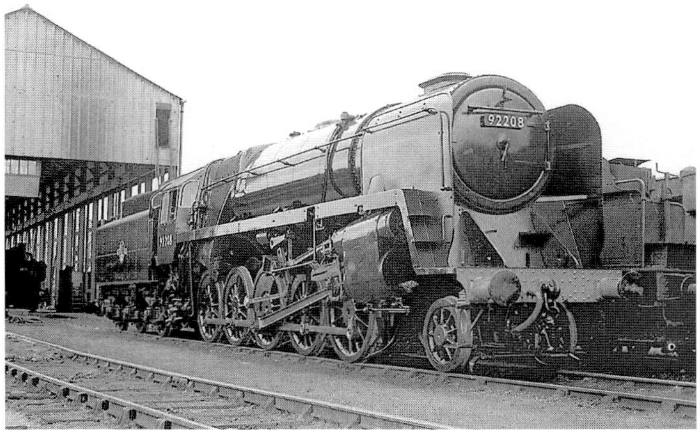

Figure 22
92208 is ex-works at Swindon on 7th June 1959; it was delivered to traffic four days later and operated from Laira MPD until reallocated to Southall in March 1960. 92208 was one of the WR-based 9Fs transferred to the LMR north west area in October 1963 where it later exchanged its BR1G tender for a BR1C type. *(RCTS Collection)*

Figure 23
Saltley-based 92129 is here being serviced at Cricklewood in early 1962. The engine has likely worked in on one of the overnight fitted freights from Birmingham Lawley Street. According to the record 92129, unusually, appears to have spent some three months on Derby Works in early 1961 for what was termed a Light Casual repair, having completed over 107,000 miles. *(RCTS Collection)*

Figure 24
92161 (Newton Heath) is seen in a line at an unidentified location in the early 1960s. Originally a Westhouses engine, 92161 was soon transferred to Newton Heath (June 1958). At the same time, Newton Heath received 92015/6/7 and 92162 also from the LMR Midland Division, the first 9Fs to be allocated to the region's Central Division. 92161 remained at Newton Heath for seven years before moving on to Carlisle Kingmoor (May 1965); withdrawal was in December 1966. *(RCTS Collection)*

these two classes continued operating on both freight and passenger work as late as the mid-1970s on hilly routes in the Alps and the Appennines.

Over the years, attempts were made to interest other railway networks in the Franco-Crosti system and 'one-off' locomotives were built, for example, in Spain, Argentina and Ireland. The only other network to adopt the Crosti system for a significant number of engines was the DB in West Germany when two World War II Kriegslok Class 52 2-10-0s, 52.893 and 52.894 built by Henschel, were converted in 1951 with preheaters situated below the main boiler and renumbered 42.9000 and 42.9001. Later, in 1954, a DB Class 50 2-10-0, 50.1412, was rebuilt with a single preheater along the lines of the FS 741 Class and similar to the BR 9F design. In 1958/9, it was reported that the DB installed the Crosti system in 30 more Class 50 2-10-0s, renumbering them 50.4002-31, the original 1954 conversion taking the number 50.4001; the work was again undertaken by Henschel.

The DB 2-10-0s suffered badly from the corrosive effects of sulphuric acid being deposited in flue gas preheaters and smokebox, a problem which was to be repeated with the BR 9Fs. By the end of 1961, all the DB Crosti 2-10-0 conversions were out of action and only a few were deemed worth returning to service with new boilers and preheaters. One was converted to oil-burning with some success; despite this, the engines were all reported to have been withdrawn by the mid-1960s.

Back in Great Britain in 1951, BR still had a great deal of development work in hand to produce a Crosti design which could be accommodated within the British loading gauge; it should be borne in mind that the BR 9Fs were the first new locomotives to incorporate the system, all others to date being conversions from existing designs. The provision of two preheaters, one on each side of the boiler as in the original FS conversions was not possible owing to loading gauge restrictions. The Crosti boiler with single preheater as used in the FS 741 Class and the DB 50 Class was proposed by the Italians and accepted by BR. This required the provision of a smaller boiler (formerly BR9A then recoded BR12) rather than the BR9 carried by the standard members of the 9F class. Similarly the cylinders and reversing gear arrangement needed to be redesigned and the sandboxes relocated. Begun in early 1953, the project was undertaken with considerable resourcefulness by the Brighton Works staff in conjunction with the Società per Azioni Locomotive a Vapore Franco-Crosti of Milan, in close consultation with Dott. Ing. Piero Crosti. Three separate designs were worked up and discarded before the final parameters of the BR12 boiler were established. The original Brighton design did not have a combustion chamber; also boiler diameter at 5 ft 0³/16 in was just over 5½ in less than the BR12. The two other discarded designs incorporated high superheat arrangements resulting in steam temperatures of over 700°F as opposed to the 669°F adopted for the BR12 (the BR9 boiler carried by the standard 9Fs gave 627°F). Although the original concept had been to make as many parts as possible to be interchangeable with those of the standard 9Fs so that conversion could be effected either way dependent on results in traffic, the Crosti design was so radical that only a limited number of common parts was possible.

After protracted negotiations between BR and the Italians, agreement on royalty payments was reached in March 1953. The precise amounts were to be established by reference to average coal consumption per drawbar horsepower hour for the Crostis compared with figures from a standard 9F tested under identical conditions. Trials were to be conducted at speeds of 20mph, 30mph, 40mph and 50mph at a water feed rate of 16,000 lbs per hour on the Rugby Testing Plant. Maximum royalty payments of £800 per engine would accrue if average savings amounted to 18%; this figure was to be reduced on a pro-rata basis reaching zero if savings dropped below 12%. Discussions had been conducted in French and it is likely that the language problem contributed to a crucial misconception on the part of the Italians who had assumed tests would be conducted with a live steam injector whereas it was normal practice for BR to employ the exhaust steam injector as standard. This misunderstanding inevitably put the Crosti design at a potential savings disadvantage which in practice amounted to some 6%.

It was almost two years from the signing of the agreement that construction work at Crewe began on the Crostis, the first examples appearing in May 1955. Rather than being allocated to the WR as originally planned, all ten of the class were assigned to Wellingborough on the LMR for the Brent coal traffic. The agreed comparison trials of a Crosti against a standard 9F were a disappointment for all concerned as the computed savings in fuel amounted to little more than 7%; full details of the trials are given in Section 11.1.

It was of course anticipated that there would be teething troubles with such an unorthodox design during its first months in service. These problems began to multiply however and quickly became intractable. The result was that by the middle of 1959, the decision was taken to convert all ten of the class to the standard boiler arrangement; performance details of 92020-29 during their time as Crostis are given in Section 11.2.

As anticipated, the appearance of such an unconventional locomotive design on BR tracks caused a great deal of interest for observers. One of the authors well remembers his first sighting of one of these 'beasts'. The impression on a group of fourteen years-old enthusiasts as a brand new example appeared from under the station buildings at Luton Midland Road with the soon-to-be-characteristic thick, black smoke belching from the chimney had to be seen to be believed. It will be appreciated that the 'grapevine' had not prepared them for such a revolutionary departure from traditional design.

1.4 Design Development
Westinghouse Air Pump-fitted Engines
92060-92066, 92097-99

As a result of the successful trials with 92037 on the Tyne Dock-Consett iron ore traffic (see Section 7.1), seven engines, 92060-66, from the 1954 building programme were allocated to the NER for this service. Three more of the class, 92097-99, followed in the next programme and were all allocated to Tyne Dock MPD. The engines were authorised to be fitted with brand new Westinghouse air pumps necessary to operate the hopper doors on the new 56-ton capacity wagons specifically designed for the traffic. The first group, 92060-66, emerged from Crewe towards the end of 1955 but was temporarily allocated to Wellingborough as a replacement for that depot's Crosti allocation, away at Crewe for modification. Accordingly there was a delay of several months before the engines appeared on Tyneside. Whilst operating on the LMR, the engines displayed a conspicuous gap on the fireman's side running board which contained two empty brackets to

Figure 25 '
Westinghouse pump-fitted 92066 (Tyne Dock) climbs from Pelton Level past Tyne Dock MPD with loaded hoppers for Consett on St. George's Day, 23rd April 1960. The engine was loaned to the LMR for a short spell in the first few months of 1956, after which it operated from Tyne Dock until withdrawal in May 1965. *(C. T. Gifford)*

Figure 26
92062 takes water at the closed Consett station after working one of the iron ore trains from the Tyne Dock bunkers to the steelworks on 21st September 1965. The view shows the Westinghouse air pumps carried by 92062 for operating the doors of the hopper wagons. Record cards indicate the engine was fitted with the LNER fire hole door modification in February 1957; AWS was installed in January1960. *(Hugh Ballantyne)*

Figure 27
92060 passes South Pelaw signal box with a Tyne Dock-Consett iron ore train on 20th September 1965. The engine was one of the last of the Tyne Dock allocation to be withdrawn, succumbing just over a year later, the service being handed over to diesel operation in November 1966. *(Hugh Ballantyne)*

Figure 28
92079 was reallocated from Toton to Bromsgrove in May 1956 to take up duty as the Lickey incline 'big engine' banker in place of withdrawn ex-MR 0-10-0 58100 'Big Bertha'. By the time this view was taken (7th July 1956), the 9F had inherited 58100's famous headlamp used by the crew during the hours of darkness for safe approach to the rear of trains requiring assistance. *(Gavin Morrison)*

Figure 29
Lickey banker 9F 92079 (Bromsgrove) assists Stanier Jubilee 4-6-0 45660 *Rooke* (Bristol Barrow Road) as they tackle the incline with the 12-coach 10.30am Bristol-Newcastle express on 1st July 1961. 92079, still with single chimney, had not visited works since January 1960 (Swindon), the shot thus confirming the engine did not carry a double chimney at any time as the programme for the retro-fitting of double chimneys to WR 9Fs ceased at the end of 1960. Note the headlight is no longer in use. *(John Walford)*

accommodate the air pumps; these were duly installed over the period March to May 1956 at Crewe Works before the engines were despatched to the NER. The second group, 92097-99 fitted with the pumps from new, was delivered in June/July 1956.

The two 10 in air pumps, designed to maintain a pressure of 90 lb/sq in worked independently of each other, one to keep the hopper wagon doors closed whilst the other operated the opening mechanism of the doors as and when required; a cylindrical air reservoir was an integral part of the system and was located under the running plate close to the cab on the driver's side. Installed at Tyne Dock was a static standby compressor for use with a loaded train when no engine was available.

The 30 new wagons, mounted on two four-wheel bogies and fitted with continuous vacuum-operated brakes, were built by BR at Shildon Works to the Consett Company's specification and numbered 446000-446029; length over the buffers measured 36 ft 5 in and tare weight was slightly over 29 tons. Twenty seven of the wagons were operated in three sets of nine whilst the remainder were either on standby or undergoing scheduled maintenance in the purposely designed facility at Tyne Dock MPD.

Apart from the continuous vacuum brake pipe, each wagon was fitted with two other sets of pipes for the supply of compressed air to control the operation of the discharge doors, No. 1 to keep the doors closed and No. 2 to control their opening. The wagons had two compartments of nominal capacity 28 tons each both of which were fitted with a power

Figure 30
92079 has almost completed another banking turn as it approaches Blackwell station on 29th June 1957. Clearly visible is the cutaway portion on the tender coal retainer arranged to facilitate coaling at Bromsgrove. *(Gavin Morrison)*

door on either side. The driver controlled the discharging doors from the engine by means of a red-painted valve situated in the cab. The No. 1 position of the operating valve controlled the compressed air flow to the No. 1 pipe, designated the Constant Pressure Pipe, which kept the wagon doors closed via a 14 in stroke cylinder on each wagon; an isolating cock below the valve was kept in the closed position until the discharge doors were due to be opened. With the isolating cock then in the open position and the operating valve in the No. 2 position, compressed air flowed from the No. 1 pipe to the No. 2 pipe causing the doors to be opened via a 16 in stroke cylinder on each wagon simultaneously; a hand operated safety catch had to be released by the guard before the driver could operate the discharge mechanism.

The Tyne Dock 9Fs retained their air pumps until the end. With the exception of 92065, reallocated to Wakefield for its last few months and condemned in April 1967, the Tyne Dock engines were withdrawn between May 1965 and November 1966.

1.5 Design development: Double Chimney: New: 92165-92167, 92178, 92183-92250 Modified: 92000-92002, 92005, 92006

For well over a century after the introduction of the steam locomotive, there were no established and generally accepted criteria for arriving at the optimum dimensions of the chimney or the disposition of the latter in relation to the blastpipe for a given locomotive design. The whole process was something of an art rather than a science, individual design offices of the different railway companies having devised workable formulae by trial and error which provided a rough 'rule of thumb' method for achieving acceptable performance from their motive power.

For good steaming, it is clearly necessary to ensure sufficient air reaches the firebox such that enough coal can be burned to generate the quantity of steam needed for the work rate envisaged. This is of course achieved by exhausting the steam from the cylinders via the chimney thus inducing, or draughting, the flow of combustion products through the boiler from the firebox. To achieve optimum flow and thus maximum steam generation without reducing boiler efficiency by forcing unburned fuel through the boiler is the key objective in the art of draughting.

The major factors having an effect on draughting include:

- the weights of steam and combustion gas flows per unit of time.
- the free gas area through the boiler.
- the flow resistance through the boiler.
- the chimney choke and the blastpipe orifice areas.
- the size and shape of the chimney itself and its relation to the blastpipe cap size and shape.
- the resistance contributed by the firebed itself which is affected by the nature and quality of the fuel used to generate the steam.

Any method for developing the optimum chimney and blastpipe arrangements must take all these elements into account. Typically the initial step is to determine the minimum diameter for the blastpipe cap which is possible once the required maximum rate of steaming has been established. The latter figure may have been ascertained from the known dimensions of an existing boiler or from the proposed design requirements. Having calculated the

Figure 31
Mechanical stoker-fitted 92165 is seen on Saltley shed on 16th June 1962. Within a few weeks, having been displaced from the Birmingham-Carlisle freights by diesels, 92165 would be despatched to Bidston for working the John Summers ore trains. The mechanical stoker device was removed during a visit to Crewe Works at the end of the year. The engine was fitted with AWS apparatus in February 1961 and enjoys also the distinction of an embellished numberplate. *(Courtney Haydon)*

minimum size of the blastpipe cap, a minimum chimney choke diameter and minimum height from cap to choke can then be determined. Taking into account the loading gauge restrictions, the remaining critical dimension is the maximum possible chimney length. Experience has indicated that if this were less than 24 in, it would be unlikely that a singular circular blastpipe could be made to give really good steaming. To optimise the steaming characteristics, it would then be necessary either to compromise on the other dimensions or to consider adopting a double blastpipe and chimney arrangement. In the latter case the minimum blastpipe cap diameter would be smaller, thus allowing for a reduced length chimney whilst still giving excellent steaming characteristics.

The draughting arrangements for all the BR Standard designs benefited from the work carried out by S. O. Ell at Swindon in the late 1940s and early 1950s. The data derived from the research enabled a set of working formulae to be developed. After the design details of the Standard classes had been established, the steaming characteristics of some other classes were put under the spotlight. Considerable success was achieved with a number of designs including some pre-Grouping classes which had not been working at their full potential. Later, in 1956, an investigation was begun into one of the Standard classes which had developed a reputation for 'shy steaming', the Class 4 4-6-0s (75000-79). The obvious area to investigate was the possibility that a double blastpipe and chimney might lead to improvements. The result was the appearance of 75029 in May 1957 fitted with this modification which was subsequently carried by some other class members including all 15 of the original SR allocation.

Attention was then focused on the 9F class, possibly as part of the debate on the proposal to test a Giesl Oblong Ejector and in September 1957, 92178 duly appeared with double blastpipe and chimney in place but without smoke deflectors; it was later confirmed that deflectors would still be beneficial and 92178 was so fitted before entering service. Provisionally allocated to the Eastern Region's (ER) New England depot, 92178 was the subject of tests on the Swindon Test Plant and also controlled road trials on the WR between Stoke Gifford and Reading. These were conducted from November 1957 to February 1958 and details are given in Section 11.1 Performance. In summary, the tests were regarded as demonstrating a useful increase in power output and a saving in coal consumption which was sufficient to justify the fitting of double blastpipe and chimney to all new 9Fs from 92183 onwards. The arrangement was also applied to the three mechanical stoker-fitted variants, 92165-7 which were delivered out of numerical sequence in April/May 1958 (see Section 1.6). It will be noted that 92163/4 originally earmarked for the fitting of stokers (a plan subsequently cancelled) were also delivered out of sequence but did not receive the double exhaust arrangement.

Consideration was given to fitting earlier 9Fs with double chimneys and although the LMR and ER/NER did not undertake such a conversion programme, five WR class members were thus modified; dates of conversion were as follows.

92000: 02.60 92001: 03.60 92002: 11.60.
92005: 04.60 92006: 08.60

The long-time Lickey banker, 92079, was reported as having received a double chimney in early 1960. Although the engine was officially noted undergoing repair in Swindon Works from May 1959 to January 1960, there appears to be neither official confirmation nor photographic evidence to indicate the modification was ever carried out. Views of 92079 operating in July 1961 on the Lickey incline confirm the engine had a single chimney at that time, only a few weeks before the next recorded works visit (Wolverhampton Stafford Road, August 1961) following on from that to Swindon in 1959/60. The conclusion is that 92079 did not carry a double chimney at any time.

1.6 Mechanical Stoker-fitted Engines: 92165-92167

The idea that mechanical stokers might be considered for some of the BR Standard classes dated back to an early stage in their conception. E. S. Cox, the Executive Officer responsible for their design had recently returned from a trip to the USA where a number of railway companies were visited. Mr. Cox had been impressed with much that he had seen there which included the widespread use of mechanical stokers. His initial survey for the design project proposed that provision should be made for such a device in the designs of the larger engines, perhaps to be fitted at some future date.

There were a number of advantages anticipated by the use of mechanical stokers:

- the maximum firing rate sustainable by the average fireman was deemed to be around two tons of coal per hour. In the case of the 9Fs, this equated to some 110 lbs per square foot of grate area per hour. It was calculated that this rate equated to only around 65-70% of the maximum output of the boiler. Although an increase in firing rate would cause a significant drop in boiler efficiency by pulling through appreciable quantities of unburned coal 'fines', either present already or produced by the grinding action of the screws, the increased rate would result in the generation of around 25% more steam per hour.
- future supplies of coal could be of lower quality than currently then available. These would not only have lower calorific value but would also have a higher percentage of ash and other impurities. It would thus be necessary to transfer more coal from the tender to the firebox for a given amount of steam production, making the fireman's job even more arduous.
- the increased firing capacity of the stoker would enable speeds or loads to be increased with a resulting improvement in ton-miles per train-hour.
- the absence of fatigue in the fireman plus the reduced time

Figure 32
This 16th June 1962 view shows the inside of the cab of mechanical stoker-fitted 92165 (Saltley) with the coal feed pipe and firebox doors prominent. The firebox coal jet placement controls are seen in the top right hand corner. The cramped nature of the crew's working area can be appreciated.
(Courtney Haydon)

Figure 33
Crewe Works, 16th April 1958, with Berkley mechanical stoker-fitted 92165, soon to be allocated to Saltley. The view shows the riser conduit (complete with conveyor screw) which extends upward through the footplate to the firebox.
(W. T. Stubbs)

required for fire cleaning resulting from maximum use by the stoker of the whole grate area would enable longer runs to be made and help towards the aim of increased availability.

- the use of a mechanical stoker would enable a lighter and more uniform firebed to be carried. This in turn would allow a softer draught to be used with consequent reduction in back pressure giving improved cylinder performance.
- experience has also indicated that the ability on the stoker-fired engines to keep the fire hole door closed produced a more constant firebox temperature which was reflected in lowered boiler maintenance costs; the formation of less clinker also reduced the cost of grate repairs.

During 1949/50, results became available from tests with the former Southern Railway Merchant Navy Pacific, 35005 *Canadian Pacific,* which had been experimentally fitted with a Berkley mechanical stoker in March 1948. Even though the Pacific had 48½ square feet of grate area, it was concluded that under the normal conditions of operation, no difficulty was experienced in providing the maximum supply of steam required. Further, with typical grades of coal then in use for express passenger engine work, the mechanical stoker was less efficient than hand firing although, as anticipated, the difference was less when using inferior quality fuel.

During September 1956, with just over 100 9Fs in service and another 150 or so either being built or on order, consideration again turned to the provision of mechanical stokers for several of the class. One option was to convert up to ten existing examples as they passed through works for general overhaul, the first of which would be due by 1959 at the latest. Large-scale modifications were required however. The engines needed a different firebox backplate with repitched water stays, a support bracket on the foundation ring and a modification of the cab carrying frame. The coal bunker and access doors on the tender would need to be modified with provision for the trough roller greasing points; additionally, water capacity was reduced to accommodate the space required by the stoker components. In view of all this, it was considered more practical to incorporate the stoker device into some of the new engines still being built.

In May 1957 authorisation was given to build five mechanical stoker-fitted engines, 92163-7 at Crewe Works; within a very short period however, the number was reduced to three, 92165-7 and the latter finally appeared in April/May 1958. There remained the option of fitting mechanical stokers to other class members, dependent on satisfactory results in service.

Allocated to Saltley, 92165-7 were rostered for two fitted freight workings each way between Birmingham and Carlisle. The 230-mile route was via Sheffield, Leeds and then over the Pennines at Ais Gill summit involving a sustained climb at 1 in 100 for some 15 miles from Settle Junction to Blea Moor tunnel. The services were the 3.50am and 4.45pm from Water Orton (a through freight to Glasgow College) and the 4.03pm and 11.15pm returns from Carlisle. These freights had been handled for some years by the best of Saltley's Stanier Class 5 4-6-0s which had been limited to 43 wagons on a class 'D' timing. The new 9Fs allowed the limit to be raised to 50 wagons for class 'C' schedules (up to 42mph) and 55 wagons for class 'D'. The trio was also used on other, much shorter trips. Ideal was the out-and-home-in-a-day run to Oxford. For these short runs, there was no need to re-coal before returning to Saltley, thus reducing the risk of wrong-size fuel pieces being added to the tender. Coaling was by elevator; the tender was not filled under the main Saltley coal hopper.

It is not clear why the relatively undeveloped and somewhat complicated Berkley Mechanical Stoker was chosen over the fully evolved and widely established American Standard Stoker, already manufactured under licence in Great Britain by a subsidiary of Beyer Peacock & Co. BR's examination of the Beyer Peacock stoker showed it gave comparable results to the Berkley device. Presumably the contacts made during the experience with the Merchant Navy 35005 swayed the decision to go for the Berkley stoker; cost may also have been a factor.

The Berkley Mechanical Stoker included a number of novel features which had proved successful in operation in other countries. Total cost of the stoker and conversion was £2,400 per engine; the equipment weighed 1.9 tons, much of which was concentrated on the middle and rear pairs of coupled wheels (see Diagram D).

The device as fitted to the 9Fs was of the steam jet type consisting of four main units, i.e. the engine or power unit, tender conveyor unit, intermediate conduit and riser conduit; details are shown in Figure A. The engine which was mounted on the tender front dragbox, provided the necessary power under all conditions to supply coal to the firebox, and could be throttled down to furnish the coal as sparingly or continuously as required. It could be worked in reverse should the stoker mechanism become jammed or blocked.

The tender conveyor unit consisted of a trough, conveyor screw, crusher and gearbox. The trough was located below the coal bunker and mounted on rollers to take account of the movement between engine and tender. The power from the engine unit was transmitted to the gearbox, mounted at the rear of the conveyor unit, by a slip shaft with universal joints. The gearbox transmitted motion to the conveyor screw which carried coal from the bunker through the crusher, where it was broken down to the correct size and then fed into the intermediate conduit. The latter included a conveyor screw enclosed in a conduit or casing, which was connected to the riser by a special ball joint.

The riser conduit, which extended upward through the footplate and was secured to the back of the firebox, included another conveyor screw which was connected to the intermediate screw by a universal joint. The reverse flight of the screw at the extreme end resulted in the coal being levelled down and spread out before delivery into the firebox, thus ensuring uniform delivery of coal over the distributor plate fitted above the hooded jet plate and located at the underside of the firehole.

The jet plate was fitted in the lower portion of the mouth of the riser conduit and means were provided for easy adjustment to the correct firing angularity. The front of the jet plate had hoods above the jet orifices which allowed divergence of the steam jet before meeting the coal, thus ensuring efficient distribution over the grate. The jet plate was divided into four compartments, each controlled by a separate valve located in the jet manifold and marked to indicate which section of jets the valve controlled; Left Front, Right Front, Left Back, Right Back. Pressure gauges were located on a panel in the cab. In the right hand and left hand gauges, the black hand indicated jet pressure for the back corners and the red hand indicated jet pressure for the front of the firebox. The centre gauge showed the stoker engine pressure. The jet

FIGURE A
FEATURES OF THE BERKLEY MECHANICAL STOKER

FEATURES OF THE BERKLEY STOKER

Run-of-Mine Coal

The Berkley Stoker takes the hardest run-of-mine coal and crushes it to the proper size without powdering the coal.

Wet or Dry Slack Coal

The Berkley Stoker will handle slack coal, wet or dry.

Cab Room

The Berkley Stoker occupies a minimum amount of space in the cab, having only a riser conduit below the firedoor opening. The stoker control valve, manifold, gauge panel and stoker engine reverse lever are conveniently located in the cab.

Grate Area

The Berkley Stoker does not take up any grate area.

Fire Door

The fire door is in no way obstructed by the Berkley Stoker. It can be used the same as before the stoker was applied. The doors are equipped with *peep holes* permitting observation of the fire without opening doors and causing sudden cooling of the fire, loss of steam and damage to the tubes and firebox sheets.

Lack of Noise

The Berkley Stoker, because of its design and construction, makes *no noise.*

Compactness

The stoker engine is small and compact taking up a minimum amount of space and weighing only 590 lbs. and can be located on locomotive, on tender or rear of the gear box.

Top Deflector

The top deflector of the Berkley Stoker is an effective feature in distributing coal to the back corners of the firebox and in deflecting a large amount of fine coal into the firebed, which would otherwise be lost through the stack. It may be adjusted at the terminal or roundhouse to the position found most effective to perform its function of fine coal deflector and draft shield.

Driving Mechanism

The stoker engine crank case, cylinders and cylindrically shaped crosshead guides are cast integrally, insuring correct alignment throughout the life of the engine. All wearing surfaces are protected by renewable bushings. Its balance is such that there is no vibration throughout its speed range. It is supported on a three point sub-base which insures against strain in the engine base. The engine is thoroughly lubricated by an efficient splash system and requires only *nine quarts* of oil to fill it. Leakage is guarded against by oil seals.

Long Life and Low Maintenance Cost

The Berkley Stoker is *simple* in *design* with all wearing parts made of special steel; the gears are heat treated, properly lubricated and sealed with oil seals, which insure long life with a minimum of maintenance.

The manufacturer's claims for the Berkley stoker.

BERKLEY STOKER ARRANGEMENT AND LUBRICATION

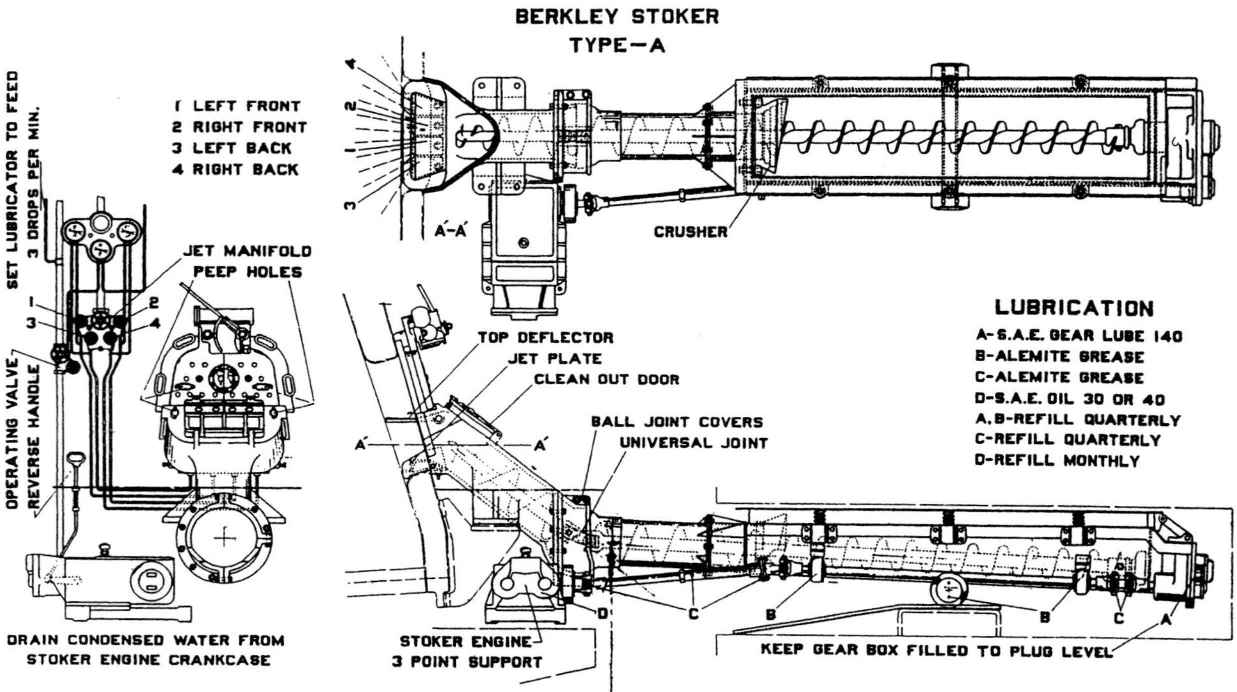

CAN BE LOCATED ON LOCOMOTIVE, TENDER OR REAR OF GEAR BOX

Figure 34
Giesl Oblong Ejector-fitted 92250 rests at its home shed of Severn Tunnel Junction on 2nd August 1964. The engine retained the ejector device through to withdrawal at the end of 1964.
(RCTS Collection)

casting was protected from the heat of the fire by an apron held in place by a removeable pin.

With this form of stoker, it was possible to adjust independently the coal feed and the steam jet pressure and thus obtain an even distribution of coal in the firebox under all conditions. The locomotive could be fired, with difficulty, by hand through the highly pitched butterfly door should the stoker mechanism fail or when it was necessary to correct the firebed after removal of clinker. Hand firing might also be necessary when working on comparatively short journeys where time would be insufficient to allow correct setting of the coal feed and jet pressures of the stoker.

For trouble-free performance on the road, the stoker needed to be supplied with coal in the appropriate physical form. If the pieces were too large, the mechanism tended to jam and it was not always easy to clear the blockage despite repeated reversal of the screw. On the other hand if the pieces were too small or dusty, the coal blown into the firebox by the steam jets ended up passing through unburned or piling up against the brick arch where it fused into a semi-solid intractable mass. Screened nuts or cobbles made the best fuel for the purpose but were not always available. To convert standard motive power depot coal into a suitable physical form frequently required two enginemen some two and a half hours to break up enough material for the 230 mile Birmingham-Carlisle run, a distinctly tedious and unproductive activity. Even with such preparation, there were many instances of blockage in the delivery system in service. A particularly harrowing incident is recorded in Mr. T. E. Essery's book **Firing Days at Saltley** where one of the mechanical stoker engines was hand-fired for most of a northbound journey following a major screw blockage.

For these reasons in the summer of 1961, BR took the decision in principle to terminate the mechanical stoker experiment. Towards the end of the year, all three engines were noted lifeless on Saltley depot, their Carlisle freight turns in the process of being taken over by BR/Sulzer Peak Type 4 diesels. There was a late reprieve in May 1962 for 92167 however when it went to Tyne Dock for trial on the Consett iron ore trains. No Westinghouse air pump equipment was fitted so the engine was mainly involved in banking duties from South Pelaw Junction to South Medomsley. It was reported that the exhaust from 92167 when ascending the incline was spectacular even by Tyne Dock-Consett standards. In June/July 1962, 92165/6 with stokers still in place were transferred to Bidston to work on the Shotton ore trains; 92167 was also allocated there by the end of the year. All three engines passed through Crewe Works (November 1962 to January 1963) for what was designated Light Casual repair, at which stage the mechanical stokers were removed.

Details of testing and performance of the stoker-fitted 9Fs are given in Section 11.1 Performance.

1.7 Giesl Oblong Ejector: 92250

As noted in Section 1.5, Double Chimney, the proper scientific study of blastpipe and chimney design with the aim of improving draughting and thermal efficiency came rather late in the life of the steam locomotive. Successful developments included the Kylchap double draughting arrangement and the Lemaître multiple-jet blastpipe with large diameter chimney as fitted to some Southern Railway classes. The guiding principle was the multiplication of the blast cones by increasing their surface area in order to achieve a lower cut-off percentage for a given amount of work. This lowers the terminal exhaust pressure at the chimney whilst retaining an adequate draught and hence providing a useful saving in fuel costs.

The last significant development in this process was the Giesl Oblong Ejector, a blastpipe and chimney configuration, devised by Dr. Adolph Giesl-Gieslingen of the Vienna Technical University in collaboration with the OBB (Austrian Federal Railways) and the Schoeller-Bleckmann Steel Company of Vienna which manufactured and offered the Giesl ejector as a prefabricated unit.

The essence of the development was the provision of a blastpipe and chimney each having a narrow, oblong configuration. The blastpipe tapered up to the narrow slot where, instead of either an ordinary single or double jet, the

Figure 35
On 1st August 1964, 92130 (Carlisle Kingmoor) heads north over Beattock summit with a Class 'D' fitted freight from Carlisle. Kingmoor 9Fs worked into Scotland on a regular basis until steam was officially banned from the Scottish Region in August 1967. Even then, the odd 9F appearance was made in the Motherwell area as late as November of that year. *(Courtney Haydon)*

steam passed through a number of ovoid orifices (usually seven), arranged in a fan-like configuration, the size of which could be altered by adjusting two steel strips. The resulting seven steam jets diverged from the base to fill a long chimney outlet area which tapered outward toward the top.

The theoretical basis for the device was what Dr. Giesl-G. termed the 'True Ejector', i.e. an ejector in its most efficient form, containing a mixing and a diffusing cone with a type of choke between them. Early investigation by the inventor focused on comparing two different blastpipe and chimney configurations representing opposite ends of the spectrum. These are displayed in Figure B, published earlier in *The Locomotive*, August 1956, p.145. In one case, designated Style I and popular in North America, the blastpipe nozzle was located within the entrance to the cylindrical lower part of the chimney. Here the chimney is of sufficient length so as to achieve a rapid, virtually complete mixture of steam and gas. In Style II, the chimney entrance was placed high above the blastpipe nozzle, as favoured by continental European practice so that the mixing of steam and gas is virtually complete before entering the chimney.

The main aspect of the study was to calculate how much of the initial energy in the steam as it exhausted from the nozzle was lost by 'shock' occurring as the slower moving combustion gases struck the steam. Until the steam and gases were thoroughly mixed, the flow of the combined stream was inevitably impeded by turbulence. Results shown in the graph in Figure B indicate that Style I is much better in this respect, with a shock loss of some 20% or less; the Style II configuration cannot achieve a shock loss of much below 70%, reaching a minimum of 66% when the ratio of gas to steam weight is only 2:1; experience had indicated that the latter figure is close to the absolute minimum for good combustion in an efficient boiler. Style 1 is virtually independent of the gas to steam ratio.

A further advantage for Style I is also apparent from the graph. By introducing intermediate nozzles between the single exhaust nozzle and the chimney, still lower shock losses can be achieved on condition that each of the configurations is long enough to allow rapid and complete mixture of each steam jet and that part of the gas stream associated with it. Further experimentation showed that the increased height required, taking into account the greater wall friction resulting from the faster flow, made an intermediate nozzle advantageous only if equipped for spreading the steam and gas mixture so as to fill a chimney which tapered out to a much greater degree than usual; this was necessary to avoid an undesirable reduction in flow area within the chimney. Additional tests indicated that the inlet level of the chimney should be placed slightly above the outlet of the exhaust nozzle to achieve optimum results; the ensuing gap also allowed easier access for clearing the nozzle of carbon deposit.

In Style I, as the graph in Figure B displays, the combined mixture of steam and gases has to flow at a high velocity if a

FIGURE B
GIESL OBLONG EJECTOR DEVELOPMENT:
COMPARISON OF TWO STYLES OF BLASTPIPE AND CHIMNEY ARRANGEMENT

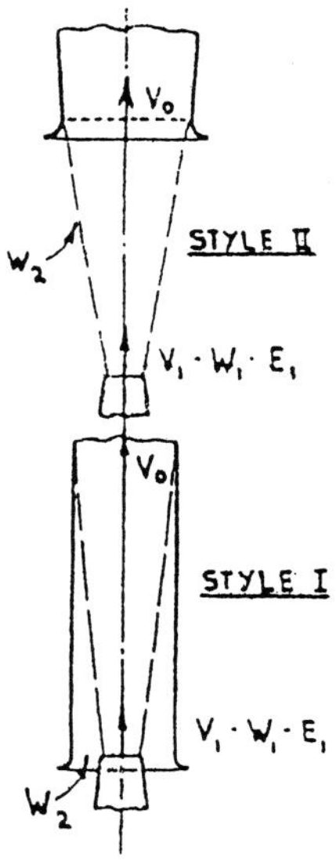

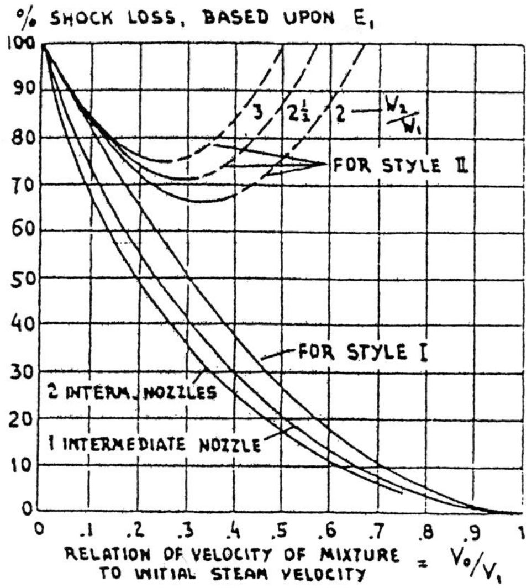

Fig. 1. Calculated Shock Loss During the Entrainment Process Definition of Terms

W_1 Weight of Nozzle Steam, lb/sec.
W_2 Weight of Smokebox Gas, lb/sec.
V_1 Velocity of Nozzle Steam, ft/sec.
V_0 Velocity of Mixture ft/sec.
E_1 Kinetic Energy in Nozzle Steam. ft.lb/sec.

Fig. 2. Extreme styles of exhaust arrangements:

Style 1: the mixing of gas and steam takes place within a chimney portion of constant cross-sectional area

Style II: The steam mixes with the gas within the smokebox; the mixing process is virtually completed when steam and gas enter the chimney.

Giesel Oblong Ejector Development

Diagram of Blast Nozzles, Chimney and Damper in Longitudinal Section of Locomotive Smokebox Fitted with Giesl Ejector

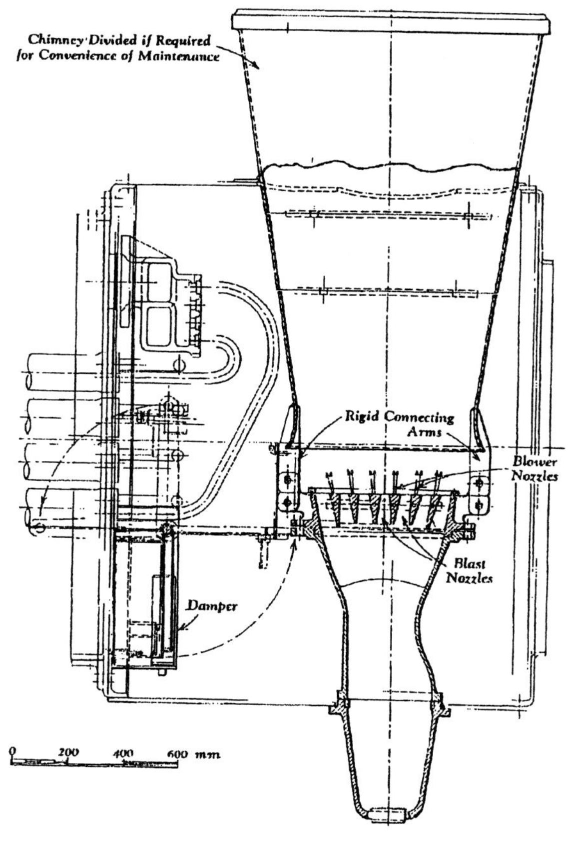

FIGURE C
COMPARISON OF BLASTPIPE ARRANGEMENT FOR DOUBLE CHIMNEY 9F 92178 AND GIESL OBLONG EJECTOR 92250

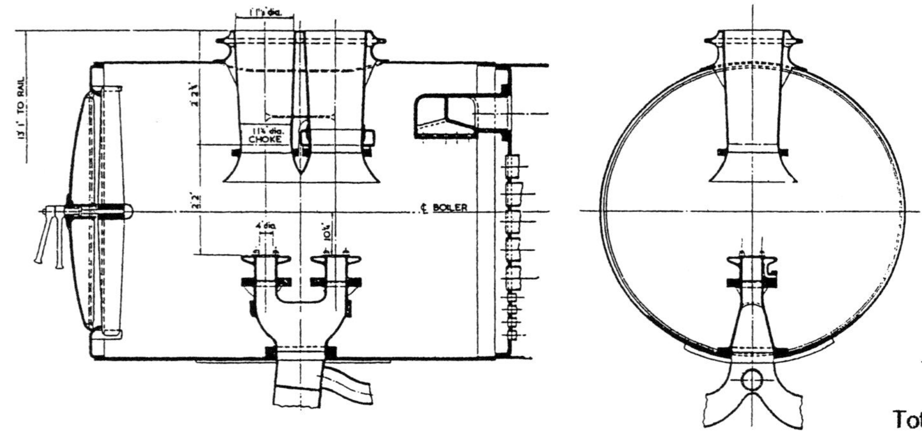

Total Nozzle Area: 25.1 sq. in.
Total Choke Area: 199 sq. in.
Total Chimney Top Area: 271 sq.

Double Blastpipe and Chimney Draught Arrangement

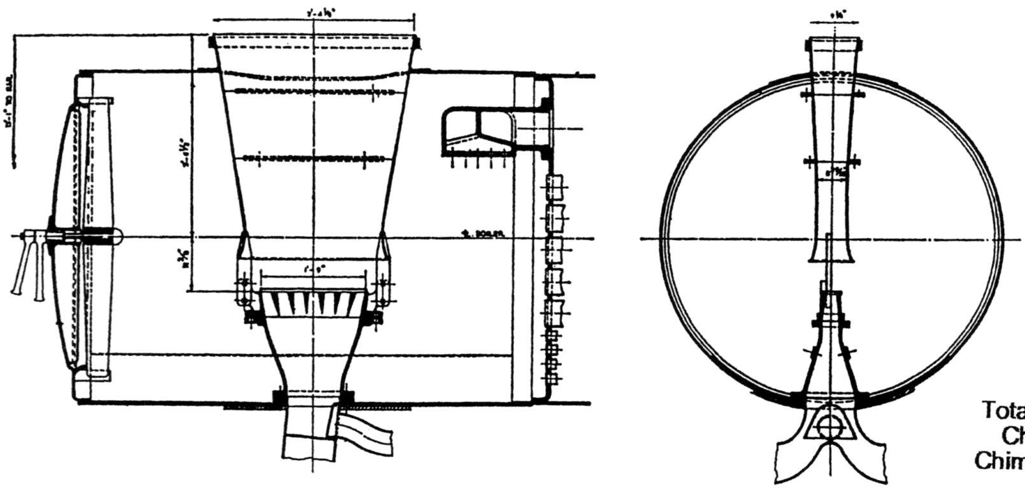

Total Nozzle Area: 302 sq. in.
Choke Area: 150.5 sq. in.
Chimney Top Area: 370 sq. in

Giesl Oblong Ejector Draught Arrangement

low shock loss is to be obtained. However, for high overall efficiency, the energy loss on exit from the chimney must be moderate so as not to increase back pressure. In practice, the velocity of the steam/gas mix must be brought down to one half or less in the type of effective diffuser as represented by the diverging portion of the chimney. To achieve an acceptable exit velocity for the mix, such a chimney would have to be of a considerable height, breaching the loading gauge by a wide margin.

Theoretically, to reduce the height requirement, the logical step would be to employ a multiplicity of narrow chimneys each with its own exhaust nozzle. In this way the advantages of the reduction in shock loss at the mixing stage of the steam and gases could be retained without losing the benefit of the minimal effect on back pressure afforded by an acceptable chimney exit loss. The individual chimneys could then be arranged in a fan-like configuration put close together such that their adjacent walls would intersect. In practice, these intersecting walls were omitted and the individual chimneys were merged into a single one of elongated cross-section whilst retaining the multiple blastpipe jets. In this way, the distinctive shape of the Giesl Oblong Ejector evolved, see Figure B. The lower diagram here shows a longitudinal section of a locomotive smokebox fitted with a typical ejector and was first published in *Engineering,* Vol. 187, 17th April 1959, p.510.

A comparison between the Standard 9F double chimney layout and that of the Giesl ejector is given in Figure C which also includes technical details of nozzle, choke and chimney top areas. A key feature of the ejector assembly was the substantial connecting arm arrangement between the blastpipe nozzle and the chimney. This made for a very precise and enduring alignment, a point not always appreciated as critical in conventional draughting arrangements and a more than likely reason why locomotives of the same class sometimes had very different steaming characteristics in service. For accessibility and ease of maintenance in the smokebox area, the chimney was divided into two or three parts for speedy dismantling and reassembly.

In its simplest form, the Giesl Ejector was intended for replacing the conventional blastpipe and chimney on both new and existing locomotives, conversion of an existing boiler front end being a relatively simple matter; experience had indicated that there was no sign of wear even after 300,000 miles of running.

Also developed along with the ejector was a modification which enhanced its performance; this was known as the Giesl-Altmann Superheater Booster. It was a feature of modern boilers that they were designed for low gas-flow resistance. The low back pressure resulting from the use of the Giesl Ejector enabled a selective throttling of the boiler tubes to improve the gas flow to the superheater and thus raise the overall efficiency of the locomotive. The consequent resistance to the gas flow through the boiler barrel was readily compensated for by the ejector's high pumping efficiency. The smoke tubes below the superheater were throttled by a damper which was left closed during operation of the locomotive; the upper tubes were restricted individually, either by means of heat resisting rings fitted inside them at the firebox end or by suitable throttling devices at the smokebox end. This move made it possible to control the gas flow through the firebox and boiler and hence the amount of heat transmitted to the superheater elements, allowing for extra fuel savings typically of the order of 10-15% and additional superheat of between 10 degrees and 65 degrees Celsius.

In summary, the benefits claimed for the Giesl Oblong Ejector were:

1. greater mechanical simplicity than a conventional front end and easier maintenance.
2. optimum combustion and minimum back pressure resulting in fuel economy, increased power and minimum exhaust noise and smoke.
3. minimum wear to chimney because of perfectly centred flow.
4. accessibility of all boiler tubes for cleaning from smokebox end resulting from less space taken up by narrow chimney.
5. incorporation of effective spark arresters may be possible as required without affecting the engines' steaming performance.

Tests in Austria and on the German Federal Railway had shown that for a given draught through the boiler smokebox tubes, the Giesl Ejector achieved a reduction in back pressure of 75% as compared with the best orthodox chimney and blast nozzle arrangement. In the event, trials with 9F 92250 at Rugby Testing Station in 1959 fitted with a Giesl Ejector were a considerable disappointment, showing only a marginal increase in efficiency compared with the same engine tested whilst fitted with double blastpipe and chimney; details are given in Section 11.1.

2. Dimensions and Data

2.1 Standard: 92000-92019, 92030-92250

The parent office for the design of the Class 9Fs was Brighton with certain sections being designed at Derby, Doncaster and Swindon. Various features and details of the design were common with those of the other British Railways Standard types. Principal dimensions and axle loads are given in Diagrams A1 to A4 which reproduce BR Standard Drawing Nos. SL/9R/1 illustrating a 9F attached to a BR1G tender (A1), SL/9R/3 with BR1F tender (A2), SL/9R/4 BR1C tender (A3) and SL/9R/5 BR1B tender (A4); other data are listed in Tables 2.1 and 2.2.

Boiler

The boiler was similar in many respects to the wide firebox types fitted to the Britannia Class 7 and Clan Class 6 Pacifics. Full details are given in Table 2.1 and Section 3.

Regulator

The decision was taken at an early stage in the design of the 9Fs to dispense with the heavy and expensive Melesco multivalve smokebox regulator used on the Pacific classes. This had been considered desirable for the 4-6-2s in an effort to reduce the tendency of this wheel arrangement type to slip on starting away. The standard 9F had an Adhesion Factor of 4.38 compared with the lower figures of 4.23 for the Class 7 Britannia Pacifics and 3.78 for the solitary Class 8, 71000 *Duke of Gloucester* ; in contrast the Class 6 Clan Pacific figure at 4.63 was higher than that of the 9F. As a further comparison, 4.22 was the figure for the proposed and rejected Class 8 2-8-2 referred to in Section 1.1. Adhesion Factor is the ratio of the total weight on an engine's coupled wheels to its tractive effort, both measurements in lbs. The greater the value of this factor then the more sure-footed the engine should be on starting. The 4-6-0 design was regarded as particularly reliable in this respect and the Class 5 version of this type in the Standards series had an Adhesion Factor of 4.97.

The alternative choice of regulator for the 9Fs was the sliding grid type, with both the main and pilot valves sited horizontally to enable the steam inlet to be placed as high as possible above the water level in the very squat dome. This was necessary as, due to the high pitch of the boiler, the dome had to be of minimal height for clearance reasons. The regulator rod from the cab was on the outside of the boiler on the driver's side and was divided into two lengths at a central rocking lever situated on the side of the firebox which compensated for relative thermal expansion. This was in contrast to that on the BR Standard Pacifics where the rocking lever for the smokebox regulator was sited on the boiler. The regulator operating gear entered the boiler transversely, passing through a stuffing box on the side of the barrel. The sliding grid regulator type did however lead to early problems in service and was subsequently modified, see Section 9.

Firebox

The firebox, positioned above the 5 ft diameter coupled wheels, was necessarily limited in its depth in order for the engine to comply with the loading gauge; it was hence more shallow than those designed for the BR Standard Pacifics whose trailing wheels were only 3 ft 3½ in diameter. The firebox was of the Belpaire type, 7 ft 5½ in long at the bottom with a maximum outside width of 7 ft 0⅛ in giving a grate area of 40.2 sq ft. The outer steel plate was ½ in thick and the wrapper plate of the copper inner firebox was ⅝ in thick. The throat plate was of the sloping pattern with combustion chamber provided, while the backplate also sloped.

All the firebox water space stays, except those in the rows nearest to both the firebox back plate and throat and tube

Figure 36
92211 is under assembly in Swindon Works 'A' Shop on 26th July 1959; it was delivered to Old Oak Common in September 1959. Record cards indicate there were no more visits to Swindon Works, Light Intermediate overhauls being carried out at Crewe. 92211 was withdrawn in May 1967 from Wakefield shed. *(Philip J. Kelley)*

Table 2.1
BR Standard Class 9F 2-10-0s: Boiler Dimensions and Proportions Comparison with BR Standard Pacifics

Class			70000	92000	92000 ¶	72000	71000
Boiler Dimensions							
BR Designation			BR1	BR9	BR9	BR2	BR13
Boiler Barrel Outside Diameter		max.	6' 5½"	6' 1"	6' 1"	6' 1"	6' 5½"
		min.	5' 9"	5' 9"	5' 9"	5' 4"	5' 9"
Firebox Outside		length	7' 0½"	7' 5½"	7' 5½"	6' 9"	8' 0⅛"
		max. width	7' 9"	7' 0⅛"	7' 0⅛"	7' 0"	7' 9"
Tubes small		outside diameter	2⅛"	2"	2"	2⅛"	2⅛"
		number	136	138	138	108	136
large		outside diameter	5½"	5¼"	5¼"	5½"	5½"
		number	40	35	35	35	40
Superheater Elements		outside diameter	1⅜"	1⅜"	1⅜"	1⅜"	1⅜"
Length between tubeplates			17' 0"	15' 3"	15' 3"	17' 0"	17' 0"
Heating Surface	Tubes	sq. ft.	2,264	1,836	1,836	1,878	2,264
	Firebox	sq. ft.	210	179	179	195	226
	Total	sq. ft.	2,474	2,015	2,015	2,073	2,490
	Superheater	sq. ft.	677	535	535	592	691
Grate Area		sq. ft.	42.0	40.2	40.2	36.0	48.6
Working Pressure		p.s.i.	250	250	250	225	250
Firebox Volume		cu. ft.	273	213	213	248	296
Water Surface at half-glass		sq. ft.	122	115	115	115	127
Volume of Steam above half-glass		cu. ft.	148	109	109	146	153
Boiler Proportions							
Free area through Tubes	large	sq. ft.	4.13	3.10	3.10	3.62	4.13
	small	sq. ft.	2.66	2.35	2.35	2.11	2.66
	Total	sq. ft.	6.79	5.49	5.49	5.73	6.79
Area through large Tubes as % of Total			60.9	56.9	56.9	63.2	60.9
Total free area as % of Grate Area			16.2	13.7	13.7	15.9	14.0
Area /Surface ratio		large tubes	1/420	1/447	1/447	1/420	1/420
		small tubes	1/435	1/415	1/415	1/435	1/435
Steam pipe in boiler		Bore	7"	7"	7"	7"	7"
	Cross sectional area	sq. in.	38.5	38.5	38.5	38.5	38.5
Regulator Full Open	Area	sq. in.	48.8★	22.2†	22.2†	37.0★	52.9★
Superheater Elements	Total area	sq. in.	39.3	32.5	32.5	34.4	37.2
Steam Pipes to cylinders	Total area	sq. in.	56.5	56.5	56.5	56.5	84.8 (3)
Blast pipe cap	Diameter		5⅜"	5¼" ††	4" (2) ø	5¼"	4" (2)
	Area	sq. in.	22.7	22.7	12.6 (2)	21.6	12.6 (2)
Chimney Throat	Diameter		1' 3⅝"	1' 3¼"	1' 0" (2)	1' 3⅝"	1' 0" (2)
	Area	sq. ft.	1.29	1.27	0.69 (2)	1.29	0.78 (2)
Throat area as % of Grate area			3.09	3.16	3.43	3.57	3.22
Height between blast pipe cap and chimney throat			2' 10¾"	2' 4⅞"	2' 2"	3' 0½"	2' 6⅛"
Taper of chimney			1 in 14	1 in 14	1 in 14.3	1 in 14	1 in 13.9

¶ Double Blastpipe and Chimney ★ Multiple valve regulator † As modified †† As modified: originally 5⅜"
ø For Mechanical stoker-fitted engines, figure is 3⅞"

plates were of Monel metal, fitted with steel nuts inside the firebox. Monel metal is a corrosion resistant alloy containing copper and nickel available in a number of ratios, typically 40:60, together with smaller quantities of metals such as iron, manganese and aluminium added to the alloy to confer enhanced anti-corrosion performance. Stays in the extreme rows were made of copper and riveted in order to facilitate caulking of the joints between the plates; the roof, longitudinal and transverse stays were of steel. On the first 20 engines, the lagging of both the firebox and the boiler consisted of fibreglass mattresses, chosen for their lower cost and weight compared with the standard asbestos types then on offer. Previous experience on the SR's Merchant Navy Pacifics however had indicated that fibreglass was not as durable as asbestos in this application and when a more lightweight form of the latter at a cost comparable to that of the fibreglass became available, it was used on subsequent batches of 9Fs including the Crosti boiler variants.

Grate and Ashpan

The rear half of the grate was horizontal with the front portion sloping. The grate had twelve rocking sections, each fitted with twelve grid type fire-bars, which were divided longitudinally so that the six right-hand and six left-hand sections could be manipulated together independently of the sections on the other side. The gear at the footplate was so arranged that full travel could be used for dropping the fire when standing over a pit; a limited movement of the rocking sections could also be made to break up clinker and eliminate ash whilst running.

For the self-emptying ashpan, which again was limited in its allowable depth because of its siting over the trailing pair of coupled wheels, the sides were designed in such a way as to give the steepest possible angle from the outside edges of the wide firebox to the central hopper portion between the frames to assist clearance of the ash. In practice, the angle proved not to be steep enough however and led to accumulation of ash at the sides of the pan, resulting in the air spaces between the firebars regularly becoming clogged. Later, small side doors were adopted at the front and back of the pan to allow the ash to be raked clear; care was needed in this operation to prevent dust and ash contaminating the adjacent side rod bearings. Photographic evidence indicates the ashpan door modification was introduced from 92087 onwards with earlier engines being modified as they passed through works for general overhaul; the 9Fs were often noted operating with these ashpan doors open.

Two hopper doors were provided at the base of the ashpan between the frames. Front and rear damper doors were fitted to regulate the air flow to the grate; the full open area was two square feet at each end. These doors were controlled by handwheels in the cab which operated screwed spindles. Operation of the hopper doors, which could only occur with the engine stationary, was carried out at ground level using a removable key which also served for working the rocking grate.

On the forward lower corner of both cabsides was a hinged flap used for allowing access to a washout plug situated in the bottom corner of the firebox. This regularly became jammed with coal dust and other adventitious material and was very often observed in the partially open position during running. In the early 1960s at least five engines (Doncaster-based 92171/5/6/90, 92201) had the flap replaced by a sliding plate arrangement, presumably in an attempt to reduce draughtiness in the cab when operating GN line fast fitted freights.

Superheater

The superheater had 35 ball-joint type elements 1⅜ in outside diameter and 9 swg (standard wire gauge) thick to the Superheater Company's design, arranged in five rows of seven with a cast iron header of orthodox type.

Clack Valves

Two standard clack valves were arranged for top feed and were placed approximately at 30 degrees on either side of the vertical centre line on the front barrel ring. They delivered the feed water on to two inclined deflectors which directed it around the barrel, clear of the tube bank.

Steam Manifold

The steam manifold, incorporating separate shut-off valves to each auxiliary steam supply, was mounted on the top of the firebox outside the cab. This manifold also formed the mounting for the whistle valve which was operated by means of a Bowden cable. The whistle was of the single note type. The steam manifold could be operated by means of a main stop valve, the handle for which was extended into the cab. This valve when closed, cut off the steam to all the auxiliaries, except the boiler pressure gauge. Two standard water gauges of the tube type were fitted on the firebox backplate. The two Ross 'Pop' safety valves were mounted on a recessed seating on the top of the rear barrel ring just behind the dome. Records indicate that 'Everlasting' continuous blowdown gear was fitted to LMR-based 92045-9 and to 20 ER-based engines, 92140-9, 92168-77 from new. The rest of the class had manually operated blow-down apparatus as standard. The continuous gear was later applied as a modification to others of the class, including it is believed to the whole of the LMR-based allocation, although records are incomplete on this point (see Section 9).

Smokebox

A cylindrical smokebox rolled from ⅜ in thick steel plate rested on a fabricated saddle which also formed a rigid stay between the two outside cylinders. Self-cleaning apparatus was provided, consisting of a nearly vertical plate in front of the tubes and a horizontal table plate so arranged as to conduct the gases downwards and to the front of the smokebox. A wire gauze screen placed across the gas passage to the chimney prevented the emission of large particles of unburned fuel. The original blast pipe design had a single exhaust nozzle of 5⅜ in later modified to 5¼ in diameter and the four Cardew blower nozzles were incorporated in the cap. It has been reported that the machining of some of the 9F smokebox saddles of the Swindon production lots was carried out at the Hunslet Engine Co. at Leeds.

Although Riddles could have insisted on either the Crewe-type chimney or his trademark WD stovepipe, the 9F design was similar to that of the Class 7 Britannia Pacifics, its distinctive LYR style unmistakable; drawings do exist of a 9F with a WD style Austerity chimney however (see Diagram E). The LYR choice was influenced, it was said, by E. S. Cox, Executive Officer responsible for design and a former Horwich man. There have been reports that Riddles later sought to reimpose the Austerity chimney on the 9Fs. This suggestion is not supported by Cox in a fulsome tribute to his

Figure 37
On 3rd June 1966, 92011 climbs towards Lambrigg on the WCML with a northbound goods; the banker on this occasion is Fairburn 2-6-4 tank engine 42210. 92011, looking slightly abandoned with neither front numberplate nor shedplate, was a Birkenhead engine after having been at Annesley for the 'windcutter' services for much of its working life. *(Hugh Ballantyne)*

Figure 38
One month before withdrawal, 92012 (Carlisle Kingmoor) heads a short southbound Class 'F' mixed freight past Scout Green on 20th September 1967. *(Rodney Lissenden)*

old boss after the death of Riddles at the grand age of 91 on 15th June 1983. (see *Steam World* No. 30, September 1983, p. 16). In any event, Riddles had retired by the time the first 9F was completed and 92000 emerged from Crewe in January 1954 with the handsome LYR chimney in place.

Main Frames

The heavy, rigid and robust frames of the 9Fs consisted of 1¼ in thick frame plates spaced by vertical stretchers at intervals throughout the length. Horizontal plate stretchers extended rearwards from the saddle, continuously to the ashpan at a level just above the horn spaces, whilst at the bottom of the rigid frame, cross stretchers were formed integrally with the vertical stretchers. The frame plates were located in the planes of the centre lines of the axleboxes. The welded-in hornblocks, which were symmetrical and of horseshoe form, were provided with manganese liners, approximately ¼ in thick, on the guide faces. All coupled axleboxes featured underhung laminated springs without compensation. In earlier engines, from 92000-19 and from 92030-85, the steel hornblocks were welded to the frame.

For the Crosti variants, 92020-9, and all Crewe-built engines from 92097 onwards, the practice of riveting cast steel horns to the frames was adopted, the only purpose for this change, it was reported, being to provide increased employment for the Crewe Works steel foundry. The bottom edges of the frameplates were stiffened by means of steel castings of inverted 'T' form, which were cast integrally with the spring hanger brackets and contained the registers for the hornstays. These castings were riveted to the frame by means of the same rivets which engaged the lower cross stretchers. When the hornstays were in position, the frame plates had what was virtually a continuous bottom flange. Between the fourth and fifth pairs of coupled wheels and over the horn gap for the latter, the frame had to be cut away to clear the firebox; to retain an adequate strength as a beam at this point, stiffening plates were riveted to each side of the main frame plates.

Axleboxes and Bearings

The coupled-wheel axleboxes were steel castings, with tight-fitting steel keeps at the bottom to maintain parallelism of the manganese steel lined guide faces. Plain bearing axleboxes were employed throughout the engine (but not on the tender wheels which were equipped with roller bearings). The plain bearing consisted of a pressed-in horseshoe, brass lined with white metal. An oil tray bolted to the keep under the journal contained a worsted pad, to distribute the lubricant, oil being fed to the tray from a mechanical lubricator.

Roller bearing axles, as fitted to earlier batches of the Class 7 Britannia Pacifics and some Class 5 4-6-0s, had potentially a much longer operating life and lower maintenance requirements compared with plain axles and were initially considered for the 9Fs. They were rejected as unjustifiable, however, based on experience with ten examples of a later batch of Britannia Pacifics which were experimentally fitted with plain bearings. Results here indicated no disadvantages compared with the earlier roller bearing-fitted engines, confirming Riddles' view that the steel axlebox described above would be robust and largely trouble-free in service. The plain bearing axlebox was considerably lower in capital cost than a roller-bearing box and represented a significant weight saving; moreover, it did not involve the high degree of accuracy required during manufacture of the engine which in this case of course had no fewer than five pairs of wheels coupled together in the frame and would have presented a tricky task for the works assembly teams. The choice of plain bearings was vindicated by the fact that the 9Fs rode smoothly, even at speeds up to 90mph on occasion, with no sign of adverse effects in their axleboxes; the shorter operating life of the plain box was also of no detriment considering the lifetime of even the longest serving 9F was still very much less than the 45 years originally envisaged.

The pony truck axleboxes were white-metalled bronze castings and were not mechanically fed with lubricant. Laminated coupled wheel bearing springs with plates of carbon steel were fitted throughout and rectangular tension spring hangers having cotters for adjustment were provided.

Cylinders and Valve Gear

The two 20 in (diameter) x 28 in (stroke) cylinders, placed outside the frames, were steel castings fitted with cast iron liners to the steam chest and cylinder barrel. Both the cylinders and piston valves were very similar in dimensions to those used on the Britannia Pacifics. The same patterns could not be used during manufacture however as it was necessary to increase the lateral distance between the two cylinders by some 2 in for two reasons:

(1) extra side play was needed in the coupled-wheel axleboxes to allow the engine to negotiate the specified minimum curve radius.

(2) the crosshead had to clear the leading end of the first side rod when the latter was moving in the top quarter.

The modified pattern was preferred to the alternative method of solving the problem which would have been to insert space plates or distance pieces at suitable points; the latter approach was rejected for reasons of weight and expense. The piston valves had a nominal diameter of 11 in and were driven by Walschaerts valve gear giving a maximum travel in forward gear (78% cut-off) of 7⅞ in with a steam lap of 1 1/16 in and a lead of ¼ in. In full reverse gear, a travel of 7 in produced 75% cut-off. The piston heads on the first 20 locomotives to appear, 92000-19, were of the box pattern type made as a steel casting and fitted with two rings and a bronze spring-loaded slipper, designed to carry the weight of the piston and minimise wear between the piston head and the cylinder barrel. Later engines had a light forged steel piston head which was flash-butt welded to the piston rod and reduced the reciprocating weight marginally. Slidebars of the three-bar type were provided in conjunction with an underhung crosshead.

Lubrication of the cylinders and piston valves was by means of atomised oil fed from a mechanical lubricator. The lubricator also fed the piston rod packing and the valve spindle rear bush. A minor variation from 92030 onwards was the larger gap in the running valance; this was required fully to clear the lubricator. The mechanical drive itself from the expansion link to the valve motion remained the same with circular section driving rods. The valve gear was lubricated mainly by grease and consisted of plain bearing joints, except in the case of the return crank, which was provided with self-aligning ball bearings. Coupling rods were of fish-bellied plain cross section rather than the I-section (or fluted) type, the latter having been prone to bending and breakage in some of the earlier Standard designs; main rods were still of the I-section type.

Table 2.2
BR Standard Class 9F 2-10-0s
Comparison of Cylinder and Valve Gear Dimensions with BR Standard Two-Cylinder Pacifics

Class		**70000**	**92000**	**72000**
Cylinder and Valve Gear Dimensions				
Cylinders: Diameter x Stroke	in.	20 x 28	20 x 28	19½ x 28
Piston Swept Volume (One cylinder)	cu. in.	8,796	8,796	8,362
Clearance Volume as % of Piston Swept Volume		10.3	10.3	10.8
Maximum Piston Thrust	lb.	78,540	78,540	67,196
Steam Chests				
Volume between Valve Heads	cu. in.	4,558	4,558	4,558
Volume as % of Piston Swept Volume		51.8	51.8	54.5
Piston Valves	Diameter	11”	11”	11”
	Steam Lap	1 11/16”	1 11/16”	1 11/16”
	Lead	¼”	¼”	¼”
	Exhaust Clearance		Nil	Nil Nil
Maximum Travel of Valves		7.73”	7.87”	7.73”
Maximum Cut-off %		78.0	78.0	78.0
Travel at 20% Cut-off		4.05”	4.06”	4.05”

Table 2.3
BR Standard Class 9F 2-10-0s
Balancing Data Comparison with BR Standard Two-Cylinder Pacifics

Class		**70000**	**92000**	**72000**
Revolving Masses: Weight per Cylinder lb.	lb.	1,500	2,040	1,500
Reciprocating Masses:				
Total Weight per Cylinder	lb.	846	865	846
Percentage Balanced		40	40	40
Unbalanced Weight per Cylinder	lb.	508	519	508
Ratio of Unbalanced Reciprocating Weight per Cylinder to Total Weight of Locomotive		1/414	1/374	1/390
Hammer Blow at 5 Wheel Revolutions per second				
Per Wheel	tons	2.12	0.78	2.12
Per Axle	tons	2.55	1.56	2.55
Per Rail	tons	5.50	3.38	5.50
Whole Locomotive	tons	6.60	6.77	6.60

The cylinder cocks were steam operated. Full cylinder and valve gear dimensions are given in Table 2.2. It is understood that Caprotti gear was under consideration at one point for a final batch of 9Fs which was proposed but not sanctioned.

Reversing Gear

The reversing gear consisted of a screw located at the reversing shaft with the nut acting directly upon the reversing shaft arm. A tubular shaft connected the screw to the hand wheel in the cab, which was of the end-on type driven through bevel gearing.

The reversing shaft emerged from the cab on the driver's side at an angle of approximately two degrees and passed through the running plate at about one third of the length from the cab to the cylinder. For the footplate crew and maintenance staff attending to the pipework adjacent to the cab the circular housing for the shaft was not an ideal platform to achieve stable footing. On the WR but not apparently on any other region, the authorities regarded this as an unacceptable hazard and authorised the fitting of a narrow rectangular metal plate, supported by three, (sometimes four) struts, which ran from the point where the reverser passed through the running plate to a location directly under the footstep on the side of the firebox in front of the cab thus making access to the manifold pipes inherently safer.

The modification was applied to the last of the 9Fs built at Swindon, 92220 *Evening Star* from new and may also have been fitted to other examples from the same batch during construction, possibly beginning with 92218. No official reference to this modification has been traced but over half the original WR 9F allocation acquired the fitting during the period from early 1960 to mid-1963, probably as they passed through Swindon Works.

Engines known to have been modified include the following; there may have been others:

92000/1/2/5/6/79,

92204/8/9/11-5/7-20/3-6/8/33/4/40/1/3-6/50

Photographic evidence from 1964 onwards indicates the following engines did not carry the modification, in most cases as a result of transfer from the WR before the work could be undertaken:

92004/7, 92203/5/6/27/31/9/42/8/9.

Wheels

The five pairs of coupled wheels were 5ft in diameter, somewhat larger than those normally associated with a heavy freight locomotive; the tyres were secured to the cast steel centres by 'Gibson' rings. Tyre profiles, with parameters as specified by the Association of Railway Locomotive Engineers (ARLE) for both the pony truck and the coupled wheels are illustrated in Appendix 5. The method of balancing followed a principle not previously employed in the UK, in which the rotating masses were fully balanced in the normal way but the reciprocating masses, consisting of rod, piston and crosshead plus part of the connecting rod, were statically balanced to the equivalent of 40%, by placing lead weights in the coupled wheels in the same phase on both sides of the engine. This left the fore-and-aft balance of the locomotive the same as if the normal procedure were followed, namely of making the reciprocating mass balance coincide with the rotating mass balance. Within this procedure, there remained an unbalanced couple which, however, was no larger than that tolerated in three-cylinder locomotives without reciprocating balance and was so small that its effect in practice was negligible. The new system had the advantage that it significantly reduced the 'wheel' hammer blow (but not the 'axle' hammer blow); in the case of the 9Fs this arrangement saved approximately two hundredweight of balance weight. The weights themselves consisted of plates clamped on each side of the coupled wheel spokes to form pockets into which lead was inserted. From 92050 onwards, the original method of securing the return crank to the big end, Gresley LNER style, was modified in favour of the four stud method consistent with LMS practice.

Route Availability for the 9Fs was officially designated on the WR, ER/NER and SR. For the WR, the authorisation was for the intermediate level 'Blue Route' lines, confirmed by the application of the 'Blue Spot' underneath the running number on the cabside. On the ER/NER, although axleweight may have placed 9Fs into either the RA7 or RA8 categories, potential problems with the ten-coupled wheel base at certain complex junctions with diamond or double-slip crossings led cautious authority to classify 9Fs as RA9, the highest category, in company with the Class A1, A2, A3 and A4 Pacifics and the Class W1 4-6-4. The SR route authorisation applying from January 1960 are listed in Section 7.1. No specific route restrictions for the LMR-based 9Fs have been traced. It is assumed that the class would have been treated in the same way as the similarly axle-loaded Stanier 8F 2-8-0s in this respect with due regard given to the possible long wheel base effect on branch lines and sidings with tight curves.

Steam sanding was provided for both the leading pair and main driving (third) pair of coupled wheels for running in the forward direction whilst for running in reverse, only the third pair had sanders. Three sandbox filler access points were situated on the fireman's side above the running plate, one adjacent to the smokebox, one above the gap between the second and third coupled wheels and the other above the fourth coupled wheel. The main driving pair of coupled wheels were flangeless of 5¾ in width and the second and fourth pair were provided with thin flanges; for full dimensions, see Appendix 5. The coupled wheelbase was 21 ft 8 in allowing a minimum track radius of approximately 400 ft, or 300 ft in sidings when driven 'dead slow'; on uneven curves, the centre drivers tended to drop off the rails, a typical feature of flangeless tread drivers. The pony truck with 3 ft diameter wheels was generally of similar design to that used on the BR Standard tender locomotives. It had helical bearing springs in two nests, each nest consisting of two springs, one within the other, arranged on either side of each axlebox. The load was transmitted to the axlebox by means of a yoke and shoe. Side movement was controlled by double helical springs and a spring-loaded frictional retarding gear acted upon the front and rear faces of the truck centre to damp out oscillation and assist the locomotive in negotiating diamond crossings.

Cab and Tender

The cab followed the same general layout as that used on the other Standard tender locomotives. It was a welded structure bolted on to a fabricated platform which was in turn bolted to the main frames and included the pedestal which carried the brake valve, blower and sanding valves. All the driving controls were grouped to give easy access from the driving position, which was on the left-hand side. Seats with back rests were provided for both driver and fireman and hinged side

Figure 39
Crosti boiler 92024 and 92021 are running northwards light engine past Elstree and Borehamwood on 16th July 1955. The pair had been delivered new to Wellingborough shed a few weeks earlier. Conversion to conventional operation was carried out in February and June 1960 respectively. 92024 was subsequently fitted with the only spare main boiler (no preheater) in November 1961.
(Philip J. Kelley)

windscreens were fitted on the outside of both sides of the cab.

One live steam and one exhaust steam injector were fitted to the right-hand side of the locomotive and were attached to a bracket carried off the frame below the cab. The steam and water controls for these injectors were grouped within easy reach of the fireman.

Unlike some earlier Standard designs in which the whole of the footplate was on the engine, the tenders carried by the 9Fs all had fall plates. These were hinged from the front of the tender to rest on the rearward extension of the cab floor; gangway doors were fitted between engine and tender. Different types of tender were fitted to different production batches of the locomotives to suit the operating requirements of the regions to which they were initially allocated. Details of tender types and numbers and their allocation to individual locomotives together with information on later changes where known are given in Section 4.

Brakes

Steam brakes were provided on both engine and tender, actuated in unison, and could be operated either directly by means of a graduable steam brake valve, or in conjunction with the vacuum brake. The coupled and tender wheels were braked by means of a single block on each wheel.

ATC and AWS Equipment

The WR 9F allocation was equipped with the region's ATC (Automatic Train Control) apparatus. For the WR 9Fs built at Swindon, 92203-20, this was fitted and commissioned during construction. For the two batches of WR engines built at Crewe, 92000-7 and 92221-50, the apparatus was installed at Crewe and commissioned during early visits to Swindon Works. Some of these visits, but not all, were recorded in the Engine History and Engine Record Cards, see Table 8.2. The two 9Fs, 92008/9, originally destined for the WR but diverted to the LMR, were also fitted with WR ATC gear at Crewe; this was removed during subsequent works visits. The Lickey banker, 92079, was also fitted with ATC apparatus, probably during its first visit to Swindon Works (May 1959) after transfer to the WR in 1958; some former WR-based 9Fs had their ATC gear removed after their later reallocations to the LMR and NER.

The WR ATC gear for the 9Fs consisted of a battery box located under the cab on the driver's side and connected to the detector shoe via a conduit pipe tucked away under the running plate. For Crewe-built engines, the conduit passed across the base of that portion of the running plate valance cut away to allow access to the lubricator; for the Swindon-built 9Fs, the conduit was dipped slightly to pass under the gap. The arrangement was completed by the addition of the brake valve, a circular device located on the vacuum ejector which was situated on the boiler between the smoke deflector and the clack valve; a detector shoe protective plate was not fitted.

Later, the BR AWS (Automatic Warning System) equipment was fitted to a number of the 9F class; details where known are given in Table 9.1. AWS was similar in principle to ATC. It comprised a battery and an adjacent cylindrical vacuum reservoir situated under the cab on the driver's side, a conduit to the contact shoe as for ATC but in this case continuing for the full length of the running plate beyond the cylinder as the AWS shoe was located further forward compared with the ATC shoe position; the conduit was 'dipped' to pass under the lubricator. A protective plate was attached by brackets to the buffer beam behind the front coupling chain; this was sometimes referred to as the 'bash' plate.

Carriage Warming Apparatus

Although none of the 9Fs were fitted with steam pipes for train heating during their BR service, provision was made for this option during construction. This consisted of two small holes drilled near the base of the buffer beam on the driver's side, approximately one third of the distance from the coupling chain to the buffer; corresponding holes were made on the fireman's side of the tender buffer beam, which also had a small half-moon-shaped cut-out directly between and under the two holes. This modification was specified for the front buffer beam of the Swindon-built WR-based 9Fs but Swindon-built engines for the ER, 92087-96, 92178-202, also had this feature. The first 9Fs built by Crewe and intended for the WR, 92000-9, did not have the half-moon feature on the front buffer beam but photographic evidence indicates that, except for the first two engines, the second batch, 92221-50, did receive the modification. Some half-moon engines, e.g. 92087, seem to have exchanged their front buffer beams for the standard type during works visits, as confirmed by photographs.

Smoke Deflectors

The provision of smoke deflectors for a freight engine in Great Britain was unusual if not unique. It was probably considered necessary as the high pitch of the boiler, required to clear the five pairs of 5 ft coupled wheels, inevitably allowed for only a small squat chimney, a type often associated with drifting smoke problems. Certainly in the case of the double chimney 9Fs, with their inherently softer exhausts, the deflectors would likely have bestowed a significant advantage in clearing smoke and steam. For the Crosti boiler engines, only a few weeks' experience had demonstrated the need to fit the final chimney with a deflector (see Section 9). Following conversion to standard operation however, the Crostis, still without the benefit of deflectors, did not appear to have chronic problems with drifting smoke and steam.

One curious feature on some 9Fs, mainly WR-based or a few regular visitors to the region, was the observation that the central portion of the smoke deflector's horizontal hand rail often showed a pronounced downward distortion, especially on the fireman's side. One theory is that this was an unofficial method (to which 'authority' had turned a blind eye) of preventing the rail from obscuring the crew's vision of colour light signals when travelling along certain parts of the route system. It will be recalled that many WR-based Britannia Pacifics had their deflector hand rails replaced by hand grips at suitable points around the edge of the deflectors following the accident with 70026 *Polar Star* at Milton, near Didcot on 20th November 1955; the obscuring of signals by the hand rails was said to have been a contributory cause of the disaster. If the speculation is correct, it may have been that the hand rails on the 9Fs were not regarded as presenting a significant hazard in this respect bearing in mind their freight trains moved at much lower average speeds compared with those of the Britannia passenger workings. With the crew having more time to sight individual signals, it was perhaps not considered necessary to replace the rails with hand grips.

2.2 Crosti Boiler: 92020-92029

Brighton was the lead drawing office for the design of the Crosti engines with some components designed at Derby, Doncaster and Swindon. The general layout of the Crostis was made with as few variations as possible from the standard Class 9F, the aim being to facilitate possible conversion either way in the light of experience. The ten locomotives involved in the Crosti initiative, 92020-9, were built at Crewe; Figures D to H show details of the layout of the components referred to below.

Heat from Exhaust Steam

In the Franco-Crosti system, the feed water entered the main boiler from the preheater drum at a temperature only marginally less than that of the water already in the boiler. In this way, a large amount of heat of combustion was utilised which would otherwise have been wasted. More heat savings were made by means of a jacket fed with exhaust steam which encircled part of the preheater drum; additionally, heat was extracted, as in the case of the standard engines, by the use of an exhaust steam injector.

The water circuit was as shown in Figure E. The cold water feed from the tender was forced through a clack valve on the firebox end of the preheater, either directly by means of a feed pump or after mixing with steam in an injector. The water in the preheater, which was at approximately boiler pressure, was displaced by fresh feed entering and moving up towards the hot end, whence it passed by way of pipes to the main boiler clack valves. The main boiler was of the normal type, having no special features, except that for a given power output, it could generally be made a good deal smaller than the boiler of the corresponding standard locomotive.

The principle of the preheater was one of 'contraflow', i.e. the hot gases and cold water flow in opposite directions. This enabled the maximum amount of heat to be extracted from the gases since the temperature differential between gases and water was at the minimum possible at each stage and tended to be more or less uniform; this arrangement allowed the coldest water to be heated by the coldest gases at the remote end of the preheater and likewise the hottest water, in the vicinity of the front smokebox, being heated by the hottest gases.

It was anticipated that economies would arise not only from the heat extracted from the gases and the exhaust steam otherwise lost through the chimney but also from the incidental increase in combustion efficiency which would result from the reduced quantity of coal burned. One slight disadvantage however was that the gases required more energy to pull them through both banks of tubes, main boiler and preheater, tending to necessitate a higher blastpipe pressure which caused a marginal loss of cylinder efficiency.

The attractive feature of the Franco-Crosti system was its simplicity, all the advantages of feed-water heating being obtained without the use of any additional moving part on the locomotive.

As noted in Section 1.3, there were various ways in which the preheater drum, or drums, could be accommodated on the locomotive frame. The most common method in continental Europe was where two drums were placed one on each side of the boiler, with the two final chimneys emerging on either side of the barrel just in front of the firebox. The direction of the gases is thus reversed at the front smokebox and thereafter they travel rearwards thus completing a double path. The British loading gauge is very restrictive and with a locomotive of the size of the 9F it was physically impossible to arrange the drums in this configuration. Instead, one drum only was provided, placed between the frames underneath the main boiler barrel, the centreline of the drum sloping downwards to the rear, see Figure E. The drum had a final smokebox, located just in front of the throatplate of the main boiler; the blast chamber and final chimney were placed on the right hand (fireman's) side of the barrel, just ahead of the firebox, see Figure F.

FIGURE D
CROSTI BOILER: DIAGRAM SHOWING LAYOUT OF PREHEATER DRUM

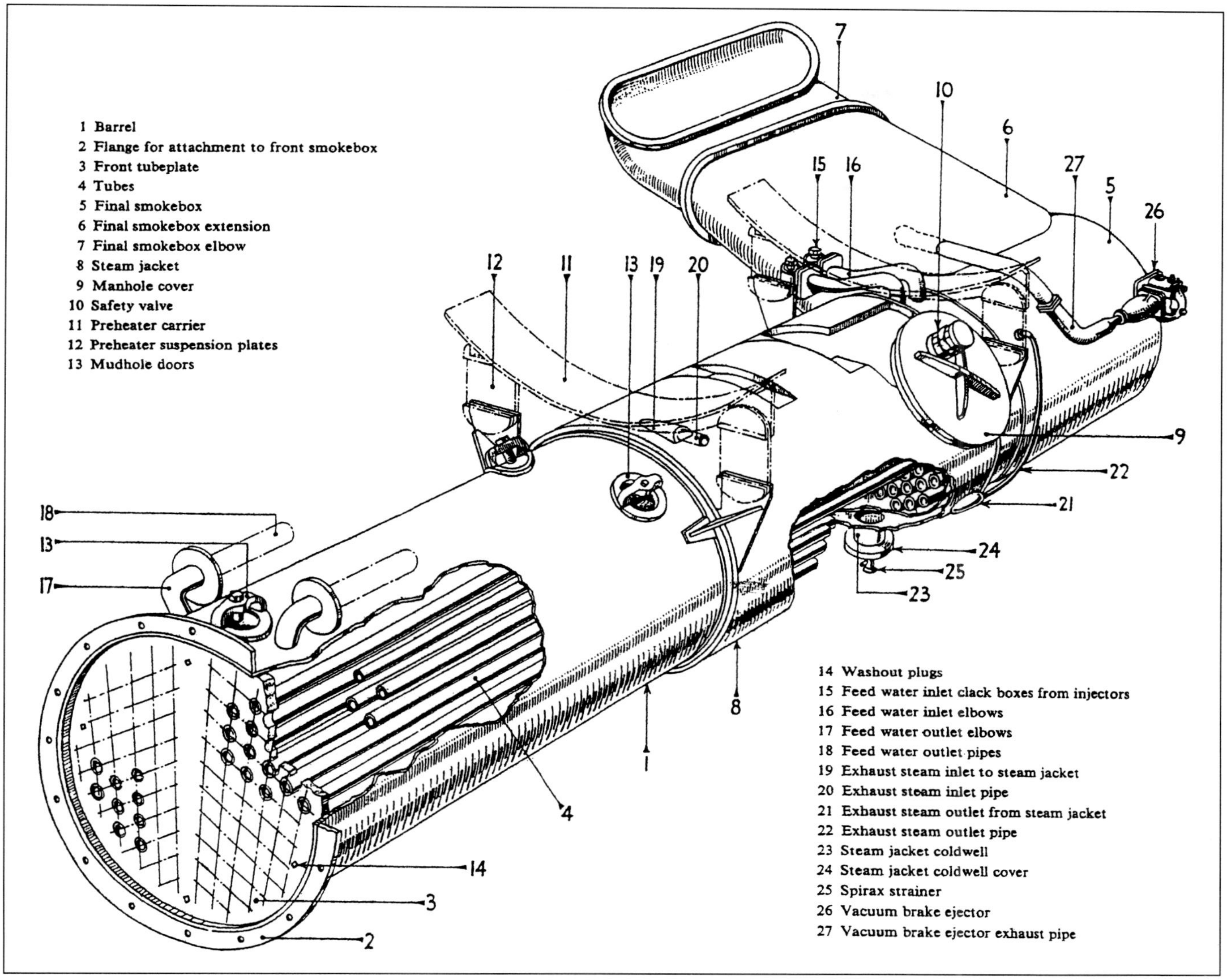

FIGURE E
CROSTI BOILER: DIAGRAM SHOWING GAS AND WATER FLOW

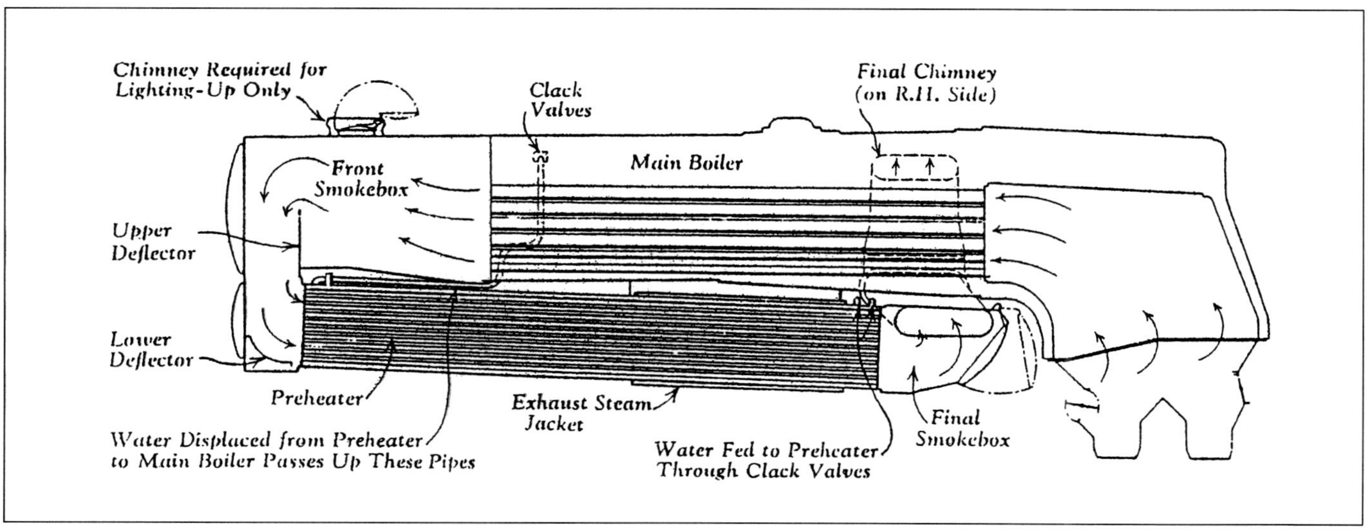

FIGURE F

CROSTI BOILER: SIDE VIEW SHOWING FINAL SMOKEBOX AND CHIMNEY ARRANGEMENT

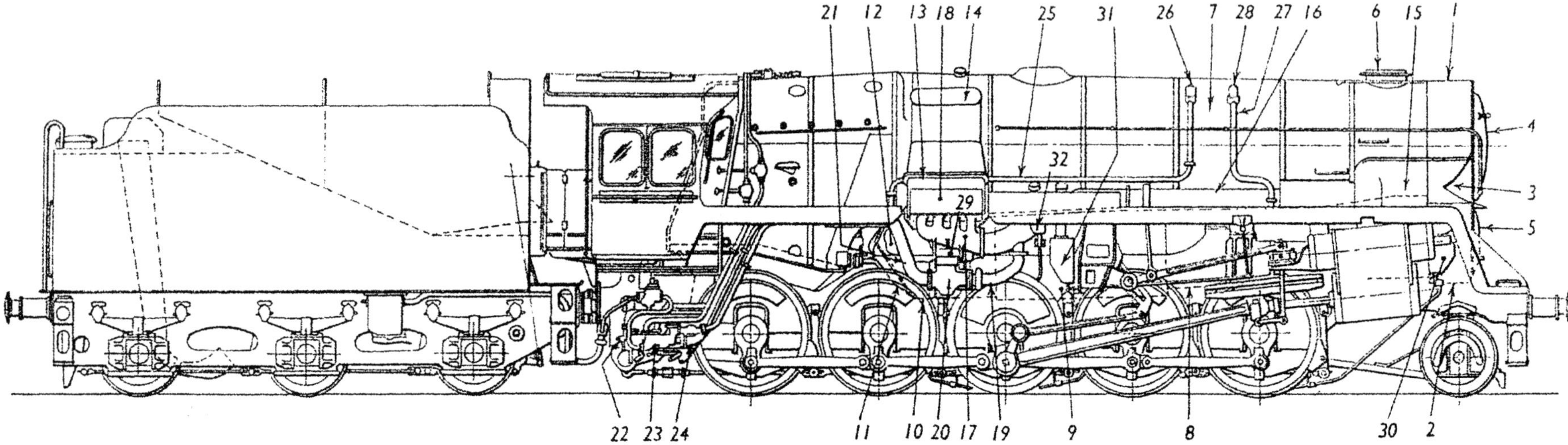

1. Front smokebox.
2. Front smokebox extension.
3. Front smokebox side pocket.
4. Front smokebox large door.
5. Front smokebox small door.
6. Chimney, for lighting up only.
7. Main boiler.
8. Preheater.
9. Preheater steam jacket.
10. Final smokebox.
11. Final smokebox door.
12. Final smokebox extension.
13. Final smokebox elbow.
14. Final chimney.
15. Casing over steam and exhaust pipes.
16. Casing over exhaust pipes.
17. Manifold for blast pipe nozzles.
18. Cover for access to blast pipe nozzles.
19. Exhaust steam to grease separator.
20. Grease separator for exhaust steam injector.
21. Exhaust steam pipe to exhaust steam injector.
22. Exhaust steam injector.
23. Live steam injector.
24. Two-way valve connected to live steam injector.
25. Delivery pipe from two-way valve to main boiler.
26. Clackbox for above pipe (right-hand side only).
27. Delivery pipe from preheater to main boiler, on both sides.
28. Clackbox for above pipe, on both sides.
29. Supporting bracket for final chimney and grease separator.
30. Sandbox, leading coupled wheels, forward running, on both sides.
31. Sandbox, driving coupled wheels, forward running, on both sides.
32. Sandbox, driving coupled wheels, backward running, on both sides.

Figure 40
92210 heads the ten-coach 7.45am Bradford Forster Square-Bournemouth West near Horsington (Templecombe) at 4.12pm on 21st July 1962. 92210 remained a WR engine all its working life which amounted to little more than five years. *(E. W. Fry)*

Figure 41
92110 (Kirkby-in-Ashfield) drifts downhill towards Barrow Hill with an up coal train on 11th July 1964. 92110 spent much of its working life on MML coal traffic but was moved to the north west (first Newton Heath, then Carlisle Kingmoor) for three years before withdrawal at the end of 1967. 92110 was one of a number of LMR 9Fs not to have had its lamp brackets repositioned by this date. *(Courtney Haydon)*

Figure 42
92094 is under construction in Swindon 'A' Shop in January 1957. The engine spent most of its working life allocated to Annesley shed for the 'windcutter' service between there and Woodford Halse before transfer to Merseyside in May 1965. 92094 survived until May 1968 when it was withdrawn from Speke Junction MPD. *(G. Wheeler)*

Boiler

Dimensions and technical details of the BR12 Crosti boiler and preheater are given in Section 3.2 and Table 3.1.

Regulator

The modified version of the regulator as described in Section 9 was fitted to the Crosti engines from new.

Firebox, Grate and Ashpan

The firebox was 7ft 5½in long at the bottom with a maximum outside width of 7 ft 0⅛ in, giving a grate area of 40.2 sq ft as with the standard 9F. All other firebox, grate and ashpan details were as described in Section 2.1 for the standard boiler engines; the lagging for both the firebox and the boiler consisted of lightweight asbestos mattresses rather than the fibreglass used on the first 20 9Fs.

Front Smokebox

The front smokebox was a welded chamber rigidly attached to the front of the main boiler barrel; the latter rested on main supports under the front barrel ring and was there rigidly attached to the frame. Expansion of the front smokebox was freely permitted forwards and expansion brackets carried the weight on to the front ends of the frame plates. The gases entering the front smokebox from the boiler tubes passed through to the front of the chamber and over a vertical deflector plate which was provided to trap the smokebox char. They then passed downwards into a pocket which formed the entrance to the preheater tubes, fitted with the lower deflector which was curved to lead the gases into the preheater tubes.

Two smokebox doors were fitted; the upper one, being the larger, provided general access to the front tubeplate of the main boiler. When it was open, the centre portion of the vertical deflector plate, which was hinged, could be lowered to form a platform over which any accumulation of char could be swept out. This procedure was necessary as the Crostis were not fitted with self-cleaning smokeboxes. The lower door was for access to the front tubeplate of the preheater but before this could be reached it was necessary to remove the curved deflector plate. Both doors were secured by screwed-down steel clamping 'dogs'. The approximate positions of these were: main boiler, 12, 2, 4, 6, 8 and 10 o'clock, and preheater, 2, 4, 8 and 10 o'clock. The externally-mounted tube cleaner pipe and valve terminated at a point close to the 10 o' clock position. Two foot steps were fitted at the base of the smoke box for the main boiler for access to lamp brackets.

The forward chimney was only required for producing a draught for lighting-up purposes and was therefore fitted with a door which was closed for normal running and secured by means of a central dart. A hand rail on the fireman's side, adjacent to the chimney and parallel to the boiler length, was provided for the safety of the crew when adjusting the door and was accessed via a prominent foot step on the side of the smokebox.

Superheater

The superheater header, of orthodox design, was accommodated in the front smokebox and there were 28 elements of the bifurcated type, 1¼ in outside diameter and 9 swg thick, with the Superheater Company's design of ball end. The main steam pipes to the cylinders passed forwards to the front of the box and then downwards, passing out horizontally from the 'ears' of the box through the glands which allowed free expansion of the box forwards in relation to the steam pipes.

Preheater

Dimensions and technical data for the preheater are given in Section 3.2 and Table 3.1.

Final Smokebox

This was rigidly attached to the rear end of the preheater drum and was of welded construction; it had a door at its rear end, hinged at the top and was secured to its asbestos-packed seating by metal 'dogs'. A catch was fitted for holding the door open when washing out and cleaning the inside of the smokebox. The final smokebox which is shown in Figure G had a tubular extension to the right side of the locomotive leading to the blast chamber, or elbow, which housed the four blastpipe nozzles; a cross-section of one of these is shown in Figure H. The blast chamber was placed on the right of the locomotive so as not to interfere with the driver's view ahead. The fireman's view was, however, slightly more obstructed than on a standard locomotive. The oval shaped chimney was attached to the top of the blast chamber and passed upwards, inclined towards the centre of the locomotive. It was extended to the maximum the loading gauge would permit in such a way as to enable the exhaust to clear station awnings as far as possible. To reduce corrosion in the final smokebox, blast chamber and chimney, the whole of the inner surface of these components was treated by the 'Calorization' process, which consisted of the application of a mix of aluminium and aluminium oxide to a specified thickness.

To carry the weight of the blast chamber, a substantial bracket from the main frame was provided, the chamber resting on this through a sliding bearing to allow for expansion of the preheater; this bracket also carried the grease separator for the exhaust injector. The chimney was located laterally by means of a pin-jointed stay from the boiler barrel. At the base of the blast chamber was an exhaust manifold which was connected at its front end to the combined exhaust steam pipe from the cylinders. The manifold carried the four blast-pipe nozzles of 2½ in diameter, which were mounted in a straight line so as to exhaust into the oval chimney. Each nozzle had a spherical mounting so that it could be adjusted to direct its

FIGURE G
CROSTI BOILER: DIAGRAM SHOWING FINAL SMOKEBOX, BLASTPIPES AND CHIMNEY

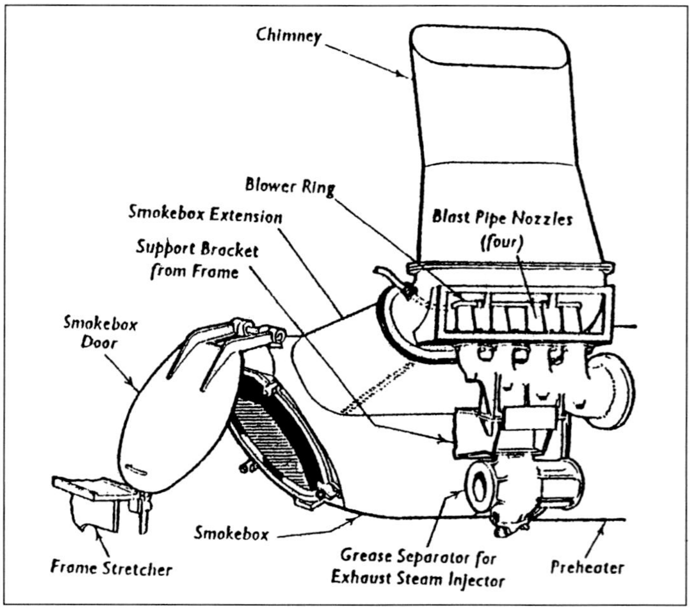

FIGURE H
CROSTI BOILER: CROSS-SECTION THROUGH ONE OF THE FOUR BLASTPIPE NOZZLES

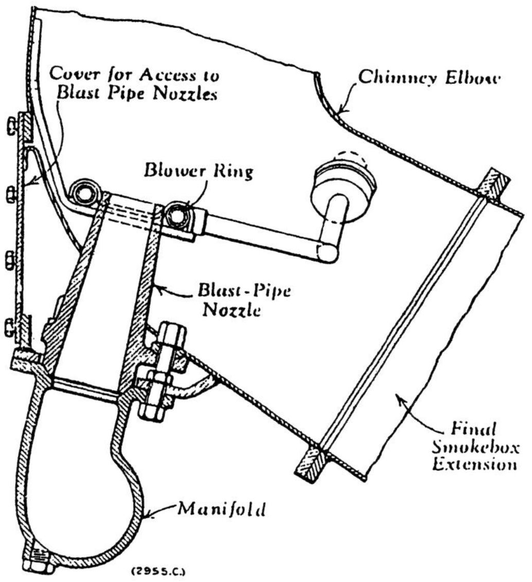

steam jet correctly into the chimney. A removable plate on the outside of the blast chamber provided access to the nozzles for the removal of carbon deposits as necessary.

The exhaust steam from the cylinders, instead of passing directly into the base of the blastpipe in the front smokebox as on an orthodox locomotive was carried back in two long pipes which on the right hand side passed directly from the cylinders to the blast chamber; that on the left hand side passed back and was directed under the boiler barrel to join the other pipe just before entering the blast chamber. As in the case of the boiler and firebox, the lagging of the preheater consisted of lightweight asbestos mattresses, covered by the normal clothing sheets. The front smokebox was provided with clothing sheets but no lagging material was interposed. The steam jacket of the preheater was dealt with similarly. The Crostis were provided from new with 'Everlasting' blowdown apparatus which was manually operated; continuous blowdown was later fitted to all the Crostis, see Section 9.

Frames

The frames followed as closely as possible those of the standard 9F. They consisted of 1¼ in plates rigidly stayed by means of vertical and horizontal stretchers, some of which had to be modified slightly to accommodate the preheater. As in the case of the standard engine, the frame plates were located in the planes of the centre-lines of the coupled axleboxes, with the hornblocks of symmetrical horseshoe form welded in. The smokebox saddle had been eliminated and in its place there was a large stretcher, shaped to fit under the preheater. The front of the main boiler was carried on a saddle riveted to the barrel near the front tubeplate and supported on a T-shaped flange welded to the top edge of the main frame plates.

Axleboxes and Bearings

Plain bearing axleboxes were used throughout the engine; details were the same as on the standard 9Fs and are given in Section 2.1; as with all BR Standard tenders, the BR1B type carried by the Crosti 9Fs was fitted with Timken roller bearing axles; full details of the BR1B tender are given in Section 4.

Cylinders and Valve Gear

The two cylinders, with a diameter of 20 in and a stroke of 28 in, were steel castings fitted with cast-iron liners to the cylinder barrel and steam chest. The cylinders were similar to those of the standard 9F but with the exhaust passages arranged to connect with the exhaust steam pipes described earlier which pass along each side of the engine to the final smokebox.

The Walschaerts valve gear was identical to that of the standard engines except that the reversing shaft ran parallel to the running plate instead of at an angle and was positioned higher, so that it could pass between the main boiler and the preheater, necessitating a longer lifting link. Piston valve, and lubrication details were the same as for the standard engines and are given in Section 2.1.

Wheels

Coupled wheel and pony truck details as well as the method of balancing the reciprocating masses were the same as in the standard engines and are given in Section 2.1.

Steam sanding was provided but because of the presence of the preheater between the frames, it was necessary to find alternative positions for the sandboxes. This resulted in a return to the practice of arranging individual sand boxes for each feed. The leading sandboxes were placed ahead of the cylinders and these fed the leading wheels in the forward direction. The main driving wheels (middle pair) had both front and rear sanders and the boxes for these were mounted outside the frames, below the platform.

Cab and Tender

To permit access to the part of the platform on the fireman's side between the cab and the blast chamber/side chimney, a long step was fitted below the cab side with sunken hand rails fitted to the side of the cab just below the window. In addition, a hand rail, known as a grab handle, was provided adjacent to the cab's forward window and followed the profile of its rear edge. This allowed safe access from the footplate to the isolated part of the platform; safety considerations meant that access was restricted to times when the locomotive was not in motion.

The Crostis were equipped with the BR1B tender, details of which are given in Section 4.

Brakes

Steam brakes were fitted on both engine and tender. The engine had one brake cylinder operating on the front two pairs of coupled wheels and another on the back three; the tender had one brake cylinder. The brakes could be operated by a graduable steam brake valve, or in conjunction with the vacuum brake on the train.

Other Design Details

Comparative dimensions of the standard 9F compared with the Crosti variant are given in Table 3.1. Other design particulars not mentioned in this Section are common to both types and are given in Section 2.1.

3. Boilers

3.1 Standard Boilers

The original proposal in the Standard locomotive programme for the heavy freight design was the 2-8-2 type which would have utilised the BR1 boiler design, the same as that carried by the Class 7 Britannia Pacifics. Following adoption of the 2-10-0 type however, the need for placing the firebox above trailing pairs of coupled wheels of 5 ft diameter meant it was not possible to use any of the existing Standard boilers whilst still conforming to the loading gauge. A new boiler with a working pressure of 250 lbs/sq in and featuring a wide firebox thus had to be developed and was something of a hybrid of the Britannia Pacific (BR1) and Clan Pacific (BR2) boilers. The new boiler, designated BR9, was carried by all but ten members of the 9F class, the remaining engines being the Crosti variants, 92020-29, which were fitted with yet another new boiler originally designated BR9A, later recoded BR12; details of the latter are given in Section 3.2.

The smokebox end of the BR9 boiler barrel was the same diameter as that of the Britannia BR1 boiler and used the same flanging blocks for the smokebox tubeplate. The BR1 boiler was bigger however, widening from 69 in at the front end to 77½ in at the firebox end compared with the BR9's 69 in to 73 in respectively. For the BR9's throat and firebox tubeplates the same press blocks were used as for the Class 6 Clan Pacifics' BR2 boiler which widened to 73 in from 64 in.

The BR9 boiler shell itself was of high tensile steel plate, the barrel consisting of two rings, the rear ring carrying all of the 4 in taper, symmetrical top and bottom. The plates from which the barrel rings were rolled were 19/32 in and ⅝ in thick respectively. The drumhead type smokebox tubeplate was ¾ in thick and there were 35 large flue tubes, 5¼ in diameter outside, 7 swg thick and 138 small tubes 2 in diameter outside, 11 swg thick. The length between the tubeplates was 15 ft 3 in. The boiler was carried on the frames by a saddle fitted to a cross stretcher close to the front tubeplate. At the back end, expansion blocks, fitted to extensions integral with the foundation ring, rested on suitable frame stretchers at both ends of the firebox.

The footplating along the sides of the boiler was carried on brackets fitted to the boiler shell by means of studs and, further forward, on brackets fitted to the smokebox. Boiler dimension details are given in Tables 2.1 and 3.1.

Theoretically the BR9 boiler was inferior to the Britannia's BR1 with regard to the free gas/grate area and firebox/grate area ratios. Plant tests however indicated the BR9 was slightly more efficient at what was regarded as the upper limit for manual firing, a coal burning rate of 3,000 lbs per hour. Maximum evaporation rate was slightly less at 29,000 lbs per hour compared with the BR1's 31,500 lbs per hour, reflecting the difference in grate area, 40.2 sq ft for the BR9 compared with 42.0 sq ft for the BR1.

Including 12 spares, a total of 253 BR9 boilers were built, 198 (10 spare) at Crewe and 55 (two spare) at Swindon; Crewe provided the flanged plates for all 253 boilers. New boiler construction continued at Crewe until May 1962, some three and a half years after their last engine 92250 was turned out. Swindon ceased BR9 boiler construction in May 1960, just two months after 92220 *Evening Star* was completed. Details of initial boiler allocation (including the Crostis) are given in Table 3.2, together with an indication of the manufacturing cost per boiler, where traceable, for each batch of 9Fs; the significantly higher cost for the Swindon-built

Figure 43
One of the Woodford Halse-Annesley 'wind-cutter' empties (Class 'EUB') with 92030 (Annesley) in charge is approaching Belgrave & Birstall on 31st August 1961. The engine looks smart following a repaint at Crewe where it underwent a Heavy General overhaul with boiler change a few weeks earlier after completing nearly 200,000 miles in service.
(C. R. Berridge)

Table 3.1
BR Standard Class 9F 2-10-0s
Alternative Crosti Boiler Proposals Compared with Standard BR 9 Boiler

Design Office Scheme	Milan Crosti	Brighton Crosti Original	Brighton Crosti High Superheat A	Brighton Crosti High Superheat B	Brighton Crosti Final	Brighton Standard
Date	1951	1951	Proposed	Proposed	1955	1954
BR Designation	-	-	-	-	BR12	BR9
Boiler Presure psi.	250	250	250	250	250	250
Combustion Chamber	No	No	Yes	Yes	Yes	Yes
Barrel						
Minimum diameter	5' 1⅛"	4' 11¹¹⁄₁₆"	4' 11⅝"	4' 11⅝"	4' 11⅝"	5' 9"
Maximum diameter	5' 2¼"	5' 0¹³⁄₁₆"	5' 7½"	5' 7½"	5' 7½"	6' 1"
Tube length	16' 5"	16' 5"	16' 5"	16' 5"	16' 5"	15' 3"
Flues	22 x 6⅙"	28 x 5½"	38 x 5⅛"	38 x 5⅛"	28 x 5½"	35 x 5¼"
Tubes	63 x 2½"	60 x 2⅜"	45 x 2⅜"	45 x 2⅜"	60 x 2⅜"	138 x 2"
Superheater	Schmidt	Bifurcated	Bifurcated	Bifurcated	Bifurcated	Schmidt
Elements	1⁹⁄₁₆"	1¼"	1"	1⅛"	1¼"	1⅜"
Preheater						
Diameter	2' 7⅞"	2' 8⅝"	2' 8⅝"	2' 8⅝"	2' 8⅝"	-
Length	20' 0"	19' 3"	19' 3"	19' 3"	19' 3"	-
Tubes	108 x 2"	90 x 2¼"	90 x 2¼"	90 x 2¼"	90 x 2¼"	-
Heating Surface (sq ft)						
Tubes	1,249	1,274	1,299	1,299	1,274	1,836
Firebox	150	150	158	158	158	179
Evaporative	1,399	1,424	1,457	1,457	1,432	2,015
Preheater	1,186	1,078	1,078	1,078	1,078	-
Superheater	413	425	422	503	411	535
Grate Area (sq ft)	40.2	40.2	40.2	40.2	40.2	40.2
Free Gas Area (sq ft)						
Boiler	4.54	4.59	5.02	4.80	4.59	5.49
Preheater	1.80	2.00	2.00	2.00	2.00	-
Estimated Steam Temperature (°F)	641	669	711	705	669	627

Data Source: NRM York

boilers compared with those from Crewe will be noted.

The record of boilers subsequently carried by individual class members is incomplete; available information from Engine History Cards and Engine Record Cards is given in Table 3.3. Some members of the class had very short lives, barely lasting long enough to undergo a heavy general overhaul when the majority of boiler changes were usually made; in these cases it is likely that a number of engines carried the same boiler for the whole of their working lives.

3.2 Crosti Boilers

The backplate of the main boiler and the layout of the controls were identical to those of the standard 9Fs. Elsewhere the boiler was different, being smaller in diameter but otherwise similar in principle, with a Belpaire firebox, a combustion chamber, regulator in the dome and superheater.

As with the standard 9F, the boiler was made from high tensile steel plate, the barrel consisting of two rings, the rear one tapered. The front and rear barrel rings were rolled from plate of ½ in and ⁹⁄₁₆ in respectively. The outside diameter of the boiler barrel was 4 ft 11⅝ in, increasing to 5 ft 7½ in at the firebox end, compared with 5 ft 9 in and 6 ft 1 in respectively for the standard engine. The length between tubeplates was greater (16 ft 5 in instead of 15 ft 3 in) for the Crosti. The smokebox tubeplate was of the drumhead type, ¾ in thick. Compared with the standard 9F boiler, the Crosti boiler had fewer large flue tubes (28 x 5½in outside diameter, 7 swg thick versus 35 x 5¼ in, same outside diameter) and very many fewer small tubes (60 x 2⅜ in outside diameter, 11 swg thick as opposed to 138 x 2 in, same outside diameter). One spare Crosti boiler was authorised under the 1957 Spare Boiler Programme but not built until late 1961; it did not incorporate a preheater.

Preheater

The preheater, shown in Figure D, was a welded drum 2 ft 7⅞ in diameter inside, containing 90 steel tubes of 2¼ in outside diameter, 19 ft. 3 in between tubeplates. It was riveted

Table 3.2
BR Standard Class 9F 2-10-0s
Initial Boiler Allocation

Locomotive Number	Boiler Number Nominal Allocation (1)	Date of Boiler Construction	Boiler Built at	Cost (£)
92000-92019	1128-1147	10.53-08.54	Crewe	5,245 av.
92020-92029	1148-1157 (2)	02.55-05.55	Crewe	4,895
92030-92049	1410-1429	09.54-01.55	Crewe	5,351 av.
92050-92086	1430-1466	06.55-06.56	Crewe	5,351 av.
92087-92096	1467-1476	05.56-02.57	Swindon	7,124
92097-92177	1644-1724	05.56-01.58	Crewe	6,276 av.
92178-92202	1725-1748,1877(3)	06.57-10.58	Swindon	8,299
92203-92220	1749,1879-1896(3)	12.58-11.59	Swindon	8,746
92221-92250	1912-1941	01.58-11.58	Crewe	6,415
Spare Boilers	1876	05.57	Crewe	(4)
	1877 (3)	07.57	Crewe	8,299
	1901-1902	02.59	Crewe	(4)
	1903 (2)	10.61	Crewe	(4)
	1907	05.59	Crewe	(4)
	1908	05.60	Crewe	(4)
	1944-1945	06.61-07.61	Crewe	(4)
	1946-1947	03.60-04.60	Swindon	(4)
	1950	05.62	Crewe	(4)
	1951	03.62	Crewe	(4)

1 Not all allocated in sequence; see Table 3.3
2 BR12 (Crosti) boilers, originally designated BR9A
3 Crewe spare 1877 was sent to Swindon where it was put new on to 92198 in October 1958. Swindon 1896, originally allocated to 92220 effectively became a spare and was sent to Darlington where it replaced Swindon 1727 on 92180 in February 1960.
4 Information not traced

Figure 44
92150 (Saltley) is on shed at Carlisle Durran Hill around 1959 having worked in on one of the fitted freights from Washwood Heath via the Settle & Carlisle route. The engine is attached to a BR1C tender as specified for the original allocation of standard LMR-based 9Fs. The tender depicted here is No. 1271. 92150's scheduled tender, 1C 1360, was selected for modification and use behind BR Class 4-6-2 71000 *Duke of Gloucester*. The Duke's original tender 1E 1271 was modified to a 1C type and attached to 92150, retaining its serial number. The 1C serial number 1360 was applied to a later tender and allocated to 92162. Of the other original LMR 9Fs, the Crosti boiler engines (92020-9) had the BR1B tender and the mechanical stoker-fitted engines (92165-7) carried the BR1K type. Later, 9Fs from both the ER and WR were reassigned to the LMR and in most cases retained their original tenders, BR1F and BR1G types respectively.
(Bill Hamilton)

Figure 45
Here is a view of tender BR1F No. 1178 attached to 92088 (Annesley) at New England on 24th February 1957. Both the boiler and tender originally designated for 92088 were fitted to 92089 which also entered service four weeks earlier than 92088, strongly suggesting that their identities were transposed at an early stage during construction. *(A. R. Goult)*

Figure 46
BR1G tender No. 952 is seen paired with 92003 (Newport Ebbw Junction) at Gloucester Horton Road on 21st September 1957. This engine was used in firehole door trials with 92000 in 1956. The latter was fitted with the LNER-type letterbox door and heat radiation effects on the firemen compared. It was concluded that no advantage would be served by adopting the LNER-type door for the WR allocation. *(A. R. Goult)*

Figure 47
Mechanical stoker-fitted 92166 (Saltley) awaits its next duty at Durran Hill on 16th August 1958. The BR1K tender (No. 1376) seems to have been furnished with an excess of 'large' coals which would likely give problems for the mechanical stoker on the return ride to Birmingham. *(Bill Hamilton)*

Table 3.3
Standard Cl. 9F 2-10-0s: Record of Boilers Fitted

Engine No.	Boiler No.	Date
92000	1128	05.01.54 N
	1459	02.03.60
	1439	09.03.63
92001	1129	12.01.54 N
	1675	20.04.60
	★	28.08.64
92002	1130	16.01.54 N
	1947	01.12.60
92003	1131	25.01.54 N
	1946	10.01.61
92004	1132	30.01.54 N
92005	1133	05.02.54 N
	1131	20.05.60
92006	1134	10.02.54 N
	1908	21.09.60
92007	1135	18.02.54 N
92008	1136	01.03.54 N
	1413	05.11.60
92009	1137	12.03.54 N
	1901	16.04.59
	★	03.04.65
	★	21.05.66
92010	1138	13.05.54 N
	1424	05.05.61
92011	1139	19.05.54 N
	1414	09.11.57
92012	1140	31.05.54 N
	1876	01.08.57
	1926	23.11.62
92013	1141	23.04.54 N
	1410	23.10.61
92014	1142	18.05.54 N
	1139	30.11.57
	1663	13.09.63
92015	1143	25.09.54 N
	1907	05.12.59
92016	1144	07.10.54 N
	1465	05.12.61
92017	1145	13.10.54 N
	1143	19.05.60
92018	1146	21.10.54 N
	1461	30.12.61
92019	1147	25.10.54 N
	1683	16.06.60
92020	1148	18.05.55 N
92021	1149	18.05.55 N
	1157	??.08.62
92022	1150	18.05.55 N
92023	1151	20.05.55 N
	★	27.09.61
92024	1152	06.06.55 N
	1903	16.11.61
92025	1153	17.06.55 N
	1152	16.01.62
92026	1154	17.06.55 N
	1149	??.09.62
92027	1155	25.06.55 N
	1154	27.10.62
92028	1156	06.07.55 N
	1152	??.06.58
	1153	20.02.62
92029	1157	08.07.55 N
92030	1410	03.11.54 N
92030	1420	12.08.61
(cont.)	1146	20.05.64
92031	1411	11.11.54 N
	1433	31.05.61
92032	1412	17.11.54 N
	1145	06.08.60
92033	1413	19.11.54 N
	1147	03.09.60
92034	1414	02.12.54 N
	1140	23.08.57
	1725	04.11.60
92035	1415	03.12.54 N
	1419	25.08.60
92036	1417	03.12.54 N
	1140	22.04.61
92037	1418	08.12.54 N
	1422	29.10.60
92038	1419	14.12.54 N
	1441	03.06.60
92039	1416	17.12.54 N
	1418	04.02.61
92040	1421	23.12.54 N
	1732	04.06.60
92041	1422	31.12.54 N
	1423	18.10.60
92042	1423	12.01.55 N
	1421	08.07.60
92043	1424	18.01.55 N
	1412	10.02.61
	1438	27.03.63
92044	1425	29.01.55 N
	1142	26.09.58
	1743	03.06.61
92045	1426	09.02.55 N
	1951	??.04.62
92046	1427	11.02.55 N
92047	1428	18.02.55 N
	1137	06.11.59
92048	1429	26.02.55 N
	1136	13.01.61
92049	1420	10.03.55 N
	1467	19.05.61
92050	1430	19.08.55 N
	1476	19.10.62
92051	1431	22.08.55 N
	1944	24.06.61
92052	1432	26.08.55 N
	1460	10.10.62
92053	1433	17.09.55 N
	1429	24.03.61
92054	1434	21.09.55 N
	1453	30.05.62
92055	1435	22.09.55 N
	1428	13.05.60
92056	1436	14.10.55 N
	1684	29.09.60
92057	1437	11.10.55 N
92058	1438	13.10.55 N
	1687	??.10.62
92059	1439	20.10.55 N
92060	1440	05.11.55 N
	1443	29.04.59
92061	1441	12.11.55 N
	1687	10.03.60
92062	1442	19.11.55 N
	1645	03.08.62
	★	02.05.64
92063	1443	25.11.55 N
	1425	06.02.59
	1922	26.06.63
92064	1444	02.12.55 N
	1646	26.09.59
	1742	13.01.62
92065	1445	10.12.55 N
	1440	15.06.59
	1695	04.11.61
92066	1446	15.12.55 N
	1444	26.11.59
	1456	13.06.63
92067	1447	20.12.55 N
	1451	16.11.61
92068	1448	29.12.55 N
	1420	03.08.62
92069	1449	31.12.55 N
	1648	23.03.63
92070	1450	14.01.56 N
	1431	03.03.62
	1144	??.??.64
92071	1451	21.01.56 N
	1431	31.08.61
	1709	20.11.63
92072	1452	01.02.56 N
	1945	23.08.61
92073	1453	09.02.56 N
	★	??.??.61
92074	1454	18.02.56 N
	1138	03.07.61
	1919	28.11.64
92075	1455	01.03.56 N
92076	1456	06.03.56 N
	1876	20.03.63
92077	1457	13.03.56 N
	1657	23.02.63
92078	1458	21.03.56 N
	★	??.02.65
92079	1459	29.03.56 N
	1128	04.01.60
	★	28.11.64
92080	1460	14.04.56 N
92081	1461	23.04.56 N
	1452	17.10.61
92082	1462	03.05.56 N
	1469	08.12.61
92083	1463	11.05.56 N
	1646	23.08.63
92084	1464	19.05.56 N
	1425	17.09.63
92085	1465	26.05.56 N
	1411	29.09.61
92086	1466	06.06.56 N
	1747	15.08.63
92087	1467	29.08.56 N
	1436	06.03.61
92088	1469	24.10.56 N
	1454	28.09.61

Table 3.3
Standard Cl. 9F 2-10-0s: Record of Boilers Fitted

Engine No.	Boiler No.	Date	Engine No.	Boiler No.	Date	Engine No.	Boiler No.	Date
92088	1708	16.12.64	92119	1666	12.01.57 N	92159	1706	27.11.57 N
(cont.)				*	21.02.64	92160	1707	29.11.57 N
92089	1468	26.09.56 N	92120	1667	28.01.57 N	92161	1708	17.12.57 N
	1462	10.03.62		1450	28.04.62		1431	26.02.64
92090	1470	08.11.56 N	92121	1668	08.02.57 N	92162	1709	19.12.57 N
	1664	07.12.62	92122	1669	18.02.57 N		1659	21.09.63
92091	1471	27.11.56 N		1648	18.04.64	92163	1710	24.03.58 N
92092	1472	13.12.56 N	92123	1670	26.02.57 N	92164	1711	01.04.58 N
	1915	16.03.63		*	30.04.66	92165	1712	17.04.58 N
92093	1473	15.01.57 N	92124	1671	02.03.57 N	92166	1714	24.05.58 N
	1472	06.06.63		1680	04.11.63		1715	24.08.64
92094	1474	04.02.57 N	92125	1672	09.03.57 N	92167	1713	09.05.58 N
	1430	26.01.63		1719	29.08.63	92168	1715	20.12.57 N
92095	1475	06.03.57 N	92126	1673	18.03.57 N		1139	11.12.63
	1950	??.05.62		1475	31.08.62	92169	1716	27.12.57 N
92096	1476	02.04.57 N	92127	1674	29.03.57 N	92170	1718	31.12.57 N
	1426	23.06.62		1474	25.04.63	92171	1717	01.02.58 N
92097	1644	27.06.56 N	92128	1675	05.04.57 N	92172	1719	29.01.58 N
	1446	22.12.59		1649	03.01.64		1412	11.06.63
	1646	28.04.62	92129	1676	10.04.57 N	92173	1720	10.02.58 N
	1458	05.03.65	92130	1677	15.04.57 N		1442	23.08.63
92098	1645	04.07.56 N		1652	28.09.63	92174	1721	10.02.58 N
	1446	01.06.62	92131	1678	25.04.57 N		1679	10.12.63
92099	1646	23.07.56 N		1660	08.11.63	92175	1723	21.02.58 N
	1445	04.09.59	92132	1679	29.04.57 N	92176	1722	04.03.58 N
92100	1647	30.07.56 N		1463	09.10.63	92177	1724	12.03.58 N
	1672	16.10.63	92133	1680	22.05.57 N	92178	1725	28.09.57 N
92101	1648	13.08.56 N		1444	28.08.63		1415	06.10.60
	1471	03.11.62	92134	1681	24.05.57 N	92179	1726	07.10.57 N
92102	1649	15.08.56 N	92135	1682	11.06.57 N	92180	1727	08.11.57 N
	1466	05.10.63	92136	1683	18.06.57 N		1896	26.02.60
92103	1650	18.08.56 N		1902	02.01.60	92181	1728	22.11.57 N
	1667	21.07.62	92137	1684	24.06.57 N	92182	1729	03.12.57 N
92104	1651	24.08.56 N		1435	02.07.60		1720	28.11.63
	1655	29.05.63	92138	1685	25.06.57 N	92183	1730	20.12.57 N
92105	1652	07.09.56 N	92139	1686	28.06.57 N	92184	1731	10.01.58 N
	1923	13.09.63	92140	1687	05.07.57 N	92185	1732	15.01.58 N
92106	1653	12.09.56 N		1644	04.02.60		1727	13.04.60
	1738	23.10.63	92141	1688	29.07.57 N	92186	1733	27.01.58 N
92107	1654	20.09.56 N		1691	08.05.62	92187	1734	12.02.58 N
	1414	26.06.62	92142	1689	29.07.57 N	92188	1735	27.02.58 N
	*	15.01.66	92143	1690	10.08.57 N	92189	1736	14.03.58 N
92108	1655	12.10.56 N	92144	1691	19.08.57 N	92190	1737	28.03.58 N
	1470	29.03.63		1440	29.03.62	92191	1738	15.04.58 N
92109	1656	15.10.56 N	92145	1692	26.08.57 N	92192	1739	01.05.58 N
	1698	18.11.63		1688	06.06.62	92193	1740	23.05.58 N
92110	1657	23.10.56 N	92146	1693	05.09.57 N		1142	06.10.61
	1918	21.11.62		1933	01.05.63	92194	1741	10.06.58 N
92111	1658	06.11.56 N	92147	1695	14.09.57 N	92195	1742	27.06.58 N
	1947	02.01.64		1417	08.07.61		1740	02.12.61
92112	1659	17.11.56 N	92148	1694	21.09.57 N	92196	1743	15.08.58 N
	1930	03.08.63	92149	1696	01.10.57 N		1416	08.04.61
92113	1660	24.11.56 N	92150	1697	05.10.57 N	92197	1744	11.09.58 N
	1473	07.09.63	92151	1698	09.10.57 N	92198	1877	06.10.58 N
92114	1661	29.11.56 N		1464	08.10.63	92199	1745	29.10.58 N
	1653	23.01.64	92152	1699	16.10.57 N	92200	1746	18.11.58 N
92115	1662	12.12.56 N	92153	1700	21.10.57 N	92201	1747	05.12.58 N
	1448	23.11.62	92154	1701	28.10.57 N		1449	11.05.63
92116	1663	22.12.56 N	92155	1702	05.11.57 N	92202	1748	27.12.58 N
	1674	21.06.63	92156	1703	15.11.57 N	92203	1749	06.04.59 N
92117	1664	27.12.56 N	92157	1704	20.11.57 N		1666	29.07.64
	1654	13.10.62	92158	1705	22.11.57 N		1670	31.12.66
92118	1665	28.12.56 N		1457	25.04.63	92204	1879	21.04.59 N

Table 3.3
Standard Cl. 9F 2-10-0s: Record of Boilers Fitted

Engine No.	Boiler No.	Date	Engine No.	Boiler No.	Date	Engine No.	Boiler No.	Date
92205	1880	01.05.59 N	92225	1916	20.06.58 N	92240	1936	02.03.62
92206	1881	06.05.59 N		1941	11.08.64	(cont.)		
92207	1882	01.06.59 N	92226	1917	26.06.58 N	92241	1932	06.10.58 N
92208	1883	11.06.59 N		1130	12.10.61		1890	08.01.62
	1928	25.06.62	92227	1919	03.07.58 N	92242	1933	13.10.58 N
92209	1884	26.06.59 N	92228	1918	12.07.58 N		1438	06.02.63
92210	1885	07.08.59 N		1891	27.09.62	92243	1934	21.10.58 N
92211	1886	08.09.59 N	92229	1920	18.07.58 N	92244	1935	28.10.58 N
92212	1887	22.09.59 N	92230	1921	01.08.58 N		1931	23.05.62
	1924	02.04.62		1883	29.08.62	92245	1936	04.11.58 N
	1901	02.09.65	92231	1922	01.08.58 N		1917	06.12.61
92213	1888	22.10.59 N	92232	1923	06.08.58 N	92246	1937	20.11.58 N
92214	1889	30.10.59 N		1134	14.04.61		1913	12.07.62
92215	1890	17.11.59 N	92233	1924	11.08.58 N	92247	1938	02.12.58 N
	1923	27.10.61		1925	30.01.62	92248	1939	05.12.58 N
92216	1891	01.12.59 N		1645	13.11.64	92249	1940	10.12.58 N
	1935	07.08.62	92234	1925	19.08.58 N		1446	11.12.65
92217	1892	22.12.59 N		1133	15.08.61	92250	1941	16.12.58 N
92218	1893	18.01.60 N		*	10.10.66		1443	20.03.64
92219	1894	27.01.60 N	92235	1926	22.08.58 N			
92220	1895	25.03.60 N		1937	17.09.62			
92221	1912	30.05.58 N	92236	1927	04.09.58 N			
92222	1913	02.06.58 N	92237	1928	09.09.58 N			
	1932	25.04.62		1887	08.05.62			
92223	1914	06.06.58 N	92238	1929	22.09.58 N			
92224	1915	16.06.58 N	92239	1930	25.09.58 N			
	1921	10.10.62	92240	1931	01.10.58 N			

KEY
- N Fitted from New.
- * Information not traced.
- ?? Query on date of fitting.

Figure 48
92166 still with mechanical stoker is again seen at Carlisle, this time at Kingmoor shed on 27th July 1961, having worked in from Birmingham on a Class 'C' freight. In contrast to the view in Fig. 47, the BR1K (No. 1376) tender is fuelled up with suitably small sized coal pieces for the return journey to Washwood Heath. Also in view are a Hughes-Fowler Crab 2-6-0 and a Stanier Class 5 4-6-0.
(RCTS Collection)

by means of a circular flange to the front smokebox and was carried also by diaphragm plates suspended from the main boiler barrel. The preheater tubes provided 1,021 sq ft of heating surface and the exhaust steam jacket (described below) 57 sq ft making a total of 1,078 sq ft for the preheater. Together with the heating surfaces of the main boiler (1,274 sq ft) the firebox (158 sq ft) and superheater (411 sq ft) this gave a total heating surface for the Crosti engines of 2,921 sq ft. The preheater was supplied by Babcock and Wilcox Ltd.

Elbows were welded to the top of the barrel at the front, to which were connected the feed pipes to the main boiler. Clack valves were placed on the rear end of the preheater barrel and were fed by the injectors. A large manhole was provided for access to the preheater for the inspection of the inner surfaces when the tubes were removed; the cover was fitted with a safety valve set to 275 lb/sq in, to prevent the possibility of excessive pressure in the preheater.

The rear portion of the preheater was enveloped in a jacket into which was passed a small quantity of exhaust steam drawn from the left-hand cylinder exhaust pipe. This entered at the top of the front of the jacket and was intended to impart heat to the feed water in the preheater after which it would condense. To take away any air which accumulated from the steam, outlets were provided towards the bottom of the jacket at the rear end and these passed to the final smokebox, where the draught was designed to be sufficient to suck out the air and promote a small circulation of the steam through the jacket. A sump at the bottom of the jacket was fitted with a 'Spirax' steam trap to take away the condensate.

The boiler was fed by two injectors, one exhaust and one live, mounted exactly as in the case of the standard 9Fs. The exhaust injector was a Davies and Metcalf type K with 11 mm cones. The live steam injector was of a BR standard pattern with 10 mm cones. Both were mounted on the right side and normally delivered water direct to the preheater but in an emergency, water could be fed directly to the boiler by unsealing and turning a two-way valve fitted in the live steam injector delivery pipeline. This directed the feed into a pipe leading to a separate clack valve on the front barrel ring. When the water was fed to the preheater, it displaced a similar volume of water which passed through the outlet pipes connected to the two normal top-feed clack valves fitted to the front barrel ring of the main boiler.

Figure 49
92100 (Leicester Midland) heads an eastbound freight through Stamford station on 23rd January 1965. The engine was to take part in the exodus of MML freight power to the north west, in this case to Birkenhead, a few months later. 92100 acquired the BR1F tender during its Heavy General overhaul visit to Crewe from August to October 1963. *(Courtney Haydon)*

4. Tenders

A total of five different designs of tender were carried by the 9Fs; details are given in Table 4.1. The type of tender provided was dependent on where the engines were to be deployed, each region adopting the appropriate design for the duties it had in mind. The exception to this was the BR1K type used on the mechanical stoker-fitted engines, 92165-7.

All BR Standard tenders had six 3 ft 3½ in diameter wheels and their axles were provided with British Timken roller bearing axleboxes placed outside the wheels. External feed water sieve boxes were fitted on each side of the tender to collect any particles of foreign matter which might otherwise be detrimental to the operation of the injectors. The sieves could be withdrawn for cleaning without the necessity of emptying the tank.

All tenders had standardised coupling and connecting arrangements and, again with the exception of the BR1K, could be readily exchanged as required. On removal of the mechanical stokers from 92165-7, the BR1K tenders were modified to the BR1C pattern. Apart from those carried by the NER allocation, 92060-6 and 92097-9, all tenders carried water pick-up apparatus. Coupling of the tender to the engine was by means of a drawbar having plain eye ends, the end in the fabricated dragbox on the engine having an elongated hole. Central curved rubbing blocks were provided on both engine and tender; under normal conditions these ran ¼ in. apart. Two spring-loaded buffers were fitted to the tender dragbox and pressed against the flat rubbing plates on the engine dragbeam.

It was planned that tenders were to be manufactured at the same works as the engine to which they were to be paired; it was reported however that some if not all tenders for the last batch of 9Fs to be built at Swindon were constructed at Ashford Works.

The tender type allocation by region is listed below: full dimensions are given in Diagrams A1 to A4, B, C & D.

BR1B	LMR (Crosti); NER
BR1C	LMR (Standard)
BR1G	WR
BR1F	ER
BR1K	LMR (Mechanical Stoker)

The Crosti engines, 92020-9 delivered to the LMR, were equipped with a BR1B tender. This design had less coal capacity than the BR1C type carried by the standard members of the LMR allocation and reflected the expectation that the Crosti design would result in an overall lower fuel consumption for the duties envisaged. The BR1B tender could in theory be converted into the BR1C type and vice versa by adjusting the coal space panel. The position of the latter enabled the two types to be readily distinguished, the panel being nearer the front of the tender in the case of the BR1B type.

The BR1G tender had an inset coal bunker to improve the crew's view when running in reverse. This feature was employed on the WD 2-8-0s and 2-10-0s and had been a characteristic of continental European practice for many years.

A 6,000 gallon tender had been proposed for five engines

FIGURE J
BR 6,000 GALLON TENDER: PROPOSED DESIGN

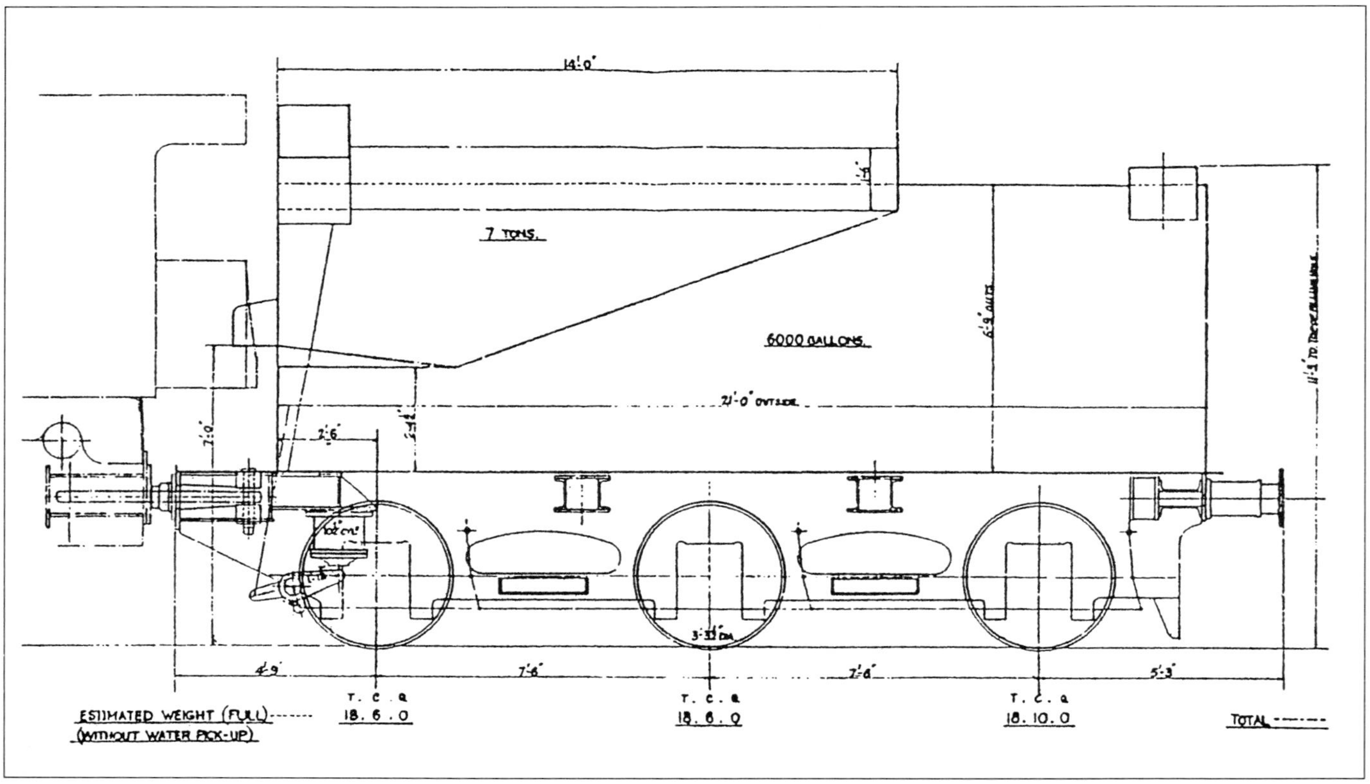

Figure 50
The shortened coal bunker on 92060's BR1B tender compared with that on the BR1C type is clearly visible as the engine heads through South Pelaw Junction towards Consett with a load of iron ore from Tyne Dock in 1965.
(J. W. Armstrong Trust)

Figure 51
92130 appears impatient to begin the next working from its home shed of Carlisle Kingmoor on 18th October 1965. The engine exchanged its BR1C tender for 92070's BR1F type in October 1960. Kingmoor's 9Fs were the only ones regularly rostered for duties into Scotland. Other sheds' 9Fs occasionally strayed north of the border for example those from Tyne Dock which lent one or two of its allocation to Heaton for ECML work at various times.
(Les Elsey)

Figure 52
Recently-restored 92212 with BR1F tender awaits departure from Loughborough on the Great Central preserved line in 1996.
(J. B. Arnold)

originally intended for the SR. The higher water capacity was deemed necessary for greater operating flexibility in view of the lack of water trough facilities on the SR. The proposed design, which resembled the BR1G type, differed from the other Standard tenders in that it had a 15 ft as opposed to a 14 ft wheel base to keep the weight per foot run to a comparable level. A drawing of the design is reproduced in Figure J. The intention had been to utilise redundant roller bearings already supplied for the cancelled Manchester-Sheffield-Wath EM2 electric locomotive order. In the event, the proposed SR 9F allocation was itself cancelled, the engines being redirected to the LMR and the project went no further than the drawing board; details of the 6,000 gallon tender are given in Table 4.1.

In some of the earlier tender designs for the Standard classes i.e. types BR1, BR1A and BR2, the conventional tender fall plate was omitted. This resulted in very draughty conditions on the footplate and fall plates were reintroduced for all later Standard tender designs including those carried by the 9Fs. The tenders were fitted with gangway doors between engine and tender; coal bunker access doors were also provided.

The initial tender allocation for each engine is given in Table 4.1.

Some engines were not fitted with the tender types authorised on the original order. These were as follows:

Tender Type as Originally Ordered and Actually Fitted

Engine Nos.	Original Order	Actually Fitted
92000-09	BR1A	BR1G
92010-14	BR1A	BR1F
92015-19	BR1A	BR1C
92020-29	BR1A	BR1B
92030-44	BR1C	BR1F
92045-59	BR1F	BR1C
92060-66	BR1C	BR1B
92077-86	BR1B	BR1C
92165-67	BR1C	BR1K

The proposed allocation for the initial group, 92000-29, was the WR and SR. The SR allocation was cancelled (see above and Section 7.1) and further changes left the WR with only eight of the first batch, 92000-7. Problems with the draughtiness of the BR1A type referred to earlier led to its modification to incorporate a fall plate, the new design being coded BR1G, the type fitted to all the intended WR 9F allocation. From new, all BR1G tenders carried by the 9Fs included foot stands on the rear top to enable the fireman to stand safely whilst filling the tank. Some half dozen BR1G tenders were later modified by the addition of hind footsteps (see Section 9).

The 92010-4 and 92015-9 groups went to the ER and LMR respectively and carried each region's specified tender, BR1F for the ER and BR1C for the LMR; the Crostis, 92020-29, were equipped with the lower coal capacity BR1B type rather than the draughty BR1A.

The 92030-44 and 92045-59 tender reallocation apparently resulted from a change in engine allocation priority between the ER and LMR. In the case of the NER group 92060-6, it was realised that the intention to deploy the engines mainly on short haul duties i.e. the Tyne Dock-Consett iron ore traffic, meant that a reduced coal capacity would suffice and the BR1B type was thus substituted for the BR1C.

The LMR eventually took delivery of 92077-86 and the stoker-fitted 92165-7, the former group carrying the LMR's BR1C standard type whilst the latter group had the BR1K type modified from the BR1C design to incorporate the engine of the mechanical stoker.

Tender changes were made from time to time and many were entered on the Engine History Cards and Engine Record Cards. Such changes were not always officially documented however and photographic evidence together with observers' records have been consulted to help in

Table 4.1
BR Standard Class 9F 2-10-0s: Initial Tender Allocation

Tender Type (Total built for 9Fs)	Tender Side	Water Capacity gallons	Coal Capacity tons	Weight in Working Order tons	Initial Operating Region	Allocated to Engine Numbers	Tender Serial Numbers	Tender Notes
BR1B (20)	Flush	4,725	7	51.25	LMR NER NER	92020-29 92060-66 92097-99	969 - 978 1149 -1155 1307 -1309	NER allocation tenders not fitted with water pick-up apparatus.
BR1C (85)	Flush	4,725	9	53.25	LMR LMR LMR LMR LMR LMR	92015-19 92045-59 92077-86 92100-39 92150 92151-64¶	964 - 968 1134 -1148 1166 -1175 1310 -1349 1271 1360 -1373	92150 was allocated tender BR1E 1271 (ex-71000 *Duke of Gloucester*) modified to a 1C type which retained its serial number. Tender numbers for 92151-64 were not allocated in sequence; see below.
BR1F (85)	Flush	5,625	7	55.25	ER ER ER ER ER ER ER ER ER	92010-14 92030-44 92067-76 92087-96 92140-49 92168 92169-77 92178-99 92200-02	959 - 963 1119 -1133 1156 -1165 1176 -1185 1350 -1359 1374 1378 -1386 1388 -1409 1410 -1412	Highest Standard tender water capacity. The only other Standard class to be allocated this type of tender were the Class 5 4-6-0s 73110-19.
BR1G (58)	Inset at top	5,000	7	52.50	WR LMR WR WR	92000-07 92008-09 92203-20 92221-50	949 - 956 957 - 958 1510 -1527 1532 -1561	
BR1K (3)	Flush	4,325	9	52.35	LMR	92165-67	1375 -1377	For Berkley mechanical stoker.
Proposed (-)	Inset at top	6,000	7	55.10 (estimated)	-	-	-	Intended for SR; cancelled when SR locomotive allocation redirected to LMR; no water pick-up apparatus.

¶ Tender numbers for 92151-64 allocated in the order: 1361-1371, 1360, 1372-1373. See text and Table 4.2 for details.

Figure 53
92071's home shed of Annesley provides a resting place on 24th June 1962. Earlier, in January, it acquired BR1C tender No. 1340, originally paired with 92130, giving up a BR1F type to 92070. *(Eric Fry)*

Figure 54
The boiler for 92210, No. 1885, is seen on its frames in Swindon 'A' shop on 3rd May 1959. 92210 was delivered to Cardiff Canton in August 1959 and withdrawn just over five years later in November 1964. *(E. W. Fry)*

Figure 55
92231 is pictured at its home shed of Eastleigh on 16th May 1961. It has been allocated along with other WR 9Fs for the Fawley-Bromford Bridge oil traffic. 92231 had undergone a Heavy Intermediate overhaul at Eastleigh Works, having covered some 78,500 miles since delivery. Any repainting appears to have been confined to the smokebox area. The extra lamp brackets halfway up the smokebox door are for the SR disc route markers; the WR-style lamp brackets remain in place. *(P. J. Cupper)*

producing a more comprehensive picture; a list of tender changes derived from the various sources is given in Table 4.2.

Reported modifications to tenders during service were few. Record Cards indicate that in the late 1950s, a number of BR1F tenders were provided with a Briquette Tube Feeder in connection with the BR on-board water softening system. There may have been others so treated however, as some reports suggest the official record is incomplete and most if not all the BR1F tenders carried by the 9Fs were thus modified.

The modification consisted of fitting a cylindrical container in the tender's water space into which chemical briquettes were inserted. The chemicals prevented solids already present in the boiler water feed from being deposited as scale on the interior surfaces of the boiler; the system inhibited corrosion of boiler tubes and plates and extended the period between boiler washouts The blowdown apparatus ensured sludge deposits were largely dispersed before they could cause boiler priming. In the vast majority of cases the BR1F tenders officially recorded as thus modified were carried by engines which at some stage had been allocated to Annesley MPD where the local water supply was known to have a very high hardness factor. In many contemporary photographs of Annesley engines, the areas adjacent to the cylinders, safety valve and other areas on the engines' boilers are coated with much calcareous white deposit.

In the majority of cases, the modification appears to have been carried out during brief visits to Stratford Works; dates of the visits where known are listed in Table 8.2. A list of the tenders known to have been modified is given below:

BR1F Tenders Fitted with Briquette Tube Feeders

Tender	Paired with Engine
959-963	92010-4
1119-22/26	92030-33/37*
1132	92043
1156-1165	92067-76
1176-1185	92087-96
1405/6	92195*/96*

* Not allocated to Annesley at any time.

In connection with water softening experiments at Annesley, 92088 was reported to have undergone trials with the French TIA *(Traitement Intégrale Armand)* system successfully used on the SR. The indications are that the BR briquette method was cheaper to operate and more robust in service however and was the preferred option; 92088's tender (BR1F 1178) converted from the TIA system is included in the above list.

In June 1956, a leading axle taken from a BR Standard tender was found to be cracked as a result of corrosion fatigue. The problem appeared to be confined to the BR1 and BR2 types on which the shovelling plate and brake cylinder drains discharged over the axle. A programme to install a protection shield was authorised to be carried out as engines passed through works; It is possible that some 9F tenders were thus modified. This programme was discontinued in October 1964 with an unknown number of tenders still to be treated.

The Record Cards for tenders BR1F 959-963, as carried by 92010-14 are endorsed with the information 'Heating Gear Fitted'. It is not known for certain but this may possibly refer to a modification to prevent the external tender mounted water sieves freezing up in winter weather, a fault to which the Standard tenders were prone.

Table 4.2
BR Standard Class 9F 2-10-0s: Record of Tenders Fitted

Loco. No.	T	Tender No. & fitting date		Loco. No.	T	Tender No. & fitting date		Loco. No.	T	Tender No. & fitting date		Loco. No.	T	Tender No. & fitting date	
92000	1G	949	01.54	92035	1F	1124	12.54	92069	1F	1177	11.65	92094	1C	1174	12.66
	1G	1513	03.60	92036	1F	1125	12.54	(cont.)	1F	1161	02.66	(cont.)			
92001	1G	950	01.54		1F	1397	04.61	92070	1F	1159	01.56	92095	1F	1184	03.57
	1F	★	09.64°	92037	1F	1126	12.54		1C	1340	10.60		1F	1160	12.63
92002	1G	951	01.54		1F	1128	11.55		1F	1158	01.62		1G	957	09.64
92003	1G	952	01.54	92038	1F	1127	12.54	92071	1F	1160	01.56	92096	1F	1185	04.57
92004	1G	953	01.54		1F	1123	05.62		1F	1158	01.61		1F	959	10.60
92005	1G	954	02.54		1F	1399	06.65		1C	1340	01.62		1F	1122	05.61
92006	1G	955	02.54	92039	1F	1128	12.54	92072	1F	1161	02.56	92097	1B	1307	06.56
92007	1G	956	02.54		1F	1126	11.55	92073	1F	1162	02.56		1B	1149	12.60
92008	1G	957	03.54	92040	1F	1129	12.54		1F	961	09.58	92098	1B	1308	07.56
	1F	1160	09.64	92041	1F	1130	12.54		1F	1182	11.59		1B	1155	03.63
92009	1G	958	03.54	92042	1F	1131	01.55		1F	1179	10.60		1B	1153	07.64
	1C	967	04.55		1F	1394	02.63	92074	1F	1163	02.56	92099	1B	1309	07.56
	1G	958	04.55	92043	1F	1132	01.55		1F	1157	12.57		1B	1151	04.60
	1C	1168	05.56		1F	1178	06.60		1F	1182	11.63		1B	1309	07.60
92010	1F	959	05.54	92044	1F	1133	01.55	92075	1F	1164	03.56	92100	1C	1310	07.56
	1F	1163	05.58	92045	1C	1134	02.55	92076	1F	1165	03.56		1F	1386	10.63
	1F	962	03.61		1C	1317	05.62	92077	1C	1166	03.56	92101	1C	1311	08.56
92011	1F	960	05.54	92046	1C	1135	02.55		1C	1373	07.63		1G	1560	04.67
92012	1F	961	05.54	92047	1C	1136	02.55	92078	1C	1167	03.56	92102	1C	1312	08.56
	1F	1162	09.58	92048	1C	1137	02.55	92079	1C	1168	03.56	92103	1C	1313	08.56
	1C	★	04.67°		1C	1341	05.60		1G	958†	05.56		1C	1317	★
92013	1F	962	04.54		1C	1140	11.60		1G	949	01.60	92104	1C	1314	08.56
	1F	1183	09.60	92049	1C	1138	03.55		1G	958†	01.60		1C	1271	08.61
92014	1F	963	05.54	92050	1C	1139	08.55	92080	1C	1169	04.56	92105	1C	1315	09.56
	1C	1323	03.64		1C	1329	09.61		1C	1372	07.64	92106	1C	1316	09.56
	1F	1119	03.64	92051	1C	1140	08.55	92081	1C	1170	04.56		1C	1144	05.62
92015	1C	964	09.54		1C	1341	11.60		1C	1330	02.60		1C	1328	07.67
92016	1C	965	10.54	92052	1C	1141	08.55	92082	1C	1171	05.56	92107	1C	1317	09.56
92017	1C	966	10.54		1B	969	11.59		1B	971	10.59		1C	1134	05.62
92018	1C	967	10.54	92053	1C	1142	09.55	92083	1C	1172	05.56	92108	1C	1318	10.56
	1G	958	04.55	92054	1C	1143	09.55		1C	1176	12.61	92109	1C	1319	10.56
	1C	967	04.55	92055	1C	1144	09.55		1F	★	08.64°		1C	1329	09.61
	1C	1148	08.65		1C	1316	05.62	92084	1C	1173	05.56		1C	1139	09.61
92019	1C	968	10.54	92056	1C	1145	10.55		1C	1142	01.66	92110	1C	1320	10.56
92020	1B	969	05.55	92057	1C	1146	10.55	92085	1C	1174	05.56		1C	1322	11.61
	1C	1141	11.59		1C	1175	01.61		1F	1181	12.66	92111	1C	1321	11.56
	1C	1349	07.64		1F	1177	01.62	92086	1C	1175	06.56	92112	1C	1322	11.56
92021	1B	970	05.55	92058	1C	1147	10.55		1C	1146	01.61		1C	1320	11.61
	1G	1551	02.65		1B	★	04.67°		1F	1176	02.61	92113	1C	1323	11.56
92022	1B	971	05.55	92059	1C	1148	10.55		1C	1172	12.61		1F	1119	03.64
	1C	1171	10.59		1C	1326	04.65°		1C	1169	01.67		1C	1323	03.64
92023	1B	972	05.55	92060	1B	1149	11.55	92087	1F	1176	08.56	92114	1C	1324	11.56
	1C	1334	10.60		1B	1307	12.60		1C	1146	03.61	92115	1C	1325	12.56
	1G	1537	01.65	92061	1B	1150	11.55	92088	1F	1178	10.56	92116	1C	1326	12.56
92024	1B	973	06.55		1B	1152	05.62		1F	1121	06.60		1C	1148	04.65
	1G	1560	01.65	92062	1B	1151	11.55	92089	1F	1177	09.56		1C	967	08.65
	1F	1157	12.65		1B	1309	04.60		1F	1181	12.60	92117	1C	1327	12.56
92025	1B	974	06.55		1B	1151	07.60		1F	1163	03.61	92118	1C	1328	12.56
92026	1B	975	06.55	92063	1B	1152	11.55	92090	1F	1179	11.56		1G	★	07.67°
92027	1B	976	06.55		1B	1150	05.62		1F	1182	10.60	92119	1C	1329	01.57
92028	1B	977	07.55	92064	1B	1153	12.55		1F	1157	11.63		1C	1319	09.61
92029	1B	978	07.55		1B	1155	07.64		1G	1560	12.65	92120	1C	1330	01.57
92030	1F	1119	11.54	92065	1B	1154	12.55		1C	1311	04.67		1C	1170	02.60
	1F	963	03.64	92066	1B	1155	12.55	92091	1F	1180	11.56		1C	1344	06.60
92031	1F	1120	11.54		1B	1308	03.63?	92092	1F	1181	12.56	92121	1C	1331	02.57
92032	1F	1121	11.54	92067	1F	1156	12.55		1F	1177	12.60	92122	1C	1332	02.57
	1F	1132	07.60	92068	1F	1157	12.55		1C	1175	01.62	92123	1C	1333	02.57
92033	1F	1122	11.54		1F	1163	12.57		1C	1325	★	92124	1C	1334	03.57
	1F	959	05.61		1F	959	05.58	92093	1F	1182	01.57		1B	972	09.60
92034	1F	1123	12.54		1F	1185	10.60		1F	961	11.59	92125	1C	1335	03.57
	1F	1394	09.61	92069	1F	1158	12.55	92094	1F	1183	02.57	92126	1C	1336	03.57
	1F	1123	10.61		1F	1160	01.61		1F	962	09.60	92127	1C	1337	03.57
	1F	1127	05.62		1F	1184	12.63		1F	1181	03.61		1C	1376	08.67

Table 4.2
BR Standard Class 9F 2-10-0s: Record of Tenders Fitted

Loco. No.	T	Tender No.	& fitting date
92128	1C	1338	04.57
92129	1C	1339	04.57
92130	1C	1340	04.57
	1F	1159	10.60
92131	1C	1341	04.57
	1C	1137	05.60
92132	1C	1342	04.57
92133	1C	1343	05.57
92134	1C	1344	05.57
	1C	1170	06.60
	1C	1372	09.60
	1C	1169	07.64
92135	1C	1345	06.57
92136	1C	1346	06.57
92137	1C	1347	06.57
92138	1C	1348	06.57
92139	1C	1349	06.57
	1C	1141	09.64
92140	1F	1350	07.57
	1F	1400	05.65
92141	1F	1351	07.57
	1F	1359	08.65
92142	1F	1352	07.57
92143	1F	1353	08.57
92144	1F	1354	08.57
92145	1F	1355	08.57
	1F	1395	04.62
	1F	1125	06.64
92146	1F	1356	09.57
92147	1F	1357	09.57
92148	1F	1358	09.57
92149	1F	1359	10.57
	1F	1351	08.65
92150	1C	1271	10.57[1]
	1C	1314	08.61
92151	1C	1361	10.57
92152	1C	1362	10.57
	1C	1365	03.63
92153	1C	1363	10.57
92154	1C	1364	10.57
	1C	1373	03.61
	1C	1166	07.63
92155	1C	1365	11.57
	1C	1362	03.63
92156	1C	1366	11.57
	1C	1371	07.64
92157	1C	1367	11.57
92158	1C	1368	11.57
92159	1C	1369	11.57
92160	1C	1370	11.57
	1G	*	11.64
92161	1C	1371	12.57
	1C	1366	07.64
92162	1C	1360	12.57
92163	1C	1372	03.58
	1C	1170	09.60
92164	1C	1373	04.58
	1C	1364	03.61
92165	1K	1375	04.58
92166	1K	1376	05.58
	1C	1337	08.67
92167	1K	1377	05.58
92168	1F	1374	12.57[2]
92169	1F	1378	12.57
92170	1F	1379	12.57
92171	1F	1380	02.58
	1F	1125	04.61
	1F	1395	06.64
92172	1F	1381	01.58
92173	1F	1382	02.58
92174	1F	1383	02.58
92175	1F	1384	02.58
	1F	1407	08.61
92176	1F	1385	03.58
	1F	1380	04.61
92177	1F	1386	03.58
92178	1F	1388	09.57
92179	1F	1389	10.57
	1F	1410	11.65
92180	1F	1390	11.57
92181	1F	1391	11.57
92182	1F	1392	12.57
92183	1F	1393	12.57
92184	1F	1394	01.58
	1F	1123	09.61
	1F	1394	10.61
	1F	1131	02.63
92185	1F	1395	01.58
	1F	1355	04.62
	1F	1406	02.65
92186	1F	1396	01.58
	1F	1401	04.61
92187	1F	1397	02.58
	1F	1401	04.61
92188	1F	1398	02.58
92189	1F	1399	03.58
	1F	1123	06.65
92190	1F	1400	03.58
	1F	1385	05.61
92191	1F	1401	04.58
	1F	1400	04.61
	1F	1350	05.65
92192	1F	1402	05.58
92193	1F	1403	05.58
	1F	1406	02.61
	1F	1355	02.65
	1F	1384	09.65
92194	1F	1404	06.58
92195	1F	1405	06.58
92196	1F	1406	08.58
	1F	1403	04.61
92197	1F	1407	09.58
	1F	1384	07.61
	1F	1355	09.65
92198	1F	1408	10.58
92199	1F	1409	10.58
92200	1F	1410	11.58
	1F	1389	11.65
92201	1F	1411	12.58
92202	1F	1412	12.58
92203	1G	1510	04.59
92204	1G	1511	04.59
	1G	1535	11.62
92205	1G	1512	05.59
92206	1G	1513	05.59
	1G	1542	11.59
92207	1G	1514	06.59
92208	1G	1515	06.59
92208 (cont.)	1G	1537	03.63
	1C	1334	01.65°
92209	1G	1516	06.59
92210	1G	1517	08.59
92211	1G	1518	09.59
92212	1G	1519	09.59
	1F	1182	04.67
92213	1G	1520	10.59
	1G	1539	11.59
92214	1G	1521	10.59
	1G	1519	04.67
92215	1G	1522	11.59
	1G	1538	07.60
	1G	1537	10.61
	1G	1515	03.63
	1B	977	03.67°
92216	1G	1523	12.59
92217	1G	1524	12.59
92218	1G	1525	01.60
	1G	1520	09.62
	1C	*	08.66°
92219	1G	1526	01.60
92220	1G	1527	03.60
92221	1G	1532	05.58
92222	1G	1533	06.58
92223	1G	1534	06.58
92224	1G	1535	06.58
	1G	1554	10.62
	1G	1552	08.66
92225	1G	1536	06.58
92226	1G	1537	06.58
	1G	1538	10.61
92227	1G	1538	07.58
	1G	1522	07.60
92228	1G	1539	07.58
	1G	1520	11.59
	1G	1525	09.62
92229	1G	1540	07.58
92230	1G	1541	08.58
92231	1G	1542	08.58
	1G	958	10.59
	1G	949	01.60
92232	1G	1543	08.58
92233	1G	1544	08.58
	1G	1551	01.62
	1B	970	02.65
92234	1G	1545	08.58
92235	1G	1546	08.58
	1G	1561	06.62
92236	1G	1547	09.58
92237	1G	1548	09.58
92238	1G	1549	09.58
92239	1G	1550	09.58
92240	1G	1551	10.58
	1G	1544	03.62
	1C	*	10.90°
92241	1G	1552	10.58
92242	1G	1553	10.58
92243	1G	1554	10.58
	1G	1511	11.62
92244	1G	1555	10.58
92245	1G	1556	11.58
92246	1G	1557	11.58
92247	1G	1558	12.58
92247 (cont.)	1G	1554	08.61°
92248	1G	1559	12.58
92249	1G	1560	12.58
	1B	973	01.65
92250	1G	1561	12.58
	1G	1546	06.62

KEY

T: tender type

* : no information

†: modified

° by this date

[1] see Table 4.1 for detail

[2] ran as 1F1377 from Dec. '57 to May '58

NOTES

1K tenders modified to 1C at time of mechanical stoker removal (see text).

92240
BRIC tender carried in preservation is newly constructed 1C type retaining the original 1G number.

5. Construction Costs

Comparison of the Authorised Cost, the Record Card Final Cost and the Official Final Cost per engine are given in Table 5.1. From the first batch delivered by Crewe in 1954 to the last batch from that works in 1958, manufacturing cost inflation was almost 26%; it should be borne in mind however that the 1958 batch was furnished with the double draughting arrangement and other refinements (see Section 1). It will be noted that the Official Final Costs for the Swindon-built batches were between 10% and 18% higher per engine than those at Crewe for engines turned out over comparable periods.

The Crosti-boilered examples, 92020-9, and the mechanical stoker versions were each around £2,000 more expensive to put into traffic compared with the conventional engines delivered during the same period. The engines fitted with Westinghouse air pumps for the Tyne Dock-Consett traffic also incurred greater costs, some £600 each in the case of 92060-6 and about £1,000 per engine for 92097-9 compared with their Crewe-built standard contemporaries.

With regard to the 1953 and 1954 manufacturing programmes, the authorised costs were reasonably accurate compared with the final costs, with the exception of the Crosti-boilered batch 92020-29 which were just over 7% too low. For the 1956 standard batches however, the figure of £23,000 per engine was clearly a significant underestimate. It is not clear why this figure was a reduction on the 1953/4 figures. According to the official BR correction factors normally applied for yearly monetary inflation, price variances etc., the unit cost figure for 1956 should have been of the order of £26,550. The 1957 and 1958 authorised unit costs were similarly too low at 6.8% for the Crewe-built examples and 18.4% for each of the Swindon batch; the higher cost of the Swindon-built engines is largely attributed to the higher cost of the boilers.

Quotations in 1955 for the supply of 35 locomotives each from North British Locomotive Co. and the Vulcan Foundry referred to in Section 1.2 were respectively £30,058 and £31,268 for each locomotive. These figures, more than 20% higher than the contemporary Crewe Works quotation, were deemed too high to be worth further negotiation.

It is of interest to compare the manufacturing costs of the 9Fs with those of the LMS Stanier Class 8F 2-8-0s in the 1930s and 1940s. The 2-8-0s were built at several non-LMS works as part of the World War Two effort and representative costs per engine are given below; again Swindon charges were the highest.

Works	**Date**	**Record Card Final Cost (£)**
Crewe LMS	06.35	7,053
Crewe LMS	09.42	8,355
Eastleigh SR	01.43	12,159
Doncaster LNER	06.43	11,754
Horwich LMS	01.44	10,944
Swindon GWR	03.44	12,514
Brighton SR	06.44	12,093
Darlington LNER	01.45	11,754

Figure 56
Crewe-built 92097 calls at Coleham shed, Shrewsbury during a running-in turn from the works in June 1956. Fitted with Westinghouse air pumps and allocated to Tyne Dock, 92097 performed mainly on the Consett ore workings until withdrawal in October 1966. *(D. Tyreman Collection)*

Table 5.1
BR Standard Class 9F 2-10-0s
Manufacturing Cost Comparison

Programme Year	Locomotive Number	Delivery Year	Authorised Cost (£)	Record Card Final Cost (£)	Official Final Cost (£)
1953	92000-07	1954	23,500	23,316	23,975
	92008-09	1954	23,500	23,226	23,882
	92010-14	1954	23,500	23,178	23,828
	92015-19	1954	23,500	23,221	23,655
	92020-29 (1)	1955	23,853 (2)	26,593	25,584
1954	92030-44	1954/5	23,500	21,799	23,266
	92045-49	1955	23,500	21,799	23,266
	92050-59	1955	23,500	22,841	24,343
	92060-66 (3)	1955	23,500	(4)	24,945
	92067-76	1955/6	23,500	23,062	24,563
	92077-86	1956	23,500	22,842	24,343
	92087-96 (5)	1956/7	23,500	30,193	29,699
1956	92097-99 (3)	1956	23,000 (6)	(4)	27,362
	92100-34	1956/7	23,000 (6)	24,541	26,344
	92135-39	1957	23,000 (6)	26,036	27,871
	92140-49	1957	23,000 (6)	(4)	27,871
	92150-64	1957/8	23,000 (6)	26,036	27,871
	92165-67 (7)(8)	1958	29,000	29,995	30,308
	92168-77	1957/8	23,000 (6)	26,036	27,871
	92178-202 (5)(9)	1957/8	28,277 (2)	(4)	32,845
1957	92203-20 (5)(8)	1959/60	28,277 (2)	30,960	33,497
1958	92221-50 (8)	1958	28,277 (2)	28,365	30,200

KEY
(1) Fitted with Crosti boiler.
(2) Representative Departmental First Cost. This included the full share of overhead and administrative costs but did not include interest on capital expenditure authorised during construction. The Representative Departmental First Cost for the non-Crosti boiler engines in the 92000-96 series was, at £22,263, some £600 per engine lower than that for the Crostis.
(3) Fitted with Westinghouse Air Pumps.
(4) Information not traced; it is assumed the Official Final Cost and the Record Card Final Cost are the same.
(5) 92087-96, 92178-92220 built at Swindon, remainder of class built at Crewe
(6) Artificially low authorisation cost reported; see text, Section 5.
(7) Fitted with Berkley Mechanical Stoker.
(8) Fitted with double blastpipe and chimney as delivered
(9) Fitted with double blastpipe and chimney as delivered (except 92179-82)

Figure 57
Prior to being repainted green and named *Evening Star,* 92220 is seen in black livery at Swindon 'A' Shop in February 1960.
(G. Wheeler)

Figure 58
After a Heavy General overhaul and boiler change, 92025 (Wellingborough) awaits resteaming outside Crewe Works paint shop on 14th January 1962. Alongside is Britannia Pacific 70022 *Tornado* (Carlisle Kingmoor); both engines were withdrawn from service in 1967, 92025 in November and 70022 in December.
(RCTS Collection)

Figure 59
The last-built 9F 'panned'! 92220, *Evening Star* nears Midford on the S&DJR single line section from Bath Junction with the 3.35pm Bristol-Bournemouth West on 14th September 1963. 92220 now carries the electric warning flashes on the boiler and smoke deflectors, probably as a result of its previous duties from Oxford which involved regular visits to Crewe where it would encounter lines equipped with 25kV overhead electric power cables.
(Hugh Ballantyne)

Figure 60
92040 poses outside the paint shop at Crewe Works in August 1963. New England was host to 92040 for over eight years from where it was used mainly on the Ferme Park mineral traffic. Although carrying a New England shedplate, 92040 was nominally a Colwick engine by this time; AWS was installed in December 1959. 92040 is one of the GN line 9Fs for which no example of an appearance on passenger work has been traced to date. *(Eric Fry)*

Figure 61
Having just been reallocated to Immingham from New England, 92038 reposes on Doncaster shed in July 1963; 92038 had run well over a quarter of a million miles in service by this date.
(RCTS Collection)

Figure 62
92200 (Doncaster) is depicted at its home shed in May 1962; the Darlington-style large cab numbers with the absence of the power classification will be noted in comparison with the Crewe-style finish applied to 92038 in Figure 61.
(RCTS Collection)

6. Liveries

All but one of the 9Fs were delivered in the BR freight engine plain black livery. There were minor variations with the cabside and tender insignia however. After March 1957, engines built new or repainted received the second BR crest (popularly known as the 'ferret and dartboard') on the tender, usually of the larger size instead of the earlier Lion and Wheel ('cycling lion') emblem.

The one exception to the black livery was 92220 *Evening Star,* the last steam engine built by British Railways which was displayed at the naming ceremony at Swindon Works on 18th March 1960 in full Swindon-style lined-green livery complete with the celebrated Great Western copper capped chimney. The engine had been routinely finished in the standard black livery in the early part of February and had languished on works whilst its repainting and celebrity status were being arranged.

In the standard BR green livery specification, working from the outside edge, the linings for the tender and cabside consisted of a ⅛ in wide orange line then a ½ in green gap followed by a 1 in wide black line, completed by a symmetrical repeat of the green gap and orange line. The boiler casing bands were similarly treated whilst the cylinder casings had orange lines of ⅛ in width inset from the edges. The treatment of the lining on *Evening Star's* running plate was different from that on the Standard Pacifics. The latter had an orange line round the inner edges of the plate to form a panel whereas on *Evening Star* the orange line was confined to the lower edge of the running plate (see Appendix 9 for further livery details).

It was natural that *Evening Star* would come in for special treatment during its lifetime and it had more than its fair share of repaints. In May 1961 for example, it appeared in spotless 'exhibition finish' along with BR Class 8 Pacific 71000 *Duke of Gloucester* at Marylebone goods yard to celebrate the Golden Jubilee of the Institution of Locomotive Engineers; its state implied an early repaint despite being little more than a year old.

Regarding the style of cabside numbers and classification lettering, Crewe practice was to use the standard 8 in numerals with the full '9F' logo; there was a least one instance however of a Crewe ex-works engine with the simple '9' in place (92097, April 1963 after a Heavy Casual overhaul). In some cases during repaints, mainly on plain black unlined engines such as the 9Fs, Crewe apparently adopted the technique of repainting the original numerals by hand brush, possibly with the help of stencils as guides, rather than using new transfers; these engines were repainted but not revarnished. For later repaints, Crewe may have 'painted round' the emblem and crest transfers as routine, particularly from 1964 onwards.

For new 9Fs destined for the Western Region, photographic evidence indicates that Crewe did not routinely apply the GWR/WR 'Blue Spot' route authorisation code below the numerals. However, ex-works views of the newly-delivered 92250, the last steam engine produced at Crewe in December 1958 do show the 'Blue Spot' in place. In addition to the coloured disc route code, WR engines were also given a power classification letter approximately proportional to the tractive effort which was carried within the coloured spot; in the case of the 28XX 2-8-0s, for example, the power class was 'E'. The WR-based 9Fs' category would have been designated 'Special' since their tractive effort exceeded 38,000 lbs. It is not clear however whether any of the BR Standard designs operating on the WR were categorised in this way. In any event, no photographic evidence has been traced to indicate any reference was ever made to this classification within the 'Blue Spot' in the case of the 9Fs.

Figure 63
92002 is outside Swindon Works on 26th May 1954 where it is awaiting modifications to the regulator and braking systems for later trials. The engine was fitted with a double chimney at Swindon in November 1960.
(Hugh Ballantyne)

Figure 64
Longmoor, 8th June 1968; David Shepherd's 92203, newly purchased from RR stands in the shed yard just after being named *Black Prince*; a red lining has been applied to its black livery. *(Hugh Ballantyne)*

Figure 65
Near Bassaleg Junction on 7th March 1958, 92000 (Newport Ebbw Junction) banks an ore train from Newport Docks towards Ebbw Vale steel works; note the familiar 'NOT IN COMMON USE' GWR brake. *(R. K. Taylor)*

Gorton, Derby and Rugby had a hand in repairing 9Fs for certain periods (see Section 8 for details). Only Light Casual and Light Intermediate repairs were carried out as a rule which would not have involved a repaint in all cases; it is likely that Crewe practice was adopted regarding cabside markings.

A curious feature of the numerals applied at Swindon was the use of standard 8 in characters of two different thicknesses. Often these different styles were used on the same engine and were unmistakable when used alongside each other in the same cabside number. There does not appear to have been a pattern in which some figures were always thicker than others; presumably this feature was the result of old stocks of numerals being used up from time to time. Towards the end of the final 9F building programme, certain digits had reverted to the thinner type, first the '0', then the '2' and so on such that by the time 92220 appeared only the '9' remained thicker; the absence of an outer black line to these transfers was noticeable on 92220. For the cabside class designation, Swindon applied only the figure '9' for the whole of the period of responsibility for 9F manufacture and repairs. It has not been possible to confirm whether the 9F tenders supplied to Swindon by Ashford Works for the final engines were fully painted before arrival.

On delivery, the Timken roller bearing axle box covers on the engines' tenders were finished in black. Later, the covers were painted yellow to distinguish them from the plain bearing types; later still when the maintenance specification was altered, a horizontal red stripe was added across the centre line of the yellow box covers to indicate that no routine lubrication was required.

It was a custom in WR works for the paint shop teams to 'sign' their work by hand-painting in small characters about five millimetres high on the tenders of the engines on which they had worked. The legend was usually applied to the bottom right hand corner of the left hand side of the tender. 92245 was noted on the 14th January 1962 thus adorned at Old Oak Common MPD, having completed a Heavy Intermediate overhaul at Swindon in December 1961. In this case the legend read '29/11/61-W' and referred to the date of painting followed by the initial of the paint team leader. It is not clear whether such dates were applied to locomotives built or repaired at Swindon for other regions.

Records show that Caerphilly, Oswestry and Wolverhampton Stafford Road carried out repairs on 9Fs but all were of the Casual or Intermediate type probably not requiring a repaint. It is likely that Swindon practice would have been followed, although the use of numerals of different thickness was apparently confined to Swindon.

Darlington overhauled the ER/NER allocation until September 1962 where 10 in. widely spaced large size numerals were routinely used. The practice was to omit the cabside power class logo at least until about 1961; the convention of painting the logo on the front buffer beam as with some other classes was not followed for the 9Fs as judged by photographic evidence. Similarly no photographs have been traced of a 9F with the old LNER route availability code 'RA9' painted on the cab side.

All the engines in the first Tyne Dock allocation, (92060-66), visited Gateshead Works for repairs in 1956/7 but it is likely that no repaints took place there as the engines were only a few months old at the time. Similarly visits to Stratford Works in 1955 and 1957 were for casual repairs or tender modifications not involving repaints.

A number of 9Fs were dealt with at Eastleigh Works from January 1961 to August 1964. With the exception of the NER allocation, repairs were carried out on 9Fs from all regions in addition to those allocated to the SR. Where repaints were undertaken, photographic evidence suggests Eastleigh may in a number of cases have simply repainted the existing numerals, either 8 in or 10 in; the adoption of the full '9F' classification logo appears to have been the norm as and when applied.

The Crosti boiler 9Fs, 92020-9, after conversion to conventional operation, were unofficially down-rated to 8F (see Section 9). Despite this, it has not been possible to trace any views of class members with the elusive '8' or '8F' legend on the cab side.

Variations

As with many steam engines surviving into the mid-1960s, theft of numberplates was commonplace and the 9Fs suffered their fair share of this practice. Where numberplates were replaced it was with wooden plaques or in some cases the number was simply chalked on; for shedplates, the legend was usually painted on.

Colour-backed numberplates were also seen on one or two 9Fs in the latter days of steam on BR. Examples are:

92006 (light blue). This background colour (or carmine red in some cases) is usually associated with engines allocated to the Scottish Region (ScR) although none of the class was ever allocated to that region. In the mid-1960s however some 9Fs were at Carlisle Kingmoor, by then an LMR depot but formerly an ScR depot some years before the 9Fs arrived. 92006 was not allocated to Carlisle Kingmoor at any time although may have been an occasional visitor when at York (September 1963-October 1966).

92063 (orange). Allocated to the NER's Tyne Dock MPD for virtually all of its life, the engine was noted on enthusiasts' specials with this adornment.

In a very few cases, shed names were painted on to the bufferbeams of some 9Fs. Examples from photographs include:

92006 York
92063 Tyne Dock
92113 Birkenhead
92139 Saltley

The power classification '9F' also appeared on some engine buffer beams; these include (with dates): 92010 (27.07.55); 92063 (16.11.65) and 92139 (13.11.65).

From April 1960, the month after the last 9F was put into traffic, BR authorised the fitting of warning flashes to engines working over lines equipped with overhead electric wires. This was the response to a number of incidents where footplate staff had been seriously injured or worse during routine duties such as lamp changing and tender filling.

The whole class was fitted with the flashes which depicted a bolt of lightning in red on a white background affixed at key points on the engine. Typically these were at the base of the smoke deflectors, on the first boiler ring near to the clack valve, on the firebox next to the cab and on the rear of the tender adjacent to the top corners. For the NER-based engines at Tyne Dock, a further flash was situated about halfway up the side of the smoke deflector, located near the deflector edge but inside the hand rail perimeter. For the Crosti boiler engines, which were not fitted with smoke deflectors, the forward flashes were located on the sides of the frames adjacent to the steps above the buffer beam.

Figure 66
92078 (Toton) wheels an up mixed freight towards Elstree tunnel on 26th September 1959. The engine would complete almost 23,000 miles that year, making a grand total of almost 100,000 miles since delivery. 92078 was one of the first 9Fs to be intentionally employed on passenger work when it took over a Scouts Jamboree special from Dover to Sutton Park at Cricklewood on 30th July 1957. AWS was fitted in January 1963. *(Courtney Haydon)*

Figure 67
Crosti boiler 92023 approaches Pontefract Baghill from the south on 19th April 1958 with the daily iron ore train from the Wellingborough area to Cargo Fleet (Middlesbrough). The engine came off at Skelton Sidings, York where an NER engine took over. Up until 1957, the Beyer Garratts worked this train on most occasions, after which both 8F 2-8-0 and 9F power shared the duty. *(Peter Cookson)*

7. Allocation and Duties

7.1 Delivery Period, January 1954 - April 1960

The 30 engines in the 1953 building programme, 92000-29, were originally allocated by Region as shown:

WR	(20)	92000-19
ER	(5)	92020-24
SR	(5)	92025-29

Early reports suggested that the SR engines were to be fitted with Westinghouse air brakes for working through continental traffic between London and Dover. In connection with this proposal WD 2-10-0 90757, on temporary transfer to England from Grangemouth, first to Doncaster and then to the WR in August/September 1952 was diverted to Ashford depot on the SR at the end of September. The engine was noted at work on the continental freights between Dover and Bricklayers Arms and also on the Tonbridge-Redhill line; 90757 returned to Grangemouth in October 1952. Although unusual, this was not the first time WD engines had operated on the SR. Some 50 Class 8F 2-8-0s had been distributed between Bricklayers Arms, Hither Green, Redhill and Feltham for several post-World War Two years, the last group leaving for the LMR, mainly Central Division depots, in July 1951.

By October 1953, the proposed distribution of the 9Fs had been revised and amended:

WR	(20)	92000-09
		92020-29
ER	(5)	92010-14
LMR	(5)	92015-19

It will be noted that the SR's allocation of five engines had now been reassigned to the LMR, the case for the use of 9F power on the SR presumably not regarded as justified. The WR still had an allocation of 20 of the new engines, the last ten of which, 92020-29, were due to be fitted with the Crosti boilers.

On delivery, the allocation had been revised yet again, the LMR now being the region destined to receive the Crosti engines, which still had the running numbers 92020-9: the last two engines, 92008/9, of the remaining batch nominally in the WR allocation were also redirected to the LMR; distribution was as follows:

WR	Newport Ebbw Jct. Note: it appears that the first four, 92000-03 were sent to Wellingborough on loan from the WR, a move which was later reported as cancelled.	(8)	92000-07
LMR	Wellingborough	(17)	92008-09 92015-19 92020-29
ER	March	(5)	92010-14

Running-in turns from Crewe included trips to Gorton (92001/2 in February 1954) and goods workings both north of Crewe and also on the Chester-Whitchurch line. The Gorton visits were probably for weighing purposes as the former GCR works, although smaller than Crewe, had superior facilities for weighing larger engines. Before despatch to the WR, 92007 was at the former LNER depot at Bidston for trials on the iron ore workings from the docks to Shotton Steel Works normally the province of Stanier or Robinson 2-8-0s. On 9th and 10th March, 92007 worked test trains on the severely graded line. On this 13-mile route, the principal incline is the half mile at 1 in 100, steepening to 1 in 75 near Heswall, approximately halfway, after which there is a descent at 1 in 100. The hilly nature of the line restricted the 2-8-0 power to 10-12 wagons whereas 92007 was successfully able to tackle 13 loaded wagons (1,070 tons in total) on one trip and later a 15-wagon train of 1,200 tons; brake vans were included with all trains. The success of 92007 in these trials led to the allocation of three 9Fs, 92045-47, in June 1956 (see later).

The first of the Newport Ebbw Junction allocation was received at the depot in February 1954. Some of the class (92000-3) were noted at Wellingborough, presumably on the temporary loan noted above, before despatch to the WR and 92001/2 passed through Oxley en route to Swindon Works from Shrewsbury on 2nd February; 92000-7 all visited Swindon for the fitting of WR ATC apparatus before beginning work in South Wales. By 11th February, 92000/1/3/4/5 were at Ebbw Junction although 92004/5 distinguished themselves by colliding with each other at the depot on their first day, fortunately without serious damage. On 8th and 9th February, 92001 was sent for clearance tests with a view to using the class on the iron ore traffic between Newport Docks (Rogerstone) and the Ebbw Vale Steel Works. Gradients on this route are severe, the stretch between Aberbeeg and Ebbw Vale climbing at 1 in 52/85 for most of the way up the valley. Single 9Fs were noted on these duties on 12th and 16th February whilst on 19th a train of 44 wagons had a 9F at both front and rear. The previous maximum (unassisted) load had been 18 wagons only.

On 17th February, another incident occurred at Ebbw Junction depot when the driver was unable to close the regulator on his 9F. A serious incident was avoided only because there were no other engines in the path of the runaway; the engine was subsequently despatched to Swindon Works for attention. This was a foretaste of things to come and as a result of the continuing problems with brakes and regulators (see Section 9), the WR allocation spent much of 1954 out of action. By mid-July, all except 92002 were stored out of service, 92001 minus its dome cover inside Ebbw Junction depot whilst 92000/3-7 were outside with sacking securely fastened over their chimneys.

Swindon Works carried out a number of successful test runs following modifications to 92002 over the summer and by the end of September, the engine was noted operating the ore trains from Newport. Other members of the class were still to be seen languishing at Ebbw Junction depot at this time, all with dome covers removed and some with their motion dismantled. Over the next few weeks, the remaining stored engines were despatched to Swindon for modification with 92000 being noted in 'A' shop on 31st October whilst 92001/6 were in the works yard and 92003 on the Triangle. In the early weeks of 1955, 92000-7, were back in regular service on the Ebbw Vale iron ore traffic as well as appearing on other duties such as coal train workings at Severn Tunnel Junction. With all eight of Ebbw Junction's 9Fs now at work, a similar number of the depot's 28XX 2-8-0s were released to Cardiff Canton. Ebbw Junction's 9Fs were not confined to

Figure 68
92014 is in Willesden shed roundhouse in June 1954 where it is being prepared for display at the International Railway Congress Exhibition. *(G. Wheeler)*

Figure 69
92014 shares the limelight with 71000 *Duke of Gloucester* in Willesden roundhouse on 3rd June 1954 during the International Railway Congress Exhibition. *(RCTS Collection)*

the South Wales area however as by the end of May 1955, several of the class had been reported at Hereford working freights over the North and West route towards Shrewsbury.

Both 92008/9, having originally been intended for the WR, were equipped with GWR-style lamp brackets and the BR1G tender specified by the WR for all its allocation. Presumably because of the problems being experienced at Ebbw Junction, the two engines were diverted to the LMR at Wellingborough where they were noted on 45/55 wagon mineral workings to Brent sidings in London by early May. Before this, 92009 managed to reach Carlisle on 7th April on a running-in turn, returning next day on the 3.10pm Carlisle-Wigan freight. 92008 was also noted on a WCML freight passing through Rugby and Watford on 8th May; both 92008/9 were frequently observed on such workings through to Willesden in June and July. In September and October 1954 Wellingborough was allocated a second batch of 9Fs, 92015-9, which with the exception of 92015 were immediately put to work on the Brent coal traffic. The latter engine was loaned to Rugby Testing Station in October and November in connection with the tests to resolve the sticking regulator problem (see Section 9). Other duties took the engines north, 92016/8 being observed at Coalville on the Leicester-Burton branch towards the end of October. The arrival of the 9Fs at Wellingborough resulted in its remaining Beyer Garratt allocation being transferred to Toton or Hasland. Despite this move, Garratts still regularly appeared on the Brent traffic from Toton until gradually displaced from this duty some months later by the arrival of Toton's own 9F allocation. By the middle of 1955, the Garratts were being withdrawn as and when their boilers became due for heavy repair.

In contrast to the situation in South Wales, the Wellingborough 9Fs were putting up a creditable performance on the Brent coal traffic and were well liked by crews. A further batch of standard 9Fs, 92045-9, arrived at Wellingborough in February and March 1955 (see later). However, the same welcome was not accorded to the next batch of the class received at Wellingborough, the Crosti-boilered variants, 92020-9. These ten engines, built out of numerical sequence, were allocated over the May-July 1955 period, again being assigned to the Brent coal traffic and by early July all except 92023 (see later) were regulars at Cricklewood. The Crostis displaced ten Stanier Class 8F 2-8-0s from Wellingborough to other Midland Division depots, namely Kettering, Toton, Canklow, Cricklewood or Stourton. These moves enabled the latter depots to release the same number of Swindon-built Stanier Class 8F 2-8-0s to Bristol St. Philips Marsh, Banbury, Newton Abbot and Worcester on the WR. This arrangement was at the request of the WR which preferred not to receive more 9Fs following their poor reception at Ebbw Junction. The WR utilised the 8Fs on fast fitted freights and regularly obtained around 30,000 miles per year from each engine on average, roughly twice the average mileage the WR achieved with their first batch of 9Fs (see Section 11.2).

Within a short period however, crews operating the Crostis were raising serious complaints about what they regarded as unpleasant and inherently unsafe working conditions. The side chimney was situated on the fireman's side and the drifting smoke frequently made it difficult for him to perform his usual role of maintaining a lookout for signals. The cab itself was frequently enveloped in choking exhaust fumes and it was reported that the crews became covered in grime after only a few miles' running. In late 1955 and early 1956, the Crostis were back at Crewe for the fitting of smoke deflectors to the side chimney in an attempt, only partially successful, to alleviate the drifting exhaust problem (see Table 9.2).

Before this, however, 92023 was despatched to Rugby Testing Station at the end of May 1955. The engine was due to leave Crewe on the night of 27th/28th May, but was sent 24 hours earlier in anticipation of the serious two-week rail strike planned for June; the engine was taken into the test plant within two hours of arrival at Rugby. Later, 92023 was involved in three weeks of road testing between Durran Hill, Carlisle and Hurlford on the G&SWR Nith Valley route; details of the tests are given in Section 11.1. Because of their

Figure 70
Only three months old, 92041 (New England) accelerates a Ferme Park coal train through the southern suburbs of Peterborough on 30th March 1955; the engine was later fitted with AWS (December 1959). At its height, the Ferme Park service saw departures from New England approximately every twenty minutes.
(RCTS Collection)

Figure 71
With steam to spare, 92080 (Wellingborough) trundles a long southbound freight over the easy gradients of the MML near Napsbury on 26th March 1960. The engine looks in need of a works visit which duly occurred a couple of months later when it was despatched to Crewe for a Light Casual repair having achieved almost 120,000 miles in service since delivery. *(Courtney Haydon)*

novel features, the Crostis were sometimes appropriated by shedmasters to test their capabilities. One example was on 24th September 1955 when 92029 made the first reported appearance of a Crosti at Coventry where it worked in with the 1.56am goods from Crewe. After unsuccessful attempts to accommodate it on the 60ft turntable there, the engine was despatched to Nuneaton for turning. On arrival however, the engine was borrowed by Nuneaton to work the 6.06 pm (SO) Hawkesbury Lane - Banbury goods, returning through Coventry in the early hours of Sunday morning on a return train of empties. 92029 was still in the area during the following week, being noted under repair at Nuneaton on 2nd October. It was reported that the unusual appearance of the engine caused much local comment, including a press report and a photograph in the local newspaper. Later 92028 made what was reported to be the first appearance of the class on the SR when it was despatched to Brighton, the principal design works for the 9Fs, on 8th September for inspection by the staff the following day; the engine travelled via the West London line and Clapham Junction, returning two days later by the same route. 92028 was turned on the Preston Park-Hove triangle since it was not permitted to enter Brighton MPD yard.

Although initial indications were that Cambridge was to host one or two of the class, in the event, all five of the first ER 9Fs, 92010-4, were allocated to March in April and May 1954. It was reported that the engines were inspected at Doncaster before despatch to March and that this procedure applied to all ER-based 9Fs on delivery to traffic. 92013 was immediately loaned to Rugby Testing Station, being despatched direct from Crewe Works to Rugby and entering the plant on 1st May 1954. Later towards the end of September, the engine was involved in road trials over Ais Gill on the Settle and Carlisle line and did not appear at March until October (see Section 11.1 for test details). 92014 was also on loan but for a much shorter period when it was exhibited at Willesden MPD from 25th May to 4th June along with several other Standard class steam locomotives and other motive power in connection with the International Railway Congress meeting in London. Running-in turns from Crewe now included trips into Yorkshire. Both 92010/2 were observed at Mirfield, in May and June respectively, the latter paying a visit to Patricroft MPD on 2nd July.

At first, the March allocation appeared to do little or no work, 92010/1 being noted out of steam at the depot on 5th June. Later, trial trips to Cambridge were organised followed by regular workings to Temple Mills on Class 'H' freights and on 27th July, 92010/4 were observed at Ely on separate down goods workings. Initially, line restrictions were applied to the 9Fs, presumably due to their lengthy wheel base. Permission was given to work between Whitemoor Yard at March and Temple Mills (Stratford) via Ely and between Temple Mills and Stratford MPD. Maximum speed allowed was 50mph with a further restriction of 10mph over Bridge 1393 between Lea Bridge and Tottenham South Junction. Maximum loading was 'equal to 59 heavies' subject to established line limitations. Observers confirmed that the 9Fs could be found on the following Class 'H' workings in the early days:

Figure 72
Approaching the end of its first year in service, 92083 passes Glendon & Rushton station near Kettering with a lengthy London-bound coal train on 24th April 1957. 92083 was withdrawn from Birkenhead MPD in February 1967 and sold for scrap to A. Draper at Hull in the following July.
(RCTS Collection)

Figure 73
Newly ex-works 92049 has arrived at Rugby on 24th March 1955 with a train of engines recently overhauled at Bagnall's Works at Stafford. The engines are WD 2-10-0 600 *Gordon* and USA S160 2-8-0 700 *Major General Carl R. Gray Jnr.* both destined for the Longmoor Military Railway in Hampshire.
(D. Tyreman Collection)

Figure 74
On 26th September 1959, 92107 (Wellingborough) ambles up the MML at Elstree with a train load of coal for the capital. The engine's cumulative mileage was approaching 90,000 at this time as recorded during a visit to Crewe Works for a Light Casual overhaul in the following December.
(Courtney Haydon)

Whitemoor-Temple Mills
2.00am; 2.25am (MX); 2.50am (MO);
10.15am (SX); 12.30pm; 10.50pm (SO).

Temple Mills-Whitemoor
3.05am; 12.40am (SX); 9.45am (SX);
4.55pm (SO); 7.45pm (SO).

Park Yard-Whitemoor
9.25am (SX); 10.00am (SO).

Whitemoor-Cambridge
9.35am (SX).

Cambridge-Whitemoor
12.52pm (SX).

Later the 9Fs were noted mainly on the Whitemoor-Temple Mills traffic although restrictions were eased for the class to run on three more routes, between Hitchin and Cambridge, Ely and Haughley, March and Peterborough North. In the latter case, the 9Fs were excluded from the No. 1 platform line at Peterborough East and subject to a five mph speed restriction over Bridge 1838 between there and Whittlesea.

By the end of 1954, March's 9Fs were regularly working the maximum permitted 59 wagons and brake between Whitemoor and Temple Mills, some ten wagons more than the maximum load for a WD 2-8-0. Return trains of empties were permitted up to a load of 75 wagons and soon 92010 was reported as running some 2,500 miles in a month on these workings. From August 1954 to January 1956, 92014 was allocated to Stratford, operating on similar duties as before but from the London end. March 9Fs were also used regularly on a variety of freight workings to Doncaster via the GN & GE Joint line through Spalding, Sleaford, Lincoln and Gainsborough.

A total of 67 engines, 92030-96, was included in the 1954 building programme. The original allocation plan was for 15 engines to the LMR, 35 to the ER, seven to the NER and the remaining ten to the WR; individual engines were to be assigned as follows:

LMR	(15)	92030-44
ER	(35)	92045-59
		92067-76
		92087-96
NER	(7)	92060-66
WR	(10)	92077-86

Various changes were proposed, however and on delivery, actual allocation was as follows, the ten WR engines now being redirected to the LMR:

ER	New England	(10)	92030/4-42
	March	(5)	92031/2/3/43/4
	Doncaster	(18)	92067-76
			92087-94
	Annesley	(2)	92095/6
LMR	Wellingborough	(10)	92045-9/82-6
	Toton	(15)	92050-9/77-81
NER	Tyne Dock	(7)	92060-6

The first 15 of the batch, 92030-44, originally allocated to the LMR but reassigned to the ER were distributed between New England (10) and March (5). 92031/2/3 spent very little time at March before transfer to New England and in the case of 92032/3, in such apparent haste that it would appear the engines had been wrongly allocated in the first place. 92030 arrived at New England on 12th November 1954 after running-in from Crewe which involved a trip to Edge Hill on 6th November. On 18th 92030 hauled a coal train to Ferme Park, Hornsey, returning the same day with 70 empty wagons. The trial was somewhat thwarted by foggy weather, 92030 being held for some time 'on the block' southbound at Cambridge Junction, Hitchin. On resumption of its journey, the train was diverted via the Hertford loop, in spite of the fact that the class had not been officially authorised to run on the route. Five more trials were arranged with Class 'H' freights over the week ending 27th November when braking tests were conducted at Huntingdon and Tempsford.

Works running-in turns saw 92035 at Farnley Junction on 12th December where it was booked to work a parcels train to Widnes and 92039 on the Chorley-Blackburn line substituting for the usual Carlisle Upperby engine on a mid-morning freight on 15th December. On the latter date also, 92034 was noted double-heading an LNWR Super D 0-8-0 at Watford Junction.

As more of the class arrived at New England further trials continued from Mondays to Fridays for at least the first three weeks of December. Up trains consisted of 45 loaded wagons, leaving New England at 5.50am arriving Hitchin at 7.40am, departing 8.36am and arriving at Ferme Park by 10.10am. The return journey with 60 empty wagons was faster, leaving Ferme Park at 11.15am, Hitchin at 12.50pm and arriving back at New England at 2.35pm. Further braking trials were arranged at Huntingdon, Tempsford and Wood Green. For the five miles mainly at 1 in 200/330/200 from Hatfield to Potters Bar, 16 minutes were allowed. On the down journey, the 15½ miles from Huntingdon to Peterborough were scheduled at 26 minutes. The engines were not popular with the crews at first with the usual complaints about poor brakes; on the first run, 92030 was reported to have overshot the appointed stopping place by some 1,000 yards. Also of residual concern was the draughtiness of the cabs, despite the fact that all 9F batches had tenders modified with the addition of a fall plate to combat the problem (see Section 4).

The braking problem by now resolved, the New England 9Fs were then almost exclusively deployed on the coal traffic to Ferme Park. The plan was to accelerate trains to a three and a half hour timing each way on Class 'E' timings so that the New England crews could work to London and back in a day's duty. Until that time the up runs could take up to five and a half hours under Class 'H' lights. Crews were obliged to return 'on the cushions' to stay within the standard working day length, although in many cases remanning at Hitchin enabled a return working to be fitted in within the day's duties. Until the arrival of more 9Fs, the class shared the Ferme Park duties with WD 2-8-0s and the LNER 2-8-0s. The latter classes had been the mainstay of the service for many years but most were now transferred from New England. The 9Fs were also noted on other duties from time to time. Examples were on 12th August 1955, when 92041 was in charge of a Welwyn-Colwick freight whilst on 28th, a down empty coaching stock special to Leicester ran as class 'E' with 92031. Later on 19th December, 92041 was used on the 11.10am Hitchin-Cambridge and 4.54pm return freights.

In 1955, members of the New England allocation were

Figure 75
The procession of up coal trains continues on 26th September 1959 as Wellingborough's 92083 passes Elstree & Borehamwood with a long rake of wagons. 92083 was loaned to Annesley for work on the 'windcutters' for a few weeks from November 1960. *(Courtney Haydon)*

Figure 76
92102 (Leicester Midland) hurries northwards past Wolverton with a train of empty hoppers on 21st July 1962. This working was probably the return leg of the daily coal hopper train from Toton to the Stonebridge Park power station in north London. *(Courtney Haydon)*

Figure 77
92060 (Tyne Dock) leaves Tyne Dock Bottom with an ore train for Consett in 1965; a Cl.08 0-6-0 diesel shunter provides banking assistance. The busy Tyne Dock port complex extends across the whole of the background. *(P. J. Robinson)*

Figure 78
Banked by another Tyne Dock 9F 92062, 92060 passes Annfield East with a Consett ore train in May 1965. The ore must be one of the denser grades as none of it is visible in the hoppers. *(P. J. Robinson)*

some of the first of the class to be observed on passenger work. Perhaps the first occasion was on 7th May, FA Cup Final day, when the 14-coach 11.50am Harrogate (and Hull) express due into Kings Cross at 4.50pm, came to a gentle halt at Hitchin South shortly before 5.00pm with 92031 in charge. The engine had taken over from ailing Gateshead A1 Pacific 60154 *Bon Accord* at Biggleswade, a few miles further north but was now deemed unfit to proceed; B1 4-6-0 61093 took over for the remainder of the run to Kings Cross. Of the second batch of 9Fs allocated to March, 92031/2/3/43/4, only the last two were still there by the beginning of 1957. The new engines continued on the Temple Mills and Cambridge line duties and were occasionally reported on the ex-GN line in the London area. Later, on 7th September 1955, a 9F was again in charge of a passenger train when 92044 of March depot was noted at Newport (Essex) with the 10.52am Bishops Stortford-Cambridge local. By the middle of 1957 all the remaining March 9Fs had been transferred to Annesley or New England as part of a reorganisation of freight power on the ER, 92011/2 departing as early as September 1955; there were no further allocations of 9Fs to March.

In addition to the five 9Fs, 92045-9, received in February/March 1955, Wellingborough acquired another batch, 92082-6, in May and June 1956. Both groups were employed on the Brent coal traffic resulting in the displacement of more Stanier Cl. 8F 2-8-0s, this time to Nottingham, Leicester Midland, Hasland, Kirkby-in-Ashfield, Derby or Saltley; again this allowed a few Swindon-built Stanier 8Fs to transfer to the WR. The Beyer Garratts, so long a feature on the Brent duties were now something of a rarity. Running-in turns for the 9Fs at this time included freights from Crewe South to Bescot, whilst on 24th March, 92049 was observed at Rugby hauling two engines, (WD 2-10-0 No. 600 *Gordon* and USA S160 2-8-0 No. 700 *Major General Carl R. Gray Jnr.*) back to the Longmoor Military Railway after overhaul at W. G. Bagnall's works at Stafford, On 26th May, 92084 was noted on a track-laying train between Rhyl and Llandudno Junction, the furthest excursion along the north Wales main line reported for the class to that date. The Wellingborough 9Fs also began to appear on the Midland West of England main line, one example being 92045 which was observed at Westerleigh sidings, Bristol in mid-November after arriving with a coal train. One other duty for Wellingborough's 9Fs was the regular traffic from the Midlands to Cargo Fleet on Teesside which LMR engines worked as far as York.

From August 1955 92047 was loaned to Bidston depot after the successful trials with 92007 on the John Summers (Shotwick) iron ore workings from Bidston docks in March 1954. This was followed in May 1956 by 92045/6, again on loan; all three 9Fs were officially allocated to Bidston in June 1956. Although 92007 had demonstrated that fifteen of the 88ton loaded hoppers plus brake could easily be handled, the standard maximum wagon load was limited to eleven. This was decreed as a precaution against the possibility of runaways on the descent from Heswall to Shotwick as the vehicles were not vacuum brake fitted; in fact they were the heaviest regular unfitted mineral workings on BR. Careful control was thus necessary on the descent as the only brakes that could be applied during running were the engine's steam brake and those of the guard's van; even so, over-runs at Shotwick were not unknown. It was reported that the crews were very appreciative of the modern footplate fittings and layout but considered the LNER Robinson 2-8-0s to have been lighter on coal and water in proportion to loads carried. Stanier Class 8F 2-8-0s were occasionally borrowed from Birkenhead in the absence of any of Bidston's 9Fs for overhaul at Crewe.

In mid-August 1955, one of the original Wellingborough allocation, 92008 was despatched to Bromsgrove for trials on the Lickey bank on the ex-MR West of England main line south of Birmingham. The engine designed for these duties, the celebrated 'Big Bertha', 0-10-0 58100, had become due for major repairs (including boiler replacement) which were assessed as uneconomic. The first choice as replacement was LNER Beyer Garratt, Class U1 2-8-0 + 0-8-2T, 69999. This engine had been made redundant from its banking duties on the Worsborough incline following the electrification of the ex-GCR Manchester-Sheffield route. The Garratt had been modified by conversion to oil-burning but despite extensive trials had not proved a success at the Lickey due to steaming problems and manoeuvring difficulties as a result of its length; the engine was even turned during its stay in order to position the cab closer to the rear of the train to be banked. 92008 took over the banking duties from 58100 on 15th August 1955 but stayed only 10 days returning on the 10.25am Water Orton-Leicester freight on 24th August. 92008 was however reported a success at Bromsgrove and on withdrawal of 58100 in May 1956, another 9F, 92079, subsequently adopted the mantle of Lickey Banker 'Big Engine' and stayed until October 1963.

Fifteen 9Fs from the 1954 building programme were allocated to Toton, the first group, 92050-9, from August to October 1955 with 92077-81 arriving in March and April 1956 after being observed on running-in turns to Birkenhead and Huddersfield. More Beyer Garratts were now withdrawn and a number of Swindon-built Stanier Class 8Fs displaced, the WR again being the beneficiary. 92050 was loaned to Rugby Testing Station and later to Carlisle Kingmoor until December in connection with comparison trials with Crosti-boiler 9F 92023. Toton used the new engines on the Brent coal traffic, displacing the few remaining Beyer Garratts from these workings and by the end of the year, the latter had almost disappeared from the Brent run. As an alternative duty, the Garratts began to appear on the Toton-Willesden mineral traffic from mid-November which also featured some of the new 9Fs. WCML Garratt power was to prove short-lived at this time however as by April 1956 they had been ousted completely from these workings by 9Fs and Stanier 2-8-0s. Whilst in the London area, Toton's 9Fs could occasionally be noted on Euston empty coaching stock workings and also on West London line freights from Willesden to the SR.

A letter published in *Backtrack* magazine, March/April 1993 (Vol. 7, No. 2) p. 107 from Mr. Ian R. Canavan of Coventry listed details of some of the 9F workings between Toton and Willesden/Cricklewood; the Willesden workings varied little between 1955 and 1960. Details for the summer of 1958 were given as follows:

Southbound

5.05am Beeston-Sudbury via Rugby
5.00am Toton-Sudbury via Rugby
5.30am Toton-Sudbury via Rugby
8.50am Toton-Sudbury via Rugby
12.25pm Toton-Sudbury via Market Harbro'
5.10pm Toton-Sudbury via Market Harbro'
8.10pm Toton-Sudbury via Market Harbro'

Figure 79
Another view of the Wellingborough-Cargo Fleet iron ore train at Pontefract Baghill, this time in early 1956 with 92062 in charge. The engine was nominally allocated to Tyne Dock at this time but along with other Tyne Dock 9Fs was on loan to Wellingborough in place of the latter depot's Crosti boiler engines away at Crewe for modification. It will be noted that the Westinghouse air pumps are not yet in place; these would be fitted at Crewe Works before the engines were despatched to the NER later in the year. *(Peter Cookson)*

Figure 80
Banked by a Type 4 diesel, 92065 blasts up past Oxhill with an ore train for Consett in 1965. *(J. W. Armstrong Trust)*

Figure 81
92065 heads a Consett ore train up through Oxhill in May 1965. This engine, the last survivor of the Tyne Dock allocation, was the only one not to be withdrawn from the depot; instead it was reallocated to Wakefield in November 1966, complete with air pumps and withdrawn the following April. *(J. W. Armstrong Trust)*

other duties; on 21st March for example 92061 was noted as far as West Thurrock Junction on the ex-LT&S line with a train of bulk soda ash wagons for Hedley's Soap Works, the engine being turned on the Tilbury triangle for the return journey. The engines also appeared in the Sheffield area with a weekday Wellingborough-Rotherwood freight and were occasionally employed on the daily iron ore working from the Wellingborough area to Cargo Fleet (Middlesbrough) as far as York, a former Beyer Garratt duty. Before release by the LMR, 92062/3 and 92064/5/6 spent a few weeks from February 1956 at Westhouses and Toton respectively eventually arriving at Tyne Dock in April and May; a further three 9Fs from a subsequent batch, 92097-99, were received at Tyne Dock a few weeks later in June and July bringing the total for the Consett operations to ten.

The first 9F to tackle the Tyne Dock-Consett workings was 92037 which had been sent on loan from New England for trials in June 1955, almost one year before the arrival of the permanent allocation. The engine had caused a few headaches for the operating staff en route to the NER as the class had not been authorised to use certain crossings on account of its lengthy wheel base. The trials were deemed a complete success resulting in the Class 9Fs being earmarked for the Consett duties as soon as practicable.

One of the first sightings of the new engines on the Consett duties was 18th May 1956 when 92061 hauled the eight-wagon 5.20pm ore train departure from Tyne Dock. Observers reported much slipping on the fierce 1 in 40 gradient from Tyne Dock Bottom towards the engine shed yard despite banking assistance from a Class 3F J25 0-6-0. On the same stretch on 19th June, 92065 came to a stand with nine hoppers again in spite of banking assistance, on this occasion provided by a Class 2F J72 0-6-0 tank engine; the 9F was eventually assisted up the bank by a Class 8F Q7 0-8-0 heading the following train. After a few weeks at Tyne Dock, 92065 was reported to have been despatched to Gateshead Works for tyre reprofiling following problems with slipping and wheel lock during braking; the record confirms a visit in August 1956; 92064 was also at Gateshead in September, perhaps for the same reason. By the end of the summer however, the Tyne Dock crews had got the measure of their new charges and were speaking highly of their capabilities. The 9Fs were considered by some to steam better than the Q7 0-8-0s and the O1 2-8-0s which had previously performed these duties. The latter were then usually to be seen on banking and standby duties; on the arrival of 92097-99, some of the Q7s not fitted with air pumps (63461/2/4/8/70/1/2) were transferred to Blaydon at the end of July.

The transfer of ore from ships on the River Tyne to the Consett Steel Works had been the subject of reorganisation in a joint initiative by the Tyne Improvement Commission, British Railways and the Consett Iron Company; the project was begun in 1951 and completed two years later. The Tyne Commission provided the dockside facilities, which included huge cranes sited at the quay-side being used to transfer the ore from ocean-going vessels to belts which conveyed it to a massive bunker. From here the ore was discharged by gravity into bogie wagons waiting directly underneath. British

FIGURE K
GRADIENT PROFILE: OUSTON SIGNAL BOX TO CONSETT NORTH SIGNAL BOX

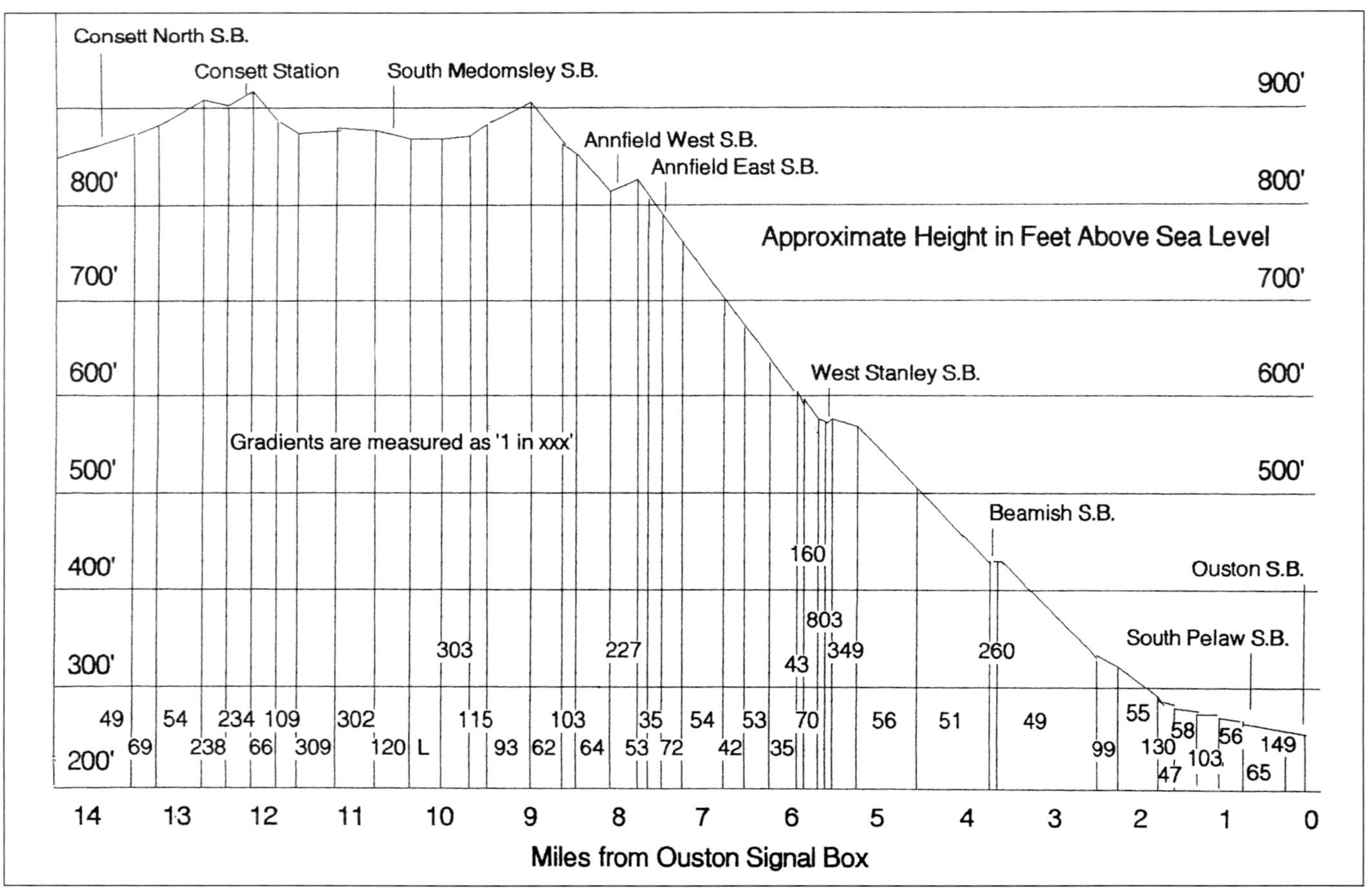

Figure 86
Six-month-old 92123 (Wellingborough) rumbles a northbound freight through Kettering station on 17th August 1957. 92123 was withdrawn in October 1967 and cut up at T. W. Ward's yard in Beighton (Sheffield) in February 1968.
(RCTS Collection)

Figure 87
92127 (Wellingborough) emerges from the 353 yard Wing tunnel south of Manton on the Melton Mowbray-Kettering line with an up Class 'H' mixed freight about 1957/8.
(RCTS Collection)

Railways built a fleet of 30 such wagons each capable of carrying up to 56 tons of ore dependent on the bulk volume of such material. This varied significantly from source to source, the Scandinavian ore, for example, being much denser than that originating from West Africa. The 36 ft 5 in long wagons had two sections each with a capacity of 28 tons and a tare weight of just over 29 tons. When fully loaded with the denser ores, each wagon weighed around 85 tons. Before the 9Fs arrived, the traffic was operated by five O1 2-8-0s (63712/55/60, 63856/74) and the same number of Q7 0-8-0s (63460/3/5/9/73), each fitted with air pumps. Following displacement by the 9Fs, the Q7s and O1s still occasionally appeared as lead engine on the workings until the air pumps were removed from the Q7s in the 1957-59 period and the O1s were withdrawn at the end of 1962.

On arriving at Consett, the normal procedure was that trains ran on to a new gantry installed by the Consett Iron Company. The ore was discharged from the full length side doors of the wagons which were automatically opened by air pressure from one of the Westinghouse pumps carried by the train engine. The empty train was then reversed along the second side of a triangle where the engine took water ready for the return journey; departure was via the third leg of the triangle.

The previous maximum train load (for the O1s and Q7s) was eight ore wagons plus brake van. After initial trials, the 9Fs were allowed nine wagons which together with the brake typically amounted to around 800 tons. Three trains were operated, allowing three wagons spare for maintenance at any one time. Provision was made in the timetable to schedule trains at approximately 1¾ hour intervals with a journey time of 1 hr 51 min outward to Consett and a 1 hr 11 min return

Figure 88
92086 (Wellingborough) heads a train of steel products south of Pontefract on 30th April 1958. The train has been identified as possibly the late-running 5.40am Skelton Sidings-Beighton Class 'H'. *(Peter Cookson)*

for the 23.6 route miles. The climb from Tyne Dock Bottom to the engine shed required banking assistance usually by Class 3F J25 0-6-0s, Class 2F J72 0-6-0 tank engines or sometimes an 0-8-0 until displaced by Cl. 08 diesel shunters in the early 1960s. The banker propelled the brake van on to the rear of the train once it was clear of the loading bunker. The next stage of the route from Pontop Crossing to South Pelaw Junction on the ECML was relatively level but was subject to restrictions and delays due to the presence of several level crossings on busy roads. From South Pelaw Junction, there was a formidable climb of almost nine miles past Beamish, West Stanley and Annfield, a portion of which was at 1 in 35/56 (see Gradient Profile, Figure K). Banking assistance was provided from South Pelaw Junction to South Medomsley and the 9Fs shared these duties with the remaining Q7 0-8-0s, O1 2-8-0s and WD 2-8-0s. The climb to Consett could present considerable operating problems especially in bad weather. The combination of gradients, line curvature and pw slacks of typically 10-15mph caused by mining subsidence occasionally led to trains stalling despite the presence of the banker. For safety reasons, the South Pelaw Junction-South Medomsley stretch of line was equipped with a total of 15 sets of catch points to ensure runaways were derailed before a major incident could occur.

During busy periods, around 14 ore trains per day were booked over the route, some wagon sets making up to five return trips in a 24-hour period, a distance of some 230 miles. Annual tonnages of ore varied from 0.6 million in 1962 to over 1.3 million in 1956 dependent on demand for steel products. Iron ore was not the only material worked up to Consett by the 9Fs. Coal and later fuel oil were also delivered by rail in addition to other materials required in the steel manufacturing process. It is interesting to note that a significant proportion of the output from Consett was sent in the form of steel billets and ingots to South Wales via the ex-GCR line through Annesley and Woodford Halse, the route of the speedy loose-coupled freights, known as the 'windcutters', powered by a stud of 9Fs based at Annesley (see later).

In the early 1960s, the timetable showed the first departure from Tyne Dock at 6.40am with workings every 1¾ hours until 4.30pm. Two other workings, at 6.20pm and 7.20pm were run as required. The Pontop Crossing-South Pelaw Junction section ran on a two-shift system only and was closed from 8.00pm to 6.00am. If additional services were required between these times, the trains were run via Felling, Gateshead and Low Fell.

Tyne Dock's 9Fs were not confined exclusively to the Consett workings. They could be found from time to time on various mineral workings in the north east as well as on the ECML between York and Edinburgh on both fitted freights and mineral workings. It was reported that one or two of the allocation went as far afield as Glasgow with fitted freights on occasion.

The next ER depot to receive batches of 9Fs was Doncaster from December 1955. 92037 from New England had been used during the previous September for clearance tests in the Doncaster area following its trials on the NER Tyne Dock-Consett workings. The first allocation, 92067-76, was received from Crewe during the period December 1955 to March 1956, to be augmented later by the first Swindon-built examples, 92087-94, arriving from August 1956 to February 1957. Running-in turns for the Crewe batch involved visits to Nuneaton and Market Harborough (92071), Rugby (92073), and Heaton Norris and Mirfield (92072). Doncaster put the class to work on the regular freights to Whitemoor via the GN & GE Joint line through Lincoln and also on the coal trains to New England via Boston. By the end

Figure 89
92084 (Wellingborough) is in charge of a southbound coal train near Harringworth on the Nottingham-Kettering line in September 1956. After Wellingborough, 92084 was allocated to Kettering, Speke Junction and Birkenhead before withdrawal in November 1967.
(RCTS Collection)

Figure 90
92134 (Wellingborough) emerges from Knighton tunnel south of Leicester London Road station with coal for the London area in August 1961. The track branching in the foreground is the line to Coalville and Burton-upon-Trent which is joined at Saffron Lane Junction. The engine is the only single chimney example of a 9F to have been preserved. It spent much of its life on MML mineral traffic, transferring to Birkenhead in April 1965. *(C.R. Berridge)*

of March 1956, the first batch was making regular appearances at Brigg on the Gainsborough-Barnetby line with freights to and from Immingham Docks. Doncaster 9Fs were also frequent visitors to York where they could be seen alongside Wellingborough-based class members which regularly appeared on mineral freights from the Midlands.

The second batch delivered to Doncaster, 92087-94, stayed for only a few months however, as early in 1957 they were transferred along with the rest of the Doncaster allocation to Annesley as part of a reorganisation of freight power on the ER. The ex-Doncaster 9Fs (92067-76, 92087-94) were not the only class members reallocated to Annesley at this time; a further four engines (92010/3/4/43) were drafted in from March in January/February 1957 and later, in May/June, six more 9Fs (92011/2/30-3) were received from New England. Together with 92095/6 delivered new from Swindon in March and April 1957, Annesley then had a total complement of 30 9Fs. As part of the reorganisation, Annesley's O1 2-8-0s were moved to March which in turn relinquished WD 2-8-0s to Doncaster to replace the 9Fs despatched to Annesley.

The main reason for the drafting of so many 9Fs to Annesley was the decision by the ER to improve the efficiency of the intensive freight service between Annesley and Woodford Halse yards. These loose-coupled freights were very strictly pathed and timed, the need to make up lost time from the inevitable delays at various stages resulting in speeds of 60mph or more being recorded on a regular basis. This gave rise to the nicknames 'windcutters' or 'runners' for this service.

The GC line had been heavily used by freight traffic for many years including a large number of services run as fast

Figure 91
Pictured at its home depot of Cricklewood on 11th August 1957 is 92112, one of two 9Fs sent new to the shed in November 1956, the other being 92111. Both were transferred to Wellingborough in April 1959. 92112 was withdrawn from Birkenhead in November 1967 and later stored at Carlisle Kingmoor before being sold to G. H. Campbell at Airdrie for scrap in March 1968.
(RCTS Collection)

Figure 92
92136 (Saltley) starts the ascent of the Lickey Incline at Bromsgrove with a short freight on 13th June 1964. 92136 was one of the few 9Fs which remained allocated to the same shed for the whole of its working life; the others were 92142/3 (New England), 92168-70/2/4/5/7 (Doncaster) on the ER and 92097-9 (Tyne Dock) on the NER. When Bromsgrove was under the control of the LMR, 92136 had occasionally been borrowed for 'Big Engine' Lickey banker duties when 92079 was away at works for repair. *(Courtney Haydon)*

Figure 93
92045 climbs Hale Bank with a test train of 19 loaded ICI hopper wagons (1,300tons gross) on the 11.04am Tunstead-Oakleigh Sidings (Winnington) on 15th January 1957. Along with 92046/7, the engine was allocated to Bidston at the time for working iron ore hoppers from the docks to John Summers steelworks at Shotton.

(J. B. Arnold)

Figure 94
It is 21st July 1960 and 92125 (Wellingborough) hurries the 6.55pm Dringhouses-Washwood Heath Class 'C' express goods north of Pontefract Baghill; this working was usually rostered for a 9F at that time. The single line in the foreground is the branch to Pontefract Monkhill (ex-LYR).

(Peter Cookson)

fitted freights. Through freight workings to the south were facilitated by the link from Woodford Halse to South Wales and to the south and south west via Banbury.

There were four main traffic streams:

- general merchandise from the north east to Banbury, the south coast and the London area.
- steel traffic from Scunthorpe and the north east to South Wales.
- fish trains from Humberside to South Wales and the south west.
- huge quantities of coal from the Yorkshire and East Midlands coalfields to South Wales and to southern England via Reading or to the south west via Swindon; these trains were run loose-coupled.

The mainstay of the freight operation was the coal traffic. The coalfields forwarded their production to the Annesley freight yards where the wagons were marshalled for despatch to Woodford Halse and further sorting. Before World War Two the Annesley-Woodford Halse freights involved a few lodging turns but the majority entailed crew changes at Leicester South Goods. Here Annesley crews relinquished their southbound trains to Woodford Halse men who handed over the northbound freights to the Annesley crews; this allowed out and home runs to be completed within the shift time allowance for both sets of men.

Lodging turns ceased during World War Two, and in order to increase the efficient operation of the service, the LNER instituted a new out and home arrangement in 1947 with 40 or more freights scheduled in each direction per day operated by Class O1/O4 and WD 2-8-0s. Local crews took the loaded trains forward from Annesley Yard to Bulwell Common where the rostered out and home crews took over. The latter had signed on at Bulwell, the area where almost all of them lived, thus saving travelling time to and from Annesley depot. The 60-mile or so journey to Woodford Halse usually took under three hours in either direction. On arrival, the Annesley crews handed over their engine to Woodford Halse men for transfer to the shed for servicing. Meanwhile a fresh engine would be provided for the return to Annesley. Turn round time would be of the order of an hour, thus allowing Annesley crews to sign off at Bulwell within the specified working shift. On a round-trip mileage of just over 134 miles, the scheme enabled a saving of over 50 sets of intermediate relief crews and increased the average of train miles per train hour from 10.2 to 20.6.

A decade later in early 1957, when the newly allocated 9Fs began to take over from the 2-8-0s on these intensive freight workings, their increased power allowed significant acceleration of the service. Out and home workings now started at Annesley depot itself, eliminating the need to change crews at Bulwell Common. The time saved also allowed crews on arrival at Woodford Halse to take the engines to the shed and pick up a fresh engine themselves, again contributing to the increased efficiency of the operation.

The use of the 9Fs allowed the loads to be increased as well as reducing transit time. For southbound trains from Annesley, the 9Fs could take up to 55 loaded mineral wagons (as opposed to the 45 allowed for the 2-8-0s), 60 loaded goods wagons (55), and 70 empties (60). The trains ran loose-coupled under a Class 'H' headcode and the schedule called for an average speed of slightly less than 25mph. For 9F-powered northbound freights, unbraked and running as Class 'E', scheduled speeds were around 30mph on average with 52 loaded mineral wagons allowed, 57 loaded goods wagons or 65 empties. Yard to yard timings for southbound workings were typically 2 hr 40 min whilst in the opposite direction, 2 hr 15 min was allowed. Such an intensive service could see almost 2,000 wagons per day being dealt with at Woodford Halse.

The 106 engines authorised in the 1956 building programme were delivered from June 1956 to December 1958. Distribution was between three regions, ER (45), LMR (58) and the NER (3) with individual depot allocations as shown.

Figure 95
92142 (New England) rolls a northbound parcels train through Essendine between Peterborough and Grantham on 19th August 1959. The engine was allocated to New England for the whole of its working life. 92142 was fitted with LNER-type fire hole doors from new.
(RCTS Collection)

Figure 96
Doncaster's 92177 nears High Dyke, south of Grantham, with a down Class 'C' fitted freight on 23rd April 1959. The engine was another ER-based 9F which was allocated to one depot for the whole of its working life (just over six years). 92177 was among the first group of 9Fs to be withdrawn (May 1964).
(RCTS Collection)

NER		
Tyne Dock	(3)	92097-9
	Total 3	
LMR		
Toton	(12)	92100-4 92109/10/28 92153/6-8
Wellingborough	(14)	92105-8/21-7 92154/9/60
Cricklewood	(2)	92111/2
Westhouses	(11)	92113-20/50/61/2
Saltley	(17)	92129-39/51/2/5 92165-7
Kettering	(1)	92163
Leicester Midland	(1)	92164
	Total 58	
ER		
New England	(21)	92140-9 92178-88
Doncaster	(21)	92168-77 92192-92202
Mexborough	(2)	92189/90
Darnall	(1)	92191
	Total 45	

The arrival of three more Westinghouse air pump-fitted engines, 92097-9, at Tyne Dock by the end of July 1956 completed the allocation of 9Fs to this depot. The engines spent most of their time on the Consett iron ore workings but, as before, at holiday times or when the steel plant was less busy, some of the Tyne Dock allocation were borrowed by other depots. In early August 1958 for example, Heaton found work for three of the class on freights to Tweedmouth and Edinburgh, 92060 being noted north of the border on 14th August. At the same time, Gateshead used 92098 and 92061 on a class 'D' freight to Neville Hill on 1st and 2nd of the month respectively. Also on 2nd August, 92063 worked into Carlisle from Newcastle on the 8.15am Newcastle-Heads of Ayr holiday special, returning from Carlisle on the 11.15am parcels. Later, in March 1959, Thornaby had temporary use of 92061/2/6/99 for freights from Teesside to Dringhouses and Neville Hill. No additional 9Fs were allocated to the NER until the mid-1960s when some ex-SR and ex-WR engines were at York for around three years and then at Wakefield for a short period before the demise of steam on the NER.

The majority of engines from the 1956 building programme were destined for the LMR Midland Division with Toton and Wellingborough picking up a further twelve and fourteen examples respectively. With more 9Fs at its disposal, Toton began to use the engines on duties other than the Brent coal traffic, one example being freights to Buxton where in November 1957, 92054/9 and 92128 were noted on an afternoon freight from Sheffield, returning on a similar working next day. Toton continued to use 9Fs on the WCML traffic to Willesden, which in turn used the engines on a variety of workings including empty stock duties during layovers. On 23rd March 1957, for example, 92101 was observed removing the stock of the 9.42am relief from Birmingham New Street out of Euston. On 10th February, both 92048/53 were put in charge of works trains over the electric lines at South Kenton and Willesden Junction respectively. Similarly, one Willesden duty was to provide the pilot at Broad Street during the morning peak period to release engines from the 9.01am and 9.48am arrivals from Tring. This role was usually performed by a 4-6-0, 2-6-0 or 2-8-0 but on 6th August 1958, Toton's 92078 was turned out for the job. Toton 9Fs were also used along with Cricklewood and Wellingborough 9Fs on transfer freights from the LMR to Norwood Junction and Hither Green on the SR over the West London Joint line.

During the period December 1958 to April 1959, Toton 9Fs were used in tandem in dynamometer car tests for accelerated mineral freight trials running to Class 'C' timings between Toton and Brent. 92153/6 were known to be involved as was 92094, transferred for the period from Annesley. It was reported that speeds of up to 70mph were regularly attained.

The 9Fs now began to dominate the mineral traffic on the

MML south of Wellingborough even displacing a number of Stanier 8F 2-8-0s; they were also more frequently to be seen on Class 'D' and Class 'E' freights. The rapidly dwindling band of Garratts was by this time seldom seen in the London area, the remaining class members by then allocated to Hasland near Chesterfield, where they could be observed on freights on the Erewash Valley line and to the Gowhole marshalling sidings, west of Chinley. The 9Fs played their part in a substantial increase in rail traffic, especially freight, on the MML at this time. This occurred as a result of the Suez Canal Crisis of September/October 1956. The waterway had been temporarily closed due to military conflict, resulting in a serious disruption in fuel oil supplies to Europe from the Middle East. This led to a period of fuel rationing for both commercial and private motor vehicles thus pushing more business on to the railways until restrictions were eased in the spring of 1957. Over this period, there were many examples of 9Fs double-heading long trains of northbound empty coal wagon trains as the operating authorities dealt with large numbers of unbalanced workings.

The LMR 9Fs were also frequently seen to be helping out when engines failed on passenger duties. On 18th March 1957, for example, the 10.15am St. Pancras-Manchester arrived at Derby Midland approximately one hour late with Jubilee 4-6-0 45561 *Saskatchewan* and 92052 as pilot. The Jubilee had stopped at Hathern with injector trouble, eventually struggling to Sheet Stores Junction, Trent where the 9F was attached; Standard Class 5 4-6-0 73065 took over from the pair at Derby.

Other LMR depots to receive 9Fs at this time were Cricklewood, Kettering, Saltley, Leicester Midland and Westhouses. Cricklewood received newly-built 92111/2 plus 92108 (ex-Wellingborough) and 92110 (ex-Toton) in November 1956; a regular working for these engines was the 7.10pm Leicester-Brent merchandise freight as well as the Brent coal traffic. On 5th January 1957, 92111 was working the 2.20am Cricklewood-Wellingborough Class 'H' freight when it was in collision with the rear of the 1.27am Class 'F' from Brent to Corby at Luton. Goods lines were both blocked from 4.00am to 1.30pm causing lengthy delays to overnight freight traffic from the north; 92111, with only just over 5,000 miles on the clock, spent almost three weeks under repair at Crewe Works. Other observations included 92110 on 4th April 1959 with a special London to Bury freight at Elland on the Calder Valley line whilst the repaired 92111 was used on one of the return empty 'beer trains' from London to Burton-upon-Trent on 1st March 1958. The engine returned next day with the the 4.50pm partially-fitted beer train from Burton to Cricklewood, one of two regular evening workings supplying the thirsty capital, the other departing Burton at around 7.00pm. This traffic was routed by way of what is now the heart of the National Forest, traversing the Burton-Leicester branch through Moira, Ashby-de-la-Zouch and Coalville; Leicester was avoided by using the southbound curve at Knighton Junction.

Kettering received 92105/6 from Wellingborough in November 1956 and later in March 1958, 92163 new from Crewe. In addition to MML duties, Kettering's 9Fs were also engaged in moving the local iron ore traffic. 92106 was observed for example, on 23rd February 1957 heading an iron ore train towards York on the Normanton-Castleford line; the engines were also used on similar workings to the Gloucester and Newport areas.

In January 1957, it was arranged to try a 9F on the ICI hopper traffic from Tunstead to Winnington (Northwich). A preliminary run was made on Monday 13th, when 92045 of Bidston depot worked the 6.45am empty hoppers to Tunstead and returned on the 11.04am with 16 loaded hoppers, repeating the exercise the following day. On Wedneday 15th, the day the actual test run was made, the load was increased to 19 wagons in both directions (approx. 1,300 tons). The outcome was successful, 92045 coping with the extra load without any problems. In the event, Northwich did not receive an allocation of 9Fs however, the main reason being that other work from the depot did not warrant the services of 9F power. The hopper traffic continued to be operated mainly by Stanier Class 8F 2-8-0s until dieselisation; 9Fs did deputise on occasion however when either 8Fs or diesels were unavailable.

The first batch of new 9Fs at Saltley, 92129-39, was allocated in the period April-June 1957 although the first three were soon moved to Toton; towards the end of the year the depot received 92151/2/5 new from Crewe. Saltley was already host to 92109/21 which were in use in place of Class 5 4-6-0s on the 5.15pm Class 'D' Water Orton-Leeds and the 4.15am Class 'D' Leeds-Washwood Heath freights during April. The new engines began to appear on other workings including the 5.50am Washwood Heath-Bristol returning on the 5.30pm Bristol-Water Orton; the 6.30pm Washwood Heath-Westerleigh; the 7.35pm Avonmouth-Lawley Street returning on the next day's 11.18am Washwood Heath-Westerleigh; the 9.10am Bromford Bridge-Toton returning on the 5.22pm Toton-Washwood Heath and the 1.50am Birmingham-Westerleigh, working back with the 8.55am Avonmouth-Birmingham; these duties were previously rostered for Stanier Class 8F 2-8-0s. The 9Fs were also observed working the 1.00am Lawley Street-Brent Class 'H' which when running late was often combined with the 3.10am Rowsley-St. Pancras Class 'E' at Luton, the train going forward double-headed with the Crab 2-6-0 off the Rowsley freight. Saltley 9Fs occasionally featured on the 8.52pm Washwood Heath-Redditch and the 12.18am return. The Barnt Green-Ashchurch line saw its first Saltley 9F on 1st May 1957 when 92109 worked the 8.25am freight from Evesham to Selly Oak. Later in 1957, the new 2-10-0s were successfully tried out on Saltley's turns to Carlisle Durran Hill with the Birmingham-Glasgow fast fitted freights, 92134/7/9 being observed on these workings in September and October. The 11.22pm Leeds-Washwood Heath fitted freight was also often worked by a Saltley 9F at this time. Other duties included deputising for 92079 the Lickey banker which was in Crewe Works during August 1957 for a Light Intermediate overhaul. Noted at Bromsgrove at this time were 92133/6 and 92138, each one spending about a week there on banking duties.

The last of the new 9F allocation to arrive at Saltley were the mechanical stoker-fitted trio, 92165-7, which appeared in April and May 1958. For crew training purposes, the engines were confined at first to local runs to Bordesley Junction on the WR and also the 9.42am Class 'H' from Bromford Bridge to Branston near Burton-upon-Trent, returning on the 2.15pm from Horninglow Bridge, north of Burton. The engines had been earmarked for Saltley's fitted freight turns to Carlisle via Leeds and the Settle route. These workings were the longest and most arduous freight runs on the BR network which is why they were considered ideal to test the qualities

Figure 97
92196 (Doncaster) was one month old when it was exhibited at Noel Park Goods Yard, Wood Green during the celebrations for the 750th anniversary of the Borough Charter (12th - 14th September 1958). 92196 was reallocated to Immingham in February 1959 for the express fish traffic from Grimsby and withdrawn at the end of 1964. *(Rodney Lissenden)*

of the mechanical stoker device. The main jobs were to substitute for the Stanier Class 5 4-6-0s on the 4.45pm Class 'C' Water Orton-Glasgow College as far as Carlisle returning on the next day's 4.03pm Class 'C' Carlisle Durran Hill-Washwood Heath and the 3.50am Water Orton-Carlisle returning at 11.15pm from Carlisle. By September, 92166 was away under test at Rugby and did not reappear for many months. The engines were not entirely successful owing to chronic problems with the provision of suitably sized coal; details of the experience with the mechanical stoker 9Fs are given in Sections 1 and 11. It is believed that a move was discussed in late 1958 to transfer the mechanical stoker trio to Toton for trials on the Brent mineral traffic; no reports of the engines operating on these duties have been traced however. One move which did take place was when 92166 was temporarily exchanged with Newport Ebbw Junction's 92248 in September 1959 and used for several months on trials on the Ebbw Vale iron ore traffic (see Section 9).

Leicester Midland was home to 92164 fresh from Crewe in April 1958. By this time, the depot was already operating 92109/21, both on its books from August 1957 and had also received 92100-4/28 from Toton in March 1958. As well as southbound coal traffic, duties included fitted freights to the south Yorkshire area, particularly the 4.00 pm to Normanton. The depot's 9Fs often appeared on the 9.50am (SO) Leicester-Blackpool North holiday special in the 1958 summer timetable (see Table 7.2). Due to a shortage of power on the Great Central line, 92164 was one of several Leicester Midland engines loaned to Leicester Central MPD during the summer of 1958; 92164 was frequently employed on passenger work on the ex-GC line at this time, see Table 11.28.

It was observed that Leicester 9Fs had a tendency to wander off the beaten track, occasionally being noted in the Stockton area on the 4.45pm freight from Haverton Hill to Dringhouses (York). This service was run in connection with ICI chemical traffic and featured 9Fs from other LMR depots such as Saltley and Wellingborough from time to time. Similarly 92121 was observed at Goole on 10th February 1959 with a cargo of motor cars from the Vauxhall plant at Luton.

Westhouses MPD was situated near Alfreton on the Erewash Valley main line where its main function was to service the local coal mining industry. Eight 9Fs, 92113-20 arrived from November 1956 to January 1957 displacing Stanier Class 8F 2-8-0s from heavy coal haulage duties from the numerous pits in the area. Other workings included visits to Gowhole marshalling sidings west of Chinley with freights from Avenue sidings, Chesterfield to the Manchester area, mineral workings to York and also the daily Westhouses-Aston freight. Saltley often appropriated Westhouses 9Fs for other work during layovers. On 28th December 1956 for example, 92114 was noted on a Droitwich-Washwood Heath train of empty mineral wagons. One of the allocation, 92116, was involved in an incident in the Birmingham area on 30th January 1958. In thick fog, a mobile crane travelling along the main road collided with the railway overbridge at Chester Road station on the Sutton Coldfield branch just as the engine was approaching with a northbound freight. 92116 and its train were sent back to Erdington goods yard where they were detained for several hours before being allowed to continue across the bridge. On 10th June 1958, 92113 was noted coupled with Wellingborough's 92080 to a dynamometer car on a fitted coal train heading out of Nottingham towards Staythorpe power station near Newark. Westhouses 9Fs were regularly employed on summer Saturday holiday specials to Blackpool and north Wales in 1958 (see Table 7.2).

Other LMR depots to receive an allocation of 9Fs at around this time were Burton-upon-Trent, Newton Heath and Rowsley. Burton was host to 92009/53 from September 1957. Their usual duties for this short period were the 8.25pm Burton-Leeds fitted freight, returning next day on the 8.50am Leeds-Rotherham Masborough and the 5.45pm Staveley-Wichnor Junction. The 9Fs were not well received at Burton as they were too big to go inside the shed and had to be worked on outside; moreover, they could be turned only on the Branston triangle. Thus it was no surprise when Burton's 9Fs were moved on to Saltley in March 1958.

From June 1958, five 9Fs, 92015-7 and 92161/2 were transferred on loan from Saltley and Westhouses to Newton Heath, the first 9Fs to be assigned to the LMR Central Division. The engines became officially allocated in September and were employed on the fitted freight traffic from Ancoats Yard to Rowsley over the Peak Forest line and

Figure 98
On a hot August day, there is no smoke visible from 92218 (Bristol St. Philips Marsh) as it toils up to Dainton tunnel with a down goods to Tavistock Junction on 5th August 1960. The engine's tender (No. 1525) had a modification carried out at Old Oak Common in August 1961 (see Section 9) whereby additional tender rear steps were installed for safety reasons. *(Hugh Ballantyne)*

Figure 99
92228 is pictured on shed at Severn Tunnel Junction on 15th September 1963. The engine was allocated to Banbury for over eight years from new and was transferred to Speke Junction in October 1966 only to be withdrawn early in the New Year. *(Courtney Haydon)*

to Carlisle via the Settle & Carlisle route. Later as more 9Fs were received at Newton Heath, they were noted regularly working coal trains in and out of Yorkshire. They also were reported hauling special trains of long-welded rails to various destinations from the then new welding facility at Castleton near Rochdale.

At weekends in summer, Newton Heath's 9Fs were used for passenger excursion and holiday specials to north Wales and the Lancashire coast resorts including Isle of Man boat trains from Fleetwood (see Section 7.3). Further afield, 92015 was noted at Embsay on the MR line to Ilkley on 18th February and 6th March 1959 heading special ballast trains to Edge Hill and Prestwich respectively from the private sidings of the Skipton Rock Company.

In November 1959, Rowsley received six 9Fs from Saltley, 92008/9/48-51. The engines were employed on both mineral and fitted freights to the Manchester area (Ardwick, Heaton Mersey and Gowhole sidings), as well as to Garston Docks on Merseyside. Southwards there were turns to Beeston and also a daily Class 'E' express freight to Washwood Heath; another duty in the early days was the 4.10pm freight to Stockport via Buxton. Later the 9Fs began to share with Rowsley's Standard Class 5 Caprotti 4-6-0s the two daily fitted freights to Brent sidings, returning on similar traffic from Somers Town goods depot, St. Pancras. Rowsley's 9Fs were also deployed from time to time as bankers for freights on the 15-mile 1 in 100/90 climb to Peak Forest

All but three of the ER's 9F allocation from the 1956 programme were divided equally between New England (92140-9/78-88) and Doncaster (92168-77/92-9, 92200/1/2). The remaining engines were allocated to Mexborough (92189/90) or Sheffield Darnall (92191) in March and April 1958. The latter two allocations turned out to be only temporary and all three were on Doncaster's books by the end of May. It is not clear why Mexborough and Darnall were assigned a 9F allocation. As ex-GCR depots, the original plan may have been to share some of the few Annesley 9F northbound workings but by this time the latter depot was under the control of the LMR whilst Mexborough and Darnall remained in the ER's Sheffield district.

The first batch of the New England contingent, 92140-9, was delivered from July to October 1957. During running-in from Crewe, 92141 was noted working light engine over Shap summit and back on 30th July and was in charge of the 5.15pm Carlisle-Crewe fitted freight from Carnforth. On 8th September, 92146 was observed piloting an 8F 2-8-0 past Menai Bridge with a breakdown train from the Holyhead direction. The new engines assumed the duties of some of the earlier New England 9F allocation which had been transferred to Annesley in May and June 1957. The second batch, 92178-88, arrived over the period September 1957 to February 1958, ex-Swindon Works. Of these, 92178 was the first 9F to be fitted with a double chimney following experiments at Swindon; the double chimney became standard on the 9Fs from 92183 onwards. By this time, the 9Fs had a major share of the Ferme Park coal traffic having displaced K3 2-6-0s, WD 2-8-0s and the occasional V2 2-6-2 from these duties. An innovation in the 1957/8 winter timetable however resulted in the 9Fs being rostered for several ECML Class 'D' fitted freights together with appearances on the Hull fish traffic. In the case of the latter workings, the 5.30pm and 5.58pm up fish vans from Humberside and the 8.25am Kings Cross-New Clee fish empties featured a 9F from time to time. Similarly the 6.50pm Kings Cross-Worksop Class 'D', booked to run via Hertford North was regularly 9F-hauled, as was the daily pick-up freight from Welwyn Garden City. The 9Fs began to be used on ecs trains also, 92183 being observed on a down working on 13th January 1958.

New England 9Fs were involved in the Hitchin accident of Wednesday 19th November 1958 when at around 4.30am in thick fog 92187 working the 3.25am Class 'E' down coal empties from Ferme Park ran at about 15mph into the rear of the 2.28am empties from Ferme Park in the charge of stable mate 92145. The latter train was moving away from Hitchin South signals after stopping to ensure the road was clear, 92187 making short work of the brake van and several trucks. The other wagons remained intact on the line with the exception of those immediately next to 92145 which were forced forward and upward. In so doing they demolished the down signal gantry which was left slewed across part of the wreckage on the down slow line.

At the same time Copley Hill's V2 2-6-2 60885 working the 10.35pm Ardsley-Ferme Park Class 'D' freight was approaching on the up main line and ran into the wreckage, derailing and careering forward some 40 yards before coming to a halt at an angle of approximately 45 degrees. On the adjacent up slow line was L1 tank engine 67785 from Hitchin shed waiting to cross over to the down slow road. The L1 sustained the full impact of the derailed vans from the Leeds train, was knocked over on to its side and almost totally covered by wreckage. Miraculously there were no fatalities but the incident had completely blocked all roads causing severe traffic disruption. Up passenger trains were diverted to the GE line, most terminating at Stratford, the passengers conveyed into Liverpool Street by a shuttle service of Southend electric trains. Breakdown cranes, from Peterborough, hauled by K3 2-6-0 61979 and from Kings Cross in the charge of L1 tank engine 67774, were quickly on the scene and clearance gangs worked all through Wednesday. By early Thursday morning, all lines were open in time for the first workmen's trains. 92187 suffered little more than the loss of its front buffers and a slightly bent front end; the engine spent nearly a month in Darlington Works under repair. In the subsequent inquiry, the blame was placed entirely on the unfortunate driver of 92187 for not keeping a proper lookout.

The Doncaster engines also arrived in two batches, 92168-77 from December 1957 to March 1958 and 92192-92202 from May to December 1958. The class was employed on similar workings to those relinquished by the earlier allocation which had been transferred to Annesley in February and March 1957. In addition, they began to appear on duties such as the 4.30am Class 'H' New England-Ranskill and the 2.55pm Class 'C' New England-York. On 25th January 1958, 92170 broke new ground by working the 1.40pm Class 'D' Doncaster-Holloway East goods and was also observed on the return working, the 7.03pm (MX) Clarence Yard-Hull Class 'D' on 7th February. As a result of the 9F influx at Doncaster, seven of the depot's O2 2-8-0s were placed in store.

Doncaster 9Fs, already a regular sight at York, also worked north to Newcastle-upon-Tyne, 92175 being noted there on the 1.20pm Heaton-York Class 'D' freight on 14th March 1958. Apart from the Tyne Dock engines, 92060-6/97-9, 9Fs had not been common on Tyneside but now started to be frequent visitors. Also on 14th March, Toton's 92052 was observed heading the 9.15pm Heaton-Kings Cross Class 'C' whilst 92035 of New England arrived with an evening freight

Figure 100
92116 (Westhouses) was turned out for a bank holiday Monday special (7th August 1961) seen here north of Pontefract. Although the reporting number suggests the destination to be either Leicester or Liverpool, the train has been identified as a Leicester London Road-Scarborough excursion. *(Peter Cookson)*

from the south; the following week, (on 19th March) 92157 of Toton was a guest at Gateshead depot. By midsummer, Doncaster 9Fs were regular visitors to Newcastle, some even penetrating further north, e.g. 92191 on a Heaton-Tweedmouth freight on 25th August, whilst five days earlier, 92172 worked an afternoon two-coach special from Newcastle to Carlisle.

In early May 1958, Doncaster 9Fs were involved in trials with special vacuum-fitted mineral trains. It is believed that this initiative was connected with the inauguration of the new Palace Gates automated fuel depot for the distribution of domestic coal earlier in the year. It was anticipated that the facility would handle well over 1,000 tons of coal per week when fully commissioned. On 2nd May 92173 headed a train of 40 such 16ton loaded wagons, known as 'minfits', from Doncaster Loversall Carr to Kings Cross Goods; the train had a total weight of some 850 tons. The journey was scheduled to take four and a half hours inclusive of a two-minute stop at New England South to change crews. 92173 ran on the main line except between Huntingdon South and Sandy. Despite three checks for permanent way work, the train arrived five minutes early. Intermediate passing times were of interest, the train topping Stoke Bank ten minutes after passing through Grantham and reaching Werrington Junction, 25.9 miles from Grantham 32 minutes later; it is likely speeds somewhat in excess of 60mph were achieved after Stoke summit. A similar test was carried out on 8th May this time with 92174 in charge and scheduled times for this run have been recorded. Departure from Doncaster was at 9.00am, Retford passed at 9.26am, Grantham at 10.21am with the New England stop from 11.05 to 11.07am; arrival at Kings Cross was on time at the scheduled 1.32pm.

The experimental train with 92197 in charge was also tried out on a Doncaster-Watford coal duty in 1958 which led to Doncaster 9Fs being increasingly used in the early months of 1959 on the (unfitted) Welham Junction-Watford coal duty, long the preserve of WD 2-8-0s from Colwick. The train travelled via Market Harborough and Northampton, arriving at Watford just before midnight. The engine then went on shed until 10.08am next day whence it ran light engine to Headstone Lane. Here it took on a pickup goods to Sudbury (Willesden Yard's reception sidings) calling at Harrow and North Wembley. It then retired to Willesden shed, returning north with the late evening Willesden-Colwick coal empties. Some of the class noted on the duty were 92172 (24th March, 1st and 14th April), 92173 (25th March) and 92197 (15th April). The diagram operated Tuesdays to Fridays and sometimes Saturdays. For Monday's duty, Willesden usually supplied an LNWR 0-8-0 which arrived on Watford depot on Sunday.

Unusual Doncaster 9F movements in early 1959 saw several engines appearing on Saltley shed after working in on freights from south Yorkshire. No regular duties were reported but the 9Fs may have been used as substitutes for engines working from other depots. A month later, on 24th February, 92202 was observed hauling Bo-Bo electric locomotive E5002 new from Doncaster Works to the SR; progress was rather slow as speed was restricted to a 20mph maximum.

Figure 101
92231 (Eastleigh) leaves Southampton with the 5.17pm Bournemouth stopper during 1963 and poses a lamp bracket puzzle. The top bracket appears to have been removed while the two mid-smokebox door brackets still incorporate both the SR(BR) and WR varieties; another mystery! *(G. Wheeler)*

Figure 102
92211, temporarily allocated to Westbury for the Fawley-Bromford Bridge oil traffic, dozes at its home shed on 18th June 1961. Later the same month, 92211 was loaned to the SR and then officially transferred to Eastleigh in July for the same duty. The regular-size but irregularly spaced numerals on the cabside are thought to be unique on a 9F. *(Courtney Haydon)*

The GN line 9Fs were increasingly to be found on ecs duties during 1958 and were also frequently scheduled for passenger duties (see Table 7.1). Doncaster 9Fs shared with B1 4-6-0s the 9.35am Delaval Sidings-Holloway East Goods, which for many years had been a Pacific working. On 12th July, 92178 (New England) and 92191 (Doncaster) both worked down ecs trains of 12 bogies each. Later, on Tuesday 5th August, an enormous ecs train consisting of three sets of eight-car Kings Cross suburban 'quad-art' stock were returned to London by 9F haulage after being used on several Nottingham-Skegness day excursions during the Bank Holiday weekend. Also in early August, 9Fs began to be rostered for the 12.35pm Kings Cross-York parcels train, 92141 and 92194 being observed during the week ending 9th of the month.

The 9Fs continued to deputise for failed engines on passenger work. On Saturday 26th July 1958, for example, B16 4-6-0 61426 had failed at Pilmoor with the 7.53am Filey Holiday Camp special to Glasgow. 92174 had been despatched from York and completed the diagram by working to Newcastle and then back to Scarborough on the 4.40pm arrival from Glasgow via the Gilling branch. The engine turned on the triangle at Filey Holiday Camp and then worked the ecs to York en route to Doncaster. Later, on 13th October, 92173 arrived at York an hour or so late on the down "Talisman", Kings Cross-Glasgow. The engine had replaced Kings Cross A4 Pacific 60025 *Falcon* at Newark and was in turn replaced by Heaton's A1 Pacific 60127 *Wilson Worsdell* at York.

Other depots on the ER receiving 9Fs at this time were Grantham, Frodingham and Immingham. Grantham was host to 92187/8 from June to September 1958. There does not appear to have been much suitable work for the engines at Grantham, the only reported regular duty being the 5.15am Kings Cross to York parcels and the engines were quickly returned to New England. Similarly seven 9Fs, 92034/5, 92184/9/90/7/8 were transferred to Frodingham from New England and Doncaster in January and February 1959. The engines were needed to cover increased ballast train tonnage from Scunthorpe to the south via Boston in connection with engineering works in the London area. Frodingham's 9Fs worked to Barnetby and Immingham but were not greeted with much enthusiasm, as they were reported to be suffering from serious faults such as leaking fireboxes and tube plates. All seven engines were returned to their respective depots in April or June 1959.

The six engines transferred from Doncaster and New England to Immingham in February or April 1959, 92039, 92193-6, 92202 were better received. Three of the class were required for the afternoon and evening fish trains to London. The depot lavished care and attention on their 9Fs, reportedly keeping them in immaculate condition with silver painted smokebox door hinges and centre boss. The London trains were worked over the GN East Lincolnshire line through Louth and Boston. The 5.30pm and 5.58pm departures from New Clee sidings east of Grimsby docks were the fast services whilst the 7.00pm was a slow working dropping vans off at various points en route to the capital. The 9Fs could also be observed on the 5.13pm express fish to Manchester Ashton Moss and occasionally on the 6.25pm to Leicester Central. The London trains were made up to 50 vans although each may have carried only a few hundredweight of fish as each merchant tended to specify a van exclusively for his own use resulting in more than one vehicle going to the same destination. Under these conditions, the traffic became increasingly uneconomic and was discouraged from the early 1960s onwards.

The ER 9Fs continued to visit Tyneside with fitted freights from the south after periods of absence, their appearances usually being associated with shortage of V2 2-6-2 power. By June 1959, New England had only one regular freight turn to Newcastle, the 1.15am Kings Cross-Niddrie to and from Peterborough, returning on the 6.05pm Niddrie-Kings Cross. This had been a V2 2-6-2 turn for many years but was worked by 92186/7 alternately throughout June and July. The depot had begun to use 9Fs in place of its V2s on fast fitted freight work when it had been realised that the 9Fs were well capable of running to the 60mph schedules required. This released the V2s for passenger duties at times of Pacific shortages.

The 9Fs were also in great demand for display at exhibitions during 1958/9. Examples were: 92192 at Sheffield Blast Lane goods depot on 16th August 1958; 92166 at Derby Works Annual Flower Show and Open Day on 30th August 1958; 92196 at Noel Park goods yard, Wood Green (on the occasion of the 750th anniversary of the Borough Charter) from 12th to 14th September 1958; 92201 at Lincoln on the opening of the Holmes goods depot on 16th January 1959 and 92200 at Peterborough again for the official opening of a new goods depot on 13th July 1959.

The 48 engines in the 1957 and 1958 building programmes were all allocated to the WR. The 1958 programme was for 30 engines, 92221-50, which had all been delivered from Crewe some four months before Swindon produced the first of the eighteen engines, 92203-20, in the 1957 programme. The delay in the Swindon deliveries was the result of the works resources being committed to the building of the first Cl.42 Warship B-B diesel hydraulic locomotives, D800-32. The final Swindon-built 9F, the celebrated 92220 *Evening Star,* the last steam engine to be built by BR, was in fact turned out in the same month, March 1960, as D817 *Foxhound* and D818 *Glory.*

The Crewe engines, delivered over the period May to December 1958, were allocated as shown:

Banbury	(11)	92221-30/50
Newport Ebbw Junction	(10)	92237-44
		92248/9
Old Oak Common	(3)	92245-7
Pontypool Road	(6)	92231-6
	Total	30

The Swindon deliveries appeared from April 1959 to March 1960 and were distributed as follows:

Banbury	(2)	92212/5
Cardiff Canton	(5)	92210/4/6/7/20
Laira	(2)	92208/9
Old Oak Common	(1)	92211
St. Philips Marsh	(8)	92203-7/13/8/9
	Total	18

Banbury received Crewe-built 92221-30/50 from May to December 1958 with Swindon's 92212/5 appearing in September and November 1959. The 9Fs displaced 28XX and WD 2-8-0s from some of the iron ore workings to South Wales which by the early 1960s required five engines to be rostered daily for services to Cardiff, Margam near Port

Talbot and Severn Tunnel Junction. The iron ore traffic had been routed via Leamington Spa, Hatton and Honeybourne Junction until 1960. During that year a new east to south double-track curve had been constructed at Stratford linking the Stratford-upon-Avon and Midland Junction line (S&MJ) to the WR's Birmingham-Cheltenham line. This construction not only saved some 27 route miles but also avoided the formidable Hatton Bank, some four miles at a ruling gradient of 1 in 110 just north of Leamington Spa. Crews were changed at Honeybourne, the trains then heading for South Wales via Gloucester and Newport. These duties were shared with 9Fs, 28XX and WD 2-8-0s from Newport Ebbw Junction.

Banbury 9Fs regularly worked to the London area and were also noted on the exchange freights to Woodford Halse. On 15th November 1958, 92224 was reported at Birkenhead with the 7.45pm freight to London and the class soon became frequent performers on freights to the Chester area. In 1959, Banbury's 92250 was selected for trials with the Giesl Oblong Ejector, (see Section 11.1 for test details) and was away at Rugby Testing Station from April to September. After its return 92250 was noted working on the iron ore traffic to South Wales and to Bilston in the West Midlands before reallocation to Ebbw Junction a few weeks later.

The ten new 9Fs allocated to Newport Ebbw Junction 92237-44/8/9 arrived in the period from September to December 1958. They were the first 9F additions to the depot's books since the original allocation, 92000-7, in early 1954. The majority of the new 9Fs did not remain long at Ebbw Junction, 92237 together with 92003/5 from the 1954 batch moving to Cardiff Canton whilst 92238-41/4 were all at Old Oak Common by the end of 1958. Duties for Ebbw Junction's remaining 9Fs included fitted freights to the London area, (via both the Severn Tunnel and Gloucester routes), sharing in the Banbury iron ore traffic, the exchange workings to Woodford Halse via the ex-S&MJ line and freights to and from Avonmouth Docks. It was around this period that the depot's 9Fs began to venture further afield when on 20th November 1958, 92006 was reported at Taunton heading the 8.10am freight from Bassaleg, returning on the afternoon coal empties from Newton Abbot next day.

During this period, one of Canton's newly acquired 9Fs, 92003, was involved in the collision at Highworth Junction east of Swindon in the early hours of 12th November 1958. The 12.01am Bristol East Depot-Reading freight, headed by 47XX 2-8-0 4707 and carrying mainly tobacco products from the W. D. and H. O. Wills factory, had overrun the up loop. Six wagons immediately behind the tender were derailed, fouling both the up and down main lines. Almost immediately the 12.45am Paddington-Carmarthen newspaper train with Castle 4-6-0 5009 *Shrewsbury Castle* in charge ran into the debris, sustaining considerable damage. Soon afterwards a fully fitted freight, the 10.50pm Cardiff to Paddington hauled by 92003 on the up main line, collided with the wreckage. 4707's crew, having quickly freed themselves from the rubble, had managed to warn the Southall driver on the 9F by means of a red light. An emergency brake application was made but not in time to prevent the second collision. Amazingly, there were no fatalities. The 9F was travelling relatively slowly, still picking up speed from the crew change and water stop at Swindon, otherwise the consequences could have been much more serious. All up and down lines were blocked for most of the following day whilst the wreckage was cleared. Externally

Figure 103
92100 (Westhouses) takes a breather on shed at Eastleigh on 14th June 1961. The engine is probably visiting on an oil tank empties working from the Midlands. Only one boiler change was recorded for 92100 (October 1963 at Crewe) when it also acquired a BR1F tender in exchange for its original BR1C type. 92100, along with 92101, were the first 9Fs to be fitted from new with LNER-type fire hole doors in an attempt to combat firebox glare during night time operation. *(Courtney Haydon)*

Figure 104
Bristol Barrow Road's 92221 is on shed at Eastleigh on 3rd February 1962. 92221 was one of the few 9Fs to be given a Heavy Intermediate overhaul at Caerphilly Works, completed in the previous December when the engine had achieved almost 85,000 miles in traffic. When allocated to Laira in summer 1959, 92221 was used on passenger workings between Plymouth, Bristol and Paddington. *(Courtney Haydon)*

Figure 105
92205 (Eastleigh) coasts into Southampton Central with the 10.57am Salisbury-Portsmouth & Southsea parcels on 9th February 1961. The SR-based 9Fs were often used on such services when not engaged in the oil tanker traffic from the Esso refinery at Fawley. 92205 is pictured only a few weeks after transfer from the WR; the additional lamp brackets on the smokebox door, required for the SR route disc system, are not yet in place. *(Courtney Haydon)*

Figure 106
Sunday 10th March 1963 sees 92206 (Eastleigh) at rest at its home depot. Stablemate 92205 is next in line and allows a comparison of the top lamp bracket location between the two engines; for 92206, the bracket is on the smokebox door whilst for 92205, the smokebox rim has been used. Later, 92205 lost its upper bracket after transfer to the NER in September 1963, probably for safety reasons when operating on electrified lines. Although an SR engine, the battery box below the cab sheet and the conduit clearly present along the base of the running plate confirm 92206 still has at least some of its WR ATC apparatus in situ. *(Rodney Lissenden)*

92003 appeared to have suffered little more than a buckled right hand side smoke deflector and the loss of the right hand gridiron but according to the official record was nevertheless out of action for some three months receiving attention at Swindon Works.

By October 1959, one of Saltley's 9Fs fitted with Berkley mechanical stoker, 92166, had arrived at Newport Ebbw Junction on loan from the LMR. The engine had already spent a few weeks at Cardiff Canton, although details of its duties there have not been traced; Ebbw Junction's 92248 had been sent on loan to Saltley in exchange for 92166. Ebbw Junction used 92166 on some main line and local freight duties but chiefly on the iron ore trains from Newport Docks to the Ebbw Vale steel plant; details of the trials are given in Section 9; 92166 returned to Saltley in February 1960.

Old Oak Common received four new 9Fs, Crewe-built 92245-7 in November/December 1958 and 92211 from Swindon Works in September of the following year. Arriving at the same time as the Crewe engines were seven more 9Fs, 92229/30/8-41/4, reallocated from Banbury and Ebbw Junction. It was reported that Old Oak's 9Fs were to take over the duties of the depot's 47XX 2-8-0s although withdrawal of the latter class did not commence until May/June 1962. The 9Fs worked fast freights to Bristol, Plymouth (Tavistock Junction), South Wales and the Birmingham area. One regular working was an overnight fitted freight to Carmarthen Junction, thence light engine back to Llanelli shed, returning east on the 4.00pm freight from Llandilo Junction to Acton via Gloucester and Swindon. Old Oak's 9Fs were also often used on passenger trains during the summer of 1959, see Section 7.3 for details.

Eight of the new Swindon-built 9Fs, 92203-7/13/8/9, were allocated to Bristol St. Philips Marsh arriving during the period April 1959-January 1960. Their duties included fitted freights to London, Plymouth, South Wales and Salisbury. The 4.35pm Plymouth Millbay-Paddington parcels was a St. Philips Marsh turn at this time and its 9Fs made regular appearances on this duty. Other depots' 9Fs were also noted on the service from time to time; on 24th June 1959, for example, Ebbw Junction's 92006 piloted by Modified Hall 4-6-0, 7916 *Mobberley Hall,* were observed double-heading the train over the south Devon banks. SPM's 9Fs were also frequently used on passenger work in the summer of 1959, mainly on holiday specials to South Wales and the south west.

Reports in August 1958 indicated that ten 9Fs were to be allocated to Pontypool Road depot for freight working to Shrewsbury and Chester on the North-and-West route. In the event, only five appeared, 92231-6 in August and September, the balance redirected to Newport Ebbw Junction. Within a few months however, Pontypool Road's 9Fs had all been transferred to Cardiff Canton, 92236 via Ebbw Junction in October/November and the remainder via Severn Tunnel Junction in January/February 1959. No 9Fs were subsequently allocated to Pontypool Road and it was not until 1964 that Severn Tunnel Junction received another batch of 9Fs.

Cardiff Canton was allocated five new Swindon-built 9Fs,

Figure 107
92203 (Bath Green Park) sets off from Bournemouth West with the 7.25pm for Bristol Temple Meads on 18th June 1960. Following successful trials three months earlier, 92203-6 were drafted to Green Park for the summer season, displacing the S&DJR 7F 2-8-0s from the holiday special passenger traffic to Bournemouth. Although in service for less than nine years, records indicate that 92203 carried no fewer than three different boilers during its career. The engine was withdrawn in November 1967 and is now preserved. *(Courtney Haydon)*

Figure 108
92006 comes on to the double track section at Midford with the 7.43am (SO) Bradford Forster Square-Bournemouth West on 26th August 1961. After its summer stint on the S&DJR, the engine returned to Newport Ebbw Junction in September. Two years later, 92006 was one of a group of WR and SR-based 9Fs which were sent to the NER at York. 92006 was modified with a double chimney at Swindon in August 1960 during a Heavy General overhaul.
(Hugh Ballantyne)

92210/4/6/7/20, over the period August 1959 to March 1960. Before their arrival the depot had already been operating four 9Fs from November 1958 (92003/5, 92236/7) with another batch (92231-5) allocated there in February 1959. The class was used on freight duties to Banbury, displacing 28XX and WD 2-8-0s. The engines were also deployed on long distance freights to Oxley, Saltney (Chester), Woodford Halse, Honeybourne Junction, Hackney and Tavistock Junction (Plymouth), all of which had previously been rostered for 28XX 2-8-0s, 43XX 2-6-0s or Hall 4-6-0s; where trains were routed through the Severn Tunnel, the 9Fs were restricted to a 455-ton loading. The first reported sighting of a 9F at Plymouth was in February 1959 when Canton's 92235 headed a late evening Cardiff-Hackney freight and was then rostered for the following day's 2.30pm Hackney-Tavistock Junction. On 2nd July 1959, 92003 reached Salisbury on the 4.20am Class 'D' freight from Cardiff whilst in the following month Canton 9Fs were reported to be visiting York on a series of unidentified special workings, possibly via the ex-GCR route; 92005 and 92232/3/5 were the engines noted. Canton's 9Fs were also frequently to be seen on the Cardiff-Portsmouth passenger trains as far as Salisbury, especially 92220 *Evening Star,* which became a regular on the 10.30am from Cardiff during the summer of 1960.

Swindon-built 92208/9 were allocated to Laira in June 1959, the same month in which five more of the class, 92221-5, were reallocated to Laira from Banbury; 92209 did not stay long and had moved to Cardiff Canton by the end of August. The engines were used on freight work to the Bristol area, South Wales and London as well as parcels and passenger duties. On 6th October 1959, for example, 92223 was noted at Newton Abbot on a Tavistock Junction-Avonmouth express freight.

Delivery of the 9Fs Completed

By the end of March 1960, all the 9Fs had been delivered and were allocated to just four regions, the ER, NER, LMR and WR. The original intention to deploy five of the class on the SR for continental goods traffic between Dover and London had not been followed through. Despite this, 9Fs could still be seen on SR metals on a regular basis, mainly on fitted freights to Southampton from the Birmingham area and on cross-London freight traffic from the LMR and ER to Hither Green and Norwood Junction. On 24th April 1957, 92127 (Wellingborough) was despatched to Feltham for clearance tests on the turntable there, the aim being to explore the option of through working of mineral trains from the Midlands; until then, engines were changed at Cricklewood. The only region where the 9Fs were rarely seen at this time was the Scottish Region (ScR) although it was the occasional host to some of the Tyne Dock allocation. Later, LMR-based 9Fs would become regular visitors there when allocated to Carlisle Kingmoor from the mid-1960s.

As noted earlier, in September 1955 it was arranged for one of the Crosti engines to penetrate deep into SR territory when 92028 ran via the West London line to Brighton for inspection by the works staff who had been involved at the design stage. As it was not permitted to enter the loco yard at Brighton, the engine was turned on the Preston Park-Hove triangle. This was one of a number of restrictions initially decreed by the SR for the class, presumably on account of the design's long coupled wheel base. In early 1957 it was reported that 9Fs were not to be permitted over the SR except for 92015-9, 92023/41/6/50 and 92052 upwards. This favoured group was allowed to work, subject to specified restrictions, between Kew East Junction and Clapham Junction via Barnes; Clapham Junction and Hither Green sidings via Brixton or Lewisham; Brixton and Herne Hill; Latchmere Junction and Norwood Yard via Clapham Junction, Balham and West Norwood or Selhurst. It is not clear why the other 9F class members were prohibited as there does not appear to be a common denominator among the engines selected. About a year later, restrictions were further eased with the select group now allowed between South Acton Junction and Feltham Yard; between Kew East Junction and Feltham Yard and into Stewarts Lane motive power depot.

Figure 109
On 3rd July 1965, Saltley's 92028 takes a breather at Bristol Barrow Road shed; the view clearly shows the peculiar front end left after removal of the Crosti preheater. The upper lamp bracket has been repositioned towards the driver's side and the centre lower bracket realigned accordingly. This was LMR practice introduced to reduce the risk of enginemen inadvertently coming into contact with overhead cables after 25kv electrification of the WCML had begun in the late 1950s. *(Courtney Haydon)*

In January 1960, the following, more comprehensive route restriction list was issued by the SR and applied to the whole class:

Western Section

Permitted - most main line and secondary routes east of Exeter including the S&DJR: the earlier speed restriction for 9Fs of 45mph between Templecombe & Broadstone Junction was amended to 50mph in June 1960.
- branches to Lymington Pier and Fawley.

Prohibited - entry to Waterloo station.
- Fratton and Portsmouth line.
- Swanage branch.
- Netley, Ringwood, Stockbridge and Fordingbridge lines.
- all routes west of Exeter.

Central Section

Permitted - main lines to Brighton, Newhaven and Eastbourne.
- coast line from Hastings to Havant.
- South Croydon to Lewes via Oxted.
- Edenbridge Town and Uckfield (inc. Tunbridge Wells West).
- cross country route between Tonbridge and Reading.

Prohibited - Dorking North and mid-Sussex route.
- Hurst Green, East Grinstead and Haywards Heath routes.

Eastern Section

Permitted - all trunk lines.
- Paddock Wood and Strood.

Prohibited - Ashford to Minster via Canterbury.
- Ashford and Hastings line.
- Tonbridge and Hastings line.
- entry to Cannon Street station.

About two years later, in connection with the proposed working of oil tank traffic from the Fawley refinery to the Midlands over the ex-Didcot, Newbury & Southampton route, 9Fs were permitted to operate between Shawford Junction near Winchester and Enbourne Junction near Newbury.

7.2 From April 1960 to Withdrawal

Southern Region

In October 1960, the WR transferred two 9Fs to Westbury, 92205/6. They had been delivered to Bristol St. Philips Marsh in Spring 1959 and had spent the summer of 1960 on the S&DJR operating from Bath Green Park. The reallocations were made in connection with one of BR's first contracts with an oil company to move petroleum products from refineries on the coast to storage areas and distribution points inland. The Esso Company had a refinery at Fawley on the Solent near Southampton and needed to move large tonnages of fuel each week to its Bromford Bridge distribution centre near Birmingham. The route was via Salisbury, Westbury, Bristol and the ex-MR West of England main line to Birmingham, at first with an engine change at Westbury. Return workings often produced an LMR 9F, examples being 92077 (Toton) which appeared on 26th October and 92132 (Wellingborough) two days later.

Although the Bromford Bridge trains typically loaded to around 1,200 tons northbound, it was clear that a 9F would have no problem in taking the train through from Southampton to the Midlands and in December 1960 the pair were sent on loan to the SR along with 92231 (Bristol Barrow Road); official transfer to Eastleigh was confirmed in January 1961. In addition to eliminating the need for an engine change, the move also opened up the possibility of running the trains via the Didcot, Newbury & Southampton line,

Figure 110
Eastleigh's 92231 approaches Southampton Central with an up mixed freight on 23rd April 1963. The engine has lost its top lamp bracket and now carries the configuration as displayed in Figure N, Profile D. 92231 and the rest of the Eastleigh 9F allocation were moved to Feltham in the following month and then transferred to the NER at York in September 1963.
(C. R. Berridge)

thence via Oxford, Honeybourne Junction and Bordesley which would avoid the congested Bristol area. A trial run was made on 10th December 1960 with a return freight working from Bevois Park near Northam to Didcot but although the class was finally permitted to use the route by year end, it was not until May 1962 that running by this route was frequently reported. Later, in July 1961, the WR was induced to part with two more of the class; 92211 (Old Oak Common) and 92239 (Southall), were sent to Eastleigh, again on loan, and again officially via Westbury; the latter allocation was probably a paper transfer. Some sources suggest SR ownership of the pair was not officially confirmed until December 1962. Eastleigh's 9Fs were also used on other oil trains, one established duty being a through service to Newport (South Wales), the return working of which often produced one of Newport Ebbw Junction's 9Fs; regular services to Scunthorpe (Scanton Sidings) via the ex-GCR route and another to Northampton as far as Oxford also featured SR 9Fs. There were additional oil trains to Spondon near Derby on which an engine change was reported to be made in the Bristol area and also to Denham (Bucks); non-oil tank freights included services to Washwood Heath and Tyseley.

It should be noted that for safety reasons, oil tank traffic operating on BR with steam power had 'buffer' wagons inserted between the locomotive and its train. This was strictly observed with fully loaded silver-painted tanks (i.e. those containing highly volatile products such as petroleum and Kerosene) but perhaps less so for empty silver tanks and for the black-painted tanks (heavy oils and diesels of low volatility).

The loaded oil tank trains, double-headed by tank engines, usually a Class H16 4-6-2 and either a Class 2 or a Class 3 2-6-2 were worked from Fawley to Totton or Millbrook Yard where the 9Fs took over. Later when the DN&S line rather than the Bristol route was used, the changeover occurred at Eastleigh East Yard and Allbrook Junction signal box in the up and down directions respectively. By early 1962, the nominally two trains per day Bromford Bridge service now required an additional train for three days of the week. Not unexpectedly, this increase taxed the motive power resources at Eastleigh and there were many instances of LMR 9Fs, Stanier Class 8F 2-8-0s and Class 5 4-6-0s recorded on these trains. The occasional Patriot, Jubilee or rebuilt Royal Scot Class 4-6-0 was also used but not on the DN&S route from which these classes were officially barred.

Eastleigh's 9Fs were noted on other duties from time to time. In 1961/2, there were appearances on the Exeter-Salisbury line with Meldon quarry stone trains and on 22nd September 1962, 92231 was observed at Exeter Central heading the 3.05pm stopping service from Salisbury.

At the end of the summer timetable in September 1962, regular use of Cl.33 Type 3 diesels (D65xx) on passenger work ceased as these locomotives were not fitted for steam heating. Some of these diesels were now switched to working the Fawley-Bromford Bridge trains via the DN&S line as far as Oxford. This move did not make Eastleigh's 9Fs immediately redundant as, apart from deputising for diesel failures, they were also noted working sugar beet trains from Eastleigh to Didcot during October. Towards the end of the year the 9Fs were observed on local freights, for example the 1.30pm Bournemouth Central-Bevois Park and could also be

Figure 111
92220 *Evening Star* was just four months old when it passed Bathampton station with the 10.30am Cardiff-Portsmouth (WR Reporting No. 058) on 16th July 1960. The engine became a regular on this duty after Whitsun 1960 (29th May) for much of the summer. *(Hugh Ballantyne)*

Figure 112
On 29th September 1962, Bristol Barrow Road's 92221 approaches Kingham with a regular 9F duty at the time, an Esso Bromford Bridge-Fawley Refinery empty oil tanks working. 92221 was the first of the final batch of 9Fs from Crewe; delivered in May 1958 to Banbury, it was withdrawn after just seven years' service in May 1965. *(Hugh Ballantyne)*

seen on the regular banana traffic to the Midlands and the north from Southampton Docks via the DN&S line.

Early in 1963, it was reported that WR crews were training on the Cl.33s with a view to permitting through running to Bromford Bridge. By the end of May this had been fully instituted and five or more Cl.33s could regularly be viewed overnight on Saltley depot. Eastleigh's 9Fs still often appeared at Saltley however, having worked through from Southampton with a regular bulk cement train to Washwood Heath via the usual WR route.

In May 1963, Eastleigh's allocation of 9Fs, still limited to the original five, 92205/6/11/31/9, was transferred to Feltham from where the engines began to take over former Class S15 4-6-0 duties. These included the early morning Clapham Junction-Eastleigh stock train and also the 5.05pm Southampton Terminus-Wimborne passenger service, probably the only non-freight duty in the country regularly rostered for a 9F outside the S&DJR system. Other duties at Feltham involved working freights between London and Eastleigh; Feltham and Reading. The 9.00pm freight arrival at Brighton from Eastleigh, officially a Feltham S15 duty, produced 92239 on 18th June, the first reported visit to the seaside town of a 9F in ordinary traffic.

In September 1963, Feltham's 9Fs were moved to York in exchange for an equivalent number of Standard Class 5 4-6-0s, 73167-71 from the NER Leeds area. No further 9Fs were allocated to the SR after this time, although occasionally as a result of diesel failure, they appeared on the Bromford Bridge oil trains, one example being 92047, allocated to Birkenhead, noted ex-works on 4th February 1965 at Oxford with a southbound working.

Other regions' 9Fs continued to appear on the SR however, mainly on fitted freights to Eastleigh from the Birmingham area. Typical duties were the 1.10am Washwood Heath-Eastleigh and the return 9.20pm Eastleigh-Lawley Street. The appearances were sometimes in connection with visits to Eastleigh Works for scheduled overhauls performed there for 9Fs until May 1965. Similarly there were two daily fitted freight workings from Severn Tunnel Junction to Chichester reported in June 1965. Usually worked by WR-based 9Fs, they arrived at 5.05am and 11.55am. One of the 9Fs returned to the Bristol area on the 5.58pm Chichester-Washwood Heath empties.

The SR also had its share of enthusiasts' specials featuring 9F power, as for example on 3rd April 1964, when 92220 *Evening Star* worked forward from Three Bridges to Paddington with a special from Southampton Docks.

Western Region

In April 1960, the WR allocation of 2-10-0s was 57 engines, distributed as follows:

Banbury	(13)	92212-5/21/2/3
		92226/7/8/32/3/4
Bromsgrove	(1)	92079
Cardiff Canton	(11)	92003/5, 92209/10/6/9
		92220/31/6/7/48
Ebbw Junction	(13)	92000/1/2/6/7, 92225/9/30/5
		92242/3/9/50

Laira	(1)	92224*
Old Oak Common	(9)	92211/38-41/4-7
St. Philips Marsh	(6)	92203-6/17/8
Southall	(3)	92004, 92207/8
Total		57

* transferred to Southall in June.

The 9Fs' duties on the WR continued much as before, Southall being the only depot where the class had not previously been allocated. The 9F trio, 92004, 92207/8, had arrived there in February and March 1960, with a further five engines, 92224/6/38/9/40, also present on the depot's books by the end of September, making a total of eight. By the end of November however this figure had dropped to six, with a further reduction to three by January 1962. The 9Fs were mainly used on fitted freights to Bristol and South Wales. LMR 9Fs, mainly from Saltley, regularly appeared off freights from the Midlands for servicing at Southall in the early 1960s and continued to do so after the WR Wolverhampton and Shrewsbury Districts were incorporated into the LMR Birmingham and Chester Divisions respectively from 9th September 1963.

In 1964, significant changes took place at Southall following the introduction of Cl.47 Type 4 diesels on the Paddington-Birmingham-Wolverhampton line. This move released a number of Western Cl.52 Type 4 diesel-hydraulics for services to the west and South Wales. As part of their rosters the Cl.52s worked evening or overnight goods turns, thus rendering some of Southall's steam allocation redundant. The shed's 9F complement was back to eight by this time; four were transferred to Ebbw Junction, 92210/29/50, in May and 92207 in November. Southall took over the steam duties and surviving steam allocation from Old Oak Common when the latter closed on 22nd March 1965; this did not include any 9Fs as Old Oak had lost the last of its allocation of the class in September 1963. With the run-down of steam workings on the WR towards the end of 1965, the remaining 9Fs at Southall, 92216/46, were transferred to Severn Tunnel Junction in August. LMR 9Fs could still be observed on shed, however, usually having worked in on freights to Acton or Old Oak Common or on coal trains from the Midlands to West Drayton power station. On 7th November for example, although the shed had lost the remainder of its engine allocation in the previous month, it was still open for servicing and 92152 (Saltley) and 92203 (Banbury) were present. These visits officially ceased when steam was eliminated from the WR at the end of 1965.

A significant development occurred in June 1960 when four Bristol St. Philips Marsh 9Fs, 92203-6, were allocated to Bath Green Park for the summer traffic over the Somerset & Dorset Joint line to Bournemouth. A test run had been made earlier in the year on 29th March when 92204 took a train of ten coaches and a van, weighing some 350 tons, on a return trip from Bath to Bournemouth. Despite poor weather on the day, near gale force winds, driving rain and a sprinkling of snow over the Mendips, 92204's progress was outstanding, the engine breasting Masbury summit (1 in 50/60) in fine style in both directions without pilot or banking assistance. The complete success of the test run led to the transfer of 92203-6 for the duration of the summer timetable from June to September 1960; it was reported that the engines were fitted at Swindon with the customary S&DJR line Whitaker tablet exchange apparatus for single line working before taking up their duties at Bath. This device was mounted on the tender behind the base of the front hand rail.

The first appearances of Bath's 9Fs involved two diagrams:

(1) an early morning Bath-Bournemouth freight; the "Pines Express" in both directions linking Manchester London Road (now Piccadilly) and Liverpool Lime Street with Bournemouth West often loading to twelve coaches, 400 tons and more; the 7.35pm Bournemouth-Bath freight.

(2) the 9.03am Bristol-Bournemouth from Bath, the 3.53pm Bournemouth-Templecombe followed by a Templecombe-Bath freight.

Apart from the "Pines Express" the 9Fs' summer Saturdays regular appearances on the S&DJR route included the following services:

- 7.35am (SO) Nottingham Midland-Bournemouth,
- 7.40am (SO) Bradford Forster Square-Bournemouth,
- 9.35am (SO) Sheffield Midland-Bournemouth,
- 8.16am (SO) Bournemouth-Liverpool Lime Street,
- 8.40am (SO) Bournemouth-Bradford Forster Square,
- 9.55am (SO) Bournemouth-Leeds City.

The advent of the 9Fs transformed the summer Saturday service on the S&DJR, eliminating the need for piloting over the Mendips in most cases and demonstrating a significant reserve of power to assist in recovering time from the often late arrivals of southbound traffic at Bath. One example was the exploits of 92001 on 26th August 1961 when, with the ten coaches of the 7.47am (SO) Bradford Forster Square-Bournemouth, the skilful crew was reported to have converted a 53-minute late departure from Bath to a hardly credible half minute early arrival at Bournemouth. It is clear that this would not have been possible without some smart work by the operating authorities, given the significant amount of single line working on the route.

In the first season, summer 1960, the use of the 9Fs without pilots on heavy trains such as the "Pines Express" did take its toll on the engines' firebrick arches however, as indicated by the daily availability statistics. The very high firebox temperatures reached on these heavy duties contributed to the frequent incidences of the arches collapsing. In subsequent seasons, the use of concrete brick arches in place of the original brick arches significantly improved the 9Fs' availability.

The S&DJR route was no stranger to the operation of freight engines on the summer Saturday traffic, having utilised the eleven Class 7F 2-8-0s, 53800-10, for a number of years. The 9Fs did not completely displace the 7Fs from these duties, 53801 being noted on 26th August, with the 11.12am Bournemouth West-Sheffield and 53807 on the same day's Exmouth-Cleethorpes through service which came on to the S&DJR from the SR main line at Templecombe. In fact the Class 7F 2-8-0s were still to be seen on passenger work as late as 28th July 1962 when no fewer than four of the class were observed at Bath, on three departures and one arrival. It was reported that if the 9Fs had not proven to be a success on the S&DJR in 1960, an alternative option in subsequent summer seasons might have been the redeployment of up to five Standard Class 6 Clan Pacifics which had become redundant on the ScR during 1961. [Note: five of the fifteen engines from the cancelled Clan Pacific order (1954) were said to have been destined for the S&DJR line]. In the event, the WR authorities preferred to stay with the 9Fs, supplemented by 7F 2-8-0 participation as required. In any case by this time it was probable that the WR had taken the decision in principle to close the S&DJR route, such that the expense of further

Figure 113
92224 draws out of Midsomer Norton on 7th September 1963 with the 9.03am Bristol-Bath Green Park; 92220 *Evening Star* was also drafted on to the S&DJR at the same time. The two 9Fs handled local passenger work and freights only; the through holiday express traffic had been re-routed via Oxford, Basingstoke and Southampton beginning with the 1963 season.
(Hugh Ballantyne)

Figure 114
92007 (Bristol Barrow Road) drifts down the Lickey incline into Bromsgrove with a southbound coal train on 13th June 1964. This engine had no less than four reallocations and a spell in store during the 10 months before withdrawal in December 1965.
(Courtney Haydon)

Figure 115
With less than a year of its BR working life remaining, 92220 *Evening Star* (Cardiff East Dock) leaves Worcester Shrub Hill on 12th May 1964 with a Class 'C' freight. Details of the preservation saga associated with *Evening Star* are given in Section 13.
(C. R. Berridge)

Figure 116
During the great winter freeze of 1962/3, 92239 (Eastleigh) drifts on to the Westbury line at Bathampton Junction with a Salisbury-bound goods train on 26th January 1963. Three months later, 92239 would receive its only Heavy General repair (Crewe), having achieved some 100,000 miles in traffic.
(Hugh Ballantyne)

Figure 117
92242 (Newport Ebbw Junction) stands at Cardiff General station in August 1963 with a westbound Class 'H' empty oil tank freight. Six months earlier, the engine had completed a Heavy Casual repair with boiler change at Crewe Works. 92242 was withdrawn in May 1965 after six and a half years of service.
(Peter Cookson)

Figure 118
92224 (Banbury) reposes on shed at Cardiff East Dock on 19th June 1965. The reconfigured lamp bracket arrangement and 'T-piece' platform under the smokebox door confirm the engine is now LMR-based. 92224 is probably engaged on the Midlands-South Wales iron ore traffic at this time. The engine was placed in store for several months by the WR and LMR in 1964 and 1966 respectively, finally transferring to Warrington in August 1966 from where it was withdrawn just over a year later.
(Courtney Haydon)

Figure 119
92237 (Cardiff Canton) storms out of Salisbury with a freight from the Western Region for Eastleigh on the last day of 1960. Delivered to Newport Ebbw Junction new from Crewe in September 1958, 92237 was withdrawn in September 1965 after just over seven years service. Lord Nelson 4-6-0 30859 *Lord Hood* is in the adjacent platform awaiting departure with an express for the Southampton via Redbridge route. *(Courtney Haydon)*

testing was not justified.

At the end of the summer 1960 timetable, 92203-6 did not return to St. Philips Marsh but had been reallocated to other WR depots by the end of September. 92203/4 went to Old Oak Common and Southall respectively whilst 92205/6 were sent to Westbury for the Fawley-Bromford Bridge oil tanker traffic and were eventually transferred to the SR at Eastleigh. The two other St. Philips Marsh 9Fs, 92217/8, had remained allocated to the Bristol shed over the summer period where their duties had included some passenger workings, see Table 7.1. They then moved to Old Oak Common in September; after this, there were no further allocations of 9Fs to St. Philips Marsh.

Meanwhile back on the S&DJR, through Saturday holiday specials continued to use the route for two more years and 9Fs were allocated for the duration of both summer timetables, 92000/1/6 and 92212 in 1961 with 92001, 92210/20/33/45 in 1962. Continuing a long established tradition when holiday traffic was at its height (usually July and August) the operating authorities were not above using 'foreign' engines to supplement the fleet at Bath and 9Fs were no exception. Examples noted in July 1961 were on the 9.55am (SO) Bournemouth-Leeds City with 92152 (Saltley) on 15th, 92078 (Toton) on 22nd and 92059 (Toton) on 29th.

The year 1962 was the final summer of scheduled summer Saturday holiday trains on the S&DJR although not the end of through passenger train working as a number of excursions and special trains continued using the route for at least one more season. Having brought the up train into Bath on the morning of 8th September 1962 the last day of the summer timetable, 92220 *Evening Star* headed the last 'Pines Express' to leave Bath in the afternoon, the twelve-coach train leaving amidst a cacophony of exploding detonators. At Evercreech Junction, a pine wreath was attached to the smokebox door for the final stages of the run to Bournemouth.

Although the through holiday services had been withdrawn the previous year, two 9Fs, 92220/4, were allocated to Bath Green Park for a few weeks in August 1963. Bath was temporarily short of power at the time as several engines were under repair and the 9Fs had been provided as alternatives to the Class 5 4-6-0s originally requested. The engines were entirely unsuitable for the new role which they were to perform, ie local freights and three (or four) coach local passenger trains. As anticipated they proved uneconomical on fuel on passenger services and were inconvenient to use on other than through freights between Bath and Bournemouth as they were too long to be turned on the table at Evercreech Junction North Signal Box resulting in some tender-first running. In this regard, the BR1G inset tender was less of a hindrance than the flush-sided variety carried by most of the class. Both 92220/4 had left the S&DJR by early October as they had no train heating facilities and could not be used on passenger work after September.

Again in May 1964, Bath found itself short of power and requested the loan of a Class 5 4-6-0 for a few weeks. Once more none was available and two 9Fs, 92214/26 were supplied instead, both on loan from Newport Ebbw Junction. 92214 remained at Bath until the end of June mainly on passenger work after which it was returned to its home depot. The other 9F, 92226, spent little or no time on the S&DJR proper but instead was used to work freights northward on the Midland main line, appearing from time to time on the 6.25pm freight from Bath to Avonmouth; 92226 was returned to Ebbw Junction after only three weeks. According to the record, Bath was host to 92209/43 in November 1965. 92209 was officially withdrawn at the end of the year but 92243 was noted hauling the LCGB's "Mendip Merchantman Rail Tour" on 1st January 1966 from Highbridge to just beyond Bristol where it appears finally to have expired.

Towards the end of 1960, several 9Fs were allocated to Bristol Barrow Road for the first time and by January 1961, five were present, 92004/7/10, 92221/48; 92231 was also originally included in the group but stayed only a few weeks before transfer to the SR in December 1960. Regular duties were the haulage of freights from Avonmouth Docks to the Birmingham area with one of the first diagrams commencing with the 10.00pm Avonmouth-Bromford Bridge fitted freight. The engines also penetrated further north when for example, on 30th March 1961, 92007 was observed at Belper with a northbound oil tank train and two days later at Skelton Junction, Timperley with the 2.55pm Class 'C' Brunswick-Washwood Heath fitted freight. By the summer of 1961, oil traffic from Avonmouth to Bromford Bridge had increased to the extent that extra services were needed. 9Fs were noted on the newly scheduled 11.00am (SX) and 11.30pm (FSX) northbound Class 'D' workings and the 10.40am and 8.05pm Class 'C' returns. The class also featured on the 7.15pm Bradford-Westerleigh Class 'C', the 7.33pm Avonmouth-Birmingham Lawley Street and the 9.20pm Edinburgh Lothian Road-Stoke Gifford fitted freights. Barrow Road retained an allocation of 9Fs until almost the end of steam on the WR, the remaining engines being either withdrawn (92235) or transferred, either to Cardiff East Dock (92248) or Gloucester Horton Road (92000/7, 92238) during 1965; 92209/43 were reallocated to Bath Green Park in November 1965 before withdrawal at the turn of the year.

Bromsgrove continued to be the base for the Lickey banking engines into the early 1960s. The designated 9F, 92079, was still in place and typically on summer Saturday afternoons made about half a dozen round trips assisting heavy northbound holiday specials among its other duties. With the steady increase in dieselisation of the passenger services however, it was concluded that the Cl.45 and Cl.46 Type 4 diesels should readily be able to negotiate the Lickey incline without the need for assistance when handling the normal load formations on the route. On 20th September 1961, trials took place using Cl.45 Peak Type 4 D40 with a dynamometer car and 16 coaches of approximately 550 tons tare weight. The then resident banker 92234, substituting for 92079 in Wolverhampton Works for a Heavy Intermediate overhaul, followed the test trains up the hill at some 30-50 yards distance as a precaution against possible problems; similar tests were conducted on the following day with freight vehicles. The trials were successful but it was necessary to repeal statutory restrictions requiring mandatory rear-end assistance on Lickey ascents before dispensing with the bankers' services. With such restrictions eventually lifted, diesel-hauled passenger traffic usually tackled the incline without assistance; regular banking continued for freight traffic, including the heavy Fawley-Bromford Bridge oil trains.

Other 9Fs were allocated to Bromsgrove in place of 92079 when it was moved to Birkenhead in October 1963. 92223 was the first replacement but was withdrawn by the WR in February 1964 following a periodical examination which disclosed severe scoring of both cylinders; 92230 was despatched from Ebbw Junction as replacement. 92223 was

Figure 120
92070 (Birkenhead) waits for the road to go on shed at Oxford on 30th October 1965. Originally an ER-based engine, 92070 was reallocated from Doncaster to Annesley in early 1957. A year later, Annesley became an LMR depot and 92070 spent the rest of its short life at a variety of LMR sheds. *(Courtney Haydon)*

Figure 121
92000 (Tyseley) waits on Oxford shed in 1962 for its return freight working to the Birmingham area. The engine was one of the few WR-based 9Fs to undergo repair at the LMR's Gorton Works (November 1962). *(G. Wheeler)*

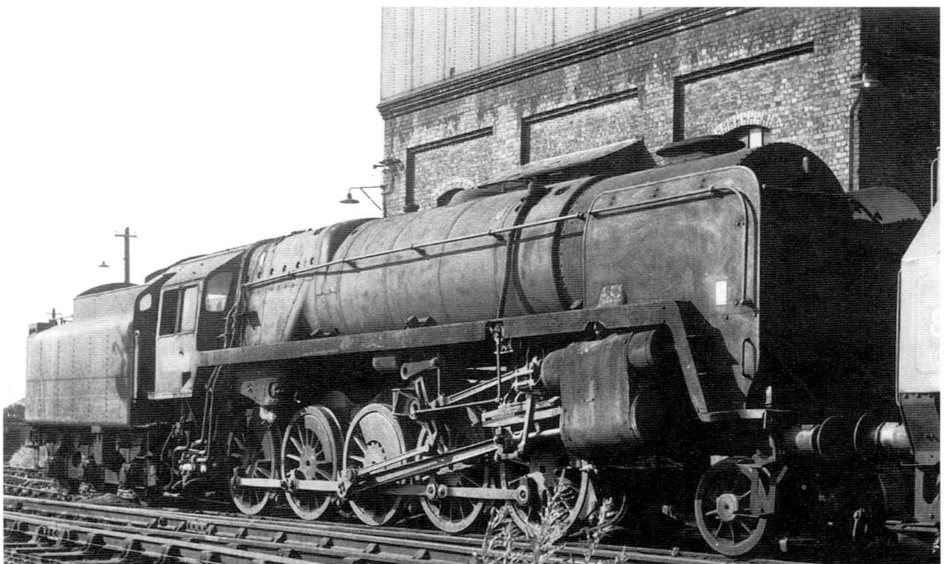

Figure 122
A derelict-looking 92000 is fading fast at its 'graveyard allocation' home shed of Gloucester Horton Road on 20th June 1965; it was withdrawn the following month. 92000 acquired its double chimney at Swindon in February 1960. *(Courtney Haydon)*

Figure 123
92067 (Annesley) heads a Banbury-bound freight past Chalcombe Road on 12th October 1963. The engine was subsequently allocated to Banbury (June 1965) on closure of the ex-GCR route and was nominally transferred to Carlisle Kingmoor for a short period before withdrawal in November 1966. The record indicates 92067 had only one Heavy General overhaul (October 1961 at Crewe) and appears to have been withdrawn at the time the next one was due. *(Rodney Lissenden)*

Figure 124
92036 of New England shed heads a very mixed freight past Oakleigh Park on the GN main line on 31st May 1962. A year later, the engine was transferred to Colwick along with several other New England 9Fs. 92036 was fitted with AWS apparatus in November 1959; it was one of the second batch of ER-based 9Fs to be withdrawn (December 1964) after almost exactly 10 years' service. *(Courtney Haydon)*

subsequently reinstated and allocated to Tyseley by the LMR in May 1964; despite languishing in a siding on Merseyside for a period, it was one of the last 9Fs to remain in service operating from Carlisle Kingmoor and later Carnforth until April 1968. Although steam banking was still in place at the beginning of the 1964 summer timetable, trials with Cl.37 Type 3 diesel D6938, rather than a Cl.35 Hymek Type 3 diesel hydraulic originally planned, were commenced in July and by the end of the month, 92230 was out of use on Bromsgrove shed. The depot was closed in September 1964 and from this time, banking was usually only scheduled for freight trains. These duties were performed by four Cl.37s supplied by Cardiff Canton, maintained at Worcester and exchanged every two weeks, although later, in 1967, the earlier plan to use Hymek diesel hydraulics was resurrected.

Cardiff Canton was host to eleven 9Fs in April 1960, 92003/5, 92209/10/6/9/20/31/6/7/48. The celebrated 92220 *Evening Star* was inevitably something of a 'part-timer' at Canton as it was in constant demand for enthusiasts' specials and the like. One example was on 19th May when it headed an excursion from Paddington to Stratford-upon-Avon and back via Oxford; the engine was also among the exhibits on display at the Derby Works open day on 26th August 1961. Duties for Canton's 9Fs were much as described earlier with *Evening Star* settling down to a regular diagram, Mondays to Fridays, (summer timetable) as far as Salisbury, with other of the depot's 9Fs appearing on the roster when 92220 was unavailable; details are as shown:

10.30am	Cardiff-Portsmouth passenger as far as Salisbury.
4.17pm	Salisbury-Bristol passenger.
10.50pm	Bristol-Cardiff Class 'C' freight.

At weekends, 92220 was often used on trains to Swansea and Fishguard. For a brief period in June and July 1960, the engine also appeared on passenger services to and from Paddington, including the 7.43am from Cardiff, the up "Red Dragon" and the down "Capitals United Express", apparently keeping the schedules with ease, regaining fifteen minutes of lost time on the up "Dragon" on 1st July for example. 92220 was later banned from these workings once 'higher authority'

Figure 125
92140 bustles down the GN main line with a heavy fitted freight on 30th July 1960. Apart from a 'graveyard' move to Langwith Junction a few months before withdrawal, the engine spent all its life allocated to New England. The 55 9Fs on the ER allocation each ran 33,200 miles on average in 1960, the highest of all the regions for that year; the total mileage was boosted by such duties as this. *(Courtney Haydon)*

became aware of these exploits. As with other 9Fs however, the engine continued to appear from time to time on passenger duties when express power was unavailable, for example on 17th June 1961 when it was entrusted with the "Merchant Venturer" from Paddington to Bristol.

In September 1962, to allow for the construction of the new diesel facilities on the site of the former steam roundhouse at Cardiff Canton, the depot's 9F allocation, (92003, 92208/10/6/9/36/7/41/4/6) was transferred to Cardiff East Dock. The latter depot had been all-diesel for some time but now reverted to steam, its allocation of diesel shunters being moved to Cardiff Cathays. Handling of the 9Fs at East Dock presented immediate problems as coaling facilities had been designed to service nothing larger than 56XX class 0-6-2 tank engines and the depot had no turntable. With the arrival of a number of Cl.35 Type 3 Hymek diesel hydraulics at Canton during 1962, the 9Fs now lost their Salisbury workings and were confined to freight duties apart from occasional passenger work on summer Saturday holiday extras. From February 1964, it was reported that 9Fs from Cardiff East Dock (and Neath, see later) were regular daily visitors through Stourbridge Junction on block freight trains from South Wales.

Rail traffic from the Shell and BP refinery at Llandarcy amounted to eight block tank trains each day at this time, three for Rowley Regis, three for Llanwern and two for Ebbw Vale. All except the Ebbw Vale trains were brake fitted throughout; 9Fs from East Dock, Ebbw Junction and the LMR were observed on these workings. Also around this time, there was a large increase in the volume of bulk oil traffic from Milford Haven. One train, the 5.00pm to Coleshill near Birmingham, began in early 1964 as a conditional working but quickly became a heavily loaded

Figure 126
92201 (Doncaster) rattles past Essendine with a cement train on 17th August 1961. The hinged flap on the forward lower corner of the cabside has been replaced with a sliding plate arrangement *(P. H. Wells)*

Figure 127
92174 slumbers on shed at Derby on 3rd October 1965. Despite looking capable of many more years' service, it was withdrawn a few weeks later from Doncaster shed where it had been allocated all its working life; 92174 was cut up at T. W. Ward's scrapyard at Killamarsh in May 1966. *(Courtney Haydon)*

daily service. Although it was rostered for Hymek haulage as far as Cardiff, where a Western Cl.52 was rostered to take over, 9Fs from Neath, Ebbw Junction and the LMR covered the duty for the first weeks.

The steel billet traffic from Briton Ferry (ex-Margam Steel Works) also showed a dramatic increase in early 1964. The service to Langley Green which had begun on a three times per week basis was increased to two trains per day with 2.00pm and 4.30pm departures and a conditional path available at 6.30pm for a third train as required; again 9Fs from East Dock and other WR depots as well as the LMR were regular performers on these trains in the early months of 1964. Later in the year, diesels began to take over these duties and many others; one instance was the rostering of a Canton Hymek on a new oil tanker service from Llandarcy to Soho Pool Wharf (Birmingham) in April. Despite this, LMR and other WR depots' 9Fs continued to appear on the block workings until the spring of 1965 when Cl.47 diesels became the regular haulage power. Cardiff East Dock depot was closed in August 1965 by which time its five remaining 9Fs were either withdrawn (92219) or transferred to Severn Tunnel Junction (92007, 92209) or Newport Ebbw Junction (92243/4).

Also observed on the Llandarcy and Briton Ferry block freights to the Midlands were the three 9Fs, 92216/22/5, transferred to Neath in October and November 1963. As diesels gradually took over these services, reorganisation of the remaining available steam power did not require a 9F allocation at Neath and the trio was reallocated in 1964 to Ebbw Junction (92225 in May) and Southall (92216/22 in September).

The Newport Ebbw Junction 9F duties continued much as before. Five of the original allocation, 92000/1/2/6/7, were still in place in April 1960 supplemented by eight engines from later batches, 92225/9/30/5/42/3/9/50 making a total of thirteen. The Giesl Oblong Ejector engine, 92250, was initially engaged mainly on the Western Valley iron ore traffic from Newport Docks to the Ebbw Vale Steel Works but was later deployed on Class 'D' fitted goods services from Newport to London. In January 1963, Ebbw Junction's 9F allocation was 17 engines: 92002/5/6, 92209/14/22/3/5/6/9/30/3/5/8/42/9/50. Later 92005 was observed on the Associated Portland Cement Works traffic from Heywood Road Junction, Westbury to Exeter Central via Taunton and Exeter St. Davids in June 1963. In July, a number of Cl.37s were received by Ebbw Junction and, amongst other duties, were used in place of the 9Fs on the Ebbw Vale iron ore traffic. In July 1963, it was reported that eighteen freight diagrams had been allocated to the Type 3 diesels which were now permitted to traverse virtually all routes in South Wales. By the end of the year, a dozen redundant 9Fs had been reallocated from Ebbw Junction to depots as diverse as e.g. York, Newton Heath and Southall; in addition, 92223 was sent to Bromsgrove as replacement for Lickey banker 92079, now transferred to Birkenhead. Ebbw Junction retained a small but varying allocation of 9Fs almost until the end of steam on the WR, the last four being transferred in October 1965 either to Bristol Barrow Road (92235/43) or Gloucester Horton Road (92230/44).

Thirteen 9Fs, 92212-5/21/2/3/6/7/8/32/3/4, were operating from Banbury depot in April 1960 on the South Wales iron ore traffic and on fitted freights to London and the Midlands as before. From 1st January 1963, when the WR Wolverhampton and Shrewsbury districts were incorporated in the LMR Birmingham and Chester Divisions respectively, the 9Fs remaining at Banbury, 92213/5/27/8/47, along with the rest of its allocation were absorbed into LMR stock. Shortly afterwards, in March 1963, Banbury's remaining 28XX Class 8F 2-8-0s were returned to the WR at Southall in exchange for 9Fs from Barrow Road and Old Oak

Common depots; the additional allocation of 92004, 92203/4/17/8 brought the total of 9Fs at Banbury to ten. Now part of the LMR operation, Banbury depot was included in the routine transfer of 9Fs within the region. In August 1964 a batch was received from Saltley and Tyseley (the former WR depot transferred to the LMR along with Banbury at the beginning of 1963). Later, in June 1965, eight of the class, 92013/30/3/67/73/4/87, 92132, made redundant at the time of the closure of the GCR line as a through route for freights, arrived from Annesley.

Towards the end of 1963, Banbury's 9Fs began to appear on freight workings to Redhill although their appearances were reported to be short-lived, ceasing by the beginning of 1964. Otherwise workings were mainly to the Midlands (including the Stourbridge Junction-Wolverhampton line) but also to the WR London area until the nominal end of steam on that region in December 1965. By the summer of 1966, dieselisation of the southern part of the LMR was almost complete, triggering the exodus of much steam power to the Midlands and the north west areas of the Region. Banbury's 16 remaining 9Fs, 92004/13/30/67/73, 92128/9/32, 92203/13/8/24/7/8/34/47 were reallocated to the above two areas over the period August to October 1966, some after an earlier period of storage.

In April 1960, Old Oak Common was operating nine 9Fs, 92211/38-41/4-7, mainly on fitted freights to Bristol, South Wales, Plymouth and the Midlands although the engines were occasionally still employed on passenger work during busy summer weekends. By January 1963, the allocation was down to five, 92203/4/17/8/43; these would be transferred during the year, the first four to Banbury in March and 92243 to Cardiff East Dock in September.

Other depots to operate 9Fs towards the end of steam on the WR were Westbury, Oxford, Tyseley, Severn Tunnel Junction and Gloucester Horton Road. Westbury was host to four 9Fs, 92205/6/21/3, for a brief period towards the end of 1960. This was in connection with the start of the oil tank traffic from Fawley (near Southampton) to Bromford Bridge distribution depot in Birmingham. Trains were routed via Bristol at first although later took the ex-DN&S route as described in the SR notes in this section. It was clear that a more efficient operation would be achieved by reallocating the engines to the SR and 92205/6 were soon at Eastleigh whilst 92221/3 were sent to other WR depots. In July 1961, 92211/39 were also reported allocated to Westbury but for less than a month before moving on to Eastleigh to assist with the increase in oil traffic volume.

Oxford received five 9Fs, 92001, 92220/4/44/5, in

Figure 128
92038 ambles through the north London suburb of New Southgate, southbound with a surprising collection of wooden-bodied coal wagons on 5th June 1962. The engine was fitted with AWS in January 1960. Here still a New England engine, 92038 was transferred to Immingham about a year later from where it was used on the express fish traffic.
(Courtney Haydon)

Figure 129
92197 (Immingham) is off its beaten track at Sundon, north of Luton on 8th September 1962. A derailment at Offord on the GN main line had occurred the previous day causing the diversion of some GN line traffic; other ER-based 9Fs noted on the MML that day were 92141 on the Cliffe-Uddingston cement train and 92198 on a fitted freight.
(Rodney Lissenden)

October 1962 although three of the group were transferred almost immediately to other WR depots, leaving only 92220/4 on the shed's books. On 1st October a fitted freight service conveying new cars to Scotland from the Cowley factory near Oxford was introduced and worked by one of the newly allocated 9Fs as far as Crewe. The engine returned from Crewe with a train of commercial vehicles and tractors from the new B.M.C. (British Motor Corporation) plant at Bathgate to Morris Cowley. Another regular duty to Crewe and back often featured 92220 *Evening Star;* this was the 1.40pm Morris Cowley-North Mersey Class 'D' freight and the return working from Aintree sorting sidings. In the summer of 1963 these services were accelerated and upgraded to Class 'C' using Crewe-based Britannia Pacific power at which time Oxford's 9Fs were transferred to Bath Green Park.

Three 9Fs, 92000, 92212/34, were allocated to Tyseley in July/August 1962; by the time the LMR took over the depot in January 1963, 92000 had been replaced by 92001. The engines were used mainly on the frequent Class 'F' freight workings to Banbury from Washwood Heath and were reported also on the freights from Bordesley to Stoke Gifford near Bristol. The 1.10am to Southampton and the 2.50am to Basingstoke also featured 9F power from time to time and were a convenient means of forwarding class members from various LMR depots to Eastleigh Works for light and intermediate overhauls which the works undertook for LMR-based 9Fs from May 1962 to February 1965. By the end of November 1963, Tyseley was operating a further five 9Fs, 92002/85, 92204/15/7, making eight in total. The same number (albeit a different group of engines) was present in early August 1966 at which time the 9Fs had become redundant as a result of dieselisation. By year end, the remaining engines had been reallocated to Saltley (92002, 92223), Wakefield (92001, 92215), Carnforth (92087, 92118, 92212) and Speke Junction (92204).

In 1964 Severn Tunnel Junction was allocated two batches of 9Fs displaced by diesels from nearby depots, 92214/26/50 from Newport Ebbw Junction in July and 92236/7/42/3 from Ebbw Junction and Cardiff East Dock in October. The engines were reported in use on local mineral workings but within twelve months, most had been either transferred, withdrawn or put in store in the shed yard. Another batch of

Figure 130
92060, fitted with Westinghouse air pumps, spreads a pall of black smoke over the countryside as it pounds towards Consett with a load of iron ore from Tyne Dock on 21st August 1965. A diesel gives rear end assistance.
(Courtney Haydon)

Figure 131
Later in the day on 21st August 1965, 92060 clatters back downhill towards the short tunnel at Stanley with iron ore empties for Tyne Dock.
(Courtney Haydon)

Figure 132
92143 trundles through Hadley Wood with a northbound GN line freight in the deep freeze of 19th January 1963. Allocated to New England for the whole of its life. 92143, along with all the other ER 9Fs from 92140 onwards, was fitted with LNER-type fire hole doors from new; AWS was installed in April 1960. *(Courtney Haydon)*

Figure 133
92148 (Langwith Junction) heads an up GC line freight through Mansfield on 6th February 1965. Recently transferred from Staveley Barrow Hill, whose shedplate it still carries, 92148 is probably bound for Annesley Yard where much of its cargo will be sent on to Woodford Halse via one of the legendary but soon to be withdrawn 'windcutters'; AWS was fitted to 92148 from January 1960.
(Courtney Haydon)

six 9Fs arrived in July/August 1965 but in October 1965, two months before the end of steam on the WR, all the shed's remaining 9Fs were withdrawn (92216) or transferred, either to Bristol Barrow Road (92209) or Gloucester Horton Road (92007, 92246/50).

Gloucester Horton Road did not receive its first 9F allocation until February 1965 with the appearance of 92000/7, 92238 from Bristol Barrow Road. A further batch, 92007 (returning after spending three months allocated to South Wales sheds from July) plus 92230/44/6/50 arrived in October from Newport Ebbw Junction and Severn Tunnel Junction. In fact there was little or no suitable work for the class at Gloucester and the move was essentially a 'graveyard' allocation where the engines were stored prior to withdrawal and despatch to breakers' yards.

The WR's remaining seven 9Fs, 92007, 92209/30/43/4/6/50, were all withdrawn in December 1965, with the exception of 92243. The engine had an apparent stay of execution when it was observed still active on the S&DJR on 1st January 1966 at the end of which it was condemned. This date was the last day of the accountancy period ending 13/65 which may have been the source of confusion regarding 92243's actual withdrawal date.

December 1965 was officially the last month of steam working on the WR, the exception being the S&DJR route where legal processes and delays in providing an alternative road service postponed closure formalities until early March 1966. 'Foreign' steam continued to appear on the WR however as a series of observations at Cheltenham on the former MR Birmingham-Bristol line during 1965 noted regular appearances of LMR 9Fs, Class 8F 2-8-0s and Class 5 4-6-0s on freights and parcels services until Easter, after which, visits became progressively fewer and had virtually ceased by the end of October.

Eastern and North Eastern Regions

The ER and NER had a combined total of 65 9Fs in April 1960, 55 on the ER and 10 on the NER, distributed as shown:

ER		
New England	(30)	92034-8/40/1/2/4 92140-9/78-88
Immingham	(6)	92039, 92193-6, 92202
Doncaster	(19)	92168-77/89-92/7/8/9, 92200/1
Total	55	
NER		
Tyne Dock	(10)	92060-6/97/8/9
Total	10	

It is worth noting that a number of route restrictions still applied to the class on the ER at this time. For example, 9Fs were allowed between Barnetby and Lincoln but not double-headed whereas in the city of Lincoln itself they were officially prohibited between Pelham Street Junction and Durham Ox Junction.

In April 1960, New England had the largest allocation of 9Fs on the ER, 30 engines, 92034-8/40/1/2/4, 92140-9/78-88. The class still virtually monopolised the Ferme Park coal workings but were also increasingly observed on fast freight duties. More than half the country's cement was produced in the ex-LT&SR Thameside area at the time and northbound traffic was such that a new service was introduced in the summer of 1960, train number 260 'C', consisting of fifteen fitted bulk Presflo cement wagons. This service, the 11.25am from West Thurrock Junction, ran every weekday to Cambuslang except Wednesdays when Leith was the destination. This was the longest regular block freight working of its day and New England 9Fs were rostered as far as York; train transit time to Scotland was around sixteen hours. The return working from Cambuslang was at 8.15pm, terminating at Palace Gates during the week and at New England on Sundays; other ER depot 9Fs were noted on the service, for example Immingham's 92193 on 26th June with the return empties. Later, in July 1960, 9Fs replaced New England's A2 Pacifics on the regular freight working to Heaton. The 9Fs often returned south from Heaton on the 6.05pm Niddrie-Kings Cross Class 'C'; examples were 92184 and 92185 on 1st and 9th July respectively; these moves provided a welcome release for the A2s to passenger duties. A potentially hazardous event took place on 28th December 1961 when confusion on the ex-LT&SR section resulted in an ER 9F and a WR 28XX 2-8-0 being mistakenly put on each other's trains. The 2-8-0 managed to reach Harlow Mill on the Cambridge line before being stopped; no out of gauge incidents with the 28XX were reported. New England 9Fs were also noted as substitutes when failures occurred on the ER with the pairs of SR-based Cl.33 diesels rostered to work as far as York on the cement trains to Uddingston (Glasgow) from Cliffe near Gravesend on the south bank of the Thames estuary.

The increase in the Ferme Park coal traffic in late 1961 and early 1962 led to a power shortage at New England. Rather than transfer the 9Fs from their fast freight duties, it was reported that K3 2-6-0s and V2 2-6-2s from New England plus a number of Class O2 2-8-0s borrowed from Doncaster and Retford were used as stopgaps.

By the middle of 1963 however, much of the New England 9F work had been taken on by diesels and in June over half the allocation was moved to either Colwick or Immingham. By January 1964, the depot's 9F allocation was fifteen, 92140-6/9/71/6/8-82, whilst one year later only three of these remained, 92142/3/81, all stored unserviceable to be withdrawn in the following month, February 1965; there were no further allocations of 9Fs to New England.

The six 9Fs at Immingham in April 1960, 92039, 92193-6, 92202 were augmented by two more examples, 92148/97, in June and September respectively. Principal duties were still the Grimsby fish trains but an additional working beginning in spring 1959 on Tu/Thu/Sat was the Fison's ammonium nitrate solution tanker traffic between the company's plant at Stanford-le-Hope on the ex-LT&SR line and Immingham. The 9.25pm departure from Stanford called at Grassmoor Junction, Whitemoor from 1.51am to 2.05am to change crews whilst the return 8.00pm from Immingham on Wed/Fri/Mon made a similar stop at Whitemoor from 11.00pm to 11.50pm.

The three ex-GN East Lincs. line Grimsby fish trains remained steam hauled until late 1964, the 5.30pm and 7.19pm to London being 9F turns supplied by Immingham and New England respectively; the 6.20pm to March, where it divided into several portions, was worked by an Immingham Britannia Pacific. Late in 1964 Cl.47 Type 4 diesels began to make occasional appearances on these workings although the majority were still 9F-hauled. In January 1965 Immingham was host to nine 9Fs, 92035/7, 92147/84/5/93/4/7, 92202, although three were in store unserviceable. In the first few weeks of 1965, the diesels began

Figure 134
92190 stands alongside Class O4/8 2-8-0 63818 at Doncaster shed on 2nd May 1965; the 9F's boiler appears to dwarf that of the O4. 92190 acquired AWS apparatus in September 1959 but still retains the original 'lug-type' foot rests positioned below the smokebox door; many class members had been fitted with the 'T-piece platform' alternative, regarded as providing a much safer footing when carrying out lamp changes and attending to smokebox maintenance. 92190 was withdrawn in October 1965 and used on Doncaster shed as a stationary boiler for a time; 63818 survived until April 1966. *(Courtney Haydon)*

Figure 135
Westinghouse air pump-fitted 92061 drifts downhill near Stanley past a delightful NE signal box with a Consett Steelworks-Tyne Dock train of empty hopper wagons on 21st August 1965. The engine was withdrawn just over a year later. The whitened smokebox door hinges appear to have been a tradition at Tyne Dock. The allocation there was equipped with BR1B tenders which were similar to the BR1C type but with less coal space as can be seen by the more forward position of the divider. *(Courtney Haydon)*

Figure 136
92065 (Tyne Dock) heads a Consett iron ore train through South Pelaw Junction in May 1965. An English Electric Type 4 (Cl.40) diesel awaits the call for banking assistance in the spur beyond the signal box. Another EE Type 4 wanders back down to Tyne Dock on the adjacent track with a train of empty ore hoppers from Consett. *(J. W. Armstrong Trust)*

Figure 137
An immaculately turned-out 92099 (Tyne Dock), complete with commemorative wreath on the smokebox door, operates the Alnmouth-Alnwick service on the last day of steam passenger working, 18th June 1966. The engine was withdrawn just over two months later. *(E. E. Smith)*

Figure 138
92065 blasts through Consett station in May 1965 with iron ore for the steel plant. The engine received its AWS apparatus in October 1960. *(J. W. Armstrong Trust)*

Figure 139
On arrival at the Consett steel works, 92065 propels its load of ore hoppers on to the gantry for the discharging of the contents into reception bunkers. *(J. W. Armstrong Trust)*

Figure 140
92060 leaves Tyne Dock with loaded iron ore hoppers for Consett; a J94 0-6-0 saddle tank provides banking assistance. The heaped hoppers indicate this particular batch of ore is of the lower density type. The string of hoppers on the left await their turn for the trip to Consett while the wagons on the right illustrate the extent of the timber 'pit prop' (colliery gallery roof support) trade through the dock. *(J. W. Armstrong Trust)*

Figure 141
92065 passes the site of Pelton station with a Tyne Dock-Consett ore train in May 1965. The engine has received the LMR lamp bracket reconfiguration following a visit to Crewe Works from May to September 1964; the top bracket has however been left in place. *(J. W. Armstrong Trust)*

Figure 142
During a period of reduced activity at the Consett steel works, 92062 (Tyne Dock) finds other employment as it passes through Newcastle Central in the summer of 1962 with a Class 'D' fitted freight. *(N. H. Ling)*

Figure 143
92026 (Wellingborough) is on shed at Cricklewood on 15th June 1963. Like most of the former Crosti boiler engines, 92026 ended its days at Birkenhead, the exceptions being 92027/8 which were withdrawn from Speke Junction and Saltley respectively. *(Rodney Lissenden)*

to take over the fish traffic and three of the depot's 9Fs, 92037, 92184/5, were withdrawn in February followed by most of the remaining allocation during the rest of the year. 92035 was still active in December 1965 when on 18th it was observed in place of two Cl.20 Type 1 diesels on a Class 7 Immingham-Colwick freight; the 9F had the return working on the same day. By early 1966, fish transport by rail from Grimsby was in severe decline, lost to road distribution, only one train of fifteen wagons being required for the London traffic.

In April 1960, the Doncaster allocation of nineteen engines, 92168-77/89-92/7/8/9, 92200/1, continued to be used on mineral traffic and fast freight work on the GN section including regular visits to York, Tyneside, Humberside and the London area. As with many engine classes having a large allocation at one depot, the Doncaster's 9Fs tended to stray on to other parts of the BR system. They were regularly noted on trans-Pennine freight services through Huddersfield, the LNWR line from Yorkshire to Stockport and Manchester; this route was also a convenient means of reaching the LMR works at Crewe or Gorton which took over the routine overhauls of the ER and NER 9Fs from August 1962. Doncaster 9Fs were also regularly observed on the LMR in the Burton-upon-Trent and Birmingham areas with fitted freights in the early 1960s. The ER 9Fs were frequently called on to perform a similar role to that of the LNWR Super 'D' 0-8-0s in LMS and early LMR days, i.e. the heavy freight engine 'of last resort' where a weighty or unusual load was to be moved. Examples were on 30th and 31st May 1960 when 92188 (New England) and 92202 (Immingham) respectively arrived at Skegness, the first reported appearances of the class there, to move long rakes of empty coaching stock from their winter storage on the branch. Similarly on 23rd July 1960, it was Doncaster's 92192 which was observed at Newark with the 3.00am special Class 'C' fitted freight from Bradford on its way to Dover via Hither Green conveying a train of 45 wagons loaded with farm tractors for export.

In an effort to speed up the conveyance of mineral freight on the GN line, further loading trials were conducted, during the two weeks beginning 4th December 1961, between Doncaster and New England. The object of the tests was to determine whether the presence of a 'head' of fitted mineral wagons next to the engine would result in shorter stopping times when approaching adverse signals, thus allowing the trains to be run safely at higher average speeds. The maximum consignment for each train was fifteen loaded 16ton fitted mineral wagons immediately behind the tender followed by 50 similar but loose-coupled wagons; two 20-ton brake vans and a dynamometer car completed the formation. For the purposes of the trials, the performance of 9F 92200 was compared with that of a WD 2-8-0, a V2 2-6-2 and a B1 4-6-0, the trains all being scheduled to run in Class 'H' (Class 8) timings. The tests were successful and later, similar trials with diesel types were undertaken. The incorporation in loaded mineral trains of the small 'head' of continuously braked wagons allowed the creation of a new 7* freight classification on the ER. This, together with the increased availability of diesel power resulted in higher speeds, improved punctuality and increased line capacity for the heavy mineral traffic from the East Midlands coalfield to Humberside, East Anglia, London and SR destinations; the new arrangements were introduced during the 1962/63 winter timetable.

On 7th September 1962, a derailment occurred at Offord

Figure 144
92124 (Wellingborough) charges through Kilnhurst Central with failed Peak Type 4 diesel D78 in tow on 31st August 1963. 92124 acquired the BR1B tender from Crosti boiler 92023 in September 1960 in exchange for its BR1C type during the period when the Crosti was in store at Wellingborough awaiting conversion. 92124 is one of the select band of 9Fs that had powered a named train; it was in charge of "The Robin Hood" from north of Bedford to St. Pancras, following a failure on 2nd June 1960. *(Courtney Haydon)*

Figure 145
92158 (Toton) snoozes on Willesden shed on 14th July 1963 probably after arriving on a coal train from the East Midlands. 92158 has received the realigned lamp bracket configuration but the footstep lugs below the smokebox have yet to be replaced by the safer 'T-piece' platform. *(Mike Burnett)*

near Huntingdon on the ex-GN main line. A1 Pacific 60123 *H.A. Ivatt* (Ardsley) was working the 8.50pm Kings Cross (Goods)-Leeds when it ran into the rear of the 8.25pm Kings Cross (Goods) to Newcastle (Forth) headed by a 9F. The latter was undamaged but the incident proved fatal for the Pacific which was withdrawn the following month. Until the blockage was cleared, some GN line traffic was diverted to the Midland main line to St. Pancras; three freights hauled by 9Fs, 92141 (on the Cliffe-Uddingston cement train) and 92197/8 (fast fitted), were noted passing Wellingborough on 8th September.

During 1963, Doncaster's 9Fs were being superseded on some of their traditional jobs by Type 2 and Type 4 diesels and by January 1964, the depot's allocation was down to eight of the class, 92168/9/70/2-5/7, the balance having been moved to Colwick, Immingham or New England. Within six months, four of this group, 92169/70/5/7 had been condemned and were withdrawn in May, the first of the class (along with 92034, 92171/6 ex-New England) to be consigned to the breakers' yards. With the exception of 92034, each had completed less than seven years service; the withdrawn Doncaster engines were replaced by transfers from Immingham (92039, 92200/1) and Colwick (92190) in June.

Early in 1965, Doncaster 9Fs were still observed at York but their visits to Tyneside were becoming less frequent. In the ex-GN southern area, steam had become increasingly less common south of Hitchin during 1964. 9Fs from Doncaster and other ER depots continued to appear in London well into 1965 however on the Millerhill (Edinburgh)-Hornsey stock train, rostered for diesel power but occasionally producing steam engines; Doncaster's 92183 and 92172 were recorded on this service on 2nd and 5th July respectively. In January 1966 however, only six 9Fs were at Doncaster, 92146/72/3/82/3, 92201; one engine, 92190, withdrawn in October the previous year was reported to have been used for a time at the shed as a stationary boiler.

Frodingham received its second batch of 9Fs, 92192/8/9, in November 1963 but the class was not a success there, the only remaining steam duties reported to be mainly trip workings for which the class was inherently unsuitable;

92198/9 were withdrawn in August 1964 with 92192 following in February 1965.

Displaced by diesels, some nineteen 9Fs were transferred to Colwick from Doncaster and New England during 1963; arriving in June were 92036/9-42/4 and 92148/83-8 with 92189-92/8/9 appearing in September. The class was used on mineral workings to Doncaster and to Welham Junction near Market Harborough. Until early 1963 9Fs were not permitted to run over the bridge which carried the Nottingham Victoria-Grantham branch over the Newark-Welham line at Bottesford Junction. This restriction precluded their use on mineral freights from Colwick to New England and Whitemoor. Following the closure of the section between Bottesford North and South Junctions in 1962, the track was recovered and the former bridge filled in. This allowed a higher route classification to be authorised for the Nottingham-Grantham line permitting the use of 9Fs on the mineral traffic to Whitemoor and the ex-GN main line to London. Although thirteen 9Fs were still at Colwick in January 1964, only two remained twelve months later, 92187/8, both of which were stored unserviceable and withdrawn in February. A further influx of 9Fs to Colwick occurred in October 1965 when eleven of the class, 92042 and 92141/4/5/6/8/73/9/82/9/91 were nominally transferred. This seemed to be a paper exercise only as, within a few weeks, most had been withdrawn and the others reallocated to Doncaster or Immingham.

The former MR depot at Staveley Barrow Hill was host to four 9Fs, 92040/1/4 and 92148 transferred from Colwick in September 1964. Again the class was found unsuitable for the depot's colliery trip working duties and had been moved on to Langwith Junction by the end of January 1965, to be replaced by WD 2-8-0s.

Following the closure of New England to steam in January 1965, the depot's active 9F allocation was transferred to Langwith Junction which, apart from receiving the Staveley Barrow Hill quartet also acquired class members from Colwick in the same month. A total of nineteen 9Fs were on Langwith's books from January 1965, 92038/40/1/2/4, 92140/1/4/5/6/8/9/78/9/80/2/9, 92191/5; four more, 92039, 92173/86, 92200, arrived from Doncaster in the following June. The 9Fs took over many of the remaining steam duties at the depot displacing most of the allocated 2-8-0s of both the LNER O4 and WD varieties which went into store or were withdrawn. Some of the O4s were retained however for coal trip workings as, although run-down, they were preferred to the 9Fs for working colliery sidings with poorly maintained track, the long wheel base of the 9Fs tending to straighten out some of the yard curves causing great difficulty. Eleven of Langwith Junction's 9Fs were withdrawn as the year 1965 progressed with an equal number of survivors transferring to Colwick in October.

In 1966, steam was well on the way to being eliminated from the ER and by 26th March, the 36 remaining steam engines on the region had been concentrated at Doncaster; apart from the five 9Fs, 92146/72/82/3, 92201, there were seven B1 4-6-0s, 19 WD 2-8-0s and five O4/8 2-8-0s; the 9Fs had all been withdrawn by the end of the following month.

On the NER, the original allocation of ten 9Fs, 92060-6/97-9 remained at Tyne Dock, still mainly working the Consett iron ore trains in April 1960. With the exception of 92065 which went to Wakefield for a few months following full dieselisation of this traffic in November 1966, all were retained at the depot until withdrawal. As noted in Section 1.6, one of the three mechanical stoker-fitted 9Fs, 92167 displaced by Type 4 diesels at Saltley in late 1961, was sent to Tyne Dock in May 1962 for trials on the Consett workings. The engine was not fitted with air pumps and was hence confined to banking duties from South Pelaw Junction to Medomsley. It was reported that the heavy black exhaust when 92167 was banking at full throttle on the route may have been awe-inspiring but simply demonstrated an essentially uneconomic use of fuel. The mechanical stoking device, designed for best results on long distance working was, not surprisingly, regarded as more trouble than it was worth; 92167 had returned south by the beginning of November 1962.

With the increasing availability of diesels on the NER in 1962, Cl.46 D171 (46034) was given a trial run on the iron ore workings on 28th September. Nine wagons, the same number as that handled by the 9Fs, were taken up to Consett without the aid of a banker in 78 minutes compared with the scheduled time of 104 minutes for a 9F. Minor modifications were reported to be necessary to the Type 4's air brake equipment to keep the wagon doors closed and a 9F was used at Consett to operate the door-opening equipment. Despite this success, no further tests with diesels were undertaken until 5th September 1963 when two Clayton Cl.17s, D8500/1, on loan from the ScR were tried out; in the event D8500 was replaced by D8536 for almost all of the trials. These locomotives were not deemed powerful enough and the 9Fs continued on the traffic, suitable alternative diesel power apparently not being made available. It is probable that the low mileage productivity of the motive power on the route was a factor in such a decision.

In 1963, demand for steel from the Consett plant was at a low ebb and in December, Tyne Dock was able to loan five 9Fs to Heaton to cover diesel failures on freight traffic in the extremely cold weather. Apart from workings to York and Tees Yard, 92061 was a rare sight north of Newcastle when used on a special freight from Heaton to Millerhill on 21st of the month; stablemate 92097 was pressed into service on ecs duties between Heaton and Newcastle on Christmas Eve.

In December 1964, provision of the bankers for the South Pelaw Junction-Medomsley section was transferred from Tyne Dock to Tyne Yard and a Cl.40 allocated to the role. Crews found the Type 4s roughly equal to the 9Fs but regretted they could not be 'flogged' as hard on the steep gradients into Consett in adverse weather conditions. By the end of January 1965, BR Sulzer Cl.24 Type 2s, modified to operate the power door wagons and working in tandem or multiple with no banker, had taken over some of the Consett duties. The traffic remained mainly steam-hauled by 9Fs however until mid-1966. By this time ten Cl.24 Type 2 diesels, D5102-11 (24102-11) had been fitted with special air pump equipment at Crewe for operating the wagon doors. For other traffic to Consett, such as the coal workings, Cl.37 Type 3s were regularly used.

Before their replacement, Tyne Dock's 9Fs were naturally in demand for enthusiasts' specials. The RCTS "North Eastern No. 2" rail tour of Saturday 10th April 1965, for example visited Consett with 92097 in charge; on the return to Darlington, the engine in immaculate condition was still able to demonstrate a good turn of speed, passing Ferryhill at 58½mph and reaching 65½mph before being stopped by signals just before Darlington. Later, 92099 again beautifully turned out, was in charge of some of the Alnwick-Alnmouth locals on the last day of steam passenger working, 18th June 1966.

The end for the 9Fs on the Consett route came on 19th November 1966. With two extra brake vans attached to carry enthusiasts, "The Tyne Docker", the last steam-hauled iron ore train from Tyne Dock to Consett was worked by 92063, the reign of the 9Fs on this traffic having spanned just over a decade. From then on the service was fully dieselised and trains were re-routed via Boldon Colliery, Pelaw, Greenfield, Birtley and Ouston Junction regaining the original line at South Pelaw.

In the early 1960s, York appeared chronically short of heavy freight power, numerous LMR-based 9Fs being borrowed for workings to Tyneside during layovers. In September 1963 however, York received its own allocation of the class, three, 92005/6, 92221 from the WR and five, 92205/6/11/31/9 from the SR, in exchange for BR Standard Class 5 4-6-0s from other NER depots. The class was observed on freight workings to Tyneside, Humberside and across the Pennines via both the Standedge and Calder Valley routes. York 9Fs also took their turn on the famous York-Manchester Red Bank empty stock train, usually double-heading with an engine from another class. From December 1963, they also took over the regular merchandise freight traffic from Dringhouses to Woodford Halse, formerly Class B16 4-6-0 and latterly Class B1 4-6-0 or Class V2 2-6-2 duties, until withdrawal of through freights from the ex-GC route in March 1965. The first of the York 9Fs to be withdrawn was 92221 in May 1965. The allocation was still active however, with 92005 reported on a Colwick-Hull petrol empties on 25th June 1965 just weeks before its own withdrawal and 92239 on the Craigentinny-Hornsey stock train on 7th October; the latter, not in the best of condition, failed at Grantham and was towed back to Doncaster next day to be withdrawn the following month. Similarly 92205/6 were observed at Skelton Junction, Timperley during September and October 1966 with mixed goods workings to and from the Warrington and Merseyside areas. York lost four of its allocation of 9Fs, 92006, 92205/6/11, to Wakefield in October; the remaining two, 92231/9, were withdrawn in November.

Apart from Tyne Dock and York, the only other NER depot to receive an allocation of 9Fs was Wakefield. There was a suspicion that the depot was being used as a dumping ground for exhausted class members as no fewer than ten examples were received in October/November 1966 from a diversity of sheds and incidentally, displaying the full gamut of tender varieties with the exception of the the BR1K mechanical stoker variants which had all been converted to BR1C types by this date. Present were 92001, 92215 from Tyseley, 92006, 92205/6/11 from York, 92030, 92150 from Saltley, 92065 from Tyne Dock (reportedly with air pumps still attached) and 92135 from Croes Newydd; none lasted more than a few months and all had been withdrawn by the end of June 1967. Duties included freights to the Stockport area, where 92006 and 92135 were noted in November and also the Stanlow-Neville Hill oil tank train on which 92206 was observed on 14th January 1967. Steam still predominated on the Wakefield-Goole line freights well into 1967 where at least 75% of the traffic was reported to be steam-hauled by 9Fs, Stanier and WD 2-8-0s, supplemented by Stanier Class 5 and B1 4-6-0s. The Wakefield to Santon (Scunthorpe) ballast empties and the return loaded train also continued to be steam operated in early 1967, 9Fs again sharing the duty with 2-8-0s and 4-6-0s. The remaining 9F allocation at Wakefield, 92135, 92205/15, was condemned on 8th June 1967, representing the end of the class on the NER.

London Midland Region

In April 1960 the distribution of the 129 9Fs allocated to the LMR was as shown:

Annesley	(28)	92010-3/30-3/43 92067/8/9/71-6 92087-96
Bidston	(3)	92045/6/7
Kettering	(4)	92105/6/60/3
Leicester Midland	(16)	92101-4/8-12/9-23/8/64
Newton Heath	(5)	92015/6/7/161/2
Rowsley	(6)	92008/9/48-51
Saltley	(15)	92014/70, 92135-9 92150/1/2/5/7 92165-7
Toton	(7)	92077/8 92129/30/53/6/8
Wellingborough	(37)	92018-29/52-6/8/9/80-6 92107/18/24-7/32/3/4/54/9
Westhouses	(8)	92057/100/13-7/31
Total	129	

Note: 92057 (Westhouses) and 92129 (Toton) transferred to Cricklewood one month later in May 1960.

Midland Main Line (MML)

Wellingborough was host to 37 9Fs in April 1960, over a quarter of the total LMR allocation. Adding this figure to the allocation of 9Fs operating from Kettering, Leicester Midland and Toton almost doubled the number of the class regularly to be seen operating on the MML. Not all the Wellingborough allocation was fully available for service, however, as the depot still had all the Crosti-boiler engines 92020-9 on its books at this time. Only four of these engines, 92024/5/6/8, had been converted to standard operation by April 1960, the remainder being either in store or seeing little active service. Despite their nominally lower power rating (unofficially down graded to 8F status) the former Crostis were used interchangeably with the standard class members, 92025 being observed regularly on the 6.40am Corby-Poplar freight from April. 92021/7/9 were back in service later in 1960 and 92020/3 in 1961 but it was not until June 1962 before the last conversion, 92022, was completed (see Table 9.2). As with other 9Fs allocated to the Midland line, the former Crostis were used on freights in other regions. For example 92021 was observed working the 12.40pm Heaton-Dringhouses Class 'C' freight on 25th February 1961. Here the former Crosti was in illustrious company as two weeks later the same service had A3 Pacific 60103 *Flying Scotsman,* typical of the normal power for this duty; 92021 had presumably been appropriated by York for a previous northbound service during a layover after a regular working from the Midlands.

The major role for the 9Fs on the MML continued to be the hauling of coal from the East Midlands to Brent sidings in London. New duties emerged from time to time. One example was the conveyance of new Vauxhall motor cars from Chiltern Green, just south of Luton, to a distribution depot in Glasgow. Sidings at 'the Green' had been converted into a ramp loading facility. Empty car-flats were brought to the

Figure 146
92032, on an Annesley-Woodford Halse 'windcutter' running under Class 'H' lights, passes Annesley stablemate 92093 north of Leicester Central on 31st August 1961. Both engines survived into 1967, 92032 succumbing in April and 92093 in September. 92032 had recently returned from a Light Casual repair having covered some 225,000 miles since delivery.
(C. R. Berridge)

Figure 147
92092 hurries through the northern suburbs of Leicester with an up GC line Class 'C' freight on 31st August 1961. Made redundant from Annesley in May 1965, 92092 was transferred to Birkenhead from where it was withdrawn in October 1966.
(C. R. Berridge)

Figure 148
92093 (Annesley) eases an up coal train past Worksop Sidings on 17th October 1964. This service was probably one of the celebrated GC line 'windcutters' linking Annesley Yard with Woodford Halse. The engine shows ample evidence on its boiler of the limescale problem which was a feature of the water supply at Annesley depot. After closure of the GC line services in June 1965, 92093 was reallocated to Kirkby-in-Ashfield. *(Courtney Haydon)*

sidings from Wilstead and after loading, taken to Harpenden. The first train to Glasgow left at 8.00pm on 25th April 1960 hauled by Wellingborough's 92126.

The car-flats train ran most evenings in the wake of the down "Condor" which also featured 9F power from time to time. The latter train was a fast fitted container service introduced on 16th March 1959, running from Hendon to Gushetfaulds goods depot in Glasgow via Leeds and the Settle & Carlisle route. The train was made up of roller-bearing flat wagons rostered for haulage by a brace of Cl.28 1,200hp Metrovick Co-Bo diesels (D57xx). Freight containers collected during the afternoon were scheduled to be at their destination during the following morning at a charge of £16 for a small container and £18 for the larger variety. Departure from Hendon was 7.23pm (M-F), 7.50pm (Su) and from Glasgow 7.50pm (FSX); arrivals were 5.15am Gushetfaulds and 5.40am Hendon.

It took some time for the service to become established and for a few months, a single Cl.28 was sufficient for handling typically 13 wagons. Later, several bogie vans were included in the formation at the front, presumably to popularise the service by offering to handle less than full container loads; by mid-1960, traffic had improved to such a level that two Cl. 28s were the usual power. Although twenty of the latter machines had been delivered by the end of October 1959, they did not enjoy the highest reputation for reliability and steam power was often used as a replacement. In the event of diesel failure, two Class 5 4-6-0s were specified as the alternative but 9Fs were much in evidence as substitutes. In June 1960 for example, 92133 was noted on the down train on 14th, with 92055 and 92081 on 16th and 17th respectively. Eventually the Cl.28s were replaced by other Type 2 diesel classes, Cl.25 and Cl.27.

Dieselisation of MML mineral traffic was also being considered in late 1959. From December of that year until February 1960, brake tests on accelerated loose-coupled mineral trains were carried out between Toton and Brent using Toton's 92153 in comparison with one of the original Peak Type 4 BR Sulzer 2,300hp diesel units (later Cl.44) then on loan to Derby from the WCML.

Up to the end of 1960, the Midland line 9Fs had regularly appeared on parcels and fitted freights but in the new year, an additional number of rebuilt Royal Scot Class 7P 4-6-0s was drafted on to the route having been displaced from the WCML by dieselisation. The Scots took over from Jubilee 4-6-0s which in turn were then used in place of the 9Fs on fast freights and parcels traffic.

By the summer of 1961, passenger duties on the Midland line were dominated by Peak Type 4 class diesels, which also appeared on the "Condor" freight service on occasion. The 9Fs were now rare on "Condor" outings but continued to share the mineral traffic with Stanier Class 8F 2-8-0s. A traffic survey of the railways of Rutland (through which ran the St. Pancras-Nottingham line) for the six months ended October 14th 1961 reported that the majority of the locally originating freight traffic was iron ore from the extensive workings in the area. Most of these trains and also the large volume of through coal traffic were worked by 9Fs together with Stanier and WD 2-8-0s; the engines were mainly from sheds at Wellingborough, Kettering, Nottingham and Toton.

In April and May 1962, a significant increase in the number of diesel-hauled freights was reported on the Midland line, with more to follow with the arrival of further batches of BRC&W Cl.27 Type 2 diesels (D53xx/D54xx) at Cricklewood over the summer period. Along with pairs of the latter class, 9Fs were involved in tests with fully fitted mineral trains in the Loughborough area during August 1962; one example was the train consisting of 70 21ton wagons plus testing vehicle and a brake observed being double-headed by 92153/8 on 19th August.

The mineral traffic was still mainly in the hands of 9Fs and 8Fs at this time. Failure of Type 4 diesels, generally operating on intricate cyclic diagrams often resulted in the appearance of 9Fs and Class 5 4-6-0s on fitted freights. Observations at Luton on 11th July for six hours from 10.00am confirmed that virtually all the freight workings had 9F power with only one Stanier Class 8F 2-8-0, one Class 5 4-6-0 and one Peak Type 4 diesel appearing on such duties. The increased use of brake tenders, often propelled in front of diesels, to improve their stopping power on heavy freights began to occur during 1962 challenging the reign of steam on the mineral traffic. By mid-October, Peak Type 4 D65 (45111) was reported to be regularly working coal trains from Wellingborough to Brent. In September 1962 a redistribution of steam power on the LMR was implemented. The aim was to employ more economically the Stanier and Standard Class 5 4-6-0s and the 9Fs and Stanier Class 8F 2-8-0s made redundant through dieselisation. As a result, all the Jubilee 4-6-0s at Burton-upon-Trent and the LNER B1 4-6-0s at Woodford Halse were replaced by Class 5 4-6-0s. The 9Fs were reassigned to work many of the duties previously carried out by the 8F 2-8-0s. This led to the transfer of some 22 of the latter class to Annesley which in turn allowed for the withdrawal of a similar number of LNER 2-8-0s.

In January 1963, the allocation of 9Fs on the Midland Main Line was as follows:

Kettering	(5)	92105/6/25/60/3
Leicester Midland	(13)	92101/2/3/8-12 92119-23
Toton	(10)	92052/3/5/9/77/8 92130/53/6/8
Wellingborough	(24)	92019-27/80-4/6 92117/24/6/7 92132/3/4/54/9
Total	52	

Steam was now disappearing from freight traffic on this route and the usual processions of mineral trains and empties were now in the charge of paired Type 2 diesels with 4-6-0s appearing occasionally on fitted freights in place of Type 4 diesels. By October, only a handful of 9Fs and Stanier 8F 2-8-0s reached the capital on a typical day. The pre-Christmas traffic on the line was exceptionally heavy in 1963 however and steam returned in force during late November and December, 8Fs and 9Fs almost monopolising the heavy freights. Sunday working was instituted to cope with the backlog and there were many unbalanced light engine movements working north, especially on Monday mornings. By the end of January 1964, the boom had subsided and the vast majority of freights were back to diesel haulage.

In January and February 1964, Wellingborough lost its allocation of 9Fs mainly to Kettering; they were replaced by a similar number of 8F 2-8-0s from other Midland Division depots. Duties for the Kettering 9F allocation at this time included the 9.15am Cardiff-Corby through train of empty iron ore hoppers, routed via Gloucester, Swindon, Oxford and Northampton.

Figure 149
Line-up at Barrow Road shed Bristol on 9th October 1965. In the centre is 92135 (Saltley) with Stanier Class 8F 2-8-0 48460 (Stourbridge Junction) and 92235, transferred to Barrow Road from Newport Ebbw Junction in the same month and withdrawn in November. 92135 later moved to the NER along with several other 9Fs and was withdrawn in June 1967; the 8F survived until October 1967.
(Courtney Haydon)

Figure 150
92104 is between jobs at Westhouses MPD, its home depot, on 9th June 1963. The engine had completed a Heavy General overhaul with boiler change at Crewe Works a few weeks earlier. 92104 was withdrawn in February 1967 and cut up at A. Draper's yard in Hull five months later.
(RCTS Collection)

Figure 151
92009 approaches Elstree & Borehamwood on the MML with a down fitted freight on 13th August 1960. 92009 was originally intended for service on the WR and had been equipped with WR ATC apparatus and BR1G tender during construction at Crewe Works. The BR1G tender was exchanged for the BR1C type paired with 92079 when the latter was transferred to Bromsgrove for Lickey banker work in May 1956. By 1960, 92009 was allocated to Rowsley and was regularly used on the shed's fitted freight diagrams to London rather than on the coal and mineral workings traditionally associated with 9Fs on this route.
(Courtney Haydon)

Figure 152
92058, then allocated to Westhouses, leans to the curve at Kettering with an up coal train on 11th May 1963. The adjacent 9F is 92106 lazing at its home shed.
(Courtney Haydon)

Figure 153
92112 trundles a load of iron ore through Birmingham Snow Hill in 1965. The engine carries no shedplate but its allocation is almost certainly Birkenhead to where it was moved in April of that year from Leicester Midland. The ore may be bound for the steel works at Bilston near Wolverhampton, Banbury-based 9Fs being the usual power for such workings. 92112 was one of a pair (with 92111) which were delivered new to Cricklewood in November 1956 and had later operated on MML mineral freights based at Wellingborough and Leicester.
(C. R. Berridge)

Figure 154
Having recently been outshopped from Crewe after a Heavy Intermediate overhaul, 92054 (Speke Junction) may be on a running-in turn as it passes Kidderminster with a northbound Class 'D' freight in August 1965. The engine was one of the last 9Fs in service and was occasionally observed on mineral trains at Skelton Junction, Timperley (see Appendix 1) in 1967/8 as well as on WCML fast fitted freights.
(C. R. Berridge)

From mid-March 1964 onwards, fewer and fewer 8Fs and 9Fs were to be observed on MML mineral trains, although these classes continued to substitute for failed diesels. In early April, there was a further step towards the elimination of steam from the Midland line when virtually all of the remaining steam-hauled Toton-Wellingborough-Brent mineral traffic was handed over to Peak Type 4 haulage (Cl.44, 45, 46) or, increasingly, to a single Type 2 diesel heading a maximum of 50 wagons. By this time the 9F class was becoming a rarity on the route, with the remaining fast fitted freights still in the hands of 4-6-0s. Following the usual increase in passenger traffic in the summer of 1964, some diesels were drafted off freight work leading to the appearance of around three or four Cl. 8Fs or 9Fs and perhaps a solitary Standard Class 5 4-6-0 on mineral workings each day.

The Toton 9F allocation was still employed on duties other than MML work in 1964 and regularly appeared on mineral freights to the Birmingham area as well as on colliery trip workings in the East Midlands.

Meanwhile, 9Fs continued to perform their usual rescue acts for diesel failures. On 22nd August 1964 for example, the 8.04am Leeds-St. Pancras express reached Bedford behind 92119, towing Type 4 D80 (45113) whilst 92125 went through Bedford on a normally Type 4 powered fast freight early the same day. As a result of the removal of the large turntable at Wellingborough at this time, turning was then carried out at Bedford and 9Fs began to appear there more frequently. One continuing steam working was the delivery of coal to the new bulk fuel and household coal concentration depot at Luton which was in full operation towards the end of the summer.

Towards the end of 1964, 9Fs could still be seen occasionally, particularly during the hours of darkness. Facilities for steam servicing were withdrawn from Cricklewood on 13th December 1964 but this did not stop the odd 9F and other steam power reaching Brent; examples were 92123, observed on an up freight on 14th December and 92100 appearing on 19th.

In the period February-April 1965, the remaining 9Fs at Midland line depots (Kettering, Leicester Midland and Toton) were transferred from the MML, mainly to Warrington or Birkenhead. Until then the Luton coal traffic had still featured 8F and 9F power whilst on 31st March 1965 92109, still on Leicester Midland's books for a few more weeks, was observed hauling the 5.15am Wellingborough-Brent coal train. The only mineral train regularly steam powered at this time was the Wellingborough-Bedford Goldington power station traffic. The reason for this was the initial reluctance of the civil engineer to permit the use of Type 4 diesels over the River Ouse bridge. There were usually three trains of coal per day, six days per week for this service and normal power was the Stanier Class 8F 2-8-0; 9Fs occasionally appeared however, with 92028 (Saltley) and 92101/67 (Birkenhead) being observed in September 1965. By January 1966, the civil engineer had relented and Type 4 diesels were permitted across the bridge. From February, the traffic was taken over by Type 4 and Cl.27 Type 2 diesels.

The 9Fs seemed unwilling to abandon the route however as despite the fact that there were no coaling facilities south of Leicester, 92122 (Birkenhead) was noted on an up freight from Toton at Bedford as late as April 1966.

Earlier, in October and November 1963, another depot in the East Midlands, Kirkby-in-Ashfield, had received its first 9F allocation (from Kettering, Wellingborough and Leicester Midland) and was destined to retain a nominal allocation of 9Fs longer than other Midland Division sheds. (Note: 92088 was given what could be described as a 'rogue' transfer to Toton in June 1965 three months after the last of the depot's 9Fs had transferred to Warrington; the engine was put into store however and reallocated to Birkenhead the following month). Kirkby's 9Fs substituted for a similar number of Stanier Class 8F 2-8-0s on colliery trip and mineral freight duties to Toton marshalling yards, as well as to the Chesterfield and Sheffield areas. The shed received another batch of 9Fs in April 1964, mainly from Rowsley at the time of the closure of the latter depot, so that by May 1964 the depot was operating some fifteen 9Fs:

92008/18/20/6/50/1/2/6/76/7
92110/1/4/27/59

As early as June 1964 however, Kirkby began to lose its allocation of 9Fs and all had departed for Newton Heath or Speke Junction by the end of the year. By early 1965 the mineral freights in the area were being taken over by Cl.25 Type 2s from Toton and the trip workings by Cl.47 Type 4s from the new Tinsley diesel depot at Sheffield. Despite this, Kirkby received a further batch of 9Fs in June 1965, 92032/72/5/93/5 and 92154. Displaced from Annesley following the withdrawal of the freight services from the GC line, these engines were immediately put into store and by May 1966 had all been withdrawn or transferred to the LMR north western area, having done little or no work at Kirkby.

Other LMR Lines

The 9Fs at Annesley continued on the intensive 'windcutter' service to Woodford Halse during the early 1960s and by January 1963, the allocation had increased to 30 engines:

92010-4/30-3/43/57
92067/8/9/71-6/87-96

In February it was rumoured that the 9Fs were to be replaced by Type 4 diesels but this move did not materialise. Also featuring 9F power, along with other types, were the through fitted freights from Dringhouses to Woodford Halse, Banbury, Bristol and Cardiff which were still routed via the GC line. Other regular workings for Annesley 9Fs were a daily Dringhouses-Marylebone freight and the twice weekly Class 'C' Guinness train from Newcastle to the Park Royal brewery near Acton. Annesley's 9Fs were also used on mineral workings to Doncaster and Welham Junction near Market Harborough.

By 1964, as a result of rationalisation following the Beeching Report on the future of British Railways, it was clear that the writing was on the wall for the GC line. In March 1965 all GC line merchandise freight services were diverted through Birmingham, from where traffic for the south west went via the ex-MR line to Bristol whilst the London area freights used the ex-WR main line, leaving only the 'windcutters' operating north of Woodford Halse. The end of the 'cutters' came when all freight services on the route were withdrawn on 14th June 1965; from that date Woodford Halse Yard was closed, the Annesley marshalling yards having already ceased operation. Over the period May-August, the bulk of Annesley's 9F allocation was either placed in store or dispersed, the majority moving to Birkenhead, Banbury or Kirkby-in-Ashfield. By the end of October, only two 9Fs remained on Annesley's books, 92043/96, both officially in store; they eventually found a home at Carlisle Kingmoor in January 1966.

Figure 155
92054 (Speke Junction) rattles a southbound train of oil tank empties through Oxenholme on 8th July 1967. The line to the left is the branch to Kendal and Windermere.
(RCTS Collection)

Figure 156
92054 (Wellingborough) is pictured on shed at Speke Junction on 17th June 1962. The engine lasted almost until the end of steam and was withdrawn from the same shed in May 1968. 92054 has probably been running-in from an HG repair at Crewe from where it was returned to traffic at the end of the previous month.
(Courtney Haydon)

Figure 157
Converted ex-Crosti 92023 basks in the summer sunshine at Carlisle Kingmoor on 8th August 1964. The engine is here fitted with a BR1C tender rather than its original BR1B type. Still present on the cabside is the hand-rail used to access the running-plate between the cab and the Crosti side chimney before the latter was removed; the foot-rail has already gone. 92023 was a regular performer on the Hardendale quarry trains for the Ravenscraig steel works near Motherwell at this time; the Britannia Pacific in the background is 70041 *Sir John Moore*.

(Courtney Haydon)

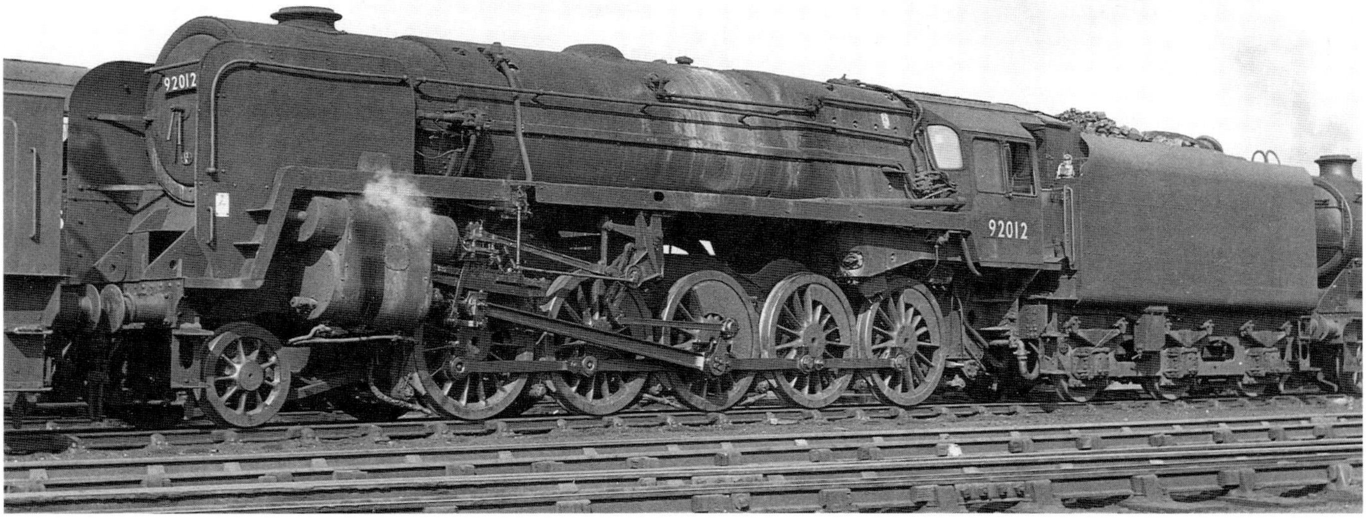

Figure 158
92012 is seen on shed at Carlisle Kingmoor on 8th August 1964. At Kingmoor, the engine was used on WCML work and was one of the few 9Fs ever to work regularly in Scotland. The modified method of securing the return crank to the big end with four studs, LMS-style, is clearly visible. 92012 had recently made a visit to Crewe Works which appears to have dispensed with the classification mark usually found on the cabside above the running number.

(Courtney Haydon)

Figure 159
92017 (Carlisle Kingmoor) arrives at Falkland Yard, Ayr in August 1964 with a train load of steel pipes for a new water main to serve the new industrial complex in the vicinity of Irvine New Town. *(Bill Hamilton)*

The 15 9Fs at Saltley in April 1960, 92014/70 and 92135-9/50/1/2/5/7/65-7, continued on similar duties as before. It was reported that one of Saltley's mechanical stoker-fitted 9Fs, 92167, made its first appearance on the MML to London as late as February 1960. On 9th, it was observed heading the 5.42pm Glasgow-St. Pancras Class 'C' fitted freight but failed at Elstree on 17th with a defective stoker when working the 10.10am Brent-Wellingborough mineral empties. Apart from the Carlisle fitted freights, Saltley 9Fs had other long distance workings to the north. For some time they had made frequent appearances at York on mineral workings but during the autumn of 1960, they began to penetrate further into NER territory, regularly being observed at Heaton with train loads of steel from the Birmingham area; previously the LMR engines had been changed at York.

In the spring of 1961, Saltley 9Fs began to reach Tyneside quite regularly on a York Type 4 diesel diagram, presumably appropriated by the depot during layovers as substitutes for diesel failures. The diagram involved working the 3.10am Whitemoor-Niddrie Class 'C' from York Skelton sidings to Heaton, returning on the 12.40pm Heaton-Dringhouses Class 'C'. The Saltley 9F arrived in York on the 10.15am Rotherham Masborough-Dringhouses Class 'C' and was rostered to return south with the Gateshead Park Lane-Washwood Heath fitted freight next day. Later, LMR 9Fs including Saltley-based engines continued to appear regularly in the north east at the then newly opened Tyne Yard, again mainly as a result of engine shortages at York; one example was 92138, observed there on 26th October 1963.

The long distance Water Orton-Carlisle/Scotland freights with which Saltley's mechanical stoker-fitted engines had been associated since their allocation in 1958 were given over to Type 4 or Type 2 diesel power by the end of summer 1961, although 9Fs continued to appear when deputising for failures. They were regularly used on out and home turns through to Oxford but apart from this, there was little suitable work for these engines after the dieselisation move and all three spent some time in late 1961 out of action at Saltley. Other possible uses were considered for these engines and as noted earlier, 92167 was loaned to Tyne Dock from May to October 1962 for trials on the Consett iron ore workings but was not deemed a success. The other two stoker engines 92165/6 were moved to Bidston in June 1962 again for trials on iron ore workings, in this instance the heavy traffic from Bidston Dock to the John Summers steel plant at Shotwick. By early 1963, the stoker trio, 92165-7, had been converted to conventional operation and were all at Bidston; the engines were replaced at Saltley by 9Fs from other LMR Midland Division depots.

Freights south from Birmingham also saw Saltley's 9Fs in action. The class naturally featured on the Midland West of England main line to Bristol but were also noted on services

Figure 160
Strange thing to find at a bus stop. 92249 (Carlisle Kingmoor) is on shed at Lower Darwen on 11th April 1965. It exchanged its BR1G tender for the BR1B type from ex-Crosti boiler 92024 in January 1965. The two small holes drilled near the base of the bufferbeam between the coupling chain and the buffer on the driver's side were provided for all 9Fs during construction to allow for carriage warming apparatus to be installed if required. In the event, none of the 9Fs received such apparatus during their BR service. Note also the 'half moon' cut out just below and between the two holes, specified for later batches of WR-based 9Fs; for background details, see Section 2.1. *(Courtney Haydon)*

to the SR and the London area of the WR. As early as November 1959, 92157 had been observed on a freight at Eastleigh and the class' appearances there continued in connection with the Fawley refinery-Bromford Bridge oil traffic until dieselisation of the service in 1963. By mid-1960, LMR 9Fs including Saltley engines were often to be seen in the Reading area on freights to and from Birmingham. The class shared the freight workings to the WR with Class 5 and Class 7P engines from Saltley during the summer of 1961. Typical duties were the 12.15pm (SX) Class 'D' Washwood Heath-Eastleigh as far as Oxford, returning on the 4.40pm Hinksey-Water Orton Class 'D'; the 2.50am (SX) Washwood Heath-Basingstoke Class 'C', again to Oxford, returning light engine if no suitable working service was available. It was reported that Saltley 9Fs were regular visitors to South Wales in the summer of 1961, appearing on the 8.30am Washwood Heath-Severn Tunnel Junction duty which they shared with Class 6P/5F Hughes-Fowler Crab 2-6-0s. Later in 1963, 9Fs and 8Fs from Saltley and other LMR depots were observed on freights to the Port Talbot and Swansea areas, returning to the Midlands with train loads of steel bars; these workings continued into 1965. The two former Crosti-boiler engines on Saltley's books at this time, 92028/9, were used turn and turn about with the 9Fs, despite their nominally lower power rating. On 5th November 1964 for example, 92028 was noted on the former WR main line between Birmingham and Chester with the 3.00pm Crewe-Banbury fitted freight whilst on 21st of the month 92029 headed the 3.25am Carlisle-Oxley on the same route.

In January 1963, Saltley's allocation of 9Fs had increased to nineteen, 92008/28/9/85, 92107/18/28/9/35-9/50/1/2/5/7/64. Visits to Reading, Didcot Moreton Yard and the WR London area continued, increasing in frequency after the transfer of some of the GC line traffic to the WR in March 1965. In London, the 9Fs appeared at places such as Acton and Old Oak Common freight depots and were serviced at Southall shed. These freights were rapidly dieselised in the run up to the withdrawal of steam from the WR at the end of 1965.

On 24th April 1965, Saltley's 9F complement was down to twelve engines, 92029, 92125/35-9/50/1/2/5/64. Until the autumn of 1965, freights in the West Midlands, although theoretically rostered for diesel power in some cases, continued to be hauled by 9Fs, 8Fs and Class 5 4-6-0s. By May 1966, however, sufficient diesels had been made available for this traffic and the Saltley 9F allocation was gradually dispersed during the rest of the year. Five went to Wrexham Croes Newydd and two to Wakefield. The remainder were either withdrawn or transferred to the LMR north west lines, mainly Birkenhead or Speke Junction, with one each to Carlisle Kingmoor and Carnforth; it is worth noting that one of the original Saltley engines, 92136, had remained allocated to that depot all its working life, June 1957 to October 1966.

In April 1960, Rowsley's allocation of 9Fs, 92008/9/48-51 was still deployed on freights to the Manchester, Liverpool and London areas. By January 1963, with reallocations and additions, the number had increased to eight, 92018/48-51/6, 92113/4. The engines were increasingly used on the London freights in place of Caprotti Standard Class 5 4-6-0s and from time to time appeared on Tyneside on fitted freights, examples of many LMR-based 9Fs borrowed by York during layovers after hauling freights to Dringhouses and Skelton sidings. Rowsley's 9Fs were also occasionally noted on the Tunstead (Peak Forest)-Northwich ICI hopper trains normally worked by Stanier Class 8F 2-8-0s; these workings were dieselised in August 1964. By the time the shed closed in April 1964, Rowsley had fourteen of the class, 92008/9/12/8/22/48-51/6/76 and 92114/27/59, on its books. On closure, these engines were reallocated to Kirkby-in-Ashfield, Kettering or Toton, whilst the shed was retained as a stabling point for banking engines for the 15-mile stretch at 1 in 100/90 up to Peak Forest summit.

The Westhouses 9Fs continued on coal haulage duties in the Chesterfield area, the allocation totalling nine engines in January 1963, 92009/54/8/70 and 92100/4/15/6/31. Although throughout 1963 virtually all unfitted and mineral freights in the area were steam-hauled, complete dieselisation of this traffic was imminent by year end. From June to November 1964, Westhouses lost most of its 9Fs to Carlisle Kingmoor or Speke Junction and by mid-1965 the remainder had been moved to Merseyside or Newton Heath.

In April 1960, Bidston depot was still host to 92045-7 for the John Summers' steel works traffic and in June 1962, two mechanical stoker-fitted 9Fs, 92165/6 displaced by dieselisation in the LMR Midland Division were received from Saltley. The latter were not modified to conventional operation until year end, at which time the other member of the stoker trio, 92167, was also allocated to Bidston, having been modified at Crewe before being put back to work. Bidston depot was closed in February 1963 with 92045-7 and 92165-7 transferred to Birkenhead which then took over the John Summers' workings.

The Bidston 9Fs were the first to be allocated to Birkenhead but by the end of 1963 a further four had arrived. These included two ex-Crosti engines, 92028/9 and the former Lickey banker, 92079, displaced from Bromsgrove by impending dieselisation. A steady stream of additional 9F allocations to Birkenhead occurred during 1965. A high proportion were engines made redundant from the LMR Midland Division, large areas of which had been given over to diesel operation by this time.

By August 1965, some 55 9Fs were allocated to Birkenhead:
92011/4/20/1/3/4/6/32/45-8/57/9/69/70/9/82-6
92088/9/90/2/4, 92100-9/11/2/3/20-3/7/31/3/4
92157/9/62/3/5/6/7

Birkenhead continued to supply steam power for the John Summers' iron ore workings until these were taken over by Type 4 diesel power in 1967. As late as Sunday 22nd October however, this line was exclusively steam worked with four 9Fs, 92002/94, 92167 and 92234 handling all the traffic, each engine making two return trips to Shotwick from the docks. On the last day of steam operation at Birkenhead, Monday 6th November 1967, 92203, beautifully turned out by the shed staff and carrying the headboard 'Summers Ore' worked the last steam-hauled Bidston-Shotwick ore train, with Sir Richard Summers on the footplate; 92203 performed admirably and standby engine 92167 was not required. Cl.47 Type 4 diesels were rostered to take over these workings from that date.

Apart from the ore traffic and freights to Chester and the Shrewsbury area, one of the class' main duties at Birkenhead was the working of the numerous oil tank trains originating from the refineries at Stanlow (Ellesmere Port). British Rail had negotiated contracts for this traffic during the late 1950s, the background to which is described in the SR notes in this

Figure 161
On 30th October 1965, Banbury-based 92074 is coupled to an ex-GWR 2-6-2 tank engine as they head for the motive power depot through the rather dilapidated station at Oxford. 92074 was one of the quintet of Saltley 9Fs transferred to Wrexham Croes Newydd shed during 1966 for work on the Brymbo steel works branch; the initiative was not successful as the 9F ten-coupled wheelbase tended to straighten out the curves on the branch, leading to a number of partial derailments.
(Courtney Haydon)

Figure 162
In the twilight of steam power on the WCML, an unidentified 9F struggles up Shap with a northbound Class 'F' freight on 20th September 1967; the banker is a Standard Class 4 4-6-0. *(Rodney Lissenden)*

Figure 163
92021 (Carlisle Kingmoor) stands in the up loop at Shap summit with a Class 'C' freight on 25th July 1964. A year later 92021 was reallocated to Birkenhead and withdrawn when the latter shed was closed to steam in November 1967.
(Rodney Lissenden)

Figure 164
Every picture tells a story. 92118 (Carnforth) struggles with a southbound Class 'E' freight near Ais Gill summit on 21st September 1967. The engine appears to be the victim of the less than fully comprehensive maintenance policy adopted for steam power towards the end of its reign on British Railways. *(Rodney Lissenden)*

section. A steady procession of these trains bound for the then West Riding of Yorkshire via the ex-CLC line could be observed on most days with destinations which included Liversedge near Huddersfield as well as Neville Hill and Hunslet in Leeds. Other services were to Colwick and Tuxford in the East Midlands, the Albion oil terminal in Birmingham and also northwards to the Carlisle area. The scope and frequency of these workings can be appreciated by reference to Appendix 1, 'Observations of Standard Class 9F 2-10-0s at Skelton Junction, Timperley, June 1966-May 1968'. This data, supplied by Mr. Alan Porter provide a valuable record of the last two years of steam workings at this busy junction, almost three quarters of the 9F sightings being Birkenhead engines mostly engaged on oil traffic movements.

By 1st January 1967, Birkenhead had no fewer than 59 9Fs on its books although some were in poor shape mechanically whilst others had but a few weeks of life left before withdrawal:
92002/11/4/20/1/3/4/6/9/32/45-9/69/70/3/9
92082/3/4/6/8/9/90/4, 92100-9/11/2/3/20-3/7
92131/3/51/2/7/9/60/2/3/5/6/7, 92203/34

From the end of March 1967 Type 4 diesels were increasingly to be seen on the oil tanker traffic, although Birkenhead 9Fs were still noted on workings to Yorkshire as late as the end of October. Meanwhile, withdrawal of the depot's 9Fs gathered pace, with three of the class from Speke Junction, 92022/5, 92119, being sent as replacements. In the weeks before the closure of Birkenhead depot in November 1967, the vast majority of its remaining 9F allocation was withdrawn with only a handful surviving for transfer to Carlisle Kingmoor (92119), Speke Junction (92069/94, 92160/5) or Carnforth (92088, 92167). Full dieselisation at Birkenhead occurred on 6th November 1967 but a number of withdrawn 9Fs were cleared on 29th October. At 8.00am, 92084 was observed hauling 92045 and 92106/31 away whilst an hour later, 92021 left with 92127/51 in tow. On Sunday 5th November, 92024 and 92101/13 were taken away to Speke Junction behind D1710 (later 47121), assisted in the rear by Stanier Class 8F 2-8-0 48465. This left only 92167 and 92203, retained in connection with the final steam-hauled Shotwick ore train described earlier and Stanier Class 5 4-6-0 44913 as the last representatives of the once large steam allocation at Birkenhead.

The Newton Heath quintet, 92015/6/7, 92161/2, received in 1958, were still in place in April 1960, and remained on their regular duties from the Manchester area to the Peak Forest line and Carlisle. The engines were also noted on cross-Pennine freights to the Huddersfield area and in 1962 workings included the Carlisle Durran Hill-Oldham Glodwick Road empty vans train which ran via the Settle route, Manchester Victoria and Ashton-under-Lyne. In September of that year, 92015/6/7 were reallocated to Bolton where they were rostered for the 8.20pm Bolton-Moston Exchange sidings and the evening Ancoats-Heysham freight.

There were also reported appearances on merchandise goods traffic between Lancashire and Scotland, sharing the work with Stanier Class 5 4-6-0s and Hughes-Fowler Crab Class 6P/5F Moguls. The trio did not appear to find favour at Bolton as they had been returned to Newton Heath by the end of 1962 in exchange for Class 5 4-6-0s.

In October 1963, a further three 9Fs, 92208/33/49, displaced from the WR by dieselisation were allocated to Newton Heath and in the following year, yet more of the class arrived, this time displaced by diesels from the LMR Midland Division, mainly Kirkby-in-Ashfield. Two former Crostis, 92022/6, were included in the new allocation and tended to be employed on local turns such as cross-Manchester transfer freights; for the others, duties now included former WD 2-8-0 freight workings along the Calder Valley line to the Healey Mills area. Another regular 9F turn was the Bolton-Goole class 'D' fitted freight, shared with B1 4-6-0s and Crab Moguls. On 24th April 1965, Newton Heath had some sixteen 9Fs on its books;

92016/8/22/6/50/1/2/6/77/80/1,
92110/4/59/61/2

From mid-1965 onwards, as dieselisation encroached, the shed gradually lost its 9F allocation either to the breakers' yards or to other LMR North Western Area depots, Birkenhead, Carlisle Kingmoor, Speke Junction or Carnforth, the last two engines, 92016/52, departing in June 1967.

The first three 9Fs to be allocated to Speke Junction, 92054, 92115/58, arrived in June 1964 and by the year end, eleven more of the class displaced from the LMR Midland Division were operating from the depot; now included were:

92008/20/5/7/54/84/9,
92104/11/5/7/27/31/58

Along with the Birkenhead allocation, Speke Junction's 9Fs were noted on the block oil tanker workings from Stanlow (Ellesmere Port), the car body trains from Halewood to Bathgate (as far as Carlisle) and also on the Tunstead (Peak Forest)-Runcorn ICI limestone hoppers from time to time (see Appendix 1). Other 9F-hauled tanker traffic was from Falwood sidings (adjacent to St. Michaels) to Preston, Salford and Holywell power stations, the latter often double-headed by 9Fs. In 1964, the new Preston-Lancaster M6 motorway was being constructed and beginning in June, bulk cement wagon trains were run two or three times per week to Lancaster Castle down yard. These trains were usually 9F powered with Speke Junction engines participating, although Cl.40 Type 4 diesels or a pair of Class 5 4-6-0s were also noted. To replace transferred or withdrawn engines, other 9F allocations were made to Speke Junction between June 1965 and January 1968.

In the latter days of steam, 9Fs were in demand in the north west for enthusiasts' rail tours and Speke Junction's engines were no exception. On 14th October 1967, for example, 92091 visited Liverpool Exchange with a Liverpool-Carlisle tour. Castle 4-6-0 7029 *Clun Castle* took over at Preston for the run over Shap, returning over the Settle & Carlisle line to Hellifield. From here, 92091 again was in charge for the return to Liverpool via Blackburn and the Bolton triangle.

In 1967, a regular turn for Speke Junction 9Fs was the 4.44 pm Brunswick-Lostock Hall gas works class 'D' tanker freight. This usually consisted of twenty vehicles and ran twice per week. Until March, the route was via Widnes, St. Helens and the main line, the 9Fs usually double-heading with a Speke Junction Stanier Class 5 4-6-0. The freight was later diverted via Gateacre, Aintree and the ex-LYR line to Preston. The return working was the 8.25pm Lostock Hall-Garston Speke sidings empty tanks. As late as 27th November 1967, five 9Fs were observed serviceable on shed at Speke Junction and there were also appearances on the Colne-Red Bank stock train, 92054 for example, being observed on the duty on 4th January 1968. Still at Speke Junction, 92160 appeared on the last day of steam operation at Skelton Junction, 4th May 1968, carrying the headboard "Last Steamer on the CLC". By the end of May 1968 however, the remaining allocation had been withdrawn apart from 92160 which was sent to Carnforth.

Warrington was late in receiving its first allocation of 9Fs, 16 engines being transferred in March 1965 from the LMR Midland Division depots of Toton (7), Kettering (5) and Leicester Midland (4) as follows:

92048/9/53/5/8/9/70/8/86,
92116/9/24/6/56/60/3

The engines replaced Stanier Jubilee 4-6-0s which were either put into store or withdrawn. Warrington 9Fs could be observed on freights on the Ditton Junction-Broadheath line and also on the Tunstead-Runcorn ICI hoppers and the regular Arpley-Dewsnap (Guide Bridge) freights (see Appendix 1). Other workings included the Northenden-Purfleet "Presflo" cement empties on which 92055 was noted at New Mills Junction on 1st May. There were also frequent visits to the Chester area with general freight and also block oil tank workings.

Although reduced, the Warrington allocation still amounted to ten 9Fs on 1st January 1967:

92055/8/78, 92119/26/32/56, 92218/24/7

During the period March to October, however, the engines were either withdrawn or transferred to Speke Junction or Carlisle Kingmoor. Before transfer, 92058 took part in the RCTS Wrexham, Mold and Connah's Quay Centenary Tour of 29th April 1967, where on the return leg from Bidston to Crewe, the engine was reported as attaining a maximum of 64mph between Mouldsworth and Delamere.

The Carlisle area regularly saw Saltley Class 9Fs on the fitted freights from Birmingham beginning in the spring of 1957; before that in November 1955, 92023/50 were briefly stationed at Carlisle Kingmoor in connection with test runs to Kilmarnock. It was not until May and June 1964 however that several of the class were allocated to Carlisle Kingmoor. At the end of July, the following thirteen engines were on the books, displaced by diesels from Kettering, Newton Heath, and Toton:

92009/10/2/5/7/9/21/3/4,
92130, 92208/33/49

Among the first duties for Carlisle's 9Fs were the limestone traffic workings from the Hardendale quarry at Shap to the steel plant at Ravenscraig near Motherwell. Early sightings in Scotland were in June, with 92130 noted on 6th heading towards Mossend through Motherwell and on 24th, 92249 double-headed a northbound freight in tandem with A2 Pacific 60535 *Hornet's Beauty*, an engine previously more at home on the East Coast route but allocated to Polmadie from September 1963 until withdrawal in June 1965. Other 9F duties on the Caledonian Railway main line included fitted freights and parcels trains to Perth as well as to the Glasgow area. Later in August 1966, the engines had a regular block soda ash working twice weekly between Wallerscote (Cheshire) and Larbert; this train had usually been operated

Figure 165
Under the wires on 29th April 1967. 92058 (Warrington) heads north near Sandbach with an RCTS special, the Wrexham, Mold and Connah's Quay Centenary Tour.
(Courtney Haydon)

Figure 166
92058 clatters through Delamere on the W. M. & C. Q. special on 29th April 1967. *(John K. Morton)*

Figure 167
On Saturday 16th July 1960, 92018 (Wellingborough) is pulling out of Pontefract Baghill on the 7.25am York-Sheffield Midland stopper, extended to Bristol on summer Saturdays. The engine on this turn was usually a Stanier Jubilee 4-6-0 but occasionally produced a Class 5 4-6-0 or a 9F. 92018 was one of the engines used on the Toton-Brent accelerated mineral train trials in 1955, substituting for 92009 which 'retired hurt' with damaged motion after a serious bout of slipping at Kettering on one of the earlier runs. *(Peter Cookson)*

Figure 168
92049 (Saltley) rolls M298, the 8.20am (SO) Kings Norton-Scarborough down the 1 in 150 towards Pontefract Baghill on 30th August 1958. 92049 was still involved in passenger train working as late as November 1964, when it was reported on one occasion as having piloted an ailing BR Pacific 72006 *Clan Mackenzie* from Warrington to Crewe with the 8.05am Blackpool Central-Euston. *(Peter Cookson)*

Figure 169
New England's 92036 passes Stevenage with a northbound train of empty stock on 9th September 1961. Having completed a Heavy General overhaul with boiler change in the previous May, 92036 was later recorded as paying a visit to Eastleigh in September 1964 for an unspecified repair. The engine was withdrawn by the end of 1964 after ten years' service. *(C. R. Berridge)*

Figure 170
92001 (Bath Green Park) breasts Masbury summit at 3.17pm on 29th July 1961 with the ten-coach 9.35am Sheffield Midland to Bournemouth West. On this date, the train was an 'All-Standard' affair as power for the first leg from Sheffield to Bath was BR Class 5 4-6-0 73016 of Millhouses shed. 92001 had been fitted with a double chimney at Swindon Works in March 1960. *(E.W. Fry)*

Figure 171
Shortly before an 'official' LMR ban on the working of passenger trains by 9Fs 'except under unavoidable circumstances', 92154 (Wellingborough) heads up the Midland Main Line near Elstree & Borehamwood with the 8.55am (SO) Manchester Central-St. Pancras express on 12th September 1959. Almost all of the original LMR 9F allocation had been recorded on passenger work at some stage in their careers, as listed in Table 7.1. The main exceptions were some of the Crosti boiler engines and the mechanical stoker trio, 92165-7. 92154 was still defying officialdom as late as summer 1964 when as an Annesley engine it was rostered for several GC line holiday specials. *(Courtney Haydon)*

with Type 4 diesel power during the earlier part of the year.

Carlisle's 9Fs were also often used on empty coaching stock work; for example on the Saturday of August Bank Holiday weekend 1964, 92249 was observed at Law Junction in charge of one of several such workings in connection with the end of Glasgow Fair; similarly on the same date, 92015 spent part of the day on ecs duties at Glasgow Buchanan Street.

Despite the large amount of freight conveyed on the ex-G&SWR line to Glasgow via Dumfries, Carlisle's 9Fs were not regularly reported in use on this route. The 9Fs did appear in south west Scotland from time to time however on special workings. In August and September 1964, a new water main was being laid from south Ayrshire to serve new industries in the vicinity of Irvine New Town. On two successive Saturdays a train load of steel pipes was worked into Falkland Yard, Ayr for this purpose; the first visit of the class was by 92233 followed a week later by 92017. Other visits to the area included a former Crosti 92021 in October 1964 when it was observed at Ayr on a Stranraer-bound empty coaching stock special and an unidentified arrival at Stranraer with a sugar beet train from Carlisle in October 1966; on 17th of the same month, 92096 was observed on Ayr shed after working a mixed freight into Falkland Yard.

Towards the end of steam, Carlisle's 9Fs along with other class members from Lancashire depots became the mainstay of the principal heavy freight workings on the WCML between Carlisle and Crewe. The 9Fs were also used on freights to Lancashire and Cheshire via the Settle & Carlisle route. In the latter case, one of the class' main duties was the anhydrite traffic from the British Gypsum quarry at Long Meg (situated between Little Salkeld and Lazonby & Kirkoswald stations) to the United Sulphuric Acid Corporation's plant at Widnes on Merseyside, routed via Hellifield, Blackburn and Lostock Hall. These trains were made up to around twenty wagons with a trailing load of some 700 tons. 9Fs continued on the Long Meg workings for most of 1967; observations on 2nd June for example included 92056 and 92223 on the 9.20am and 1.15pm from Long Meg respectively whilst 92009 was noted on the 10.45am from Widnes. From 15th October, however, the anhydrite trains were dieselised on Sundays with the weekday trains soon following suit. 9Fs still appeared occasionally on extra workings and as substitutes for failed diesels; one example was 92233 which was observed on an up special on 29th November 1967. Carlisle's 9Fs were used on other freight duties on the Settle & Carlisle route, regularly featuring on the 1.30pm Leeds Hunslet-Carlisle fitted goods amongst others in 1967.

On the Waverley route from Carlisle to Edinburgh, it was reported in January 1965 that a new block oil train had commenced running from Milford Haven to Thornton (TuThSO). A diversity of motive power was used on this working, from an A4 Pacific to a Cl.47 Type 4 diesel with unidentified 9Fs noted on 16th and 21st of the month respectively. Carlisle-Millerhill freights also featured the 9Fs, a regular duty being the 1.35pm (SX) Class 'H' from Millerhill. During the last half of August, the 2.10pm to Millerhill had 92076 (20th), 92019 (24th) and 92130 (25th); 9Fs visiting Edinburgh were usually serviced at Haymarket. The class continued working several of these freights on a regular basis until the new year when a reorganisation of goods workings on the Waverley route was implemented on 31st January 1966. All surviving steam workings were eliminated at this time, their duties being rostered for Haymarket diesels of Type

Figure 172
92238 (Gloucester Horton Road) makes heavy weather of the 1 in 50 climb from Lyncombe Vale, Bath between Devonshire and Combe Down tunnels with the ten-coach (360tons gross) Warwickshire Railway Society 'Eastleigh via S&DJR Tour' on 12th June 1965. 92238 was suffering from a broken cylinder cover which meant a stop to raise steam at Binegar. An eight-minute late departure from Bath was followed by a 44-minute late arrival at Bournemouth Central.

(Hugh Ballantyne)

2 and Type 4 (Cl.40 and Cl.47).

On 1st January 1967, Kingmoor's allocation of 9Fs had reached 24 as shown:

92004/9/12/5/7/8/9/51/6/71/4/6/80/93/6,
92110/4/25/9/37, 92208/23/33/49

On 26th March, 92009 was observed on a rail tour returning from Carlisle to Glasgow via Dumfries, a speed of 66mph being reported at Gretna Junction. The (TuThO) Whitehaven-Gartsherrie freight was regularly hauled by either a 9F piloted by a Class 5 4-6-0 or by two Class 5 4-6-0s as late as May 1967. As the year progressed however, the 9Fs' duties were increasingly taken over by diesels, the twice weekly Wallerscote-Larbert soda ash train becoming Type 4-hauled in July and, as noted above, the Long Meg anhydrite traffic given over to diesels in the autumn. Although it was decreed that all steam penetration to the ScR should cease during August, 9Fs continued to appear at Mossend with one unidentified engine being noted there on 15th November 1967. By the last day of the year, Kingmoor's allocation of 9Fs had dwindled to six engines, 92004/9, 92218/23/33/49, the rest having been withdrawn. With no more suitable work available, these survivors were transferred to Carnforth (92004/9, 92223) and Speke Junction (92218/33/49) in January 1968.

One other depot to play host to 9Fs for a short period was Croes Newydd at Wrexham. In an effort to eliminate banking engines on the climb to the local steel works at Brymbo, Stanier Class 8Fs were tried out with 48165 and 48665 being observed on this traffic in December 1965. To test the possibility of tackling higher tonnage train loads, it was later decided to evaluate some redundant 9Fs on these duties and in due course (over the period May-August 1966), 92029/74 and 92125/35/7 arrived from Saltley. The 9Fs were not a success on the Brymbo traffic as although they were well able to handle the loads involved, their long wheel base caused problems with the permanent way, resulting in distortion of the track leading to partial derailment on some of the tighter curves; by the end of the year, all five had been transferred. Whilst at Croes Newydd the class had a hand in freights and oil tank traffic to Chester, Birkenhead and the Birmingham area.

Carnforth received its first 9Fs, displaced from Saltley and Tyseley by diesels, in November 1966 when 92087, 92118/28 and 92212 arrived. The engines were used on freights, both mineral and fitted, to the Leeds and Sheffield areas and also on the Heysham-Leeds Neville Hill oil tanker traffic. The depot continued to receive more 9Fs when other depots were either closed or could find no suitable work for their 9Fs; nine of the class 92004/9/16/77/88/91, 92160/7 and 92223 arrived from Birkenhead, Carlisle Kingmoor, Newton Heath and Speke Junction between March 1967 and May 1968, The depot could be considered a 'graveyard' posting for the class as none survived to be reallocated to other sheds, the last ones, 92077 and 92160/7 being withdrawn in June 1968.

The last duties for Carnforth's 9Fs were two oil tank workings, the 6.40am Heysham-Ecclesfield (Sheffield) and the 12.06pm Heysham-Leeds Neville Hill. These heavy trains were usually piloted and on 4th June 1968 for example, 92160 was on the 6.40am together with Stanier Class 5 4-6-0 45445 whilst 92167 was assisted by a Type 2 diesel on the 12.06pm. On the latter train, double-heading would be continued to Kirkstall where the Type 2 diesel would be detached and run light to Holbeck whilst the 9F went on to Neville Hill where it waited for the return working. The oil tanks were taken by pairs of diesel shunters to Hunslet East to discharge their load and then returned to Neville Hill for the trip back to Heysham. The 9Fs at Carnforth were not in the best of condition by this time. Indeed 92167 was reported to be running as a 2-8-2 for a short period before withdrawal, having managed to drop one of its connecting rods on a Neville Hill working on 12th June. On further examination, 92167's boiler was also found to be defective and the engine was condemned forthwith. 92160 thus remained the sole

Figure 173
Masquerading as a 2-8-0 (or is it a 2-2-2-2-2?), 92002 (Tyseley) is under repair at Stourbridge Junction on 25th July 1964. No mention of this repair has been traced on the Engine History and Record Cards. This is not unusual as comprehensive record keeping on all except works visits had virtually ceased for steam locomotives by this time. *(Courtney Haydon)*

survivor of the class in BR service and was itself withdrawn from Carnforth a few days later.

7.3 9F 2-10-0s on Passenger Work

As with many freight engine classes, the 9Fs were occasionally called on to assist when locomotive failures occurred on passenger workings. Early examples were 92031 coming to the rescue of A1 Pacific 60154 *Bon Accord* on the 11.50am Harrogate-Kings Cross at Biggleswade on 7th May 1955 and 92044 deputising for an L1 2-6-4 tank engine on the 10.52am Bishops Stortford-Cambridge on 7th September in the same year (see Section 7.1).

In the summer of 1957 however reports began to appear of the intentional rostering of 9Fs for passenger duties. The practice began on the LMR where, at the time before the era of widespread private car ownership and overseas package holidays, the heavy programme of summer Saturday holiday traffic from the Midlands and the north to the coastal resorts of Lancashire, north Wales, the West Country and the south frequently stretched motive power resources to the limit. Much unsuitable power such as Class 4F 0-6-0s was regularly pressed into service, often on quite heavy trains. On these occasions the steady increase in lost time inevitably led to chaotic operating situations at busy junctions when pathways were lost; the timetable, it was said, was all but abandoned at the height of the season at some locations. The use of 9Fs on this traffic began to occur on a regular basis within a few weeks of the inception of the 1957 summer timetable. One of the first of the class to be used was Crosti-boiler 92022 with the 3.02pm Sheffield Midland-York on 27th July. Later in August and into September, the LMR used 9Fs on passenger workings from the Leicester and Birmingham areas to Blackpool and to the south Devon coast as far as Bristol; similarly on the main line to St. Pancras, 9Fs were employed on several specials and excursions in August. Appearances were much fewer on the WCML, although later, Midlands-based 9Fs were used on through trains to the SR from the East Midlands to the Kent and Sussex coasts via Willesden Junction where SR power, usually 4-6-0, took over. The reserves of power held by the 9Fs helped to reduce the number of lost minutes booked to engines, and even allowed time to be regained in some cases, contributing to an overall improvement in punctuality during the summer of 1957.

The use of 9Fs ceased during the following months as the engines were not fitted with train heating apparatus. In summer 1958 however, the 9Fs were back in force on the weekend holiday traffic on the LMR. As an example, the observations by Mr J. B. Arnold in Table 7.2 record the appearances of the class at Baguley, Cheshire in 1958 on four summer Saturday holiday specials from Yorkshire or the East Midlands for which 9Fs were regularly rostered. The GCR route, much of which came under the control of the LMR in February 1958, also saw 9Fs on passenger duties as did the ECML from Kings Cross. On these routes, however, 9F activities were not confined to specials and excursions. The class put up startling performances on some prestigious trains such as "The Master Cutler" (Marylebone-Sheffield) on the GC route in July where 92164 was reported as reaching 86mph near Nottingham and an up Edinburgh express on the ex-GN line where 90mph was recorded with 92184 between Grantham and Kings Cross during August (see Section 11.3).

High speeds for 9Fs were reported also on freight as well

Figure 174
92123 (Leicester Midland) is undergoing a Light Casual overhaul at Crewe Works on 11th August 1963. When allocated to Wellingborough in 1958, 92123 was used several times on MML passenger work. The engine was later transferred to Birkenhead (April 1965) and withdrawn in October 1967 after less than eleven years' service. *(Mike Burnett)*

Table 7.1
BR Standard Class 9F 2-10-0s
Examples of Observations on Passenger Work

Engine	Allocated Depot	Date	Recorded Observation for whole or part of Journey
92000	Bristol Barrow Road	08.08.64	10.50am Exeter-Bradford Forster Square relief
92001	Tyseley	07.08.65	11.10am Bournemouth-Newcastle via GCR route
92002	Tyseley	20.08.66	10.54am Poole-Newcastle via GCR route
92003	Cardiff Canton	12.08.61	9.05am Swansea-Kingswear
92004	Bristol Barrow Road	28.01.61	am Cardiff-Portsmouth
92005	Cardiff Canton	13.08.60	train B78 Cardiff-Bristol
92006	Bath Green Park	09.09.61	9.25am Bournemouth-Manchester, Pines Express
92007	Severn Tunnel Junction	18.08.65	1.10pm Paddington-Wolverhampton Low Level (R)
92008	Saltley	24.08.57	3.50pm Bristol-Bradford Forster Square
92009	Saltley	15.08.59	8.50am Derby Midland-Llandudno
92010	Annesley	02.08.58	6.00am Nottingham Victoria-Marylebone
92011	Annesley	11.07.58	am Bradford Exchange-Marylebone, "South Yorkshireman"
92012	Annesley	Summer 1959.	GC line holiday reliefs
92013	Annesley	??.08.60	Marylebone-Leicester Central relief
92014	*	*	*
92015	Newton Heath	??.08.58	am Manchester Exchange-North Wales
92016	Newton Heath	28.06.58	am Manchester Victoria-Southport
92017	Newton Heath	18.06.60	am Todmorden-Southport excursion
92018	Wellingborough	19.08.61	12.25pm Manchester Central-St. Pancras (R)
92019	Wellingborough	05.09.59	am Sheffield Midland-Blackpool North excursion
92020	*	*	*
92021	*	*	*
92022	Wellingborough	27.07.57	3.02pm Sheffield Midland-York
92023	Wellingborough	04.11.61	8.21am Nottingham Midland-St. Pancras
92024	Wellingborough	05.08.57	8.25am Leicester London Road-Scarborough
92025	Wellingborough	09.08.58	12.37pm Newcastle-Bristol relief
92026	Saltley	08.04.61	pm Portsmouth-Bristol (4.15 pm ex-Salisbury)
92027	Wellingborough	03.01.61	10.05pm (02.01) Edinburgh Waverley-St. Pancras sleeper
92028	Saltley	01.09.64	7.30am Gloucester-Bristol local
92029	*	*	*
92030	Annesley	08.08.64	am Skegness-Leicester Central
92031	New England	07.05.55	11.50am Harrogate-Kings Cross (R)
92032	*	*	*
92033	Annesley	30.08.63	8.15am Nottingham Victoria-Marylebone
92034	New England	22.07.61	12.30pm Kings Cross-Newcastle (R)
92035	*	*	*
92036	New England	09.08.58	1.45pm Kings Cross-Peterborough
92037	*	*	*
92038	New England	22.02.61	Edinburgh Waverley-Kings Cross, "Night Scotsman" (R)
92039	*	*	*
92040	*	*	*
92041	New England	09.09.61	9.30am Glasgow Queen Street-Kings Cross (R)
92042	New England	23.07.60	10.56am Newcastle-Filey Holiday Camp relief
92043	*	*	*
92044	March	07.09.55	10.52am Bishops Stortford-Cambridge local
92045	*	*	*
92046	*	*	*
92047	*	*	*
92048	Saltley	03.08.57	11.55am Leicester London Road-Paignton
92049	Saltley	30.07.57	11.20am St.Pancras-Catterick Camp army cadet special
92050	Toton	10.08.57	8.50am Sheffield Midland-Blackpool North
92051	Saltley	04.08.58	6.55pm St. Pancras-Leicester London Road
92052	Toton	10.08.57	am Coalville-Blackpool North
92053	Wellingborough	23.07.60	am York-Marylebone special.
92054	Wellingborough	12.09.59	7.45am Paignton-Newcastle
92055	Toton	10.08.57	8.10am Sheffield Midland-Blackpool North
92056	Toton	10.08.57	4.45pm Bristol-Derby Midland
92057	Cricklewood	06.08.60	9.20am Bradford Forster Square-Paignton
92058	Wellingborough	13.10.59	5.30pm Bedford-St. Pancras
92059	Toton	29.07.61	9.55am Bournemouth West-Leeds (S&DJR section)
92060	*	*	*
92061	*	*	*
92062	*	*	*

Table 7.1
BR Standard Class 9F 2-10-0s
Examples of Observations on Passenger Work

Engine	Allocated Depot	Date	Recorded Observation for whole or part of Journey
92063	Tyne Dock	02.08.58	8.15am Newcastle-Heads of Ayr (to Carlisle)
92064	*	*	*
92065	*	*	*
92066	Tyne Dock	10.09.60	10.12am York-Yarmouth/Lowestoft
92067	Annesley	20.08.63	7.40am Nottingham Victoria-Rugby
92068	Annesley	21.04.64	5.15pm Nottingham Victoria-Marylebone
92069	Annesley	19.07.58	Bradford Exchange-Marylebone, "South Yorkshireman"
92070	Saltley	11.06.60	8.50am Derby Midland-Llandudno
92071	*	*	*
92072	*	*	*
92073	Annesley	19.09.59	am Blackpool-Glasgow St. Enoch relief (to Kilmarnock)
92074	*	*	*
92075	Annesley	08.08.58	Huddersfeld-Marylebone, "South Yorkshireman" relief
92076	Annesley	05.08.58	Bradford Exchange-Marylebone, "South Yorkshireman"
92077	Toton	11.07.59	7.30am Newcastle-Paignton
92078	Toton	30.07.57	am Dover-Sutton Park, Scouts Jamboree special, from Cricklewood
92079	Bromsgrove	*	Note: Lickey banker engine (May 1956-October 1963)
92080	Toton	05.08.57	8.15am St. Pancras-Nottingham Midland
92081	Wellingborough	30.07.60	9.50am Leicester London Road-Blackpool North
92082	Wellingborough	05.09.59	10.40am Sheffield Midland-Llandudno
92083	Birkenhead	24.08.65	am Nottingham Victoria-Marylebone
92084	Wellingborough	31.07.60	3.50pm Marylebone-Nottingham Victoria
92085	Birkenhead	07.05.65	8.15am Nottingham Victoria-Marylebone
92086	Wellingborough	30.08.56	St. Pancras-Glasgow St. Enoch, "Thames Clyde Express" (R)
92087	Annesley	30.09.60	Glasgow St. Enoch-St. Pancras, "Thames Clyde Express"
92088	Annesley	06.08.60	am Newcastle-Swansea via GCR route.
92089	Annesley	11.06.62	6.15pm Hucknall Central-Leicester Central (Air Display special)
92090	Annesley	??.07.58	am Nottingham Victoria-Ramsgate
92091	Speke Junction	14.10.67	Liverpool-Carlisle rail tour (L'pool-Preston & Hellifield-L'pool legs)
92092	Annesley	19.05.64	6.15pm Nottingham Victoria-Rugby
92093	Annesley	23.07.60	am Dundee-Marylebone special
92094	Annesley	23.08.58	Gloucester-Bristol local
92095	Annesley	26.07.58	8.35am Newcastle-Bournemouth via GCR route
92096	*	*	*
92097	Tyne Dock	10.04.65	RCTS North East Rail tour No. 2; Newcastle-Darlington via Consett
92098	*	*	*
92099	Tyne Dock	18.06.66	Alnmouth-Alnwick locals on last day of steam passenger service
92100	Leicester Midland	07.08.58	Chesterfield-Ashburys excursion (for Belle Vue Pleasure Park)
92101	Toton	24.08.57	5.25pm Birmingham New Street-Worcester
92102	Leicester Midland	15.08.59	am Filey-Kings Norton
92103	Leicester Midland	06.09.58	9.50am Leicester London Road-Blackpool North
92104	Leicester Midland	08.08.59	am Paignton-Bradford Forster Square relief
92105	Kettering	30.07.60	10.05am Bournemouth West-Derby Midland
92106	Kettering	03.08.57	10.50am Paignton-Nottingham Midland
92107	Wellingborough	10.08.57	9.50am Leicester London Road-Blackpool North
92108	Leicester Midland	04.04.61	10.30am Bradford Forster Square-St. Pancras
92109	Leicester Midland	10.08.57	2.20pm Blackpool North-Sheffield Midland
92110	Wellingborough	01.08.59	1.00am Leicester London Road-Portsmouth
92111	Cricklewood	??.08.58	up MML relief for St. Pancras
92112	Wellingborough	22.08.59	7.36am Sunderland-Bristol
92113	Westhouses	16.08.58	8.00am Sheffield Midland-Kingswear
92114	Westhouses	01.08.59	3.50pm Bristol-Bradford Forster Square relief
92115	Westhouses	09.07.60	pm W496 Colwyn Bay-Sheffield Midland
92116	Westhouses	21.06.58	10.10am Sheffield Midland-Bangor
92117	Westhouses	14.06.58	12.15pm Nottingham Midland-St. Pancras
92118	Saltley	25.08.62	12.45pm Bristol-Sheffield Midland
92119	Westhouses	23.08.58	6.22pm Euston-Bletchley local
92120	Saltley	05.09.59	10.15am Teignmouth-Bradford Forster Square
92121	Leicester Midland	09.08.58	9.50am Leicester London Road-Blackpool North
92122	Wellingborough	01.08.58	12.25pm Leicester London Road-St. Pancras relief
92123	Wellingborough	02.08.58	1.00am Leicester London Road-Portsmouth
92124	Wellingborough	02.06.60	8.15am Nottingham Midland-St. Pancras, "Robin Hood" (R)
92125	Wellingborough	04.07.58	8.30am Manchester London Road-Marylebone

Table 7.1
BR Standard Class 9F 2-10-0s
Examples of Observations on Passenger Work

Engine	Allocated Depot	Date	Recorded Observation for whole or part of Journey
92126	Wellingborough	02.08.57	10.30pm Leicester London Road-Paignton
92127	Wellingborough	23.07.60	8.00am Derby Midland-Bristol
92128	Leicester Midland	14.06.58	6.40am Leicester London Road-Paignton
92129	Toton	Summer 1958	St. Pancras line relief ?? (one single unconfirmed observation)
92130	Toton	26.07.58	7.30am M936 Swinton-Bangor relief
92131	Toton	17.08.57	8.10am Sheffield Midland-Blackpool North
92132	Annesley	15.08.64	10.48am Eastbourne-Sheffield Victoria via GCR route
92133	Saltley	25.08.57	Birmingham New Street-Nottingham Midland football special
92134	Wellingborough	16.08.58	10.22am Leicester London Road-St. Pancras
92135	Wakefield	25.03.67	Glasgow St. Enoch-St. Pancras, "Thames Clyde Express" relief (R)
92136	Saltley	29.08.59	10.55am Paignton-Nottingham Midland
92137	Saltley	06.08.60	3.00pm Derby Midland-Bristol
92138	Saltley	29.07.61	7.00am Cleethorpes-Sidmouth/Exmouth
92139	Saltley	14.06.58	6.35am Walsall-Kingswear
92140	*	*	*
92141	New England	03.07.64	am Manchester Exchange-Bangor special (running-in ex-Crewe)
92142	New England	11.08.57	9.50am St. Pancras-Glasgow, "Thames Clyde Express" relief
92143	New England	undated	train with Cl. A headlamps (at Milford Junction, Yorks ?)
92144	New England	17.08.58	7.15pm Kings Cross-Peterborough
92145	*	*	*
92146	*	*	*
92147	*	*	*
92148	New England	02.08.58	11.00am Kings Cross-Glasgow Queen Street (R)
92149	New England	18.07.59	10.40am Kings Cross-Newcastle
92150	Westhouses	21.06.58	10.40am Sheffield Midland-Llandudno
92151	Saltley	26.07.58	10.40am Sheffield Midland-Llandudno
92152	Saltley	15.07.61	9.55am Bournemouth-Leeds (S&DJR section)
92153	Toton	11.06.60	am Rotherham-Southport excursion
92154	Annesley	29.08.64	am Bradford Exchange-Poole via GCR route
92155	Saltley	15.06.58	am Cudworth-Blackpool North excursion
92156	Toton	18.07.58	St Pancras-Glasgow St. Enoch, "Thames Clyde Express" (R)
92157	Toton	14.06.58	8.00am Derby Midland-Bristol
92158	Toton	28.06.58	10.40am Sheffield Midland-Llandudno
92159	Wellingborough	??.07.59	am south west-north east holiday extra (via Derby and Sheffield)
92160	Kettering	08.08.64	am Torquay-Bradford Forster Square relief
92161	Newton Heath	28.06.58	2.10pm Rhyl-Oldham (Mumps)
92162	Newton Heath	28.06.58	am Kearsley-Rhyl (Bolton Wakes Week relief)
92163	Kettering	11.05.60	1.57pm Sheffield Midland-St. Pancras
92164	Leicester Midland	21.07.58	Bradford Exchange-Marylebone, "South Yorkshireman"
92165	*	*	*
92166	*	*	*
92167	*	*	*
92168	Doncaster	18.05.60	6.53am Kings Cross-Cambridge (R, propelled)
92169	Doncaster	13.09.58	9.30am South Shields-Manchester Victoria/Exchange
92170	Doncaster	28.08.59	7.20am Sheffield Victoria-Kings Cross "Master Cutler Pullman" (R)
92171	*	*	*
92172	Doncaster	30.08.58	10.20am Bristol-Newcastle
92173	Doncaster	13.10.58	down "morning Talisman" Kings Cross-Glasgow Queen Street (R)
92174	Doncaster	26.07.58	7.53am Filey Holiday Camp-Glasgow (to Newcastle) (R)
92175	Doncaster	22.08.59	8.30am Cardiff-Newcastle (via Birmingham New Street)
92176	Doncaster	29.06.63	am Glasgow Queen Street-Scarborough relief (from Newcastle)
92177	Doncaster	25.07.59	11.15am Newcastle-Llandudno
92178	New England	13.03.63	12.45pm Hull-Kings Cross (R) running tender first
92179	New England	22.08.58	7.25am Peterborough-Hitchin, then 9.28 am Hitchin-Kings Cross
92180	New England	30.07.60	9.20am South Shields-Kings Cross
92181	New England	13.03.63	12.45pm Hull-Kings Cross (see also 92178) (R)
92182	New England	19.08.61	10.40am Kings Cross-Newcastle
92183	New England	08.08.59	1.45pm Kings Cross-Peterborough
92184	New England	16.08.58	1.10pm Edinburgh-Kings Cross (from Grantham)
92185	*	*	*
92186	New England	17.08.58	pm Kings Cross-Newcastle (?)
92187	New England	25.07.59	am Kings Cross-Newcastle (?)
92188	*	*	*
92189	*	*	*

Table 7.1
BR Standard Class 9F 2-10-0s
Examples of Observations on Passenger Work

Engine	Allocated Depot	Date	Recorded Observation for whole or part of Journey
92190	Doncaster	23.08.58	1.45pm Kings Cross-Peterborough (?)
92191	Doncaster	06.08.60	4.30pm Marylebone-Nottingham
92192	*	*	*
92193	Doncaster	09.08.58	train 477 (relief to 8.35 am Newcastle-Bournemouth ?)
92194	*	*	*
92195	Doncaster	16.08.58	3.00pm Kings Cross-Newcastle
92196	Doncaster	??.08.58	1.45pm Kings Cross-Peterborough
92197	*	*	*
92198	*	*	*
92199	Doncaster	19.08.61	12.40pm Kings Cross-Leeds
92200	*	*	*
92201	*	*	*
92202	*	*	*
92203	Bristol St. Philips Marsh	15.08.59	1.25pm Paddington-Kingswear
92204	Bristol St. Philips Marsh	08.08.59	7.30am Penzance-Wolverhampton Low Level
92205	Bristol St. Philips Marsh	04.07.59	7.35am Plymouth-Paddington
92206	Eastleigh	26.08.61	10.32am Bournemouth West-Manchester Victoria (from Bath)
92207	Bristol St. Philips Marsh	27.06.59	9.20am Swansea-Brockenhurst
92208	Southall	13.08.60	9.05am Swansea-Kingswear
92209	Laira	03.07.59	7.55am (MFO) Camborne-Bristol
92210	Southall	06.04.64	10.20am Swansea-Paddington
92211	Feltham	??.06.63	5.05pm Southampton Terminus-Wimborne
92212	Tyseley	21.07.62	9.10am Birmingham Snow Hill-Penzance
92213	Banbury	11.08.62	11.40am Cardiff-Birmingham Snow Hill
92214	Bath Green Park	20.06.64	3.40pm Bournemouth-Bath
92215	Banbury	Summer 1960	Train with Cl. A headlamps at Bristol TM
92216	Cardiff Canton	13.08.60	7.30am Newcastle-Paignton
92217	Bristol St. Philips Marsh	18.06.60	2.25pm Paignton-Sheffield Midland
92218	Bristol St. Philips Marsh	23.07.60	7.55am Rotherham-Paignton relief
92219	Cardiff Canton	09.07.60	3.25pm Carmarthen-Cardiff
92220	Cardiff Canton	18.06.60	7.43am Cardiff-Paddington
92221	Laira	08.08.59	12.05pm Paddington-Plymouth
92222	Laira	11.07.59	11.00am Newquay-York
92223	Laira	05.09.59	8.05am Newquay-Newcastle
92224	Laira	20.06.59	10.20am Penzance-Swansea
92225	Laira	11.07.59	8.05am Newquay-Newcastle
92226	Banbury	15.08.59	10.40am Paddington-Paignton
92227	Cardiff Canton	21.07.62	pm Worcester-Gloucester local
92228	Banbury	22.08.66	4.38pm Marylebone-Nottingham Victoria
92229	Old Oak Common	15.08.59	3.45pm Paddington-Fishguard
92230	Old Oak Common	08.08.59	1.25pm Paddington-Kingswear
92231	Feltham	10.06.63	5.05pm Southampton Terminus-Wimborne
92232	Cardiff Canton	11.07.59	9.05am Swansea-Kingswear
92233	Cardiff Canton	01.08.59	9.30am Paignton-Swansea
92234	Birkenhead	05.03.67	enthusiasts' specials Birkenhead Woodside-Chester
92235	Cardiff Canton	08.08.59	Cardiff-Newquay
92236	*	*	*
92237	Cardiff Canton	20.08.60	8.30am Pembroke Dock-Birmingham Snow Hill
92238	Old Oak Common	09.07.60	12.40pm Newquay-Cardiff
92239	Old Oak Common	22.08.59	11.50am Paddington-South Wales relief
92240	Old Oak Common	08.08.59	8.48am Hastings-Wolverhampton Low Level
92241	Old Oak Common	06.08.60	10.40am Minehead-Paddington
92242	*	*	*
92243	Newport Ebbw Junction	29.07.61	9.05am Swansea-Kingswear
92244	Old Oak Common	08.08.59	9.00am Margate-Wolverhampton Low Level
92245	Old Oak Common	25.07.59	pm Paddington-Weston super Mare
92246	Old Oak Common	11.07.59	6.18pm Gloucester-Cardiff semi-fast
92247	Old Oak Common	22.08.59	9.10am Birmingham Snow Hill-Pembroke Dock
92248	Bristol Barrow Road	19.08.61	8.30am Paignton-Derby Midland relief
92249	Newport Ebbw Junction	04.07.59	6.53am Bassaleg -Paddington
92250	Severn Tunnel Junction	19.09.64	7.30am Gloucester-Bristol local

Key (R): Rescue engine *: no passenger workings traced

Figure 175
92122 is ex-works after a Heavy General overhaul at Crewe Works in April 1964. A Leicester Midland engine at the time, it was transferred to Birkenhead a year later and withdrawn in the 'Great Birkenhead 9F Cull' of November 1967.
(J. B. Arnold)

as passenger workings. One example was in the early 1960s when a 9F was apparently clocked at 86mph working a train of some 22 empty car-flats between Weaver Junction and Crewe.

Such speeds were viewed with a certain amount of uneasiness by the operating authorities. Ninety miles per hour for a 9F meant that its five foot diameter driving wheels were turning at 8.4 revolutions per second equating to a mean piston speed of 2,352 feet per minute, both figures very high in comparison with typical speeds recorded for express passenger designs. Appendix 2, 'Maximum Reported Speeds for Various Steam Locomotive Classes', compares data for driving wheel revolutions per second and mean piston speeds at the rail speeds quoted. It is noteworthy that for a 9F at 90mph, these figures are comparable with those achieved by the LNER A4 Pacific 4468 *Mallard* during its record breaking 126mph run down Stoke Bank in 1938, i.e. 8.82 driving wheel revs. per second and 2,293 feet per minute mean piston speed; it is perhaps worth noting that, unlike *Mallard*, the 9F did not have to be replaced before the train reached Kings Cross. These exploits inevitably resulted in increased piston ring and cylinder wear on the 9Fs involved. Further speeds of this magnitude were strongly discouraged and a maximum of 60mph decreed. In March 1959, the LMR even went as far as to ban the use of 9Fs on passenger work 'except in emergencies'. Nevertheless, 9Fs continued to feature on many LMR holiday specials in the summer of 1959, although ECML line appearances between Kings Cross and Newcastle were reported to be much reduced.

In summer 1959, the WR began to use its increased allocation of 9Fs on passenger duties. Engines newly delivered to Bristol St. Philips Marsh and Laira were provided as power for holiday specials serving the south Devon and Cornish resorts, in the latter case as far as Plymouth only; Cardiff Canton and Old Oak Common frequently supplied class members for holiday traffic from South Wales and Paddington. Freight engines had of course been regularly used by the WR on such work at busy summer weekends for many years. These were usually the 2-8-0s of the 47XX class but 28XX 2-8-0s, often South Wales-based, were also to be observed at peak times pounding up to Whiteball summit from Taunton with heavy trains for the south west.

In 1960, WR 9Fs were much less common on passenger work perhaps because of the exploits of 92220 *Evening Star* in the early weeks of the summer timetable. As noted earlier, the engine had been used by Cardiff Canton as a substitute for a failed Britannia Pacific on the up "Red Dragon" and down "Capitals United" express on 27th June; speeds in the eighties were reported and the engine kept good time. Further outings occurred in July and perhaps would have continued. However, the practice of using 92220 on these duties came to the attention of higher authority when on one occasion an unscheduled water stop was reported to have been made at Reading on an up service. The subsequent enquiry and the realisation that speeds in the eighties could be a regular requirement on such services in the event of operating delays resulted in a much restricted use of 9Fs on WR passenger work from then on.

One route on which the WR 9Fs were used from the summer of 1960 was the S&DJR which had become part of the region's remit in February 1958. The engines were particularly suited to hauling the heavy summer Saturday traffic over this undulating line and the authorities sanctioned their use on the route, confident that the maximum mph were rarely higher than the mid-sixties typical of some fast freight duties on which 9Fs were employed on other parts of the region and elsewhere.

LMR, ER and NER 9Fs could still be observed on holiday special work in 1960 and 1961. However, the advent of more diesel power allowed the reallocation of some express passenger steam classes to depots such as Saltley, generally reducing the incidence of the 9Fs on passenger workings on the LMR from about 1962 onwards. Similarly, the regular Westhouses and Toton 9F summer Saturday workings from Sheffield to north Wales were taken over by Brush Cl.31 Type 2 diesels in the summer 1962 timetable. One exception to this development was the GCR route where the class continued to be used on Marylebone-Nottingham services and through holiday specials to Bournemouth as late as 1966 (see Section 11.3 for a log of one such working).

On the SR in the summer of 1963, when five 9Fs were briefly allocated to Feltham, one of the regular duties for the 9Fs was reported to be the 5.05pm local passenger service from Southampton Terminus to Wimborne. It has not been possible to confirm whether the SR used any of the class on Bournemouth line holiday specials for the Midlands and north at this time.

Some examples of observations of 9Fs recorded on passenger duties are given in Table 7.1. It will be noted that some 206 individual engines (over 82% of the class) were traced as having made an appearance on a passenger train at least once in their short lives. Indeed it is likely that almost all were engaged in such work at some time, particularly the LMR and ER allocations. Rather than quote one of the many passenger workings for the various Bath Green Park (S&DJR) allocations in the 1960-65 period in Table 7.1, other sightings have been included where possible; the 9F passenger workings on the S&DJR are covered in Section 7.2.

There were several groups which appear to have missed out during the passenger working era. These were the engines normally confined to specific heavy freight work such as iron ore haulage. For the LMR trio at Bidston, 92045/6/7, no passenger workings have been discovered. Similarly for the ten NER Tyne Dock engines, 92060-66/97/8/9, there are several instances where no record of passenger work has been traced. It is perhaps not surprising that no reports have been forthcoming of the use of the Saltley-based mechanical stoker-fitted engines on passenger work as by the time they were released from the Carlisle freight turns, the heyday of 9F passenger work on the LMR was almost over.

Table 7.1 confirms that the 9F class was engaged on passenger work for most of its life and was a particular feature on the GCR route during 1965/6 in the run-up to its closure. In the years up to the summer of 1957, the 9Fs' appearances mainly involved being drafted as substitutes for failures whereas towards the end of steam the class was in demand for enthusiasts' specials. For almost the decade in between, 1957 until 1966 however, 9Fs were regularly rostered for timetabled passenger work and were well appreciated in the role by both crews and operating authorities alike; a truly versatile class.

7.4 Allocations

The 9Fs were allocated to a variety of MPDs and at one time or another could be observed anywhere between Perth, Plymouth, Fishguard and Thames Haven. Individual depots which had a 9F allocation at some point are listed below. Some depots were subject to a change in regional control when hosting the 9F class and have been quoted under both Regional owners where this occurred.

LMR

Annesley	Banbury
Bidston	Birkenhead
Bolton	Bromsgrove
Burton-upon-Trent	Carlisle Kingmoor
Carnforth	Cricklewood
Croes Newydd *	Derby
Grimesthorpe	Kettering
Kirkby-in-Ashfield	Leicester Midland
Newton Heath	Northampton
Rowsley	Saltley
Speke Junction	Toton
Tyseley	Warrington
Wellingborough	Westhouses
Willesden	Woodford Halse

Note : * Wrexham

ER

Annesley	Colwick
Darnall	Doncaster
Frodingham	Grantham
Immingham	Langwith Junction
March	Mexborough
New England	Staveley
Barrow Hill	Stratford

WR

Banbury	Bath Green Park
Bristol St. Philips Marsh	Bristol Barrow Road
Bromsgrove	Cardiff Canton
Cardiff East Dock	Gloucester Horton Rd
Laira	Neath
Newport Ebbw Jct.	Old Oak Common
Oxford	Pontypool Road
Severn Tunnel Jct.	Southall
Swindon	Tyseley
Westbury	

NER

Tyne Dock	Wakefield
York	

SR

Eastleigh	Feltham

Apart from the above locations, a number of 9Fs were nominally 'allocated' to either Rugby Testing Station or Swindon Test Plant at various times, see Section 11.1.

Full allocation history for the 9Fs is given in Table 7.3.

Figure 176
92085 (Kettering) approaches St. Albans City on 1st April 1961 with a London-bound coal train. Four months later, the engine received a Heavy General repair by which time, it had completed some 142,000 miles mainly on MML mineral workings. After withdrawal in December 1966, 92085 was purchased by Woodham Bros. and was a candidate for preservation. No viable scheme materialised however and the engine was cut up in July 1980. *(Courtney Haydon)*

Figure 177
92225 (Newport Ebbw Junction) undergoes a Heavy Casual repair at Swindon Works on 26th July 1964. Record cards indicate the engine had been out of action from January and would not be released to traffic for another month; lengthy stays in Swindon Works appear to have been the norm for the BR Standard classes; the adjacent 9F is probably 92223, which records indicate was in works during the same period. *(Courtney Haydon)*

Table 7.2
BR Standard Class 9F 2-10-0s
Summer Saturday Timetable 1958
Observations at Baguley (Cheshire)
Four Holiday Specials Regularly Rostered for BR Standard Class 9F 2-10-0 Power

Train	M5 8.50 am Sheffield Midland- Blackpool Central Usual load: 9 coaches 288 tons tare			M9 9.50 am Leicester (London Road)-Blackpool North Usual load: 9 coaches 288 tons tare			M66 10.10 am Sheffield Midland- Bangor Usual load: 10 coaches 320 tons tare			M78 10.40 am Sheffield Midland- Llandudno Usual load: 10 coaches 320 tons tare		
Date in 1958	Engine	Shed	Pass☆ Time	Engine	Shed	Pass☆ Time	Engine	Shed	Pass☆ Time	Engine	Shed	Pass☆ Time
14.06	92151	21A	10.22	†	†	†	†	†	†	†	†	†
21.06	92117	18B	10.25	†	†	†	92116	18B	11.57	92150	18B	12.13
28.06	92157	18A	10.26	†	†	†	92053	21A	11.40	92158	18A	12.08
05.07	92113	18B	10.21	92101	15C	12.43	92150	18B	11.43	92119	18B	12.09
12.07	†	†	†	92102	15C	12.45	†	†	†	†	†	†
19.07	92114	18B	10.21	92102	15C	12.46	†	†	†	†	†	†
26.07	92113	18B	10.18	92107	15A	12.49	92152	21A	11.55	92151	21A	12.06
02.08	92114	18B	10.18	92100	15C	12.49	†	†	†	92116	18B	12.08
09.08	92104	15C	10.21	92121	15C	12.51	92119	18B	11.41	92078	18A	12.43
16.08	92055	15A	10.18	92128	15C	12.48	92136	21A	11.38	92009	21A	12.17
23.08 ★	†	†	†	†	†	†	†	†	†	†	†	†
30.08	92120	18B	10.27	92128	15C	12.47	92136	21A	11.39	92114	18B	12.15
06.09	†	†	†	92103	15C	12.42	92056	15A	11.47	92164	15C	12.12

Notes:

☆ Passing times are for Skelton Junction
★ All services diverted from CLC route due to flooding at Northenden following previous afternoon's storm.
† Service either not observed, not 9F-powered or not running on that date.

Shed key:
15A Wellingborough; 15C Leicester Midland; 18A Toton; 18B Westhouses; 21A Saltley

Table 7.3
BR Standard Class 9F 2-10-0 Allocation History

92000 1.54 Newport Ebbw Junction; 6.61 Bath Green Park; 9.61 Banbury; 3.62 Old Oak Common; 7.62 Tyseley; 11.62 Bristol Barrow Road; 2.65 Gloucester Horton Road; 7.65 WR Store; 7.65 Withdrawn.

92001 1.54 Newport Ebbw Junction; 6.61 Bath Green Park; 11.61 Cardiff Canton; 6.62 Bath Green Park; 10.62 Oxford; 11.62 Tyseley; 2.66 LMR Store; 8.66 Tyseley; 10.66 Wakefield (O/L); 11.66 Wakefield; 1.67 Withdrawn.

92002 1.54 Newport Ebbw Junction; 5.63 Tyseley; 7.64 Banbury; 11.64 Tyseley; 11.66 Saltley; 12.66 Birkenhead; 11.67 Withdrawn.

92003 1.54 Newport Ebbw Junction; 11.58 Cardiff Canton; 9.62 Cardiff East Dock; 3.65 Withdrawn.

92004 1.54 Newport Ebbw Junction; 9.59 Cardiff Canton; 2.60 Southall; 11.60 Newport Ebbw Junction; 1.61 Bristol Barrow Road; 3.63 Banbury; 10.66 Carlisle Kingmoor; 1.68 Carnforth; 3.68 Withdrawn.

92005 2.54 Newport Ebbw Junction; 11.58 Cardiff Canton; 5.61 Newport Ebbw Junction; 9.63 York; 8.65 Withdrawn.

92006 2.54 Newport Ebbw Junction; 6.61 Bath Green Park; 9.61 Newport Ebbw Junction; 9.63 York; 10.66 Wakefield; 4.67 Withdrawn.

92007 2.54 Newport Ebbw Junction; 12.60 Bristol Barrow Road; 2.65 Gloucester Horton Road; 7.65 Cardiff East Dock; 7.65 Severn Tunnel Junction; 10.65 Gloucester Horton Road; 11.65 WR Store; 12.65 Withdrawn.

92008 3.54 Wellingborough; 6.57 Saltley; 11.59 Rowsley; 1.62 Toton (O/L); 2.62 Rowsley; 6.62 Saltley; 7.63 Rowsley; 4.64 Kirkby-in-Ashfield; 12.64 Speke Junction; 8.67 Warrington; 10.67 Withdrawn.

92009 3.54 Wellingborough; 6.57 Saltley; 9.57 Burton; 3.58 Saltley; 10.58 Annesley (O/L); 11.58 Saltley; 11.59 Rowsley; 6.62 Saltley; 7.62 Westhouses; 10.63 Rowsley; 4.64 Kettering; 6.64 Carlisle Kingmoor; 1.68 Carnforth; 3.68 Withdrawn.

92010 5.54 March; 1.57 Annesley; 3.63 Wellingborough; 6.63 Leicester Midland; 3.64 Newton Heath; 6.64 Carlisle Kingmoor; 4.66 Withdrawn.

92011 5.54 March; 9.55 New England; 5.57 Annesley; 8.65 Birkenhead; 11.67 Withdrawn.

92012 5.54 March; 9.55 New England; 5.57 Annesley; 7.63 Rowsley; 4.64 Kettering; 6.64 Carlisle Kingmoor; 10.67 Withdrawn.

92013 4.54 March; 4.54 Rugby Testing Station (O/L); 10.54 March; 1.57 Annesley; 10.59 Woodford Halse (O/L); 10.59 Annesley; 6.65 Banbury; 9.66 Saltley; 10.66 Withdrawn.

92014 18.5.54 March; 19.5.54 Willesden Exhibition (O/L); 6.54 March; 8.54 Stratford; 1.56 March; 2.57 Annesley; 4.60 Saltley; 9.60 Toton; 7.61 Cricklewood; 10.61 Annesley; 5.65 Birkenhead; 10.67 Withdrawn.

92015 9.54 Wellingborough; 10.54 Rugby Testing Station (O/L); 11.54 Wellingborough; 12.57 Saltley; 6.58 Newton Heath (O/L); 9.58 Newton Heath; 9.62 Bolton; 12.62 Newton Heath; 6.64 Carlisle Kingmoor; 4.67 Withdrawn.

92016 10.54 Wellingborough; 12.57 Saltley; 6.58 Newton Heath (O/L); 9.58 Newton Heath; 9.62 Bolton; 12.62 Newton Heath; 6.67 Carnforth; 10.67 Withdrawn.

92017 10.54 Wellingborough; 12.57 Saltley; 6.58 Newton Heath (O/L); 9.58 Newton Heath; 9.62 Bolton; 12.62 Newton Heath; 6.64 Carlisle Kingmoor; 12.67 Withdrawn.

92018 10.54 Wellingborough; 12.57 Cricklewood; 1.58 Wellingborough; 3.62 Rowsley; 4.64 Kirkby-in-Ashfield; 9.64 Newton Heath; 8.66 Carlisle Kingmoor; 4.67 Withdrawn.

92019 10.54 Wellingborough; 12.57 Cricklewood; 1.58 Wellingborough; 1.62 Toton; 3.62 Wellingborough; 3.62 Rowsley; 4.62 Wellingborough; 1.64 Kettering; 6.64 Carlisle Kingmoor; 6.67 Withdrawn.

92020 5.55 Wellingborough; 4.59 LMR Store; 3.61 Wellingborough; 10.63 Kirkby-in-Ashfield; 9.64 Speke Junction; 1.65 Birkenhead; 10.67 Withdrawn.

92021 5.55 Wellingborough; 4.59 LMR Store; 4.60 Wellingborough; 1.64 Kettering; 6.64 Carlisle Kingmoor; 7.65 Birkenhead; 11.67 Withdrawn.

92022 5.55 Wellingborough; 5.59 LMR Store; 3.62 Wellingborough; 7.63 Rowsley; 4.64 Kettering; 6.64 Newton Heath; 2.66 Speke Junction; 2.67 Birkenhead; 11.67 Withdrawn.

92023 5.55 Wellingborough; 5.55 Rugby Testing Station (O/L); 11.55 Carlisle Kingmoor (O/L); 12.55 Wellingborough; 4.59 LMR Store; 6.61 Wellingborough; 7.63 Kettering; 5.64 Carlisle Kingmoor; 7.65 Birkenhead; 11.67 Withdrawn.

92024 6.55 Wellingborough; 8.59 LMR Store; 1.60 Wellingborough; 1.64 Kettering; 5.64 Carlisle Kingmoor; 7.65 Birkenhead; 11.67 Withdrawn.

92025 6.55 Wellingborough; 4.59 LMR Store; 2.60 Wellingborough; 1.64 Kettering; 4.64 Annesley; 11.64 Speke Junction; 2.66 LMR Store; 2.66 Speke Junction; 9.66 LMR Store; 10.66 Speke Junction; 2.67 Birkenhead; 11.67 Withdrawn.

92026 6.55 Wellingborough; 3.61 Saltley; 4.61 Wellingborough; 7.63 Kettering; 11.63 Kirkby-in-Ashfield; 9.64 Newton Heath; 5.65 Birkenhead; 11.67 Withdrawn.

92027 6.55 Wellingborough; 4.59 LMR Store; 8.60 Wellingborough; 1.64 Kettering; 4.64 Annesley; 11.64 Speke Junction; 8.67 Withdrawn.

92028 7.55 Wellingborough; 8.59 LMR Store; 8.59 Wellingborough; 12.60 Kettering; 10.62 Saltley; 11.63 Birkenhead; 4.64 Saltley; 3.65 Banbury; 7.65 Saltley; 10.66 Withdrawn.

92029 7.55 Wellingborough; 6.59 LMR Store; 6.60 Wellingborough; 12.60 Kettering; 10.62 Saltley; 11.63 Birkenhead; 4.64 Saltley; 5.66 Croes Newydd; 8.66 Saltley; 12.66 Birkenhead; 11.67 Withdrawn.

92030 11.54 New England; 5.57 Annesley; 6.65 Banbury; 10.66 Saltley; 10.66 Wakefield (O/L); 11.66 Wakefield; 2.67 Withdrawn.

92031 11.54 March; 3.55 New England; 5.57 Annesley; 6.65 Westhouses; 6.65 LMR Store; 7.65 Newton Heath; 1.67 Withdrawn.

92032 11.54 March; 11.54 New England; 5.57 Annesley; 6.65 Kirkby-in-Ashfield; 6.65 LMR Store; 7.65 Birkenhead; 4.67 Withdrawn.

92033 11.54 March; 11.54 New England; 6.57 Annesley; 6.65 Banbury; 7.65 Northampton; 9.65 Withdrawn.

92034 12.54 New England; 1.59 Frodingham; 4.59 New England; 6.63 Immingham; 3.64 ER Store; 5.64 Withdrawn.

92035 12.54 New England; 1.59 Frodingham; 4.59 New England; 6.63 Immingham; 1.66 ER Store; 2.66 Withdrawn.

92036 12.54 New England; 9.62 Doncaster; 6.63 Colwick; 11.63 New England; 1.64 Colwick; 6.64 New England; 11.64 ER Store; 12.64 Withdrawn.

92037 12.54 New England; 6.63 Immingham; 1.65 ER Store; 2.65 Withdrawn.

92038 12.54 New England; 6.63 Immingham; 6.64 ER Store; 6.64 New England; 1.65 Langwith Junction; 4.65 Withdrawn.

92039 12.54 New England; 2.59 Immingham; 9.61 New England; 9.62 Doncaster; 6.63 Colwick; 11.63 Immingham; 6.64 Doncaster; 6.65 Langwith Junction; 10.65 Withdrawn.

92040 12.54 New England; 6.63 Colwick; 9.64 Staveley Barrow Hill; 1.65 Langwith Junction; 8.65 Withdrawn.

92041 12.54 New England; 6.63 Colwick; 9.64 Staveley Barrow Hill; 1.65 Langwith Junction; 8.65 Withdrawn.

92042 1.55 New England; 6.63 Colwick; 1.65 Langwith Junction; 10.65 Colwick; 12.65 Withdrawn.

92043 1.55 March; 2.57 Annesley; 6.65 LMR Store; (12.65 Burton but still officially in Store); 1.66 Carlisle Kingmoor; 7.66 Withdrawn.

92044 1.55 March; 6.57 New England; 9.62 Doncaster; 6.63 Colwick; 9.64 Staveley Barrow Hill; 1.65 Langwith Junction; 4.65 Withdrawn.

92045 2.55 Wellingborough; 2.56 Toton; 5.56 Bidston (O/L); 6.56 Bidston; 2.63 Birkenhead; 9.67 Withdrawn.

92046 2.55 Wellingborough; 2.56 Toton; 5.56 Bidston (O/L); 6.56 Bidston; 2.63 Birkenhead; 10.67 Withdrawn.

92047 2.55 Wellingborough; 8.55 Bidston (O/L); 6.56 Bidston; 2.63 Birkenhead; 11.67 Withdrawn.

92048 2.55 Wellingborough; 1.56 Toton; 6.57 Saltley; 11.59 Rowsley; 4.64 Toton; 3.65 Warrington; 5.65 Birkenhead; 9.67 Withdrawn.

92049 3.55 Wellingborough; 1.56 Toton; 6.57 Saltley; 11.59 Rowsley; 4.64 Toton; 3.65 Warrington; 12.65 LMR Store; 2.66 Birkenhead; 11.67 Withdrawn.

92050 8.55 Toton; 9.55 Rugby Testing Station (O/L); 11.55 M&EE Derby Works (O/L); 11.55 Carlisle Kingmoor (O/L); 12.55 Toton; 3.57 Rugby Testing Station (O/L); 5.57 Toton; 11.59 Saltley; 11.59 Rowsley; 4.64 Kirkby-in-Ashfield; 10.64 Newton Heath; 2.66 Speke Junction; 8.67 Warrington; 9.67 Withdrawn.

92051 8.55 Toton; 11.55 Wellingborough (O/L); 12.55 Toton; 6.57 Saltley; 11.59 Rowsley; 4.64 Kirkby-in-Ashfield; 10.64 Newton Heath; 12.65 Carlisle Kingmoor; 10.67 Withdrawn.

92052 8.55 Toton; 3.58 Wellingborough; 5.61 Saltley; 6.61 Toton; 10.61 Annesley (O/L); 3.62 Toton; 3.62 Rowsley; 4.62 Toton; 7.63 Rowsley; 7.63 Toton; 8.63 Wellingborough; 10.63 Kirkby-in-Ashfield; 10.64 Newton Heath; 6.67 Carlisle Kingmoor; 8.67 Withdrawn.

92053 9.55 Toton; 9.57 Burton; 3.58 Saltley; 11.59 Wellingborough; 9.62 Toton; 3.65 Warrington; 2.66 Withdrawn.

92054 9.55 Toton; 3.58 Wellingborough; 9.62 Leicester Midland; 12.62 Westhouses; 6.64 Carlisle Kingmoor; 6.64 Speke Junction; 2.66 LMR Store; 2.66 Speke Junction; 5.68 Withdrawn.

92055 9.55 Toton; 3.58 Wellingborough; 9.60 Toton; 3.61 Bidston (O/L); 4.61 Toton; 3.62 Rowsley; 4.62 Toton; 7.62 Wellingborough; 9.62 Toton; 3.65 Warrington; 12.65 LMR Store; 01.66 Warrington; 10.67 Speke Junction; 12.67 Withdrawn.

92056 10.55 Toton; 3.58 Wellingborough; 9.60 Toton; 3.62 Saltley; 5.62 Wellingborough; 9.62 Rowsley; 4.64 Kirkby-in-Ashfield; 10.64 Newton Heath; 8.66 Carlisle Kingmoor; 11.67 Withdrawn.

92057 10.55 Toton; 1.60 Westhouses; 5.60 Cricklewood; 10.61 Annesley; 4.63 Toton; 10.63 Saltley (O/L); 11.63 Saltley; 4.64 Birkenhead; 10.65 Withdrawn.

92058 10.55 Toton; 3.58 Wellingborough; 9.60 Toton; 7.62 Westhouses; 4.64 Leicester Midland; 3.65 Warrington; 6.67 Speke Junction; 8.67 Carlisle Kingmoor; 11.67 Withdrawn.

92059 10.55 Toton; 3.58 Wellingborough; 9.60 Toton; 3.65 Warrington; 5.65 Birkenhead; 9.66 Withdrawn.

92060 11.55 Tyne Dock; 12.55 Wellingborough (O/L) ; 3.56 Tyne Dock; 10.66 NER Store; 10.66 Withdrawn.

92061 11.55 Tyne Dock; 12.55 Wellingborough (O/L); 4.56 Tyne Dock; 9.66 Withdrawn.

92062 11.55 Tyne Dock; 12.55 Wellingborough (O/L); 2.56 Westhouses (O/L); 4.56 Tyne Dock; 6.66 Withdrawn.

92063 11.55 Tyne Dock; 12.55 Wellingborough (O/L); 2.56 Westhouses (O/L); 5.56 Tyne Dock; 11.66 Withdrawn.

92064 12.55 Tyne Dock; 12.55 Wellingborough (O/L); 2.56 Toton (O/L); 5.56 Tyne Dock; 11.66 Withdrawn.

92065 12.55 Tyne Dock; 12.55 Wellingborough (O/L); 2.56 Toton (O/L); 5.56 Tyne Dock; 11.66 Wakefield; 4.67 Withdrawn.

92066 12.55 Tyne Dock; 12.55 Wellingborough (O/L); 2.56 Toton (O/L); 5.56 Tyne Dock; 5.65 Withdrawn.

92067 12.55 Doncaster; 2.57 Annesley; 6.65 Banbury; 7.66 LMR Store; 10.66 Carlisle Kingmoor; 11.66 Withdrawn.

92068 12.55 Doncaster; 2.57 Annesley; 7.65 LMR Store; (12.65 Derby but still officially in Store); 1.66 Withdrawn.

92069 12.55 Doncaster; 2.57 Annesley; 5.65 Birkenhead; 11.67 Speke Junction; 5.68 Withdrawn.

92070 1.56 Doncaster; 2.57 Annesley; 4.60 Saltley; 9.60 Toton; 6.62 Westhouses; 3.63 Wellingborough; 5.63 Leicester Midland; 3.65 Warrington; 5.65 Birkenhead; 11.67 Withdrawn.

92071 1.56 Doncaster; 2.57 Annesley; 7.65 Newton Heath; 12.65 Carlisle Kingmoor; 11.67 Withdrawn.

92072 2.56 Doncaster; 2.57 Annesley; 6.65 Kirkby-in-Ashfield; 6.65 LMR Store; 1.66 Withdrawn.

92073 2.56 Doncaster; 2.57 Annesley; 6.65 Banbury; 9.66 Birkenhead; 11.67 Withdrawn.

92074 2.56 Doncaster; 2.57 Annesley; 6.65 Banbury; 12.65 Saltley; 5.66 Croes Newydd; 12.66 Carlisle Kingmoor; 4.67 Withdrawn.

92075 3.56 Doncaster; 2.57 Annesley; 4.63 Toton; 10.63 Annesley; 6.65 Kirkby-in-Ashfield; 6.65 LMR Store; 1.66 Kirkby-in-Ashfield; 3.66 Carlisle Kingmoor; 9.66 Withdrawn.

92076 3.56 Doncaster; 2.57 Annesley; 10.63 Rowsley; 4.64 Kirkby-in-Ashfield; 10.64 Newton Heath; 1.65 Carlisle Kingmoor; 2.67 Withdrawn.

92077 3.56 Toton; 8.63 Wellingborough (O/L); 10.63 Kirkby-in-Ashfield; 6.64 Newton Heath; 3.67 Carnforth; 6.68 Withdrawn.

92078 3.56 Toton; 3.65 Warrington; 5.67 Withdrawn.

92079 3.56 Toton; 5.56 Bromsgrove; 10.63 Birkenhead; 11.67 Withdrawn.

92080 4.56 Toton; 3.58 Wellingborough; 7.63 Kettering; 6.64 Newton Heath; 8.66 Carlisle Kingmoor; 5.67 Withdrawn.

92081 4.56 Toton; 12.58 Annesley; 4.59 Toton; 11.59 Saltley; 11.59 Wellingborough; 7.63 Kettering; 6.64 Newton Heath; 2.66 Withdrawn.

92082 5.56 Wellingborough; 1.62 Toton (O/L); 3.62 Wellingborough; 2.63 Annesley; 2.63 Saltley; 11.63 Birkenhead; 11.67 Withdrawn.

92083 5.56 Wellingborough; 11.60 Annesley (O/L); 3.61 Wellingborough; 2.63 Annesley; 3.63 Wellingborough; 1.64 Kettering; 10.64 Leicester Midland; 1.65 Annesley; 5.65 Birkenhead; 2.67 Withdrawn.

92084 5.56 Wellingborough; 1.64 Kettering; 9.64 Speke Junction; 1.65 Birkenhead; 11.67 Withdrawn.

92085 5.56 Wellingborough; 12.60 Kettering; 10.62 Saltley; 11.63 Tyseley; 9.64 Willesden; 12.64 Birkenhead; 12.66 Withdrawn.

92086 6.56 Wellingborough; 1.64 Kettering; 10.64 Leicester Midland; 3.65 Warrington; 6.65 Birkenhead; 11.67 Withdrawn.

92087 8.56 Doncaster; 2.57 Annesley; 6.65 Banbury; 7.65 Northampton; 9.65 Tyseley; 11.66 Carnforth; 2.67 Withdrawn.

92088 10.56 Doncaster; 2.57 Annesley; 5.63 Toton; 8.63 Annesley; 6.65 Toton; 6.65 LMR Store; 7.65 Birkenhead; 11.67 Carnforth; 4.68 Withdrawn.

92089 9.56 Doncaster; 3.57 Annesley; 2.63 Leicester Midland; 9.64 Speke Junction; 1.65 Birkenhead; 2.67 Withdrawn.

92090 11.56 Doncaster; 3.57 Annesley; 5.65 Birkenhead; 5.67 Withdrawn.

92091 11.56 Doncaster; 3.57 Annesley; 7.65 Speke Junction; 2.66 LMR Store; 2.66 Speke Junction; 5.68 Carnforth; 5.68 Withdrawn.

92092 12.56 Doncaster; 3.57 Annesley; 5.65 Birkenhead; 10.66 Withdrawn.

92093 1.57 Doncaster; 3.57 Annesley; 6.65 Kirkby-in-Ashfield; 6.65 LMR Store; 1.66 Carlisle Kingmoor; 9.67 Withdrawn.

92094 2.57 Doncaster; 3.57 Annesley; 12.58 Toton; 4.59 Annesley; 5.65 Birkenhead; 11.67 Speke Junction; 5.68 Withdrawn.

92095 3.57 Annesley; 6.65 Kirkby-in-Ashfield; 6.65 LMR Store; 5.66 Warrington; 10.66 Withdrawn.

92096 4.57 Annesley; 10.65 LMR Store; (12.65 Derby but still officially in Store); 1.66 Carlisle Kingmoor; 2.67 Withdrawn.

92097 6.56 Tyne Dock; 10.66 Withdrawn.

92098 7.56 Tyne Dock; 7.66 Withdrawn.

92099 7.56 Tyne Dock; 9.66 Withdrawn.

92100 7.56 Toton; 3.58 Leicester Midland; 12.59 Toton; 1.60 Westhouses; 3.63 Wellingborough; 5.63 Leicester Midland; 4.65 Birkenhead; 5.67 Withdrawn.

92101 8.56 Toton; 3.58 Leicester Midland; 1.60 Wellingborough; 4.60 Leicester Midland; 4.65 Birkenhead; 10.67 Withdrawn.

92102 8.56 Toton; 3.58 Leicester Midland; 4.65 Birkenhead; 11.67 Withdrawn.

92103 8.56 Toton; 3.58 Leicester Midland; 4.65 Birkenhead; 5.67 Withdrawn.

92104 8.56 Toton; 3.58 Leicester Midland; 4.62 Westhouses; 12.64 Speke Junction; 5.65 Birkenhead; 2.67 Withdrawn.

92105 9.56 Wellingborough; 11.56 Kettering; 3.63 Wellingborough; 1.64 Kettering; 10.64 Leicester Midland; 4.65 Birkenhead; 1.67 Withdrawn.

92106 9.56 Wellingborough; 11.56 Kettering; 10.64 Leicester Midland; 4.65 Birkenhead; 7.67 Withdrawn.

92107 9.56 Wellingborough; 12.61 Saltley; 11.63 Banbury; 9.64 Willesden; 12.64 Birkenhead; 2.67 Withdrawn.

92108 10.56 Wellingborough; 11.56 Cricklewood; 4.59 Wellingborough; 3.60 Leicester Midland; 2.62 Wellingborough; 9.62 Leicester Midland; 4.65 Birkenhead; 11.67 Withdrawn.

92109 10.56 Toton; 3.57 Saltley; 6.57 Wellingborough; 8.57 Leicester Midland; 11.63 Annesley; 4.64 Leicester Midland; 4.65 Birkenhead; 11.67 Withdrawn.

92110 10.56 Toton; 11.56 Cricklewood; 4.59 Wellingborough; 3.60 Leicester Midland; 7.62 Wellingborough; 9.62 Leicester Midland; 11.63 Kirkby-in-Ashfield; 9.64 Newton Heath; 5.65 Carlisle Kingmoor; 12.67 Withdrawn.

92111 11.56 Cricklewood; 4.59 Wellingborough; 3.60 Leicester Midland; 11.63 Kirkby-in-Ashfield; 9.64 Speke Junction; 1.65 Birkenhead; 10.67 Withdrawn.

92112 11.56 Cricklewood; 4.59 Wellingborough; 3.60 Leicester Midland; 7.62 Wellingborough; 7.62 Leicester Midland; 4.65 Birkenhead; 11.67 Withdrawn.

92113 11.56 Westhouses; 6.60 Toton; 3.61 Bidston (O/L); 4.61 Toton; 4.62 Rowsley; 2.64 Wellingborough; 2.64 Toton; 10.64 Annesley; 6.65 Westhouses; 6.65 LMR Store; 7.65 Birkenhead; 10.67 Withdrawn.

92114 11.56 Westhouses; 6.60 Toton; 4.62 Rowsley; 4.64 Kirkby-in-Ashfield; 9.64 Newton Heath; 5.65 Carlisle Kingmoor; 7.67 Withdrawn.

92115 12.56 Westhouses; 6.64 Carlisle Kingmoor; 6.64 Speke Junction; 2.66 Withdrawn.

92116 12.56 Westhouses; 3.63 Wellingborough; 2.64 Kettering; 3.65 Warrington; 11.66 Withdrawn.

92117 12.56 Westhouses; 10.61 Annesley; 3.62 Westhouses; 3.62 Rowsley; 4.62 Wellingborough; 2.64 Kettering; 10.64 Speke Junction; 12.67 Withdrawn.

92118 12.56 Westhouses; 11.59 Wellingborough; 1.62 Saltley; 7.64 Banbury; 11.64 Tyseley; 11.66 Carnforth; 5.68 Withdrawn.

92119 1.57 Westhouses; 1.59 Cricklewood; 4.59 Leicester Midland; 3.65 Warrington; 6.67 Speke Junction; 6.67 Birkenhead (O/L); 8.67 Carlisle Kingmoor; 9.67 Withdrawn.

92120 1.57 Westhouses; 10.58 Annesley (O/L); 11.58 Westhouses; 12.58 Saltley; 11.59 Wellingborough; 3.60 Leicester Midland; 11.60 Annesley; 10.61 Leicester Midland; 4.65 Birkenhead; 7.67 Withdrawn.

92121 2.57 Wellingborough; 3.57 Saltley; 6.57 Wellingborough; 8.57 Leicester Midland; 4.65 Birkenhead; 7.67 Withdrawn.

92122 2.57 Wellingborough; 3.60 Leicester Midland; 7.62 Wellingborough; 9.62 Leicester Midland; 4.65 Birkenhead; 11.67 Withdrawn.

92123 2.57 Wellingborough; 3.60 Leicester Midland; 4.65 Birkenhead; 10.67 Withdrawn.

92124 3.57 Wellingborough; 2.64 Kettering; 3.65 Warrington; 12.66 Withdrawn.

92125 3.57 Wellingborough; 12.60 Kettering; 11.63 Saltley (O/L); 12.63 Saltley; 5.66 Croes Newydd; 12.66 Carlisle Kingmoor; 12.67 Withdrawn.

92126 3.57 Wellingborough; 2.64 Kettering; 3.65 Warrington; 8.67 Withdrawn.

92127 3.57 Wellingborough; 7.63 Rowsley; 4.64 Kirkby-in-Ashfield; 10.64 Speke Junction; 1.65 Birkenhead; 8.67 Withdrawn.

92128 4.57 Toton; 3.58 Leicester Midland; 6.62 Saltley; 7.64 Banbury; 9.66 Saltley; 11.66 Carnforth; 11.67 Withdrawn.

92129 4.57 Saltley; 6.57 Toton; 7.59 Kettering; 2.60 Toton; 5.60 Cricklewood; 10.61 Annesley; 12.61 Saltley; 7.64 Banbury; 7.66 LMR Store; 9.66 Carlisle Kingmoor; 7.67 Withdrawn.

92130 4.57 Saltley; 6.57 Toton; 5.64 Carlisle Kingmoor; 6.66 Withdrawn.

92131 4.57 Saltley; 6.57 Toton; 1.60 Westhouses; 12.64 Speke Junction; 5.65 Birkenhead; 9.67 Withdrawn.

92132 4.57 Saltley; 12.57 Wellingborough; 2.64 Kettering; 2.64 Annesley; 6.65 Banbury; 8.65 Northampton; 9.65 Banbury; 2.66 LMR Store; 8.66 Warrington; 10.67 Carlisle Kingmoor; 10.67 Withdrawn.

92133 5.57 Saltley; 12.57 Wellingborough; 2.64 Leicester Midland; 4.65 Birkenhead; 7.67 Withdrawn.

92134 5.57 Saltley; 12.57 Wellingborough; 2.64 Leicester Midland; 4.65 Birkenhead; 12.66 Withdrawn. Preserved.

92135 6.57 Saltley; 5.66 Croes Newydd; 10.66 Wakefield (O/L); 11.66 Wakefield; 6.67 Withdrawn.

92136 6.57 Saltley; 10.66 Withdrawn.

92137 6.57 Saltley; 8.66 Croes Newydd; 12.66 Carlisle Kingmoor; 9.67 Withdrawn.

92138 6.57 Saltley; 8.66 Speke Junction; 7.67 Withdrawn.

92139 6.57 Saltley; 12.66 Speke Junction; 8.67 Carlisle Kingmoor; 9.67 Withdrawn.

92140 7.57 New England; 1.65 Langwith Junction; 4.65 Withdrawn.

92141 7.57 New England; 9.62 Doncaster; 3.63 New England; 1.65 Langwith Junction; 10.65 Colwick; 12.65 Withdrawn.

92142 7.57 New England; 12.64 ER Store; 2.65 Withdrawn.

92143 8.57 New England; 1.65 ER Store; 2.65 Withdrawn.

92144 8.57 New England; 9.62 Immingham; 3.63 New England; 1.65 Langwith Junction; 3.65 ER Store; 4.65 Langwith Junction; 10.65 Colwick; 12.65 Withdrawn.

92145 8.57 New England; 1.65 Langwith Junction; 10.65 Colwick; 12.65 Immingham; 2.66 Withdrawn.

92146 9.57 New England; 1.65 Langwith Junction; 10.65 Colwick; 12.65 Doncaster; 4.66 Withdrawn.

92147 9.57 New England; 3.63 Immingham; 4.65 Withdrawn.

92148 9.57 New England; 6.60 Immingham; 9.61 New England; 3.63 Doncaster; 6.63 Colwick; 9.64 Staveley Barrow Hill; 1.65 Langwith Junction; 10.65 Colwick; 12.65 Withdrawn.

92149 10.57 New England; 1.65 Langwith Junction; 3.65 ER Store; 4.65 Langwith Junction; 6.65 Withdrawn.

92150 10.57 Westhouses; 2.59 Saltley; 5.64 Tyseley; 6.64 Saltley; 10.66 Wakefield (O/L); 11.66 Wakefield; 4.67 Withdrawn.

92151 10.57 Saltley; 11.66 Birkenhead; 4.67 Withdrawn.

92152 10.57 Saltley; 11.66 Birkenhead; 11.67 Withdrawn.

92153 10.57 Toton; 10.63 Westhouses; 6.65 Speke Junction; 1.66 LMR Store; 7.66 Speke Junction; 1.68 Withdrawn.

92154 10.57 Wellingborough; 5.58 Annesley (O/L); 9.58 Wellingborough; 2.64 Annesley; 6.65 Kirkby-in-Ashfield; 6.65 LMR Store; 7.65 Speke Junction; 7.67 Withdrawn.

92155 11.57 Saltley; 8.66 Speke Junction; 11.66 Withdrawn.

92156 11.57 Toton; 3.65 Warrington; 7.67 Withdrawn.

92157 11.57 Toton; 2.59 Saltley; 4.64 Birkenhead; 8.67 Withdrawn.

92158 11.57 Toton; 9.63 Westhouses; 6.64 Speke Junction; 7.66 Withdrawn.

92159 11.57 Wellingborough; 12.58 Cricklewood; 12.58 Wellingborough; 2.64 Rowsley; 4.64 Kirkby-in-Ashfield; 9.64 Newton Heath; 5.65 Birkenhead; 7.67 Withdrawn.

92160 11.57 Wellingborough; 9.58 Kettering; 3.65 Warrington; 12.65 LMR Store; 2.66 Birkenhead; 11.67 Speke Junction; 5.68 Carnforth; 6.68 Withdrawn.

92161 12.57 Westhouses; 6.58 Newton Heath (O/L) 9.58 Newton Heath 5.65 Carlisle Kingmoor; 12.66 Withdrawn.

92162 12.57 Westhouses; 6.58 Newton Heath (O/L); 9.58 Newton Heath; 5.65 Birkenhead; 11.67 Withdrawn.

92163 3.58 Kettering; 6.59 Leicester Midland; 11.59 Kettering; 3.65 Warrington; 6.65 Birkenhead; 11.67 Withdrawn.

92164 4.58 Leicester Midland; 6.62 Saltley; 7.66 Withdrawn.

92165 4.58 Saltley; 6.62 Bidston; 2.63 Birkenhead; 11.67 Speke Junction; 3.68 Withdrawn.

92166 5.58 Saltley; 9.58 Rugby Testing Station (O/L); 5.59 Saltley; 9.59 Cardiff Canton (O/L); 10.59 Newport Ebbw Junction (O/L); 2.60 Saltley; 6.62 Bidston (O/L); 7.62 Bidston; 2.63 Birkenhead; 11.67 Withdrawn.

92167 5.58 Saltley; 5.62 Tyne Dock (O/L); 10.62 Saltley; 12.62 Bidston (O/L); 1.63 Bidston; 2.63 Birkenhead; 11.67 Carnforth; 6.68 Withdrawn.

92168 12.57 Doncaster; 6.65 Withdrawn.

92169 12.57 Doncaster; 3.64 ER Store; 5.64 Withdrawn.

92170 12.57 Doncaster; 1.64 ER Store; 5.64 Withdrawn.

92171 2.58 Doncaster; 11.63 New England; 4.64 ER Store; 5.64 Withdrawn.

92172 1.58 Doncaster; 4.66 Withdrawn.

92173 2.58 Doncaster; 6.65 Langwith Junction; 10.65 Colwick; 12.65 Doncaster; 3.66 Withdrawn.

92174 2.58 Doncaster; 12.65 Withdrawn.

92175 2.58 Doncaster; 2.64 ER Store; 5.64 Withdrawn.

92176 3.58 Doncaster; 11.63 New England; 2.64 ER Store; 5.64 Withdrawn.

92177 3.58 Doncaster; 2.64 ER Store; 5.64 Withdrawn.

92178 9.57 New England; 11.57 Swindon Testing Plant (O/L); 3.58 New England; 1.65 Langwith Junction; 8.65 ER Store; 10.65 Withdrawn.

92179 10.57 New England; 1.65 Langwith Junction; 4.65 ER Store; 5.65 Langwith Junction; 10.65 Colwick; 11.65 Withdrawn.

92180 11.57 New England; 1.65 Langwith Junction; 4.65 Withdrawn.

92181 11.57 New England; 1.65 ER Store; 2.65 Withdrawn.

92182 12.57 New England; 1.65 Langwith Junction; 10.65 Colwick; 12.65 Doncaster; 4.66 Withdrawn.

92183 12.57 New England; 6.63 Colwick; 1.65 Doncaster; 4.66 Withdrawn.

92184 1.58 New England; 1.59 Frodingham; 6.59 New England; 6.63 Colwick; 11.63 New England; 1.64 Immingham; 1.65 ER Store; 2.65 Withdrawn.

92185 1.58 New England; 6.63 Colwick; 11.63 New England; 1.64 Immingham; 1.65 ER Store; 2.65 Withdrawn.

92186 1.58 New England; 6.63 Colwick; 1.65 Doncaster; 6.65 Langwith Junction; 8.65 Withdrawn.

92187 2.58 New England; 6.58 Grantham; 9.58 New England; 6.63 Colwick; 1.65 ER Store; 2.65 Withdrawn.

92188 2.58 New England; 6.58 Grantham; 9.58 New England; 6.63 Colwick; 1.65 ER Store; 2.65 Withdrawn.

92189 3.58 Mexborough; 3.58 Grimesthorpe; 4.58 Darnall; 5.58 Doncaster; 1.59 Frodingham; 4.59 Doncaster; 9.63 Colwick; 1.65 Langwith Junction; 10.65 Colwick; 10.65 ER Store;12.65 Withdrawn.

92190 3.58 Mexborough; 4.58 Darnall; 5.58 Doncaster; 1.59 Frodingham; 4.59 Doncaster; 9.63 Colwick; 6.64 Doncaster; 10.65 ER Store; 10.65 Withdrawn.

92191 4.58 Darnall; 5.58 Doncaster; 9.63 Colwick; 1.65 Langwith Junction; 10.65 Colwick; 12.65 Withdrawn.

92192 5.58 Doncaster; 9.63 Colwick; 11.63 Frodingham; 1.65 ER Store; 2.65 Withdrawn.

92193 5.58 Doncaster; 2.59 Immingham; 5.64 ER Store; 6.64 Immingham; 6.65 Withdrawn.

92194 6.58 Doncaster; 2.59 Immingham; 12.65 Withdrawn.

92195 6.58 Doncaster; 2.59 Immingham; 5.64 ER Store; 6.64 New England; 1.65 Langwith Junction; 5.65 Withdrawn.

92196 8.58 Doncaster; 2.59 Immingham; 10.64 ER Store; 12.64 Withdrawn.

92197 9.58 Doncaster; 2.59 Frodingham; 4.59 Doncaster; 9.60 Immingham; 9.65 Withdrawn.

92198 10.58 Doncaster; 2.59 Frodingham; 6.59 Doncaster; 9.63 Colwick; 11.63 Frodingham; 6.64 ER Store; 8.64 Withdrawn.

92199 10.58 Doncaster; 9.63 Colwick; 11.63 Frodingham; 6.64 ER Store; 8.64 Withdrawn.

92200 11.58 Doncaster; 9.63 Immingham; 6.64 Doncaster; 6.65 Langwith Junction; 10.65 Withdrawn.

92201 12.58 Doncaster; 9.63 Immingham; 6.64 Doncaster; 3.66 Withdrawn.

92202 12.58 Doncaster; 4.59 Immingham; 12.65 Withdrawn.

92203 4.59 Bristol St. Philips Marsh; 6.60 Bath Green Park; 9.60 Old Oak Common; 3.63 Banbury; 9.66 Birkenhead; 11.67 Withdrawn. Engine preserved.

92204 4.59 Bristol St. Philips Marsh; 6.60 Bath Green Park; 9.60 Southall; 11.60 Old Oak Common; 3.63 Banbury; 9.63 Tyseley; 8.66 Speke Junction; 12.67 Withdrawn.

92205 5.59 Bristol St. Philips Marsh; 6.60 Bath Green Park; 9.60 Westbury; 12.60 SR O/L; 1.61 Eastleigh; 5.63 Feltham; 9.63 York; 10.66 Wakefield; 5.67 NER Store; 6.67 Withdrawn.

92206 5.59 Bristol St. Philips Marsh; 6.60 Bath Green Park; 9.60 Westbury; 12.60 SR O/L; 1.61 Eastleigh; 5.63 Feltham; 9.63 York; 10.66 Wakefield; 5.67 Withdrawn.

92207 6.59 Bristol St. Philips Marsh; 2.60 Southall; 11.64 Newport Ebbw Junction; 12.64 Withdrawn. Engine preserved.

92208 6.59 Laira; 3.60 Southall; 12.61 Cardiff Canton; 9.62 Cardiff East Dock; 10.63 Newton Heath; 6.64 Carlisle Kingmoor; 11.67 Withdrawn.

92209 6.59 Laira; 8.59 Cardiff Canton; 5.61 Newport Ebbw Junction; 9.63 Cardiff East Dock; 5.65 WR Store; 6.65 Southall; 7.65 Cardiff East Dock; 7.65 Severn Tunnel Junction; 10.65 Bristol Barrow Road; 11.65 Bath Green Park; 12.65 Withdrawn.

92210 8.59 Cardiff Canton; 9.60 Bristol Barrow Road; 7.62 Bath Green Park; 8.62 Cardiff Canton; 9.62 Cardiff East Dock; 12.63 Southall; 5.64 Newport Ebbw Junction; 11.64 Withdrawn.

92211 9.59 Old Oak Common; 6.61 Westbury; 7.61 SR O/L; 7.61* Eastleigh; 5.63 Feltham; 9.63 York; 10.66 Wakefield; 5.67 Withdrawn. * Some sources suggest official confirmation delayed until 12.62.

92212 9.59 Banbury; 6.61 Bath Green Park; 9.61 Newport Ebbw Junction; 7.62 Tyseley; 11.66 Carnforth; 1.68 Withdrawn. Engine preserved.

92213 10.59 Bristol St Philips Marsh; 11.59 Banbury; 10.66 Carlisle Kingmoor; 11.66 Withdrawn.

92214 10.59 Cardiff Canton; 11.59 Banbury; 12.61 Newport Ebbw Junction; 5.64 Bath Green Park; 6.64 Newport Ebbw Junction; 7.64 Severn Tunnel Junction; 7.65 WR Store; 8.65 Withdrawn. Engine preserved.

92215 11.59 Banbury; 9.63 Tyseley; 10.66 Wakefield (O/L); 11.66 Wakefield; 5.67 NER Store; 6.67 Withdrawn.

92216 12.59 Cardiff Canton; 9.62 Cardiff East Dock; 10.63 Neath; 9.64 Southall; 8.65 Severn Tunnel Junction; 10.65 Withdrawn.

Figure 179
92077 languishes at its home shed, Kirkby-in-Ashfield on 8th February 1964. This was one of the last three members of the class in service, being withdrawn from Carnforth with 92160 and 92167 in June 1968, two months before the end of steam on BR. 92077 was fitted with AWS apparatus a year earlier complete with protective plate behind the coupling link. *(Courtney Haydon)*

The availability of mileage figures for the 92100-39 and 92150-64 batches at the Heavy General stage is limited. Reference to Table 11.16 accompanying Section 11.2 however confirms that by the end of 1960, the average figures per engine ('000s) were 114.2 for the former batch and 91.0 for the latter batch.

The Crosti-boilered engines, 92020-9 were a special case, entering and re-entering Crewe Works for various adjustments and modifications (see Section 9.2) resulting in a lower annual average mileage than the standard-boilered engines before their first major repair. The 'availability for work' figures were lower in the case of the Crostis compared with the conventional 9Fs. This is attributed in part to their extra time on works and in part to the fact that they were almost universally disliked by crews who apparently took every opportunity to fail them in favour of a non-Crosti alternative of almost any class of comparable power rating. Eventually, the Crostis were converted to the standard boiler arrangement, having achieved just under 81,000 miles on average before the conversion carried out under a variety of designations, from LC to HG. Thereafter 92020-9 were treated in the same way as the standard engines in overhaul scheduling. Few mileage figures for the Crostis at the second major repair stage have been traced. With reference to data available up to mid-1961 however, an estimate has been made based on an average of 25,000 per year after conversion; this indicates a cumulative average mileage of around 125,000 to second major repair.

Data on the trio of 9Fs, 92165-7, fitted with the Berkley mechanical stokers, is incomplete with very little mileage information. No reference to a heavy overhaul for 92167 has been traced, although 92165/6 were recorded respectively as having a Light Intermediate (from April 1965) and a Heavy Casual (from April 1964) overhaul at Crewe. The mechanical stokers were removed from the trio in the period November 1962-January 1963 at Crewe during what was termed Light Casual overhauls.

For the ER allocation, the story is similar to that for the LMR engines. The first major overhaul, usually Light Intermediate, was again undertaken at between two and a half and three and a half years after delivery. Mileages run by this time were of the same order as on the LMR although in the case of the 92168-92202 batch the average is almost 100,000 miles. This probably reflected the use of the class by the ER on longer distance fast fitted freights for a greater proportion of their time compared with the main LMR duties which were mainly slow heavy mineral workings.

General overhauls for the ER-based engines were carried out between four and six years after delivery with mileages again similar to those achieved by the LMR allocation. By the time general overhauls were due for the 92168-92202 batch, only three, 92177/83/9, had been completed at Darlington according to the official record before the LMR was assigned ongoing responsibility for the role, the work being undertaken at Crewe.

The ten 9Fs allocated to the NER, 92060-6 and 92097-9, were also repaired at Darlington. Heavy Intermediate or General overhauls were carried out between three and four years after delivery but average mileages up to this time were generally lower than on the ER and LMR as their main duties

Table 8.2
BR Standard Class 9F 2-10-0s: Record of Repairs

NOTE: See end of Table for key to column headings

No.	1	2	3	4	5
92000	U	S	20.10.54 - 05.11.54	15	★
	'U	Ej	22.09.55 - 11.11.55	44	★
	U	S	03.05.56 - 10.05.56	07	★
	U	S	01.08.56 - 08.08.56	07	★
	LC	S	06.10.56 - 18.12.56	59	★
	'U	Ej	24.02.59 - 18.03.59	20	★
	HG	S	11.08.59 - 03.03.60	176	78.6
	'U	Ba	04.10.61 - 08.11.61	31	★
	'U	Ba	31.01.62 - 17.02.62	16	★
	'LC	Go	12.11.62 - 25.01.63	65	★
	'***HC***	C	31.01.63 - 09.03.63	33	143.2
	'LC	Br	30.07.63 - 28.10.63	77	★
	'U	Br	30.12.63 - 22.01.64	21	157.9
	'U	Br	30.05.64 - 02.07.64	29	★
92001	'U	Ej	25.07.55 - 26.08.55	29	★
	LC	S	09.09.57 - 14.10.57	31	★
	HI	S	28.09.59 - 20.04.60	177	79.4
	LC	Cy	17.02.61 - 10.03.61	19	★
	'U	Cc	06.12.61 - 04.01.62	25	★
	'U	Ty	13.05.63 - 28.06.63	41	★
	HI	C	27.05.64 - 28.08.64	81	★
	LC	C	03.05.65 - 04.06.65	29	★
92002	'U	S	12.05.54 - 09.09.54	104	★
	'U	Ej	08.11.55 - 05.01.56	51	★
	LC	S	25.01.57 - 21.05.57	103	★
	LC	S	04.11.58 - 20.01.59	69	★
	'U	Ej	19.03.59 - 06.04.59	16	★
	'U	Ej	28.07.59 - 18.08.59	18	★
	HG	S	20.07.60 - 01.12.60	116	85.7
	'U	Dy	23.12.62 - 28.03.63	83	★
	'U	Ty	01.05.63 - 24.05.63	21	★
	HC	C	13.09.63 - 23.10.63	35	★
	CL	C	25.03.64 - 14.05.64	44	★
	★	C	02.65	★	★
	★	C	04.66	★	★
	★	C	07.65	★	★
92003	U	S	29.10.54 - 18.11.54	18	★
	U	Ej	05.01.56 - 15.02.56	36	★
	LC	S	14.05.57 - 31.07.57	68	41.1
	CR	S	13.11.58 - 09.03.59	108	★
	U	Ej	07.10.59 - 31.10.59	22	★
	'U	So	20.11.59 - 08.12.59	16	★
	HG	S	07.09.60 - 10.01.61	108	92.3
	LC	Cy	25.06.62 - 06.07.62	11	★
	'U	Oo	04.02.63 - 05.04.63	53	★
	'LC	S	28.11.63 - 20.12.63	21	160.0
	'U	Ce	03.04.64 - 15.05.64	37	★
92004	U	S	03.11.54 - 17.01.55	65	★
	U	S	16.03.55 - 25.03.55	09	★
	'U	Ej	16.02.56 - 10.03.56	21	★
	HC	S	30.10.56 - 18.02.57	97	★
	CR	Cy	11.10.57 - 25.10.57	13	★
	HI	S	18.03.59 - 07.09.59	149	69.2
	'LC	W	04.03.61 - 12.05.61	60	★
	LC	E	03.01.62 - 27.01.62	22	123.6
	'U	Br	30.05.62 - 14.06.62	14	★
	'U	Br	11.10.62 - 27.10.62	15	★
	CA	C	05.11.64 - 23.12.64	42	★
	★	C	??.10.66 - ??.11.66	★	★
92005	★	S	??.11.54 - 05.12.54	★	★
	'U	Ej	14.03.56 - 28.03.56	13	★
	CR	S	24.07.57 - 14.10.57	71	★
	'U	Ej	12.11.57 - 05.12.57	21	★
	HI	S	15.12.59 - 20.05.60	136	92.4
	'U	Cc	21.09.60 - 14.10.60	21	★
	'U	Cc	06.05.62 - 24.05.62	16	★
	'U	Ej	27.07.62 - 31.08.62	31	★
	'U	Ej	02.04.63 - 01.05.63	26	★
	'U	Gl	17.05.63 - 31.05.63	13	★
	★	C	09.65	★	★
92006	★	S	10.54	★	★
	'U	Ej	15.03.56 - 18.05.56	56	★
	LC	S	09.11.57 - 13.12.57	30	★
	'U	Ej	24.10.58 - 08.11.58	14	★
	'U	Ej	20.12.58 - 08.01.59	17	★
	HG	S	23.02.60 - 21.09.60	182	91.3
	'U	Ej	21.08.62 - 06.09.62	15	★
	'U	Ej	10.12.62 - 23.02.63	66	★
	'U	Ej	01.07.63 - 29.07.63	25	★
	U	C	11.09.64 - 23.01.65	116	★
	I	C	06.08.65 - 02.10.65	50	★
92007	'U	Ej	17.10.55 - 08.11.55	20	★
	'U	Ej	16.02.56 - 15.03.56	25	★
	LC	S	31.12.56 - 12.04.57	89	★
	'U	Ej	27.01.58 - 14.02.58	17	★
	HI	S	04.05.59 - 08.10.59	136	73.1
	'U	Ej	01.09.60 - 19.09.60	16	★
	'LC	Cy	24.03.61 - 28.04.61	31	★
	'U	Br	30.10.61 - 20.12.61	45	★
	'LC	C	21.01.63 - 21.03.63	52	★
	'U	Oo	13.12.63 - 30.01.64	42	164.6
92008	NR	C	08.03.54 - 15.03.54	07	0.1
	NM	C	01.06.54 - 17.06.54	15	4.7
	LC	C	23.08.54 - 01.09.54	09	10.0
	LI	C	12.11.57 - 06.12.57	26	92.9
	HG	C	11.10.60 - 05.11.60	23	174.3
	LC	C	10.10.63 - 15.11.63	32	★
	LC	C	14.02.64 - 13.03.64	25	★
	LC	C	09.10.64 - 27.11.64	41	★
	LC	C	13.05.65 - 27.05.65	13	★
92009	NC	C	12.05.54 - 28.05.54	15	3.8
	NR	De	25.01.55 - 01.02.55	07	18.8
	NC	C	25.07.55 - 12.08.55	17	35.6
	LI	C	01.05.57 - 05.06.57	31	75.7
	HG	C	13.03.59 - 16.04.59	30	132.8
	HC	C	30.01.61 - 10.03.61	35	191.0
	★	W	??.61	★	★
	LC	C	19.02.63 - 16.03.63	23	★
	LC	C	18.07.63 - 24.08.63	33	★
	HI	C	05.03.65 - 03.04.65	26	★
	HC	C	06.04.66 - 21.05.66	40	★
	★	C	11.66	★	★
92010	LC	C	05.10.54 - 02.12.54	51	9.3
	BQ	St ?	08.57	★	★
	'LI	C	11.06.58 - 17.07.58	32	90.6
	'LC	Ru	25.03.59 - 10.04.59	15	123.7
	'***HG***	C	11.03.61 - 05.05.61	48	203.3
	★	C	05.63	★	★
92011	BQ	St	08.57	★	★
	G	Da	19.09.57 - 09.11.57	45	75.8
	'LC	C	14.10.58 - 06.12.58	47	112.9
	'LC	C	15.12.59 - 29.01.60	40	151.2
	★	C	12.63	★	★
	★	C	07.65	★	★
92012	LC	C	03.03.55 - 16.04.55	39	15.0
	G/BQ	Da	07.06.57 - 01.08.57	48	★
	NC	Da	13.01.58 - 14.01.58	02	★
	LI	C	27.10.58 - 22.11.58	24	117.4
	HC	C	09.01.61 - 15.02.61	33	205.5
	HG	C	29.10.62 - 23.11.62	23	★
	★	C	05.64	★	★
	HI	C	19.10.65 - 04.12.65	41	★
92013	LC	Da	22.04.55 - 26.05.55	30	17.0
	BQ	St	06.08.56 - 06.08.56	01	★
	'HG	C	23.06.58 - 19.09.58	77	78.8
	'NC	C	20.04.59 - 05.06.59	41	107.6
	'***HG***	C	09.09.61 - 23.10.61	38	185.6
	★	C	11.63	★	★
	★	C	04.65	★	★
	★	C	01.66	★	★

Table 8.2
BR Standard Class 9F 2-10-0s: Record of Repairs

No.	1	2	3	4	5
92014	LC	St	12.55	★	★
	LC	Ma	11.56	★	★
	CL	Da	01.03.57 - 27.03.57	23	70.4
	BQ	St	28.05.57 - 28.05.57	01	★
	G	Da	23.10.57 - 10.12.57	42	85.5
	LC	C	29.09.58 - 18.10.58	17	121.5
	LC	C	22.01.59 - 21.02.59	27	131.5
	LC	Go	16.08.60 - 10.09.60	23	179.5
	LC	Go	10.01.62 - 10.02.62	28	★
	NR	Go	05.03.62 - 24.03.62	18	★
	HG	C	25.07.63 - 13.09.63	44	★
92015	LI	C	09.10.57 - 09.11.57	28	76.9
	HG	C	02.11.59 - 05.12.59	30	130.6
	CL	Go	30.01.63 - 28.03.63	50	★
	HI	C	04.01.65 - 06.02.65	30	★
92016	LI	C	02.12.57 - 28.12.57	24	88.5
	HC	C	10.11.60 - 16.12.60	32	158.2
	HG	C	27.10.61 - 05.12.61	34	★
	LC	C	29.05.64 - 23.07.64	44	★
	LI	C	15.03.66 - 16.04.66	28	★
92017	LC	C	03.02.56 - 06.03.56	28	31.2
	LI	C	25.03.58 - 25.04.58	28	86.2
	HG	C	19.04.60 - 19.05.60	27	137.6
	★	W	01.61	★	★
	HC	C	14.11.61 - 12.12.61	25	★
	LI	C	18.03.65 -25.04.65	33	★
	LC	C	26.05.66 - 21.06.66	23	★
92018	LC	C	17.04.56 - 19.05.56	29	35.7
	LI	C	03.06.58 - 24.06.58	19	89.7
	HC	C	04.05.60 - 10.06.60	33	141.7
	LC	C	21.12.60 - 21.01.61	28	159.4
	HG	C	24.11.61 - 30.12.61	32	★
	LI	C	11.08.65 - 17.09.65	33	★
92019	HI	C	26.09.57 - 26.10.57	27	80.5
	TU	Ds	24.10.58 - 06.11.58	12	★
	HG	C	13.05.60 - 16.06.60	30	★
	CL	Go	03.09.62 - 09.11.62	59	★
	HI	C	19.10.64 - 05.12.64	42	★
92020	NC	C	19.07.55 - 20.09.55	55	0.2
	NC	C	17.11.55 - 18.11.55	02	3.9
	NC	C	22.11.55 - 28.11.55	05	4.4
	LC	C	13.03.56 - 05.04.56	21	10.9
	LC	C	05.10.56 - 01.11.56	24	21.7
	HC	C	25.06.57 - 03.08.57	35	37.2
	LI	C	06.08.58 - 11.09.58	32	61.5
	NC	C	24.09.58 - 29.09.58	05	62.1
	HG	C	27.03.61 - 07.06.61	63	70.1
	LC	C	08.01.63 - 07.02.63	27	★
	LC	C	25.07.63 - 17.08.63	20	★
	LI	C	10.01.66 - 26.02.66	42	★
92021	LC	C	04.11.55 - 28.11.55	22	8.5
	LC	C	23.03.56 - 01.05.56	34	15.8
	LC	C	28.08.56 - 27.09.56	27	21.2
	LC	C	07.08.57 - 24.08.57	16	39.7
	HI	C	10.09.58 - 08.10.58	26	62.0
	LC	C	26.04.60 - 07.06.60	36	68.6
	LC	De	19.11.60 - 09.02.61	73	83.2
	HG	C	15.06.62 - 29.09.62	92	★
	I	C	24.06.65 - 12.08.65	43	★
92022	LC	C	16.01.56 - 09.02.56	22	9.8
	LC	C	22.03.57 - 17.04.57	23	37.4
	HI	C	12.06.58 - 04.07.58	20	60.0
	HC	C	03.04.62 - 20.06.62	68	★
	HI	C	10.05.65 - 16.06.65	33	★
92023	LC	C	05.01.56 - 01.02.56	24	8.7
	LC	C	25.09.56 - 17.10.56	20	23.2
	LC	C	10.01.57 - 02.02.57	21	27.6
	CR	C	11.03.57 - 30.03.57	18	28.5
	LC	C	05.09.57 - 28.09.57	21	37.8
	HI	C	05.09.58 - 29.09.58	21	59.6

No.	1	2	3	4	5
92023	***HC***	C	19.06.61 - 27.09.61	87	69.8
(cont.)	LC	C	16.09.63 - 26.10.63	36	★
	LI	C	05.05.65 - 02.06.65	25	★
	LC	C	25.11.65 - 01.01.66	33	★
92024	NR	C	30.12.55 - 04.02.56	32	10.0
	LC	C	10.04.56 - 09.05.56	26	14.1
	HC	C	07.03.57 - 10.04.57	30	36.1
	LC	C	02.58	★	★
	HI	C	01.05.58 - 14.06.58	39	61.5
	LC	C	12.12.58 - 21.01.59	35	71.8
	HC	C	29.12.59 - 20.02.60	47	88.0
	HG	C	13.10.61 - 16.11.61	30	★
	LC	C	27.08.63 - 20.09.63	22	★
	LC	C	06.12.63 - 15.01.64	35	★
	HC	C	02.09.64 - 14.10.64	37	★
	LI	C	26.05.65 - 25.06.65	27	★
92025	NC	C	06.06.55 - 07.07.55	28	0.1
	LC	C	02.12.55 - 29.12.55	24	10.9
	LC	C	02.08.56 - 15.10.56	65	27.5
	LC	C	19.09.57 - 19.10.57	27	47.8
	LI	C	10.02.60 - 08.04.60	51	67.5
	HG	C	20.10.61 - 16.01.62	76	★
	LI	C	22.04.65 - 04.06.55	38	★
92026	LC	C	15.11.55 - 30.12.55	40	9.7
	HC	C	04.01.57 - 30.01.57	23	35.1
	LC	C	14.08.57 - 11.09.57	25	48.3
	HI	C	28.02.58 - 02.04.58	29	58.5
	LC	C	15.06.59 - 11.09.59	77	81.4
	LC	C	17.10.60 - 18.11.60	29	110.2
	HG	C	22.06.62 - 06.10.62	92	★
	★	C	05.64	★	★
	LC	C	09.02.66 - 26.03.66	41	★
92027	NC	C	18.11.55 - 03.12.55	16	9.9
	LC	C	27.02.56 - 16.03.56	17	15.2
	HC	C	21.02.57 - 22.03.57	26	38.3
	LI	C	07.01.58 - 08.02.58	29	58.3
	LC	C	28.08.60 - 15.10.60	42	91.4
	HG	C	30.08.62 - 27.10.62	51	★
	LC	C	29.04.65 - 31.05.65	28	★
92028	LC	C	14.12.55 - 08.02.56	49	★
	LC	C	16.04.57 - 16.05.57	27	★
	LC	C	18.10.57 - 09.11.57	25	★
	HI	C	25.06.58 - 12.08.58	42	★
	LC	C	02.09.59 - 03.12.59	80	100.3
	HG	C	16.01.62 - 20.02.62	31	★
	LC	C	03.04.64 - 14.05.64	36	★
	LC	E	10.09.64 - 07.10.64	24	★
92029	NC	C	19.07.55 - 20.09.55	55	★
	LC	C	23.01.56 - 23.02.56	28	★
	LC	C	01.03.57 - 30.03.57	26	★
	LC	C	02.02.59 - 25.02.59	23	79.2
	HC	C	03.06.60 - 06.08.60	56	★
	HG	C	06.06.62 - 16.08.62	62	★
	T	C	18.08.65 - 30.09.65	38	★
92030	NC	Da	13.06.57 - 19.06.57	05	★
	BQ	St	26.07.57 - 26.07.57	01	★
	LI	Da	17.01.58 - 20.02.58	30	94.8
	AD	Da	03.03.58 - 03.03.58	01	★
	LC	C	17.04.59 - 14.05.59	24	141.2
	NC	De	15.12.60 - 20.12.60	05	187.3
	'HG	C	26.06.61 - 11.08.61	44	199.0
	HC	C	07.02.62 - 16.03.62	33	★
	HC	C	10.04.64 - 20.05.64	35	★
	HC	C	20.08.65 - 30.09.65	36	★
92031	LC	C	12.01.55 - 26.02.55	40	2.7
	CR	Da	24.06.55 - 14.07.55	24	14.1
	BQ	St	30.05.57 - 30.05.57	01	★
	LI	C	07.07.58 - 27.08.58	45	97.1
	HG	C	28.04.61 - 31.05.61	29	204.9
	NR	C	16.11.61 - 29.11.61	12	★

Table 8.2
BR Standard Class 9F 2-10-0s: Record of Repairs

No.	1	2	3	4	5
92031	HI	C	31.12.63 - 31.01.64	28	★
(cont.)	NR	C	06.02.64 - 19.02.64	12	★
92032	NC	Da	06.06.57 - 13.06.57	07	★
	BQ	St	29.07.57 - 31.07.57	03	★
	'LI	C	18.03.58 - 18.04.58	28	95.7
	'LC	Ru	27.01.59 - 13.02.59	14	131.3
	'LC	C	29.07.59 - 18.09.59	45	150.9
	'HG	C	20.05.60 - 06.08.60	68	178.8
	'LC	C	13.06.61 - 07.08.61	48	224.9
	★	C	02.64	★	★
	★	C	04.65	★	★
	★	C	01.66	★	★
92033	NC	St	19.07.55 - 21.07.55	03	★
	NC	St	17.10.55 - 18.10.55	02	★
	NC	Da	24.05.57 - 29.05.57	05	★
	BQ	St	12.08.57 - 12.08.57	01	★
	LI	C	06.05.58 - 30.05.58	22	94.3
	'LC	Ru	06.02.59 - 20.02.59	13	124.2
	HG	C	04.08.60 - 03.09.60	27	170.3
	LC	C	06.01.61 - 01.02.61	23	179.2
	LC	C	11.05.61 - 06.06.61	23	191.6
	LC	C	26.04.62 - 25.05.62	26	★
	LC	C	24.01.63 - 28.02.63	31	★
	NC	C	02.09.65 - ??	★	★
92034	NC	Da	10.08.55 - 23.09.55	38	★
	NC	Da	10.05.57 - 16.05.57	06	★
	LI	Da	23.06.57 - 23.08.57	54	67.5
	NC	Da	09.10.59 - 17.10.59	08	★
	HG	Da	15.09.60 - 04.11.60	44	157.6
	LC	Da	01.06.62 - 14.08.62	64	209.9
	★	C	12.63	★	★
92035	NC	Da	01.05.57 - 06.05.57	05	★
	LI	Da	22.08.57 - 03.10.57	37	82.3
	LC	Da	03.06.58 - 04.07.58	28	101.3
	NC	Da	07.12.59 - 11.12.59	05	★
	HG	Da	29.06.60 - 25.08.60	50	159.7
	AD	Da	14.09.60 - 05.10.62	19	★
	LC	C	04.04.63 - 15.05.63	36	250.4
	CR	C	11.03.64	★	★
92036	CR	Da	07.05.55 - 23.05.55	14	10.5
	NC	Da	02.04.57 - 08.04.57	06	★
	LI	Da	26.03.58 - 02.05.58	33	94.5
	NC	Da	17.11.59 - 27.11.59	10	★
	LC	Da	27.01.60 - 17.03.60	44	158.6
	HG	Da	01.03.61 - 22.04.61	46	183.8
	AD	Da	15.05.61 - 19.05.61	05	
	★	E	09.64	★	★
92037	LC	Da	03.12.55 - 03.12.55	01	27.6
	BQ	Da	18.03.57 - 21.03.57	04	★
	LI	Da	22.01.58 - 13.03.58	44	88.4
	NC	Da	18.09.59 - 28.09.59	09	★
	HG	Da	19.08.60 - 29.10.60	62	164.1
	★	C	02.61	★	★
	LC	C	10.09.63 - 22.10.63	37	★
92038	LI	Da	05.02.58 - 28.03.58	45	90.1
	NC	Da	12.01.60 - 20.01.60	08	★
	HG	Da	28.04.60 - 03.06.60	32	167.4
	AD	Da	27.06.60 - 29.06.60	03	★
	LC	C	19.11.62 - 04.01.63	41	249.2
92039	NC	Da	09.02.57 - 15.02.57	06	★
	LI	Da	12.09.57 - 19.10.57	33	77.7
	NC	Da	06.05.59 - 13.05.59	07	★
	NC	Da	17.08.59 - 26.08.59	09	★
	HG	Da	02.12.60 - 04.02.61	56	168.2
	AD	Da	05.04.61 - 22.04.61	15	★
	W	Do	24.07.61 - 24.07.61	01	★
92040	LI	Da	13.12.57 - 31.01.58	50	87.8
	NC	Da	02.12.59 - 08.12.59	06	★
	HG	Da	25.04.60 - 04.06.60	36	161.7
	LC	Da	14.10.60 - 17.12.60	56	173.6

No.	1	2	3	4	5
92040	LC	C	12.07.63 - 08.08.63	24	★
92041	NC	Da	23.01.57 - 25.01.57	03	★
	LI	Da	28.02.58 - 03.04.58	30	93.1
	NC	Da	14.12.59 - 23.12.59	09	★
	HG	Da	20.07.60 - 18.10.60	78	172.2
	AD	Da	14.12.60 - 17.12.60	04	★
	HI	C	29.11.62 - 16.02.63	69	245.2
92042	LI	Da	14.04.58 - 20.05.58	32	95.7
	CR	Da	22.12.58 - 20.01.59	26	113.1
	★	Da	01.59	★	★
	HG	Da	24.05.60 - 08.07.60	39	166.4
	LI	C	03.01.63 - 09.02.63	33	256.8
	★	C	08.64	★	★
92043	LC	Ma	16.06.56	★	★
	NC	St	06.56	★	★
	NC	Da	20.12.56 - 29.12.56	09	★
	BQ	St	18.06.57 - 19.06.57	02	★
	LI	C	05.05.58 - 03.06.58	26	86.0
	'LC	Ru	24.02.59 - 06.03.59	10	122.9
	LC	Go	25.07.60 - 13.08.60	18	173.3
	HG	C	04.01.61 - 10.02.61	33	184.8
	NC	C	16.03.61 - 27.03.61	10	187.9
	HC	C	21.11.62 - 18.01.63	53	★
	HC	C	08.02.63 - 27.03.63	41	★
92044	LC	C	18.03.55 - 29.04.55	37	2.6
	NC	St	27.06.55 - 29.06.55	03	★
	NC	St	10.10.55 - 12.10.55	03	★
	LC	Da	22.10.56 - 26.11.56	31	40.3
	NC	St	08.02.57 - 23.02.57	14	★
	NC	Ma	15.06.57 - 15.06.57	01	★
	G	Da	21.08.58 - 26.09.58	32	90.1
	HG	Da	01.05.61 - 03.06.61	30	185.3
	HC	C	21.02.63 - 04.04.63	37	238.5
92045	'HC	C	10.08.57 - 27.09.57	42	51.2
	'LI	C	12.12.58 - 13.01.59	28	72.5
	'LC	C	24.02.60 - 07.04.60	38	91.4
	HG	C	??.04.62 - ??.05.62	★	★
	★	Go	10.62	★	★
	LC	E	20.10.64 - 04.12.64	45	★
92046	★	C	11.55	★	★
	'LC	C	03.11.56 - 28.12.56	48	40.6
	FB	C	24.04.57 - 08.06.57	40	44.8
	'LC	C	12.06.57 - 11.07.57	26	44.9
	'LI	C	10.02.59 - 26.03.59	39	73.6
	'LC	C	13.02.61 - 30.03.61	46	109.9
	★	C	06.64	★	★
92047	'LC	C	28.06.55 - 02.07.55	05	13.5
	'LC	C	03.10.56 - 10.11.56	34	31.5
	FB	C	28.03.57 - 08.05.57	36	37.4
	'HI	C	26.07.57 - 31.08.57	32	41.0
	'LC	C	14.10.57 - 14.11.57	28	43.2
	'LC	C	29.01.58 - 22.03.58	46	47.0
	'HG	C	09.09.59 - 06.11.59	51	71.4
	'HC	C	20.02.61 - 12.04.61	45	99.2
	★	C	12.64	★	★
92048	LI	C	25.09.57 - 24.10.57	26	68.1
	LC	C	19.08.59 - 19.09.59	28	120.8
	HG	C	01.12.60 - 13.01.61	38	154.9
	LC	Go	12.03.62 - 14.04.62	30	★
	LC	C	08.11.62 - 11.12.62	29	★
	LI	C	04.05.66 - 11.06.66	34	★
92049	LI	C	17.10.57 - 16.11.57	27	67.9
	HG	C	19.04.61 - 19.05.61	27	156.2
	LC	Go	13.08.62 - 05.09.62	21	★
	NC	C	09.01.63 - 26.01.63	16	★
	I	C	02.06.65 - 31.07.65	52	★
92050	LC	C	06.02.57 - 01.03.57	21	★
	D	C	18.11.57 - 14.12.57	24	★
	LC	C	26.03.58 - 17.04.58	20	★
	LC	C	15.01.60 - 13.02.60	26	★

Table 8.2
BR Standard Class 9F 2-10-0s: Record of Repairs

No.	1	2	3	4	5
92050 (cont.)	LC	Go	04.04.62 - 19.04.62	14	★
	HG	C	13.09.62 - 19.10.62	32	★
	LC	C	07.06.65 - 09.08.65	55	★
92051	LI	C	06.11.58 - 29.11.58	21	★
	HG	C	15.05.61 - 24.06.61	36	★
	LI	C	07.12.64 - 16.01.65	36	★
92052	TU	Ds	19.06.58 - 04.07.58	14	★
	HC	C	04.04.60 - 06.05.60	29	★
	LC	C	09.11.60 - 13.12.60	28	★
	HG	C	07.09.62 - 10.10.62	29	★
	LI	C	30.03.66 - 18.05.66	43	★
92053	LC	C	25.10.55 - 08.11.55	13	★
	LI	C	06.02.59 - 07.03.59	26	★
	HG	C	25.01.61 - 24.03.61	51	★
	NR	C	01.09.61 - 22.09.61	19	★
	NR	C	18.06.62 - 21.06.62	04	★
	NC	C	07.01.63 - 21.01.63	13	★
	NC	C	10.02.64 - 20.03.64	35	★
	LC	E	20.10.64 - 04.12.64	40	★
92054	TU	De	28.07.58 - 19.08.58	20	66.3
	LI	C	04.02.59 - 28.02.59	22	80.0
	LC	Go	23.05.61 - 16.06.61	22	153.0
	HG	C	30.03.62 - 30.05.62	53	★
	HI	C	03.07.65 - 01.08.65	25	★
92055	'NC	Wl	23.08.58 - 02.09.58	09	79.5
	'HG	C	22.03.60 - 13.05.60	46	128.4
	★	C	12.64	★	★
92056	LC	C	02.06.58 - 05.06.58	04	68.6
	HG	C	17.08.60 - 29.09.60	38	133.5
	NR	C	01.11.60 - 15.11.60	13	★
	LC	Go	11.12.61 - 19.01.62	35	170.7
	LC	C	30.07.63 - 28.08.63	26	★
	LC	E	25.08.64 - 29.09.64	31	★
92057	LI	C	31.03.59 - 04.05.59	30	93.6
	CL	Go	09.01.62 - 11.02.62	29	★
	HG	C	15.08.62 - 22.09.62	33	★
92058	LI	C	25.06.58 - 02.08.58	34	76.9
	HC	C	16.05.60 - 24.06.60	35	136.4
	HG	C	10.10.62 - 14.11.62	31	★
	HI	C	06.06.66 - 30.07.66	48	★
92059	'NC	Wl	11.10.58 - 22.10.58	09	82.2
	'LC	C	20.04.60 - 25.06.60	58	126.2
	'LC	De	09.10.61 - 25.10.61	15	163.1
	★	C	08.64	★	★
92060	NC	Ga	17.01.57 - 28.01.57	10	★
	G	Da	23.03.59 - 29.04.59	33	78.3
	LC	Da	11.08.60 - 07.10.60	50	★
	HC	Da	10.03.61 - 20.06.61	88	131.5
	HG	C	15.07.63 - 29.08.63	40	162.0
	U	C	27.11.64 - 02.01.65	33	★
92061	NC	Ga	29.01.57 - 07.02.57	09	★
	LC	Da	14.10.58 - 07.11.58	22	★
	G	Da	21.01.60 - 10.03.60	43	100.0
	G	Da	31.05.62 - 14.08.62	65	158.0
	NC	C	15.10.64 - 14.11.64	27	★
	LC	C	15.10.64 - 18.11.64	30	★
92062	NM	Ga	12.02.57 - 14.02.57	03	★
	LC	Da	29.07.58 - 03.10.58	58	★
	LC	Da	10.03.59 - 21.04.59	37	★
	HI	Da	08.12.59 - 20.01.60	38	87.2
	AD	Da	16.02.60 - 07.03.60	18	★
	NC	Da	22.03.60 - 01.04.60	10	★
	LC	Da	29.04.60 - 23.06.60	48	★
	G	Da	05.04.62 - 03.08.62	104	162.5
	AD	Da	28.08.62 - 17.09.62	18	★
	LC	Da	09.08.63 - 03.10.63	48	★
	HG	C	28.02.64 - 02.05.64	56	★
92063	NC	Ga	19.02.57 - 26.02.57	07	★
	★	Ga	??.09.57	★	★
	★	Ga	??.12.57	★	★

No.	1	2	3	4	5
92063 (cont.)	***G***	Da	05.01.59 - 06.02.59	29	78.5
	HI	Da	11.08.60 - 29.10.60	69	115.0
	G	Da	22.05.63 - 26.06.63	31	152.0
	UN	C	26.08.65 - 23.10.65	51	★
	CA	C	?? 11.65 - 25.11.65	★	★
92064	'LC	Ga	12.09.56 - 01.10.56	17	★
	G	Da	18.08.59 - 26.09.59	35	82.5
	NC	Da	25.07.61 - 04.08.61	10	★
	G	Da	20.11.61 - 13.01.62	48	148.0
	I	C	16.11.64 - 22.12.64	32	★
	NC	C	06.06.66 - 02.07.66	24	★
92065	LC	Ga	16.08.56 - 31.08.56	14	★
	G	Da	04.05.59 - 15.06.59	37	85.6
	LC	Da	13.10.60 - 15.12.60	55	★
	G	Da	07.09.61 - 04.11.61	51	155.7
	CA	C	28.05.64 - 30.09.64	108	★
92066	NC	Ga	26.02.57 - 12.03.57	13	★
	LC	Da	14.08.58 - 11.09.58	25	★
	G	Da	13.10.59 - 26.11.59	39	86.4
	HC	C	10.08.62 - 22.09.62	38	154.0
	HC	C	08.05.63 - 13.06.63	32	★
92067	NC	Da	23.11.56 - 29.11.56	06	★
	BQ	St	06.06.57 - 06.06.57	01	★
	'LI	C	15.10.58 - 12.11.58	25	86.6
	HG	C	11.10.61 - 16.11.61	32	★
	LC	C	13.12.63 - 22.01.64	35	★
	LC	C	24.11.64 - 02.01.65	35	★
92068	BQ	St	??.05.56	★	★
	NC	Da	22.10.56 - 25.10.56	04	★
	LI	C	05.09.58 - 30.09.58	22	71.2
	LC	C	25.10.60 - 25.11.60	28	154.5
	HG	C	19.06.62 - 03.08.62	43	★
	LC	C	14.11.63 - 11.12.63	24	★
92069	NC	Da	10.10.56 - 15.10.56	05	★
	BQ	St	23.05.57 - 23.05.57	01	★
	LI	C	20.03.58 - 24.04.58	31	56.8
	LC	C	10.02.61 - 25.03.61	38	174.4
	NM	C	14.04.61 - 26.04.61	11	★
	HG	C	01.02.63 - 23.03.63	44	★
	HI	C	20.06.66 - 18.08.66	52	★
92070	NC	Da	30.10.56 - 02.11.56	04	★
	BQ	St	30.04.57 - 02.05.57	03	★
	LI	C	27.10.58 - 24.11.58	25	87.1
	★	C	09.60	★	★
	HG	C	30.01.62 - 03.03.62	29	★
	HC	C	??.64	★	★
92071	NC	Da	28.09.56 - 04.10.56	06	★
	BQ	St	21.05.57 - 21.05.57	01	★
	LI	C	18.12.58 - 12.01.59	22	88.8
	HG	C	03.08.61 - 31.08.61	25	191.5
	HG	C	04.10.63 - 20.11.63	41	★
	HC	C	21.12.65 - 05.02.66	41	★
92072	NC	Da	19.09.56 - 22.09.56	04	★
	BQ	St	19.07.57 - 19.07.57	01	★
	LI	C	05.08.58 - 29.08.58	22	75.4
	HG	C	18.07.61 - 23.08.61	32	196.5
	HC	C	19.09.63 - 31.10.63	37	★
92073	NC	Da	10.09.56 - 13.09.56	04	★
	BQ	St	03.05.57 - 04.05.57	02	★
	'LI	C	22.08.58 - 07.10.58	40	85.7
	'LC	C	18.12.59 - 04.03.60	67	138.8
	HG	C	??.61	★	★
	★	C	??.03.65 - ??.04.65	★	★
92074	NC	Da	25.08.56 - 04.09.56	09	★
	BQ	St	25.07.57 - 25.07.57	01	★
	LI	C	01.10.58 - 30.10.58	26	76.5
	HG	C	31.05.61 - 03.07.61	29	186.1
	HC	C	28.09.64 - 28.11.64	54	★
92075	NC	Da	20.08.56 - 25.08.56	06	★
	BQ	St	29.08.57 - 29.05.57	01	★

Table 8.2
BR Standard Class 9F 2-10-0s: Record of Repairs

No.	1	2	3	4	5
92075	’LI	C	24.09.58 - 29.10.58	31	84.6
(cont.)	’LC	C	12.10.60 - 05.01.61	74	166.8
92076	NC	Da	29.07.56 - 10.08.56	11	★
	BQ	St	07.06.57 - 07.06.57	01	★
	LI	C	30.05.58 - 02.07.58	29	67.3
	LC	Ru	10.03.59 - 25.03.59	14	101.8
	LC	Go	18.02.61 - 18.03.61	25	183.0
	CA	C	16.11.61 - 13.12.61	24	★
	LC	C	05.01.62 - 09.02.62	31	★
	HG	C	08.02.63 - 20.03.63	35	★
	LC	C	08.03.65 - 01.04.65	22	★
92077	NC	C	03.04.56 - 23.04.56	18	★
	LI	C	04.05.59 - 01.06.59	25	75.6
	HC	C	22.06.61 - 11.08.61	44	134.7
	★	C	02.62	★	★
	HG	C	22.01.63 - 23.02.63	29	★
	HC	C	14.03.66 - 15.04.66	29	★
92078	’LC	C	31.12.56 - 15.01.57	14	22.3
	’LC	C	16.12.59 - 16.01.60	28	96.2
	LC	C	26.01.63 - ??	★	★
	HG	C	02.65	★	★
92079	NM	De	07.05.56 - 12.05.56	06	2.5
	LI	C	16.08.57 - 28.09.57	38	32.1
	LC	C	27.02.58 - 29.03.58	27	★
	HC	S	15.05.59 - 04.01.60	202	62.3
	’HI	W	30.08.61 - 24.11.61	75	100.1
	I	C	01.10.64 - 28.11.64	51	★
92080	’NC	Ds	02.07.58 - 10.07.58	08	★
	’LC	C	24.05.60 - 01.07.60	34	118.6
	’HG	C	09.61	★	★
	★	C	05.64	★	★
	★	C	04.65	★	★
92081	’LI	C	08.09.58 - 11.10.58	30	71.3
	’LC	C	22.02.60 - 29.04.60	57	117.4
	HG	C	06.09.61 - 17.10.61	36	163.1
	★	C	02.62	★	★
	★	C	11.63	★	★
92082	BW	De	21.05.58 - 06.06.58	15	55.5
	LC	C	26.09.60 - 22.10.60	24	115.9
	HG	C	02.11.61 - 08.12.61	32	★
	HC	C	17.02.64 - 28.03.64	36	★
	NR	C	19.05.64 - 19.06.64	28	★
92083	BW	Ds	21.05.58 - 10.06.58	18	54.9
	LC	C	10.08.60 - 09.09.60	27	118.8
	HC	C	19.01.62 - 24.02.62	32	★
	HG	C	18.07.63 - 23.08.63	32	★
92084	BW	Ds	06.06.58 - 16.06.58	09	★
	LI	C	14.10.59 - 13.11.59	27	94.0
	LC	Go	29.03.62 - 16.05.62	42	★
	HG	C	12.07.63 - 17.09.63	58	★
	CA	C	31.03.65 - 20.04.65	18	★
92085	TU	Ds	10.06.58 - 19.06.58	09	★
	LC	Go	13.06.60 - 05.07.60	20	114.4
	HG	C	24.08.61 - 29.09.61	32	142.0
	HC	C	07.04.64 - 20.05.64	38	★
	LC	C	24.09.65 - 16.10.65	20	★
92086	TU	Ds	16.06.58 - 04.07.58	17	★
	LC	C	29.02.60 - 24.03.60	22	105.5
	LC	C	16.01.61 - 17.02.61	29	132.6
	HG	C	24.06.63 - 15.08.63	46	★
92087	BQ	St	26.06.57 - 26.06.57	01	★
	LI	C	01.12.58 - 24.12.58	21	77.4
	HG	C	23.01.61 - 30.03.61	35	170.3
	LC	C	24.05.61 - 12.06.61	17	178.5
	LC	C	05.03.63 - 05.04.63	28	★
	LC	C	13.10.64 - 04.12.64	46	★
	CA	C	10.02.66 - 23.03.66	36	★
92088	CR	Da	04.01.57 - 17.01.57	12	3.9
	BQ	St	21.05.57 - 21.05.57	01	★
	LI	C	27.11.58 - 23.12.58	23	72.2
92088	LC	C	08.03.60 - 09.04.60	29	117.1
(cont.)	***HG***	C	22.08.61 - 28.09.61	33	167.8
	HI	C	12.10 64 - 16.12.64	57	★
92089	BQ	St	14.06.57 - 14.06.57	01	★
	LI	C	23.12.58 - 22.01.59	27	69.1
	LC	Go	04.04.61 - 03.05.61	26	★
	HG	C	31.01.62 - 10.03.62	34	★
	LC	C	22.05.63 - 15.06.63	22	★
92090	LC	Da	08.04.57 - 03.05.57	23	9.3
	BQ	St	11.05.57 - 13.05.57	03	★
	LI	C	20.02.59 - 25.03.59	29	78.5
	LC	Go	07.11.60 - 01.12.60	22	140.3
	HG	C	31.10.62 - 07.12.62	33	★
	HC	C	03.12.63 - 24.01.64	46	★
	LC	C	25.05.64 - 10.07.64	41	★
	LI	C	21.12.65 - 12.02.66	47	★
92091	BQ	St	26.06.57 - 27.06.57	02	★
	’LI	C	18.01.59 - 21.02.59	30	82.5
	NC	Ds	??.01.61	★	153.7
	’LC	Go	06.10.61 - 28.10.61	20	177.4
	★	C	??.05.65	★	★
	★	C	??.01.66	★	★
92092	BQ	St	21.06.57 - 22.06.57	02	★
	LI	C	30.09.58 - 01.11.58	29	72.8
	HC	C	19.10.60 - 18.11.60	27	155.6
	LC	C	06.01.61 - 24.01.61	16	157.5
	LC	Go	05.03.62 - 31.03.62	24	★
	HG	C	08.02.63 - 16.03.63	32	★
92093	BQ	St	14.05.57 - 14.05.57	01	★
	LI	C	01.10.58 - 23.10.58	20	72.0
	LC	C	24.11.59 - 02.01.60	35	114.5
	LC	C	29.04.60 - 06.06.60	33	124.9
	HC	C	18.12.61 - 27.01.62	36	★
	HG	C	30.04.63 - 06.06.63	33	★
	LC	C	04.01.65 - 13.02.65	36	★
	LI	C	22.02.66 - 01.04.66	34	★
92094	BQ	Do	01.03.57 - 15.03.57	13	★
	LC	C	29.06.59 - 15.08.59	42	67.4
	LC	C	05.10.60 - 05.11.60	28	118.3
	LC	Go	21.11.61 - 13.01.62	47	★
	HG	C	27.12.62 - 26.01.63	27	★
	LC	C	10.03.64 - 23.04.64	39	★
	HI	C	01.07.65 - 20.08.65	43	★
	LC	C	19.10.65 - 06.11.65	17	★
	NR	C	04.01.66 - 12.01.66	08	★
92095	BQ	St	15.07.57 - 15.07.57	01	★
	’LC	C	29.03.58 - 17.05.58	43	45.3
	’LI	C	05.02.59 - 23.04.59	67	76.1
	’LC	C	24.06.60 - 17.09.60	74	126.5
	’LC	Go	09.11.60 - 07.12.60	25	135.8
	★	C	??.04.62 - ??.05.62	★	★
	★	C	06.64?	★	★
92096	BQ	St	25.05.57 - 25.05.57	01	★
	LI	C	21.10.58 - 15.11.58	24	70.3
	CR	C	19.02.59 - 07.03.59	15	80.2
	LC	C	30.12.59 - 30.01.60	28	106.7
	HC	C	19.07.61 - 24.08.61	32	168.6
	CR/***HG***	C	25.04.62 - 23.06.62	53	★
	HI	C	17.08.65 - 04.10.65	42	★
92097	NC	Ga	07.03.57 - 22.03.57	14	★
	G	Da	29.10.59 - 22.12.59	47	77.1
	G	Da	27.02.62 - 28.04.62	53	142.4
	CL	C	18.07.62 - 20.08.62	29	★
	HC	C	11.03.63 - 18.04.63	34	★
	I	C	22.12.64 - 05.03.65	64	★
92098	NC	Ga	21.03.57 - 05.04.57	14	★
	HI	Da	01.09.59 - 22.10.59	45	77.2
	G	Da	22.03.62 - 01.06.62	62	139.0
	AD	Da	18.06.62 - 28.06.62	10	★
	AD	Da	30.07.62 - 17.08.62	16	★

Table 8.2
BR Standard Class 9F 2-10-0s: Record of Repairs

No.	1	2	3	4	5
92098	UN	C	17.08.64 - 22.10.64	58	*
(cont.)	CA	C	31.10.64	*	*
92099	NC	Ga	04.04.57 - 16.04.57	11	*
	G	Da	21.07.59 - 04.09.59	40	71.0
	NC	Da	15.08.61 - 24.08.61	09	*
	LC	Go	10.09.62 - 20.11.62	62	142.0
	NR	Go	03.12.62 - 14.12.62	11	*
	UN	C	07.01.64 - 15.02.64	35	*
	CA	C	15.02.65 - 13.03.65	24	*
92100	LC	Go	04.08.60 - 24.08.60	18	108.9
	HC	C	16.08.61 - 21.09.61	32	128.2
	HG	C	13.08.63 - 16.10.63	56	*
	LC	C	09.09.64 - 24.10.64	40	*
92101	CR	C	20.08.56 - 23.08.56	04	0.2
	LC	C	28.09.60 - 29.10.60	28	115.3
	HG	C	25.09.62 - 03.11.62	35	*
	*	C	01.66	*	*
92102	CR	C	29.03.57 - 03.05.57	31	18.1
	LC	C	27.04.60 - 27.05.60	27	104.3
	LC	Go	19.02.62 - 24.03.62	30	*
	HG	C	22.08.63 - 05.10.63	39	*
	LC	C	16.04.64 - 19.05.64	29	*
	CA	C	11.05.65 - 21.05.65	10	*
92103	LC	C	20.08.57 - 14.09.57	23	28.0
	LC	C	21.12.59 - 09.01.60	18	92.8
	HG	C	28.05.62 - 21.07.62	48	*
	LC	C	13.08.63 - 17.09.63	31	*
92104	CR	C	10.12.56 - 27.12.56	16	7.4
	CR	C	11.11.57 - 30.11.57	18	32.3
	LC	Go	28.08.60 - 17.09.60	18	111.4
	HC	C	25.08.61 - 30.10.61	57	137.9
	HG	C	05.04.63 - 29.05.63	47	*
	LC	C	16.06.64 - 07.08.64	46	*
92105	TU	Ds	26.08.58 - 09.09.58	13	50.5
	LC	C	09.12.59 - 02.01.60	22	84.2
	NR	C	04.01.60 - 09.01.60	06	*
	LC	C	15.02.62 - 16.03.62	26	*
	HG	C	12.07.63 - 13.09.63	55	*
92106	TU	Ds	21.10.58 - 30.10.58	09	50.9
	LC	Go	15.06.60 - 08.07.60	21	100.2
	NR	Go	24.09.60 - 29.10.60	31	105.1
	LC	Go	31.05.62 - 13.08.62	68	*
	HG	C	20.09.63 - 23.10.63	29	*
92107	TU	Ds	23.06.58 - 11.07.58	17	*
	LC	C	04.12.59 - 02.01.60	26	90.6
	LC	C	06.04.61 - 12.05.61	32	129.7
	HG	C	30.05.62 - 26.06.62	25	*
	LC	C	13.02.63 - 28.02.63	14	*
	LC	C	03.02.65 - 20.03.65	40	*
	HI	C	30.11.65 - 15.01.66	41	*
92108	LC	C	18.01.60 - 19.02.60	29	93.8
	LC	Go	18.06.62 - 24.08.62	59	*
	HG	C	25.02.63 - 29.03.63	29	*
92109	LI	C	21.01.59 - 12.02.59	20	58.0
	LC	Go	28.05.62 - 06.07.62	35	*
	HG	C	16.10.63 - 18.11.63	29	*
92110	LC	Go	11.04.60 - 12.05.60	28	93.9
	LC	C	14.09.60 - 14.10.60	27	103.7
	HG	C	24.10.62 - 21.11.62	25	*
	HI	C	19.04.66 - 26.05.66	33	*
92111	CR	C	21.01.57 - 13.02.57	21	5.1
	LC	C	29.01.60 - 27.02.60	26	84.5
	NC	Ds	19.12.60 - 07.01.61	18	111.0
	LC	C	17.01.62 - 23.02.62	33	*
	HG	C	21.11.63 - 02.01.64	37	*
92112	CR	C	20.10.58 - 13.12.58	48	55.1
	LC	Wl	07.12.60 - 12.12.60	05	113.6
	LC	Go	16.11.61 - 22.12.61	32	*
	HG	C	13.06.63 - 03.08.63	45	*
	NC	C	04.67	*	*
92113	LC	Go	05.01.61 - 16.02.61	37	94.4
	HG	C	26.07.63 - 07.09.63	38	*
	LC	C	27.01.65 - 27.02.65	28	*
92114	LC	C	13.04.60 - 20.05.60	33	81.4
	HG	C	13.12.63 - 23.01.64	36	*
92115	'LC	Go	25.05.60 - 24.06.60	27	88.1
	'LC	C	26.09.60 - 12.11.60	42	94.9
	'HG	C	17.10.62 - 23.11.62	33	*
92116	***G***	C	31.05.63 - 26.06.63	23	*
	LC	E	17.12.64 - 08.01.65	23	*
92117	LC	C	02.06.60 - 06.07.60	30	*
	HG	C	11.09.62 - 13.10.62	29	*
	LC	C	13.11.64 - 19.12.64	32	*
	HC	C	09.11.65 - 11.12.65	29	*
92118	*	S??	02.62	*	*
	*	C	04.62	*	*
	*	C	02.64	*	*
	*	C	05.66	*	*
92119	LC	C	09.06.59 - 01.07.59	20	*
	HC	C	25.09.61 - 27.10.61	29	*
	HG	C	21.01.64 - 21.02.64	28	*
92120	LC	Go	24.05.60 - 15.06.60	20	*
	CA	C	25.01.61 - 03.03.61	33	*
	HG	C	23.03.62 - 28.04.62	32	*
	LC	C	31.12.62 - 19.01.63	18	*
92121	LC	C	18.01.61 - 21.02.61	30	112.6
	LC	C	02.08.61 - 23.08.61	19	123.2
	LI	C	21.02.64 - 04.04.64	38	*
92122	TU	Ds	20.09.58 - 09.10.58	17	49.7
	LC	Go	18.06.60 - 09.08.60	45	105.9
	LC	C	19.11.62 - 05.01.63	42	*
	HG	C	04.03.64 - 18.04.64	40	*
92123	TU	Ds	14.09.58 - 27.09.58	12	47.8
	HC	C	30.08.60 - 30.09.60	28	107.5
	LC	C	12.09.61 - 12.10.61	27	137.0
	LC	C	28.11.61 - 21.12.61	21	*
	LC	C	23.07.63 - 16.08.63	22	*
	*	C	??.04.64 - ??.05.64	*	*
	LI	C	05.08.64 - 15.08.64	10	*
	LC	E	10.64	*	*
	HC	C	18.03.66 - 30.04.66	38	*
92124	BW	Ds	21.05.58 - 30.05.58	09	*
	LC	C	18.12.58 - 01.01.59	13	52.5
	LC	Go	11.08.60 - 03.09.60	21	108.4
	HC	C	13.04.61 - 11.05.61	25	125.3
	HG	C	25.09.63 - 04.11.63	35	*
	LC	C	06.08.65 - 11.09.65	32	*
92125	NC	C	13.05.58 - 03.06.58	19	37.1
	TU	Ds	14.11.58 - 26.11.58	11	54.3
	LC	C	12.09.60 - 12.10.60	27	113.9
	LC	C	09.11.61 - 13.12.61	30	*
	HG	C	26.07.63 - 29.08.63	30	*
92126	TU	Ds	28.07.58 - 12.08.58	14	43.8
	LC	Go	23.09.60 - 26.10.60	29	112.0
	HG	C	01.08.62 - 31.08.62	27	*
	LC	C	17.04.64 - 21.07.64	82	*
92127	TU	Ds	11.10.58 - 22.10.58	10	48.5
	LC	Go	12.09.60 - 12.10.60	27	106.2
	LC	C	29.08.61 - 04.10.61	32	134.2
	HG	C	22.03.63 - 25.04.63	30	*
92128	LC	Go	25.07.60 - 13.08.60	18	93.0
	NR	Go	27.09.60 - 03.11.60	33	96.1
	LC	C	28.11.62 - 07.01.63	35	*
	HC	C	20.11.63 - 03.01.64	39	*
92129	LC	De	13.12.60 - 14.03.61	79	107.2
	LC	C	22.02.62 - 28.03.62	30	*
	LI	C	30.01.64 - 14.03.64	39	*
92130	LC	C	28.10.60 - 05.12.60	33	92.8
	HG	C	01.08.63 - 28.09.63	51	*
92131	LC	C	10.05.60 - 21.06.60	37	80.0

Table 8.2
BR Standard Class 9F 2-10-0s: Record of Repairs

No.	1	2	3	4	5
92131	LC	C	16.09.60 - 11.10.60	22	83.4
(cont.)	LC	Go	11.10.62 - 25.10.62	14	*
	HG	C	30.09.63 - 08.11.63	35	*
	LC	C	14.05.64 - 08.07.64	48	*
92132	'TU	Ds	20.09.58 - 10.10.58	18	48.5
	LC	C	11.11.59 - 05.12.59	22	84.8
	HC	C	15.05.61 - 20.06.61	32	126.5
	HG	C	01.08.63 - 09.10.63	60	*
	LC	C	15.12.64 - 23.01.65	35	*
92133	TU	Ds	14.08.58 - 26.08.58	11	44.8
	LC	C	07.09.60 - 08.10.60	28	107.9
	NR	C	18.10.60 - 21.10.60	04	*
	LC	C	07.09.61 - 09.10.61	28	136.0
	HG	C	25.07.63 - 28.08.63	30	*
	*	C	06.64	*	*
	LC	C	12.02.65 - 20.03.65	32	*
92134	CR	C	26.08.57 - 14.09.57	18	8.0
	TU	Ds	28.07.58 - 08.08.58	11	33.8
	LC	C	12.12.60 - 24.01.61	38	111.0
	LC	Go	04.09.62 - 18.10.62	39	*
	LC	C	24.07.63 - 17.08.63	22	*
	HI	E	22.07.64 - 08.09.64	42	205.0
	*	C	05.65	*	*
92135	NC	C	17.06.58 - 07.07.58	18	33.2
	LI	C	18.09.59 - 17.10.59	26	77.4
	LC	De	08.12.59 - 02.03.60	74	79.5
	LC	C	08.02.61 - 14.03.61	30	115.3
	LC	C	28.11.62 - 09.01.63	37	*
	LC	E	24.06.64 - 27.08.64	56	*
92136	NC	C	06.05.58 - 29.05.58	21	32.2
	HC	C	26.11.59 - 02.01.60	33	87.8
	NC	Cc	13.03.60 - 30.03.60	18	*
	LC	Go	05.04.62 - 19.05.62	39	*
92137	LC	C	07.05.58 - 28.05.58	19	32.8
	HG	C	18.05.60 - 02.07.60	40	105.6
	LC	C	06.02.61 - 02.03.61	22	129.2
	LC	Go	19.10.62 - 20.12.62	54	*
	*	C	04.64	*	*
	LI	C	18.06.65 - 10.08.65	46	*
	*	Os	11.66	*	*
92138	LC	C	01.07.58 - 07.08.58	33	32.7
	LC	C	21.06.60 - 06.08.60	41	102.1
	HI	C	15.01.63 - 23.02.63	33	*
	HI	E	30.07.64 - 22.09.64	47	*
	*	C	07.65	*	*
92139	'LC	C	08.07.58 - 14.08.58	33	36.5
	'LC	C	09.06.60 - 26.07.60	41	101.6
	*	C	08.64	*	*
	*	C	02.65	*	*
	*	C	09.65	*	*
92140	***G***	Da	09.01.60 - 04.02.60	23	93.4
	LC	C	14.11.62 - 18.12.62	30	205.4
	*	E	07.64	*	*
92141	LI	Da	30.10.59 - 08.12.59	34	91.7
	G	Da	03.04.62 - 08.05.62	31	187.9
	'LC	C	23.11.62 - 14.12.62	28	201.2
	'LC	C	11.06.64 - 27.06.64	15	*
92142	LI	Da	05.02.60 - 24.03.60	42	92.3
	LC	Go	03.09.62 - 31.10.62	51	191.4
92143	LI	Da	19.02.60 - 05.04.60	40	94.2
	CL	Da	23.01.61 - 22.03.61	51	130.1
	LC	Go	18.09.62 - 07.12.62	70	186.4
92144	LI	Da	06.10.59 - 14.11.59	35	87.3
	G	Da	19.02.62 - 29.03.62	34	184.2
	AD	Da	02.04.62 - 04.04.62	03	*
	AD	Da	09.04.62 - 27.04.62	17	*
92145	LI	Da	27.08.59 - 10.10.59	39	72.3
	CR	Da	24.02.61 - 25.03.61	26	131.8
	G	Da	17.04.62 - 15.06.62	52	170.4
	'LC	C	05.10.62 - 20.10.62	14	179.9
92146	CR	Da	26.05.59 - 17.06.59	20	69.7
	LI	Da	13.04.60 - 01.06.60	43	102.2
	AD	Da	13.06.60 - 25.06.60	11	*
	AD	Da	04.07.60 - 28.07.60	22	*
	HG	C	02.04.63 - 01.05.63	26	198.4
92147	CR	Da	15.04.59 - 22.05.59	33	55.4
	NC	Da	26.08.59 - 03.09.59	08	*
	G	Da	08.06.61 - 08.07.61	27	*
92148	LI	Da	14.12.59 - 29.01.60	41	91.4
	*	C	03.62	*	*
	'LC	C	27.07.62 - 24.08.62	25	174.9
	'HG	C	15.01.63 - 30.01.63	14	198.1
92149	HI	Da	21.06.60 - 18.08.60	51	103.8
	AD	Da	26.08.60 - 12.09.60	15	*
	CL	Go	07.02.63 - 05.04.63	50	198.8
92150	HC	C	17.06.60 - 05.08.60	43	82.2
	LC	C	22.09.61 - 24.10.61	28	120.6
	LC	E	18.05.62 - 19.05.62	02	*
	LI	C	25.01.63 - 27.02.63	29	*
	*	C	06.64	*	*
	LC	E	19.10.64 - 20.11.64	29	*
92151	LC	Go	09.12.60 - 21.01.61	38	102.5
	HG	C	31.07.63 - 08.10.63	60	*
92152	'LC	Go	29.08.60 - 30.09.60	29	98.5
	*	C	02.62	*	*
	*	C	04.63	*	*
	LC	E	24.12.64 - 17.02.65	48	203.0
92153	LC	C	07.10.59 - 07.11.59	28	48.9
	'LC	Wl	21.03.61 - 27.03.61	06	89.7
	LC	Go	13.09.61 - 23.09.61	10	99.7
	LC	Go	05.11.62 - 25.01.63	71	*
	LC	C	04.06.63 - 22.06.63	17	*
	LC	C	04.11.63 - 20.11.63	15	*
	LI	E	18.03.65 - 05.05.65	42	*
	NR	E	26.05.65 - 01.06.65	06	*
92154	TU	Ds	14.11.58 - 23.11.58	08	40.4
	LC	Go	05.05.60 - 28.05.60	21	83.5
	LC	Go	26.06.61 - 19.08.61	48	115.3
	LC	Go	15.05.62 - 04.07.62	44	*
	HC	C	26.07.63 - 28.08.63	29	*
	LC	C	27.04.64 - 01.07.64	57	*
	HC	C	08.06.66 - 10.08.66	55	*
92155	LC	C	01.06.59 - 27.06.59	24	57.3
	LC	C	30.11.60 - 31.12.60	28	100.8
	NR	C	02.01.61 - 18.01.61	15	*
	LC	C	08.01.63 - 02.02.63	23	*
	LC	C	20.03.63 - 13.04.63	22	*
	CA	C	07.02.64 - 12.03.64	35	*
	LC	E	22.02.65 - 09.04.65	41	191.0
92156	LC	C	02.07.59 - 18.08.59	41	42.6
	LC	Go	24.01.61 - 25.02.61	29	83.3
	LI	C	12.03.64 - 08.05.64	50	*
	LC	E	08.10.64 - 23.10.64	16	*
92157	LC	Go	07.11.60 - 17.12.60	36	93.7
	LC	C	23.01.62 - 24.02.62	29	*
	*	C	12.63	*	*
	LI	C	14.08.64 - 15.01.65	133	*
92158	LC	Go	18.04.61 - 15.05.61	24	*
	HG	C	26.03.63 - 25.04.63	27	*
92159	TU	Ds	05.09.58 - 27.09.58	20	27.3
	LC	C	03.03.61 - 05.04.61	29	106.2
	LC	C	17.04.61 - 20.04.61	04	106.7
	LC	C	28.11.61 - 05.01.62	34	*
	HG	C	25.11.63 - 09.01.64	40	*
92160	'LC	C	27.01.58 - 15.02.58	18	4.8
	'NC	Wl	31.05.58 - 11.06.58	10	*
	'LC	C	29.10.60 - 09.01.61	62	86.0
	*	C	04.61	*	*
	*	C	11.64	*	*
	*	C	05.66	*	*

Table 8.2
BR Standard Class 9F 2-10-0s: Record of Repairs

No.	1	2	3	4	5
92161	LC	C	14.10.59 - 07.11.59	22	44.1
	LC	Go	09.05.61 - 03.06.61	23	83.3
	LC	Go	01.04.63 - 13.05.63	37	★
	HG	C	27.01.64 - 26.02.64	27	★
92162	LC	C	21.03.61 - 26.04.61	32	81.8
	HG	C	31.07.63 - 21.09.63	46	★
92163	CR	C	14.04.58 - 01.05.58	16	1.7
	TU	Ds	04.11.58 - 13.11.58	09	17.4
	LC	C	03.11.61 - 07.12.61	30	★
	LC	C	29.11.62 - 23.01.63	48	★
	LC	C	26.02.63 - 16.03.63	17	★
	LC	C	13.02.64 - 25.03.64	36	★
	LI	C	11.06.66 - 18.06.66	07	★
92164	LC	Go	14.03.61 - 12.04.61	26	94.3
	HC	C	24.04.63 - 24.05.63	27	★
92165	LC	C	04.01.61 - 16.02.61	38	79.7
	LC	C	15.11.62 - 20.12.62	31	★
	LI	C	21.04.65 - 14.06.65	47	★
	LC	C	22.07.65 - 26.08.65	27	★
92166	★	C	08.59	★	★
	LC	C	10.12.62 - 15.01.63	32	★
	HC	C	29.04.64 - 24.08.64	101	★
92167	’LC	Ru	25.02.59 - 13.03.59	15	32.9
	’LC	C	25.10.60 - 13.01.61	70	75.8
	★	C	12.61	★	★
	LC	C	02.12.62 - 07.01.63	31	★
	★	C	08.63	★	★
	★	C	10.64	★	★
92168	NC	Da	18.09.59 - 29.09.59	10	★
	LI	Da	05.07.60 - 02.09.60	52	88.1
	’HG	C	01.11.63 - 11.12.63	35	★
	’LC	E	02.02.65 - ??	★	★
92169	’NC	Da	15.10.59 - 26.10.59	10	★
	’LI	Da	25.04.60 - 15.06.60	45	87.4
	AD	Da	27.06.60 - 05.07.60	08	★
	’TM	C	14.02.64 - ??	★	★
	★	C	01.65	★	★
92170	’NC	Da	29.09.59 - 07.10.59	08	★
	’LI	Da	10.05.60 - 24.06.60	40	83.9
	’AD	Da	06.09.60 - 08.10.60	29	★
	’NC	C	12.12.63 - ??	★	★
92171	’NC	Da	08.12.59 - 16.12.59	08	★
	’LI	Da	31.01.61 - 23.03.61	45	94.5
92172	NC	Da	24.11.59 - 01.12.59	07	★
	LI	Da	25.10.60 - 02.12.60	34	87.1
	HG	C	16.05.63 - 11.06.63	23	★
	HC	E	09.12.64 - 10.02.65	55	★
92173	NC	Da	27.10.59 - 09.11.59	12	★
	LI	Da	03.11.60 - 21.12.60	42	98.2
	HG	C	18.07.63 - 23.08.63	32	★
	LC	Ho	25.03.64 - 24.04.64	27	★
92174	NC	Da	16.10.59 - 31.10.59	14	★
	LI	Da	21.11.60 - 07.01.61	42	98.1
	HG	C	24.10.63 - 10.12.63	41	★
92175	NC	Da	26.10.59 - 05.11.59	10	★
	LI	Da	21.06.61 - 16.08.61	49	95.6
92176	NC	Da	28.10.59 - 09.11.59	11	★
	LI	Da	01.02.61 - 30.03.61	50	96.5
	AD	Da	04.04.61 - 05.04.61	02	★
	’ET	C	06.02.64 - ??	★	★
92177	NC	Da	11.03.60 - 21.03.60	09	★
	LI	Da	09.11.60 - 04.01.61	49	96.3
	G	Da	30.05.62 - 28.06.62	26	141.2
	’NC	C	10.01.64 - ??.03.64	★	★
92178	***LI***	Da	10.08.60 - 06.10.60	50	98.3
	LC	Da	21.10.60 - 03.11.60	12	★
	HG	C	12.11.63 - 01.01.64	44	★
92179	LI	Da	22.03.60 - 06.05.60	40	99.5
	’LI	Go	20.09.62 - 07.12.62	68	186.0
	LC	E	16.12.64 - 26.02.65	63	229.5
92180	***G***	Da	21.01.60 - 26.02.60	32	85.1
	LC	C	24.12.62 - 25.01.63	29	181.0
92181	LI	Da	16.06.60 - 15.08.60	51	101.9
	LC	Da	26.10.61 - 09.11.61	13	148.1
	HI	C	04.01.63 - 09.02.63	32	187.4
92182	NC	Da	25.08.59 - 02.09.59	08	★
	LI	Da	02.09.60 - 21.10.60	43	105.6
	HG	C	23.10.63 - 28.11.63	32	★
92183	NC	Da	03.09.58 - 10.09.58	07	★
	LI	Da	04.08.60 - 17.09.60	39	100.9
	LC	Da	01.11.61 - 15.12.61	39	142.9
	HC	Da	05.04.62 - 05.07.62	79	152.2
	HC	C	19.11.63 - 02.01.64	39	★
92184	’LI	Da	06.04.60 - 27.05.60	45	86.9
	’HG	C	20.12.62 - 25.01.63	32	188.4
	’LC	E	25.09.64 - 29.10.64	30	★
92185	***G***	Da	07.03.60 - 13.04.60	33	90.4
	LC	Go	31.12.62 - 22.02.63	47	198.4
	★	C	02.64	★	★
92186	LI	Da	02.06.60 - 27.07.60	48	104.6
	HC	C	20.12.62 - 25.01.63	32	189.8
92187	NC	Da	08.08.58 - 15.08.58	07	★
	NC	Da	09.10.58 - 28.10.58	17	★
	CR	Da	05.12.58 - 02.01.59	25	24.1
	HI	Da	15.03.61 - 27.04.61	38	125.0
	AD	Da	08.05.61 - 15.05.61	07	★
	’HG	C	18.09.63 - 25.10.63	33	★
92188	LC	Da	08.07.58 - 08.08.58	28	14.0
	NC	Da	21.12.59 - 02.01.60	12	★
	LI	Da	08.12.60 - 21.01.61	39	108.4
	AD	Da	03.61	★	★
	LC	C	03.02.64 - 13.02.64	10	★
92189	’NC	Da	14.08.59 - 25.08.59	10	★
	LI	Da	15.01.61 - 17.02.61	40	98.3
	’G	Da	30.05.62 - 06.07.62	33	132.2
	’LC	C	06.06.63 - 30.07.63	47	★
92190	CR	Da	28.08.58 - 03.10.58	32	14.7
	NC	Da	24.08.59 - 01.09.59	08	★
	HI	Da	24.03.61 - 13.05.61	44	96.5
	LC	Da	08.08.61 - 28.09.61	45	103.6
	CL	Go	04.10.62 - 28.11.62	48	128.3
92191	’NC	Da	29.01.60 - 06.02.60	08	★
	’LI	Da	21.03.61 - 29.04.61	35	107.8
	★	Da	??.11.61 - ??.12.61	★	★
	’LC	Go	08.01.63 - 13.03.63	56	147.6
	’LC	C	12.07.63 - 21.08.63	35	★
92192	CR	Da	06.11.58 - 28.11.58	20	22.0
	’NC	Da	16.10.59 - 30.10.59	13	★
	’LI	Da	23.05.61 - 05.07.61	38	105.9
	’HG	C	19.06.63 - 14.08.63	49	★
92193	NC	Da	28.10.58 - 04.11.58	07	★
	NC	Da	22.06.59 - 24.06.59	03	★
	NC	Da	10.08.59 - 27.08.59	16	★
	LC	Da	11.12.59 - 09.02.60	52	57.5
	NC	Da	21.03.60 - 25.03.60	07	★
	LC	Da	24.03.61 - 07.04.61	13	98.5
	G	Da	05.09.61 - 06.10.61	28	108.2
	LC	C	24.09.62 - 13.10.62	18	141.3
92194	NC	Da	11.06.59 - 16.06.59	05	★
	NC	Da	02.09.59 - 10.09.59	08	★
	NC	Da	21.01.60 - 11.03.60	44	★
	LI	Da	03.10.61 - 18.11.61	41	109.2
	AD	Da	22.03.62 - 02.04.62	10	★
92195	NC	Da	02.07.59 - 06.07.59	04	★
	NC	Da	22.09.59 - 01.10.59	10	★
	G	Da	24.10.61 - 02.12.61	35	107.3
92196	NC	Da	27.07.59 - 06.08.59	10	★
	G	Da	14.02.61 - 08.04.61	47	108.3
	AD	Da	15.05.61 - 30.05.61	14	★
92197	NC	Da	15.01.60 - 22.01.60	07	★

Table 8.2
BR Standard Class 9F 2-10-0s: Record of Repairs

No.	1	2	3	4	5
92197	LI	Da	05.06.61 - 29.07.61	43	84.4
(cont.)	LC	E	19.03.65 - 05.05.65	41	⋆
92198	NC	Da	15.03.60 - 25.03.60	10	⋆
	LI	Da	05.03.62 - 18.04.62	39	106.7
92199	NC	Da	19.04.60 - 27.04.60	08	⋆
	LI	Da	28.12.61 - 09.02.62	38	108.7
92200	NC	Da	01.09.59 - 11.09.59	10	⋆
	LI	Da	15.09.61 - 03.11.61	43	94.9
	HC	C	20.06.63 - 09.08.63	44	⋆
92201	NC	Da	07.09.59 - 16.09.59	09	⋆
	NC	Do	22.10.59 - 29.10.59	07	⋆
	LI	Da	27.02.62 - 06.04.62	34	104.3
	LC	Go	25.02.63 - 15.03.63	17	⋆
	HC	C	09.04.63 - 11.05.63	29	125.1
92202	NC	Da	29.05.59 - 03.06.59	05	⋆
	NC	Da	14.09.59 - 22.09.59	08	⋆
	LI	Da	11.01.62 - 01.03.62	43	105.7
92203	'U	Sp	02.06.59 - 18.06.59	15	⋆
	⋆	S	11.60	⋆	⋆
	'U	So	18.03.61 - 02.04.61	13	⋆
	'U	Oo	02.08.61 - 12.09.61	36	⋆
	'U	So	25.10.61 - 22.12.61	51	⋆
	'U	Oo	31.05.62 - 17.06.62	15	⋆
	LC	C	16.11.62 - 19.12.62	29	91.4
	LC	Ba	14.05.63 - 27.05.63	12	⋆
	LC	C	22.08.63 - 26.09.63	31	⋆
	⋆	S	12.63	⋆	⋆
	HC	C	04.05.64 - 29.07.64	75	⋆
	HC	C	19.10.66 - 31.12.66	64	⋆
92204	'U	So	02.05.61 - 16.05.61	13	⋆
	'U	Oo	24.09.61 - 10.10.61	14	⋆
	'U	Oo	02.05.62 - 16.05.62	13	⋆
	HI	S	28.06.62 - 01.11.62	109	103.2
	LC	C	12.07.63 - 03.08.63	20	⋆
92205	'U	Sp	25.01.60 - 11.02.60	16	⋆
	LC	E	05.09.61 - 23.09.61	17	69.2
	LC	E	09.10.62 - 10.11.62	29	95.4
	CA	C	30.07.64 - 15.08.64	15	⋆
	I	C	09.02.65 - 23.03.65	37	⋆
92206	'U	Na	21.09.59 - 23.09.59	03	⋆
	'U	La	20.10.59 - 20.11.59	28	⋆
	PV	Br	12.09.60 - ??	⋆	⋆
	LC	E	13.01.61 - 03.02.61	19	73.0
	LI	E	17.05.62 - 09.06.62	21	81.2
	LC	E	27.12.62 - 19.01.63	21	93.1
	CA	C	11.09.64 - 23.01.65	116	⋆
	⋆	C	07.65	⋆	⋆
92207	U	La	28.01.60 - 11.02.60	13	⋆
	U	Cy	20.05.61 - ??	⋆	⋆
	'U	So	16.01.62 - 12.02.62	24	⋆
	'LC	C	14.09.62 - 21.12.62	85	⋆
	'LC	C	07.03.63 - 20.04.63	39	⋆
	'U	So	06.05.64 - 29.05.64	21	⋆
92208	'U	S	08.12.59 - 11.12.59	04	⋆
	'U	So	31.08.60 - 30.09.60	27	⋆
	HI	S	12.04.62 - 25.06.62	64	78.5
	HI	C	12.01.66 - 11.03.66	51	⋆
92209	'U	Cc	20.07.60 - 04.08.60	14	⋆
	'U	W	27.01.61 - 22.02.61	23	⋆
	'U	Ej	18.05.61 - 12.07.61	48	⋆
	'HI	S	12.08.62 - 28.11.62	144	76.1
92210	'LC	Os	11.10.61 - 03.01.62	73	⋆
	'U	So	31.08.62 - 25.09.62	22	⋆
	'LC	C	12.11.62 - 15.01.63	56	⋆
	'U	Sj	30.04.64 - 11.06.64	37	⋆
92211	'U	Ws	29.06.61 - 18.07.61	17	⋆
	LC	E	13.10.61 - 04.11.61	20	58.9
	LC	C	29.06.62 - 10.08.62	37	⋆
	LC	C	04.03.63 - 30.03.63	24	⋆
	I	C	23.12.64 - 16.03.65	72	⋆
92211	U	C	08.08.66 - 21.09.66	39	⋆
92212	'U	Sj	23.06.60 - 22.07.60	26	⋆
	'U	Ba	12.09.60 - 02.10.60	18	⋆
	'U	Bg	26.05.61 - 27.07.61	54	⋆
	HC	S	06.11.61 - 02.04.62	128	49.4
	LI	C	23.06.64 - 20.08.64	51	⋆
	HC	C	22.06.65 - 02.09.65	61	⋆
92213	'LC	Cy	27.05.60 - 21.06.60	22	⋆
	'U	Sj	12.06.61 - 19.09.61	86	⋆
	'U	Wr	28.12.61 - 23.01.62	23	⋆
	'U	Ba	07.05.62 - 25.05.62	17	⋆
	'U	Sj	07.01.63 - 04.02.63	25	68.3
	'U	Ba	07.05.63 - 05.06.63	26	⋆
	LC	C	29.07.63 - 28.08.63	27	⋆
	'U	Gl	26.09.63 - 22.10.63	23	⋆
92214	⋆	S	??.11.60 - ??	⋆	⋆
	'U	Ba	16.03.61 - 21.04.61	32	⋆
	'U	Ba	26.04.61 - 10.05.61	13	⋆
	'U	Ba	27.06.61 - 11.07.61	13	⋆
	'U	Ej	01.03.62 - 15.03.62	13	⋆
	'U	Gl	30.04.62 - 26.05.62	24	⋆
	'U	Ej	13.11.62 - 30.11.62	16	⋆
	NC	Cy	23.01.63 - 21.02.63	26	⋆
	'U	Ej	27.02.63 - 02.04.63	30	⋆
	LC	C	17.06.63 - 30.07.63	38	⋆
	'U	Ej	27.02.64 - 12.03.64	13	⋆
92215	***'HC***	S	10.05.61 - 27.10.61	147	44.1
	CA	Go	07.03.63 - 17.04.63	36	⋆
	CA	C	03.06.63 - 19.07.63	41	⋆
92216	'U	Gl	20.07.61 - 18.08.61	26	⋆
	'HC	S	04.04.62 - 07.08.62	108	73.6
	'LC	C	02.10.62 - 13.12.62	63	⋆
92217	'U	Oo	24.03.61 - 11.04.61	16	⋆
	'LC	W	11.07.61 - 19.09.61	61	⋆
	'U	Oo	13.11.61 - 03.12.61	18	⋆
	'U	Gl	18.01.62 - 08.02.62	19	⋆
	'U	Oo	01.06.62 - 20.06.62	17	⋆
	LC	C	14.11.62 - 20.12.62	32	⋆
92218	'U	Oo	01.06.61 - 30.06.61	26	⋆
	'U	Oo	04.10.61 - 30.10.61	23	⋆
	LC	S	15.12.61 - 08.03.62	72	⋆
	'U	Oo	07.05.62 - 22.05.62	14	⋆
	LC	C	12.06.63 - 19.07.63	33	⋆
	⋆	C	05.66	⋆	⋆
92219	'U	Cc	09.09.60 - 24.09.60	14	⋆
	⋆	S	??.08.61 - ??.10.61	⋆	⋆
	'U	Ty	28.03.62 - 13.04.62	15	⋆
	'U	Ce	13.12.62 - 13.01.63	27	⋆
	'LC	C	18.03.63 - 06.04.63	20	⋆
92220	U	S	09.60	⋆	⋆
	'U	S	15.04.61 - 02.05.61	15	⋆
	'U	Gl	09.07.62 - 03.08.62	23	⋆
	'U	Ox	27.12.62 - 27.01.63	27	⋆
	'LC	C	05.02.63 - 02.03.63	23	⋆
	LC	S	26.02.64 - 24.03.64	24	⋆
	⋆	C	12.66	⋆	⋆
	CR	C	01.67	⋆	⋆
92221	'U	W	18.02.59 - 17.03.59	24	⋆
	'U	Ba	06.06.59 - 26.06.59	18	⋆
	U	La	20.10.59 - 20.11.59	28	⋆
	'U	Ba	30.05.60 - 04.07.60	31	⋆
	'U	Br	22.05.61 - 12.06.61	19	⋆
	'HI	Cy	25.07.61 - 08.12.61	118	84.6
	'U	Br	16.05.63 - 05.06.63	18	⋆
92222	'U	Ba	21.04.59 - 19.05.59	25	⋆
	U	Oo	29.10.59 - 16.11.59	16	⋆
	'U	Ba	07.05.60 - 21.05.60	13	⋆
	'U	Ej	31.10.60 - 17.11.60	16	⋆
	'U	Ej	13.12.60 - 31.01.61	43	⋆
	'U	Gl	19.05.61 - 10.06.61	20	⋆

Table 8.2
BR Standard Class 9F 2-10-0s: Record of Repairs

No.	1	2	3	4	5
92222	'U	Ej	02.08.61 - 12.09.61	36	★
(cont.)	***'HI***	S	20.12.61 - 25.04.62	109	78.5
	'U	Ej	09.10.63 - 31.10.63	20	★
	LC	S	10.03.64 - 16.04.64	33	★
92223	AT	S	16.09.58 - 19.09.58	04	★
	'U	Ba	28.01.59 - 13.02.59	15	★
	'U	Ws	11.11.59 - 01.12.59	18	★
	'U	Ba	05.04.60 - 26.04.60	19	★
	HC	S	13.10.60 - 15.02.61	107	49.4
	LC	Go	12.10.62 - 10.01.63	78	★
	HI	S	22.05.64 - 24.12.64	186	90.0
	'LC	C	25.07.66 - 08.09.66	40	★
92224	AT	S	23.09.58 - 13.10.58	18	★
	'U	Ba	26.02.59 - 18.03.59	18	★
	U	La	22.01.60 - 09.02.60	16	★
	LC	S	23.04.60 - 26.05.60	29	★
	'U	Ba	28.07.61 - 11.09.61	39	★
	'HI	S	05.06.62 - 10.10.62	112	95.9
	'U	Ox	02.11.62 - 16.11.62	13	★
	'U	Ox	02.03.63 - 11.04.63	35	★
	CA	C	26.03.65 - 28.04.65	29	★
92225	'U	Sp	29.07.59 - 18.08.59	18	★
	U	La	14.09.59 - 02.10.59	15	★
	U	Ta	24.12.59 - 11.01.60	16	★
	'U	Ej	13.03.61 - 06.04.61	22	★
	'HI	Cy	23.06.61 - 20.10.61	103	84.1
	'U	Ej	31.10.61 - 18.11.61	17	★
	'LC	Cy	13.03.62 - 04.05.62	46	★
	'U	Ej	19.12.62 - 12.01.63	22	★
	'U	Ej	16.04.63 - 04.05.63	17	★
	'U	Gl	19.07.63 - 19.08.63	27	★
	'HC	S	23.01.64 - 11.08.64	173	★
92226	'U	Ba	02.06.59 - 17.06.59	14	★
	U	Ba	30.09.59 - 24.10.59	22	★
	'U	Ba	02.12.59 - 23.12.59	19	★
	'U	Ej	03.01.61 - 26.01.61	21	★
	'U	Ej	22.02.61 - 10.03.61	15	★
	'HI	S	22.03.61 - 12.10.61	176	63.8
	'U	Oo	15.03.62 - 03.04.62	18	★
	'U	Ej	14.08.63 - 16.09.63	29	★
92227	'U	Wr	11.07.58 - 08.08.58	25	★
	AT	S	08.10.58 - 09.10.58	02	★
	'U	Ba	26.02.59 - 18.03.59	18	★
	'U	Ba	11.09.59 - 28.09.59	15	★
	'U	Ba	06.10.59 - 20.10.59	13	★
	'U	Ba	24.12.59 - 07.01.60	13	★
	'U	Ba	07.05.60 - 30.05.60	20	★
	LC	S	11.07.60 - 13.10.60	82	★
	HI	W	26.01.62 - 01.06.62	109	79.7
	'U	Dt	24.01.63 - 26.03.63	53	★
	LC	C	04.09.63 - 12.10.63	34	★
	CA	C	15.04.64 - 25.06.64	62	★
	LI	C	01.03.66 - 20.04.66	44	★
92228	'U	Ba	29.04.59 - 18.05.59	17	★
	U	Ba	08.10.59 - 31.10.59	21	★
	U	W	??.60	★	★
	'HC	S	14.07.60 - 19.01.61	164	★
	HI	S	15.05.62 - 27.09.62	117	92.6
	'U	Sj	27.12.62 - 04.02.63	34	★
	'LC	C	08.11.65 - 23.12.65	40	★
92229	'U	Sa	07.08.58 - 10.09.58	30	★
	'U	Ej	20.08.60 - 10.09.60	19	★
	'HI	Cy	25.09.61 - 02.02.62	113	78.4
	'U	Ej	02.11.63 - 02.01.64	53	★
92230	AT	S	15.08.58 - 09.09.58	22	★
	'U	Ba	26.02.59 - 18.03.59	18	★
	'U	Oo	06.04.59 - 24.04.59	17	★
	★	S	02.61	★	★
	'U	Ej	12.09.61 - 07.10.61	23	★
	'HI	S	06.04.62 - 29.08.62	126	88.5
92230	'U	Gl	09.02.63 - 28.03.63	41	★
(cont.)					
92231	AT	S	17.10.58 - 21.10.58	04	★
	U	Wr	11.59	★	★
	HI	E	20.03.61 - 06.05.61	42	78.5
	'U	Gl	28.07.61 - 21.08.61	21	★
	HG	C	04.03.63 - 04.04.63	28	★
	U	C	21.09.64 - 07.11.64	42	★
	NR	C	12.11.64 - 13.11.64	02	★
92232	U	Ba	16.10.59 - 30.10.59	13	★
	U	Ba	26.01.60 - 01.03.60	31	★
	U	W	??.60	★	★
	HC	S	10.12.60 - 14.04.61	108	69.3
	'U	Cc	06.04.62 - 05.05.62	26	★
	LC	Go	15.10.62 - 19.12.62	56	★
	'U	Ce	18.03.63 - 03.04.63	15	★
	'U	Oo	30.08.63 - 25.09.63	23	★
	LC	S	23.01.64 - 17.04.64	74	129.2
92233	AT	S	22.10.58 - 24.10.58	03	★
	U	Ba	18.11.59 - 07.12.59	17	★
	LC	Cy	08.08.60 - 07.10.60	53	★
	'U	Cc	08.06.61 - 23.06.61	15	★
	HI	S	19.10.61 - 30.01.62	89	88.1
	'U	Ej	26.02.63 - 15.03.63	16	★
	LC	C	02.12.63 - 18.01.64	42	★
	HC	C	15.09.64 - 13.11.64	52	★
	LI	C	08.02.66 - 05.03.66	23	★
	NR	C	21.03.66 - 30.03.66	09	★
92234	AT	S	27.10.58 - 31.10.58	05	★
	'U	Pr	02.12.58 - 17.12.58	14	★
	'U	Ba	02.10.59 - 21.10.59	16	★
	'U	Ba	19.11.59 - 03.12.59	13	★
	'U	Ba	26.02.60 - 15.03.60	16	★
	LC	Cy	27.10.60 - 11.11.60	14	★
	HI	S	18.04.61 - 15.08.61	103	69.0
	LC	C	23.05.63 - 15.06.63	21	★
	HC	C	04.10.63 - 29.11.63	49	★
	LI	C	03.06.65 - 07.07.65	30	★
	HC	C	02.08.66 - 10.10.66	60	★
92235	LC	Cy	18.05.60 - 31.05.60	12	★
	'U	Sj	21.11.60 - 14.12.60	21	★
	'U	Gl	26.07.61 - 24.08.61	26	★
	'HI	S	04.05.62 - 17.09.62	117	95.9
	'U	Gl	12.06.64 - 05.08.64	47	★
92236	U	Dt	29.10.59 - 27.11.59	26	★
	'U	Cc	03.08.60 - 17.08.60	13	★
	'HI	Cy	06.12.61 - 10.04.62	109	107.5
	'U	Ce	26.10.62 - 21.11.62	23	★
	'U	Gl	22.09.63 - 21.10.63	25	★
92237	U	Cc	01.12.59 - 14.12.59	12	★
	'U	Cc	22.07.60 - 06.08.60	14	★
	'U	Cc	30.08.61 - 17.09.61	16	★
	'HI	S	04.01.62 - 08.05.62	107	105.8
	'U	Ce	27.09.63 - 17.10.63	18	★
	'U	Ce	03.11.63 - 28.11.63	22	★
	'U	Gl	14.04.64 - 27.05.64	38	★
92238	'U	Ly	07.02.59 - 17.03.59	33	★
	U	Oo	28.11.59 - 14.12.59	14	★
	'U	Oo	24.05.60 - 13.06.60	18	★
	'U	Oo	20.08.60 - 09.09.60	18	★
	'U	So	08.04.61 - 24.04.61	14	★
	'HI	Cy	21.06.61 - 01.12.61	141	78.6
	★	S	??.03.64 - ??.04.64	★	★
	LC	E	11.06.64 - 01.07.64	18	★
92239	AT	S	13.11.58 - 18.11.58	05	★
	'U	Oo	13.02.59 - 18.03.59	29	★
	LC	W	06.01.61 - 10.02.61	31	★
	LC	E	17.11.61 - 16.12.61	26	89.4
	LC	E	16.02.62 - 24.02.62	08	89.6
	LC	E	17.05.62 - 19.05.62	03	89.9

Table 8.2
BR Standard Class 9F 2-10-0s: Record of Repairs

No.	1	2	3	4	5
92239 (cont.)	‘HG	C	03.04.63 - 04.05.63	28	★
	★	C	10.63	★	★
92240	AT	S	19.11.58 - 21.11.58	03	★
	'U	Ly	30.12.58 - 13.01.59	13	★
	HI	S	17.11.61 - 02.03.62	91	94.1
	'U	So	06.02.63 - 07.03.63	26	★
	LC	C	16.07.63 - 17.08.63	27	★
	LC	E	20.08.64 - 04.09.64	14	★
92241	'U	Oo	14.09.60 - 13.10.60	26	★
	'U	Gl	25.02.61 - 24.03.61	24	★
	'U	Dt	21.04.61 - 22.05.61	27	★
	'HI	S	03.07.61 - 08.01.62	163	85.6
	'U	Gl	28.11.62 - 01.02.63	56	★
	'U	Ce	04.11.63 - 16.12.63	37	★
92242	'U	S	04.12.58 - 10.04.59	111	★
	'U	Ej	17.11.60 - 02.12.60	14	★
	'U	Gl	21.08.61 - 03.10.61	38	★
	'LC	Go	04.10.62 - 21.12.62	68	★
	'HC	C	01.01.63 - 06.02.63	32	80.9
92243	U	Ej	19.02.60 - 11.04.60	45	★
	'U	Ej	08.10.60 - 07.11.60	26	★
	'U	Ej	19.08.61 - 07.09.61	17	★
	'HI	S	21.05.62 - 02.11.62	143	80.8
	'U	Oo	11.12.62 - 31.03.63	95	★
	'U	Ce	10.04.64 - 02.06.64	46	★
92244	U	So	04.01.60 - 12.02.60	35	★
	'U	Cc	09.11.60 - 29.11.60	18	★
	'U	Cc	22.05.61 - 11.06.61	18	★
	'U	So	24.08.61 - 13.10.61	44	★
	★	S	12.61	★	★
	'HI	S	20.02.62 - 23.05.62	80	86.1
92245	'U	Ba	26.02.59 - 18.03.59	18	★
	'U	Oo	12.06.59 - 29.06.59	15	★
	U	Oo	13.12.59 - 04.01.60	19	★
	'U	Oo	18.08.60 - 09.09.60	20	★
	'U	S	06.03.61 - 31.05.61	75	★
	'HI	S	06.07.61 - 06.12.61	132	74.2
	'U	Sg	20.02.62 - 10.03.62	17	★
	'LC	Cy	13.04.62 - 24.04.62	10	★
	'U	Ox	27.12.62 - 01.02.63	32	★
92245 (cont.)	'U	So	30.07.63 - 21.08.63	20	★
92246	U	Oo	20.11.59 - 11.12.59	19	★
	'U	So	31.08.60 - 14.09.60	13	★
	'U	Oo	01.10.60 - 15.10.60	13	★
	'U	Cc	20.10.60 - 11.11.60	20	★
	'U	Cc	23.11.60 - 20.12.60	24	★
	LC	Cy	??.12.60 - 28.01.61	★	★
	'U	Cc	10.04.61 - 26.04.61	15	★
	'U	Cc	31.05.61 - 19.06.61	17	★
	'HI	S	04.04.62 - 12.07.62	86	89.7
	'U	Hd	11.01.63 - 30.03.63	68	★
	'U	S	18.07.63 - 29.08.63	37	★
	'U	So	07.12.63 - 03.01.64	24	121.3
	'U	So	30.01.64 - 27.02.64	25	★
	★	C	07.65	★	★
92247	'U	Oo	18.02.59 - 17.03.59	24	★
	'U	So	06.11.59 - 27.11.59	19	★
	'U	So	02.11.60 - 21.12.60	43	★
	'U	Oo	01.07.61 - 18.07.61	15	★
	'LC	Os	11.11.61 - 09.02.62	78	★
	★	C	08.62	★	★
	★	C	06.63	★	★
	★	C	06.65	★	★
92248	'U	Ej	02.06.60 - 23.06.60	19	★
	'U	Br	15.03.62 - 04.04.62	18	★
	'U	Br	21.04.62 - 24.05.62	29	★
	'U	Br	28.09.62 - 12.10.62	13	★
	'LC	C	02.04.63 - 11.06.63	61	★
	'U	Br	04.05.64 - 02.06.64	26	★
92249	'U	La	06.08.60 - 25.09.60	43	★
	'U	Ej	11.05.61 - 27.05.61	15	★
	'U	Ej	15.09.61 - 02.10.61	15	★
	'U	Ej	11.01.63 - 01.02.63	19	★
	LI	C	25.03.63 - 19.04.63	23	93.4
	★	C	07.65	★	★
	'HI	C	27.10.65 - 11.12.65	39	★
92250	'U	Ej	25.01.61 - 22.02.61	25	★
	'LC	C	14.12.62 - 15.01.63	29	80.7
	'HC	S	24.12.63 - 20.03.64	77	98.5

Key

Note: ★ indicates information not traced

Column 1. Repair Classification

Repairs in heavy italics eg. ***HG*** indicate a boiler change was made at this overhaul.

Data taken from Engine Record Cards except for repairs marked (') where Engine History Cards are the source.

AD	Adjustment (equivalent to NR)
AT	WR ATC apparatus fitted
BQ	Briquette Tube Feed water softener fitted
BT	Boiler Tube Repairs
BW	Boiler Water Tubes
CA	Casual
CL	Casual Light
CR	Collision Repair
D	Derailment
ET	Engine Tyre Turning
FB	Firebox fracture repair
G	General
HC	Heavy Casual
HG	Heavy General
HI	Heavy Intermediate
I	Intermediate
LI	Light Intermediate
LC	Light Casual
NC	Non Classified
NM	Non Classified (Modification)
NR	Non Classified Rectification Engine Order often recorded as 'NC (Rect.) EO'
PV	Pistons and Valves
R	Repair
T	Tyre Repair
TM	Tubes and Mouthpiece
TU	Tubes
U	Unclassified
UN	Unscheduled Repair
W	Weighing exercise

Column 2. Repair Location

Ba	Banbury MPD	La	Laira MPD
Bg	Bath Green Park MPD	Ly	Llanelly MPD
Br	Bristol Barrow Road MPD	Ma	March MPD
C	Crewe Works	Na	Newton Abbot MPD
Cc	Cardiff Canton MPD	Oo	Old Oak Common MPD
Ce	Cardiff East Dock MPD	Os	Oswestry Works
Ck	Carlisle Kingmoor	Ox	Oxley MPD
Cy	Caerphilly Works	Pr	Pontypool Road MPD
Da	Darlington Works	Ru	Rugby Works
De	Derby Works	S	Swindon Works
Do	Doncaster MPD	Sa	Salop MPD
Ds	Derby MPD	Sg	Stourbridge Junction MPD
Dt	Didcot MPD	Sj	Severn Tunnel Junction MPD
Dy	Duffryn Yard MPD	So	Southall MPD
E	Eastleigh Works	Sp	Bristol St. Philips Marsh MPD
Ej	Ebbw Junction MPD	St	Stratford Works
Ga	Gateshead Works	Ta	Taunton MPD
Gl	Gloucester Horton Road MPD	Ty	Tyseley MPD
Go	Gorton Works	W	Wolverhampton Stafford Road Works
Hd	Hereford MPD	Wl	Wellingborough MPD
Ho	Horwich Works	Wr	Worcester MPD
Kt	Kettering MPD	Ws	Westbury MPD

Column 3. Date of Repair

The data was taken from the Engine Record Cards (ERCs) where these are available and record the month of Works entry.

For repairs marked (') in Column 1 the data was taken from the Engine History Cards (EHCs).

The ERC dates specify the period of time the engine was actually on Works whereas the EHC refers to the period between being taken out of traffic and being released by Works. The release dates on both cards almost invariably coincide.

Column 4. Weekdays Out Of Service

Number of days out of service for that particular repair excluding Sundays.

Column 5. Mileage from New at Start of Repair ('000s)

Except where errors in the record have occurred, the date taken out of traffic on the EHCs is earlier than that on the ERCs, ranging from several days in most instances to a number of weeks in others. In the case of some WR repairs undertaken at Swindon, the difference could be of the order of two months or more.
Weekdays Out Of Service data, see Column 4, obtained from EHCs is thus not strictly comparable with that from ERCs and should be taken as a guide only.

Figure 180
92012 (Carlisle Kingmoor) approaches Shap station with a southbound Class 'F' mixed freight on 11th June 1965. From transfer to Carlisle one year earlier, the engine was employed mainly on such WCML freight work until withdrawal in October 1967. 92012 and 92073 exchanged their BR1F tenders at about the time of their visits to Crewe Works for Light Intermediate overhauls in October 1958. *(Rodney Lissenden)*

Figure 181
92001 has been fitted with the Whitaker Tablet Exchange equipment for single line working. Here the fireman is ready with the catcher set for the tablet pick-up, as the ten-coach 7.43am Bradford Forster Square-Bournemouth West eases towards Bath Junction signal box on 14th July 1962, the last summer of through holiday express working on the S&DJR. 92001 was fitted with a double chimney at Swindon in March 1960 and was still employed on passenger train working (GCR line) in August 1965; the S&DJR headlamp code will be noted.
(Hugh Ballantyne)

Table 8.3
British Railways Steam Locomotive Repair Classification

Repair Type	Designation	Description of Work Carried Out	Status
General (G) †	Heavy (H)	Boiler Change All mechanical parts stripped, repaired or renewed as necessary to enable engine to run to next Intermediate or General overhaul	Mileage 'made good'
Intermediate (I)	Heavy (H) or Light (L) depending on work done as defined in Ministry of Transport Classification (see below)	Boiler not changed but such repairs to be carried out to it and all mechanical parts as will ensure mileage approx. equal to average for the class between consecutive General and Intermediate repairs will be attained before next scheduled General or Intermediate repair	Mileage 'made good'
Casual (C)	Heavy (H) or Light (L) depending on work done as defined in Ministry of Transport Classification (see below)	Repair or replace those parts which have become defective due to failure or mishap making engine unserviceable. No work carried out on other components	Mileage NOT 'made good'
Non-Classified (NC)		Repairs necessary as defined for Casual repairs but not covered by Ministry of Transport Heavy or Light classification. No work carried out on other components	Mileage NOT 'made good'

Key: † General: Darlington Works appears in some cases to have classified Heavy General overhaul as 'G' rather than 'HG'

Table 8.4
Ministry of Transport Steam Locomotive Repair Classification and Specification

Heavy Repairs	Light Repairs
(1) Engine re-boilered (2) Boiler taken out of frame for heavy repair Any two of the following (3) Fitting of new tyres to four or more wheels (4) Fitting new cylinders (5) Fitting new axle or axles, engine or tender (6) Re-tubing of boiler (7) Turning up wheels or refitting axleboxes; or motion and brake-work stripped and overhauled (8) Repairing of boiler on frame with not less than 50 stays renewed Note: the two items in (7) would not, taken together, constitute a heavy repair	(1) Fitting new axle or axles, engine or tender (2) Taking out and replacing 50 or more boiler tubes (3) Taking out and replacing four or more superheater tubes (4) Taking down and replacing superheater header (5) Renewal of piston valve liners or piston valves (6) Fitting new tyres to one or more wheels (7) Turning up four or more wheels and refitting axleboxes (8) Complete overhaul of one or more valve gears (9) Fitting patch on boiler or firebox (10) Renewing 30 or more firebox stays (11) Fitting four or more new axleboxes or engine axlebox brasses (12) Welding, patching or straightening frame or renewing buffer beam (13) Re-boring cylinders and re-facing ports (14) Taking off and repairing tanks

Note on Mileage 'made good'
It will be noted in the work specified in Table 8.4, constituting either a Heavy or Light repair, that no indication is given of the extent if any to which mileage run in traffic has been 'made good'. A locomotive for example which has its boiler lifted for attention to some leaking rivets behind the frames or for any other reason, however incidental, is automatically classified as having had a heavy repair, although no work may have been done on the tyres, axleboxes, frames or motion. In such circumstances the mileage run by the locomotive since previous repairs has not been 'made good' and it is not necessarily fit for a further full average period in traffic.

were the short-haul iron ore traffic from Tyne Dock to Consett for the steel works. With the exception of 92066, the NER allocation was given a second heavy overhaul at Darlington, such work then being transferred to Crewe; for 92063, the ERC states that it received a General overhaul at Darlington in May 1963, some eight months after such work was supposed to have been reassigned to Crewe. After responsibility for 9F repairs was transferred from Darlington, no record of NER engines visiting Eastleigh for repairs has been traced. This may have been because the expertise for overhauling the Westinghouse air pumps now resided at Crewe, the works where the equipment was originally fitted.

For the first batch of 9Fs allocated to the WR, 92000-7, the first major repair was either a Heavy Intermediate or Heavy General carried out on average at just over 80,000 miles from new. (Note: the data here includes that for 92079, the Lickey banker, transferred to the WR from February 1958). Two significant points are of note here. The first is that it took nearly twice as long for the engines to run over 80,000 miles in service compared with the subsequent two WR batches, 92203-20 and 92221-50. This can be attributed to their use mainly on the Newport Docks-Rogerstone-Ebbw Vale iron ore traffic which, as in the case of the Shotton and Consett workings noted earlier, were short-haul in character resulting in annual mileages of around 15,000 or less.

The second point is the length of time the engines were resident on Swindon Works, a duration of some 153.6 days on average for the first heavy repair compared with 45 days or less at Darlington or Crewe. This did not appear to accord with the modified system for controlling the intake of engines for repairs at Swindon, introduced in July 1955. Under these proposals, 9Fs were scheduled to be fairly rare birds in works; details of shopping periods for the main heavy freight classes and numbers expected to be on works at any one time are given as follows:

Class	Shopping Period from Last Service	Target Number for Class on Works at any one time
BR 9F 2-10-0	34 months	0.5*
WD 2-8-0	80k miles	3
28XX 2-8-0	36 months	12
47XX 2-8-0	100k miles	1
ROD 2-8-0	60k miles	2
72XX 2-8-2T	42 months	4
42XX 2-8-0T	36 months	11
5205 2-8-0T	36 months	6
LMS 8F 2-8-0	22 months	†
LNWR 0-8-0	24 months	†

Key:
k thousands
* i.e. a 9F representative not always expected to be present on works.
† WR-based class member overhauls usually carried out at LMR works.

For the WR allocation, the LMR was responsible for major repairs by the time the engines were due for the next heavy overhaul and most were carried out at Crewe with a few, mainly light, repairs at Gorton and Eastleigh. Both light and heavy intermediate repairs for the SR's small allocation of only five engines 92205/6/11/31/9 in the early 1960s were dealt with at Eastleigh initially but again later repairs were assigned to Crewe. The SR-allocated 9F data is similar to that of the later WR batches which reflects the fact that they were operated by the WR until transfer; the much reduced works dwell time at Eastleigh compared with Swindon is apparent.

It appears that the BR policy from the middle of 1962 onwards was for 9F repairs to be increasingly focused on Crewe, although some work was still carried out at Gorton and Eastleigh. Average dwell time on works for the five years from autumn 1963 was similar to that for the earlier years; details are given in Table 8.6. Figures for Swindon Works for the 1961-2 period are also included. Most of the work carried out there was for Heavy Intermediate repairs during 1962; again the comparatively lengthy dwell time will be noted. After 1962, very little work is recorded at Swindon on 9Fs.

Overall, several points are apparent from the data. Except in the special case of the Crosti-boilered engines, the length of stay on works for overhauls carried out at Crewe was almost invariably lower than that for other regions. In particular, the Swindon figures indicate a much longer dwell time in works. In fairness, it should be noted that much of the WR information for the 92203-50 batches is derived from EHC data which as noted above may have included a quite lengthy period when the engine was officially 'stopped for works' but could nevertheless have been used in revenue service before eventually being taken into Swindon, Caerphilly or Wolverhampton Stafford Road. This is not however the case for the first batch of WR engines, 92000-7, (plus 92079), all relevant quoted data for which was obtained from the ERC; this shows a stay on Swindon Works of more than 150 working days on average for heavy overhauls.

Certainly in the case of the LMR, the policy was to restrict the amount of repair work on an individual engine to the minimum necessary to allow it to run the full period before the next scheduled service. Time on works was thus reduced to a minimum as were unit repair costs. WR practice was different, with Swindon carrying out a very thorough repair each time a major service was due, the aim being to achieve virtually trouble free operation apart from the usual minor problems until the next scheduled major repair. The much increased 'downtime' at the WR works however made for overall lower productivity for individual engines. Another factor may have been the lack of enthusiasm for the Standard types in general on the WR possibly resulting in the assignment of a lower priority for repairs to the BR Standards compared with 'home-grown' classes; other Standard types, e.g. the WR-based BR Class 5 4-6-0s were also noted for suffering lengthy spells on Swindon Works.

Table 8.7 shows representative repair costs per mile for the 9Fs in comparison with other Standard Classes for the year 1957. Boiler costs for the 9Fs are the highest of the six quoted examples which probably reflects the extra expense associated with the Crosti-boiler engines. The higher boiler costs resulting from operation in harder water areas where more frequent boiler washouts and extra maintenance are required may also have been a factor; some engines had been operating since January of that year from Annesley depot, whose water supply was exceptionally hard.

As a guide to the extent of the work carried out for each category of repair, Table 8.3 summarises the BR Steam Locomotive Repair Classification whilst Table 8.4 details the Ministry of Supply Locomotive Repair Classification and Specification applicable after the formation of British Railways in 1948. It is not clear whether this protocol was strictly followed in later years.

Table 8.8 displays the BR HQ's official analysis of the 9F repair data for the years 1957, 1958 and 1960. The data again confirms the relatively low productivity of the WR-based 9Fs compared with that of both the LMR and ER/NER allocations. The modifications to the earlier Standard designs based on operating experience, e.g. plain section coupling rods and the reintroduction of fall plates for tenders were all applied to the 9Fs. The only significant teething troubles with the class were the slow-acting brakes and sticking regulator experienced with the first two lots, 92000-14 and 92015-9, immediately after delivery; the investigation and remedies are covered in Section 9.1 below. Some engines were subject to a number of other detail modifications and these are also described in that section.

Figure 182
Heading north through Kidderminster with an Evesham-Crewe Class 'D' freight, 92165 (Birkenhead) shows evidence of Crewe paint shop's work after its recently completed Light Intermediate overhaul (June 1965). The engine was one of the trio of mechanical stoker-fitted engines allocated new to Saltley for the Carlisle fast freight jobs in spring 1958. 92165 was relieved of its stoker apparatus at the end of 1962 and was one of the few survivors of the 9F cull at Birkenhead in November 1967 to enjoy a short spell at Speke Junction before withdrawal in March 1968. *(C. R. Berridge)*

Table 8.5
BR Standard Class 9F 2-10-0s
Repair Schedule Summary

Region, Works and Engine Batch	First Major Repair (nominally 'Intermediate') Sched. Repair Type	Time from Delivery average in months	Period of Works Entry from/to mo.yr/mo.yr	WooS average no. of days	Miles average to repair date ('000s)	Second Major Repair (nominally 'General') Sched. Repair Type	Time from Delivery average in months	Period of Works Entry from/to mo.yr/mo.yr	WooS average no. of days	Miles average to repair date ('000s)
WR **Swindon**										
92000-07 (1)	HI/HG	67.6	03.59-09.60	153.6	80.5	No 9F HGs at Swindon after 09.60, although HIs				*
92203-20 (2)	HG/HI/HC	33.0	05.61-06.62	116.7	70.8	& HCs were undertaken for WR a/c; for a few of				*
92221-50 (3)	HG/HI/HC	39.8	10.60-12.63	113.4	83.7	the WR a/c some heavy repairs were at Crewe. For ex-WR 9Fs re-ac. to SR, LMR or NER heavy repairs were at Crewe or Eastleigh.				*
Caerphilly										
92221-50 (4)	HI	37.8	06.61-12.61	116.8	86.6	No 9Fs received for major repairs after 12.61				*
Stafford Rd.ø										
92221-50 (5)	HI	41.0	08.61-01.62	113.5	89.9	No 9Fs received for major repairs after 01.62				*
LMR **Crewe** **LMR a/c**										
92008-19 (6)	LI/HI/HG	42.8	05.57-06.58	32.4	84.5	HG	81.5	03.59-07.63	32.6	160.7
92020-29 (7)	HC/LI/HI	41.4	01.58-06.60	34.5	61.1	HG/HI	80.4	03.61-08.62	65.2	c125.0†
92030-33/43	LI (8)	41.8	01.58-07.58	30.2	93.6	HG	73.6	05.60-06.61	40.2	187.6
92045-59	LI/HI/HC	40.6	07.57-04.60	27.7	71.7	HG	73.6	09.59-10.62	38.8	128.9¶
92067-96 (9)	LI	29.8	03.58-10.59	28.2	76.9	HG/HC	72.0	01.61-07.63	35.4	173.9¶
92100-39	Record Cards imply no scheduled Intermediate Overhaul; major repairs as required, mainly					HG/HI/LI HC & HC (10)	78.3	03.62-08.64	35.7	*
92150-64	Record Cards imply no scheduled Intermediate Overhaul; major repairs as required, mainly					HG/LI/HC HC	71.2	01.63-03.65	37.7 (11)	*
92165-67 (12)	Record incomplete, see text note					Record incomplete, see text note. Some LC/LI/HI repairs for LMR a/c were carried out at Eastleigh.				
ER a/c										
92140-49	First major overhauls at Darlington, see ER data					HG	66.5 (13)	01.63-04.63	20.0	198.3
92168-202	First major overhauls at Darlington, see ER data					HG/HI/HC	64.6 (14)	12.62-11.63	35.2	172.7
Gorton **LMR a/c**										
All batches	No scheduled intermediate overhauls at Gorton for LMR 9F a/c; some LC repairs carried out.					No scheduled general overhauls at Gorton for LMR 9F a/c; some LC repairs carried out.				*
ER a/c										
92168-202	First major overhauls at Darlington; see ER data					LI (15)	60.0	09.62	68.0	186.0
						Some LC repairs for ER a/c were carried out at Gorton				
ER **Darlington**										
92010-14 (16)	G	40.3	06.57-10.57	45.0	77.7	Second major overhaul at Crewe; see LMR data				
92030-33/43	Re-a/c to LMR before or during first major repair					Second major overhaul at Crewe; see LMR data				
92034-42/4	LI/G	37.5	06.57-08.58	36.0	86.7	HG	69.6	04.60-05.61	45.7	168.6
92067-76	Re-a/c to LMR before first major repair due					See LMR data				
92087-96	Re-a/c to LMR before first major repair due					See LMR data				
92140-49	LI/HI/G	29.7	08.59-06.60	38.7	92.1	G (17)	54.0	06.61-04.62	36.0	180.8
92168-202	LI/HI/G	34.7	01.60-03.62	41.5	99.4	G/HC(18)	51.7	04.62-05.62	46.0	141.9
						Later overhauls were all at either Crewe, Eastleigh or Gorton				
NER **Darlington**										
92060-66	G/HI	45.0	01.59-01.60	36.3	85.5	G/HC (19)	75.8 (19)	03.61-08.63	64.5	151.3
92097-99	G/HI	39.3	07.59-11.59	42.0	75.1	G	69.0	02.62-03.62	57.5	140.7
						Later overhauls were all at either Crewe or Gorton				
SR **Eastleigh**										
SR a/c (20)	HI/LI/LC	35.2	03.61-10.62	27.6	80.7	Re-a/c to NER before General repair due; all subsequent major repairs carried out at Crewe				*
	LC sometimes reclassified LI as work progressed									

Key

WooS Weekdays out of Service; LC Light Casual; LI Light Intermediate; HI Heavy Intermediate; HC Heavy Casual; G General; HG Heavy General

1 Includes 92079 transferred to WR stock 02.58;
2 Excludes 92205/6/11 transferred from WR to SR before Intermediate overhauls due.
3 Excludes 92231/9 transferred from WR to SR before Intermediate overhauls due.
4 Five locos 92221/5/9/36/8;
5 Two locos 92079, 92227;
6 First major repair excludes 92011/2/4 still on ER;
7 Crosti boiler engines;
8 First major repair for 92030 was at Darlington;
9 Excludes 92079 transferred to WR stock 02.58;
10 92134 reported to have had LI at Eastleigh, July 1964;
11 Excludes 92157 on Works for LI for 132 days from August 1964 with unspecified 'serious problem'.
12 Mechanical Stoker-fitted engines;
13 Data for two locos only 92146/8;
14 Data for thirteen locos 92168/72-4/8/81/2/4/6/7/92, 92200/1;
15 Data for one loco, 92179;
16 First major repair excludes 92010/3 already re-a/c to LMR;
17 Data for four locos, 92141/4/5/7;
18 Data for three locos, 92177/83/9;
19 Second major repair for 92066 was carried out at Crewe;
20 Five locos, 92205/6/11/31/9.

* Data not traced; estimated average mileage for LMR a/c by depot suggests figure is around 175,000 for 92100-39 batch and 165,000 for 92150-64 batch.
a/c allocation; re-a/c reallocated;
† Estimate based on average 25,000 miles per year post conversion.
¶ Figures distorted by lack of mileage data after 1961; estimates based on typical average mileage by depot indicate 145,000 would be nearer the true figure for the 92045-59 batch and 190,000 for the 92067-96 batch;
ø Wolverhampton

Figure 183
In the fierce winter conditions of 1963, 92145 eases a northbound Class 'F' freight through Peterborough North on 14th January. 92145 appears to have been an engine favoured for experimental modifications. At various times, according to record cards, it was fitted with a speedometer, SUPAPLUS fibre gland cylinder packing and steel internal steam pipes to inhibit corrosion; also installed were a soot blower and coal sprinkler. AWS was carried from October 1959. *(Courtney Haydon)*

Table 8.6
BR Standard Class 9F 2-10-0s
Time Taken to Complete Repairs
by Works and Repair Type (1963-1968)

Works	Repair Type	Dwell Time on Works (average no. of working days)
Crewe	HG	44
	HI/I	41
	LI	37
	HC	37
	LC/C	30
Gorton	LC	51
Eastleigh	HI/LI	43
	LC	33
Swindon	HI	113 †
	HC	115 †
	LC	¶

Key † Data for the period 1961-1962
Little later HI/HC work reported

¶ Little such work carried out in this period

Data source: NRM York and PRO Kew

Table 8.7
BR Standard Class 9F 2-10-0s
Representative Repair Costs (new pence) per Mile for the Year 1957
Comparison with the Larger Standard Classes

Class	Wheel Arrangement	Engine	Boiler	Tender	Total
9F (incl. Crosti engines)	2-10-0	3.77	0.64	0.35	4.76
8P Duke Of Gloucester	4-6-2	4.42	0.40	0.65	5.47
7MT Britannia	4-6-2	2.83	0.46	0.21	3.50
6MT Clan	4-6-2	3.65	0.22	0.30	4.17
5MT	4-6-0	3.47	0.36	0.42	4.25
4MT	4-6-0	3.22	0.53	0.50	4.25

Table 8.8
BR Standard Class 9F 2-10-0s
Repair History: Official BR Report for the Years 1957, 1958 and 1960 from NRM Records

Year Region and Engine Type	General Repairs						Intermediate Repairs						Intermediate Repairs			Casual Repairs				Boilers		
							To Inter from General			To General or Inter. following Inter.						Heavy		Light	Total	Total boilers fitted in all repairs inc. Gens.		
	Loco with new boiler (no.)	Loco with rep-aired boiler (no.)	Total Gen-eral repairs (no.)	Av. miles bet-ween Gen. repairs ('000s)	Av. time bet-ween Gen. repairs (mo-nths)	Av. shop time (work-ing days)	Locos (no.)	Av miles from Gen-eral ('000s)	Av. time from Gen-eral (mo-nths)	Locos (no.)	Av. miles from last Inter ('000s)	Av. time from last Inter (mo-nths)	Heavy (no.)	Light (no.)	Total (no.)	With boiler ch'nge (no.)	With-out boiler ch'nge (no.)	(no.)	Heavy & Light (no.)	Locos (no.)	Av. miles from last boiler ch'nge ('000s)	Av time from last boiler ch'nge (mo-nths)
1957																						
LM Standard	*	*	*	*	*	*	9	69.4	33.4	*	*	*	2	7	9	*	1	12	13	*	*	*
LM Crosti	*	*	*	*	*	*	*	*	*	*	*	*	*	*	*	*	4	10	14	*	*	*
E/NE Standard	1	3	4	79.0	37.0	44.0	2	80.0	33.0	*	*	*	*	2	2	*	*	3	3	4	79.0	37.0
W Standard	*	*	*	*	*	*	*	*	*	*	*	*	*	*	*	*	1	7	8	*	*	*
1958																						
LM Standard	*	1	1	78.8	51.0	69.0	25	78.7	32.1	*	*	*	*	25	25	*	*	13	13	1	78.8	*
LM Crosti	*	*	*	*	*	*	9	60.3	35.6	*	*	*	7	2	9	*	*	*	*	*	*	*
E/NE Standard	*	1	1	90.1	43.0	31.0	6	91.6	38.0	*	*	*	*	6	6	*	*	7	7	1	43.0	*
W Standard	*	*	*	*	*	*	*	*	*	*	*	*	*	*	*	*	1	7	8	*	*	*
1960																						
LM Standard	*	8	8	148.0	62.0	21.1	*	*	*	5	73.4	29.2	*	*	*	*	7	36	43	8	148.0	62.0
LM Crosti	*	*	*	*	*	*	1	67.5	56.0	*	*	*	*	1	1	*	2	3	5	*	*	*
E/NE Standard	1	11	12	129.4	49.0	44.0	18	91.9	31.0	6	75.7	27.0	3	15	18	*	*	6	6	12	129.4	49.0
W Standard	2	1	3	85.2	42.9	112.0	2	85.9	43.2	*	*	*	2	*	2	1	*	6	7	4	79.5	65.3

9. Modifications in Service

9.1 Standard Design

On arrival at Newport Ebbw Junction in early 1954, the first batch of 9Fs, 92000-7, quickly displayed two disconcerting characteristics:

(1) the slow action of the steam brakes following periods of inactivity and

(2) the tendency of the regulator valve to stick wide open.

In other words, once the engines were up and running, they were, under certain circumstances, quite difficult to stop. The brake problem was tracked down to the steam delivery to the two brake cylinders which were supplied through relatively long and narrow unlagged pipes. Following tests carried out in early July 1954 on 92002, the only WR 9F in active service at the time, it was established that the time taken to achieve brake cylinder working pressure of 230 lb/sq in from 'cold' was around 50 seconds, over twice as long as the 20 seconds recorded when the engine was 'warm'.

The problem was resolved to a large extent by increasing the bore size of the steam delivery pipe to the brake cylinders such that greater quantities of steam were supplied at a faster rate; the effectiveness was enhanced by the provision of a suitable pipe lagging. Other remedies such as increasing the brake cylinders' diameter from 9¼ in and modifying the leverage ratio of the brake assembly could possibly have improved matters further but were rejected on the grounds that this would have resulted in the braking force exceeding the engines' adhesive weight leading to the risk of derailment either of the engine or its train.

The braking problem, although much reduced by these modifications, persisted however and apparently was never fully resolved. In particular, a number of engines delivered to depots unused to their characteristics could be observed on early return visits to works for collision damage repair (see Table 8.2) until crews got the measure of them. One reported instance related to the first allocation of 9Fs to Saltley. The engines were found to be a tight fit on the roundhouse turntable and it was said that on more than one occasion, a 9F left the building with a number of bricks in the tender, having come into contact with the external wall; a joiner and bricklayer found almost continuous employment there for several weeks.

Braking problems were also experienced during the early days of the 9F workings on the S&DJR. In the booklet, **The S&D 7Fs Remembered**, published by the 73082 Camelot Locomotive Society, Mr. Peter Smith comments that although the 9Fs were intended for passenger duties on the S&DJR, the diagram covering the "Pines Express" involved hauling a freight train in each direction. The 8.10 pm Poole Yard to Bath was a particularly heavy train which usually loaded to the maximum permitted for the class of locomotive working it. On at least two occasions, the 9F working this train reportedly lost control of its load when running downhill; in neither case was reckless driving involved.

In tackling the sticking regulator problem, improved lubrication using molybdenum disulphide was tried at first but the effects wore off within a few days and it was considered impractical to specify this application as a routine service requirement. After further investigation, the problem was attributed to the horizontal configuration of the throttle in the dome which had been positioned as high as possible above the water surface, to reduce risk of priming and for which no adequate means of lubrication had been devised. The pressure of the steam resulted in the regulator being pushed down hard on its seating as the steam passed through. Apart from a return to the Melesco multi-valve throttle in the smokebox which was a non-starter due to expense and weight considerations, the only other option was a smaller sliding throttle in the dome.

To check the viability of such an alternative, it was decided to conduct tests to establish whether an appreciable reduction in the steam port entry area of the regulator, permitting the area under differential steam pressure to be correspondingly reduced, would prove detrimental to the working of the locomotive.

The method chosen was to measure the pressure drop between boiler and steam chest with the engine performing at several different steam rates over the working range. Initial road tests were carried out, again with 92002 in South Wales, from June to September 1954. Tests were made initially with the port area fully open (34.2 sq in, itself a reduction from the 42 sq in of the original design). A special restriction stop was then fitted to the regulator head so that the valve could only open to 24.3 sq in. Initial results with 92002 proved promising and in October 1954, 92015 similarly modified, was tested on Rugby Plant for two weeks. Equipment was specially made to measure the differential pressure between dome and steam chest more accurately. Six tests were conducted with the regulator fully open and five with the reduced opening. The increase in pressure drop with the latter was around 11%, equating to only one pound per square inch loss even at the maximum sustained steaming rate (29,000 lb per hour with live steam injector) of which the locomotive was capable. It was thus established that there would be no appreciable reduction in power output at any given steaming rate.

As a result, the modified regulator was adopted for all new 9Fs and installed retrospectively on the earlier engines. The latter remained stored out of service until the new regulators could be fitted, the WR engines 92000/1/3-7 at Gloucester and in South Wales and the ER group (92010-4) at March depot. Lot Number E489 (92030-49) began to emerge from Crewe in early November 1954 but information on which engine of this group was the first to receive the modified regulator from new has not been traced. It is interesting to observe that 92008/9 out of the first batch delivered from Crewe and operated by the LMR out of Wellingborough were not reported as being subject to 'show-stopping' regulator problems.

Several additional modifications were noted on the 9Fs over the years. The original hand brake arrangement on the tenders was modified to be more effective but it has not been possible to trace details of the change. On many 9Fs, mainly those given overhauls at Crewe, the original small steps at the front of the smokebox were also replaced by a continuous wide footstep, referred to by some as a 'T-piece', which was inherently safer for the crew when manoeuvring lamps and accessing the smokebox door handles. Although all the 9Fs were turned out with the small steps, the modification was begun within a few weeks of the last engine, 92220 *Evening*

Figure 184
92166 (Saltley) stands outside the paint shop at Crewe Works in September 1959 four months after being released from trials at Rugby Testing Station and just before transferring on loan to the WR for Western Valley iron ore traffic trials (see Section 9).
(G. Wheeler)

Figure 185
92248 (Bristol Barrow Road) is on shed at Eastleigh in front of the new diesel depot on 7th October 1961. The Fawley oil trains were still operating via Bristol rather than the DN&S line at this time and 92248 may have appeared on one of these workings. From September 1959, 92248 spent five months on loan to Saltley in exchange for mechanical stoker-fitted 92166 which was operating on trials from Cardiff Canton and Newport Ebbw Junction. Records indicate that 92248 did not undergo a heavy repair during its lifetime, visiting works only once (April-June 1963) for a light casual overhaul two years before its withdrawal. *(Courtney Haydon)*

Star, being released to traffic. Photogaphic evidence indicates that virtually all the LMR and NER-based 9Fs received this modification but there were a number of ER and WR-based engines which, if they had not received it by the end of 1963, were not thus modified.

The WR allocation was fitted only with the GWR style lamp brackets on delivery. The two engines, 92008/9, diverted from the WR to the LMR also carried the WR brackets but received the standard BR type in addition; 92008/9's WR brackets were removed on subsequent works visits. Later, on the LMR, in common with other classes of steam engines regularly working on the overhead electrified routes, reconfiguration of the lamp brackets was required for safety reasons. The upper bracket was lowered approximately to the level of the numberplate and displaced toward the driver's side of the smokebox, the central lower bracket being repositioned under the top bracket to maintain the correct configuration.

The four 9Fs transferred to Bath Green Park (92203-6) for the summer holiday traffic on the S&DJR in 1960 had been fitted with the WR-style lamp brackets only. This created an immediate problem, as the train reporting number boards used on the line were designed for the BR standard bracket and would not fit the WR-type. Each engine was then provided with a standard lamp bracket attached to the driver's side of the smokebox rail above the numberplate to accommodate the reporting board. For the following seasons of 9F work on the S&DJR, new boards were provided which were compatible with the WR-style brackets; 92203-6 retained their smokebox rail brackets for some time afterwards, up until withdrawal date in at least one case, that

Table 9.1
BR Standard Class 9F 2-10-0s: Detail Modifications

Modification	Locomotive Modified and Date of Modification; officially recorded dates refer to 'Period Ending'				
E3329	92010: 09.08.58	92011: 27.12.58	92012: 27.12.58	92013: 04.10.58	92014: 01.11.58
	92017: 17.05.58	92018: 12.07.58	92019: 06.11.58?	92020: 04.10.58	92021: 01.11.58
	92022: 09.08.58	92023: 04.10.58	92024: 14.06.58	92025: *	92026: 19.04.58
	92027: *	92028: *	92029: *	92033: 14.06.58	92043: 14.06.58
	92055: 21.05.60	92057: 16.05.59	92069: 17.05.58	92073: 01.11.58	92077: 13.06.59
	92081: 01.11.58	92083: 10.09.60	92086: 26.03.60	92091: 21.02.59	92094: 05.09.59
E3491	92082: 03.10.59				
E4983	92020: 30.09.67°	92033: 23.03.63	92034: 17.10.59	92035: ??.12.59	92036: 27.11.59?
	92037: ??.10.59	92038: 20.01.60	92039: 04.02.61?	92040: 08.12.59	92041: 23.12.59
	92042: 08.07.60	92043: 26.01.63	92044: 03.06.61	92049" 26.01.63	92053: 29.09.63°
	92060: 07.10.60	92061: 21.07.66°	92062: 20.01.60	92063: 29.10.60	92064: 04.08.61
	92065: 13.10.60	92066: 26.11.59?	92067: 16.1.61?	92068: 25.11.60	92069: 23.03.63
	92070: *	92071: *	92072: *	92073: *	92074: *
	92075: *	92076: 23.03.63	92077: 23.02.63	92078: 26.01.63	92087: *
	92088: *	92089: *	92090: *	92091: *	92092: 23.03.63
	92093: *	92094: 26.01.63	92095: *	92096: *	92097: 28.04.62
	92098: 22.10.59	92099: 24.08.61	92115: 19.04.63	92122: 26.01.63	92128: 07.01.63
	92135: 26.01.63	92138: 23.02.63	92140: 04.02.60	92141: 08.11.59	92142: 24.03.60
	92143: 05.04.60	92144: 14.11.59	92145: 10.10.59	92146: 17.06.59	92147: 29.10.61
	92148: 29.01.60	92149: 18.08.60	92150: 23.03.63	92155: 23.02.63	92163: 26.01.63
	92165: 10.02.61?	92166: 26.01.63	92167: 13.01.61?	92168: 29.09.59	92169: 26.10.59
	92170: 07.10.59	92171: 16.12.59	92172: 01.12.59	92173: 09.11.59	92174: 31.10.59
	92175: 05.11.59	92176: 09.11.59	92177: 21.03.60	92178: 06.10.60	92179: 06.05.60
	92180: 22.09.62?	92181: 15.08.60	92182: 01.12.59	92183: 04.08.60?	92184: 27.05.60
	92185: 13.04.60?	92186: 27.07.60	92187: 27.04.61	92188: 31.12.59	92189: 25.08.59
	92190: 01.09.59	92191: 06.02.60	92192: 30.10.59	92193: 25.03.60?	92194: 11.03.60?
	92195: 01.10.59	92196: 06.08.59	92197: 22.01.60	92198: 25.03.60	92199: 27.04.60
	92200: 03.11.61	92201: 06.04.62	92202: 01.03.62?	92205: *	92206: *
	92211: 21.03.65°	92231: *	92239: 28.02.64		
J5770	92079: 11.07.56				
R5900	92008: 28.11.57	92009: 05.06.57	92015: 30.11.57	92016: 28.12.57	92017: 17.05.58
	92018: 12.07.58	92019: 06.11.58?	92020: 03.11.56	92021: 06.10.56	92022: 20.04.57
	92023: 03.11.56	92024: 20.04.57	92025: 03.11.56	92026: 23.02.57	92027: 23.03.57
	92028: *	92029: *	92045: 05.10.57	92046: 29.12.56	92047: 01.12.56
	92049: 30.11.57	92054: 21.03.59	92055: 21.05.60	92056: 14.06.58	92057: 16.05.59
	92058: 09.08.58	92059: 16.07.60	92077: 13.06.59	92078: 26.01.57	92079: 05.10.57
	92080: 16.07.60	92081: 01.11.58	92083: 10.09.60	92084: 28.11.59	92085: 07.10.61
	92086: 26.03.60				
R8245	92010: 09.08.58	92011: 27.12.58	92012: 29.11.58	92013: 04.10.58	92014: 01.11.58
	92030: 16.05.59	92031: 06.09.58	92067: 29.11.58	92068: 04.10.58	92070: 29.11.58
	92071: 24.01.59	92072: 06.09.58	92073: 01.11.58	92074: 01.11.58	92075: 01.11.58
	92076: 09.08.58	92087: 27.12.58	92088: 27.12.58	92089: 24.01.59	92090: 18.04.59
	92091: 21.02.59	92092: 01.11.58	92093: 01.11.58	92094: 05.09.59	92095: *
	92096: 29.11.58				
R8606	92012: 21.02.59				
R9294†	92020: 17.06.61	92021: 18.06.60	92022: 14.07.62	92023: 04.11.61	92024: 27.02.60
	92025: 23.04.60	92026: 03.10.59	92027: 31.12.60	92028: 03.12.59	92029: 06.08.60
SR31 (T2337)	92205: 09.10.62	92206: 27.12.62			
WH118	92165: 20.12.62	92166: 26.01.63	92167: 02.12.62		

Key
* Believed to have been modified but date not traced.
° AWS in place by this date as indicated by observers' notes and/or photographic evidence.
? Regarded as probable period ending date but not confirmed either by EHC or ERC data.
† Official ERC 'signing off' dates

of the preserved 92203.

The five 9Fs, 92205/6/11/31/9, reallocated from the WR to the SR in the early 1960s were fitted with extra lamp brackets each side of the smokebox door and halfway up the rear of the tender to accommodate the SR route discs; the original WR brackets were retained at this stage. The evolution of the lamp/disc brackets on the SR-based 9Fs is illustrated in Figure L. Profile A shows the lamp bracket configuration on the engines as delivered to the WR. Profile B pictures the positioning of SR brackets alongside the existing WR brackets with two additional SR brackets on the smokebox door. Profile C shows the SR smokebox brackets now matched by the WR variety. Finally Profile D confirms that in most cases the WR brackets and the SR/BR-type top bracket have been removed whilst the bottom middle bracket has been repositioned to leave a configuration similar to that on the LMR-based 9Fs referred to earlier; the fireman's side redundant smokebox door bracket remained in place. The above changes were of course applied equally to the back of the engines' tenders.

Photographic evidence indicates that there were variations on these schemes. One example was the saga of 92205, which did not carry an upper lamp bracket for a period after 1963. Here the WR-style upper bracket, although originally located on the smokebox door as was usual for the WR allocation, was later positioned higher, actually on the smokebox rim. Later, this bracket was removed, probably for safety reasons when working in overhead electrification areas. As 92205 was one of the four 9Fs which spent the summer of 1960 on the S&DJR, it had been fitted with a standard BR bracket attached to the smokebox rail for affixing the reporting number board. This then became the top bracket as in the LMR reconfiguration; the smokebox door middle brackets were still in place from the engine's SR days. The smokebox rail bracket was, in turn, removed at some point when the driver's side smokebox door middle bracket would presumably have been used as substitute. Confusion could well have arisen however as photographs confirm the buffer beam central bracket realignment was not carried out at the same time, although it was altered later. A further complication occurred when it appears that 92004 received the smokebox door from one of the formerly SR-based engines still with its modified bracket configuration (minus the top bracket) in place. 92004 was on Crewe Works at the same time as 92206 during the period November-December 1964 (see Table 8.2); the presumption is that the latter engine was the likely donor.

Several modifications authorised for new 9Fs at various times were applied to most, if not all, earlier engines as they passed through works; these were:

- a wider and higher cutaway portion of the running plate valance near the cylinders introduced from 92030 onwards to allow easier access to the mechanical lubricator. In addition, photographs show 92156 with a separate extra portion cut away on the driver's side after overhaul at Crewe in 1964 and 92250 was modified with an extra-wide cutaway portion on the fireman's side probably sometime in the early 1960s.
- substitution of the Gresley LNER-style method of securing the return crank to the big end by the former LMS four-stud method as specified for new 9Fs from 92050 onwards; this modification appears to have been confined to engines overhauled at Crewe.
- provision of ashpan side and front access doors as authorised for all new engines from 92087 onwards.

The double chimney modification carried out on five WR-based 9Fs (92000-2/5/6) in 1960 is covered in Section 1.5.

An early problem in service for the 9Fs was the short life of the firebox brick arch which due to the wide and shallow nature of the firebox was only usually of the order of a few weeks. The use of a concrete mix, consisting of crushed firebrick and a cement compound as building material for the arches, extended their life for up to the six months between boiler inspections when the arch had to be removed in any case as part of the inspection process; the engine was out of traffic for slightly longer than with ordinary firebrick arch replacement to allow the concrete up to 12 hours to set.

A Note on Firehole Doors

From the crews' point of view, the 9F was an ideal engine to work on. It not only produced vast amounts of steam using coal of varying quality but also gave a smooth and stable footplate ride. Many of the fireman's controls could be operated while he was seated which had the benefit of making it easier for him to keep a good look-out for signals.

The 9F firebox was shallow and almost square in configuration. A 'big fire' was always needed and it was best to make this up to the appropriate depth before the beginning of the duty; special attention would be paid to the back corners of the box for optimal steaming rate.

However, the shallow, wide box design led to three problems when firing the 9F. The first was the significant nuisance of firebox glare when operating in the hours of darkness. The glare made it difficult under certain conditions to read the aspects of distant signals. For the driver, the problem was reduced by the installation of an upright steel plate between the firebox and brake pedestal. Similarly the replacement of the original sliding firebox door with the LNER-type letterbox door (on the ER and NER) helped to reduce the glare for the fireman but was only partially successful. Further improvement could be made by the *ad hoc* arrangement of wedging a shovel close to the water gauge glass so that the hanging blade partially masked the glare.

The second problem was the heat radiation effects on the crew. On the 9F, the fireman was of course closer to the incandescent heart of the fire than he would be with a deep, narrow firebox and the intense heat from the relatively high flat bed made it more difficult to get the coal to the furthest corners of the box. By placing several shovels full of fuel to form a heap just inside the firebox door however, it was possible to deflect or 'bounce' subsequent shovel loads off the heap towards the far corners. The ability to fire both left and right handed also helped to mitigate the heat effects. Installed on some 9Fs was a device known as an air deflector. This was designed to assist in the efficient combustion of fuel but also served to shield the fireman from some of the heat. Due to budgetary constraints, deflector plates were not fitted as standard to all 9Fs.

The third problem with the 9F's wide, shallow firebox was the proximity of the main body of the fire to the sliding firehole door which tended to expand and seize up in the intense heat. Where fitted, the air deflector mentioned above helped to reduce the effect of heat radiation on the door. Other methods used to combat the problem included spraying with water from the slacker pipe or jabbing with a piece of

FIGURE L
BR STANDARD CLASS 9F 2-10-0 SR ALLOCATION (*)
EVOLUTION OF LAMP/DISC BRACKET CONFIGURATION

Profile A
As Delivered to WR

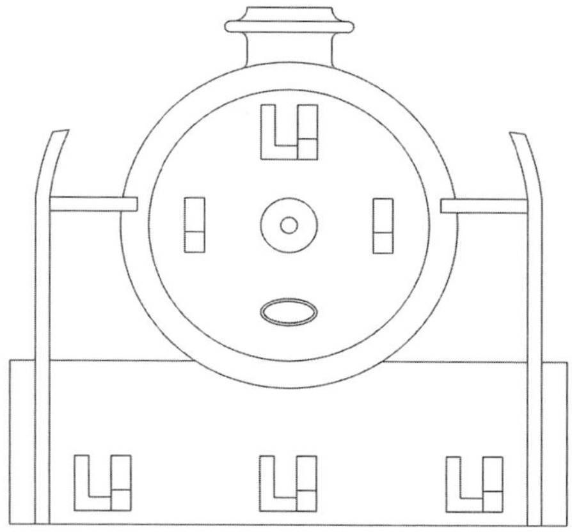

Profile B
After Transfer to SR

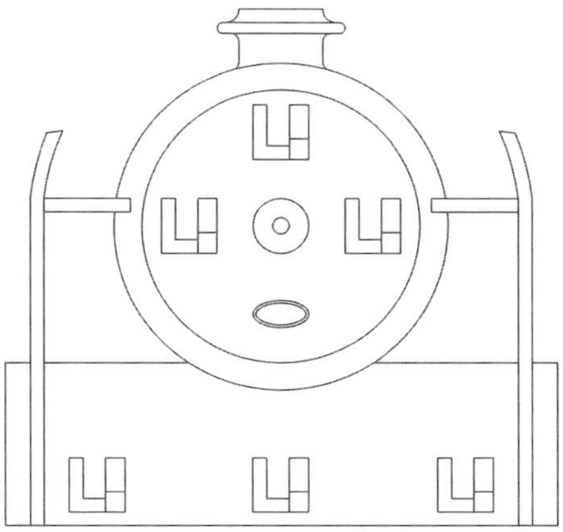

Profile C
As Observed on 92231 (May 1961)

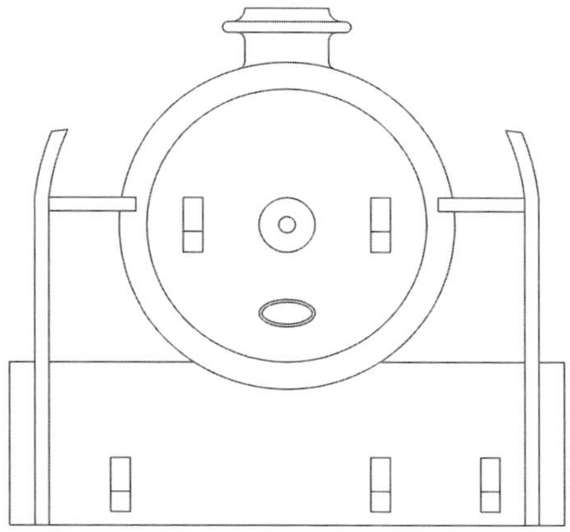

Profile D
As Observed on 92205 (November 1963)
After Transfer to NER

Key:

WR–type Lamp Bracket

SR/BR–type Lamp Bracket

* 92205, 92206, 92211, 92231, 92239

Researched by Mr.P.J.Cupper

signal rodding. The more usual method was, of course, the time-honoured process known as 'The Engineer's Reset', i.e. the conferring of a heavy blow on the offending component with a large and handy blunt instrument (generally referred to as a 'Manchester Screwdriver') such as a coal hammer. Needless to say, the failure rate of the doors under these circumstances (usual verdict: 'misadventure') was disquietingly high. The high casualty rate here was probably the main reason why the ER and NER 9Fs had their original doors replaced.

In the *Journal of the Stephenson Locomotive Society* Vol. 49, January 1973, p. 25, a letter from Mr. K. R. Phillips comments on the LNER doors fitted to the 9Fs:

"The LNER-type door....always appeared to be a larger and cruder type compared with those fitted to the ER Pacifics and V2s. One fault was that the ratchet was too small. When the trap was open, instead of being horizontal, it was at an angle; if a piece of coal touched it, it shut. Also, the inner plate of the door was too large and this prevented the trap opening to its correct position. When the fire was being cleaned or made up, it was necessary to have the door open. With the 9F, the door had to be wedged open with a spanner or coal hammer, otherwise it slowly closed and trapped the fireman's hands. None of these faults existed with the excellent ex-LNER wide fireboxes".

Record cards confirm two engines, 92100/1 were fitted with LNER type fire hole doors from new. The feature was also specified for the next batch destined for the ER (92140-49) and is believed to have been applied to the remaining ER allocation 92168-202. EHCs for ten of the original ER allocation, 92067-76, and six of the NER Tyne Dock allocation (92062/4/5/97-9) refer to the fitting of the fire hole door modification on the dates as shown:

ER

92067: 29.11.56	92068: 25.10.56
92069: 15.10.56	92070: 20.10.56
92071: 04.10.56	92072: 22.09.56
92073: 13.09.56	92074: 04.09.56
92075: 25.08.56	92076: 10.08.56

Note: Official data confirming the modification was applied to the remainder of the ER allocation has not been traced. Anecdotal evidence suggests however that all ER-based 9Fs had received it by the late 1950s. It is probable that any remaining Annesley-based 9Fs not modified by the time the depot was transferred to the LMR in February 1958 remained unaltered.

NER

92062: 14.02.57	92064: 01.10.56
92065: 31.08.56	92097: 22.03.57
92098: 05.04.57	92099: 16.04.57

Note: It is likely that the other Tyne Dock engines were similarly modified about this time.

For the NER allocation other EHC information indicates that 'weather shields' were carried by 92060. No details of this device were specified and no such reference was traced on official records of other 9Fs. Record cards confirm both coal sprinklers and soot-blowers were fitted to 92097-9; again it is probable that the first batch of Tyne Dock 9Fs (92060-6) also received these two features. The reason for fitting the coal sprinklers may have been to reduce the amount of flying coal dust entering the cab during the tender-first descent from South Medomsley to South Pelaw Junction following banking duties. In this context, it is interesting to note that photographs of 9Fs on the Tyne Dock-Consett run indicate their tenders were in many cases not fully loaded with coal, suggesting perhaps another means of reducing the flying dust problem. The soot-blowers were used to assist in decarbonising the boiler tubes, effectively a 'de-coke'.

The record also indicates that a number of ER 9Fs were fitted with coal sprinklers and soot blowers as noted below:

Coal sprinklers:	92144/5/68/77/82
Soot blowers:	92141/4/5//68/77/82

Another modification for the original NER-based engines was the reported fitting to 92097/8/9 of piston heads having three rings in an attempt to reduce piston wear resulting from the bouts of strenuous uphill activity required on the Consett run; this modification may have been applied to the rest of the Tyne Dock 9F allocation although EHCs and ERCs are mute on this point.

The engine 92141 was also fitted at some stage with the mysteriously worded 'side buffer' modification according to the EHC: it is not clear what this was or why it was fitted. 92144/5 were also reported to have had steel internal steam pipes installed to reduce corrosion potential.

Water hardness led to two other modifications on the 9Fs. Supplies at Annesley depot were especially hard and authorisation was given for the provision of two additional wash-out plugs in the boiler barrel ahead of the firebox tubeplate. Annesley-allocated 92088 was experimentally fitted with the French water softening TIA *(Traitement Intégrale Armand)* system in 1958 which was later substituted by the BR briquette method (see Section 4).

During the second half of 1958, EHCs and ERCs indicate that a number of LMR Midland Division-based 9Fs visited Derby MPD for what is described as 'Boiler Wash Tubes' work. This is likely to have been the result of the LMR's decision to suppress two firetubes in each of its 9Fs in order to install two washout plugs in the front tubeplate. The engines noted and dates of modification were as follows; dates of entry to works for this modification are given in Table 8.2.

05.58	92082/3, 92124
06.58	92052/84/5/6, 92107
07.58	92054, 92126/34
08.58	92105/33
09.58	92122/3/32/59
10.58	92019, 92106/27
11.58	92125/54/63

Speedometers were not fitted as standard to any of the 9F batches but 92013 was reported to have carried one during its road trials following its Rugby Test Plant Performance and Efficiency evaluation in 1954. ERC's indicate that both 92031 and 92145 were also fitted with speedometers at some stage.

Other detail modifications as noted in the EHCs and ERCs are given in Table 9.1. Information is incomplete as changes were not always recorded, particularly from the early 1960s onwards. The official data has been supplemented by information from observers' records. Also included are the modifications to the Lickey banker 92079 which acquired the front headlight and the steam-powered electric generator (mounted below the cab on the driver's side) of Fowler 0-10-0 58100, the former banker in use on the Lickey incline since 1919. It was reported that these items were removed from 92079 sometime during the first half of 1960 and do not appear to have been transferred to any of the subsequent bankers. The tender of 92079, BR1G/958, was also modified on the driver's side by having an opening approximately one metre in width cut from the inset coal retainer close to the spectacle plate to facilitate coaling at Bromsgrove. Official data indicates that 92079 was still paired with tender BR1G/958 from January 1960 onwards. If so, photographic evidence confirms that at some stage after reallocation from Bromsgrove to Birkenhead the opening was blanked off restoring the coal retainer to its original dimensions.

A brief description of the work involved and the official costs for the modifications are as follows.

Ref. No.	Work Specified and Costs Involved
E3329	Modified pistons for continuous blowdown valves. Cost £0 17s 6d (£0.88)
E3491	Fitting of fibreglass boiler insulation mattresses. Cost £104 11s 11d (£104.60)
E4983	Fitting of BR type ATC equipment. Cost £302 9s 0d (£302.45)
J5770	Working of Lickey Incline. Transfer of electrical equipment (headlight and wiring) from engine 58100 to 92079 and modification of tender side plate of BR1G/958 to facilitate coaling at Bromsgrove. No costs quoted.
R5900	Fitting of safety links between engine and tender. Cost £17 18s 4d (£17.92)
R8245	Fitting of continuous blowdown gear and additional washout plugs. Cost £34 18s 8d (£34.93)
R8606	Provision of chain safety device for smokebox door. Cost £0 15s 8d (£0.78)
R9294	Conversion from Crosti boiler to Standard boiler (see Section 9.2).
WH118	Removal of Berkley mechanical stoker. Cost £234 6s 8d (£234.33) derived from capital saved £1,962 13s 4d (£1,962.67) offset by a revenue charge of £2,197 0s 0d.
SR31	SR Test Number 2337. It has not been possible to trace the details of this modification which was applied to 92205/6 on transfer from the WR to the SR in December 1960; it has been suggested that it referred to the fitting of continuous blowdown apparatus but this is unconfirmed. The reference SR 31 is an arbitrary number which follows on from the series listed in **RCTS British Railways Standard Steam Locomotives, Volume Two: The 4-6-0 and 2-6-0 Classes.** Engines under test usually carried a brass plate on the cabside under the running number but it has not been possible to confirm whether these were ever carried by 92205/6; it seems unlikely.

A list of experimental fittings applied to LMR-based 9Fs (dated March 1959) is given as follows. In a number of cases, the alteration was recorded as 'deleted' suggesting the planned modification was either not carried out or subsequently terminated. The references are all prefixed 'MCL' which indicates the work was carried out at Crewe.

Mod. No.	Detail of Modification
MCL/1444	Engine and tender have parts specially treated to prevent corrosion: concluded 08.03.61. 92015-9.
MCL/1454	No details traced. 92015.
MCL/1455	Modified gangway door fastening pins. 92044 (29.01.55).
MCL/1457	Method 1. Tubes expanded in accordance with present practice, waterside with parallel hole for comparison with Methods 2 and 3, see below. 92018/9/45/9. Method 2. Tubes fireside expanded with parallel hole in both steel and copper tube plates. 92046/7/8/50. Method 3. Tubes fireside expanded with a 1-24 taper hole in copper tubeplate; and fireside expanded with parallel hole in steel tube plate. 92051/2/4. Trials concluded 25.04.61.
MCL/1460	Trial of ex-LMS type gangway doors on 9F. 92049 (no date).
MCL/1466	No details traced. 92049 (no date).
MCL/1469	Steam operated cylinder cocks and header drain fitted with 'LION' type 'U' ring. 92077/8/9. Trials concluded 03.10.62.
MCL/1470	Automatic wheel flange lubrication on leading and trailing engine wheels. 92077 (Deleted). Comparison engine: 92078 (Deleted). Trials concluded 23.02.59.
MCL/1474	UK type piston rod packing right hand side for comparison with standard packing on left hand side. 92008/15/6/8/47/8/9/53/4, 92109. Trials commenced: 92008/15/6/8: 28.12.57. 92053: 07.03.59. 92047/8/9/54: no date. 92109: 12.12.59. Trials concluded 92008/15/6/8: 17.06.60. 92047/8/9/53/4: 03.10.62. 92109: 03.10.62.
MCL/1476	Engine fitted with LNER-style fire hole door. 92100/1 (from delivery).
MCL/1481	No details traced. 92051/4: no date.
MCL/1485	No details traced. 92058: 31.01.57.
MCL/1489	No details traced. 92161: no date.
MCL/1492	No details traced. 92050: no date.
MCL/1496	No details traced. 92023: 02.02.57.
MCL/1500	No details traced. 92164: 28.09.60 (concluded).
MCL/1502	Lubrication to cylinder barrels increased to improve performance of piston rings. Existing 12 feed lubricator replaced by 16 feed lubricator. Lubricator to top of barrel doubled and atomised. Bottom doubled but not atomised. Data suggest trials carried out from engine

Figure 186
92029 (Wellingborough) calls at Nuneaton shed on 25th September 1955. The engine has worked in with the 1.56am goods from Crewe en route to its home shed after a works visit. The externally mounted tube cleaner valve, hidden behind the smoke deflector on the standard 9F, can be seen affixed to the smokebox above the handrail on the fireman's side. The Crosti is accompanied by earlier generations of freight power, Super 'D' 0-8-0s, a Class 4F 0-6-0 and a Class 8F 2-8-0.
(John S. Phillips)

Figure 187
92029 is pictured at Wellingborough MPD on 14th August 1959 after modification with a smoke deflector over the final chimney. *(Bill Hamilton)*

Figure 188
On 26th August 1962, former Crosti boiler 92029 (Kettering) has returned to its home shed after a Heavy General overhaul at Crewe Works. With the three views here, it is possible to trace the main changes in the external appearance of the engine from its original Crosti condition through to post-conversion.
(RCTS Collection)

Figure 189
92023 is out of action at Wellingborough MPD on 14th August 1959, in store in the open before conversion to conventional operation. The engine inevitably shows signs of deterioration, during storage under such conditions, including damage to the cylinder casing. *(Bill Hamilton)*

Figure 190
Wellingborough's Crosti boiler 92021 is stored at its home depot awaiting conversion to standard boiler arrangement on 30th January 1960. The side chimney on 92021 has been modified by the addition of a smoke deflector; 92021 was converted five months later. *(Courtney Haydon)*

Figure 191
Following conversion from the Crosti to the conventional boiler arrangement (September 1961), Wellingborough's 92023 pilots Stanier Class 8F 2-8-0 48193 on a PW train southwards past Long Eaton Junction on 11th May 1963. Many enginemen regarded the converted Crostis as less powerful than the standard engines, being equivalent to an 8F or even a 7F classification.
(Courtney Haydon)

delivery date to September 1960.
92163: 28.09.60 (concluded)
92164: no date
92165: 28.09.60 (concluded)
92166: no date
92167: no date.
Standard lubrication to cylinder barrels for comparison.
92161: 17.12.57
92162: 19.12.57.

MCL/1515 Driver's seat covered in black leather cloth in lieu of hide.
92072: ??.??.?? - 25.01.61
92084: 24.02.60 - 25.01.61
92135: 17.10.59 - 25.01.61
92155: 27.06.59 - 25.01.61.

MCL/1519 Flexible intermediate steam brake pipes-metallic hose: no date.
92081 with BR1C tender 1170.

MCL/1521 No details traced.
92009: 01.03.66 (concluded).

MCL/1527 No details traced.
92088: 03.10.62 (concluded).
92094: 19.04.60.

MCL/1528 No details traced.
92135: 17.10.59 - 14.09.60.

MCL/1530 Modified cylinder lubrication.
92012: 02.10.59 - 28.09.60
92074: 11.09.59 - 28.09.60
92093: 31.08.59 - 28.09.60
92108: 06.08.59 - 28.09.60
92126: 07.04.59 - 28.09.60.

MCL/1532 No details traced.
92053: 07.08.59 - 18.07.60
92090: 17.03.59 - 18.07.60
92109: 12.02.59 - 18.07.60.

MCL/1534 No details traced.
92030/87/8: no dates.

MCL/1535 No details traced.
92049: 30.05.61 - 03.10.62
92051: 28.08.61 - 03.10.62
92072: 23.08.61 - 03.10.62
92077: 18.08.61 - 03.10.62
92088: ??.??.?? - 03.10.62
92096: 23.08.61 - 03.10.62.

MCL/1538 No details traced.
92093: 05.02.62 - 03.10.62
92094: ??.??.?? - 03.10.62
92107: 17.05.61 - 03.10.62
92121: 31.10.61 - 03.10.62
92132: 26.06.61 - 03.10.62
92133: 12.10.61 - 03.10.62.

Figure 192
The last steam locomotive built for British Railways, 92220, received the name *Evening Star* at a ceremony at Swindon Works on 18th March 1960. Its first public outing was on 3rd April when it worked an LCGB rail tour, the "Six Counties Ltd". seen here at Princes Risborough.
(Courtney Haydon)

Figure 193
Ex-Crosti 92028 (Saltley) is pictured at Eastleigh on 6th May 1966. The engine was converted to standard operation in December 1959, one of the first two of the Crosti sub-class to be thus modified. LMR 9Fs had been regular visitors on through freights from the Midlands to the Southampton area for several years. 92028 has lost its smokebox numberplate and has a stencilled shedplate; records indicate that the original BR1B tender has been retained.
(Les Elsey)

Figure 194
92220 *Evening Star* storms through Axminster on 20th September 1964 with one of several "Farewell to Steam" rail tours over the Waterloo-Exeter line. This tour started at Victoria and travelled by way of Stewarts Lane, Tooting, Wimbledon, Alton, Southampton and Salisbury to visit the Lyme Regis and Seaton branches. 92220 is seen here on the return trip to Victoria via the direct route to Wimbledon and East Putney.
(Courtney Haydon)

Figure 195
Evening Star is seen at Salisbury after handing over a Cardiff-Portsmouth service to an SR engine on 17th May 1960. Although allocated to Cardiff Canton, the 86C shedplate has yet to be affixed. Note the reversing shaft cover plate, fitted from new. This modification was carried by a number of WR-based 9Fs; for details, see Section 2.1. *(G. Wheeler)*

The list of modifications traced for ER-based 9Fs is given below; DA refers to Darlington:

E/DA/L/54	Modification to firehole doors. 92030: 14.07.55.
E/DA/L/63	Internal steam brake pipes. 92039: 02.57.
E/DA/L/65	Internal steam brake pipes. 92040: 01.57, 92041: no date. Note: E/DA/L/63 and E/DA/L/65 probably refer to a similar if not the same modification.
E/DA/L/69	Modifications to valve seating. 92064: no date 92144: 01.59, 92192: 10.59.
E/DA/L/72	Cylinder lubrication modifications. 92060: 01.61, 92145: no date.
E/DA/L/76	Holder for wheel bearing springs. 92064: no date.
E/DA/L/82	Continuous footsteps for frames in front of smokebox. 92039: 02.61.
NE/DA/L/105	SUPAPLUS: Fibrous regulator gland packing. 92144/5: 05.62-10.64.

Further information on the modifications authorised for WR-based class members has been possible as a result of reports made available in the NRM at York; details are as follows. Note SW refers to Swindon.

W/SW/L/127
Purpose: Fit one 9F with LNER-type firehole door in which firing is through a hinged flap. Object is to reduce heat radiation on footplate and establish whether difficulties will be experienced when firing through the flap to back corners of firebox with WR-type firing shovel.
Authorised: 29.03.56, 92000 fitted 10.05.56.
Progress Report: 26.06.56.
Swindon drawing office representative and locomotive inspector made two trips on 92000 and also on 92003 for comparison purposes on Western Valley line iron ore trains (Rogerstone-Ebbw Vale). It was concluded that there was no reduction in heat radiation effects with the LNER-type fire doors and that with the WR-type shovel on 92000, it was impossible to fire correctly the back corners and sides of the firebox.
Experiment closed: 12.07.56.
Modification Not Adopted.

W/SW/L/150
Purpose: Fit two 9Fs (and two Standard Class 3 2-6-2 tank engines) with trailing axlebox lubrication pipes of flexible steel to Drawing SL/SW/1133 (not traced) to replace present rubber hoses which burn and need renewing every two to three months.
Authorised 09.09.57, 92001/5 fitted (17.10.57).
Progress Report: 27.01.59.
Reports over fourteen-month period confirm steel flexible pipes remained in good condition.
Experiment closed: 29.01.59.
Adopted as standard on 9Fs (and Standard Class 3 2-6-2 tank engines) on WR.

W/SW/L/163
Purpose: 92166, fitted with Berkley Mechanical Stoker,

transferred from LMR for service trials on WR on authority of British Transport Commission after test trials at Rugby. Allocation is to Ebbw Junction to be used on iron ore traffic. Running and maintenance staff to report generally on performance of the engine in service together with comments on handling and maintenance of equipment.
Authorised: 11.09.59; 92166 arrived 16.10.59.
Progress Report: 07.03.62.
92166 was in service for four months on WR with generally satisfactory performance on Western Valley iron ore traffic. Coal consumption was normal for the service but the engine required selected coals which are outside usual supplies available to WR. Ejection of fine ash in large quantities was found objectionable. Tender first working found to be the subject of strong complaint as tender type (BR1K, flush-sided) not designed to facilitate reverse working and special coaling requirements had to be provided for this engine.
Experiment closed: 07.03.62.
Fitting of mechanical stoker device not extended to WR; 92166 now returned to LMR.

W/SW/L/164
Purpose: Evaluation by running and maintenance staff of performance of 92250 fitted with Giesl Ejector.
Authorised: 09.09.57, 92250 fitted with Giesl Ejector 09.10.59.
Progress Report: 12.08.61.
92250 now in service for 21 months. Initially mainly engaged on iron ore traffic between Newport and Ebbw Vale steel works but later transferred to Class 'D' fitted freights between Newport and Paddington. Observations have given no markedly different performance than other 9Fs on similar work. Running and maintenance staff say no significant fuel saving from use of Giesl Ejector. No defects of a mechanical nature developed in the ejector but there was a need to clear the blastpipe tips of small carbon build-up at boiler washouts. Negotiations between BR and equipment supplier on-going in June 1960 but are now concluded.
Experiment closed: 17.08.61.
The Giesl Ejector will not be adopted for other WR locomotive classes. The equipment will remain fitted on 92250 until its condition necessitates replacement, when a standard arrangement will be substituted.

W/SW/L/192
Fit a total of six Standard BR tenders with hind footsteps to Sketch SK/293 (not traced) to determine if footsteps positioned on the rear buffer beam adjacent to the ladder will assist staff by providing safer and easier access to the ladder when climbing to the top of the tender than do the standard steps now fitted.
Authorised: 01.05.61.
Tenders fitted:
1510 92203 08.61 at Old Oak Common
1511 92204 08.61 at Old Oak Common
1525 92218 08.61 at Old Oak Common
1537 92215 27.10.61 at Swindon
1545 92234 15.08.61 at Swindon
1554* 92247 08.61 at Old Oak Common
* There is an anomaly here; 92247 was recorded as carrying tender number 1558 by August 1961.
Progress Report: 03.05.62.
Footsteps reported to be an improvement. Comments are that the steps 'stick out rather far' but are within the loading gauge so there is no need to authorise modifications. Agreed on 02.02.62 to recommend fitting the modified steps and that drawings should be circulated to all regions.
Experiment closed: 20.11.64.
Request for authority to make steps standard feature not granted by General Manager in view of the current policy to run-down steam.

W/SW/L/202
Purpose: To extend the life of the BR Standard regulator packing by fitting two 9Fs in the following manner:
92002 to have regulator gland packed with 1¾ in internal diameter rubber rings together with standard asbestos metallic coils in accordance with WR standard practice. 92005 to have regulator gland packed with Walkers' 'Superplas' self-lubricating fibrous packing.
Authorised: 26.02.62, 92002/5 fitted at Ebbw Junction on 31.01.62.
Progress Report: 26.09.62.

Figure 196
92013, bereft of smoke deflectors, is pictured on the rollers at the Rugby Testing Station during its Performance and Efficiency testing programme in the period May to August 1954.
(C. P. Atkins collection)

92005 ran 6,366 miles over a period of six months before the 'Superplas' regulator packing required renewal. During this period there was no additional packing required and no adjustment necessary. 92002 ran 8,866 miles over the six months. Initial WR soft packing with rubber rings required to be renewed after three months service and was found to be packed incorrectly. The second packing (correctly installed) required frequent adjustment and examinations found new packing was being added to stop leaks. 'Supaplas' packing was found to be very satisfactory and superior to WR-type packing with rubber rings. This confirms results of LMR trials which have now made 'Supaplas' regulator packing standard for their 9Fs.
Experiment closed: 26.09.62.
'Supaplas' regulator packing proposed and accepted as standard on WR.

9.2 Crosti Boiler Design

The Crosti boiler engines were subject to a number of modifications before the decision was taken to convert them to conventional operation.

Following reports of poor steaming, the draughting arrangement was redesigned and by the end of 1955, only a few months old, all ten of these engines, 92020-29, were back at Crewe Works either undergoing or awaiting this modification. Smoke deflector plates were also fitted to the side chimney during this visit to reduce the amount of smoke entering the cab; this was partially successful. A hinged plate was fitted to the side of the deflector plate to allow access to the sandbox fillers. Later, attention to preheater, blast chamber and chimney for each engine was necessary to reduce the amount of corrosion resulting from the sulphuric acid deposits produced during steaming; the dates of these modifications, carried out at Crewe from November 1955 to October 1957, are given in Table 9.2.

The Crostis were converted to conventional operation at Crewe Works during the period September 1959 to June 1962; Table 9.2 gives the conversion dates and details of the storage periods awaiting conversion for each engine. After conversion to conventional operation, the Crostis were unofficially down-rated to 8F. This rating could even have slipped into the 7F category if an *ad hoc* alteration to the tractive effort calculation formula, attempting to take into account the substantial reduction in total heating surfaces of over 40% following the removal of the preheater, were to be the only criterion employed; the conversion reference is as follows:

R9294 Conversion from Crosti boiler to conventional boiler operation.
Cost £961 14s 0d (£961.70) derived from:
Capital: -£2,152 16s 0d (£2,152.80)
Revenue:+£3,114 10s 0d (£3,114.50)
Engines 92020-9.

Photographic evidence indicates that for the first three conversions, 92024/6/8, the front window grab handle, the hand rail below the cab window and the foot rail at the base of the cab sheet were all retained. For the remainder of the conversions, the hand and grab rails were kept but the foot rail was dispensed with; 92024/6/8 also lost their foot rails during subsequent works visits. Similarly the hand rail adjacent to the forward chimney on the Crosti and its associated foot step on the side of the smokebox were removed during conversion.

The original footsteps situated under the forward smokebox door were retained on conversion but were

Figure 197
92153 (Toton) pauses at Burton Salmon to attach/detach cattle wagons to the 6.55pm Dringhouses-Washwood Heath Class 'C' express goods in the summer of 1961; the engine is in the process of shunting near Burton Salmon signal box. 92153 was at one time regarded as 'Toton's Favourite', as it always seemed to be the first choice for the various Toton-Brent mineral freight trials conducted in the late 1950s/early 1960s. *(Peter Cookson)*

supplemented by the addition of the continuous wide 'T-piece' full footstep during later works visits.

The converted Crostis also had the vacuum brake ejector repositioned to the same location as that on the standard engines i.e. at the smokebox/boiler joint on the driver's side.

Only a few other modifications have been traced in the official record; there may have been more.

Mod No.	**Detail of Modification**
MCL/1462	Improved method of holding 'GACO' packing in steam operated cylinder cocks. 92028/9 (no dates)
MCL/1475	No details traced. 92020: ??.??.?? - 16.02.59 92021: 22.09.57 - 16.02.59 92022: 18.06.58 - 16.02.59 92023: ??.??.?? - 16.02.59 92024: ??.??.?? - 16.02.59 92025: ??.??.?? - 16.02.59 92026: ??.??.?? - 16.02.59 92027: 12.04.57 - 16.02.59 92028: no dates 92029: no dates.
MCL/1496	No details traced. 92023: 02.02.57.
MCL/1515	Driver's seat covered in black leather cloth in lieu of hide. 92020: ??.??.?? - 25.01.61 92021: 17.06.60 - 25.01.61.

Table 9.2
BR Standard Class 9F 2-10-0s
Dates of Modifications Applied to Engines with Crosti Boilers (92020-92029)

No.	Delivery Date	Draughting Modifications and Addition of Smoke Deflectors to Side Chimney	Preheater Retubed	New Chimney and Renewal of Blast Chamber	Stored	Conversion from Crosti to Conventional
92020	18.05.55	11.55	11.56	08.57	05.59-03.61	06.61
92021	18.05.55	11.55	09.56	08.57	04.59-04.60	06.60
92022	18.05.55	02.56	04.57	04.57	05.59-03.62	06.62
92023	20.05.55	02.56	02.57	09.57	04.59-06.61	09.61
92024	06.06.55	02.56	04.57	04.57	08.59-01.60	02.60
92025	17.06.55	12.55	10.56	10.57	04.59-02.60	04.60
92026	17.06.55	12.55	01.57	01.57	not stored	09.59
92027	25.06.55	12.55	03.57	03.57	04.59-08.60	10.60
92028	06.07.55	02.56	05.57	05.57	08.59	12.59
92029	08.07.55	02.56	03.57	03.57	06.59-06.60	08.60

10. Names and Nicknames

The only Class 9F 2-10-0 to carry a name in BR days was 92220 *Evening Star*, the last steam engine to be built by British Railways. The name had been chosen following a competition run by the British Railways Western Region Staff Magazine in 1959/60. The naming took place at a ceremony in 'A' Shop at Swindon Works on 18th March 1960 presided over by Mr. R. F. Hanks, Chairman of the Western Area Board. Cash prizes were presented to the three entrants who had suggested the name *Evening Star*, Driver T. M. Phillips of Aberystwyth, Boilermaker J. S. Sathi of Old Oak Common shed and Mr. F. L. Pugh (an RCTS member) of the General Manager's Office, Paddington. The naming was then carried out by Mr. K. W. C. Grand, Member of the British Transport Commission. As noted in Section 6, the locomotive was finished in fully lined-out passenger green livery with a copper-capped chimney.

The opportunity was taken to stage an exhibition for the occasion where 'milestone' classes built at Swindon were represented; on view were King Class 4-6-0 6003 *King George IV*, Castle Class 4-6-0 5057 *Earl Waldegrave* and the famous 3440 *City of Truro*. Diesel construction was marked by the presence of Cl.42s D817 *Foxhound* and D818 *Glory* together with a Cl.03 diesel shunter D2136 and GWR Railcar No. 4. Somewhat bizarrely, Caledonian Railway 4-2-2 Single 123 was also on show, perhaps as an echo of the celebrated GWR broad gauge singles of the nineteenth century. Paddington guests were conveyed to and from Swindon in a special train worked by Castle Class 4-6-0 7007 *Great Western*.

Evening Star was also commemorated in the philatelic world in 1983. On 10th November of that year, the Caribbean island of Nevis issued two stamps in its 'Leaders of the World, Railway Locomotives (1st series)' set of 16. Two separate stamps were issued, each of $1 denomination, the first showing a technical drawing in bright crimson, 'new' blue and black whilst the second illustrated the engine at work and was multicoloured.

The name *Evening Star* had been used on the GWR twice before:

(1) Star Class 2-2-2 broad gauge single, built by R. Stephenson and Co., Maker's No. 265, which was delivered in July 1839 and ceased work in June 1871.

(2) Churchward Star Class 4-6-0 4002 built in March 1907 and withdrawn in June 1933.

92220's nameplates were cast in similar fashion to those of the Standard Class 7 Britannia and Class 6 Clan Pacifics, although the lettering was in the traditional GWR nameplate style. Commemorative building plates were affixed to the smoke deflectors just below the nameplate; details of the inscription are given in Figure M.

At the end of 1964 whilst *Evening Star* was allocated to Cardiff East Dock, it was discovered that the engine's nameplates had been stolen; the theft was believed to have taken place at Tyseley. Unfortunately the British Transport Police were not advised of the incident until March 1966. Despite this, four Birmingham railwaymen were successfully charged with larceny of both nameplates and numberplate. It is not clear whether these items were eventually recovered but authority was subsequently given for two more nameplates to be produced at a cost of £70 each. These are probably the nameplates that remained on the engine until a further theft occurred in March 1989 (see Section 13, Preservation).

Names for WR 9Fs ?

At the time the first batch of 9F 2-10-0s, 92000-7, was being delivered to the WR in 1954, rumours were circulating in railway enthusiast circles that the names of former broad gauge locomotives were being considered for the engines. Indeed, it has even been suggested that George Dow, who with E. S. Cox and D. S. M. Barrie, constituted the BR Locomotive Naming Committee, explored the possibility of giving the class 'powerful' names such as *Hercules*. This may have been pure speculation but in any event it is likely that the initiative would have been rejected on the grounds that it was not normal policy to name freight locomotives.

This would have reflected the situation when a similar proposal had been made in 1924 in the case of the GWR Class 7F 47XX 2-8-0s which had then only recently been introduced. Research by Mr. R. C. Riley, first published in the journal *Railway World*, Vol. 27, No. 308, January 1966 indicated that Mr. C. B. Collett, the Chief Mechanical Engineer of the GWR at the time had raised the matter with the General Manager, Sir Felix Pole. On consulting Viscount Churchill, the Chairman of the GWR, Sir Felix was advised that 'the chairman was of the opinion that the practice of naming should be confined to the engines of express passenger trains'. In view of Viscount Churchill's comments, it is ironic that both the 47XXs and 9Fs were successfully used for a number of years on the WR on summer Saturday holiday expresses. For the record, the names considered for the 47XX Class 2-8-0s in 1924 were as follows:

Behemoth	*Gladiator*	*Romulus*
Bellerophon	*Hercules*	*Tantalus*
Champion	*Mammoth*	*Thunderer*
Dreadnought	*Plutarch*	*Trafalgar*

The names had previously been borne by engines from the GWR Caesar, Premier, Pyracmon and Standard 0-6-0 goods classes. Note: the rather obscure name 'Pyracmon' refers to one of Vulcan, the Roman God of Fire's workmen, who was employed in the mythical smithy on Mount Etna in Sicily.

The name *Gladiator* was subsequently brought into use in January 1941 when a Castle class 4-6-0, 5076 *Drysllwyn Castle* was renamed. *Gladiator* commemorated one of the aircraft designs used in the defence of the Firth of Forth in Scotland in World War Two; the same type distinguished itself also in Norway and in the Battle of Malta during the same conflict.

In preservation, two 9Fs have acquired names:

92203	*Black Prince*
92207	*Morning Star*

Preservation details are given in Section 13.

In the case of 92207, there was an early suggestion that the name *Phoenix* might be more appropriate as the engine had reportedly had an uncomfortably close encounter with the breaker's torch before rescue.

Nicknames for the Standard 9Fs appear to have been few in number, the most popular being 'Spaceships', a sobriquet in use at New England MPD, for example, perhaps as early as 1955. There are several suggested origins for this nickname: (1) the 9Fs were speedy machines, 'as fast as a Spaceship'.

Note: it should be borne in mind that 90mph on an up Edinburgh express between Grantham and Peterborough is quite an achievement but falls somewhat short of the 25,000mph required to escape the pull of Earth's gravity.

(2) the noticeable 'space' between the underside of the boiler and the frame when viewed sideways, especially from a distance.

(3) the narrow, long boiler is reminiscent of a 'spaceship' laid on its side whilst being transported to its launch site.

Another ER nickname was 'Dromedaries' perhaps referring to the large 5,625 gallon BR1F tenders carried by that region's 9Fs, clearly bestowing characteristics similar to the prodigious capacity of their camel namesake to negotiate lengthy journeys without the need to stop for water. It is also possible that the term referred to the so-called 'hump' in the firebox floor.

Rail enthusiasts in the Midlands often referred to the class as 'Niner-Blinkers', a reference to the power classification, running numbers and the rather imposing smoke deflectors. During the allocation of a large number of the class to Birkenhead in the 1960s, the 9Fs were locally known as 'Birkenhead Sulzers', probably referring to their long distance workings with the Ellesmere Port oil tanker traffic, such distances usually being associated with the use of diesel power.

The 'affectionate' name for the mechanical stoker-fitted trio 92165-7 by Saltley crews was almost inevitably 'The Mechanicals'; it is envisaged that other, less polite, epithets would be used from time to time, depending on the number of coal screw delivery blockages on the fast freight turns between Birmingham and Carlisle.

It has also been reported that some Southern area enthusiasts referred to the 9Fs as '92XXXs' or simply '92 triple Xs'.

No doubt there were many other local unrecorded nicknames for the class.

No 92220 BUILT AT SWINDON
MARCH 1960
THE LAST STEAM LOCOMOTIVE FOR BRITISH RAILWAYS
NAMED AT SWINDON ON MARCH 18TH 1960 BY
K. W. C. GRAND ESQ.
MEMBER OF THE BRITISH TRANSPORT COMMISSION

FIGURE M
DETAIL OF THE COMMEMORATIVE BUILDING AND NAMING PLATES CARRIED BY 92220 *Evening Star*

Figure 198
92178, the first 9F to be fitted with a double blastpipe and chimney, is installed on the Swindon Test Plant for its trials over the period 5th November to 10th December 1957; details of the test results are given in Table 11.3. One of 92178's smoke deflectors is missing; both were removed for the road tests conducted in early 1958. *(G. Wheeler)*

11. Testing and Performance in Service

11.1 Summary of Test Results

Performance and efficiency tests were carried out on all but four of the original BR Standard tender class designs. The exceptions were the Class 6 Clan Pacifics (72XXX), the Class 3 2-6-0s (77XXX) and the two Standard designs virtually identical to earlier LMS types, i.e. the Class 4 2-6-0 (76XXX) and Class 2 2-6-0 (78XXX) where test data was already available; none of the Standard tank engine classes was tested. The tests consisted principally of verifying in practice the theoretical calculations arrived at during the design process. The aim was twofold:

- to confirm the optimum draughting arrangements to maximise efficient steam production.
- to determine the relationship between fuel consumption and the total amount of power transmitted to the cylinders and drawbar.

Initial tests were carried out on the Rugby Test Plant. These were supplemented by a series of controlled road tests to take into account factors which could not be measured on a stationary test plant such as aerodynamic and frictional losses associated with train movement in representative conditions of service.

In the case of the 9Fs, no fewer than five sub-classes were eventually to operate on BR and all were subject to test procedures; the five types were:

(1) Single Chimney
(2) Double Chimney
(3) Crosti Boiler
(4) Mechanical Stoker
(5) Giesl Oblong Ejector

Official reports were produced for four of the above types. The exception was the double chimney type; raw data exists for the latter but this was never analysed in an official report. A synopsis of the test results for all types including the double chimney variant is included below.

1. Single Chimney

Boiler and cylinder performances were first established by a total of 73 runs at the Rugby Test Plant from 7th May to 20th August 1954; 92013 was the engine selected. It was new, having been delivered to traffic on 23rd April 1954 and had run only nominal mileage before testing; new piston rings were fitted before the trials. Early on in the first series of tests, owing to steaming difficulties, the standard 5⅜ in diameter blastpipe cap was replaced by one of 5¼ in diameter.

The stationary plant tests were conducted at constant rates of combustion and of water evaporation and at constant speeds. The range covered was from 15mph to 55mph, from 15% to 60% cut-off and from 11,500 lb/hour to 29,000 lb/hour of feed water; in the majority of the tests, the regulator was fully open. The duration of tests on the plant was of the order of 60-150 minutes which compared with a period of 60-90 minutes on the road, the latter exclusive of an initial warming up period. For rates of firing significantly in excess of 3,000 lb/hour, two firemen were used to avoid undue fatigue.

Measurements consisted mainly of rates of coal and water consumption, rate of steam flow to the cylinders, steam and gas temperatures, drawbar horsepower, rate of steam production as related to the amount of air supplied, smokebox draught and resistance of the boiler to gas flow. A summary of the results compared with those of the two Pacific classes tested, Class 8 (71XXX) and Class 7 (70XXX), is given in Table 11.1. The table also includes details of IHP (Indicated Horsepower) values obtained at various speeds during testing of double chimney 9F 92178 at Swindon and a BR Standard Class 7 Britannia Pacific on the LMR.

The road tests (September/October 1954) were between Skipton and Carlisle over Ais Gill summit with LMR No. 3 Dynamometer Car and Mobile Test Units: by then 92013 had achieved some 4,250 running miles, most of it on the rollers at Rugby. Unsatisfactory results were obtained using the live steam injector due to the tendency to 'flood' the boiler at low and medium steam rates, even with the regulator at minimum feed. Large fluctuations in the boiler pressure were inevitable and satisfactorily stable conditions could not be readily established. Hence the exhaust steam injector was used for the majority of the tests and proved satisfactory at all feed rates below 10,000 lb/hour and to a maximum of 28,000 lb/hour; for higher steaming rates the feed was supplemented to a limited extent by the live steam injector.

The observed maximum rate of water evaporation was 29,000 lb/hour, the calculated maximum being just over 5% more at 30,600 lb/hour. This figure compares well with results from other wide firebox classes tested, see below:

Wide Firebox Classes
Maximum Water Evaporation Rates

	Grate Area (sq ft)	Distance between Tube-plates (ft in)	Max. Water Evap. Rate (lb/hr)	
BR Cl. 7	42.0	17' 0"	Test	30,000
			Calc.	35,000
ER Cl. V2	41.25	16' 11⅝"	Test	30,400
			Calc.	34,000
WD 2-10-0	40.0	15' 3"	Test	27,000
			Calc.	29,500
BR Cl. 9F	40.2	15' 3"	Test	29,000
			Calc.	30,600

A number of tests were conducted comparing the performance with the live steam injector and the exhaust steam injector. The latter showed a water economy of 5¾% and a corresponding coal economy, ranging from around 6¾%-8% at the maximum delivery rate of the exhaust steam injector. Blidworth Cobbles, Grade 2B were used as fuel, the average gross calorific value being 12,290 B.Th.U/lb. Boiler efficiency at 73% was comparable to those of the BR Standard Pacific designs (see Table 11.1). Although the blastpipe cap had been reduced to 5¼ in diameter, it was reported that steaming was not as free as desirable; a further reduction of blastpipe diameter to 5³⁄₁₆ in was considered to be worth a trial at some later date. Difficulty was also experienced in directing coal into the back corners of the firebox due to the shallow depth under the firedoor. During subsequent tests referred to later on the Toton-Brent route, this was overcome to some extent by cutting away the sides of the firehole baffle plate. It was also noted that considerable leakage occurred

Table 11.1
BR Standard Class 9F 2-10-0s
Performance and Efficiency Comparison with BR Standard Pacifics

Class Parameter Coal Grade	BR 9F 2-10-0 At Maximum Rate of Steam Evaporation	 At Minimum Indicated Steam Consumption	BR 7 4-6-2 Britannia Class At Maximum Rate of Steam Evaporation	 At Minimum Indicated Steam Consumption	BR 8 4-6-2 At Maximum Rate of Steam Evaporation	 At Minimum Indicated Steam Consumption
Water Evaporated lbs/hr.						
South Kirkby	-	-	30,200	19,000	32,750	22,800
Blidworth	29,000	18,850	30,000	19,000	29,000	22,800
Maximum IHP						
South Kirkby	-	-	2,220	1,575	2,630	1,980
Blidworth	2,070	1,530	2,200	1,575	2,420	1,980
Maximum DBHP						
South Kirkby	-	-	1,800	1,280	2,100	1,440
Blidworth	1,780	1,225	1,800	1,280	1,920	1,440
Steam Temperature °F						
South Kirkby	-	-	710	655	770	710
Blidworth	735	655	737	636	750	710
Steam per IHP.hr. lbs						
South Kirkby	-	-	14.4	13.3	13.0	12.2
Blidworth	14.4	13.6	14.4	13.3	12.4	12.2
Coal per IHP.hr. lbs						
South Kirkby	-	-	1.95	1.55	2.60	1.52
Blidworth	2.20	1.85	2.30	1.95	2.55	1.81
Boiler Efficiency %						
South Kirkby	-	-	68	77	50	72
Blidworth	64	73	66	72	44	68
Cylinder Efficiency %						
South Kirkby	-	-	12.9	14.2	14.5	15.7
Blidworth	12.6	13.9	12.7	14.0	15.0	15.7

Note: Calorific Values (B.Th.Us./lb: South Kirkby 13,800; Blidworth 12,600-12,800

BR Standard Class 9F 2-10-0s
Comparison of IHP (Indicated Horsepower) Values For
Double Chimney 9F 92178 and BR Britannia Class 7 4-6-2

	BR Class 9F 2-10-0 92178 WR Swindon Test Plant Data		BR Britannia Class 7 Pacific LMR Data	
Speed mph	Driving Wheel RPM	IHP	Driving Wheel RPM	IHP
20	112	1,020	91	1,030
25	140	1,060	114	1,070
30	168	1,095	136	1,100
40	224	1,148	182	1,150
50	280	1,190	227	1,185
60	336	1,205	272	1,195
65	364	1,207	295	1,200

Table 11.2
BR Standard Class 9F 2-10-0s
LMS/BR Toton-Brent Route: Testing of Loaded Mineral Trains

Year	Test Subject	Average Load tons	Route Length miles	Running Time mins.	Average Speed mph	Coal Consumed lbs/mile	Water Feed gallons/mile
1927	LNWR G2 0-8-0	938	127.5	434.9	17.6	79.0	50.0
1927	S&DJR 2-8-0	927	127.3	435.1	17.6	80.6	60.8
1930	LMS 7F 0-8-0 LS★	887	128.0	381.5	20.1	48.4	42.1
	LMS 7F 0-8-0 ACFI †	910	127.9	393.9	19.5	46.4	38.9
1931	LMS Beyer Garratt	1,301	128.5	346.9	22.2	92.4	74.2
1936	LMS Stanier 8F	1,070	127.6	401.1	19.1	66.3	51.0
1948	Exchange Trials						
	LMS Stanier 8F	1,047	127.7	484.7	15.8	79.7	60.5
	ER 01	1,061	127.8	440.3	17.4	73.0	54.4
	WD 2-8-0	1,091	128.0	440.7	17.4	84.4	62.9
	WD 2-10-0	1,047	127.9	514.1	14.9	87.1	65.2
	WR 28XX	Out of Gauge for Toton-Brent route.					
1955	BR9F 2-10-0	892	127.1	238.5	32.0	83.1	69.7
		804	127.1	239.5	31.8	78.1	66.3

Notes:

★ Live Steam Injector

† Fitted with ACFI (Societe L'Auxiliare des Chemins de Fer et de I'Industrie) feed water heating apparatus.

Data Source: NRM York

Figure 199
Following the trials on the Swindon Test Plant, double chimney 92178 is seen attached to a dynamometer car for a series of road trials between Reading and Stoke Gifford in January/February 1958 (see Table 11.4). 92178 eventually found service on the ECML operating from New England and Langwith Junction before withdrawal in October 1965. *(G. Wheeler)*

from the firebox stays and some 150 had to be caulked each weekend during the Skipton-Carlisle trials. The steam/gas draught and the blastpipe pressure cycle showed a deficiency in the amount of excess air at high steaming rates despite a satisfactory relationship between steam flow, blastpipe pressure and smokebox vacuum, as demonstrated by a falling tendency of the 'Gas Vacuum' characteristic at high steaming rates; a still higher smokebox vacuum would therefore be required for optimum efficiency..

Cylinder efficiency compared well with the highest values obtained by other BR Standard designs. Peak efficiency for the 9F was obtained at higher speeds and moderate steaming rates, ie 14.2% at 20,500 lb/hr steaming rate, compared with a maximum of 14% at 19,000 lb/hr for a BR Class 7 4-6-2. Overall efficiency in terms of coal/DBHP.hr was largely dependent on the cylinder and boiler efficiency and was particularly satisfactory in the case of the 9Fs, which had the best overall efficiency of those BR Standard classes fitted with Walschaerts valve gear.

From 7th to 17th February 1955, further road trials were carried out on the Toton-Brent route. These tests were again conducted with the LMR No. 3 Dynamometer Car with vacuum fitted 16ton loaded mineral wagons, to establish the loading level of trains which might be worked to Class 'C' timings (41.0mph Toton-Brent and 42.4mph for the return); for the purposes of the tests, the average speeds for the test schedules were relaxed to 35.2mph and 37.4mph respectively to take account of permanent speed restrictions and the need to change from the fast to the slow line and vice versa from time to time. Calculations based on the 1954 test data indicated that a load of 900 tons was feasible, assuming a steam production rate of 18,500 lb/hour, i.e. approximately 64% of the maximum available.

Footplate staff, none of whom had worked a 9F before, were not specially selected and different crews worked engines on each return run. Grade 2 coal was used, Firbeck coal at Toton, Treeton or Blidworth coal at Cricklewood. Apart from the Brent-Toton run on 15th February when the tender contained a patch filled with a high percentage of 'smalls', the fuel quality was satisfactory.

It was considered desirable to work at a consistent level of power production as required to keep Class 'C' timings. Drivers were requested to work as far as practicable with full regulator and vary the cut-off to maintain a constant rate of steam production as indicated by a meter on the footplate. The firemen were asked to use the exhaust steam injector and fire 'little and often', using no more than eight shovels of coal for each firing. No further steps were taken to control the working of the engine. On these road trials, the firing rate was not measured but water consumption was recorded in the Dynamometer Car.

Due to problems at collieries, it was not possible to provide coal loads, stone ballast being used in its place; the average gross weight of 22 tons 9 cwt per wagon with the ballast compared with 21 tons 6 cwt. with coal. The special trains ran to Class 'C' timings at 1.10pm from Toton to Brent, the return trip being scheduled at 5.45am; the load initially was 37 mineral wagons plus brake (equivalent to 41 coal-filled wagons plus brake) weighing 892 tons.

The first 9F to be provided for the tests was 92009, (ca. 18,500 miles from new) fitted with the 5⅜ in blastpipe cap; steaming on the first run was unsatisfactory and the blastpipe cap was replaced with one of 5¼ in. diameter. On the second return run from Brent on 10th February however, a serious slip occurred when leaving Kettering station and the motion was damaged. A fresh engine, 92018 with 9,312 miles on the clock was used for the remainder of the trials and the 5¼ in. blastpipe cap transferred from 92009. The riding of both engines was reported to be good up to the highest speed achieved on the tests, i.e. 60mph. Continuous blowdown was in operation on the first engine, 92009, but at the end of the trials it was found that the blowdown valve was sticking on 92018 and had not been functioning during the tests.

As noted above, the first run from Toton to Brent with the 5⅜ in diameter blastpipe cap demonstrated unsatisfactory steaming rates (minimum pressures of 160-180 lb/sq in were recorded). For subsequent runs, the use of the 5¼ in blastpipe diameter cap resulted in considerable improvement in steaming although boiler pressure fell to 220 lb/sq in at times and even 200 lb/sq in when sustained power output was required; recovery was gained only by easing the engine. Full regulator was employed wherever practicable and the general cut off on the level and easier gradients was 25%. Over 1 in 200 grades, 30%-35% cut off was used whilst the maximum at Sharnbrook bank (1 in 120) was around 40%.

Following the installation of the 5¼ in blastpipe cap, the second two return trips with the 892 ton trains (9th/10th and 14th/15th February) proved well within the capabilities of the 9F running to the required schedule, delays being attributed mainly to a series of signal checks. The tender feed rate was 18,700 lb water per hour with a corresponding coal

Figure 200
At the Rugby Testing Station in 1958, mechanical stoker-fitted 92166 awaits transfer to the rollers to begin a series of tests. Inserted between engine and tender is the *ad hoc* arrangement for delivering coal to the firebox (see Figure N). Nominally allocated to Saltley, 92166 was out of traffic on test for more than six months. *(C. P. Atkins Collection)*

Table 11.3
BR Standard Class 9F 2-10-0s
Trials on BR Standard Class 9F 2-10-0 92178 fitted with Double Blastpipe and Chimney during Tests on Swindon Test Plant, WR November/December 1957

Test Run No.	Date	Plant Mileage	Boiler/Grate Efficiencies %	Coal Burnt lb/hr.	Nominal Steaming Rate lb/hr.	Cut off %	Speed mph	Duration mins.	Boiler Pressure Average (Gauge) psi	Coal Rate lb/hr.	Water Rate lb/hr.	Equivalent Evaporation lb/hr.	Notes
1	05.11.57	46.0	Test abandoned, due to 'condition of fireman'										Runs: 1-7: blastpipe diameter 3⅞"
2	25.11.57	76.5	68.8/84.6	2,078(1)	17,000	25	30	109.4	225.4	2,456	16,030	21,990	-
3	26.11.57	54.3	67.7/82.8	2,154(1)	17,000	25	30	59.0	229.7	2,600	16,720	22,940	-
4	26.11.57	78.3	71.7/87.0	1,662(1)	*	20	30	119.6	231.1	1,910	13,180	17,860	Tender water gauge seven gallons different to water meter
5	27.11.57	94.2	66.6/82.6	2,444(1)	*	27½	35	101.6	228.7	2,960	18,520	25,680	Ash layer approx. two inches thick through length of smokebox
6	28.11.57	87.7	66.5/82.6	2,875(1)	22,000	30	40	92.2	227.3	3,480	21,700	30,160	-
7	28.11.57	93.5	72.2/87.8	1,836(2)	*	20	35	109.7	226.3	2,093	14,500	19,650	-
8	03.12.57	64.8	72.2/87.4	2,285(2)	17,000	25	30	80.2	229.2	2,615	17,720	24,560	Runs 8-17: blastpipe diameter 4⅛"
9	03.12.57	51.5	75.6/89.2	1,670(2)	*	*	*	78.9	233.3	1,874	13,590	18,460	-
10	04.12.57	39.5	Test abandoned										Due to leading brake running hot
11	05.12.57)	137.0	72.6/89.2	2,480(2)	19,200	27	35	*	228.7	2,780	19,280	26,300	-
	)	for whole											
12	05.12.57)	day	66.8/56.4	*	15,600	20	35	*	230.0	2,205	14,060	19,170	Boiler efficiency low due to clinker formation
13	06.12.57	53.5	No results recorded										-
14	06.12.57	57.3	No results recorded										-
15	09.12.57)	136.0	71.7/88.8	2,794(3)	21,000	30	40	*	228.4	3,144	21,240	29,700	-
	)	for whole											
16	09.12.57)	day	71.7/85.2	1,745(3)	14,000	20	35	*	231.5	2,047	14,130	19,320	-
17	10.12.57	71.5	77.0/91.4	1,756(3)	14,000	20	35	*	231.3	1,922	14,320	19,570	-

* Information not recorded

Key Coal Type Blidworth Grade 2 Cobbles: Calorific Value (dry) in B.Th.U./lb as indicated
(1) 13,750 (2) 13,740 (3) 13,860

Table 11.4
BR Standard Class 9F 2-10-0s
Trials with BR Standard Class 9F 2-10-0 92178 fitted with Double Blastpipe and Chimney on Road Tests from Reading to Stoke Gifford and Return, WR January/February 1958

Run No.	Date in 1958	Boiler/Grate Efficiencies %	Coal Burnt lb/hr.	Av. Boiler Pressure (Gauge) psi	Coal Rate lb/hr.	Water Rate lb/hr.	Equivalent Evaporation lb/hr.	Load tons/coaches tare-gross	DBHP¶ each day Max.	Notes
1R	28.01	No results recorded						460-490/14	810	Boiler pressure gauge not functioning
2R	28.01	No results recorded						460-490/14	810	Boiler pressure gauge still not functioning
3R	29.01	69.8/85.8	2,219(7)	200	2,587	17,400 17,000 †	24,096	630-660/19	865	-
4R	29.01	72.5/88.1	2,379(4)	194.5	2,700	18,510 18,110 †	25,693	630-660/19	865	-
5R	30.01	No results recorded						740-770/23	890	'Jimmies' in blastpipes to reduce effective diameter to 4"
6R	30.01	65.5/81.7	2,402(4)	206	2,940	18,250 17,850 †	25,394	740-770/23	890	'Jimmies' in blastpipes ¼" thick to achieve same diameter as in 5R
7R	04.02	62.4/76.6	2,903(4)	237	3,790	22,200 21,800 †	31,186	330-370/10	750	'Jimmies' in blastpipes $^{3}/_{16}$" thick
8R	04.02		(5)	Test abandoned				330-370/10	750	Engine failed to steam. On examination, about 2" of clinker cover found on grate. Stopped at Wantage Road due to excessive vibration of loco.
9R	05.02		(5)	Test abandoned						About 1½" of clinker found on grate on examination at Stoke Gifford
10R	05.02		(5)	Test abandoned						Large amount of clinker found on grate at Reading (6' x 4' x 2' 4" deep)
11R	06.02		(4)	Test abandoned						'Jimmies' in blastpipes ¼" thick. Ashpan hopper flaps 'down' Large amount of clinker found on grate at Stoke Gifford (4' x 4' x 2' deep)
12R	06.02		(4)	Test abandoned						On examination at Reading, about 25% of spaces in back half of fire grate were blocked by hard glazed clinker. Front half comparatively clear; just odd spaces here and there were blocked
13R	07.02	68.8/83.5	2,230(6)	244	2,670	17,120 16,720 †	24,026	220-250/7	660	'Jimmies' in blastpipes ¼" thick. Ashpan hopper flaps 'up'. Small amount of clinker at Stoke Gifford similar to that found on Plant trials
14R	07.02	68.3/83.0	2,244(6)	240	2,704	17,220 16,820 †	24,195	220-250/7	660	'Jimmies' in blastpipes ¼" thick. Ashpan flaps 'up'

Note: Blastpipe diameter 4⅛" for all tests except where modified by the introduction of 'Jimmies' as indicated † Steam rate to cylinders ¶DBHP: DrawBar HorsePower

Key Coal Type Blidworth Grade 2 Cobbles: Calorific Value (dry) in B.Th.U./lb as indicated
(4) 13,910 (5) 14,010 (6) 13,810 (7) 13,950

Figure 201
Mechanical stoker-fired 92166 is seen at speed on the rollers at Rugby Testing Station during trials in the autumn and winter of 1958/9. Throughout the tests, various minor modifications were made to 92166, not all of which were applied to the other two members of the mechanical stoker trio, 92165 and 92167. After it returned from Rugby, 92166 was said by some to be the best performer of the trio.
(C. P. Atkins Collection)

Figure 202
An overhead view of the Giesl Oblong Ejector fitted to 92250 at Rugby Testing Station during the trials in 1959. In April and May tests were carried out with the standard double chimney arrangement with which 92250 had been equipped during construction at Crewe Works. This was then replaced with the Giesl device for subsequent test runs from 21st May onwards.
(J. G. Glick Collection)

feed rate of 2,670 lb per hour. These rates were required for a large portion of the running time however and were clearly close to the limit of a fireman's capabilities, especially in view of the repeated signal checks and delays and the need to double-handle the coal by hauling it from the back of the tender. As a result, the final run in each direction (16th/17th February) was made with only 804 tons, (33 mineral wagons plus brake equivalent to 37 coal-filled wagons plus brake) with a tender feed rate of 17,700 lb water per hour and a firing rate of 2,500 lb per hour. These rates provided a margin for contingencies and a train of 37 x 16ton loaded wagons and brake was recommended as the maximum for Toton-Brent Class 'C' workings. Logs of three of the runs were published and are displayed in Table 11.32. For the record, the 9F performances in these tests are compared with test runs of other engine classes over the same route in Table 11.2; the significantly increased average speed with the 9F test runs is remarkable.

2. Double Chimney

Development work with the BR Standard Class 4 4-6-0 design at Swindon in the mid-1950s indicated that a steaming rate increase from 19,600 lb/hr to 22,490 lb/hr was theoretically possible by the fitting of a double blastpipe and chimney of suitable dimensions. In May 1957, Standard Class 4 4-6-0 75029 was duly modified with the double exhaust arrangement and subsequent testing confirmed a water evaporation rate of 22,400 lb/hr. This prompted an examination of the steaming characteristics of other classes including the 9Fs which during testing at Rugby with the single chimney 92013 and 92050 had been established as 29,000 lb/hr. maximum.

The first 9F to be fitted with double blastpipe and chimney was 92178. Stationary tests were carried out on the engine at Swindon Works Test Plant in November and December 1957 followed by road trials with various loadings on the Reading-Stoke Gifford section of the Paddington-Bristol main line in

January and February 1958. The results were not published in an official report but a file of raw data was brought to the attention of the authors by Mr. C. P. Atkins, Research Manager at the NRM at York. The data consists essentially of measurements taken during the seventeen test runs on the plant at Swindon together with the seven pairs of runs between Reading and Stoke Gifford. Details are given in Tables 11.3 and 11.4; a full log of one of the road test runs is given in Table 11.31, Section 11.3.

The tables readily illustrate the type of problem arising during such test work. In particular it was necessary to abandon some of the road tests due to the incidence of clinker build-up on the grate during the runs which drastically affected steaming rates and rendered much of the test data invalid. The other variable factor was the blastpipe cap dimension which was the subject of several changes, one of 4in. diameter eventually being selected as the optimum. The data on equivalent water evaporation rates indicated that 92178 was capable of producing steam at over 31,000 lb/hr, representing an increase of between 4% and 11% on the rates achieved earlier during the single chimney test engines at Rugby and on road tests on the LMR. Whether or not such a comparison was valid, given the different testing conditions on the respective plants and during the various road trials, it seemed sufficient to convince the authorities to fit all new 9Fs from 92183 onwards with the double blastpipe and chimney arrangement. Also fitted with double exhaust equipment were the three mechanical stoker engines, 92165-7, delivered out of sequence in spring 1958 although the blastpipe diameter of these engines was reduced to 3⅞ in. Some of the original WR allocation of single chimney engines were also retro-fitted with the double arrangement in 1960 (see Sections 1.5 & 9.1) but by this time the BR modernisation plan was well under way and resources for steam locomotive modification were much restricted; neither the ER, LMR nor the NER converted any of their single chimney engines to the double arrangement.

3. Crosti Boiler

In 1955, comparative tests were conducted between 92023, fitted with a Crosti boiler and 92050, fitted with a standard boiler. The trials were carried out to implement the 'Agreement' of 31st March 1953 between the Societa Anonima Locomotive a Vapore Franco of Milan, Italy and the BR Railway Executive. The protocol referred in general to a number of tests to be arranged for the purpose of determining what, if any, payments were to be made to the Italian company in respect of manufacture and use of the Crosti boilers fitted to the ten 9Fs, 92020-9.

Trials at Rugby Testing Station

Trials were conducted at the Rugby Testing Station from early June to mid-November 1955 under the joint supervision of BR and the Italians. Coal consumption per drawbar horsepower was measured at four speeds, 20, 30, 40 and 50mph at a constant rate of evaporation of 16,000 lb of feed water with the customary coal source of Blidworth Grade 2B small cobbles. The average of the four values for coal consumption for each of the two engines was taken as the basis on which any savings were to be determined. The royalty was fixed as 100% of the agreed amount of £800 per engine if the savings in coal consumption attained the level of 18%, reducing pro rata on a sliding scale to zero if the figure were 12% or less.

Figure 203
Dr. Ing. Adolf Giesl-Gieslingen stands beside ejector-fitted 92250 during preparation for its trial runs on the Test Plant at Rugby in September 1959. *(J. G. Glick Collection)*

The Crosti boiler representative, 92023 with some 80 miles on the clock, arrived at Rugby in late May direct from Crewe Works and was on the test plant from 7th June to 28th September 1955. During the first runs, it was found that the combustion of the fuel was very poor and the boiler could not be made to produce enough steam for the proposed tests to be carried out. In agreement with the Italians, successive alterations were to be made to the chimney and blastpipe nozzles until a reasonably good combustion was achieved.

The necessary measurements were made on the test plant during the course of the 79 runs conducted. At each rate of working, a careful selection was made of the results of those runs which showed the highest quality in as many respects as possible, i.e. 'first class' conditions. These included the steadiness of the pressure and water level in the boiler, the most uniform rates of coal firing and feeding of the water to the boiler, the best and most consistent analyses of the products of combustion and finally the most uniform steam and gas temperatures for the whole of the test period. The other aspect to be covered by the tests was the determination of the savings accruing from the use of the exhaust steam injector.

The same procedure was applied to the standard engine selected for the comparison, 92050. This engine was again virtually new, having been delivered into traffic on 19th August 1955 and incorporated the new blastpipe diameter of 5¼ in which was now in use for the standard 9Fs following the tests conducted with 92013 a year earlier. Engine 92050 was tested on the plant during 38 runs from 7th October to 15th November with Blidworth Grade 2B small cobbles as

Table 11.5
BR Standard Class 9F 2-10-0s
Rugby Testing Station Trials
Crosti Boiler 92023 and Standard 92050

Quantities of Coal Required to Produce 16,000 lb/hr. of Steam

Engine	92023	92050
Boiler Type	BR12 Crosti	BR9 Standard
Coal Consumption lb/hr.		
Live Injector	2,018	2,162
Exhaust Injector	1,852	2,050
Savings in Favour of Exhaust Injector %	8.23	5.18
Water Feed lb/hr.		
Live Injector	16,000	16,000
Exhaust Injector	14,880	15,320
Savings in Favour of Exhaust Injector %	7.00	4.25
Savings in Favour of Crosti Boiler Engine		
Coal Consumption		
Live Injector %	6.66	control
Exhaust Injector %	9.66	control
Water Feed		
Live Injector %	-	control
Exhaust Injector %	2.87	control

Table 11.6
BR Standard Class 9F 2-10-0s
Combined Results
from Rugby Testing Station and Road Trials
Crosti Boiler 92023 and Standard 92050

Comparison of Coal Consumption per Drawbar Horse Power Hour (DBHP.hr)

Speed mph	Coal Consumption lb/DBHP.hr			
	Crosti 92023 Live Steam	Exhaust Steam	Standard 92050 Live Steam	Exhaust Steam
20	2.3410	2.1480	2.3580	2.2360
30	2.2420	2.0580	2.2520	2.1350
40	2.3110	2.1160	2.3020	2.1820
50	2.4400	2.2340	2.3940	2.2700
Average	2.3335	2.1390	2.3265	2.2058

before but of slightly lower calorific value (12,450 B.Th.U./lb for Crosti 92023 and 12,200 B.Th.U./lb for 92050).

From the results of the plant trials, the figures derived for the quantities of coal required to produce 16,000 lb/hr of steam from each of the two engines are given in Table 11.5. The results were a disappointment for all concerned. Savings of coal in favour of the Crosti engine over the standard locomotive were no more than 6.7% when comparing live steam injection although this increased to 9.7% when the exhaust steam injection comparison was made. Both these figures fell short of the 12% required to trigger royalty payments. The only way the latter figure could be exceeded was if the Crosti exhaust injector result was compared with the standard engine's live steam injector result; in that case a saving of 14.3% in coal was evident. The latter comparison was invalid as laid down in the agreement and pro-rata royalties which would have amounted to around £300 per engine on that basis were not payable.

The greater proportional economy in water use for Crosti 92023 compared with standard 92050 when using the exhaust steam injector was considered partly the result of the exhaust steam pressure and temperature being higher on the Crosti than on 92050; this result was however mainly attributed to an adventitious difference between two nominally identical injectors.

Road Trials

The Italians, being somewhat baffled by the Rugby Test Station results, advised that the Crosti boiler could be expected to perform better in standard service conditions and although this was not part of the original agreement, BR arranged for road tests to be carried out. The chosen route was the ex-G&SWR main line between Carlisle and Hurlford (Kilmarnock); 92023 and 92050 were put through their paces in late November and early December 1955. Speeds of 20-50mph and steaming rates of 14,000 to 20,000 lb per hour were covered in the test series during which all runs were carried out using the live steam injector only. In order to make the tests as far as possible representative of actual service conditions where locomotives on freights have to stand for considerable periods, stops of ten minutes duration were arranged at Dumfries, Carronbridge and New Cumnock in each direction. Also a stop at Hurlford of two hours between outward and return runs and a certain amount of light engine running between shed and train, including turning the locomotive and dynamometer car on the triangle at Carlisle were taken into account when assessing the 'standing time'.

For the 16,000 lb/hr steaming rate when hauling empty passenger stock weighing some 600 tons, the values for the drawbar horsepower were determined as follows, using the **LMR No. 3 Dynamometer Car and Mobile Test Unit:**

Speed mph	Drawbar Horsepower (DBHP) Crosti 92023	Standard 92050
20	862	917
30	900	960
40	875	939
50	827	903
Average	866	930

The figures show that the power at the drawbar of the Crosti 92023 was 6.88% less than the standard 92050. This was attributed partly to the higher exhaust pressure of the Crosti which reduced the cylinder efficiency; the effect of this was greater than the counter effect of the more highly superheated steam from the Crosti boiler. Rolling resistance may also have been increased by the presence of the Crosti preheater between the frames, making them less rigid.

Because of the fortuitous difference in resistance to motion of the two locomotives which could not be fully established until after the tests had been completed, it was considered that the relative economy of the two engines on an Indicated Horse Power (IHP) basis should also be stated although this basis was not part of the 'Agreement'. For the same running conditions as above, the average IHPs of the two locomotives were 1,088 for the Crosti and 1,122 for the Standard compared with 866 and 930 respectively at the drawbar. On a comparative IHP basis, the Crosti was confirmed as 3.03% less powerful at the same hourly steaming rate instead of the 6.88% figure on the DBHP basis.

Rugby Test Plant and Road Trials: Combined Results for 'Agreement' Parameters

By combining the results from the test plant trials with those from the road runs, the figures for coal consumption per drawbar horsepower hour were as shown in Table 11.6.

Later, in 1957, 92050 was again put on the rollers at Rugby to resolve perceived differences between results on the stationary plant indicator diagrams and those obtained during the road tests. A total of 39 runs were made on the plant from 6th March to 26th April 1957 from which it was clear that 92050's average DBHP should have been 905 rather than the 930 figure from the dynamometer car trials used in the Crosti comparison calculations. On this basis, the Crosti 92023 would have been 4.3% less powerful than 92050, as opposed to the 6.88% figure quoted in the report. Similarly the estimated average fuel consumption of the Standard locomotive as displayed in Table 11.6 would have been 2.3945 lb/DBHP.hr (instead of 2.3265 lb/DBHP.hr) when using the live steam injector and 2.2705 lb/DBHP.hr (as opposed to 2.2058 lb/DBHP.hr) when using the exhaust steam injector.

From these and the 1955 test figures, it was therefore deduced that the average economies in fuel at the **'Agreement' steam rate to the cylinders of 16,000 lb/hour,** were as follows:

A. Crosti using Live Steam Injector compared with Standard using Live Steam Injector:
1955 figures: Crosti 0.3% less economical
1957 figures: Crosti 2.55% more economical

B. Crosti using Exhaust Steam Injector compared with Standard using Exhaust Steam Injector:
1955 figures: Crosti 3.03% more economical
1957 figures: Crosti 5.80% more economical

C. Crosti using Exhaust Steam Injector compared with Standard using Live Steam Injector.
1955 figures: Crosti 8.06% more economical
1957 figures: Crosti 10.67% more economical

Overall Test Results Summary

Summarising the results from the Testing Station and road trials combined at all the speeds and steam rates examined rather than just the 'Agreement' parameters, the final

Figure 204
92033 (Annesley) rolls a 'windcutter' train of empty mineral wagons northwards from Leicester Central on 31st August 1961. 92033 remained allocated to Annesley until the withdrawal of GC line freight services in June 1965. It did not survive much longer however, being withdrawn in the following September after successive short reallocations to Banbury and Northampton. *(C. R. Berridge)*

report indicated that on average, the following savings could be realised:

A. Crosti using Live Steam Injector compared with Standard using Live Steam Injector:
Crosti 3.93% more economical

B. Crosti using Exhaust Steam Injector compared with Standard using Exhaust Steam Injector:
Crosti 7.33% more economical

C. Crosti using Exhaust Steam Injector compared with Standard using Live Steam Injector.
Crosti 11.74% more economical.

During the road tests, with both engines using the live steam injector, the actual saving under the same conditions was found to be 7% rather than the 3.93% quoted. The additional 3% or so was accounted for by better heat retention whilst standing, resulting in a higher superheat on starting and accelerating from rest.

The Italians, although readily acknowledging the fairness of the testing, were still puzzled at the unexpected outcome. The fact that during the early negotiations on the project, Ing. Crosti and his team had not appreciated that an exhaust injector was fitted to the 9Fs as standard, resulting in an estimated inherent 6% advantage in favour of the conventional 9F, was probably the crucial point. Even so, comparison of the Crosti using the exhaust steam injector compared with the standard using the live steam injector still did not reach the 12% savings to trigger any royalty payment. The company nevetheless commissioned the eminent French locomotive engineer M. André Chapelon to analyse the huge amounts of data, some of it contradictory, produced during the trials. It was two years before M. Chapelon's report was issued, in early 1958. The fact that the report took so long to emerge was partly due to M. Chapelon's illness and partly due to the fact that no single obvious reason could be put forward as to why the exercise had not come up to expectations. The suggestion that extensive scaling inside the preheater could have accounted for the disappointing performance of the Crosti boiler was largely discounted due to the fact that 92023 had less than 100 miles on the clock before being taken in to Rugby Testing Station. Another suggestion was, as in the case of some oil-fired designs, the installation of sand guns to keep the preheater tubes free of soot deposits. This was based on the theory that soot could accumulate there, (thus reducing the extent of heat transmission), in the absence of abrasion from solid particles which scoured the main boiler tubes but which were assumed to be retained in the front smokebox. Other suggestions such as the addition of orthodox smoke deflectors and a redesign of the tender to make it more aerodynamic appeared little more than a 'clutching at straws' exercise and likely to be of marginal value. Later, Ing. Crosti even suggested the installation of a turbine driven fan to provide a strong draught with minimum back pressure. Virtually all of these proposals would have resulted in a great deal of extra expense and design work rendering the whole

FIGURE N
TEMPORARY FEED ARRANGEMENT FOR MECHANICAL STOKER TESTS
AT RUGBY TESTING STATION

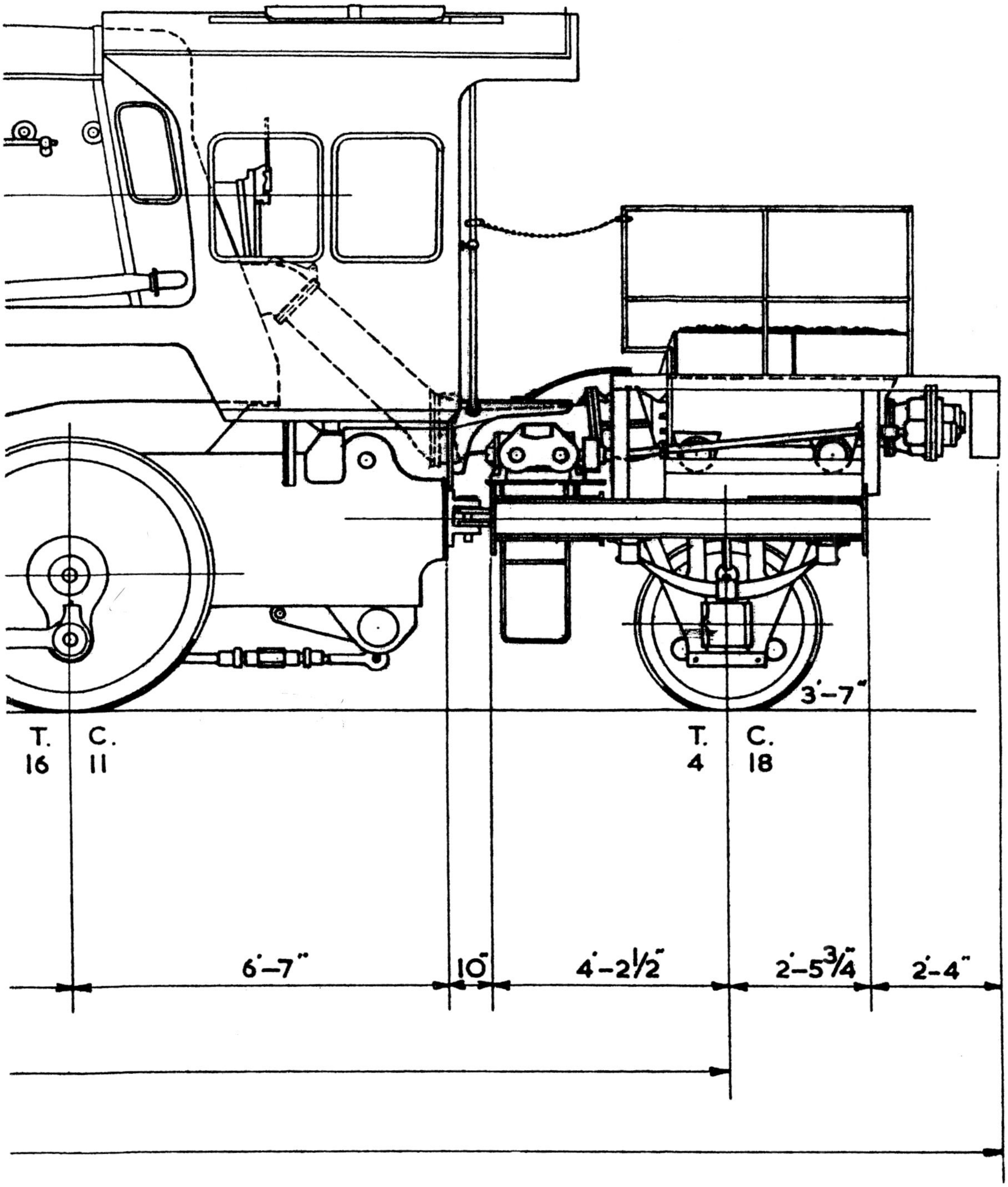

Table 11.7
BR Standard Class 9F 2-10-0s

Comparison of Double Blastpipe and Chimney Engine (92178) with Giesl Oblong Ejector Engine (92250) at a Steam Rate of 18,000 lb/hr. at 40 mph

Exhaust Type	Double Blastpipe 92178	Giesl Oblong Ejector 92250			
Coal Grade	Blidworth Grade 2	Blidworth Grade 2	Whitwick Large	Whitwick Small	Cossall Slack
Cost per ton (£)	4.40	4.40	3.74	3.40	2.87
Calorific Value (B.Th.U./lb)	12,626	12,626	10,785	10,354	10,116
Firing Rate (lb/hr.)	2,564	2,564	3,102	4,321	7,200
Fuel Cost/hr. (£)	5.04	5.04	5.18	6.56	9.23
Indicated HP	1,247	1,297	1,267	1,267	1,267
Cost per HP/hr. (p)	0.40	0.39	0.41	0.52	0.73
Relative cost per HP/hr. (%)	Control	-2.5	+2.5	+30	+83
Overall Efficiency (%)	9.9	10.3	9.7	7.3	4.5

remedial programme hopelessly uneconomic. Maintaining modified engines of such increased complexity would also have been a challenge to the operating authorities.

In a comprehensive review in the spring of 1958, the decision was taken to terminate the Crosti project and an ex-gratia payment of £1,000 was made to the Italians as a goodwill gesture. Various ideas were discussed on the best method of transforming the Crostis into reliable machines. Mechanical stokers, Giesl Oblong Ejectors and even Ing. Crosti's turbine fan were considered as options. Finally however, relying on the well tried maxim that 'simplest is best', it was decided to convert the ten engines to conventional operation and Derby Works was authorised to produce the necessary drawings to achieve this in the autumn of 1958. Nevertheless it was not until June 1962 that the last of the class, 92022, emerged from Crewe in the converted state.

4. Mechanical Stoker

The objective of fitting a mechanical stoker to three of the 9Fs, 92165-7, was an attempt to realise the full potential of the class in day-to-day operation. This was restricted by what was termed the 'fireman's limit', i.e. the amount of coal a fireman could reasonably be expected to fire continuously per hour; it was believed that a significant increase in output could be obtained without this constraint. As noted in Section 1.6, the stoker was driven by a small separate steam engine mounted on the tender and fed by steam drawn from the locomotive boiler. Coal was fed from a hopper mounted on the coal space of the tender by means of a screw through an enclosed conduit, directly on to a plate immediately inside the firehole whence it was distributed by means of steam jets arranged at various angles to ensure as far as possible all parts of the grate would be covered.

For use on the stationary plant, it was necessary to design and build a two-wheeled trolley on which to mount the stoker equipment, see Figure N. This enabled the normal fuel weighing procedures to be carried out without interruption. The trolley remained permanently attached to the engine both on the plant when the tractive effort was transmitted through the framing to the plant dynamometer and also on those occasions when it was necessary to couple the tender for transit to the local MPD.

The mechanical stoker trio were fitted with double blastpipes and chimneys following the successful testing of 92178 at Swindon in November and December 1957. Engine 92166 was selected for the trials which were conducted from 21st November 1958 to 17th March 1959 in a series of 79 runs. Early on in the trials it was found that the 4 inch diameter blastpipe caps were quite inadequate to force into the firebox the necessary air for combustion restricting the steaming rates to no higher than 16,000 lb/hr. As the simplest step, both blastpipe orifices were reduced to 3⅞ inches and these together with holes cut in the front and back of the ashpan enabled steaming rates of up to 28,000 lb/hr to be achieved with Blidworth coal.

The maximum steaming rate on a day-to-day basis in service was assumed to be 75% of the test maximum, i.e. 21,000 lb/hr. In order to establish truly comparable performances throughout a series of tests with a particular fuel, it was the practice to clean the fire after each run. However, with the objective of testing the practicability of utilising the mechanical stoker over a long non-stop run hauling a heavy freight train, a particular test was carried out using the standard Blidworth Grade 2B cobbles of uniform size and quality at a steaming rate of approximately 20,500 lb/hr. This test conformed to the 'first class' test conditions for 2 hours and 40 minutes. The engine was allowed to stand for upwards of an

Figure 205
92077 (Newton Heath) approaches Chapel-en-le-Frith with RCTS "The East Midlander No. 9" rail tour from Nottingham Midland to Crewe Works on 21st May 1966. The tour went outward via Tamworth, Walsall, Wolverhampton, Stafford (71mph maximum at Penkridge), Wellington and Market Drayton. Return was via Acton Grange Junction, Arpley, Skelton Junction, Stockport Tiviot Dale, Romiley, New Mills South Junction, Peak Forest, Matlock and Ambergate. 92077 was in good form for the trip, having been just over a month out of Crewe Works following a Heavy Casual repair. *(M. S. Welch)*

Figure 206
92077 on the RCTS "East Midlander No. 9" tour is seen at Arpley curve, Warrington on 21st May 1966. *(B. Barlow)*

Figure 207
92077 takes the returning "East Midlander No.9" tour past Buxworth on the climb to Peak Forest on 21st May 1966. *(P. J. Russell)*

hour at the conclusion of the test and, without cleaning the fire, it was possible to restart, re-establish and maintain the same steaming rate again in 'first class' test conditions for upwards of 70 minutes with no sign of fire deterioration. Such clinker as did form over the grate in no way impeded the access of sufficient air to ensure complete combustion. Total distance traversed was some 130 miles and a constant horsepower at the wheels was sustained at around 1,300. At the particular speed of the test (30mph), this figure would represent approximately 1,500 tons of train hauled on level track.

In the case of the hand-fired engine this result was produced by burning around 3,000 lb Blidworth coal per hour, whereas with the mechanical stoker locomotive, the coal consumption increased by anything up to 25%. The main reason for this increase was that by the time the Blidworth small cobbles had reached the fire bed, they had been to some extent crushed by the action of the stoker and contained up to 30% fines measuring less than 1 inch in diameter. The jet pressures in the firebox, adjusted to spread the original size cobble, would clearly be too high for optimum distribution of these fines. The result was that the latter were either carried away up the chimney as unburnt fuel or became piled up in a virtually impenetrable bank under the brick arch at the front of the grate, effectively reducing the grate area. This implied attempting to obtain the same steam output from 30 square feet or less of grate area compared with the full 40.2 square feet. Any reduction of the jet pressures merely resulted in the piling up of the larger uncrushed coal under the fire door; the net result in fire condition and its effect on performance was the same.

In order to mitigate this problem, a modification of the grate was tried in which the front half was lifted up, reducing the angle of its slope such that the 'hump' in the middle was much less pronounced. This change quickly showed considerable improvement in the fire bed, its shape and condition and enabled the maximum steaming rate to be increased to around 30,000 lb/hr with generally better combustion conditions throughout the entire range. The idea of lengthening the brick arch to reduce the extent of unburnt fuel particle ejection was not pursued. As a result of the improved combustion, it was anticipated that a maximum daily service level steaming rate of 24,000 lb/hr would be attainable. Not all of this would be 'steam-to-cylinders', of course, due to the steam demand of the mechanical stoker itself.

A comparison of the boiler efficiency of the standard hand-fired locomotive (92050) using Blidworth cobbles was made with that of the mechanical stoker-fired engine under the following three sets of conditions:

(1) the standard grate mechanical stoker-fired engine using Blidworth cobbles
(2) the modified grate mechanical stoker-fired engine using Blidworth cobbles
(3) the modified grate mechanical stoker-fired engine using a mix of coal as delivered to Rugby MPD coaling plant for freight engine use.

Table 11.8
BR Standard Class 9F 2-10-0s

Coal Consumption
Giesl Oblong Ejector Engine (92250) v. Double Blastpipe and Chimney Engine (92178)

	Specified Conditions: IHP = 1236 @ 40mph			Specified Conditions: Steam Rate = 18,000 lb/hr. @ 40mph			
Fuel & Chimney Arrangement	Firing Rate lb/hr.	lb/IHP.hr.	Difference v. Control	IHP	Firing Rate lb/hr.	lb/IHP.hr.	Difference v. Control
Blidworth Double Chimney	2,558	2.070	Control	1,236	2,558	2.070	Control
Blidworth Giesl	2,463	1.993	3.72% decrease	1,280	2,558	1.998	3.48% decrease
Whitwick Large Giesl	3,043	2.462	18.94% increase	1,258	3,102	2.467	19.17% increase
Whitwick Slack Giesl	4,191	3.390	63.77% increase	1,258	4,321	3.436	66.0% increase
Cossall Slack Giesl	6,405	5.180	150.24% increase	1,258	6,800	5.405	161.11% increase

Note. IHP: Indicated Horsepower

Compared with the hand-fired 92050, the results from all three sets of trials showed a decrease in boiler efficiency of approximately 9-12% over the working range when using the mechanical stoker. An alternative to Blidworth cobbles examined during the testing was Whitwick 1 in 'Deep Hard' slack. It was quickly found almost impossible to carry out satisfactory trials with this grade owing to the inability to establish stable 'first class' testing conditions. Coal of this quality was thus regarded as virtually useless with the 9F's type of firegrate and conventional draughting arrangements.

It was postulated that the mechanical stoker would show to better advantage if coal of a lower calorific value but of suitable size were used as basis for comparison with Blidworth cobbles since the amount the fireman could fire would produce less steam. The trials indicated that the ideal coal for use with the mechanical stoker should be screened to size 2 in by 1 in. Whilst this would have advantages in the way of performance, from the economic viewpoint any specifying of the coal in this way would raise the price of any lower calorific value coal to that approaching the Blidworth cobbles price, thus immediately outweighing the advantages. It was also borne in mind that for a given power output, more coal would be required with the mechanical stoker due not only to lower boiler efficiency but also for the need to divert some of the steam to power the stoker engine itself.

The report concluded by stating that the importance of the size of the coal for use with the mechanical stoker could not be too highly stressed from another aspect, i.e. whilst a certain amount of crushing must be accepted as inevitable, the physical form of the coal must be actually capable of being crushed. Hard coal of larger size than Blidworth cobbles would only cause jamming of the screw delivery mechanism or 'tunnelling' (lower rate of coal delivery) which would speedily result in loss of either boiler pressure or water level or both, phenomena reported as by no means uncommon in daily service conditions. As if to emphasise the point, trials conducted on the road between Saltley and Carlisle on the LMR after the Rugby tests were not satisfactory overall due mainly to the mechanical stoker not operating consistently because of the presence of oversized lumps of coal jamming the screw mechanism.

To summarise the results of the trials, it was established that when the mechanical stoker worked well, the engine was able to operate at slightly greater steaming rates than the hand-fired locomotive. In view of the much higher coal consumption with the mechanical stoker engine however, the report concluded that an economic case for converting other engines to the system could not be justified.

5. Giesl Oblong Ejector

The first approaches to BR on the possible testing of the Giesl Oblong Ejector were made in 1954. The device was the patented invention of Dr. Ing. Adolph Giesl-Gieslingen, an Austrian locomotive engineer, and had been applied to a number of engines on the OBB system in Austria and elsewhere in Europe. The opportunity was not taken up by BR at the time, perhaps because it was just about to start on the Crosti experimental programme with the Italians. The

Figure 208
92250 (Severn Tunnel Junction) is on shed at Southall on 27th June 1965. The engine was one of only two BR locomotives fitted with a Giesl Oblong Ejector (the other was SR BB Pacific 34064 *Fighter Command*) in the rather half-hearted experiment during the dying days of BR steam. 92250 was the 7,331st – and last – steam locomotive to be built at Crewe Works; a special ceremony to mark the occasion was held at Crewe on 15th December 1958. . *(Courtney Haydon)*

disappointing results of the latter project probably dampened enthusiasm for further ventures into the world of continental European steam locomotive technology. Thus it was not until early 1959 after some intense 'behind the scenes' lobbying of the BTC and its chairman Sir Brian Robertson by the Austrians and their supporters that a reluctant BR was obliged to test the idea.

Although the BR modernisation plan involving heavy commitment to dieselisation and electrification was in full progress, there was still an intensive debate about the wisdom of scrapping the steam locomotive. In particular, presentations were being made outlining the economic benefits of converting steam locomotives to oil firing whilst simultaneously installing fuel saving devices such as the Giesl Ejector. The debate was further fuelled in the early 1960s by a controversial paper by a New York engineering consultant, Mr. H. F. Brown, read at the Institute of Mechanical Engineers and entitled 'Economic Results of Diesel Electric Power on the Railways of the United States of America', (Proceedings, *Institute of Mechanical Engineers,* Vol. 175, No. 5, 1961). The gist of the paper was that rather than generating a 30% ROI (Return On Investment), the target figure at the time, the total cost of capital and maintenance of diesel locomotives on most US railroads was actually more than if the resources had been expended on development and manufacture of equivalent steam power of modern design.

It was against this background that arrangements were made between the British Transport Commission and Messrs. Schoeller-Bleckmann of Vienna, the manufacturer of the Giesl Oblong Ejector under licence from the patentee, to fit a BR Standard 9F with an example of the device and submit it to a programme of testing at Rugby. The objective was to make a direct performance and economy comparison with the standard draughting arrangements of double blastpipe and chimney as fitted to the later 9F production batches.

Figure 209
A front end view of Giesl Oblong Ejector-fitted 92250 at Southall on 27th June 1965.
(Courtney Haydon)

The two main claims for the Ejector were:

(1) a considerable reduction in back pressure at the blastpipe resulting in a significant increase in cylinder power.
(2) an enhanced ability to burn low grade coals hitherto deemed unusable as locomotive fuel.

An agreed condition was that the boiler should be able to produce not less than 21,000 lbs of steam per hour with any of the coals used.

The tests on the stationary plant were designed to obtain:

(1) a specific coal consumption figure with a standard double blastpipe double chimney locomotive at a representative rate of 18,000 lbs of steam/hr at a running speed of 40 mph using Blidworth Grade 2 coal (calorific value 12,626 B.Th.U./lb), this value to serve as a reference and to establish that the engine was similar in performance to that of previously tested engines of the same class.
(2) corresponding coal consumption figures with the same locomotive fitted with the Giesl Oblong Ejector using Blidworth Grade 2 and other selected coals.

The engine chosen for the tests was 92250 the last 9F to be built at Crewe. The engine, fitted with a double blastpipe and chimney in common with all of the last Crewe batch of 9Fs, was delivered in December 1958 and had accumulated some 6,000 miles during the three months before being taken into Rugby Testing Plant in April 1959. Thirty-two test runs were made before the double blastpipe and chimney were replaced by the Giesl Oblong Ejector. After this, a further 84 runs were made, the whole testing period beginning on 9th April and ending on 1st September 1959.

The coal grades tested were:

(a) Whitwick Deep Hard (large) having a calorific value of 10,785 B.Th.U./lb, to be broken up into the same size as the Blidworth coal.
(b) Whitwick 1 in slack, a product which had a very high dust content, calorific value 10,354 B.Th.U./lb.
(c) Cossall ¾ in slack, a product similar in characteristics to the Whitwick 1 in slack, calorific value 10,116 B.Th.U./lb.

The criterion for judging the effectiveness of the Ejector would be the achievement of financial savings of not less than

7½% over the cost of the Blidworth coal. This figure was arrived at by requiring the £500 cost of the Ejector to be recouped over two years, the savings of £250 per annum being the approximate cost of the 50 tons of coal not consumed each year by a standard 9F typically burning 670 tons per annum on an average mileage of 26,000 at 58 lb of coal per mile.

A steaming rate of 29,000 lb/hr was obtained under completely satisfactory conditions with the Blidworth coal. Similarly a figure of 24,000 lb/hr was achieved under acceptable conditions with the Whitwick Deep Hard (large) grade when reduced to the Blidworth size; this was achieved by reducing the free nozzle area through the blastpipe to 26.2 square inches compared with the 30.2 square inch figure for the Blidworth coal. It was noted that there were large void spaces in the fire with the Whitwick Deep Hard coal which tended to reduce the efficiency of steam generation. Attempts to cover such spaces with increased layers of fuel resulted in the development of an uneven firebed and an accumulation under the brick arch of a mass of coal which could not be burnt.

With the Whitwick and Cossall slack grades however, the stipulated minimum steaming rate of 21,000 lb/hr was not achieved except for short periods in transitory conditions. This failure was accounted for by the presence of substantial clinkering in the grate and the consequent gradual reduction of grate area available for burning the fuel. In addition both grades contained around 80% of fines of less than ½in. size; the overall conclusion was that such fuels were discounted as practical propositions for the firing of a 9F.

Tests were undertaken at 20, 30, 40 and 50mph through a range of steaming rates from 12,000 to 18,000 lb/hr. Examples of coal consumption figures using Blidworth cobbles for the standard double exhaust arrangement compared with the Giesl Oblong Ejector are given in Tables 11.7 and 11.8; also included are the results for the Giesl device using the other three grades of coal. The data has been extracted from BR Report No. R18 which summarises the results of the 92250 Giesl tests at Rugby. For an indicated horsepower of 1,236 at 40mph, the Giesl device shows a fuel economy of 3.72% in terms of lb/IHP.hr; the results with the other fuels however show substantial increases in the amount of coal consumed. Similarly at a steaming rate of 18,000 lb/hr at 40mph, a decrease of 3.48% in fuel consumed is noted with the Giesl device which also delivered a 3.6% increase in IHP; again fuel consumption with the other grades shows a significant increase.

Taking into account all the figures for the different steaming rates at 40mph, the overall results show that increases in IHP of 35-85 (3.5-5.1%) were made available with the Giesl draughting arrangement in place whilst at 50mph the corresponding figures were 40-110 IHP (4.8-7.25%). The increase in power was attributed almost entirely to the reduction in blastpipe pressure accorded by the Giesl Oblong Ejector.

The report concluded that, as a draughting device to reduce blastpipe pressure and hence cylinder back pressure, 92250's Giesl Oblong Ejector conferred an increase in available indicated horsepower of around 4% over that achievable by a double blastpipe fitted 9F under the conditions specified in the agreement with the Austrians. However, any claim to enable low grade small size fuels to be burned remained to be substantiated.

In the light of previous experience suggesting that small savings in fuel under plant test conditions would likely be reduced to negligible proportions in day-to-day service, the benefits of the Ejector as determined by the tests were considered insufficient for BR to authorise conversion of other 9Fs to the Giesl system. Arrangements were put in hand to return the device to the manufacturers but this was refused on the grounds that it was non-standard and hence of no intrinsic value. 92250 carried the Ejector for the rest of its life, spending much of its time at Newport Ebbw Junction mainly on the iron ore traffic to and from the Banbury area. Reports suggested that the engine demonstrated no significant fuel savings compared with its stablemates.

11.2 Service Performance Data

From its early days, BR produced annual performance statistics for its locomotive fleet. The data summarised details of the operating stock, the average annual mileage and the average amount of time under repair for each class. These figures were often referred to as the 'Miles and Days' statistics and enabled the productivity of the various classes to be compared. Productivity was defined as the number of weekdays in service out of a possible 309 days. Indications are that the figure 309 was arrived at by subtracting the number of Sundays in the year (52) from the total of 365 and also, it has been suggested, four Bank Holidays, (Good Friday, Easter Monday, Christmas Day and Boxing Day), when activity would be generally low apart from holiday excursion work at Easter. It is not clear how the incidences of leap years were dealt with; presumbably the figure of 310 was used for the number of days available.

Recording of data for the 9Fs was begun in 1955 and information by region for the class from that year to 1961 inclusive is given in Tables 11.9 to 11.13; for interest the 9F statistics are compared with those for other freight classes. When referring to mileage statistics, it is important to note that figures for individual engines do not necessarily agree precisely with the data presented for works visits in Table 8.2, Record of Repairs, Section 8. There are two different sources for mileage figures in many record cards. It is a feature of official statistics of the period that there are frequently minor discrepancies between data sets nominally referring to the same topic.

For 1955 (Table 11.9), the WR 9F allocation (92000-7) achieved the very low average annual mileage of just over 16,000. This was accounted for by the fact that the engines were all allocated to Newport Ebbw Junction at the time and were confined mainly to the short-haul Ebbw Vale iron ore traffic, allowing little scope for generating high mileages; the number of days in service at 87% however was very high, indicating that the engines were apparently doing virtually all that the WR was expecting of them. It is noteworthy that other freight engines operated by the WR such as the 28XX, 47XX and LMS 8F 2-8-0s were achieving almost double this mileage at that time. Even the few remaining Robinson-designed World War I ROD 30XX 2-8-0s, rapidly coming to the end of their long lives, managed to exceed the 9F average for the year as did the 8F and 7F 42XX and 8F 72XX tank engines whose duties were also mainly confined to short trip working.

On the ER and NER, the average mileage for the 9Fs was over 26,000, exceeded only by that of the region's LNER O1 2-8-0s. Most of the 9F work on the ER at that time was the

Figure 210
Fawley-bound empty tank wagons head south through Shawford behind 92231 (Eastleigh) on 28th July 1962. The extra SR lamp/route indicator brackets are now in place on the smokebox door. 92231 was transferred to the NER (York) in September 1963 for two years before withdrawal during which time its brackets were probably reconfigured as in Figure L, Profile D. The usual couple of wagons between the tender and first tank are there as a token precaution against possible ignition of the oil by any excess emission of cinders from the chimney.
(Courtney Haydon)

Figure 211
92062 passes South Pelaw Junction on its return to Tyne Dock from the Consett steel works with empty iron ore hoppers in the late 1950s.
(J. W. Armstrong Trust)

Figure 212
92075 (Annesley) heads an up GC line 'windcutter' freight near Rushcliffe Halt between Nottingham and Loughborough on 19th May 1964, just over a year before withdrawal of freight services from this route. Although an LMR engine, the lamp bracket reconfiguration has not yet been applied. After a spell officially in store (June 1965-January 1966), 92075 was transferred to Carlisle Kingmoor in March 1966 where it saw service on the WCML until withdrawal six months later. *(M. Mitchell)*

New England-Ferme Park mineral traffic and the Whitemoor-Temple Mills freights; the 9Fs were showing high productivity, being in use for over 80% of the possible days available for service.

For the LMR, the 26,000 annual average mileage for their 9Fs, operating from Wellingborough and Toton mainly on mineral traffic, was similar to that of the ER and NER allocation and higher than that of the various categories of 8F 2-8-0s. The annual average mileage for the LNWR 0-8-0s, usually between 19,000 and 20,000 in the early 1950s was by this time gradually reducing. It is perhaps surprising to note that the 26 Beyer Garratts still in service on the LMR at the end of 1955 were achieving over 20,000 miles per year on average, operating for a respectable 72% of the available days, the latter figure being the same as for the 9Fs. Also of interest are the figures for the Lickey banker 58100, then in its last full year of life, which show an annual mileage of around 22,000, almost six thousand more than the average for the WR 9F allocation.

The 1956 figures show the WR 9F average mileage dropping some 6% to only 15,200 for the year, a fact possibly associated with the first visits to Swindon Works for repairs. Meanwhile, the 8F freight classes on the WR increased their average annual mileage during 1956. Even the ROD 30XX figures showed improvement over the previous year in both the miles run (18,500 on average) and the number of days worked, whilst the heavy freight 42XX and 72XX tank engine mileages were about the same as in 1955. Of the freight classes quoted for the WR, only their ageing LMS Class 3F 0-6-0s and the remaining LNWR 0-8-0s had a lower average mileage than the region's 9Fs in 1956. It is likely that the wisdom of allocating 9Fs to the WR was queried at some point during this period.

On the ER and NER, the number of 9Fs doubled from year end 1955 to year end 1956. Annual average mileage dropped a little, probably associated with the inclusion of 92060-6/97-9 in use on the Tyne Dock-Consett runs. Here, even an unusually high four return trip working in one day would involve no more than 200 miles. The balance of the additional 9Fs in the region was allocated to Doncaster from where they were employed mainly on mineral workings with some on fast fitted freights.

On the LMR in 1956, the Crostis continued to perform poorly in terms of both availability and mileage compared with the standard boiler engines. The average annual mileage for the latter at nearly 25,000 was higher than any other freight class in the region; this was almost invariably the case until regular mileage monitoring ceased in 1961.

For the 9F class as a whole on BR, apart from the Crostis, typical availability figures for individual engines had settled down in the range 70-85% dependent on the schedule for works visits in any particular year.

For 1957, only LMR and ScR data has been traced. The Crosti mileage and availability figures remain low, both worse than the sole surviving Beyer Garratt; the 4F 0-6-0 and 8F 2-8-0 figures are impressive, mileage being in excess of 20,000 for both classes with availabilities similarly above 80%. It should be noted that the LMS 8F 2-8-0 figures are split into three categories, LMS-built, HMG (His/Her Majesty's Government, i.e. engines formerly owned by the War Department for use in the Second World War effort) and ORC (engines built by Other Railway Companies); in practice, there was very little difference in the performance of the three groups. On the ScR, the WD 2-10-0s returned a lower average for both 'Miles and Days' compared with their WD and Stanier 2-8-0 stablemates.

In 1958, the last year that the number of days in service was specifically monitored, the ER 9Fs retain the 'Blue Riband' for mileage and availability whilst the 39 WR engines could only muster an average mileage for the year of just over

Table 11.9

BR Cl. 9F 2-10-0s: Comparison of Annual Mileage and Availability with Other Freight Classes for the Year 1955

Region/ Locomotive Class	Oper-rating Stock 31.12.55	Average Annual Miles ('000s) 1955	Weekdays out of Service (WOOS)					In Service	
			Repairs						
			Classified Shop & Shed	Running & Exams	Total Repairs	Not Re-quired	Total WOOS	No of Days	% of Total Possible (309 days)
WR									
9F BR Standard	8	16.2	Nil	26	26	15	41	268	87
8F 28XX 2-8-0	167	28.9	18	38	56	14	70	239	77
8F WD 2-8-0	47	19.9	25	62	87	17	104	205	66
8F LMS 2-8-0	42	30.2	18	36	54	21	75	234	76
7F ROD 30XX	20	17.3	70	96	103	13	116	193	62
7F 47XX 2-8-0	9	31.1	10	68	78	16	94	215	69
7F LNWR 0-8-0	31	14.4	21	67	88	45	133	176	57
4MT 43XX 2-6-0	211	28.5	17	38	55	15	70	239	77
3MT 22XX 0-6-0	119	19.6	15	38	53	31	84	225	73
3F LMS 0-6-0	9	13.0	Nil	59	59	28	87	222	72
2F LMS 0-6-0	2	06.7	13	37	50	55	105	204	66
8F 72XX 2-8-2T	54	18.7	18	28	46	17	63	246	80
8F 42XX 2-8-0T	60	17.9	18	21	39	16	55	254	82
7F 42XX 2-8-0T	91	17.3	17	31	48	16	64	245	79
E&NER									
9F BR Standard	23	26.7	17	30	47	13	60	249	81
8F LNER O1	58	27.7	37	33	70	14	84	225	73
8F LNER O2	66	21.9	12	32	44	18	62	247	80
8F WD 2-8-0	364	23.6	20	32	52	16	68	241	78
8F WD ScR	5	17.6	50	48	98	10	108	201	65
7F LNER Q7	15	19.0	14	59	73	7	80	229	74
7F LNER O4	266	18.5	22	29	51	14	65	244	79
6F LNER Q6	120	19.7	21	40	61	10	71	238	77
5F LNER J27	115	16.9	12	28	40	14	54	255	83
5F LNER J39	263	17.9	17	49	66	19	85	224	72
4F LMS 0-6-0	13	20.4	6	35	41	18	59	250	81
Beyer-Garratt U1 2-8-0 + 0-8-2T ¶	1	10.6	Nil	106	106	57	163	146	47
LMR									
9F BR Standard	22	26.1	Nil	52	52	14	66	243	72
9F BR Crosti	10	New	*	*	*	*	*	*	*
8F LMS 2-8-0	316	23.2	13	33	46	11	57	252	82
8F LMS ex-HMG	22	22.8	17	35	52	9	61	248	80
8F LMS ex-ORC	275	23.0	12	33	45	12	57	252	82
8F WD 2-8-0	263	19.8	11	29	40	26	66	243	79
7F S&D 2-8-0	11	23.2	15	70	85	20	105	204	66
7F LNWR G2	56	17.8	18	43	61	18	79	230	74
7F LNWR G2A	185	17.7	18	40	58	15	73	236	76
7F LMS G3	38	17.6	19	36	55	26	81	228	74
4F LMS 0-6-0	693	20.5	11	36	47	14	61	248	80
4F S&D 0-6-0	11	24.6	10	56	66	18	84	225	73
3F MR 0-6-0	292	15.2	7	29	36	53	89	220	71
3F L&Y 0-6-0	136	14.0	7	27	34	60	94	215	70
3F FR 0-6-0	5	9.2	8	28	36	117	153	156	51
2F MR 0-6-0	101	13.7	7	26	33	52	85	224	73
2F GC J10	53	14.9	18	25	43	79	122	187	61
Lickey Banker	1	22.0	Nil	10	10	5	15	294	95
Beyer-Garratt 2-6-0 + 0-6-2T	26	20.4	31	44	75	11	86	223	72
ScR									
8F WD 2-10-0	25	21.3	36	74	110	12	122	189	61
8F WD 2-8-0	54	23.9	27	44	71	12	83	228	73
8F LNER O6	3	35.4	12	50	62	7	69	242	78
8F LMS 2-8-0	1	36.0	40	34	74	4	78	233	75
8F LMS ex-ORC	4	36.3	22	34	56	9	65	246	79
5F LNER J37	104	20.2	12	46	58	12	70	241	77
6F LNER J38	35	21.1	19	56	75	7	82	229	74

Key ¶ Data for 1951 * No data recorded.

Table 11.10
BR Cl. 9F 2-10-0s: Comparison of Annual Mileage and Availability with Other Freight Classes for the Year 1956

Region/ Locomotive Class	Oper-rating Stock 31.12.56	Average Annual Miles ('000s) 1956	Weekdays out of Service (WOOS)					In Service	
			Repairs						
			Classified Shop & Shed	Running & Exams	Total Repairs	Not Re-quired	Total WOOS	No of Days	% of Total Possible (310 days)
WR									
9F BR Standard	8	15.2	17	52	69	20	89	221	71
8F 28XX	167	30.7	17	37	54	4	58	252	81
8F WD ex-HMG	47	23.1	16	58	74	7	81	229	74
8F LMS 2-8-0	52	31.4	13	37	50	11	61	249	80
7F ROD 30XX	6	18.5	32	53	85	12	97	213	69
7F 47XX	9	32.8	50	32	82	5	87	223	72
7F LNWR 0-8-0	31	14.4	11	73	84	50	134	176	57
4MT 43XX 2-6-0	206	29.7	21	38	59	3	62	247	80
3MT 22XX 0-6-0	118	21.1	15	37	52	17	69	240	78
3F LMS 0-6-0	9	12.4	3	40	43	56	99	211	68
2F LMS 0-6-0	1	15.5	Nil	16	16	41	57	253	82
8F 72XX 2-8-2T	54	19.8	17	29	46	6	52	258	83
8F 42XX 2-8-0T	60	17.9	18	29	47	6	53	257	83
7F 42XX 2-8-0T	91	17.0	23	29	52	7	59	251	81
E&NER									
9F BR Standard	46	26.1	6	38	44	10	54	256	83
8F LNER O1	58	27.0	30	36	66	5	71	239	77
8F LNER O2	66	21.5	14	34	48	12	60	250	81
8F WD ex-HMG	369	24.8	16	32	48	6	54	256	83
8F LNER Q7	15	16.8	27	53	80	8	88	222	72
7F LNER O4	266	19.2	20	28	48	5	53	257	83
6F LNER Q6	120	20.0	16	39	55	6	61	249	80
5F LNER J27	115	16.9	13	22	35	10	45	264	85
5F LNER J39	262	17.5	20	46	66	21	87	222	72
4F LMS 0-6-0	16	20.1	13	26	39	8	47	263	85
LMR									
9F BR Standard	51	24.8	7	64	71	7	78	232	75
9F BR Crosti	10	21.4	50	55	105	6	111	199	64
8F LMS 2-8-0	316	21.6	12	34	46	5	51	259	84
8F LMS ex-HMG	22	22.3	13	33	46	4	50	260	84
8F LMS ex-ORC	265	23.3	12	33	45	4	49	261	84
8F WD 2-8-0	263	21.1	12	29	41	12	53	257	83
7F S&D 2-8-0	11	23.6	19	49	68	21	89	221	71
7F LNWR G2	55	18.7	15	42	57	5	62	248	80
7F LNWR G2A	181	23.4	15	43	58	7	65	245	79
7F LMS G3	32	18.5	11	34	45	16	61	249	80
4F LMS 0-6-0	682	20.7	10	34	44	5	49	261	84
4F S&D 0-6-0	11	23.1	5	60	65	12	77	232	75
3F MR 0-6-0	271	14.9	4	29	33	51	84	226	73
3F L&Y 0-6-0	118	14.6	9	29	38	45	83	211	68
3F FR 0-6-0	3	12.0	Nil	44	44	54	98	211	68
2F MR 0-6-0	88	14.6	4	29	33	26	59	250	81
2F GC J10 0-6-0	37	17.1	2	30	32	51	83	226	73
Beyer-Garratt 2-6-0 + 0-6-2T	13	20.5	18	48	66	8	74	236	76
ScR									
8F WD 2-10-0	25	18.6	55	55	110	16	126	184	59
8F WD 2-8-0	54	24.9	18	50	68	12	80	230	74
8F LNER O6	3	36.2	34	33	67	2	69	241	78
8F LMS 2-8-0	1	37.5	24	51	75	4	79	231	75
8F LMS ex-ORC	4	32.9	21	36	57	2	59	251	81
6F LNER J38	35	21.3	18	62	80	4	84	226	73
5F LNER J37	104	19.9	14	47	61	6	67	243	78

Table 11.11

BR Cl. 9F 2-10-0s:Comparison of Annual Mileage and Availability with Other Freight Classes for the Year 1957

Region/ Locomotive Class	Operating Stock 31.12.57	Average Annual Miles ('000s) 1957	Weekdays out of Service (WOOS)					In Service	
			Repairs						
			Classified Shop & Shed	Running & Exams	Total Repairs	Not Re-quired	Total WOOS	No of Days	% of Total Possible (309 days)
LMR									
9F BR Standard	85	26.1	12	46	58	7	65	244	79
9F BR Crosti	10	21.3	45	63	108	4	112	197	64
8F LMS 2-8-0	287	22.7	13	32	45	51	50	259	84
8F LMS ex-HMG	17	22.6	14	29	43	51	48	261	84
8F LMS ex-ORC	239	23.0	14	31	45	52	50	259	84
8F WD 2-8-0	144	20.7	12	30	42	11	53	256	83
7F S&D 2-8-0	*	*	*	*	*	*	*	*	*
7F LNWR G2	55	17.6	19	44	63	8	71	238	77
7F LNWR G2A	149	17.6	14	40	54	8	62	247	80
7F LMS G3	19	7.2	12	42	54	18	72	237	77
4F LMS 0-6-0	618	20.2	12	34	46	74	53	256	83
3F MR 0-6-0	225	14.4	4	30	34	49	83	226	73
3F L&Y 0-6-0	70	14.2	8	27	35	44	79	230	74
2F MR 0-6-0	72	13.8	5	29	34	29	63	246	79
2F GC J10 0-6-0	31	15.7	1	39	40	56	96	213	69
Beyer-Garratt 2-6-0 + 0-6-2T	1	24.1	Nil	41	41	9	50	259	84
ScR									
8F WD 2-10-0	25	22.5	21	63	84	13	97	213	69
8F WD 2-8-0	62	24.6	21	51	72	9	81	229	74
8F LMS 2-8-0	11	34.3	13	45	58	2	60	250	81
6F LNER J38	35	21.9	15	71	86	2	88	222	72
5F NBR J37	104	20.1	17	49	66	7	73	237	76
4F LMS 0-6-0	49	19.4	11	51	62	14	76	234	75
3F LMS 0-6-0	5	19.0	-	34	34	12	46	264	85

Key: * information not traced

20,000. Again the high mileages for the WR-based Stanier 8F and 47XX Class 2-8-0s are noteworthy. The data for the ER and NER is quoted separately for the first time and the difference in mileage between the two allocations is apparent. This is attributable to the short-haul work of the Tyne Dock engines offering little scope for high mileage compared with the ER engines which had a relatively high proportion of fast fitted freights included in their duties.

From 1959 to 1961, the annual average mileages for the 9Fs, with the exception of those in the NER, shows a consistent decline over the period although the WR had managed to get more use out of its allocation in 1959/60 compared with other years.

Only one set of data was traced for the SR 9F quintet at Eastleigh and this was for the year 1962. The respectable annual average of nearly 26,000 miles reflected the use of the engines on the oil traffic from the Esso refinery at Fawley and is similar to the figure for the Class 6F S15 4-6-0s which were much used on fitted freights between London and Southampton Docks.

Cumulative mileage figures for the 9Fs operated by the WR in the early 1960s are given in Table 11.14. Although there was a higher rate of reallocation of 9Fs on the WR compared with other regions, it is possible to deduce a correlation between the mileage record for individual engines and their allocations up to the end of 1963. The Old Oak Common and Cardiff (Canton and East Dock) duties appear to result in the relatively high mileage of over 30,000 per annum on average for several engines, reflecting their use on fast long distance freight work. Engines allocated to Banbury and Newport Ebbw Junction on the other hand tend to display much lower mileage on average at 20,000 or less, their duties being concerned with the slower movement of heavy iron ore freight.

The LMR assiduously recorded individual locomotive mileages for its allocation up until around 1960 and it is hence possible to monitor almost all of the 9F allocation individually from 1954 onwards where record cards have survived. Table 11.15 gives annual mileage and availability for each of the years 1954-1960 whilst Table 11.16 lists cumulative mileage at 31st December 1960 together with the derived annualised average mileage figure from date of delivery. Despite the general lack of record keeping from the early 1960s onwards, it has been possible to trace mileage figures for a few of the LMR allocation in their final years. These are also listed in Table 11.16; for 92008 and 92154, nominal lifetime figures compute at 300,800 and 214,000 respectively. The WR, ER and NER were less conscientious in this regard but mileage

Table 11.12

BR Cl. 9F 2-10-0s: Comparison of Annual Mileage and Availability with Other Freight Classes for the Year 1958

Region/ Locomotive Class	Oper-rating Stock 31.12.58	Average Annual Miles ('000s) 1958	Weekdays out of Service (WOOS)					In Service	
			Repairs						
			Classified Shop & Shed	Running & Exams	Total Repairs	Not Re-quired	Total WOOS	No of Days	% of Total Possible (309 days)
WR									
9F BR Standard	39	20.6	10	52	62	17	79	230	74
8F 28XX	161	28.7	13	39	52	15	67	242	78
8F WD 2-8-0	45	18.8	14	46	60	57	117	192	62
8F LMS 2-8-0	45	30.3	15	36	51	10	61	248	80
7F 47XX 2-8-0	9	31.4	50	40	90	10	100	209	68
7F S&D 2-8-0	11	21.3	21	61	82	11	93	216	70
7F LNWR 0-8-0	10	03.8	Nil	17	17	243	260	49	16
4MT 43XX 2-6-0	178	27.6	18	39	57	15	72	237	77
4F LMS 0-6-0	36	20.5	12	35	47	13	60	249	81
3MT 22XX 0-6-0	119	18.4	16	35	51	41	92	217	70
3F LMS 0-6-0	23	15.9	8	36	44	44	88	221	72
8F 72XX 2-8-2T	54	18.2	18	31	49	14	63	246	80
8F 42XX 2-8-0T	60	15.7	21	29	50	21	71	238	77
7F 42XX 2-8-0T	91	15.6	16	30	46	21	67	242	78
ER									
9F BR Standard	55	35.7	13	33	46	3	49	260	84
8F LNER O1	30	21.5	29	64	93	12	105	204	66
8F LNER O2	66	20.7	14	23	37	31	68	241	78
8F WD 2-8-0	230	22.0	21	29	50	12	62	247	80
8F LMS 2-8-0	39	19.5	12	28	40	7	47	262	85
7F LNER O4	227	16.2	22	28	50	30	80	229	74
5F LNER J39	127	16.6	11	48	59	52	111	198	64
4F LMS 0-6-0	63	19.2	8	35	43	4	47	262	85
3F LMS 0-6-0	35	14.6	5	28	33	29	62	247	80
2F LMS 0-6-0	4	14.8	5	25	30	51	81	228	74
NER									
9F BR Standard	10	21.9	10	28	38	47	85	224	72
8F LNER Q7	15	14.5	13	44	57	31	88	221	72
8F LNER 01	5	16.1	21	56	77	35	112	197	64
8F WD 2-8-0	224	22.6	12	31	43	12	55	254	82
8F LMS 2-8-0	55	21.8	15	40	55	3	58	251	81
7F LNER O4	11	14.6	16	43	59	4	63	246	80
6F LNER Q6	120	18.9	17	45	62	9	71	238	77
5F LNER J27	115	15.8	13	41	54	9	63	246	80
5F LNER J39	120	15.5	15	47	62	32	94	215	70
4F LMS 0-6-0	46	18.8	9	34	43	3	46	263	85
3F LMS 0-6-0	20	09.0	3	23	26	122	148	161	52
3F LYR 0-6-0	17	13.1	2	45	47	52	99	210	68
2F LMS 0-6-0	3	14.0	Nil	27	27	56	83	226	73
LMR									
9F BR Standard	119	29.6	12	64	76	7	83	226	73
9F BR Crosti	10	21.5	47	72	119	6	125	184	60
8F WD 2-10-0	1	27.8	16	68	84	4	88	221	72
8F LMS 2-8-0	262	22.5	13	35	48	61	54	255	83
8F LMS ex-HMG	17	21.9	14	29	43	7	50	259	84
8F LMS ex-ORC	245	23.0	12	35	47	62	53	256	83
8F WD 2-8-0	174	20.8	11	34	45	11	56	253	82
8F LNER O1	23	20.9	19	49	68	4	72	237	77
7F LNER O4	27	19.7	10	34	44	6	50	254	82
7F LNWR G2	59	15.7	8	44	52	11	7	232	75
7F LNWR G2A	146	15.7	9	44	53	11	77	232	75
7F LMS G3	20	12.4	22	22	44	15	59	198	64
5F LNER J39	31	17.9	13	55	68	7	75	234	76
4F LMS 0-6-0	554	18.8	10	37	47	9	69	240	78
3F MR 0-6-0	169	14.0	5	33	38	12	73	236	76
3F L&Y 0-6-0	58	13.3	7	28	35	41	93	216	70
2F MR 0-6-0	62	9.9	4	24	28	37	117	192	62
ScR									
8F WD 2-10-0	24	19.5	11	70	81	23	104	206	66
8F WD 2-8-0	60	22.3	18	56	74	10	84	226	73
8F LMS 2-8-0	3	25.3	Nil	83	83	5	88	222	72
6F LNER J38	35	22.1	17	62	79	5	84	226	73
5F LNER J37	104	18.6	13	52	65	7	72	238	77

figures are available, usually recorded at the start of works visits for major overhauls. Table 11.14 (referred to earlier) for the WR and Table 11.17 for the ER/NER list average mileages at specified dates based on these figures.

As a result of the LMR policy of maintaining comprehensive records, it is possible to gain a general idea of the annual average mileage of its 9Fs by allocated depot as there appeared to be a reasonably consistent 'core' allocation of specific engines in any particular year. Only data for those engines allocated for the whole of the year is included but with this reservation in mind it is still possible to discern trends. Table 11.18 shows the LMR 9F allocation by MPD for the period 1956-60 during which time eleven depots had an allocation of the class for the whole of a particular year.

The Annesley allocation consistently shows the highest annual average mileage as would be expected given the heavy use of the class on the celebrated 'windcutter' freights to Woodford Halse. In contrast, the low figure for the Bidston allocation is consistent with their main duty, the short-haul Shotwick ore traffic from Bidston Docks. Also again noteworthy is the relatively poor performance of the Crostis at Wellingborough compared with the standard engines, a situation which became decidedly worse towards the end of their lives as Crostis. The comparison of the standard allocation compared with the mechanical stoker-fitted engines at Saltley shows the preference each year for the former. The relatively low annual average mileage for the Westhouses allocation again reflects the class' usual pattern of short-haul coal workings during the week coupled with longer distance duties in 1958/9 on passenger traffic to the north Wales and Lancashire coasts in summer. The Toton and Kettering engines were mainly engaged in the mineral workings to and from London whilst the Leicester Midland and Cricklewood allocations had a greater proportion of fitted freight work. The Newton Heath and Rowsley duties for the 9Fs were a mixture of mineral and fitted freight work with the Newton Heath contingent sometimes being used on passenger work at holiday times in summer.

On the ER and NER, there were two investigations carried out into perceived problems with both regions' 9Fs, the first in March 1960 regarding what was described as 'indifferent steaming' and the other in 1962 where the incidence of fractured smokebox tubeplates was examined.

In the Darlington Works DMPO Minute No. 107, dated 1st March 1960, 'Steaming of Class 9F Locomotives', the committee chairman referred to the 55 9Fs allocated to the GN line, noting their allocation at that time was as follows:

Depot	**Single Blastpipe**	**Double Blastpipe**	**Total**
Immingham	1	5	6
Doncaster	10	9	19
New England	23	7	30

It was reported that the question of indifferent steaming of these locomotives had been outstanding for too long and definite steps would have to be taken to remedy the situation by the three traffic managers responsible. Tests and observations were to be made on the following bases.

- to ascertain whether there were any complaints regarding steaming of the locomotives fitted with double blastpipes.
- to carry out trials with different size blastpipe tops to determine a suitable dimension for single blastpipes and likewise for double blastpipe locomotives if it was established locally that the latter were giving similar trouble.
- to examine at least three or four locomotives by 'opening out specially at each depot' to ascertain piston ring wear and clearances; excessive wear on the rings may be a possible cause of the engines not steaming freely.

The three district motive power officers were asked to report on their findings by the end of April 1960.

It has not been possible to trace documentation regarding the outcome of this investigation. It is likely however that the main cause of the problem was excessive wear of the piston and valve rings, piston heads and cylinder barrels bearing in mind the high proportion of fast fitted freight work to which the ER assigned their 9Fs. The normal running mileage between piston and valve examinations was expected to be around 30,000 to 36,000, whereas for a short period in some cases, piston rings were being changed at an alarming 5,000 miles or every two months.

The 1962 investigation into the incidences of smokebox tubeplate fracture included both the ER and NER 9F allocation. No official report has been traced but some raw data exists and is reproduced here. A comprehensive summary of the performance of each boiler in terms of mileage up to and from the engine's previous major overhaul is given in Table 11.19. Similarly, an attempt was made to relate smokebox tubeplate cast numbers from the various suppliers of the original steel components, such as Appleby Frodingham and Colvilles, so that any correlation could be identified; it would appear that no such trends could be established.

It is possible to deduce mileages for individual locomotives from these figures and, with one or two exceptions, the total mileage figures from this source agree reasonably well with mileage data extracted from the Engine History and Engine Record Cards.

The results of the tubeplate fracture investigation do not appear to have been reported officially and it is possible the project was abandoned as resources became more focused on diesel and electric traction at this late stage in the life of the steam locomotive on BR. Some notes on interim conclusions however are displayed in Table 11.20. It appears that the engines employed on the Tyne Dock-Consett iron ore traffic may have been more prone to this problem than any of the other ER/NER allocation. The combination of strenuous uphill efforts with heavily loaded ore wagons followed by a drifting back down again to the coast may have been a factor.

Similar problems were reported with the LMR 9Fs 92045-7 allocated to Bidston for the John Summers' iron ore traffic in 1956/7 (and to a lesser extent with the Lickey banker 92079 by both the LMR and WR). In contrast there does not appear to have been any such complaint reported with the WR allocation based at Newport Ebbw Junction which was engaged in similar heavy ore movements.

A Note on Double Chimney 9F Performance

In the early design stages of the BR Standard classes, the provision of double chimneys was considered for the larger grate-area types but not adopted for two main reasons:

- the engines were designed to perform their normal work at low fuel combustion rates, i.e. they were relatively large for the work expected of them; hence a single blastpipe and chimney were all that was needed even for the larger grate sizes such as the 40.2 sq ft of the 9Fs.
- a double blastpipe and chimney designed for high power

Table 11.13

BR Cl. 9F 2-10-0s: Annual Mileage Compared with Other Freight Classes 1959-61

Region/ Locomotive Class	Operating Stock 31.12.59	Average Annual Miles ('000s) 1959	Operating Stock 31.12.60	Average Annual Miles ('000s) 1960	Operating Stock 31.12.61	Average Annual Miles ('000s) 1961
WR						
9F BR Standard	54	27.8	54	25.8	52	20.1
8F 28XX 2-8-0	132	25.8	118	27.4	117	27.1
8F WD 2-8-0	35	19.0	35	20.7	34	20.2
8F LMS 2-8-0	54	27.1	54	27.0	54	25.4
7F 47XX 2-8-0	9	32.3	9	33.7	9	30.9
7F S&D 2-8-0	10	21.0	9	17.6	7	17.4
4MT 43XX 2-6-0	144	26.4	120	26.9	113	23.5
4F LMS 0-6-0	30	19.6	27	19.3	27	15.8
3MT 22XX 0-6-0	92	16.9	82	17.2	73	17.1
3F LMS 0-6-0	14	16.7	9	14.0	5	12.9
8F 72XX 2-8-2T	54	16.4	54	18.2	54	16.0
8F 42XX 2-8-0T	76	15.2	60	17.0	59	14.5
7F 42XX 2-8-0T	60	15.2	74	16.6	70	15.2
ER						
9F BR Standard	55	36.8	55	33.2	55	32.3
8F LNER 01	30	22.1	30	21.0	30	20.1
8F LNER 02	66	17.4	62	21.1	56	20.6
8F WD 2-8-0	231	21.5	229	21.7	229	20.1
8F LMS 2-8-0	37	20.1	37	21.7	37	21.6
7F LNER 04	185	17.3	180	17.5	167	16.3
5F LNER J39	80	10.4	22	14.8	No allocation	
4F LMS 0-6-0	61	19.5	54	17.9	33	12.7
NER						
9F BR Standard	10	22.5	10	29.7	10	25.0
8F LNER 01	5	19.9	5	19.8	5	16.1
8F LNER Q7	15	15.0	15	15.1	15	03.6
8F WD 2-8-0	222	21.4	222	21.2	222	20.5
8F LMS 2-8-0	57	22.5	57	21.1	57	21.7
7F LNER 04	11	13.5	11	11.8	10	12.2
6F LNER Q6	120	17.2	119	17.4	118	16.1
5F LNER J27	94	16.6	93	15.7	91	14.8
5F LNER J39	120	14.7	120	14.3	100	14.9
4F LMS 0-6-0	46	17.0	45	16.1	45	14.6
3F LMS 0-6-0	11	4.1	6	6.9	6	10.2
LMR						
9F BR Standard	118	32.1	119	29.0	119	28.4
9F BR Crosti	8	5.8	3	Nil	1	Nil
9F BR Crosti Conv.	2	17.8	7	19.3	9	20.9
8F WD 2-10-0	1	18.7	1	24.3	1	31.7
8F LMS 2-8-0	262	18.7	262	24.3	262	23.2
8F LMS ex-HMG	17	24.3	17	23.1	17	24.0
8F LMS ex-ORC	236	23.5	235	24.7	235	22.8
8F WD 2-8-0	184	24.3	184	19.9	185	19.0
8F LNER O1	23	20.1	23	19.6	23	17.8
8F LNER O4	26	20.5	24	19.8	19	19.9
7F LNWR G2	41	15.4	41	12.0	26	14.8
7F LNWR G2A	96	15.5	91	12.3	62	14.4
7F LMS G3	9	16.9	5	15.6	1	11.1
5F LNER J39	29	16.9	25	15.7	17	15.6
4F LMS 0-6-0	482	18.2	444	18.9	430	17.0
3F MR 0-6-0	109	15.2	79	14.2	52	12.8
ScR						
8F WD 2-10-0	24	17.3	24	18.1	21	16.8
8F WD 2-8-0	60	21.3	60	22.8	60	22.0
8F LMS 2-8-0	3	20.3	3	35.4	3	21.2
6F LNER J38	35	20.6	35	20.2	35	22.0
5F LNER J37	101	18.2	100	18.5	95	17.3
SR (data for 1962)						
9F BR Standard	WR	WR	*	*	5	25.8
6F S15 4-6-0	*	*	*	*	41	25.3
5F Q1 0-6-0	*	*	*	*	40	16.5
4F Q 0-6-0	*	*	*	*	17	16.3

* information not traced. WR: engines operated by WR at this time.

Table 11.14
BR Standard Class 9F 2-10-0s: Original WR Allocation Cumulative & Average Miles ('000s) at Specified Dates

No.	Cumulative Mileage at quoted dates			¶ Annualised average miles at latest quoted date
	07.07.62	30.12.62	28.12.63	
92000	*	*	157.9	15.8
92001	*	131.7	143.0	14.4
92002	119.0	*	*	14.0
92003	*	*	160.0	16.1
92004	129.9	*	*	15.4
92005	†92.4	*	*	15.8
92006	†91.3	*	*	15.2
92007	*	*	164.6	16.7
92203	91.4	*	*	28.1
92204	103.2	*	*	32.2
92205	†95.4	*	*	27.8
92206	*	†93.3	*	25.5
92207	*	*	86.8	18.9
92208	79.4	*	*	25.6
92209	76.1	*	102.3	22.7
92210	*	*	114.5	25.9
92211	†58.9	*	*	28.0
92212	55.4	*	*	19.9
92213	*	68.3	*	21.4
92214	*	*	85.0	20.4
92215	*	65.5	76.5	18.6
92216	73.6	*	109.6	26.8
92217	83.7	*	*	32.9
92218	77.4	*	*	31.2
92219	*	*	117.0	29.9
92220	*	*	104.3	27.7
92221	†84.6	*	*	26.9
92222	*	*	112.2	20.1
92223	*	*	115.6	20.8
92224	*	*	119.1	21.5
92225	*	*	120.8	21.8
92226	*	*	119.3	21.6
92227	82.4	*	*	20.5
92228	92.6	*	*	23.3
92229	*	*	113.2	20.7
92230	*	*	109.0	20.1
92231	†78.5	*	*	29.9
92232	*	*	129.2	23.9
92233	100.9	*	*	25.9
92234	*	94.0	*	21.5
92235	*	*	119.7	22.4
92236	*	*	152.6	28.6
92237	*	*	145.6	27.4
92238	*	*	116.7	22.1
92239	†89.9	*	*	24.7
92240	*	*	115.0	21.9
92241	*	*	127.0	24.3
92242	*	*	99.9	19.2
92243	*	*	103.1	19.8
92244	*	*	129.8	25.1
92245	*	*	112.6	21.9
92246	*	*	121.3	23.7
92247	*	95.2	*	23.3
92248	*	*	103.9	20.5
92249	80.9	*	*	22.7
92250	*	*	98.5	19.5

Key: ¶ annualised av. miles takes account of delivery date
† Mileage dates for these engines are as follows:
92005 15.12.59 92206 31.12.62 92231 13.03.61
92006 23.02.60 92211 13.10.61 92239 19.05.62
92205 09.10.62 92221 25.07.61

Figure 213
92132 pounds through St. Albans City with a string of coal empties from the London area on 1st April 1961. In the following month, 92132 would enter Crewe Works for a Heavy Casual repair, having run over 126,000 miles in traffic since delivery four years earlier.
(Courtney Haydon)

Figure 214
Although an ER-based 9F, 92183 (New England) is seen passing Pontefract Baghill with the 6.55pm Dringhouses-Washwood Heath Class 'C' fitted freight on 16th June 1959. The engine rostered for this turn worked down to York on the 10.20am Class 'D' from Rotherham station yard and 92183 may have been used as substitute for a failure. This is one of the services which occasionally brought ER-based 9Fs to the Derby and Birmingham areas at this time.
(Peter Cookson)

Figure 215
92024 (Wellingborough) leaves Pontefract Baghill with a Leicester London Road-Scarborough special on 3rd August 1957. This was one of the few reported occasions when a Crosti boiler 9F was used on passenger work.
(Peter Cookson)

Table 11.15
BR Standard Class 9F 2-10-0s: Annual Mileage and Availability LMR Allocation 1954-1960

Engine No.	1954 miles '000s	1954 avail. %	1955 miles '000s	1955 avail. %	1956 miles '000s	1956 avail. %	1957 miles '000s	1957 avail. %	1958 miles '000s	1958 avail. %	1959 miles '000s	1960 miles '000s
92008	19.0	80	25.2	81	19.9	63	31.2	80	28.7	70	35.4	20.0
92009	20.7	88	23.5	73	23.4	70	26.9	76	31.6	84	37.5	25.9
92010	ER		ER		ER		ER		31.5	58	40.6	43.3
92011	ER		ER		ER		ER		32.9	62	36.6	33.7
92012	ER		ER		ER		ER		32.9	61	43.9	40.4
92013	ER		ER		ER		ER		19.9	42	41.0	32.6
92014	ER		ER		ER		ER		43.8	72	33.5	20.3
92015	04.6	97	25.5	80	27.3	82	23.8	72	27.6	73	24.3	33.6
92016	06.4	94	28.7	87	28.9	82	24.9	72	30.4	89	24.6	14.6
92017	05.0	78	25.6	84	24.5	72	24.2	77	26.0	80	25.4	27.9
92018	05.9	90	26.6	86	19.5	58	27.3	79	28.5	80	29.1	22.5
92019	na		na		na		na		na		na	na
92020	*		07.0	58	19.5	58	22.5	63	20.8	60	0.1	nil
92021	*		10.8	74	18.0	60	18.8	58	21.0	55	0.3	20.5
92022	*		09.8	83	23.6	72	17.9	56	21.4	65	12.0	nil
92023	*		08.7	97	18.2	65	18.0	59	22.5	70	02.4	nil
92024	*		10.0	81	21.8	67	23.7	72	16.4	51	16.2	27.0
92025	*		11.0	69	19.8	63	21.4	69	15.4	48	nil	17.9
92026	*		09.7	65	25.3	76	21.9	67	20.6	61	13.8	21.9
92027	*		11.7	75	22.7	65	23.7	72	25.8	69	07.5	05.3
92028	*		09.2	65	21.4	68	20.9	63	27.7	72	21.8	nil
92029	*		05.1	32	23.7	71	24.1	74	23.6	65	08.0	nil
92030	ER		ER		ER		ER		35.8	62	36.8	21.1
92031	ER		ER		ER		ER		35.6	62	43.2	37.6
92032	ER		ER		ER		ER		40.1	73	31.0	44.8
92033	ER		ER		ER		ER		34.8	60	36.7	21.9
92043	ER		ER		ER		ER		36.9	64	42.2	26.9
92045	*		24.4	85	18.1	60	14.7	79	15.4	87	17.6	17.5
92046	*		23.1	85	17.7	55	13.3	75	17.1	93	15.9	20.6
92047	*		18.9	88	14.4	70	12.4	64	14.8	78	14.1	22.4
92048	*		21.6	85	24.2	77	29.5	80	32.7	81	23.9	23.0
92049	*		19.3	85	25.4	80	27.5	73	30.8	82	27.2	21.4
92050	*		na		na		na		na		na	na
92051	*		na		na		na		na		na	na
92052	*		na		na		na		na		na	na
92053	*		na		na		na		na		na	na
92054	*		05.9	93	25.3	79	25.6	79	20.3	53	33.7	32.3
92055	*		07.5	98	27.9	84	27.7	81	27.1	71	32.8	30.1
92056	*		05.6	96	26.7	82	24.9	75	28.7	75	34.9	19.0
92057	*		05.8	95	29.5	86	28.1	81	24.9	73	26.7	23.2
92058	*		04.2	93	29.2	86	27.3	79	25.2	65	38.7	32.4
92059	*		05.3	99	28.0	85	28.3	85	26.2	71	30.5	23.6
92067	*		ER		ER		ER		35.7	70	43.4	34.0
92068	*		ER		ER		ER		34.1	60	44.0	30.3
92069	*		ER		ER		ER		39.9	72	41.0	40.3
92070	*		ER		ER		ER		34.8	66	38.4	37.0
92071	*		ER		ER		ER		26.8	61	40.8	41.5
92072	*		ER		ER		ER		39.2	68	44.9	42.9
92073	*		ER		ER		ER		37.8	69	41.0	40.5
92074	*		ER		ER		ER		34.9	62	43.8	45.0
92075	*		ER		ER		ER		37.2	65	40.2	34.7
92076	*		ER		ER		ER		41.5	71	44.3	40.4
92077	*		*		20.6	78	29.4	88	20.1	63	24.4	26.7
92078	*		*		22.2	89	27.4	84	23.8	76	23.0	29.5
92079¶	*		*		18.2	97	19.8	83	19.4	na	15.6	15.6
92080	*		*		20.5	87	27.9	83	23.6	65	34.4	32.1
92081	*		*		20.3	90	28.8	86	32.1	68	35.4	25.9
92082	*		*		19.8	89	29.8	80	22.1	64	27.3	23.9
92083	*		*		19.2	87	30.3	85	26.3	72	28.8	28.7
92084	*		*		18.8	88	27.5	90	27.3	89	24.3	36.1
92085	*		*		17.9	89	30.6	84	28.3	78	24.1	27.0
92086	*		*		16.8	90	31.0	85	23.1	67	32.8	28.9
92087	*		*		ER		ER		30.6	62	43.8	48.5
92088	*		*		ER		ER		35.0	67	39.8	37.9
92089	*		*		ER		ER		24.8	51	40.0	42.5
92090	*		*		ER		ER		39.5	75	36.9	30.6
92091	*		*		ER		ER		40.0	72	37.6	34.8
92092	*		*		ER		ER		35.3	65	43.1	35.8
92093	*		*		ER		ER		40.1	73	33.9	38.9

KEY

* not yet in service

ER: engine operated by the Eastern Region at this time.

na: data not traced

nil: engines stored unserviceable

avail. %: no. of weekdays (including Sats.) available for service as % of total.

miles: annual mileage in ('000s).

¶ WR loco from 02.58

Table 11.15
BR Standard Class 9F 2-10-0s: Annual Mileage and Availability LMR Allocation 1954-1960

Engine No.	1954 miles '000s	1954 avail. %	1955 miles '000s	1955 avail. %	1956 miles '000s	1956 avail. %	1957 miles '000s	1957 avail. %	1958 miles '000s	1958 avail. %	1959 miles '000s	1960 miles '000s
92094	*		*		*		ER		24.4	78	25.9	39.1
92095	*		*		*		ER		36.6	65	33.5	30.3
92096	*		*		*		ER		39.8	69	31.0	42.2
92100	*		*		11.7	86	28.3	82	31.4	88	24.0	19.9
92101	*		*		10.5	86	28.7	84	27.1	83	28.5	26.0
92102	*		*		11.6	88	25.6	74	28.7	87	30.7	28.4
92103	*		*		10.2	91	26.9	81	30.8	86	25.0	26.4
92104	*		*		07.6	68	26.5	80	29.5	85	28.8	28.3
92105	*		*		08.2	87	26.5	90	23.2	72	26.2	33.9
92106	*		*		08.3	91	26.1	90	21.9	69	31.3	21.8
92107	*		*		08.0	90	31.1	86	26.9	78	24.7	32.7
92108	*		*		07.6	97	28.3	83	27.9	77	29.8	32.0
92109	*		*		05.5	91	26.9	89	24.5	90	33.9	32.0
92110	*		*		04.6	94	28.7	88	27.2	82	26.2	21.6
92111	*		*		04.3	92	26.3	80	25.4	82	28.7	27.1
92112	*		*		03.1	100	29.9	88	22.7	76	34.3	24.8
92113	*		*		02.4	91	23.0	86	21.4	80	21.7	25.9
92114	*		*		02.1	100	22.7	85	24.1	82	26.7	27.8
92115	*		*		00.7	57	23.9	87	23.3	82	29.9	20.7
92116	*		*		na		na		na		na	na
92117	*		*		na		na		na		na	na
92118	*		*		na		na		na		na	na
92119	*		*		*		na		na		na	na
92120	*		*		*		na		na		na	na
92121	*		*		*		25.5	91	29.0	87	28.8	28.2
92122	*		*		*		28.2	87	28.6	74	36.6	26.2
92123	*		*		*		28.7	92	28.1	72	33.7	25.7
92124	*		*		*		25.7	89	26.8	65	37.9	25.7
92125	*		*		*		24.5	91	32.9	75	36.3	30.1
92126	*		*		*		24.9	89	33.2	80	32.9	27.2
92127	*		*		*		24.1	88	30.9	82	31.7	27.5
92128	*		*		*		23.0	92	28.3	84	28.1	22.8
92129	*		*		*		23.0	90	29.2	87	29.2	25.8
92130	*		*		*		22.9	91	24.4	82	26.9	20.3
92131	*		*		*		22.5	92	27.0	81	26.4	12.5
92132	*		*		*		25.3	91	30.3	80	32.0	30.2
92133	*		*		*		25.5	97	31.5	75	33.5	24.8
92134	*		*		*		18.1	80	29.1	79	35.1	28.7
92135	*		*		*		20.9	94	32.7	76	25.9	33.6
92136	*		*		*		18.9	90	35.8	84	33.2	44.2
92137	*		*		*		19.1	92	37.1	85	36.2	33.5
92138	*		*		*		13.7	68	35.7	80	39.4	31.0
92139	*		*		*		17.1	91	35.5	80	33.8	31.1
92150	*		*		*		04.1	81	22.8	83	40.2	32.1
92151	*		*		*		08.7	90	33.7	84	36.9	23.3
92152	*		*		*		07.3	95	35.4	84	34.5	28.4
92153	*		*		*		06.1	95	28.6	90	18.1	31.0
92154	*		*		*		05.3	90	38.4	81	35.1	24.7
92155	*		*		*		05.6	91	40.0	90	29.7	25.5
92156	*		*		*		03.9	91	29.9	87	20.9	27.3
92157	*		*		*		03.4	92	31.5	88	34.9	24.2
92158	*		*		*		03.5	92	30.9	89	25.4	26.2
92159	*		*		*		02.6	96	33.0	81	36.2	30.6
92160	*		*		*		03.2	91	27.9	75	32.7	22.1
92161	*		*		*		00.7	86	26.1	85	21.7	29.7
92162	*		*		*		00.5	100	26.6	89	27.4	22.4
92163	*		*		*		*		21.0	80	28.8	26.8
92164	*		*		*		*		27.6	90	30.7	29.0
92165	*		*		*		*		29.7	80	32.2	17.7
92166	*		*		*		*		12.2	92	11.2	31.7
92167	*		*		*		*		30.3	81	28.6	16.9

Table 11.16
BR Standard Cl. 9F 2-10-0s: LMR Allocation Cumulative Mileage at 31st December 1960

No.	Cumulative Mileage at 31.12.60 ('000s)	Annualised Average Mileage ('000s)	No.	Cumulative Mileage at 31.12.60 ('000s)	Annualised Average Mileage ('000s)	No.	Cumulative Mileage at 31.12.60 ('000s)	Annualised Average Mileage ('000s)
92008	179.4	26.3	92069	172.6	34.5	92116	★	★
92009	189.5	27.9	92070	165.8	33.4	92117	★	★
92010	196.1	29.6	92071	171.1	34.7	92118	★	★
92011	196.6	29.7	92072	180.2	36.7	92119	★	★
92012	205.6	31.2	92073	179.3	36.6	92120	★	★
92013	164.6	24.6	92074	173.2	35.4	92121	111.5	28.6
92014	183.1	27.6	92075	167.0	34.6	92122	119.6	30.9
92015	166.7	26.6	92076	178.0	37.0	92123	116.2	30.3
92016	158.5	25.5	92077	121.2	25.3	92124	116.1	30.3
92017	158.6	25.6	92078	125.9	26.4	92125	123.8	32.5
92018	159.4	25.8	92079	88.6	18.7	92126	118.2	31.2
92019	★	★	92080	138.5	29.4	92127	114.2	30.5
92020	69.9	12.4	92081	142.5	30.4	92128	102.2	27.4
92021	89.4	15.9	92082	122.9	26.3	92129	107.2	28.8
92022	84.7	15.1	92083	133.3	28.8	92130	94.5	25.5
92023	69.8	12.4	92084	134.0	29.0	92131	88.4	24.0
92024	115.1	20.7	92085	127.9	27.8	92132	117.8	32.1
92025	85.5	15.4	92086	132.6	29.1	92133	115.3	31.8
92026	113.2	20.4	92087	169.8	39.2	92134	111.0	30.6
92027	96.7	17.5	92088	150.2	35.9	92135	113.1	31.8
92028	101.0	18.4	92089	151.6	35.5	92136	132.1	37.3
92029	84.5	15.4	92090	144.0	34.7	92137	125.9	35.8
92030	187.3	30.4	92091	153.7	37.6	92138	119.8	34.0
92031	195.0	31.8	92092	157.5	39.0	92139	117.5	33.6
92032	204.7	33.4	92093	153.4	38.8	92150	99.2	30.7
92033	179.2	29.3	92094	126.1	32.4	92151	102.6	31.8
92043	184.8	31.0	92095	135.8	35.6	92152	105.6	32.9
92045	107.7	18.3	92096	148.9	39.7	92153	83.8	26.3
92046	107.7	18.3	92100	115.3	26.1	92154	103.5	32.7
92047	97.0	16.5	92101	120.8	27.6	92155	100.8	32.0
92048	154.9	26.6	92102	125.0	28.6	92156	82.0	26.2
92049	151.6	26.1	92103	119.3	27.3	92157	94.0	30.3
92050	★	★	92104	120.7	27.7	92158	85.9	27.7
92051	★	★	92105	118.0	27.4	92159	102.4	33.2
92052	★	★	92106	109.4	25.5	92160	85.9	27.9
92053	★	★	92107	123.4	28.8	92161	78.2	25.7
92054	143.1	27.2	92108	125.6	29.9	92162	76.9	25.3
92055	153.1	29.1	92109	122.8	29.2	92163	76.6	27.7
92056	139.8	26.8	92110	108.3	25.9	92164	87.3	31.8
92057	138.2	26.5	92111	111.8	27.0	92165	79.6	29.4
92058	157.0	30.1	92112	114.8	27.8	92166	55.1	21.2
92059	141.9	27.3	92113	94.4	23.0	92167	75.8	28.7
92067	169.4	33.6	92114	103.4	25.3			
92068	158.0	31.6	92115	98.5	24.4			

Note: Annualised Average Mileage takes into account date of delivery

BR Standard Class 9F 2-10-0s
Final Years' Mileage of Selected LMR-based Engines

Engine No.	Time Period	Accumulated Mileage During Time Period ('000s)
92008 ø	05.11.60 - 07.10.67 †	126.5
92084	17.09.63 - 24.04.67	69.0
92100	16.10.63 - 04.05.67	54.0
92101	03.11.62 - 14.09.67	86.7
92102	05.10.63 - 21.04.67	60.0
92103	21.07.62 - 03.04.67	70.0
92111	02.01.64 - 23.10.67 †	65.8
92112	03.08.63 - 13.10.67	64.5
92113	07.09.63 - 14.09.67	75.7
92131	08.11.63 - 15.09.67	69.1
92132	09.10.63 - 14.04.67	66.0
92154 ø	19.08.61 - 22.07.67 †	98.7

Key: ★ information not traced † engine withdrawn by this date ø lifetime total mileage ('000s) 92008: 300.8 92154: 214.0

Table 11.17
BR Standard Class 9F 2-10-0s: Original ER and NER Allocation Cumulative Mileage at Specified Dates

No.	Date	Mileage at Quoted Date Cumu-lative ('000s)	Annual average ('000s) †	No.	Date	Mileage at Quoted Date Cumu-lative ('000s)	Annual average ('000s) †	No.	Date	Mileage at Quoted Date Cumu-lative ('000s)	Annual average ('000s) †
ER				92089	31.12.57	44.3	35.4	92183	05.04.62	152.2	35.3
92010	31.12.57	80.7	22.3	92090	31.12.57	37.0	31.7	92184	20.12.62	188.4	38.2
92011	31.12.57	93.4	25.8	92091	31.12.57	41.3	38.1	92185	31.12.62	198.4	40.0
92012	31.12.57	88.4	24.7	92092	31.12.57	43.3	41.6	92186	20.12.62	189.8	38.6
92013	31.12.57	71.0	19.2	92093	31.12.57	40.5	42.3	92187	15.03.61	125.0	40.5
92014	31.12.57	85.5	23.6	92094	31.12.57	36.7	44.0	92188	08.12.60	108.4	39.1
92030	31.12.57	93.6	30.0	92095	31.12.57	35.4	42.5	92189	30.05.62	132.2	31.4
92031	31.12.57	78.6	25.2	92096	31.12.57	35.9	47.9	92190	04.10.62	128.3	28.3
92032	31.12.57	88.8	28.4	92140	05.11.62	205.4	38.2	92191	08.01.63	147.6	31.2
92033	31.12.57	85.8	27.5	92141	03.11.62	201.2	38.3	92192	23.05.61	105.9	34.6
92034	01.06.62	209.9	28.0	92142	03.09.62	191.4	37.7	92193	24.09.62	141.3	32.6
92035	04.04.63	250.3	30.0	92143	18.09.62	186.4	36.5	92194	03.10.61	109.2	33.0
92036	01.03.61	183.8	29.4	92144	19.02.62	184.2	40.8	92195	24.10.61	107.3	32.4
92037	19.08.60	164.1	28.9	92145	05.10.62	179.9	35.1	92196	14.02.61	108.3	43.3
92038	19.11.62	249.2	31.5	92146	02.04.63	198.4	35.7	92197	05.06.61	84.4	30.9
92039	21.12.60	168.2	27.9	92147	15.04.59	55.4	35.0	92198	05.03.62	107.7	31.5
92040	14.10.60	173.6	29.9	92148	15.01.63	198.1	37.1	92199	28.12.61	108.7	34.3
92041	29.11.62	245.2	31.0	92149	07.02.63	198.8	37.1	92200	15.09.61	94.9	33.5
92042	03.01.63	256.8	32.3	92168	05.07.60	88.1	34.4	92201	09.04.63	125.1	28.7
92043	31.12.57	78.8	26.6	92169	25.04.60	87.4	37.5	92202	11.01.62	105.7	34.5
92044	21.02.63	238.4	29.6	92170	10.05.60	83.9	35.6				
92067	31.12.57	56.3	27.6	92171	31.01.61	94.5	31.5	**NER**			
92068	31.12.57	49.6	24.8	92172	25.10.60	87.1	31.9	92060	23.03.59	78.3	23.2
92069	31.12.57	51.5	25.8	92173	03.11.60	98.2	36.0	92061	21.01.60	100.0	23.9
92070	31.12.57	55.6	28.4	92174	21.11.60	98.1	35.1	92062	10.12.59	87.2	21.5
92071	31.12.57	62.0	31.7	92175	21.06.61	95.6	28.7	92063	18.08.60	115.0	24.8
92072	31.12.57	53.2	27.8	92176	01.02.61	96.5	33.1	92064	21.08.59	82.5	22.1
92073	31.12.57	60.0	32.0	92177	30.05.62	141.2	33.6	92065	11.09.61	155.7	27.0
92074	31.12.57	49.5	26.4	92178	10.08.60	98.3	34.2	92066	13.10.59	86.4	22.5
92075	31.12.57	54.9	30.0	92179	20.09.62	186.0	37.5	92097	05.11.59	77.1	23.0
92076	31.12.57	51.8	28.3	92180	24.12.62	181.0	35.3	92098	03.09.59	77.2	24.4
92087	31.12.57	46.9	35.2	92181	04.01.63	187.4	36.6	92099	29.07.59	71.0	23.5
92088	31.12.57	37.5	31.0	92182	02.09.60	105.6	38.4				

Key † Annualised mileage taking into account date of delivery

outputs is almost inevitably a less effective draught producer when output is low. Thus for an engine normally working well within its capacity (i.e. at low combustion rates) a double chimney is not only unnecessary but could be detrimental to performance.

Test results have shown that for a given rate of steam production at speeds of up to 60mph, a double chimney gives only marginally more power at the pistons compared with a single chimney carefully designed for the specific operating requirements. For higher speeds and hence higher fuel combustion rates however, the improvement in power output for the double chimney arrangement is significant, allowing the possibility of an appreciable gain in load capacity. As noted in Section 11.1, tests at Swindon indicated that the 9Fs would benefit from the fitting of a double chimney and some 77 class members (about 30% of the total) were so fitted either from new (72) or with subsequent modification (5).

In practice, footplate crews' opinions on the effectiveness of the double chimney 9Fs tended to be polarised. Many LMR enginemen reported little or no improvement in performance whilst ER crews observed a 'startling difference' in steaming capacity compared with the single chimney versions. There were probably three main reasons for this:

- limited experience of the double chimney engines on the LMR, especially in the early years.
- differences in typical duties for the LMR engines (slow mineral freights) compared with those on the ER (ECML fast fitted freights as well as mineral traffic).
- the driving methods of individual drivers.

The last reason could well have been the most influential factor. For steam locomotives, the driver's judgement on whether he was operating his engine in an efficient manner tended to be influenced strongly by the sound of the exhaust. For a careful driver, the idea of routinely 'thrashing' his engine (*staccato* exhaust) would be quite unacceptable. A double chimney gives a much quieter exhaust for a given steam flow compared with the single chimney type and under such conditions, a driver may feel comfortable working the engine harder, thus obtaining more power from his engine than he normally would. The increased draught would require a thicker

Table 11.18
BR Standard Class 9F 2-10-0s: LMR Allocation
Average Annual Mileage ('000s) per Loco
by MPD 1956-1960
(Data for locos allocated for whole of specified year)

MPD	YEAR				
	1956	1957	1958	1959	1960
Annesley	(1)	(1)	35.5[2]	38.8	36.9
Bidston	*	13.5	15.8	15.9	20.2
Cricklewood	*	28.3	27.2	*	*
Kettering	*	26.3	22.6	29.8	26.2
Leicester Midland	*	*	26.8	30.4	29.4
Newton Heath	*	*	*	25.7	25.6
Rowsley	*	*	*	*	22.6
Saltley					
Standard	*	*	34.4	33.2	30.7
Mech. Stoker	*	*	30.0[3]	30.4[3]	22.1
Toton	27.0	27.4	27.0	25.1	26.8
Wellingborough					
Standard	23.9	30.1	29.2	32.5	28.1
Crosti boiler	21.4	21.3	21.5	07.5	09.3
Westhouses	*	23.2	24.1	26.1	20.5

Key

* no allocation for the full year

1 depot operated by ER in these years

2 ER depot until February 1958

3 data refers to two engines only, i.e. 92165, delivered in 04.58 and 92167 in 05.58. 92166 was under test at Rugby (09.58 to 05.59) and on loan to the WR from 08.59 to 02.60

fire of course, otherwise increased loss of fuel would occur by the lifting of cinders through the chimney. Failure to take this into account may be the main reason why many enginemen considered double chimney locomotives to be excessively heavier on fuel compared with single chimney types.

Thus the improvement in power output for the double chimney engines compared with the single type at higher speeds and higher fuel combustion rates could have been the main reason why footplatemen using 9Fs on fast freight work were more likely to appreciate the benefits of the double blastpipe and chimney compared with the experience of crews routinely employed on low speed mineral freight traffic.

11.3 Performance Logs

The versatile 9Fs were at home on most types of service. Observers recorded their exploits on loose-coupled mineral freights, fast fitted freights, summer Saturday holiday specials and express passenger duties including their use as substitutes for rostered locomotive failures. A number of logs are presented here covering all these aspects, including two runs with the celebrated 'windcutters' between Annesley and Woodford Halse on the GCR.

Commentary on Log Runs

Three logs originally published in **Trains Illustrated Annual,** editor G. Freeman Allen, Ian Allan 1960, describe runs with Cl. 9Fs, two with the 'windcutters' and one from Water Orton sidings to Sheffield on a Class 'C' fitted freight working to Glasgow College using one of the mechanical stoker-fitted members of the class. The logs were recorded by '45671' otherwise known as Mr. A. J. Powell who was employed in various roles on the LMR during the time when the 9Fs were designed and operated.

On the GC line from January 1957 several 9Fs were transferred to Annesley for the Woodford Halse duties and within a short time around 30 or so 9Fs were on Annesley's

Table 11.19
BR Standard Class 9F 2-10-0s
ER & NER Allocation: Boiler Mileage, April 1962

Built	Works	Boiler No.	Carried by Loco. No. @ 16.04.62	Miles to Last Major Overhaul ('000s)	Miles since Last Major Overhaul ('000s)	Total Mileage of Boiler ('000s)
1954	Crewe	1140	92036	146.7	38.0	184.7
		1142	92193	181.9	21.5	203.4
		1415	92178	148.0	59.6	207.6
		1416	92196	164.3	32.9	197.2
		1417	92147	167.4	26.9	194.3
		1418	92039	134.7	31.7	166.4
		1419	92035	160.4	63.3	223.6
		1421	92042	136.6	73.1	209.7
		1422	92037	142.8	57.9	200.7
1955	Crewe	1423	92041	185.0	62.2	247.2
		1425	92063	117.8	39.4	157.2
		1440	92144	149.4	no info.	no info.
		1441	92038	100.0	73.8	173.8
		1442	92062	75.3	69.1	144.4
		1443	92060	78.3	63.4	141.7
		1444	92066	83.0	66.4	149.3
		1445	92099	84.1	66.6	150.7
		1446	92097	86.4	66.8	153.2
1956	Crewe	1644	92140	75.6	100.5	176.1
		1645	92098	75.7	65.4	141.1
		1646	Spare	140.9	no info.	no info.
1957	Crewe	1687	92061	80.3	60.8	141.2
		1688	92141	82.6	100.8	183.5
		1689	92142	66.4	93.8	160.2
		1690	92143	77.6	83.9	161.6
		1691	Spare	78.3	109.1	187.4
		1692	92145	70.0	108.0	177.9
		1693	92146	87.2	75.9	163.0
		1694	92148	85.0	73.5	158.5
		1695	92065	160.5	8.4	168.9
		1696	92149	82.9	73.3	156.1
		1715	92168	75.7	48.1	123.8
		1716	92169	69.6	38.5	108.1
		1718	92170	74.2	38.6	112.8
1957	Swindon	1725	92034	93.7	56.1	149.9
		1726	92179	82.1	77.9	160.0
		1727	92185	79.7	89.6	169.3
		1728	92181	84.8	61.3	146.2
		1729	92182	97.9	46.7	144.6
		1730	92183	85.0	43.5	128.5
1958	Crewe	1717	92171	83.9	35.9	119.8
		1719	92172	79.0	49.6	128.6
		1720	92173	88.5	43.4	132.0
		1721	92174	79.6	40.8	120.4
		1722	92176	85.1	42.9	127.9
		1723	92175	91.0	26.9	117.9
		1724	92177	89.5	46.8	136.3
1958	Swindon	1731	92184	79.5	82.7	162.2
		1732	92040	83.0	45.5	128.5
		1733	92186	84.4	65.4	149.8
		1734	92187	99.2	32.8	132.0
		1735	92188	93.6	42.7	136.2
		1736	92189	88.2	29.8	118.0
		1737	92190	86.7	13.4	100.2
		1738	92191	93.9	18.5	112.4
		1739	92192	92.2	26.0	118.2
		1740	92195	107.3	21.5	128.8
		1741	92194	99.0	1.4	100.4
		1742	92064	109.6	3.9	113.5
		1743	92044	99.5	17.1	116.6
		1744	92197	77.4	32.3	109.7
		1745	92199	108.7	7.6	116.3
		1746	92200	87.6	6.0	93.6
		1747	92201	103.4	12.4	115.8
		1748	92202	105.6	2.9	108.5
1957	Crewe	1877	92198	97.6	0.0	97.6
1960	Swindon	1896	92180	89.0	81.0	170.0

Table 11.20
BR Standard Class 9F 2-10-0s: Investigation into Smokebox Tubeplate Defects, April 1962

Engine	Boiler	Boiler Built	Builder	Region/MPD	Class of Repair	Remarks
92097	1446	1955	Crewe	NE/Tyne Dock	General	Tubeplate severely fractured
92098	1645	1956	Crewe	NE/Tyne Dock	General	As above but not so extensive
92062	1442	1955	Crewe	NE/Tyne Dock	General	Tubeplate to be removed for examination
92141	1688	1957	Crewe	ER/New England	General	Tubeplate to be removed for examination. Main steampipe loose
92183	1730	1957	Swindon	ER/New England	Casual	Tubeplate to be removed and examined

books, allowing for a virtual monopoly of the class on this service.

In the winter 1958 timetable, there were some 26 Class 'H' trains in the up direction with an average running time from Annesley to Woodford Halse of 2 hours 39 minutes. On the down service, the empties were worked to several destinations in the Annesley area, with a running time of the order of just over two hours.

Table 11.21 gives details of the 1.38pm Class 'H' Annesley-Woodford Yard loaded to the maximum of 'equal to 60' wagons, weighing well in excess of 1,000 tons. The rostered engine, 92043, was short of steam as a result of damage to the discharge pipe from the continuous blowdown valve during disposal operations. The pipe led into the ashpan and was discharging upwards on to the underside of the grate, effectively dousing an area of the fire when the injector was on. Despite this handicap, 92043 easily kept time and would have had a punctual arrival if a bout of slipping had not been experienced in the tunnel near Staverton Road towards the end of the trip. Cut-off was between 25 and 30% for most of the journey and there was no difficulty in maintaining sufficient boiler and steam chest pressures to achieve an average speed for the run of almost 25mph with a maximum of 41mph at Rugby.

Three weeks later Mr. Powell records that he made the return trip from Woodford Yard to New Hucknall sidings with the 12.45pm Class 'E', mainly mineral empties, with the same engine 92043 as on the up run (Table 11.22). The train was comparatively light ('equal to 65 wagons') for a return empty mineral working. As far as Loughborough, it was a clear autumn afternoon but once in the Trent Valley, a dense fog was encountered which inevitably played havoc with operations. Hence Table 11.22 logs the run only as far as Arkwright Street box south of Nottingham Victoria where the train was stopped by signals.

The start was very leisurely as the curvature and embankments were such that the guard's hand signal to the enginemen, to indicate that he was safely in the van and the train complete, could not be seen until the engine had fully run one mile and was well out on Charwelton troughs. The permanent way slack at Barby for bridge works in connection with the then new M1 motorway and again beyond Rugby over the bridge crossing the WCML precluded any fast running in the early stages. From there however, speed increased on the four mile 1 in 176 climb towards Lutterworth eventually reaching 52mph down the 1 in 176 past Whetstone with steam on as far as Aylestone. Progress from Leicester was similarly energetic but by East Leake, visibility was down to 20 yards and nothing so high was repeated. The engine rode smoothly and it was only by looking back and viewing the lively riding of the four-wheeled wagons running fast was there any real impression of speed.

Saltley depot in Birmingham took delivery of three mechanical stoker-fitted 9Fs during April/May 1958. One of their main jobs was the 4.45pm Class 'C' freight from Water Orton sidings to Glasgow College as far as Carlisle, via Sheffield and Skipton, returning next day with the 4.03pm Class 'C' Carlisle Durran Hill-Washwood Heath. The schedule required the train to cover the 219 miles at an average speed of almost 34mph. The maximum load for the service with a 9F was 50 wagons which was not particularly taxing until the Settle Junction-Blea Moor tunnel stretch (15 miles at a ruling gradient of 1 in 100); this could be heavy going on a typical 'wild weather' Pennine night especially as by this stage the fireman of a non stoker-fitted engine had been shovelling for some five hours.

On the run described, the train was of medium weight with 37 wagons and a brake in the charge of 92165; the details are set out in Table 11.23. With such a moderate load, the working did not require a spectacular performance. Despite this, Driver Rossiter was well equipped with goggles as there were plenty of flying cinders in the air. The engine had a very irregular beat on one side suggesting broken piston rings and Fireman Baker could not coax the stoker to distribute the coal evenly and to his liking. The fuel was rather wet and the centre of the grate got very little coal while the part under the door collected too much; this built up into a wall of caked coal requiring constant breaking up with a dart. As a result, it was barely possible to hold a steady boiler pressure and much of the run was made with little more than 200 lb/sq in on the dial.

From Derby Midland up to Ambergate, the boiler pressure and water levels gradually fell and round the curve through Toadmoor tunnel at Ambergate, the regulator was closed to give a brief respite with the injector. After this the rest of the

Table 11.21
BR Standard Class 9F 2-10-0s

LMR: 1.38pm Class 'H' Annesley Yard-Woodford Halse
Engine: 92043 (Annesley)
Load: 56 wagons = 60 of goods
Driver/Fireman: Elnor/Storer. Recorder: Mr. A.J. Powell ('45671'). Date: Autumn 1958

Distance Miles		Sched min.	Actual m. s.	Speed mph	Boiler Pressure p.s.i.	Steam Chest Pressure p.s.i.	Cut-off %
00.0	ANNESLEY YARD dep.	0	0.00	-	210	70	45
00.4	*Annesley South Junction*	3	2.10	29	-	Shut	-
03.1	Hucknall		8.34	35	-	-	-
			sigs.				
05.6	Bulwell Common	14	14.20	12	-	-	-
06.7	*Bagthorpe Junction*	17	19.38	11	-	-	-
			sigs.				
08.9	NOTTINGHAM VICTORIA	25	27.40	20/15	220	40/90	45/30
09.7	Arkwright Street		30.07	27	180	110/140	22
13.2	Ruddington		36.57	33/30	180	140	26
15.4	*Gotham Junction*		40.59	34	200	140	26
17.9	East Leake		47.12	19/21	180	160	26
	M.p. 89½		-	20	170	Shut	-
22.4	LOUGHBOROUGH	55	57.02	38	190	120/140	30/25
24.5	Quorn		60.38	28/29	215	140	25
27.3	Rothley		66.48	25/28	190/210	165	25
30.0	Belgrave		72.24	24	190	Shut	-
			sigs.				
32.3	LEICESTER CENTRAL	78	79.13	10	215	180	28/22
33.3	*Leicester South Goods*	81	81.38	34	200	180	22
37.0	Whetstone		88.39	31/32	215	170	25
41.5	Ashby Magna	101	102.07	18/20	200/220	185	25
45.4	Lutterworth		112.12	39/29	210	90/120	25
48.6	*Shawell*		117.41	36/34	240	Shut	-
52.2	RUGBY CENTRAL	125	123.53	41/25	220	150	25
			p.w.s.	18			
			p.w.s.	24			
56.9	Braunston		135.07	27	230	190	23/25
	Staverton Road		143.41	21	210	180	28
			Slipping in tunnel				
63.9	Charwelton		155.11	18/20	230	120	25
66.3	WOODFORD YARD arr.	159	162.26	-	-	-	-

Note: Water consumption: 2,900 gallons, ie. 43.7 gallons per mile.

First published in Trains Illustrated Annual 1960, ed. G. Freeman Allen, Ian Allan, page 93.

Table 11.22
BR Standard Class 9F 2-10-0s

LMR: 12.45pm Class 'E' (Unbraked) Woodford Halse-New Hucknall Sidings
Engine: 92043 (Annesley).
Load: 45 wagons = 65 in length.
Driver/Fireman: Edwardson/Willett. Recorder: Mr. A.J. Powell ('45671'). Date: Autumn 1958

Distance Miles		Sched min.	Actual m. s.	Speed mph	Boiler Pressure p.s.i.	Steam Chest Pressure p.s.i.	Cut-off %
00.0	WOODFORD YARD dep.	0	0.00	-	245	140	45
02.3	Charwelton		8.16	24	230	170/100	27
	Staverton Road		14.10	40/42	200	Shut 70	27
09.4	Braunston		18.57	43/40	210/225	Shut 130	27
			p.w.s.	10	230	180/210	27
14.1	RUGBY CENTRAL	24	29.49	23	-	Shut	-
			p.w.s.	18	230	170	27
17.7	*Shawell*		38.29	30/32	220	170/180	27
20.9	Lutterworth		44.20	29/43	210	140/160	27
24.7	Ashby Magna	42	50.22	33/47	200	120/75	27
29.2	Whetstone		55.50	52	210	70	27
32.9	*Leicester South Goods*	55	60.56	-	-	Shut	-
33.9	LEICESTER CENTRAL	57	63.00	32	210	80/175	27
36.3	Belgrave		67.21	33/31	220	170	27
39.0	Rothley		71.42	46/43	220	130	27
41.8	Quorn		75.32	46	210	80	27
43.8	LOUGHBOROUGH CENTRAL	73	78.07	49/45	225	145	27
	M.p. 89½		-	29	215	110	27
48.4	East Leake		85.43	-	-	100	27
53.0	Ruddington		92.08	45/42	200	110	27
			sigs.	-	-	Shut	-
55.9	*Nottingham South Goods*	92	96.54	5	-	-	-
			sigs.				
56.4	ARKWRIGHT STREET arr.	-	98.23	-	-	-	-

Note: Water consumption (through to Annesley): 2,900 gallons, ie. 43.7 gallons per mile.

First published in Trains Illustrated Annual 1960, ed. G. Freeman Allen, Ian Allan, page 94.

run was taken at a moderate pace with the signal check at Sheepbridge dispelling any thoughts of rushing the five and a half miles at 1 in 100 up to Bradway Tunnel. Every now and again, Fireman Baker would place a few pieces of coal strategically where the mechanical stoker was failing to put them. On this occasion, there were no stoppages in the screw conveying the coal into the firebox which was reported by the crew as unusual. This was attributed to the presence of Mr. Powell on the footplate. It was the crew's opinion that the authorities had arranged for the coal to be hand-picked to the correct size to demonstrate the benefits of the mechanical system.

Table 11.24 gives details of a footplate run on 92031 in charge of one of the frequent New England-Ferme Park mineral workings which the 9Fs took over from LNER and WD 2-8-0 motive power in the mid-1950s. Details of the run, made by Mr. R. J. Doran, accompanied by Inspector Buxton were first published in *Railway World*, Vol. 17, No. 198, November 1956, page 281. Notes on speed, boiler pressure, steam-chest pressure and cut-offs included in the log were compiled from Mr. Doran's observations. A full note of passing times was not published but an indication of the gradient profiles at individual locations is included in the log for interest.

The train was a Class 'H' freight scheduled to depart from New England at 3.55pm and due to arrive at Ferme Park at 8.58pm, routed via the Potters Bar main line; in the event, the service was diverted via the Hertford loop (Langley Junction-Wood Green), used chiefly for freight and occasional through passenger trains. The train consisted mainly of loaded coal wagons but included four bogie bolsters containing concrete posts coupled next to the tender. 92031 was fitted with the LNER type fire door, reported to be the first 9F at New England to be so equipped.

A cut-off of 45% with gradually opening regulator got 92031's train on the move and after passing Fletton Junction,

Table 11.23
BR Standard Class 9F 2-10-0s

LMR: 4.45pm Class 'C' Water Orton-Glasgow College.
Engine: 92165 (Saltley). Fitted with Berkley mechanical stoker.
Load: 37 wagons.
Driver/Fireman: Rossiter/Baker. Recorder: Mr. A.J. Powell ('45671'). Date: not specified.

Distance Miles		Sched min.	Actual m. s.	Speed mph	Boiler Pressure p.s.i.	Steam Chest Pressure p.s.i.	Cut-off %
0.0	WATER ORTON SIDINGS	0	0.00	-	230	First Valve	60/40 35/30
				sigs. to advance starter			
04.5	Kingsbury	10	10.58	35	235	First Valve	25
08.3	Wilnecote		16.49	42	220	Shut	-
			p.w.s.				
10.2	TAMWORTH	18	20.46	24	230	First Valve	30/20
14.3	*Elford*		-	46/45	220	First Valve	15
17.9	*Wichnor Junction*	28	32.37	47	220	First Valve Shut	15
23.1	BURTON-UPON-TRENT	36	38.43	27	230	First Valve	25
27.8	Repton & Willington	42	46.31	40	210	First Valve	20
29.3	*Stenson Junction*	45	48.46	43	210	First Valve	20
32.6	*Melbourne Junction*	50	53.21	42	200	Shut	-
34.1	DERBY MIDLAND	55	56.11	13	220	First Valve	40
37.3	*Little Eaton Junction*		64.00	36	210	½	30/25
39.3	Duffield		67.19	38	200	½	25
44.0	*Ambergate South Junction*		75.04	35	190	Shut	-
44.6	*Ambergate North Junction*	70	76.25	28	210	½	25
48.1	Wingfield		82.36	35/34	200	½	25
51.6	Stretton	82	88.29	35	200	½	25
54.2	Clay Cross	89	93.17	45	200	½	25
			sigs.	-	-	Shut	-
58.3	CHESTERFIELD	97	97.48	34	-	-	-
58.8	*Tapton Junction*	98	98.54	-	-	-	-
			sigs.	21	245	½	50
62.9	*Dronfield Colliery Sidings*	108	112.04	22/20	215	½	38
65.3	Dore & Totley		118.33	42 max.	-	Shut	-
69.5	SHEFFIELD MIDLAND	120	125.44	-	-	-	-

Note: Water consumption: 3,250 gallons, ie. 46.7 gallons per mile.

First published in Trains Illustrated Annual 1960, ed. G. Freeman Allen, Ian Allan, page 95.

the controls were set in the position used for much of the run, cut-off at 25% and the regulator open sufficiently to maintain a steam-chest pressure of 180-200 lb/sq in. Speeds were typically in the range 15-35mph with slacks at Sandy and Arlesey of 5mph. A minimum of 17mph was maintained up the four and a quarter mile 1 in 200 climb from Connington South box past Abbots Ripton to Milepost 63. It was estimated that 92031's drawbar horsepower on the climb was between 700 and 800, a similar figure to that achieved for short spells during the run at around 40mph on level track; elsewhere, this power was approached but not exceeded. The Cambridge Junction water stop was reached in 116 minutes, (average speed 23mph) at 6.17pm, the late start being converted to a five minute early arrival. Some 2,250 gallons of water had been consumed or just over 50 gallons per mile.

Departure from Cambridge Junction was at 6.31pm, 21 minutes early and the three and a half mile 1 in 200 climb to Stevenage was achieved in 17 minutes with a minimum speed of 13½mph at the summit. After the diversion to the Hertford loop, the mainly 1 in 198 falling gradient allowed the train to roll along at around 35mph for some miles until a signal stop at Hertford North. On restarting, the three-mile gradient up to just beyond Bayford was completed at a minimum speed of 16mph followed by a spell of free-running at around 40mph until the signal check at Crews Hill. Ferme Park was reached at 8.10pm, 48 minutes early, the 29.6 miles from Cambridge Junction having taken 99 minutes at an average speed of almost 18mph. During the whole of the run, this duty was clearly well within the capacity of the 9F which had ridden with exemplary smoothness throughout.

Figure 217
A single chimney 9F on the S&DJR ? It must have been borrowed. 92059 (Toton) is in charge of the 9.55am Bournemouth West-Leeds near Chilcompton on 29th July 1961.
(Rodney Lissenden)

holiday season traffic. One of the engines temporarily transferred in early July was a 9F, 92164, allocated to Leicester Midland from new and only three months old. During its seven and a half weeks stay on the GC section the engine was used many times on express passenger duties. One of the most impressive performances was logged on the Leicester to Nottingham section one evening in July when 92164 was given charge of the down "Master Cutler", still then operating on the GC route from Marylebone to Sheffield: for details, see Table 11.28.

From Leicester there is an initial rise to a mile past Belgrave mainly at 1 in 176. Thereafter apart from a short climb through Rothley, the line descends towards Loughborough for six miles with gradients mainly of 1 in 176/264. Then follows a short 2¼ mile ascent at 1 in 176 past Barnston box and a 3¼ mile drop again mainly at 1 in 176 past Gotham Junction. The rest of the run to Nottingham Victoria was more or less level with a severe speed restriction at Arkwright Street preceding the curve to Weekday Cross Junction; the latter was the only permanent speed restriction on this sector.

92164 was through Loughborough in under 11 minutes at a passing speed of 79mph followed by a minimum of 69mph at Barnston summit. On the downgrade through Gotham Junction, a speed of 86mph was logged. The (un-named) driver concerned had a reputation for hard running and on another occasion in August with the same engine on the 3.20pm from Marylebone covered the 19.9 miles from Rugby to Leicester in 17½ minutes. On that occasion on the seven mile 1 in 176 descent of Ashby Magna bank, the driver timed himself at 90mph near Whetstone.

A comparison of 92164's exploits is made in the accompanying log in Table 11.28 of A3 Pacific 60107 *Royal Lancer* again with the down "Master Cutler" in the days when the route was under the control of the ER. The A3 was slower in starting but passed Loughborough at a similar pace to that of the 9F and topped Barnston summit at 69mph minimum, exactly the same as the 9F. Speed on the stretch from Gotham Junction was maintained at 85mph with arrival at Victoria a half minute or so later than 92164.

Another log timed by Mr. Frank Lodge featured a 9F on the GC route in August 1963. Here 92073 was in charge of a summer Saturday holiday special, 1O41, the eleven-coach 390 tons gross weight 9.55am Leeds-Poole. This was typical of the duty 9Fs were still called upon to perform in the early 1960s and the class could still be seen on such GC line workings as late as 1966. Although the schedule was not demanding, 92073 appeared to be rather slow off the mark achieving only 40mph on the 1 in 176 climb past Ashby Magna. The mostly downhill stretch through Lutterworth and Rugby saw speeds in the mid-60s however, reducing again to 40mph up the seven miles at 1 in 176 to Charwelton. Overall, as Mr. Lodge commented, the run was rather disappointing; perhaps by this time the 'Riot Act' had been read by the authorities regarding the tendency to push 9Fs to high speeds on passenger work; details are given in Table 11.29.

Perhaps one of the most remarkable runs recorded with a 9F was the celebrated occasion when 92184, fitted with double chimney and only some eight months old, was given charge of the 1.10pm Edinburgh Waverley-Kings Cross from Grantham on 16th August 1958, see Table 11.30. The day was a busy summer Saturday and the 9F had reached Grantham on the 1.45pm slow from Kings Cross. Top Shed had been almost bereft of engines and the only alternative had been a WD 2-8-0 which the driver had rejected in favour of the 9F. Grantham was warned that something more suitable would be required for the return leg of the roster, the up "Heart of Midlothian" relief, and had earmarked an unbalanced Kings Cross A4 for the working. In the event, the A4 had been needed for a northbound express and with nothing more suitable available, Driver Bauer was obliged to return with 92184; fortunately, experienced recorder Mr. B. C. Bailey was on board.

The start up the 1 in 200 to Stoke summit was slower than often recorded with a similarly loaded Pacific but then 92184 was given its head. By Corby Glen, 78mph was reached and this was followed by 86mph down the 1 in 200 at Little Bytham with the 90mph before Essendine. At this speed, the driving wheels were revolving at some eight and a half times per second (504 rpm). These figures compare with those for A4 Pacific *Mallard's* drivers on its record breaking 126mph run on the same stretch of nearly nine times per second (529 rpm). Not only this but 92184's average speed over the 12.5 miles from Corby Glen to Tallington was all but 85mph.

Table 11.28
BR Standard Class 9F 2-10-0s

LMR/ER Leicester Central-Nottingham Victoria

			Down Master Cutler			Down Master Cutler		
Train:			Down Master Cutler			Down Master Cutler		
Date:			July 1958			(c.1956?)		
Engine:			9F 2-10-0 92164 (Leicester GC) on loan from Leicester Midland			A3 Pacific 60107 (Leicester GC) Named *Royal Lancer*		
Load:			9 coaches, 315 tons tare, 330 tons gross			9 coaches, 314 tons tare, 330 tons gross		
Driver/Fireman:			Leicester GC crew			Leicester GC crew		
Recorder:			No information			Mr. P. R. Hardy		
Distance Miles			Sched min.	Actual m. s.	Speed mph	Sched min.	Actual m. s.	Speed mph
0.0	LEICESTER CENTRAL	dep.	0	0.00	-	0	0.00	-
2.2	Belgrave			-	-		4.46	42½
2.3	Birstall			4.05	47		-	-
5.0	Rothley			6.52	69		7.54	64
7.8	Quorn			9.11	77		10.20	75
9.9	LOUGHBOROUGH CENTRAL			10.45	79		11.55	80
12.9	Milepost 90 (*Barnston Box*)			-	69 (min.)		14.20	69
14.4	East Leake			-	72		15.39	72
16.8	*Gotham Junction*			16.11	86		17.30	85
19.0	Ruddington			17.46	82		19.00	85
21.9	Milepost 81			-	-		-	75
22.5	Arkwright Street			20.35	*		21.40	*
23.4	NOTTINGHAM VICTORIA	arr.	24½	23.12	-	24½	23.41	-
* Speed reduced by brakes			First published in Railway World, Vol. 20, No. 228, May 1959 page 242			First published in Trains Illustrated Vol. XI, No. 114, March 1958, page 129		

Table 11.29
BR Standard Class 9F 2-10-0s

LMR Leicester Central-Woodford Halse

Train		9.55am Leeds City-Poole Holiday Special		
Date		17th August 1963		
Engine		9F 2-10-0 92073 (Annesley)		
Load		11 vehicles 372 tons tare/390 tons gross		
Driver/Fireman		No information		
Recorder		Mr. Frank Lodge		
Distance Miles		Sched min.	Actual m. s.	Speed mph
00.0	LEICESTER CENTRAL dep.	0	00.00	-
01.0	*Leicester South Goods*		02.50	30
04.7	Whetstone		10.14	32
09.2	Ashby Magna		17.54	40
13.1	Lutterworth		23.08	60/54
19.9	Rugby Central		29.50	65/54
24.6	Braunston & Willoughby		34.40	62/57
27.9	*Staverton Road*		38.38	48
31.6	Charwelton		43.35	40
				50 max.
34.0	WOODFORD HALSE arr.	45	46.57	-

After the Peterborough slack, the 9F was encouraged to keep up the good work. By Holme, on level track, 72mph was achieved and the minimum speed up the four and a half miles at 1 in 200 past Abbots Ripton was 56mph. Huntingdon saw a maximum of 75mph and the small rise at St. Neots was taken at 73mph. By Tempsford, an increase to 78mph was attained after which the brakes had to be applied for a 29mph permanent way slowing at Sandy. 92184 was now six and a quarter minutes early and the remainder of the run was taken more easily with several slowings for signals. The recorder indicates that without the Sandy check and even including the leisurely running from there onwards, Hatfield could have been passed in 86½ minutes. With no higher speed than 60mph after that, Kings Cross would have been reached in about 106 minutes from Grantham or 14½ minutes less than schedule.

Unfortunately for future exploits of this nature, a party of VIPs including the General Manager were travelling with the train. Questions were asked during the following week and after this a nominal limit of 60mph was put on the 9Fs operating on the GN main line.

As a comparison with a similarly loaded A4 Pacific on the same route, a log of 60007 *Sir Nigel Gresley* on the up "Flying Scotsman" is given alongside that for 92184 in Table 11.30. In this case, the driver was the legendary Driver Bill Hoole (assisted by Fireman A. Leech) who produced a run which was regarded at the time (1954/5) as outstanding. A six-minute late start from Grantham gave the crew the incentive and after a good climb to Stoke summit, there came another hurricane descent of the bank with an average of 91mph from Little Bytham to Tallington reaching a top speed of 94mph.

Despite the excellent work of 60007 in climbing the four and a half miles at 1 in 200 to Abbots Ripton at a minimum speed of 64mph, 92184 was little more than a minute behind the A4 by Tempsford. Here the slowing for the Sandy slack precluded any further direct comparison with 60007's performance The latter had a clear run apart from a permanent way slowing near Potters Bar, reaching Kings Cross in slightly less than 102 minutes from Grantham; net time for the A4's run was estimated at 97 minutes. Nevertheless it is clear that 92184 was capable of providing a respectable challenge to the A4 Pacific on a demanding schedule with little short of 500 tons behind the tender.

Following tests on the draughting arrangements for the Standard Class 4 4-6-0s at Swindon in 1956, the first of the second batch of 9Fs built at Swindon, 92178, emerged in September 1957 fitted with a double blastpipe and chimney. Table 11.31 sets out a log made by Mr. O. S. Nock during one of the trials carried out with the WR dynamometer car and trains of empty coaching stock between Stoke Gifford and Reading. On this particular day, the down run from Reading had been a somewhat rough trip. 92178 had been fired with a Blidworth coal of rather poor quality and a layer of clinker some 1½ in. thick had formed over the fire. While the engine was being steamed hard, the clinker was carried in suspension but had severe adverse effects on steaming; much clinker had to be removed from the firebox before the return test journey to Reading quoted in Table 11.31.

The load consisted of 19 vehicles of 632 tons tare, 635 tons gross. The steam rate was set to be 22,000 lb per hour and with a clean bright fire, the going was at first very good. Up the continuous 1 in 300 to Badminton, speed rose to a

Figure 218
Langwith Junction shed yard on 6th February 1965 with 9Fs 92195 and 92180 on the left and O4/8 2-8-0s 63739 and 63861 on the right looks rather drab and depressing. Both 9Fs had been allocated to Langwith in the previous month but were withdrawn within a few weeks. The view allows comparison of the two different 9F footstep styles below the smokebox door. In view of the little work done by 9Fs allocated to this depot, it perhaps should have been renamed 'Languish' Junction as far as the class was concerned. *(Courtney Haydon)*

Table 11.30
BR Standard Class 9F 2-10-0s

ER Grantham-Kings Cross

Train:			**1.10pm Edinburgh -Kings Cross**			**Up Flying Scotsman**		
Date:			16th August 1958.			No date. (c. 1954)		
Engine:			9F 2-10-0 92184 (New England) Fitted with double chimney.			A4 Pacific 60007 (Kings Cross) Named *Sir Nigel Gresley*		
Load:			14 vehicles, 462 tons tare, 485 tons gross			13 coaches, 470 tons tare, 495 tons gross		
Driver/Fireman:			A Bauer/S. Booth (Kings Cross).			W. Hoole/A. Leech (Kings Cross)		
Recorder(s):			Messrs. Edward Bagshawe and B. D. J. Walsh.			Mr. B. C. Bailey		
Distance Miles			Sched min.	Actual m. s.	Speed mph	Sched min.	Actual m. s.	Speed mph
00.0	GRANTHAM	dep.	0	0.00	-	0	0.00	-
03.5	Great Ponton			7.43	41		-	-
05.4	*Stoke*		9½	10.28	46		9.30	44
08.4	Corby Glen			13.24	78		12.34	72
13.3	Little Bytham			17.01	86		16.14	87
16.9	Essendine		18½	19.26	90		18.34	94
20.7	Tallington		(†3)	22.08	86		21.07	85
26.0	*Werrington Junction*		28½	26.14	76		24.50	68
							p.w.s.	20*
29.1	PETERBOROUGH		33½	29.48	25*	29	28.26	25*
30.5	*Fletton Junction*			32.00	-		30.59	-
32.9	Yaxley			34.48	-		-	-
36.1	Holme			37.45	72		36.40	71
38.1	*Connington South*			39.27	70		-	-
42.0	Abbots Ripton			43.03	56		41.44	64
46.6	HUNTINGDON		52½	47.17	75	47½	45.53	76
49.5	Offord			49.30	78		-	-
53.8	St. Neots			52.53	73		51.39	72/82
58.0	Tempsford			56.17	78		-	-
				p.w.s.	29*			
61.4	Sandy		65½	59.16	-		57.33	78/80
64.4	Biggleswade			-	-		59.47	77/70
68.5	Arlesey		(†2)	67.50	59		62.57	75/80
73.6	HITCHIN		79½	73.34	47	72	66.54	75
76.9	Stevenage			77.56	44/56		69.49	62
80.5	Knebworth			-	-	79	72.53	70
82.0	*Woolmer Green*			83.39	54/76		-	-
85.2	Welwyn Garden City			-	-		76.47	75/77
87.8	HATFIELD		94½	88.41	61*	87	78.54	-
			(†1)	sigs.	30*		p.w.s.	25*
92.8	Potters Bar		101½	94.10	-	96	83.46	-
			(†4)	sigs.	24*			
96.3	New Barnet			-	-		89.18	62
103.0	FINSBURY PARK		115½	111.07	30*	112	95.41	-
				sigs.	10*		sigs.	10*
105.5	KINGS CROSS	arr.	120½	119.19	-	117	101.54	-
* Speed reduced by brakes			† Recovery time					
			First published in Trains Illustrated, Vol. XI, No 114, November 1958, page 594.			First published in Railway Magazine Vol. 101, No. 647, March 1955, page 190.		

Figure 219
92066 (with Class Q6 0-8-0 63359 beyond) awaits its fate in the scrapyard of Ellis (Metals) Ltd. at Swalwell near Gateshead on 10th August 1965; 92066 was the first of the Tyne Dock 9F allocation to be withdrawn (23rd May 1965).
(Trevor Ermel)

Figure 220
It will not be long before the gates close for the last time on the life of former mechanical stoker-fitted 92167 awaiting the cutter's torch in the scrapyard of Clayton and Davie, Dunston, Gateshead on Saturday 5th October 1968. The speed with which such a large locomotive could be scrapped is astonishing. On the following Monday, only the tender was intact. The frames had been cut but remained in situ whilst the boiler, cab and cylinders were already gone. By the end of Tuesday, the engine was no more, having been reduced to a heap of small metal pieces. Newly arrived on that day were 92077 and 92160 for which an equally speedy demise was planned. *(Kevin Hudspith)*

Figure 221
Less happy times for 92245. Withdrawn from Southall in December 1964, the engine was still languishing among the debris of Barry scrapyard a decade later on 1st March 1975; beyond is Stanier Class 5 4-6-0 45293; 92245 is now preserved. *(Courtney Haydon)*

Figure 222
92060 (Tyne Dock) and stablemate 92097 have arrived on York shed yard en route to A. Draper's scrapyard at Hull in early 1967. The engines were both withdrawn in October 1966 and cut up in April 1967.
(Peter Cookson)

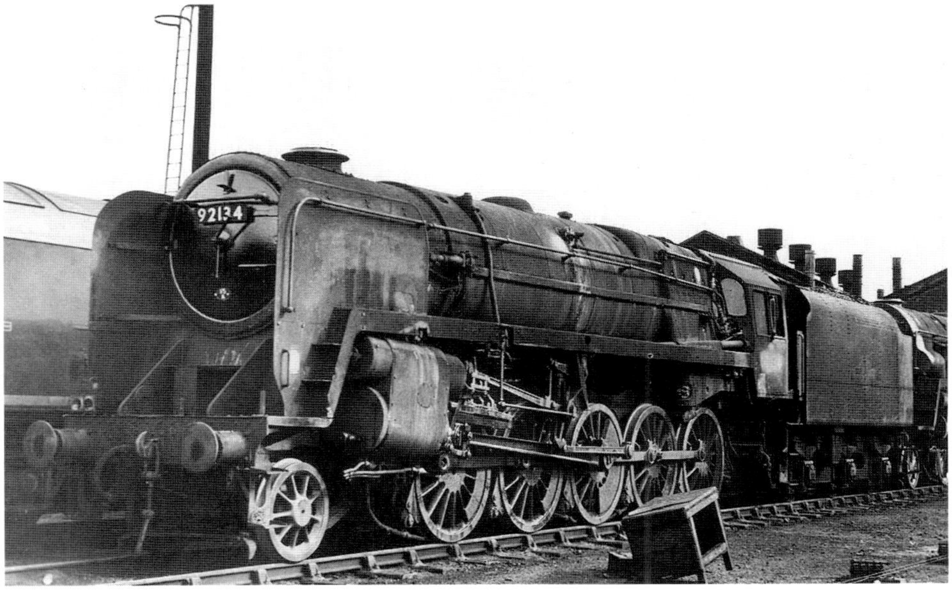

Figure 223
92134, the only preserved single chimney 9F, broods at its home shed, Wellingborough on 14th July 1963. 92134 was photographed a few days before despatch to Crewe Works for a Light Casual repair. A year later, the engine will have clocked up over 200,000 miles mainly on MML mineral workings to London. *(Courtney Haydon)*

Figure 224
Three weeks after delivery new from Crewe Works to Newport Ebbw Junction, 92240 is pictured at Gloucester Horton Road MPD on 22nd October 1958. As confirmed in this case, the WR 'Blue Spot' route availability designator carried below the cabside number was not routinely applied by Crewe paint shop for the last batch of WR 9Fs built there; the engine may have received it on a three day visit to Swindon Works during the following month. *(John S. Phillips)*

Figure 225
Rebuilt Crosti 9F 92025 (Speke Junction) starts an up coal train for Stanton ironworks from Bulwell Common down sidings on 16th September 1965. The engine was in store at Wellingborough from April 1959 to February 1960 awaiting conversion to standard boiler operation. 92025 eventually transferred to Birkenhead in February 1967 and was withdrawn during the following November. *(D. Swale)*

sustained 45mph giving an uncorrected drawbar horsepower of 1,150-1,170. After Badminton, 92178 was not allowed to attain any high speed. Sixty mph was laid down as the maximum on this particular test and once this was approached the brakes were gradually applied and the cut-off increased accordingly so as to keep the rate of steaming constant throughout; on previous runs, it was reported that 92178 had achieved speeds of almost 75mph and exhibited excellent riding qualities.

After reaching 60mph at Alderton tunnel, midway between Badminton and Hullavington, the brakes were applied and speed reduced to 21mph whilst steaming hard on a descending 1 in 300 gradient. There were further self-imposed checks later to 31mph at Wootton Bassett, 22mph at Shrivenham, 32mph at Wantage Road and 29mph before Didcot; from each of these, 92178 accelerated very freely and easily. Even before Swindon, however, the poor coal was once again having its effect and from Shrivenham to the end of the test at Milepost 45½, there was never more than 175 lb/sq in in the boiler. To keep the steaming rate constant, longer cut-offs had to be used. Just before the end of the test, 30% cut-off was required to keep the heavy train running at 62mph on level track; the boiler pressure at that point was no more than 165 lb/sq in. The approximate coal consumption had been 4,200 lb per hour, a very big increase over the 3,000 lb per hour established in earlier tests for a 9F steamed at 22,000 lb per hr. The trip highlighted the significant increase in the physical labour of firing that can be caused by indifferent fuel and the consequent rapidly deteriorating conditions in the firebox.

Table 11.32 gives performance data on the road trials between Toton and Brent in February 1955 carried out to establish loading levels for the proposed running of mineral trains to Class 'C' timings with the 9Fs then being allocated to the LMR Midland Division in increasing numbers; details of the trials are given in Section 11.1.

As noted in Section 7.3, 9F 2-10-0s were occasionally called on to rescue locomotives which had failed when working passenger trains. One such incident was recorded on 17th February 1963 by Mr. C. R. Berridge who describes the scene:

"The train was the eight-coach 6.50pm from Bristol Temple Meads to Leicester London Road with 45611 *Hong Kong* the rostered power. I was expecting trouble as the fireman was shovelling coal continuously at Bristol and complaining about it; the locomotive had been in store for

Table 11.31
BR Standard Class 9F 2-10-0s

WR Stoke Gifford-Reading

	Train:	**Dynamometer Car Test Run**		
	Date:	5th February 1958		
	Engine:	9F 2-10-0 92178 (not allocated) Fitted with double chimney.		
	Load:	19 vehicles, 632 tons tare, 635 tons gross		
	Driver/Fireman:	No information		
	Recorder:	Mr. O. S. Nock		
Distance Miles		Sched min.	Actual m. s.	Speed mph
00.0	*Stoke Gifford East Box*	0.0	0.00	-
01.6	Winterbourne		5.29	31
06.9	Chipping Sodbury		14.04	42
11.5	Badminton	20.0	20.10	45
			brakes	60 (max.)
17.3	Hullavington		26.49	37
			brakes	21
21.8	Little Somerford		34.12	60 (max.)
			brakes	-
28.6	Wootton Bassett	42.0	41.55	31
34.2	SWINDON	48.0	49.14	53
			brakes	60 (max.)
40.0	Shrivenham		57.02	22
42.5	*Knighton Crossing*		61.16	49
47.6	Challow		66.44	63
			brakes	32
51.1	Wantage Road		71.45	41
			brakes	29
58.4	DIDCOT	78.0	82.09	50½
63.0	*Milepost 48½*		87.00	62
72.8	Tilehurst		97.49	-
75.5	READING (Goods Line)	97.0	106.17	-

First published in Railway Magazine,
Vol. 107, No. 726, October 1961, page 712

some time and the coal in the tender would have deteriorated. *Hong Kong* staggered up to Fishponds and did not exceed 55mph as far as Berkeley Road where it stopped and there was a shouted conversation with the signalman. At Gloucester, there was a 9F, 92126, alongside the train, so I put my head out of the coach alongside the cab and spoke to the driver, telling him the 9F would do a lot better than the Jubilee which was hardly heating the train. He told me the 9F was going on the front of our train. I do not remember if the train was any warmer from Gloucester; this was towards the end of the great 'freeze-up' in the early weeks of 1963. Unfortunately I did not ask for the driver's name but he was from Saltley depot".

92126 set off 21 minutes late and made a leisurely run to Cheltenham with the eight coaches and *Hong Kong* in tow (estimated 380 tons gross). After this, respectable speeds of around 60mph were recorded between there and Ashchurch and at Eckington and Wadborough. Details are given in Table 11.33.

In the summer of 1960, several 9Fs were transferred to Bath Green Park for work on the S&DJR line to Bournemouth West. The line had always been challenging for the motive power used on this route, afflicted as it was with severe gradients and speed restrictions for line curvature. Until the arrival of the 9Fs, maximum loads for a single engine were restricted to eight coaches for both the Stanier and BR Class 5 4-6-0s and the Bulleid light Pacifics. On busy summer Saturdays in particular, loading almost always exceeded this number, 10 to 12-coach trains being the norm for the through holiday expresses to and from the north. Earlier in the year, tests had indicated that the 9Fs would be able to handle up to 12 coaches without assistance; Table 11.34 details just such a run made on the "Pines Express" on Friday 14th July 1961 with 92000 fitted with double chimney. Details of the run were first published in *Railway Magazine* Vol. 107, No 726, October 1961, p. 713 by Mr. O. S. Nock. The recorder was the very experienced Baron G. Vuillet accompanied by HQ locomotive Inspector Darrell Smith; the crew was the

Table 11.32
BR Standard Class 9F 2-10-0s

LMR Toton-Brent: engine 92018 (Wellingborough MPD)

Distance Miles	Train: / Date: / Load:		1.10pm Toton-Brent Test Train, 14th February 1955, 892 tons, 37 wagons (=41 coal load) Sched min.	Actual m. s.	Average Speed over preceding section mph	1.10pm Toton-Brent Test Train, 16th February 1955, 804 tons, 33 wagons (=37 coal load) Sched min.	Actual m. s.	Average Speed over preceding section mph
00.0	TOTON SIDINGS	dep.	0.0	0.00	dep. 1.08 pm	0.0	0.00	dep. 1.07½pm
03.4	*Ratcliffe Junction*		12.0	10.45	19.0	12.0	10.15	19.9
07.5	Hathern		20.0	20.30	25.2	20.0	19.15	27.3
10.3	Loughborough		24.0	27.45	23.2	24.0	26.00	24.9
17.6	*Syston North Junction*		35.0	41.45	31.3	35.0	40.00	31.3
27.5	Melton Mowbray		52.0	59.45	33.0	52.0	57.45	33.5
42.7	Manton		76.0	81.00	42.9	76.0	79.00	42.8
44.0	*Wing Sidings*		78.0	82.30	52.0	78.0	80.30	52.0
58.2	*Glendon South Junction*		101.0	108.30	32.5	101.0	105.30	34.1
60.8	KETTERING	arr.	105.0	114.15	27.6	105.0	122.30	9.2
			Av. speed from Toton 31.9mph			Av. speed from Toton 29.8mph		
00.0	KETTERING	dep.	0.0	0.00	dep. 3.14¾ pm	0.0	0.00	dep. 3.15 pm
01.2	*Kettering Junction*		3.0	4.30	16.0	3.0	4.15	16.9
06.9	Wellingborough		10.0	12.45	41.5	10.0	11.45	45.6
09.8	*Irchester South Signal Box*		15.0	16.45	43.5	15.0	15.15	49.7
13.9	Souldrop		21.0	24.30	31.7	21.0	22.00	36.4
19.0	Oakley		27.0	30.15	53.2	27.0	28.00	51.0
22.1	Bedford		31.0	35.00	39.2	31.0	32.15	43.8
39.2	Leagrave		62.0	62.30	37.3	62.0	58.00	39.8
41.8	Luton		68.0	68.00	28.4	68.0	66.45	17.8
47.4	*Harpenden Junction*		76.0	75.45	43.4	76.0	74.15	44.8
52.1	St. Albans		85.0	84.30	33.0	85.0	86.15	23.5
56.8	Radlett		93.0	97.45	21.2	93.0	97.15	25.6
65.0	Hendon		108.0	117.00	25.6	108.0	112.15	32.8
66.3	BRENT SIDINGS	arr.	113.0	124.15	10.8	113.0	117.00	16.4
			Av. speed from Kettering 32.0mph			Av. speed from Kettering 34.0mph		

Distance Miles	Train: / Date: / Load:		5.45am Brent-Toton Test Train, 15th February 1955, 892 tons, 37 wagons (= 41 coal load) Sched min.	Actual m. s.	Average Speed over preceding section mph
00.0	BRENT SIDINGS	dep.	0.0	0.00	dep. 5.45¾ pm
01.3	Hendon		6.0	4.15	18.4
09.5	Radlett		21.0	21.15	28.9
14.2	St. Albans		27.0	30.15	31.3
18.9	*Harpenden Junction*		36.0	45.15	11.8
24.5	Luton		42.0	52.30	46.3
44.2	Bedford		64.0	83.15	38.4
47.3	Oakley		68.0	89.15	31.0
52.4	*Souldrop*		76.0	96.15	43.7
57.0	Irchester Station		81.0	105.15	30.7
59.4	Wellingborough		85.0	119.15	10.3
65.1	*Kettering Junction*		94.0	130.30	30.4
66.3	KETTERING	arr.	97.0	134.45	16.9
			Av. speed from Brent 29.5mph		
00.0	KETTERING	dep.	0.0	0.00	dep. 8.10½am
02.6	*Glendon South Junction*		6.0	9.00	17.3
16.8	*Wing Sidings*		28.0	29.00	42.6
18.1	Manton		30.0	31.15	34.5
33.3	Melton Mowbray		54.0	53.45	40.5
43.2	*Syston North Junction*		73.0	75.45	27.0
50.5	Loughborough		88.0	87.45	36.5
53.3	Hathern		93.0	91.15	48.0
57.4	*Ratcliffe Junction*		99.0	98.00	36.4
60.8	TOTON SIDINGS	arr.	108.0	110.30	16.3
			Av. speed from Kettering 33.0mph		

celebrated partnership of Driver Donald Beale and Fireman Peter Smith of Branksome shed.

Weather conditions were poor on the day in question with strong westerly winds and heavy rain. The 450ton train got away from Bath 12½ minutes late and began the 1 in 50 climb to Combe Down tunnel with regulator full open and cut-off gradually increased from 35% to 42%; speed was sustained at a steady 24mph with boiler pressure maintained at 235-245 lb/sq in. Despite a loss of ½ minute from Midford to Radstock, there followed a remarkable climb to Masbury summit. Speed is severely restricted for the curve through Radstock coming right at the start of the main climb of four miles at 1 in 50-53. Moreover, the effect of the severe curves above Midsomer Norton increases the effective severity of the grades to 1 in 52½ on average for the whole four miles. From 37mph just after Radstock, speed initially fell off very slowly. Cut-off was increased to 35% approaching Midsomer Norton and nearing the straight length beyond the station, cut-off was increased further to 40% with speed still at 28½ mph; boiler pressure remained at 240 lb/sq in with water level right at the top of the glass.

The incidence of the subsequent curves brought an immediate fall in speed but the slight easing of the grade through Chilcompton station brought speed up to 30¾mph with 92000 working at 48% cut-off. Speed then actually increased to 36mph at Milepost 14¾ and was maintained up the following 1 in 60-73, the cut-off being shortened step by step to 23% by the time Binegar was passed. The last mile at 1 in 63-73 was cleared at 30mph. Baron Vuillet calculated that the average edhp during this ascent was no less than 2,000 with the indicated horsepower at 2,240; the average edhp for the entire climb worked out at 1,840. After this superb effort, the lateness on leaving Bath had been exactly halved on breasting Masbury summit.

The steep ascent of six miles at the ruling gradient of 1 in 50 to Evercreech Junction was taken cautiously but even so, the station was reached only 2¾ minutes late. The smart working at Evercreech meant the stay was cut by two minutes and the "Pines" left less than a minute late. The 1 in 166 down grade made for a very rapid start and Cole, 3.8 miles, was passed in 4 min. 55 sec. The three minute scheduled stop at Shillingstone for crossing a northbound train was exceeded by 2½ min however and the "Pines" was thus 3 min. late into Blandford. Here water was taken and a tender gauge check showed the consumption from Bath to be 3,500 gallons, an average of 66 gallons per mile and an approximate evaporation rate of 23,000 lb per hour. The six miles from Blandford to Bailey Gate is something of a switchback but the latter was passed in 7 mins 40 secs at 64mph. Speed was then reduced to 50mph for the mechanical tablet exchange at Corfe Mullen Junction and for the immediately following two miles climb at 1 in 80, the reverser was put into 45% cut-off and and regulator opened to the full. Speed was maintained at 43mph with a cylinder horsepower estimated to be 2,700; this effort gained two minutes between Blandford and Broadstone.

The fireworks were not yet over however. Because of a signal check from a preceding SR train, departure from Poole was still 2½ min late. 92000 tackled the mile or so to the foot of the initial 1½ mile 1 in 60 Parkestone-Branksome bank on full regulator and 49% cut-off. At the foot of the bank where speed had risen to 47mph, the cut-off was increased to 52%. The 1 in 60 was stormed at no lower speed than 41mph with boiler pressure still 225 lb/sq in at the summit allowing the "Pines" to regain all but 30 seconds of the lost time still outstanding on departure from Poole.

Baron Vuillet was one of the most experienced observers of locomotive performance anywhere in the world at that time. The Baron summed up his reaction to the run as "a magnificent example of skilled driving and firing, with high sustained capacity and remarkable outbursts of exceptional power showing the flexibility of the steam locomotive.....This is one of the most remarkable trips I have made on a locomotive and the Class 9 engines are certainly among the very best".

Figure 226
92220 *Evening Star,* with its York shedplate, recovers from a permanent way slack near Horton in Ribblesdale with the northbound "The Border Venturer" enthusiasts' special on Saturday 13th May 1978. *(L. A. Nixon)*

Figure 227
The scene is Longmoor on 8th June 1968. Recently purchased from BR by David Shepherd, 92203 climbs towards Weavers Down Junction with a Bulleid Society special from London to the Longmoor Military Railway. The nameplates *Black Prince* are covered prior to the naming ceremony later in the day. 92203 headed the last steam-hauled John Summers ore train from Bidston to Shotton on Monday 6th November 1967 before being withdrawn from BR service in the same month.
(Hugh Ballantyne)

Figure 228
92203 stands in Longmoor shed yard on 8th June 1968; the engine has had red lining applied to its black livery.
(Hugh Ballantyne)

Table 11.33
BR Standard Class 9F 2-10-0s

LMR Gloucester -Worcester Shrub Hill

Train	6.50pm Bristol Temple Meads-Leicester London Road
Date	17th February 1963
Engine	9F 2-10-0 92126 (Wellingborough)
Load	8 vehicles (plus failed Jubilee 4-6-0 45611 *Hong Kong*, ca 125 tons) 370 tons tare/385 tons gross
Driver/Fireman	Saltley crew
Recorder	Mr. C. R. Berridge

Distance Miles		Sched min.	Actual m. s.	Speed mph
00.00	GLOUCESTER	0	00.00	-
06.50	CHELTENHAM	11	15.50	-
00.00	CHELTENHAM	0	00.00	-
				57
07.25	ASHCHURCH	12	10.59	-
00.00	ASHCHURCH	0	00.00	-
02.00	Bredon		03.48	-
04.75	Eckington		06.36	62
05.75	Defford		07.41	61
09.00	Wadborough		11.17	-
11.50	Norton Halt		17.19	10 (p.w.s.)
				51
14.50	WORCESTER SHRUB HILL	27	24.22	-

Table 11.34
BR Standard Class 9F 2-10-0s

WR Bath Green Park-Bournemouth West

	Train:	**The Pines Express**		
	Date:	14th July 1961		
	Engine:	9F 2-10-0 92000 (Bath G. P.) Fitted with double chimney.		
	Load:	12 coaches, 416 tons tare, 450 tons gross		
	Driver/Fireman:	D. Beale/P. Smith (Branksome)		
	Recorder:	Baron G. Vuillet		
Distance Miles		Sched min.	Actual m. s.	Speed mph
00.0	BATH (GREEN PARK)	0	0.00	-
	Combe Down Tunnel (in)		-	24
04.3	Midford	10	10.10	-
10.7	RADSTOCK	19	19.40	37
12.0	Midsomer Norton		21.50	31
13.5	*Milepost 13**		25.23	22
14.5	Chilcompton		27.52	25¼
15.2	*Milepost 14¾**		29.11	36/33
17.5	Binegar		32.25	36
18.2	*Milepost 17¾* (Masbury)*	41	34.43	30
26.4	EVERCREECH JCT.	56	46.00	-
3.8	Cole		4.55	-
7.1	Wincanton		10.55	-
			Three tablet slacks	-
20.9	Shillingstone	31	31.45	-
5.5	BLANDFORD	9	9.00	-
6.1	Bailey Gate		7.40	64½
	Corfe Mullen Junction		-	50
	Summit of 1 in 80		-	43
10.9	BROADSTONE	16	14.10	-
			sigs.	-
3.4	POOLE	8	7.05	-
				47 (max.)
1.8	Parkstone		-	41 (min.)
3.1	Branksome		5.10	-
4.4	BOURNEMOUTH WEST	10	8.00	-

* Mileposts are measured from Bath Junction, 0.5 miles from Bath (Green Park).

First published in Railway Magazine,
Vol. 107, No. 726, October 1961, page 713

12. Storage, Withdrawal and Disposal

A number of 9Fs were stored prior to their withdrawal, particularly on the Eastern Region (ER) and Western Region (WR) which had aimed to dispense with steam power by the end of 1965. This objective was met on the WR (apart from the S&DJR) but 9Fs lingered on the ER until April 1966.

On the LMR, all of the Crosti boiler engines with the exception of 92026 were stored for a period before conversion to standard boiler operation, sometimes for many months. A handful of standard boiler engines on the LMR were also mothballed in a serviceable state for a few months mostly in 1965/6.

A list of engines put in store, as reported in the record cards and supplemented by information from observers' notes, is given in Table 12.1 together with known dates.

Table 12.2 lists the dates of withdrawal and places and dates of disposal; the engines were usually cut up within a few weeks of receipt on the breakers' yards, the exception of course being the legendary Barry yard of Messrs Woodhams, the source of so many preserved steam locomotives. In at least four cases, 92066/77, 92160/7, the engines were not scrapped on the premises of the buyer. The cutting up process appears to have been subcontracted to other yards; there may have been other engines in this category.

Before their removal to scrapyards, withdrawn 9Fs were usually stored at or close to their final depots with some locations such as Speke Junction, Birkenhead and Carlisle Kingmoor on the LMR hosting appreciable numbers for short periods; details are given where known.

Table 12.1
BR Standard Cl. 9F 2-10-0s 92000-92250: Official Storage Dates

No.	Dates of Storage	Status	No.	Dates of Storage	Status	No.	Dates of Storage	Status
92000	??.07.65	U	92075	14.06.65-17.01.66	S	92189	??.10.65-19.12.65	U
92001	21.02.66-04.08.66	U	92088	14.06.65-05.07.65	U	92190	??.10.65	U
92007	??.11.65-31.12.65	U	92091	03.02.66-21.02.66	U	92192	10.01.65-21.02.65	U
92020	??.04.59-??.03.61	U	92093	14.06.65-31.12.65	U	92193	11.05.64-14.06.64	S
92021	??.04.59-??.04.60	U	92095	14.06.65-25.04.66	U	92195	10.05.64-14.06.64	S
92022	??.05.59-??.03.62	U	92096	18.10.65-07.01.66	U	92196	11.10.64-06.12.64	U
92023	??.04.59-??.06.61	U	92113	14.06.65-19.07.65	S	92198	08.06.64-02.08.64	U
92024	??.08.59-??.01.60	U	92129	16.07.66-12.09.66	S	92199	14.06.64-02.08.64	S
92025	??.04.59-??.02.60	U	92132	08.02.66-03.08.66	S	92205	??.05.67-??.06.67	U
	03.02.66-21.02.66	S	92142	26.12.64-21.02.65	U	92209	??.05.65-??.06.65	U
	03.09.66-21.10.66	S	92143	03.01.65-21.02.65	U	92214	??.07.65-09.08.65	U
92027	??.04.59-??.08.60	U	92144	28.03.65-04.04.65	U	92215	??.05.67-08.06.67	U
92028	??.08.59	U	92149	28.03.65-04.04.65	U	92219	??.07.65-09.08.65	U
92029	??.06.59-??.06.60	U	92153	??.01.66-??.07.66	S	92220	3 w/e 27.03.65	U
92031	14.06.65-05.07.65	S	92154	14.06.65-05.07.65	S	92222	3 w/e 27.03.65	U
92032	14.06.65-05.07.65	S	92160	13.12.65-04.02.66	S	92224	??.07.64-??.11.64	S
92034	??.03.64-31.05.64	U	92169	15.03.64-31.05.64	U		07.02.66-03.08.66	S
92035	??.01.66-06.02.66	U	92170	12.01.64-31.05.64	U	92225	??.06.65-02.07.65	U
92036	01.11.64-??.12.64	S	92171	12.04.64-31.05.64	U	92230	??.11.65-31.12.65	U
92037	10.01.65-??.02.65	U	92175	16.02.64-31.05.64	U	92232	??.12.64-26.12.64	U
92038	14.06.64-??.06.64	U	92176	11.02.64-31.05.64	U	92236	??.02.65-21.04.65	U
92043	28.06.65-10.01.66	S	92177	16.02.64-31.05.64	U	92240	??.07.65-06.08.65	U
92049	30.12.65-14.02.66	S	92178	??.08.65-03.10.65	U	92241	??.07.65	U
92054	03.02.66-24.02.66	S	92179	11.04.65-02.05.65	U	92244	??.11.65-31.12.65	U
92055	13.12.65-31.01.66	S	92181	03.01.65-21.02.65	U	92245	??.12.64	U
92060	??.10.66-23.10.66	S	92184	10.01.65-21.02.65	U	92246	??.11.65-31.12.65	U
92067	29.07.66-29.09.66	S	92185	10.01.65-21.02.65	U	92250	??.11.65-31.12.65	U
92068	12.07.65-24.12.65	S	92187	10.01.65-21.02.65	U			
92072	14.06.65-08.01.66	S	92188	10.01.65-21.02.65	U			

Key: S Stored serviceable U Stored unserviceable

Table 12.2
BR Standard Class 9F 2-10-0s

Summary of Construction, Withdrawal, Storage and Disposal Data

Loco	To Traffic	Withdrawn	Storage Location	Sold	Cut up	Disposal
92000	05.01.54	02.07.65	GHR	08.65	11.65	Birds Commercial Motors, Long Marston
92001	12.01.54	17.01.67	WAK	05.67	05.67	Cox & Danks, Wadsley Bridge
92002	16.01.54	w.e. 11.11.67	SPJ	03.68	04.68	G.H.Campbell, Airdrie
92003	25.01.54	26.03.65	CED	05.65	07.65	J.Cashmore, Newport
92004	30.01.54	w.e. 23.03.68	CNF/SCO	06.68	07.68	J.Cashmore, Newport
92005	05.02.54	30.08.65	CRS	11.65	12.65	T.W.Ward, Beighton, Sheffield
92006	10.02.54	10.04.67	WAK	11.67	11.67	A.Draper, Hull
92007	18.02.54	31.12.65	GHR	02.66	02.66	J.Cashmore, Newport
92008	01.03.54	w.e. 07.10.67	SPJ/SCO	06.68	08.68	J.Buttigieg, Newport
92009	12.03.54	w.e. 23.03.68	CNF	06.68	07.68	J.Cashmore, Newport
92010	13.05.54	w.e. 02.04.66	CKR	06.66	06.66	Arnott Young, Carmyle
92011	19.05.54	w.e. 11.11.67	EDH	01.68	01.68	G.H.Campbell, Airdrie
92012	31.05.54	w.e. 28.10.67	CKR	02.68	02.68	J.McWilliam, Shettleston
92013	23.04.54	w.e. 01.10.66	SAL	01.67	05.67	G.Cohen, Kettering
92014	18.05.54	w.e. 14.10.67	SPJ/SCO	08.68	08.68	J.Buttigieg, Newport
92015	25.09.54	w.e. 29.04.67	CKR	09.67	11.67	J.McWilliam, Shettleston
92016	07.10.54	w.e. 21.10.67	CNF	04.68	04.68	J.McWilliam, Shettleston
92017	13.10.54	w.e. 23.12.67	CKR	04.68	04.68	Arnott Young, Parkgate (see 1)
92018	21.10.54	w.e. 22.04.67	CKR	07.67	08.67	Motherwell Machinery & Scrap Co., Wishaw
92019	25.10.54	w.e. 10.06.67	CKR	01.68	01.68	Motherwell Machinery & Scrap Co., Wishaw
92020	18.05.55	w.e. 21.10.67	SPJ/SCO	03.68	08.68	J.Buttigieg, Newport
92021	18.05.55	w.e. 11.11.67	EDH	01.68	01.68	G.H.Campbell, Airdrie
92022	18.05.55	w.e. 11.11.67	SPJ	03.68	04.68	G.H.Campbell, Airdrie
92023	20.05.55	w.e. 11.11.67	SPJ	03.68	04.68	G.H.Campbell, Airdrie
92024	06.06.55	w.e. 11.11.67	SPJ	03.68	05.68	G.H.Campbell, Airdrie
92025	17.06.55	w.e. 11.11.67	SPJ	03.68	04.68	G.H.Campbell, Airdrie
92026	17.06.55	w.e. 11.11.67	SPJ	03.68	04.68	G.H.Campbell, Airdrie
92027	25.06.55	w.e. 05.08.67	SPJ	12.67	12.67	J.Buttigieg, Newport
92028	06.07.55	w.e. 22.10.66	SAL	01.67	01.67	J.Cashmore, Great Bridge
92029	08.07.55	w.e. 11.11.67	SPJ	01.68	02.68	G.H.Campbell, Airdrie
92030	03.11.54	27.02.67	WAK	07.67	07.67	Arnott Young, Parkgate
92031	11.11.54	w.e. 07.01.67	TRP	04.67	05.67	T.W.Ward, Killamarsh
92032	17.11.54	w.e. 15.04.67	BIR/CRS	10.67	10.67	J.Cashmore, Great Bridge
92033	19.11.54	w.e. 18.09.65	CRS	11.65	12.65	T.W.Ward, Killamarsh
92034	02.12.54	w.e. 31.05.64	IMM	08.65	08.65	T.W.Ward, Killamarsh
92035	03.12.54	06.02.66	IMM	04.66	04.66	T.W.Ward, Killamarsh
92036	03.12.54	w.e. 06.12.64	NED	03.65	05.65	G.Cohen, Kettering
92037	08.12.54	w.e. 21.02.65	IMM	04.65	06.65	A.Draper, Hull
92038	14.12.54	w.e. 11.04.65	LGJ	06.65	07.65	J.Cashmore, Great Bridge
92039	17.12.54	w.e. 17.10.65	LGJ	01.66	02.66	T.W.Ward, Killamarsh; then Arnott Young, Parkgate (02.66)
92040	23.12.54	w.e. 08.08.65	LGJ	10.65	11.65	A.Draper, Hull
92041	31.12.54	w.e. 29.08.65	LGJ	09.65	11.65	J.Cashmore, Great Bridge; then T.W.Ward, Beighton, Sheffield (11.65)
92042	12.01.55	19.12.65	COL	03.66	04.66	T.W.Ward, Beighton, Sheffield
92043	18.01.55	w.e. 30.07.66	CKR	10.66	10.66	G.H.Campbell, Airdrie
92044	29.01.55	w.e. 11.04.65	LGJ	06.65	07.65	J.Cashmore, Great Bridge
92045	09.02.55	w.e. 16.09.67	SPJ/SCO	02.68	02.68	T.W.Ward, Beighton, Sheffield
92046	11.02.55	w.e. 21.10.67	SPJ	03.68	08.68	J.Buttigieg, Newport
92047	18.02.55	w.e. 11.11.67	SPJ	03.68	04.68	G.H.Campbell, Airdrie
92048	26.02.55	w.e. 16.09.67	SPJ	02.68	02.68	T.W.Ward, Beighton, Sheffield
92049	10.03.55	w.e. 11.11.67	CKR	04.68	06.68	G.H.Campbell, Airdrie
92050	19.08.55	w.e. 30.09.67	WAR/SCH	01.68	02.68	J.Buttigieg, Newport
92051	22.08.55	w.e. 22.10.67	CKR	02.68	02.68	Motherwell Machinery & Scrap Co., Wishaw
92052	26.08.55	w.e. 12.08.67	CKR	12.67	01.68	J.McWilliam, Shettleston
92053	17.09.55	w.e. 19.02.66	WAR	07.66	12.66	W.George, Station Steel, Wath then to J.Cashmore, Great Bridge (11.66)
92054	21.09.55	w.e. 04.05.68	NEH	08.68	06.68	Arnott Young, Parkgate
92055	22.09.55	w.e. 23.12.67	SPJ	03.68	04.68	T.W.Ward, Killamarsh
92056	14.10.55	w.e. 11.11.67	CKR	02.68	02.68	Motherwell Machinery & Scrap Co., Wishaw
92057	11.10.55	w.e. 02.10.65	BIR	12.65	12.65	T.W.Ward, Beighton, Sheffield
92058	13.10.55	w.e. 04.11.67	CKR	02.68	02.68	J.McWilliam, Shettleston

Loco	To Traffic	Withdrawn	Storage Location	Sold	Cut up	Disposal
92059	20.10.55	w.e. 17.09.66	BIR	01.67	01.67	A.Draper, Hull
92060	05.11.55	23.10.66	TND	02.67	04.67	A.Draper, Hull
92061	12.11.55	w.e. 04.09.66	TND	11.66	11.66	A.Draper, Hull
92062	19.11.55	w.e. 26.06.66	TND	08.66	10.66	Hughes Bolckow, Blyth
92063	25.11.55	w.e. 24.11.66	TND	03.67	04.67	T.J.Thompson, Stockton-on-Tees
92064	02.12.55	w.e. 24.11.66	TND	03.67	04.67	T.J.Thompson, Stockton-on-Tees
92065	10.12.55	w.e. 03.04.67	WAK	08.67	08.67	Arnott Young, Parkgate
92066	15.12.55	23.05.65	TND	09.65	09.65	G.Cohen, Cargo Fleet, Middlesbrough Cut up at Ellis Metals, Swalwell, Gateshead
92067	20.12.55	w.e. 05.11.66	CKR	01.67	02.67	J.McWilliam, Shettleston
92068	29.12.55	w.e. 15.01.66	CKR	04.66	04.66	Arnott Young, Troon
92069	31.12.55	w.e. 05.05.68	SPJ	10.68	10.68	Arnott Young, Parkgate
92070	14.01.56	w.e. 11.11.67	BIR/SPJ	01.68	02.68	G.H.Campbell, Airdrie
92071	21.01.56	w.e. 11.11.67	CKR	02.68	02.68	Motherwell Machinery & Scrap Co., Wishaw
92072	01.02.56	w.e. 08.01.66	KBY/BIR	06.66	06.66	T.W.Ward, Beighton, Sheffield
92073	09.02.56	w.e. 11.11.67	BIR/SPJ	02.68	02.68	G.H.Campbell, Airdrie
92074	18.02.56	w.e. 15.04.67	CKR	07.67	10.67	Motherwell Machinery & Scrap Co., Wishaw
92075	01.03.56	w.e. 17.09.66	CKR	01.67	02.67	A.Draper, Hull
92076	06.03.56	w.e. 25.02.67	SPJ/CKR	05.67	06.67	J.McWilliam, Shettleston
92077	13.03.56	w.e. 22.06.68	CNF	10.68	10.68	G.H.Campbell, Airdrie. Cut up at Clayton & Davie, Dunston, Gateshead
92078	21.03.56	w.e. 06.05.67	WAR	12.67	01.68	T.J.Thompson, Stockton-on-Tees
92079	29.03.56	w.e. 11.11.67	SPJ	03.68	04.68	G.H.Campbell, Airdrie
92080	14.04.56	w.e. 06.05.67	CKR	09.67	11.67	J.McWilliam, Shettleston
92081	23.04.56	w.e. 12.02.66	NEH/SPJ	05.66	06.66	W.George, Station Steel, Wath
92082	03.05.56	w.e. 11.11.67	SPJ	03.68	04.68	G.H.Campbell, Airdrie
92083	11.05.56	w.e. 18.02.67	BIR	07.67	07.67	A.Draper, Hull
92084	19.05.56	w.e. 11.11.67	BIR/SPJ	03.68	03.68	G.H.Campbell, Airdrie
92085	26.05.56	w.e. 24.12.66	BIR/BAR	03.68	07.80	Woodham Bros., Barry (Stored at Barry Docks until cut-up)
92086	06.06.56	w.e. 11.11.67	SPJ	03.68	04.68	G.H.Campbell, Airdrie
92087	29.08.56	w.e. 25.02.67	CKR	05.67	06.67	J.McWilliam, Shettleston
92088	24.10.56	w.e. 27.04.68	CNF	09.68	10.68	Arnott Young, Dinsdale
92089	26.09.56	w.e. 18.02.67	BIR	07.67	07.67	A.Draper, Hull
92090	08.11.56	w.e. 20.05.67	BIR	09.67	12.67	G.Cohen, Kettering
92091	27.11.56	w.e. 25.05.68	CNF	09.68	11.68	T.W.Ward, Beighton, Sheffield
92092	13.12.56	w.e. 22.10.66	BIR	02.67	04.67	A.Draper, Hull
92093	15.01.57	w.e. 02.09.67	WOR	01.68	02.68	Motherwell Machinery & Scrap Co., Wishaw
92094	04.02.57	w.e. 04.05.68	SPJ	08.68	09.68	Arnott Young, Parkgate
92095	06.03.57	w.e. 01.10.66	WAR	02.67	04.67	A.Draper, Hull
92096	02.04.57	w.e. 25.02.67	CKR	05.67	06.67	J.McWilliam, Shettleston
92097	27.06.56	w.e. 23.10.66	TND	02.67	04.67	A.Draper, Hull
92098	04.07.56	w.e. 31.07.66	TND	10.66	10.66	A.Draper, Hull
92099	23.07.56	w.e. 04.09.66	TND	11.66	11.66	A.Draper, Hull
92100	30.07.56	w.e. 13.05.67	BIR/CRS	11.67	01.68	G.Cohen, Kettering
92101	13.08.56	w.e. 14.10.67	SPJ /SCO	03.68	05.68	J.Buttigieg, Newport
92102	15.08.56	w.e. 11.11.67	SPJ	03.68	03.68	G.H.Campbell, Airdrie
92103	18.08.56	w.e. 27.05.67	BIR/SPJ	11.67	06.68	G.Cohen, Kettering
92104	24.08.56	w.e. 25.02.67	EDH	07.67	07.67	A.Draper, Hull
92105	07.09.56	w.e. 14.01.67	BIR	05.67	05.67	T.W.Ward, Killamarsh
92106	12.09.56	w.e. 29.07.67	BIR	12.67	12.67	T.J.Thompson, Stockton-on-Tees
92107	20.09.56	w.e. 25.02.67	BIR	07.67	07.67	A.Draper, Hull
92108	12.10.56	w.e. 11.11.67	SPJ	02.68	02.68	G.H.Campbell, Airdrie
92109	15.10.56	w.e. 11.11.67	NEH	02.68	03.68	G.H.Campbell, Airdrie
92110	23.10.56	w.e. 30.12.67	CKR	03.68	03.68	G.H.Campbell, Airdrie (see 2)
92111	06.11.56	w.e. 28.10.67	BIR/SPJ	02.68	02.68	T.W.Ward, Beighton, Sheffield
92112	17.11.56	w.e. 11.11.67	SPJ/CKR	03.68	03.68	G.H.Campbell, Airdrie
92113	24.11.56	w.e. 07.10.67	SPJ/SCO	03.68	08.68	J.Buttigieg, Newport
92114	29.11.56	w.e. 22.07.67	CKR	02.68	02.68	G.H.Campbell, Airdrie
92115	12.12.56	w.e. 19.02.66	BIR	06.66	06.66	W.George, Station Steel, Wath
92116	22.12.56	w.e. 12.11.66	WAR	03.67	06.67	A.Draper, Hull
92117	27.12.56	w.e. 23.12.67	SPJ	04.68	04.68	T.W.Ward, Killamarsh
92118	28.12.56	w.e. 25.05.68	CNF	09.68	09.68	T.W.Ward, Beighton, Sheffield
92119	12.01.57	w.e. 23.09.67	CKR	01.68	02.68	Motherwell Machinery & Scrap Co., Wishaw
92120	28.01.57	w.e. 08.07.67	BIR/CRS	01.68	02.68	Birds Commercial Motors, Long Marston
92121	08.02.57	w.e. 29.07.67	BIR/CRS	01.68	01.68	T.J.Thompson, Stockton-on-Tees
92122	18.02.57	w.e. 11.11.67	BIR/SPJ	02.68	02.68	G.H.Campbell, Airdrie
92123	26.02.57	w.e. 28.10.67	SPJ	02.68	02.68	T.W.Ward, Beighton, Sheffield
92124	02.03.57	w.e. 03.12.66	SPJ	04.67	04.67	T.W.Ward, Killamarsh

Loco	To Traffic	Withdrawn	Storage Location	Sold	Cut up	Disposal
92125	09.03.57	w.e. 30.12.67	CKR	03.68	04.68	Arnott Young, Parkgate (see Note 1)
92126	18.03.57	w.e. 05.08.67	CNF/WAR	01.68	01.68	J.McWilliam, Shettleston
92127	29.03.57	w.e. 19.08.67	SPJ/SCO	12.67	12.67	J.Buttigieg, Newport
92128	05.04.57	w.e. 11.11.67	CNF	05.68	05.68	J.McWilliam, Shettleston
92129	10.04.57	w.e. 01.07.67	CKR	10.67	11.67	Motherwell Machinery & Scrap Co., Wishaw
92130	15.04.57	w.e. 14.06.66	CKR	10.66	11.66	Motherwell Machinery & Scrap Co., Wishaw
92131	25.04.57	w.e. 23.09.67	BIR/SPJ	02.68	02.68	T.W.Ward, Beighton, Sheffield
92132	29.04.57	w.e. 21.10.67	CKR	01.68	02.68	Motherwell Machinery & Scrap Co., Wishaw
92133	22.05.57	w.e. 22.07.67	BIR/SPJ	12.67	01.68	T.J.Thompson, Stockton-on-Tees
92134	24.05.57	w.e. 10.12.66	BIR/BAR	05.67	-	Woodham Bros. Barry Preserved and undergoing restoration on a site near Crewe
92135	11.06.57	08.06.67	WAK	01.68	03.68	A.Draper, Hull
92136	18.06.57	w.e. 29.10.66	SAL	02.67	02.67	T.W.Ward, Beighton, Sheffield
92137	24.06.57	w.e. 09.09.67	CKR	01.68	02.68	Motherwell Machinery & Scrap Co., Wishaw
92138	25.06.57	w.e. 08.07.67	SPJ	12.67	02.68	Birds Commercial Motors, Long Marston
92139	28.06.57	w.e. 09.09.67	CKR	01.68	02.68	Motherwell Machinery & Scrap Co., Wishaw
92140	05.07.57	w.e. 11.04.65	LGJ	06.65	07.65	J.Cashmore, Great Bridge
92141	29.07.57	19.12.65	COL	03.66	04.66	T.W.Ward, Beighton, Sheffield
92142	29.07.57	w.e. 21.02.65	NED/COL	05.65	02.66	G.Cohen, Kettering
92143	10.08.57	w.e. 21.02.65	NED	05.65	05.65	G.Cohen, Kettering
92144	19.08.57	19.12.65	COL	03.66	04.66	T.W.Ward, Beighton, Sheffield
92145	26.08.57	06.02.66	IMM	04.66	04.66	T.W.Ward, Beighton, Sheffield
92146	05.09.57	w.e. 17.04.66	DON	07.66	08.66	W.George, Station Steel, Wath
92147	14.09.57	w.e. 04.04.65	DON	07.65	08.65	J.Cashmore, Great Bridge
92148	21.09.57	19.12.65	COL	03.66	04.66	T.W.Ward, Beighton, Sheffield
92149	01.10.57	w.e. 27.06.65	LGJ	10.65	10.65	T.W.Ward, Beighton, Sheffield
92150	05.10.57	17.04.67	WAK	11.67	11.67	A.Draper, Hull
92151	09.10.57	w.e. 22.04.67	BIR/SPJ	03.68	04.68	A.Draper, Hull
92152	16.10.57	w.e. 11.11.67	SPJ	03.68	03.68	G.H.Campbell, Airdrie
92153	21.10.57	w.e. 21.01.68	SPJ/SCO	04.68	06.68	J.Cashmore, Newport
92154	28.10.57	w.e. 22.07.67	SPJ	12.67	01.68	T.J.Thompson, Stockton-on-Tees
92155	05.11.57	w.e. 19.11.66	SPJ	02.67	04.67	A.Draper, Hull
92156	15.11.57	w.e. 22.07.67	WAR	03.68	03.68	A.Draper, Hull
92157	20.11.57	w.e. 19.08.67	BIR/SPJ	12.67	01.68	J.Buttigieg, Newport
92158	22.11.57	w.e. 23.07.66	SPJ	08.66	11.66	A.Draper, Hull
92159	27.11.57	w.e. 22.07.67	SPJ	12.67	01.68	T.J.Thompson, Stockton-on-Tees
92160	29.11.57	w.e. 29.06.68	CNF	10.68	10.68	G.H.Campbell, Airdrie. Cut up at Clayton & Davie, Dunston, Gateshead
92161	17.12.57	w.e. 10.12.66	CKR	05.67	05.67	Motherwell Machinery & Scrap Co., Wishaw
92162	19.12.57	w.e. 11.11.67	SPJ	05.68	05.68	G.H.Campbell, Airdrie
92163	24.03.58	w.e. 11.11.67	SPJ	05.68	05.68	G.H.Campbell, Airdrie
92164	01.04.58	w.e. 30.07.66	SAL	08.66	10.66	A.Draper, Hull
92165	17.04.58	w.e. 16.03.68	SPJ/SCO	06.68	06.68	J.Cashmore, Newport
92166	24.05.58	w.e. 11.11.67	SPJ/BIR	03.68	03.68	G.H.Campbell, Airdrie
92167	09.05.58	w.e. 29.06.68	CNF	10.68	11.68	G.H.Campbell, Airdrie. Cut up at Clayton & Davie, Dunston, Gateshead
92168	20.12.57	w.e. 27.06.65	DON	10.65	11.65	T.W.Ward, Beighton, Sheffield
92169	27.12.57	w.e. 31.05.64	DON	01.65	01.65	T.W.Ward, Killamarsh
92170	31.12.57	w.e. 31.05.64	DON	01.65	01.65	T.W.Ward, Killamarsh
92171	01.02.58	w.e. 31.05.64	NED	03.65	03.65	T.W.Ward, Killamarsh
92172	29.01.58	w.e. 17.04.66	DON	07.66	07.66	W.George, Station Steel, Wath
92173	10.02.58	w.e. 06.03.66	DON	05.66	05.66	T.W.Ward, Killamarsh
92174	10.02.58	w.e. 12.12.65	DON	05.66	05.66	T.W.Ward, Killamarsh
92175	21.02.58	w.e. 31.05.64	DON	02.65	02.65	T.W.Ward, Killamarsh
92176	04.03.58	w.e. 31.05.64	NED	03.65	03.65	T.W.Ward, Killamarsh
92177	12.03.58	w.e. 31.05.64	CRK	08.64	08.64	Crewe Works
92178	28.09.57	03.10.65	LGJ	12.65	12.65	T.W.Ward, Killamarsh
92179	07.10.57	14.11.65	COL	02.66	05.66	Hughes Bolckow, Blyth
92180	08.11.57	w.e. 11.04.65	LGJ	06.65	07.65	J.Cashmore, Great Bridge
92181	22.11.57	w.e. 21.02.65	NED	05.65	07.65	G.Cohen, Kettering
92182	03.12.57	w.e. 17.04.66	DON	07.66	07.66	W.George, Station Steel, Wath
92183	20.12.57	w.e. 03.04.66	DON	07.66	07.66	W.George, Station Steel, Wath
92184	10.01.58	21.02.65	IMM	04.65	06.65	A.Draper, Hull
92185	15.01.58	w.e. 21.02.65	IMM	05.65	05.65	A.Draper, Hull
92186	27.01.58	w.e. 29.08.65	LGJ	02.66	02.66	A.Draper, Hull
92187	12.02.58	w.e. 21.02.65	COL	04.65	05.65	A.Draper, Hull
92188	27.02.58	w.e. 21.02.65	COL	04.65	05.65	A.Draper, Hull
92189	14.03.58	19.12.65	COL	03.66	04.66	T.W.Ward, Beighton, Sheffield

Loco	To Traffic	Withdrawn	Storage Location	Sold	Cut up	Disposal
92190	28.03.58	w.e. 10.10.65	DON	01.66	01.66	T.W.Ward, Beighton, Sheffield
92191	15.04.58	19.12.65	COL	03.66	04.66	T.W.Ward, Beighton, Sheffield
92192	01.05.58	w.e. 21.02.65	DON	04.65	05.65	T.W.Ward, Beighton, Sheffield
92193	23.05.58	w.e. 13.06.65	IMM	09.65	11.65	A.Draper, Hull
92194	10.06.58	w.e. 05.12.65	IMM	03.66	03.66	Arnott Young, Parkgate (see 3)
92195	27.06.58	w.e. 09.05.65	LGJ	09.65	11.65	A.Draper, Hull
92196	15.08.58	w.e. 06.12.64	IMM	01.66	01.66	T.W.Ward, Beighton, Sheffield
92197	11.09.58	w.e. 19.09.65	IMM	12.65	01.66	T.W.Ward, Beighton, Sheffield
92198	06.10.58	w.e. 02.08.64	FRD	05.65	06.65	T.W.Ward, Beighton, Sheffield
92199	29.10.58	w.e. 02.08.64	FRD	05.65	06.65	T.W.Ward, Beighton, Sheffield
92200	18.11.58	w.e. 03.10.65	LGJ	12.65	12.65	T.W.Ward, Killamarsh
92201	05.12.58	w.e. 27.03.66	DON	07.66	07.66	W.George, Station Steel, Wath
92202	27.12.58	w.e. 19.12.65	IMM	02.66	03.66	T.W.Ward, Beighton, Sheffield
92203	06.04.59	w.e. 11.11.67	CRS	11.67	-	Sold to David Shepherd, Esq. Preserved. Preent location: Gloucestershire Warwickshire Railway
92204	21.04.59	w.e. 09.12.67	SPJ	02.68	03.68	T.W.Ward, Beighton, Sheffield
92205	01.05.59	w.e. 08.06.67	WAK	01.68	01.68	A.Draper, Hull
92206	06.05.59	w.e. 09.05.67	WAK	08.67	09.67	Arnott Young, Parkgate
92207	01.06.59	26.12.64	NEJ/BAR	02.65	-	Woodham. Bros., Barry. Preserved. Undergoing restoration at Shillingstone station, North Dorset
92208	11.06.59	w.e. 28.11.67	CKR	02.68	02.68	J.McWilliam, Shettleston
92209	26.06.59	31.12.65	BBR	02.66	03.66	J.Cashmore, Newport
92210	07.08.59	06.11.64	NEJ	02.65	03.65	J.Buttigieg, Newport
92211	08.09.59	w.e. 22.05.67	WAK	12.67	12.67	A.Draper, Hull
92212	22.09.59	w.e. 06.01.68	BAR	02.68	-	Woodham Bros., Barry. Preserved. Present location Ropley depot Mid-Hants. Railway
92213	22.10.59	w.e. 05.11.66	CKR	01.67	02.67	J.McWilliam, Shettleston
92214	30.10.59	09.08.65	STJ/BAR	09.65	-	Woodham Bros., Barry. Preserved. Present location, East Lancashire Railway Bury
92215	17.11.59	08.06.67	WAK	01.68	02.68	A.Draper, Hull
92216	01.12.59	26.10.65	OXF	12.65	04.66	J.Cashmore, Newport
92217	22.12.59	w.e. 30.07.66	TYS	08.66	10.66	A.Draper, Hull
92218	18.01.60	w.e. 04.05.68	PAT	07.68	07.68	Arnott Young, Parkgate
92219	27.01.60	09.08.65	GHR/BAR	09.65	-	Woodham Bros., Barry Preserved at Midland Railway Centre, Butterley, Derbyshire
92220	25.03.60	26.03.65	STJ/PPR CED/PRP	-	-	Preserved, National Collection, NRM York
92221	30.05.58	10.05.65	YRK	07.65	09.65	Hughes Bolckow, Blyth
92222	02.06.58	26.03.65	STL	06.65	07.65	J.Cashmore, Newport
92223 †	06.06.58	w.e. 13.04.68	CNF	09.68	09.68	Arnott Young, Dinsdale
92224	16.06.58	w.e. 30.09.67	CKR	04.68	06.68	J.McWilliam, Shettleston
92225	20.06.58	02.07.65	NEJ	08.65	09.65	J.Cashmore, Newport
92226	26.06.58	10.09.65	STJ	11.65	02.66	J.Cashmore, Newport
92227	03.07.58	w.e. 04.11.67	SPJ	01.68	01.68	T.W.Ward, Beighton, Sheffield
92228	12.07.58	w.e. 28.02.67	SPJ	05.67	06.67	T.W.Ward, Beighton, Sheffield
92229	18.07.58	06.11.64	STJ	02.65	02.65	Cox & Danks, Park Royal, North Acton
92230	01.08.58	31.12.65	NEJ	03.66	07.66	J.Cashmore, Newport
92231	01.08.58	w.e. 17.11.66	YRK	02.67	04.67	A.Draper, Hull
92232	06.08.58	26.12.64	CED	02.65	03.65	Woodham Bros., Barry
92233	11.08.58	w.e. 03.02.68	SPJ	08.68	08.68	T.W.Ward, Beighton, Sheffield
92234	19.08.58	w.e. 11.11.67	BIR/SPJ	02.68	02.68	G.H.Campbell, Airdrie
92235	22.08.58	18.11.65	OXF	12.65	04.66	J.Cashmore, Newport
92236	04.09.58	21.04.65	SDN	07.65	10.65	R.&S. Hayes, Bridgend
92237	09.09.58	10.09.65	NEJ	10.65	11.65	J.Cashmore, Newport
92238	22.09.58	10.09.65	STJ	10.65	12.65	T.W.Ward, Briton Ferry (see 4)
92239	25.09.58	17.11.66	YRK	02.67	04.67	A.Draper, Hull
92240	01.10.58	06.08.65	BAR	09.65	-	Woodham Bros., Barry Preserved on Bluebell Railway, East Sussex
92241	06.10.58	02.07.65	STL	09.65	12.65	J.Cashmore, Newport
92242	13.10.58	21.05.65	STJ	06.65	08.65	J.Cashmore, Newport
92243	21.10.58	01.01.66	BGP	03.66	04.66	J.Cashmore, Newport
92244	28.10.58	31.12.65	GHR	03.66	07.66	J.Cashmore, Newport

Loco	To Traffic	Withdrawn	Storage Location	Sold	Cut up	Disposal
92245	04.11.58	26.12.64	STL/BAR	02.65	-	Woodham Bros., Barry Preserved on Vale of Glamorgan Railway at Barry Island
92246	20.11.58	31.12.65	TYS/GHR	02.66	04.66	J.Cashmore, Newport
92247	02.12.58	w.e. 08.10.66	BIR	01.67	04.67	A.Draper, Hull
92248	05.12.58	21.05.65	CED	06.65	08.65	J.Cashmore, Newport
92249	10.12.58	w.e. 04.05.68	SPJ	08.68	09.68	Arnott Young, Parkgate
92250	16.12.58	31.12.65	GHR	03.66	07.66	J.Cashmore, Newport

Key **w.e.**: week ending; † Withdrawn by WR, 07.02.64; reinstated by LMR, ??.05.64

1. 92017 and 92125 were sent in error to Carmyle; redirected to Parkgate in April 1968.
2. 92110 also reported as sold to Arnott Young, Parkgate on same date; G.H.Campbell seems more likely.
3. 92194 also reported as sold to M.Bauer, Cleveland Dockyard, Middlesbrough on same date; Arnott Young seems more likely. Reported stored at GHR (12.65-01.66) which seems unlikely.
4. 92238 also reported as sold to J. Cashmore, Newport on same date; T.W.Ward seems more likely.

Notes: 92002/22-6/47/79/82/4/6, 92102/52/62/3/6 were moved from Speke Junction to Carlisle Kingmoor at the rate of four engines per day on 27.02.68, 28.02.68, 29.02.68 and 01.03.68, all being en route to G.H. Campbell, Airdrie.

It should be noted that the locations of the preserved 9Fs will be subject to change.

Key to Storage Locations

BAR	Barry Docks
BBR	Bristol Barrow Road
BGP	Bath Green Park
BIR	Birkenhead
CED	Cardiff East Dock
CKR	Carlisle Kingmoor
CNF	Carnforth
COL	Colwick
CRK	Crewe Works
CRS	Crewe South
DON	Doncaster
EDH	Edge Hill
FRD	Frodingham
GHR	Gloucester Horton Road
IMM	Immingham
KBY	Kirkby-in-Ashfield
LGJ	Langwith Junction
NED	New England
NEH	Newton Heath
NEJ	Newport Ebbw Junction
OXF	Oxford
PAT	Patricroft
PPR	Pontypool Road
PRP	Preston Park
SAL	Saltley
SCH	Shrewsbury Coton Hill
SCO	Shrewsbury Coleham
SDN	Swindon
SPJ	Speke Junction
STJ	Severn Tunnel Junction
STL	Southall
TND	Tyne Dock
TRP	Trafford Park
TYS	Tyseley
YRK	York
WAK	Wakefield
WAR	Warrington
WOR	Workington

13. Preservation

Nine members of the 9Fs have survived into preservation in various stages of activity; these are:

92134 92203 92207 92212 92214
92219 92220 92240 92245

Of these locomotives, one (92203) was purchased directly from BR by a private individual, one (92220) was transferred to the newly formed National Railway Museum and seven were purchased from Woodham Bros. In common with other preserved BR Standard steam locomotives, these spent more time in the scrapyard at Barry and undergoing restoration or in preservation than working on BR. Their present condition ranges from little more than a partially assembled collection of components to locomotives that are or have been certified for main line running on Network Rail and its predecessors. However, it now appears unlikely that any of the 9Fs will return to the mainline because of potential problems with check rails and high speed crossovers.

The history of each engine in preservation is given as follows.

92134

History since withdrawal

After withdrawal from service on 6th December 1966 this locomotive was sold to Woodham Bros. at Barry in May 1967 as part of a lot of five locomotives, Hughes-Fowler Crab 2-6-0s 42765 and 42859, Jinty 0-6-0T 47324 and 9Fs 92085 and 92134. These were despatched to Barry via Shrewsbury in June 1967.

Towards the end of 1979, a small group of North Yorkshire Moors Railway members began to consider the possibility of purchasing a large freight locomotive from Barry. Two members inspected the 9Fs at Barry in early 1980 and settled on 92134 as the best on hand.

A rumour that Mr. Dai Woodham had started to cut up locomotives spurred the group, now formed as a limited company, into action and the purchase was completed on 30th June 1980 at a cost of £9,000 plus VAT. No tender was available for the group to buy at that time. As part of the purchase, as many parts as possible were assembled from the other locomotives in the yard and taken to the NYMR. Transportation of the locomotive itself from Barry to the NYMR was to have taken place commencing on 22nd September 1980 at a cost of £1,950 plus VAT. However, the discovery that 92134 was fitted with blue asbestos boiler and cylinder lagging delayed transportation until after this had been removed by a specialist firm on 3rd and 4th December 1980 at a cost of £300.

92134 left Barry on 9th December 1980 and arrived at Pickering late on Friday 12th having travelled by road at a maximum speed of 12mph. It was the 116th locomotive to leave Barry scrapyard.

Progress with the restoration at the NYMR was slower than expected for various reasons. As many of those involved in the locomotive's restoration lived in Essex, it was decided to move 92134 to Shipyard Services at Brightlingsea for the restoration to continue. The engine left Pickering on 28th February 1984 and arrived at Brightlingsea on 1st March 1984. It was intended to use volunteer labour supplemented by contracting certain work to Shipyard Services and to complete the restoration in three years.

It appeared then that the available finance and volunteer manpower resources had become increasingly unequal to the task of restoration and eventually the project ground to a halt. 92134 had been partly dismantled whilst at NYMR and other components were dismantled at Brightlingsea. Inevitably once this had happened and with the passage of the years and general disinterest in the locomotive's fate, parts went missing. The locomotive had spent nearly 14 years in the sea air at Barry and was to spend another 15 years beside the sea at Brightlingsea. The salt air took its toll. At one point, the cab blew into the sea during a storm and had to be rescued. The owner of the yard came very close on a number of occasions to cutting up the remains of 92134 as space within the yard had become needed for other work.

The locomotive continued to languish at Brightlingsea until rescued by its present owners, Howard and Heather Self. Howard explains "I had always been interested in steam locomotives thanks to childhood years watching long trains of 16ton mineral wagons struggling up the 1 in 80 at the bottom of our garden in Manchester and blackening my mother's washing. Enthusiasm waned with adult preoccupations of career and other hobbies but a move to Macclesfield and my young son's attraction to Thomas rekindled my own interest and led to a visit to the Churnet Valley Railway in 1998. An offer to help was swiftly taken up and appointments as Company Secretary and, later, Director followed. I happened to mention to the Chairman in an unguarded moment that if they were ever forming a syndicate to purchase another steam locomotive, I would be interested. Such are the machinations of the steam world that two weeks later I was informed that a locomotive was available but not a syndicate! My wife and I took a deep breath and after my inspection of the 'kit of parts' and good advice from a number of people, decided to buy it". They bought 92134 in April 1999. The terms of the purchase agreement prevent the identity of the vendor being disclosed.

Initially, the frames, wheel sets and associated components went to Ian Riley at Bury, the boiler to the Churnet Valley Railway at Cheddleton and the remaining bits to Howard's barn. On completion of the contract with Ian Riley, the locomotive was moved to the LNWR Works at Crewe for the next stage of the restoration.

Since 92134 moved to Crewe, progress has been steady and very satisfactory. Steve Latham and Philip Oldfield are both well known in the heritage world and their contacts and knowledge have enabled the owners to obtain original components for the project and even trace and recover a number of items that had gone missing from the locomotive long ago. One member of the original preservation group was found to have a storeroom full of original components from 92134 which he had been keeping safely until restoration should start again.

In May 2003, 92134 returned to the erecting shop where it was built when it appeared as part of the Crewe Works open weekend. Since then much work has been done, including the completion of the motion and the reassembly and refitting of the pony truck. Work continues on the fabrication of the boiler crinolines and cladding.

92134 is the only single chimney example of the class to be preserved.

Detail Modifications

Carriage warming apparatus will be installed to enable 92134 to work passenger trains in the winter. Two live steam injectors will be fitted instead of one live and one exhaust. For the sort of work that 92134 will be doing on preserved railways, this is a more satisfactory arrangement. Coil springs will be used for the side control springs of the pony truck owing to the impossibility of obtaining replicas of the originals.

Tender Number and Type

The Engine Record Card shows that the locomotive had BR1C tender No. 1169 at its date of withdrawal (6th December 1966). However, this is recorded as being transferred to 92086 on 15th January 1967. While it is not clear which tender was transferred to 92134 in exchange (if any), it is recorded that "...a BR1C tender (No. 1344) was acquired [for 71000 *Duke of Gloucester*] instead which had been with 92134..." (Volume 1 of this series p.147). Certainly no tender was included in the purchase from Woodham Bros. as none was available at the time. However, new frames were obtained by the original purchasers and these and the wheel sets are available for future use.

Boiler Number

The group that purchased 92134 from Barry was of the opinion that it still had its original boiler, No. 1681, and this is supported by examinations of the Engine Record Cards and Engine History Sheets.

Present Location

92134 is at the LNWR Co., Crewe, about half a mile from where it was built.

Status

92134 is undergoing restoration from Barry scrapyard condition to preserved railway running order.

There are no plans to restore the locomotive to main line running order, although it is hoped that it will enter service on the Churnet Valley Railway.

92203

History since withdrawal

In early 1967, David Shepherd, inspired by the people raising funds to purchase rebuilt Merchant Navy Pacific 35028 *Clan Line*, decided that he would buy a steam locomotive of his own. Having decided to purchase a BR Standard Class 4 4-6-0 he chose 75029 on the advice of a friend at Guildford MPD. A contact at Longmoor agreed that he could stable the locomotive on the railway system there.

Before this purchase was completed, David decided to buy a 9F and was fortunate to obtain 92203 which was withdrawn from Birkenhead MPD after having been overhauled and painted specially for the operation of the last steam-hauled train of iron ore from Birkenhead Docks to John Summers Steel Works at Shotton on 6th November 1967. Luckily, 92203 was also able to be accommodated at Longmoor.

Through the good offices of Mr. D. C. R. (Bob) Mackmurdie, then Divisional Operating Superintendent at Stoke-on-Trent (and one time fireman at Kings Cross), David was put in touch with the Scrap Sales Controller at Derby and the purchase of both locomotives was completed. These two locomotives cost a total of £5,200 of which 92203 represented £3,000. A bulk purchase facilitated by the Association of Railway Preservation Societies included in addition to 75029 and 92203, rebuilt Merchant Navy Pacific 35028 *Clan Line*, unrebuilt West Country light Pacific 34023 *Blackmore Vale* and a number of other smaller locomotives and coaches.

By November 1967, 75029 and 92203 were stabled at Crewe South MPD 'for collection' by their new owner. The locomotives were handed over by Mr. George Dow, Divisional Manager, Stoke-on-Trent, at a small ceremony in the depot. After a long battle with various organisations within BR, it was agreed that the two locomotives would be allowed to travel from Crewe to the Longmoor Military Railway under their own power. The journey took place during the weekend of Saturday/Sunday 6th/7th April 1968 with an overnight stay at Cricklewood MPD.

At Longmoor, 75029 and 92203 joined the last two steam locomotives in working order (WD 2-10-0 600 *Gordon* and 0-6-0 196) and were later joined by *Clan Line, Blackmore Vale* and Ivatt Class 2 2-6-2T 41298. During the next few months, David Shepherd and the owners of the other locomotives managed to create servicing and maintenance facilities on part of the site that was now surplus to Army requirements.

92203 was named *Black Prince* by General Errol Lonsdale at an Army open day in June 1968 and distinguished itself by taking over a special train from Waterloo at Liss and working the fourteen-coach load up the bank to Longmoor Downs. On being asked why he chose the name, David said "I like it and it suits the engine". The original pair of nameplates made at Swindon and used at the ceremony were not up to standard and a fresh set replaced these later. While at Longmoor, *Black Prince* was lined out in red but soon reverted to its original unlined black.

On the closure of the Longmoor Military Railway in October 1969, it became necessary to find other accommodation for 92203 and its stablemates. The military authorities gave notice to the locomotives' owners to vacate the site by the end of March 1970 but offered a lease on an alternative site at Liss. This then became *Black Prince's* next home. Unfortunately, a small number of local residents strongly opposed the operation of the site at Liss and plans to purchase the leased site had to be abandoned. Just a few weeks before departure from the Longmoor area, *Black Prince* featured in the film *Young Winston*, the story of the early life of Sir Winston Churchill. For this, it was disguised as a South African locomotive by removing the smoke deflectors, superimposing a fibreglass chimney over its own, fitting an imitation dome on top of the boiler and the Lickey banker's headlamp to the smokebox door. The letters S.A.R. were stuck to the tender sides. Finally it was renumbered by taping over the '9' and the '3'.

The next home for 92203 was to be on a rented siding at Eastleigh. On Sunday 24th October 1971, *Black Prince,* 75029 and the accompanying rolling stock were hauled there by a Cl.47. While attention was sometimes given inside the diesel depot, a siding in the open was not an ideal stabling point in the long term. Occasional steaming in the depot area was permitted by BR. Then, on Sunday 13th May 1973, 92203 was permitted to work two well filled nine-coach trips to Romsey and back. Next came a Wirral Railway Circle charter train on Saturday 19th May 1973 which 92203 worked from Oxford to Hereford for the Bulmer's 'Cider Festival'.

While arrangements at Eastleigh continued to be amicable,

Figure 229
The major SVR embankment slip in 1983, immediately south of the new Bridgnorth by-pass bridge, was repaired with commendable speed by the date of the photograph, 18th May. The first trains over it were hauled by the SVR's distinguished visitor, 92220 *Evening Star*. It is seen here coming over with the third and last train of the day, the 3.15pm to Bewdley. *(Hugh Ballantyne)*

David Shepherd was looking for a more permanent home for his locomotives. Having decided that the site would have to be within two hours' drive of his home in Godalming, Surrey, he examined a number of sites including Ludgershall, the Meon Valley Line and Maiden Newton before a friend suggested Cranmore on the East Somerset Line which had closed to passenger traffic on 9th September 1963, eight years before David and his friends first visited the site.

After much work had been done to turn Cranmore into the home of the East Somerset Railway, 92203 left Eastleigh under its own steam, conveying Maunsell Schools 4-4-0 30928 *Stowe* and a number of other vehicles as 8Z02, 5.55pm Eastleigh depot to Cranmore on Saturday 17th November 1973, followed by 75029 with five preserved coaches.

In April 1974, *Black Prince* worked a train of loaded stone wagons totalling an estimated 1,800 tons out of Foster Yeoman's quarry at Merehead. In the following year on 20th June, a footplate ride was given to a Royal visitor when HRH Prince Bernhard of the Netherlands officially opened the East Somerset Railway. Later the same year, 92203 worked from and to Westbury with a 15-coach charter train from Bristol to Eastleigh.

In the summer of 1979, the locomotive was withdrawn from service for a boiler overhaul. After some dispute between the Western and Southern Regions as to whether such a movement could be permitted, 92203 was towed to Marchwood Army depot near Southampton where the necessary work was carried out by staff from Husband's Shipyard before the engine returned to Cranmore.

In September 1982, Foster Yeoman invited *Black Prince* to repeat its trial of strength from April 1974 at a staff open day. On this occasion, a train of 2,178 tons gross was successfully worked out of the terminal. This was claimed to be the greatest weight ever hauled in the United Kingdom by a single steam locomotive.

92203 continued working on the East Somerset Railway until 1991 after which it became widely travelled with visits to the East Lancashire Railway, Peak Rail, Mid-Hants Railway, Great Central Railway, Swanage Railway, Shotton Steel Works, Llangollen Railway, Foster Yeoman's quarry at Merehead and the Gloucestershire-Warwickshire Railway.

From December 2001 to May 2004, 92203 underwent a major overhaul at the Flour Mill, Bream, Gloucestershire. When this was completed, the engine left by road for RailFest 2004 at the National Railway Museum, York. Here it was in light steam (though stationary) for nine consecutive days. It then worked on the Churnet Valley Railway during June and July 2004 before moving on to the Gloucestershire-Warwickshire Railway again on 25th August for the GWR's "Harvest Festival of Steam" on 11th-12th September 2004. The GWR formally 'relaunched' *Black Prince* at a public ceremony on Monday 18th October 2004 in the presence of David Shepherd and television personality Alan Titchmarsh.

Prior to these two events it had become evident that all ten driving wheels needed re-tyring so the locomotive relocated again, this time to Ian Riley's workshops at Bury. On the Gloucestershire-Warwickshire website, David Shepherd was quoted as saying: "This is clearly disappointing and I wish we had fully appreciated the extent of the wear, particularly on the rear set of driving wheels before the overhaul. But I think the right decision has been reached. When work is completed, the wheels will be fit for many thousands of miles' running. Those wheels will carry *Black Prince* forward over many years to come, for future generations to enjoy".

Following this work, 92203 returned to the G-WR, made short visits to the Mid-Hants and West Somerset and North Norfolk Railways and is now expected to stay on the G-WR for the foreseeable future. However, a short visit to Foster Yeoman's Tor Works and the East Somerset Railway is planned for June/July 2008. At present, there is no plan to obtain certification for operation on Network Rail.

Detail Modifications
Carriage warming apparatus was fitted by the East Lancashire and Mid-Hants Railways in the early 1990s.

Tender Number and Type
BR1G 1510, fitted from new. This tender was modified by fitting with rear footsteps at Old Oak Common, August 1961, see Section 9.

Boiler Number
No. 1670, fitted at Crewe Works, 31st December 1966.

Present Location
Gloucestershire-Warwickshire Railway.

92207
History since withdrawal
After withdrawal from service on 26th December 1964, this locomotive was sold to Woodham Bros. on 11th February 1965 and was moved to Barry almost immediately. In 1986, it was purchased by Keith Bottomley and transported by road to the East Lancashire Railway on 22nd October 1986 in a move sponsored by Beatties, the model railway and toy retailers. Prior to this, some cosmetic restoration was carried out including the refitting of smoke deflectors. On the day before the move, 92207 was named *Morning Star* by Sir Raymond Gower, the then MP for the Vale of Glamorgan. The locomotive remained intact on the ELR until 1990 when dismantling commenced.

In 2003, 92207 was moved to Bryn Engineering, Wigan, for re-wheeling and completion of valves and cylinders. In December 2005, the locomotive was moved again, this time to Shillingstone station in Dorset to allow work to continue. New parts have been or will be made as necessary and the restoration is being carried out to allow eventual main line running.

Detail Modifications
The work is planned to include the eventual fitting of air braking, TPWS and flange lubrication.

Tender Number and Type
No tender was available at Barry so a completely new BR1G tender will be built and numbered 1514 to accord with the tender carried throughout its working life.

Boiler Number
92207 retained boiler no. 1882 from new.

Present Location
Shillingstone station, north Dorset.

Present Owner
The 92207 Railway Company Ltd.

92212
History since withdrawal
This locomotive survived almost until the end of steam on BR, being withdrawn from service in P.01/68 and subsequently sold to Woodham Bros. at Barry. It was purchased from Woodham's together with a separate Type BR1F tender by the 92212 Locomotive Company Ltd. and delivered to the Great Central Railway at Quorn on 29th September 1979; it returned to traffic on 27th September 1996.

92212 performed regularly on the Great Central Railway as well as visiting the Mid-Hants Railway in July 1998 and being a star attraction with 92203 at Foster Yeoman's 75th anniversary in June 1998. In September 1999, 92212 pulled what was claimed to be the longest freight train on a preserved railway on the GCR for a photographers' special.

Since then the locomotive has been working on the ELR, GCR, West Somerset Railway, Severn Valley Railway and from 2002 the Mid-Hants Railway. Between December 2003 and September 2004, wheels were removed and re-tyred on normal out of service days, with other major work being carried out at Ropley from March to June 2005.

Following an Extraordinary General Meeting at the Ramada Loughborough Hotel on 7th January 2006, 92212 was sold to Locomotive Services Ltd. and the 92212 Locomotive Company was then wound up.

Detail Modifications
92212 is now fitted with carriage warming apparatus, speedometer and through piping for air braking; the plan is also to fit TPWS.

Tender Number and Type
The tender is plated as BR1F 1161 and dated 1954. As the original tender was not available, this was purchased from Woodham Bros. at the same time as the engine.

Boiler Number
The boiler carried is no. 1901, fitted to this locomotive in September 1965 as deduced from the official record.

Present Location
Ropley depot, Mid-Hants Railway.

Status
Operational.

Present Owner
Locomotive Services Ltd.

92214
History since withdrawal
92214 was condemned on 9th August 1965 and remained in store at Severn Tunnel Junction MPD (86E) until October

1965, having been sold to Woodham Bros. Barry on 6th September.

The locomotive and tender were purchased on 6th March 1980 (Invoice No. 1) for the sum of £9,000 plus 15% VAT from Woodham's for preservation by the Peak 9F Loco Co. Ltd. The locomotive moved to Buxton in Derbyshire on 11th December 1980; it was the 117th to leave Barry. 92214 was subsequently moved to the Midland Railway Centre at Butterley, Derbyshire. In July 1991, ownership reverted to and is held in trust by The 9F Locomotive Charitable Trust Company.

92214 was first re-steamed in public on 4th July 2003 at Butterley. Later, in September 2004, it passed its 14-month boiler examination and was transported to the West Somerset Railway to take part in their S&D Central 150 celebrations and then their 'Autumn Gala'. Next it was transported by road to Staveley Barrow Hill roundhouse to take part in the 9th-10th October steam event there and returned to Swanwick on 20th-21st October 2004.

After working on the Midland Railway on 23rd-24th and 30th-31st October 2004, 92214 was withdrawn for a number of items to receive attention during the winter. These included boiler washout, replacing a broken driving axle spring, rebushing of a brake crossbeam, replacement of the tender-engine injector water supply hoses, cross-drilling of the driving axle and pony truck underkeep drain plugs (to make checking for water in the axle oil baths easier) bushing of both mechanical lubricator drive rods and replacement of part of the steam chest pressure gauge piping. The smokebox and firebox/grate were cleaned and both tubeplates wire-brushed and oil-sprayed. All motion was sprayed with rust preventative.

After completion of this work, 92214 was transported by road from Butterley to the East Lancashire Railway in Bury on 30th-31st March 2005 and is now in service on that railway.

Detail Modifications

Carriage warming apparatus is now fitted, with the pressure gauge mounted above the boiler pressure gauge on the fireman's side of the firebox. Similarly the steam valve is mounted on the fireman's side of the cab backhead. An electrically driven speedometer is fitted next to the steam chest pressure gauge on the driver's side; the wiring for the speedometer is taken from the driver's side leading Timken axlebox on the tender. A mechanically driven mileometer is fitted to the leading Timken axlebox cover on the fireman's side of the tender.

Other modifications include the fitting of an ashpan spray pipe. Here the feed is taken via a valve in the cab from the inside live steam injector output pipe; the feed to the ashpan spray is also taken to the coal spray in the tender. Western Region ATC apparatus is mounted on the driver's control pedestal but is non-operational.

Tender Number and Type

92214 carries BR1G tender no. 1519.

Boiler Number

The boiler no. is 1889, fitted from new.

Present Location

East Lancashire Railway, Bury.

Present Owner

The 9F Locomotive Charitable Trust Company.

92219

History since withdrawal

92219 was condemned on 9th August 1965. It was quickly sold to Woodham Bros. at Barry on 6th September and moved there later that year. The engine (only) was purchased on 6th February 1984 (Invoice no. 073) for the sum of £9,000 plus 15% VAT from Woodham's by the Peak Railway 9F Loco Co. Ltd. In June 1985, it was moved to the Peak Rail site at Buxton for cosmetic restoration, having been in bad condition on its purchase. It was then the 163rd locomotive to leave Barry after just a few months short of twenty years. It was subsequently moved in 1990 to the Midland Railway Centre at Butterley, Derbyshire. In July 1991, ownership reverted to and is held in trust by The 9F Locomotive Charitable Trust Company.

Tender Number and Type

No tender was purchased with 92219.

Boiler Number

Boiler no. 1894 remains on the engine as fitted from new.

Present Location

Swanwick Junction at the Midland Railway Centre, Butterley, Derbyshire.

Status

In store.

Steps to return to service

When 92219 was moved to Butterley, it was decided that no further restoration work would be carried out as it was originally purchased to provide a spare boiler for 92214.

Present Owner

The 9F Locomotive Charitable Trust Company.

92220 *Evening Star*

History since withdrawal

Evening Star was unique in that it was designated for preservation from the day it was built. However, this did not guarantee it an easy transition into the lovingly maintained specimen that it is today.

The withdrawal of 92220 on 26th March 1965 was precipitated by frontal damage after a collision with buffer stops. John Scholes, the Curator of Historical Relics at that time was not prepared to accept the locomotive in this condition and BR (WR) was not prepared to meet the cost of £1,029 to carry out the necessary repairs. During these discussions, it was offered to Swindon Corporation who turned it down. Consideration was then given to preserving instead a similar but undamaged example of the class. It was pointed out that *Evening Star's* importance was based on its status as the last steam locomotive built for BR as well as being a representative of a class of locomotive designed and built since nationalisation that had proved successful. However, the General Manager of the WR was adamant that he had no further need for the locomotive in its damaged state but suggested it might be worth repairing if another region would like to have it. At this stage, negotiations commenced with a

Figure 230
After a surprise stop at Ribblehead, the "Cumbrian Mountain Express" leaves with 92220 *Evening Star* in charge. The date is Easter Monday, 23rd April 1984 and judging by the shirt sleeves, 'global warming' is already making its presence felt.
(Rodney Lissenden)

Mr. Snowden, a 20 year old chef from Southall, on behalf of the GWR Trust but he was unable to raise the necessary £4,000 to finance the purchase. Further discussions took place with Captain Peter Manisty of the Association of Railway Preservation Societies to see if any other prospective purchaser could be found. Upon cancellation of the proposed sale to Mr. Snowden, the locomotive was replaced on the 'Preservation List'. During these discussions the unwanted 92220 was in store in the open at Pontypool Road. At the end of October it was allegedly moved to Radyr to be stored under cover.

Meanwhile a Mr. J. R. Green of Cooden, Sussex, had expressed his interest in purchasing the locomotive for preservation and Messrs Scholes and Green examined it at Crewe Works on 3rd November 1966 as part of the negotiations for purchase by the latter. It was made clear to Mr. Green that the BRB would not allow this or any other restored locomotive to run on BR lines.

By this time, the cost of purchase and repair was being quoted as £14,000. Negotiations were very protracted and had still not been concluded in 1968. Nevertheless, on the strength of these discussions, British Railways Workshops were persuaded to carry out repairs and restoration at Crewe Works, apparently without any formal authority for the expenditure of around £10,000. The complete repainting was carried out exactly to the original specification of the GWR-style lined passenger green and the copper cap was replaced on the chimney. On completion of this work, *Evening Star* was moved on 3rd January 1968 to the former Pullman Car Company's Works at Preston Park, Brighton, for storage pending purchase by Mr. Green. At this stage, Mr. Green signified his agreement to the proposed contract but wanted to inspect the locomotive again and later yet again. By now the Chief Legal Adviser and Solicitor to the BRB had expressed a view that this was "yet again another piece of procrastination on Mr. Green's part" but accepted that the request was reasonable. Consequently *Evening Star* was inspected again on 7th February 1969 and found to be in excellent condition, much to Mr. Green's surprise. However, a subsequent examination that year showed that rust had started to appear in a number of places.

At this stage, a number of USA prospects, including the Illinois Railway Museum, had shown interest. By now the view was being voiced that Mr. Green was unlikely to produce any money in the near future and that the opportunity should be taken to accept such an offer. Indeed, consideration was again given to locating another 9F for exhibition in the National Collection to allow *Evening Star* to be sold to the USA. After due deliberation, it was considered that none was available, those of the class remaining at Barry presumably being regarded as unsuitable.

Mr. Green was now seeking assurances that the deterioration caused by the unheated storage at Preston Park would be rectified at no cost to himself. Correspondence between the Workshops Division and the Curator of Historical Relics now became rather acrimonious. The Workshops Division maintained that the deterioration was a result of storage in unheated accommodation while Mr. Scholes demonstrated that all precautions as specified earlier by the division had been scrupulously carried out.

At the end of November, on the recommendation of the Chief Legal Adviser and Solicitor, Mr. Green was advised that unless he withdrew his latest set of suggested amendments to the draft agreement, some of which would amend clauses he had himself previously suggested, and paid the sum of £9,160, the British Railways Board would not take the deal any further. This brought a threat from Mr. Green that he would seek an injunction against the Board.

Despite the differences between British Railways Engineering Limited (as the Workshops Division had now become), and the Curator of Historical Relics, the repairs to *Evening Star's* paint work were completed (at Preston Park) by BREL staff on 17th February 1970. In the same month however, the Chief Legal Adviser and Solicitor advised that the locomotive was covered by Section 144(7) of the Transport Act of 1968 as it had been designated for "a collection maintained or proposed to be maintained by the Secretary of State". This effectively gave the Board grounds to withdraw from the negotiations with Mr. Green. On 28th April, 1970, the Chief Legal Adviser and Solicitor (CLA&S) advised Mr. Green's solicitor that "the Department of Education and Science had indicated that this locomotive is of sufficient interest to warrant preservation in a collection to be maintained or proposed to be maintained by that department and that by virtue of Section 144(7) of the Transport Act of 1968, the Board is not able to dispose of the locomotive without first offering it to the department". The department had indicated that it would not like *Evening Star* transferred to Mr. Green under the terms of the draft agreement as this would entitle him to withdraw the locomotive and move it elsewhere at the museum's expense if certain standards of maintenance were not observed. The CLA & S's letter went on to state that the BRB was not able to conclude the agreement with Mr. Green. The latter's solicitor responded that his client did not accept the situation and would seek further legal advice. However, nothing was heard from Mr. Green until September 1975 when he wrote to the Board asking for its proposals for dealing with the matter, "as it has not been formally settled". He followed this up with a writ in October 1975 but this does not appear to have been progressed. The saga did not quite finish here, as in 1982, a solicitor acting for Mr. Green's estate said that as Mr. Green was now deceased, the proceedings would be discontinued!

The delays, whether deliberate or not, resulted in 92220 being saved from the scrap heap until it passed from the British Railways Collection to the newly formed National Railway Museum.

Following an approach in April 1973 by the Rt. Revd. Eric Treacy, Bishop of Wakefield, in his capacity as President of the Keighley & Worth Valley Railway, it was agreed that *Evening Star* should go to that railway on loan until the opening of the National Railway Museum at York. The journey was scheduled to start on Thursday evening, 31st May 1973 when 92220 was to be shunted from the Old Pullman Car Shops at Preston Park to Brighton (Top Yard) prior to departure as 8X76, 10.30pm to Tyseley. The 'X' in the reporting number indicated that a number of restrictions were to apply during the journey including a requirement not to travel at more than 25mph without an examination by the accompanying CM&EE representative. The transfer was completed without incident but unfortunately, in 1974, 92220 was involved in a slight collision at Haworth. Detailed examination however showed the damage to be only nominal and no repair was necessary.

Evening Star was of course a star attraction at Shildon in 1975 for the 150th Anniversary of the opening of the Stockton and Darlington Railway and also at the Rainhill Cavalcade in 1980. After operating a programme of special trains for BR in 1976, the engine was subsequently banned from BR tracks as its flangeless centre driving wheels were now deemed to be considered to be a safety hazard. In 1981, it was retubed, overhauled and repainted while at the Great Western Society facility at Didcot from late 1979 to early 1982. This resulted in a slight displacement of the BR roundels on the tender.

Following the rescinding of the ban on *Evening Star* operating on BR track, the locomotive worked main line tours during each year from 1982 until the expiry of its boiler certificate in 1988. These included trips on the "Cumbrian Mountain Express" and the "Scarborough Spa Express" at various times during this period (see Table 13.1).

While en route by road from the NRM to the West Somerset Railway on Thursday 9th March 1989, *Evening Star's* nameplates were stolen; this was the second time such an incident had occurred (see Section 10). The brass nameplates together with a 50A shed plate disappeared from the engine at Corley services on the M6 motorway while the driver of the low-loader and his wife were having a meal in the restaurant. Police officers interviewed a number of other lorry drivers at the scene and searched a lorry which had already left the lorry park with no result. However, some three hours later the driver of the low-loader apprehended a man acting suspiciously nearby and detained him until the police took charge of him. The recovered plates continued their journey to Minehead in the cab of the low-loader but were later replaced on 92220 by a set of fibreglass replicas. The thief was subsequently fined and ordered to complete a period of community service. Since that time, *Evening Star* has been on static display in the National Railway Museum, York.

Detail Modifications

Carriage warming apparatus was fitted in 1984.

Tender Number and Type

92220 carries BR1G tender no. 1527, the one it was issued with from new.

Table 13.1
BR Standard Class 9F 2-10-0s

92220 *Evening Star*; Chronology of Main Events after Preservation

Date	Activity
1975	
August	Operated at Shildon for the Stockton and Darlington 150th Anniversary.
	From Shildon, moved to York.
1976	Operated programme of special runs for British Railways.
	Subsequently failed due to cracked/broken cylinder.
	Later prohibited from BR lines for safety reasons (concerns over flangeless wheels).
	Policy change; restrictions continued on ER but rescinded on sections of WR.
1980	
	Took part in Rainhill Cavalcade to commemorate the opening of the Liverpool and Manchester Railway.
July	Routine maintenance including tender and smokebox descaling and ultrasonic axle testing
August-November	Located at the Great Western Society (GWS) Didcot.
	Zenith Main Line Tours.
1981	Overhaul, retubing and repaint at GWS Didcot.
1982	Main Line operations.
Spring and Autumn	
1983	
May	Farewell Tour from Great Western Society to Severn Valley Railway.
August	Scarborough Spa Express duties.
1984	
April	Cumbrian Mountain Express rail tours.
August	Scarborough Spa Express duties.
1985	
March	Newcastle and Carlisle Railway 150th Anniversary Main Line rail tour.
June	GWR 150th Anniversary train.
July	Cardiff Canton Open Day; Hereford Steam Centre.
	Transfer from Hereford to York.
August	Scarborough Spa Express duties.
September	10th Anniversary Celebrations steaming in York.
1986	
April	Edinburgh-Gleneagles tour.
July and October	North York Moors Railway.
1987	
April	Scarborough-York run.
August	Scarborough Spa Express duties.
1988	
April	Settle and Carlisle line runs.
August	Visits to Scarborough, Hull and Harrogate.
	Boiler ticket expires.
1989	
March-September	West Somerset Railway.
1989 to Present	Static Display, Great Hall, NRM York.

Boiler Number
Boiler no. is 1895 fitted from new.

Present Location
The Great Hall. National Railway Museum, York. Planned to be moved to STEAM at Swindon in August 2008 in exchange for 6000 *King George V.*

Status
On static exhibition.

Steps to return to service
No plans to return to service for the foreseeable future.

Present Owners
The National Museum of Science and Industry.

92240
History since withdrawal
After spending 13 years at Barry this locomotive was purchased (without tender) for £10,500 by the Bluebell Railway of Sheffield Park, East Sussex from Woodham Bros. and became the first 9F to leave the site; it arrived on the Bluebell Railway on 5th October 1978. A new tender was constructed at Sheffield Park to the BR1C design (at the request of certain persons who had contributed to the purchase) and mounted on an underframe purchased from Briton Ferry Steelworks in South Wales. The tender is plated as BR1C no. 1551 and dated 1958. This was the number of the first tender carried by 92240 although the original was of course a BR1G type. The boiler (1936) was completely overhauled, cylinders and motion repaired and carriage warming apparatus fitted.

It was hoped that 92240 would be returned to steam in 1982 for the centenary of the opening of the Lewes & East Grinstead Railway of which the present Bluebell Railway is now the only surviving part. A boost to the restoration work came on 11th May 1980 when the 88 year-old Mr. R. A. Riddles visited the Bluebell Railway accompanied by Mr. R. C. Bond, Col. H. C. B. Rogers, Mrs. Riddles and Mrs. Bond to see the progress thus far and to unveil commemorative plaques on the locomotive. In his speech, Mr. Riddles expressed a wish to be present when the 9F returned to traffic. Sadly, however, this was not to be as he passed away at the age of 91 before restoration was completed.

Unfortunately, the needs for other locomotives to have priority for workshop space at Sheffield Park meant it was not possible to complete 92240 in time for the 1982 celebrations and it was smartened up so that it could be hauled through Horsted Keynes station by 21C123 *Blackmoor Vale*. Eventually, 92240 was moved into the works on 18th September 1987. While in the works, Carriage Warming Apparatus was installed as this would be essential for duties which would include Santa Specials during December.

92240 was steamed for the first time on the Bluebell Railway on 5th September 1990 and worked its first public passenger train - the 4.50pm from Sheffield Park to Horsted Keynes - on 15th September.

A few years later, a number of boiler stays were found to need replacement. The opportunity was therefore taken to re-certificate the boiler at this time. From entering service on the Bluebell Railway it ran some 43,132 miles until withdrawn in 2002 for its ten-year service. The mileage has included (for example) 4,721 miles on 73 days in 1998, 6,385 miles on 106 days in 2001 and 3,971 miles on 59 days in 2002 according to *Bluebell News*. While in service, 92240 was described as "a tiger of an engine.....capable of pulling the coal off the [fireman's] shovel"... but... "for all its size, an economical engine on our line" *(Bluebell News)*. 92240 is the figurehead of the Bluebell Railway's 9F Club for its junior members.

The locomotive was disguised as 92245 for a photographic charter on 13th November 2000. It was then used in the filming of 'Charlotte Gray' from 2nd-4th April 2001. It was shown being 'blown up' when working a German military train conveying tanks, lorries and ammunition through occupied France; the smokebox numberplate was clearly visible in the finished film.

Detail Modifications
Carriage warming apparatus fitted.

Tender Number and Type
BR1C no. 1551 as referred to above.

Boiler Number
92240 now carries boiler number 1936 fitted on 2nd March 1962.

Present Location
Bluebell Railway, Sheffield Park, East Sussex.

Status
On static display awaiting entry to works for overhaul. The Riddles commemorative plaques were removed for safe-keeping when the locomotive came out of service and are currently in the care of the Bluebell museum. It is hoped they will be re-applied to the locomotive when it is returned to service.

Steps to return to service
To be returned to service following completion of a pending overhaul.

Present Owner
Bluebell Railway Preservation Society.

92245
History since withdrawal
92245 was officially withdrawn on 26th December 1964 and sold to Woodham Bros., Barry, on 11th February 1965. It and nine other locomotives were purchased by the Wales Railway Centre (now defunct) with assistance from the National Heritage Memorial Fund and left the scrapyard in February/March 1988 for Cardiff Bute Road station. The locomotives were intended to be the centre-pieces of the Wales Steam Heritage Centre which would be established there. It soon became apparent that the Butetown Historical Railway Society's proposals were in conflict with those of the Cardiff Bay Development Corporation which had been set up to develop the derelict former dockland area. Relocation became a priority and eventually agreement was reached with the Vale of Glamorgan Borough Council to move to Barry Island. Work started on the new heritage centre in February 1996 and the locomotives were moved there one year later on 6th-7th February 1997. However, 92245 had spent some of the intervening time at the Western Welsh bus depot on the Atlantic Trading Estate at Sully near Barry.

Detail Modifications
None reported.

Tender Number and Type
No tender available at Woodham's when the locomotive was purchased.

Boiler
92245 carries boiler no. 1917, fitted on 6th December 1961.

Present Location
Now housed in the former EWS depot at Barry.

Status
Awaiting restoration; the engine has no tender or pony truck.

Steps to return to service
None in the foreseeable future.

Present Owner
Vale of Glamorgan District Council.

CONCLUSION

The locations for the preserved 9F locomotives are believed by the authors to be correct at the beginning of 2008. However, these can change at short notice and prospective visitors should check before making long journeys.

Restoration and operation of preserved locomotives is time-consuming and expensive. Offers of assistance will always be welcomed by their owners.

Much of the information contained in this section has been obtained from the locomotives' owners and their representatives.

The authors are very grateful for their enthusiastic co-operation and permission to quote from published works where appropriate.

A SELECTED BIBLIOGRAPHY

The Railway Magazine Gradients of the British Main Line Railways
The Railway Publishing Co. Ltd., 1947.

The Locomotive Exchanges 1870 - 1948 and New Light on the Locomotive Exchanges
Cecil J. Allen, Ian Allan, 1949 and 1950 respectively.

Trains Illustrated Annual 1960
editor G. Freeman Allen, Ian Allan.

Locomotive Panorama Vol. 1
E. S. Cox. Ian Allan, 1965.

British Railways Standard Steam Locomotives
E. S. Cox, Ian Allan, 1966, revised 1973.

The Somerset and Dorset Railway
Robin Atthill, David & Charles, 1967.

The Last Steam Locomotive Engineer: R. A. Riddles
H. C. B. Rogers, George Allan and Unwin, 1970.

Railway Histories of the World: Italian Railways
P. M. Kalla-Bishop, David & Charles (Publishers) Limited, 1971.

The BR 2-10-0 Locomotive
Brian Reed, Great Trains Part 1, New English Library, 1972.

Loco Profile No. 33: B.R. Class 9 2-10-0
Brian Reed, Profile Publications Limited, 1973.

A Lifetime with Locomotives
R. C. Bond, Goose and Son, 1975.

Steam on the Somerset and Dorset
G. A. Richardson, D. Bradford Barton, 1975.

BR Standard Class 9F:
a study of British Railways Standard Class 9F 2-10-0 heavy freight locomotive
edited by G, Weeks, D. Bradford Barton Ltd, 1975.

Locomotives Illustrated, Their Life and Times, No. 5, 9F 2-10-0s
Ian Allan, 1976.

Living with London Midland Locomotives
A. J. Powell, Ian Allan, 1977.

BR Standard Steam Album
Alan Williams, Ian Allan, 1980.

BR Standard Steam In Close-Up Volume 2
edited by Tony Fairclough and Alan Wills, D. Bradford Barton Ltd., 1981.

Steam Past Series: The Riddles Standard Types in Traffic
G. Freeman Allen, George Allen and Unwin, 1982.

Riddles and the 9Fs
H. C. B. Rogers, Ian Allan, 1982.

A Brush with Steam: David Shepherd's Railway Story
David Shepherd, David & Charles Ltd., 1983.

A Pictorial Record of British Railways Standard Steam Locomotives
E. Talbot, Oxford Publishing Co., 1982.

BR Standard Steam Locomotives
Brian Stephenson, Ian Allan, 1983.

The Standard Steam Locomotives of British Railways
Rodger P. Bradley, David & Charles Ltd., 1984.

Italian State Railway Steam Locomotives
P. M. Kalla-Bishop, Tourret Publishing, 1986.

The Last Years of the Great Central Main Line
Robert Robotham, Ian Allan, 1986.

The S&D 7Fs Remembered
compiled by P. W. Gibbs, 73082 Camelot Locomotive Society, 1986.

Austerity 2-8-0s & 2-10-0s
J. W. P. Rowledge, Ian Allan, 1987.

Barry Scrapyard: The Preservation Miracle
Alan Warren, David & Charles Ltd., 1988.

The Illustrated History of British Marshalling Yards
Michael Rhodes, Oxford Publishing Co., 1988.

Organised Chaos!
A transcription of the Bath (Green Park) Running Foreman's log book for 1960/1 with additional information.
Compiled by Brian Macdermott with text by John Barber and Peter Smith, Somerset and Dorset Railway Trust, 1989.

Experiments with Steam: Landmarks in unusual British locomotive design, 1846 - 1959
Charles Fryer, Patrick Stephens Limited, 1990.

Britannia - Birth of a Locomotive
Philip Atkins, Irwell Press, 1991.

Locomotives Illustrated No. 75, BR 9F 2-10-0s
Ian Allan, 1991.

92240 Restored
compiled by David G. Jones, Bluebell Railway Class 9F Preservation Group, 1991.

The British Railways Standard 9F 2-10-0
Philip Atkins, Irwell Press, 1993.

Heavy Freight Locomotives of Britain
Denis Griffiths, Patrick Stephens Ltd., 1993.

The 9Fs: BR's Heavy Freight Locomotives
John Scott Morgan, Ian Allan, 1994.

Firing Days at Saltley
Terry Essery, Silver Link 1994.

Steam Locomotives Compared
Terry Essery, Atlantic Transport Publishers, 1996.

The Book of the BR Standards (1 and 2)
Richard Derry, Irwell Press, 1997 (1) and 2002 (2).

Steam Locomotives 1955, 70000 - 90774. Standards and Austerities
Eric Sawford, Sutton Publishing, 1998.

The Power of the 9Fs
Gavin Morrison, Oxford Publishing Co., 2001.

The Railways of Great Britain, A Historical Atlas
Michael H. Cobb, Distributed by Ian Allan, 2003.

A Pictorial Record of British Railways Standard Steam Locomotives
Volume Two
Edward Talbot, 2004, Edward Talbot.

Locomotives in Detail No. 7. Riddles Class 9F 2-10-0
David Clarke, Ian Allan Publishing Ltd., 2007.

Reference has been made to various issues of the following journals: Bluebell News, British Railway Journal, Railnews, Railway Modeller, Railway Observer, Stephenson Locomotive Society Journal, Railway Magazine, Railway World, Trains Illustrated, Modern Railways, Steam Days, Steam World, Railways South East, British Railways Illustrated, Backtrack, Railway Locomotives.

ACKNOWLEDGEMENTS

Mr. J. B. Arnold
Mr. C. P. Atkins
Mr. B. Basterfield
Mr. W. Batterson
Mr. I. Beattie
Mr. R. Bellchambers
Mr. C. R. Berridge
Mr. M. G. C. Boatman
Mr. K. Bottomley
Mr. M. Burnett
Mr. P. J. Cupper
Mr. P. Doggett
Mr. A. Dow
Mr. W. Hamilton
Mr. A. J. Lait
Mr. F. Lodge
Mr. J. Morgan
Mr. M. Morgan
Mr. L. Nodes
Mr. D. Percival
Mr. D. Phillips
Mr. K. R. Phillips
Mr. M. Pollard
Mr. A. Porter
Mr. J. Potter
Mr. S. Potts
Mr. F. L. Pugh
Mr. M. Richardson
Mr. M. Sanderson
Mr. H. Self
Mr. David Shepherd CBE
Mr. B. Stickland
Mr. S. Summerson

DIAGRAM A1

BR STANDARD CLASS 9F 2-10-0 WITH BR1G TENDER (BR STANDARD DRAWING NO. SL/9R/1)

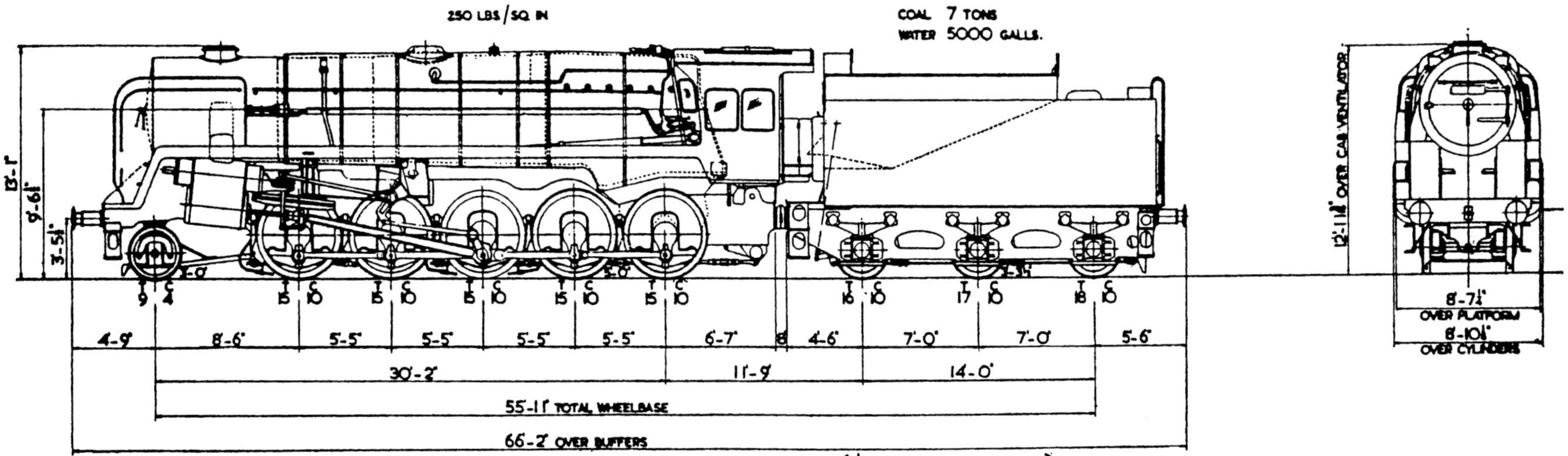

MINIMUM RADIUS CURVE WITHOUT GAUGE WIDENING 6 CHAINS (4½ CHAINS DEAD SLOW.)

BOILER BARREL DIAMETER (OUTSIDE)	5'-9" INCREASING TO 6'-1"
FIREBOX (OUTSIDE)	7'-5¼" LONG x 7'-0⅛" TO 6'-6¼" WIDE
TUBES	35 LARGE 5¼" O.D. x 7 S.W.G.
	138 SMALL 2" O.D. x 11 S.W.G.
SUPERHEATER ELEMENTS	1⅜" O.D. x 9 S.W.G.
LENGTH BETWEEN TUBEPLATES	15'-3"
HEATING SURFACES: TUBES	1836 SQ. FT.
FIREBOX	179 SQ. FT.
TOTAL EVAPORATIVE	2015 SQ. FT.
SUPERHEATER	535 SQ. FT.
FREE FLUE AREA	5·49 SQ. FT.
GRATE AREA	40·2 SQ. FT.

CYLINDERS (TWO)	20" x 28"
TRACTIVE EFFORT	39,667 LBS.
ADHESION FACTOR	4·38
BRAKE % ENGINE & TENDER	69·8
BOILER TYPE	B.R.9
TENDER TYPE	B.R.1G

WEIGHTS	FULL T	FULL C	EMPTY T	EMPTY C
ENGINE	86	14	78	0
TENDER	52	10	23	3
TOTAL	139	4	101	3

SCALE 0 2 4 6 8 10 FEET

B.R. STANDARD CLASS 9. 2-10-0 ENGINE

DIAGRAM A2

BR STANDARD CLASS 9F 2-10-0 WITH BR1F TENDER (BR STANDARD DRAWING NO. SL/9R/3)

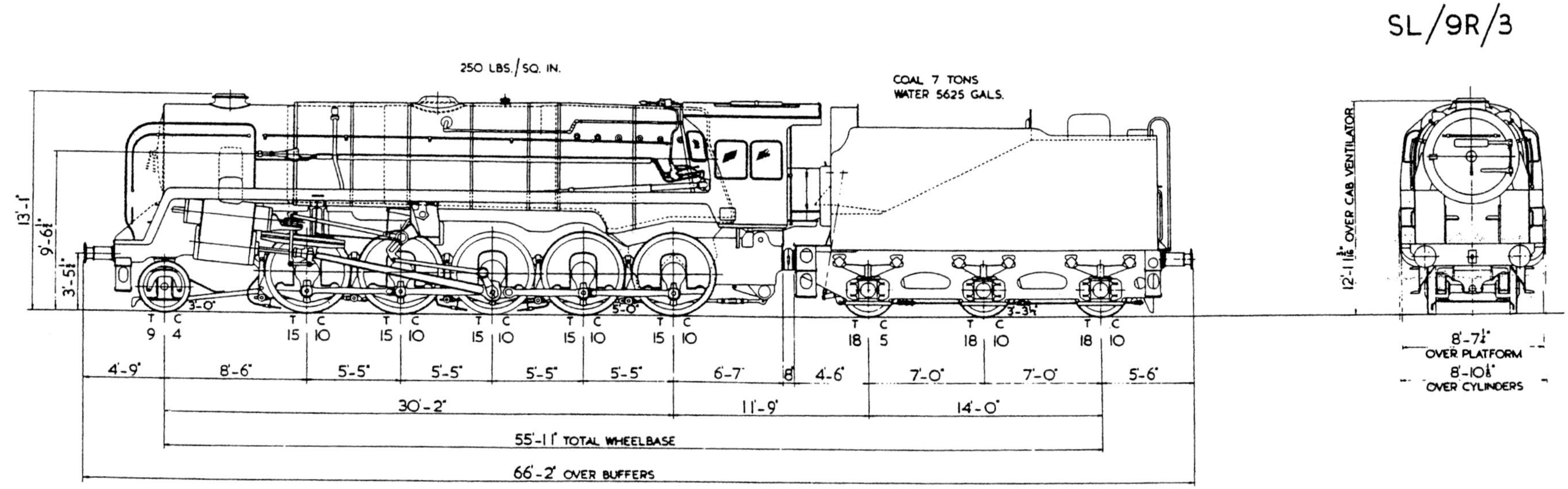

BOILER BARREL DIAMETER (OUTSIDE)	5'-9" INCREASING TO 6'-1"
FIREBOX (OUTSIDE)	7'-5½" LONG x 7'-0⅛" TO 6'-6 7/16" WIDE
TUBES	35 LARGE 5¼" O.D. x 7 S.W.G.
	138 SMALL 2" O.D. x 11 S.W.G.
SUPERHEATER ELEMENTS	1⅜" O.D. x 9 S.W.G.
LENGTH BETWEEN TUBEPLATES	15'-3"
HEATING SURFACES: TUBES	1836 SQ. FT.
FIREBOX	179 SQ. FT.
TOTAL EVAPORATIVE	2015 SQ. FT.
SUPERHEATER	535 SQ. FT.
FREE FLUE AREA	5.49 SQ. FT.
GRATE AREA	40.2 SQ. FT.

CYLINDERS (TWO)	20" x 28"
TRACTIVE EFFORT	39,667 LBS.
ADHESION FACTOR	4.38
BRAKE % ENGINE & TENDER	68.8
MINIMUM RADIUS CURVE WITHOUT GAUGE WIDENING	6 CHAINS (OR 4½ CHAINS DEAD SLOW)
BOILER TYPE	B.R.9
TENDER TYPE	B.R.1F

WEIGHTS	FULL		EMPTY	
	T	C	T	C
ENGINE	86	14	78	0
TENDER	55	5	23	3
TOTAL	141	19	101	3

SCALE 0 2 4 6 8 10 FEET

B.R. STANDARD CLASS 9. 2-10-0 ENGINE

DIAGRAM A3

BR STANDARD CLASS 9F 2-10-0 WITH BR1C TENDER (BR STANDARD DRAWING NO. SL/9R/4)

SL/9R/4.

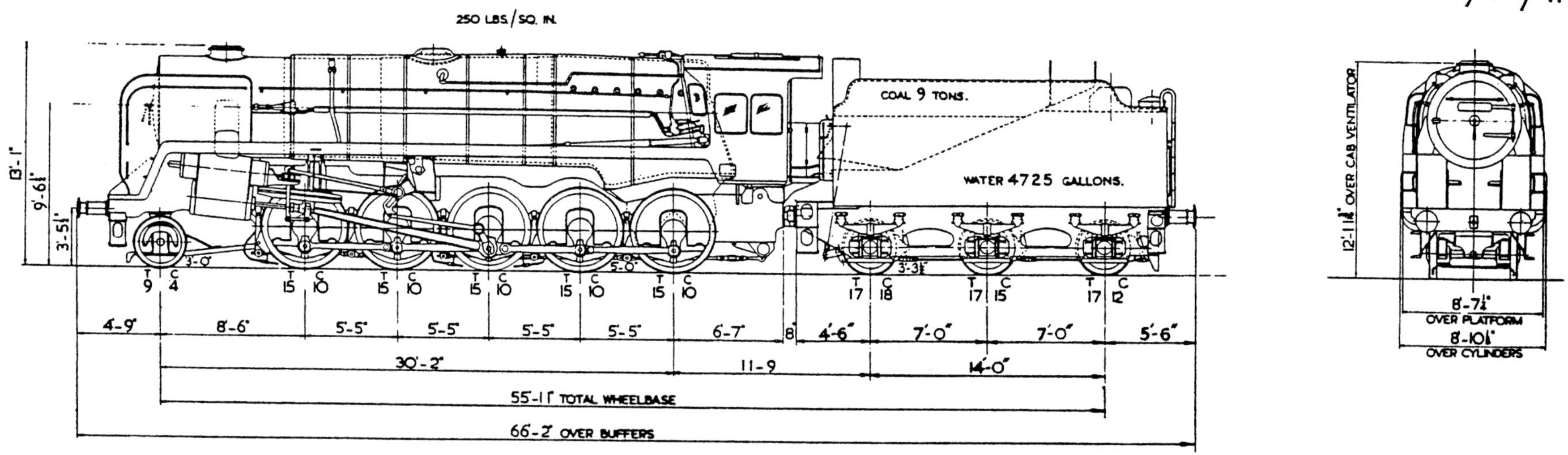

BOILER BARREL DIAMETER (OUTSIDE)	5'-9" INCREASING TO 6'-1"
FIREBOX (OUTSIDE)	7'-5½" LONG x 7'-0¼" TO 6'-6¾" WIDE
TUBES	35 LARGE 5¼" O.D. x 7 S.W.G.
	138 SMALL 2" O.D. x 11 S.W.G.
SUPERHEATER ELEMENTS	1⅜" O.D. x 9 S.W.G.
LENGTH BETWEEN TUBEPLATES	15'-3"
HEATING SURFACES: TUBES	1836 SQ. FT.
FIREBOX	179 SQ. FT.
TOTAL EVAPORATIVE	2015 SQ. FT.
SUPERHEATER	535 SQ. FT.
FREE FLUE AREA	5·49 SQ. FT.
GRATE AREA	40·2 SQ. FT.

CYLINDERS (TWO)	20" x 28"
TRACTIVE EFFORT	39,667 LBS.
ADHESION FACTOR	4·38
BRAKE % ENGINE & TENDER	69·5
MINIMUM RADIUS CURVE WITHOUT GAUGE WIDENING	6 CHAINS (OR 4½ CHAINS DEAD SLOW)
BOILER TYPE	B.R. 9
TENDER TYPE	B.R. 1C.

WEIGHTS	FULL		EMPTY	
	T	C	T	C
ENGINE	86	14	78	0
TENDER	53	5	23	3
TOTAL	139	19	101	3

SCALE

0 2 4 6 8 10 FEET

B.R. STANDARD CLASS 9. 2-10-0 ENGINE

DIAGRAM A4

BR STANDARD CLASS 9F 2-10-0 WITH BR1B TENDER (BR STANDARD DRAWING NO. SL/9R/5)

SL/9R/5.

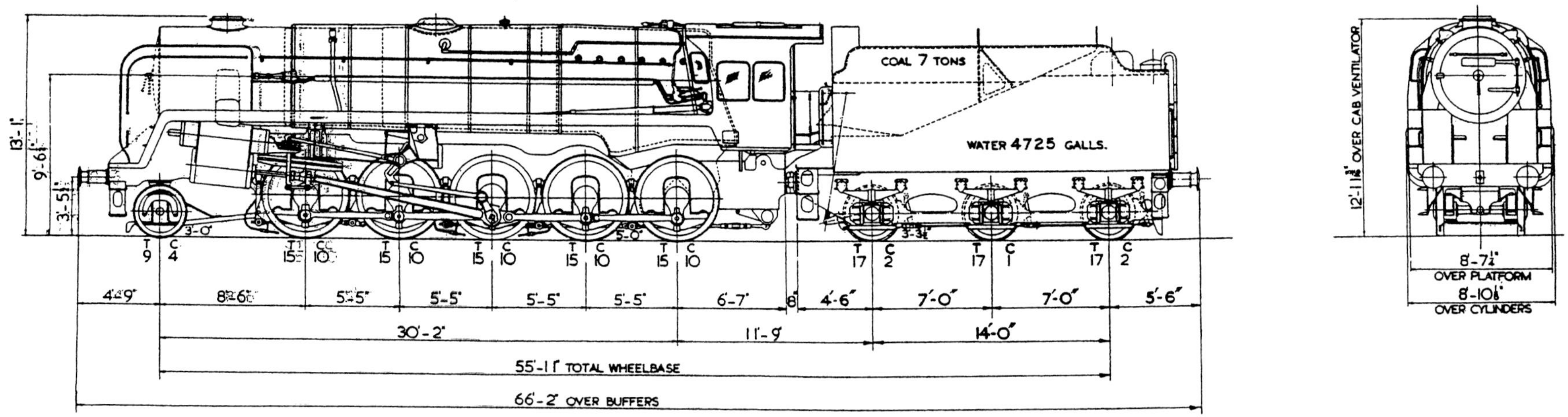

BOILER BARREL DIAMETER (OUTSIDE)	5'-9" INCREASING TO 6'-1"
FIREBOX (OUTSIDE)	7'-5¼" LONG x 7'-0⅜" TO 6'-6¾" WIDE
TUBES	35 LARGE 5¼" O.D. x 7 S.W.G.
	138 SMALL 2" O.D. x 11 S.W.G.
SUPERHEATER ELEMENTS	1⅜" O.D. x 9 S.W.G.
LENGTH BETWEEN TUBEPLATES	15'-3"
HEATING SURFACES TUBES	1836 SQ. FT.
FIREBOX	179 SQ. FT.
TOTAL EVAPORATIVE	2015 SQ. FT.
SUPERHEATER	535 SQ. FT.
FREE FLUE AREA	5·49 SQ. FT.
GRATE AREA	40·2 SQ. FT.

CYLINDERS (TWO)	20" x 28"
TRACTIVE EFFORT	39,667 LBS.
ADHESION FACTOR	4·38
BRAKE % ENGINE & TENDER	70·25
MINIMUM RADIUS CURVE WITHOUT GAUGE WIDENING	6 CHAINS (OR 4½ CHAINS DEAD SLOW)
BOILER TYPE	B.R. 9
TENDER TYPE	B.R. 1B

WEIGHTS	FULL T	FULL C	EMPTY T	EMPTY C
ENGINE	86	14	78	0
TENDER	51	5	23	3
TOTAL	137	19	101	3

SCALE

0 2 4 6 8 10 FEET

B.R. STANDARD CLASS 9. 2-10-0 ENGINE

DIAGRAM B

BR 9F 2-10-0 CROSTI BOILER: 1955 DESIGN (BR STANDARD DRAWING NO. SL/9R/2)

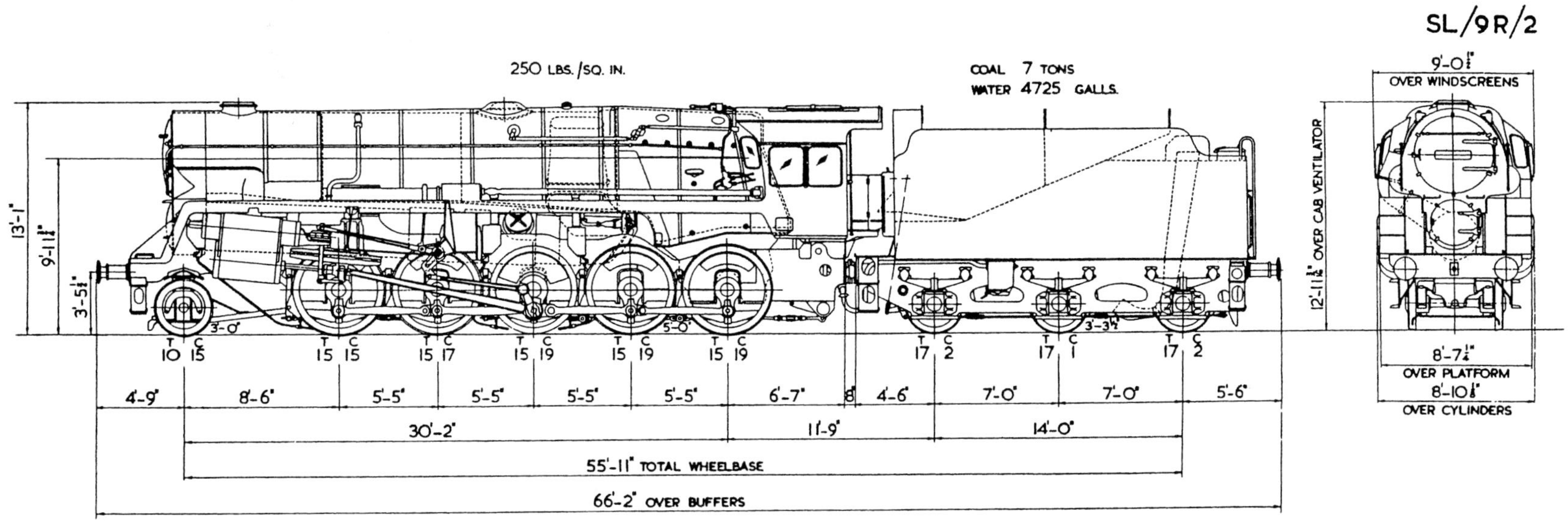

BOILER	
BARREL DIA (OUTSIDE)	4'-11⅜" INCREASING TO 5'-7½"
FIREBOX (OUTSIDE)	7'-5½" LONG x 7'-0¼" TO 6'-6¾" WIDE
TUBES	28 LARGE 5¼" O.D. x 7 S.W.G.
	60 SMALL 2⅛" O.D. x 11 S.W.G.
SUPERHEATER ELEMENTS	1¼" O.D. x 9 S.W.G.
LENGTH BETWEEN TUBEPLATES	16'-5"
PREHEATER	
BARREL DIA (OUTSIDE)	2'-8⅞"
TUBES	90—2¼" O.D. x 11 S.W.G.
LENGTH BETWEEN TUBEPLATES	19'-3"

HEATING SURFACES	
BOILER	
TUBES	1274 SQ. FT.
FIREBOX	158 SQ. FT.
TOTAL EVAPORATIVE	1432 SQ. FT.
SUPERHEATER	411 SQ. FT.
PREHEATER	
TUBES	1021 SQ. FT.
EXHAUST STEAM JACKET	57 SQ. FT.
FREE FLUE AREA (BOILER)	4·59 SQ. FT.
FREE FLUE AREA (PREHEATER)	2·0 SQ. FT.
GRATE AREA	40·2 SQ. FT.

CYLINDERS (TWO)	20" x 28"
TRACTIVE EFFORT	39,667 LBS
ADHESION FACTOR	4·48
BRAKE % ENGINE & TENDER	68·4
MINIMUM RADIUS CURVE (WITHOUT GAUGE WIDENING)	6 CHAINS (OR 4½ CHAINS DEAD SLOW)
BOILER TYPE	B.R.12
TENDER TYPE	B.R.1B.

WEIGHTS	FULL T	FULL C	EMPTY T	EMPTY C
ENGINE	90	4	82	2
TENDER	51	5	23	3
TOTAL	141	9	105	5

SCALE

0 2 4 6 8 10 FEET

B.R. CLASS 9, 2-10-0 CROSTI ENGINE

DIAGRAM C
BR 9F 2-10-0 CROSTI AFTER CONVERSION (BR STANDARD DRAWING NO. SL/9R/7)

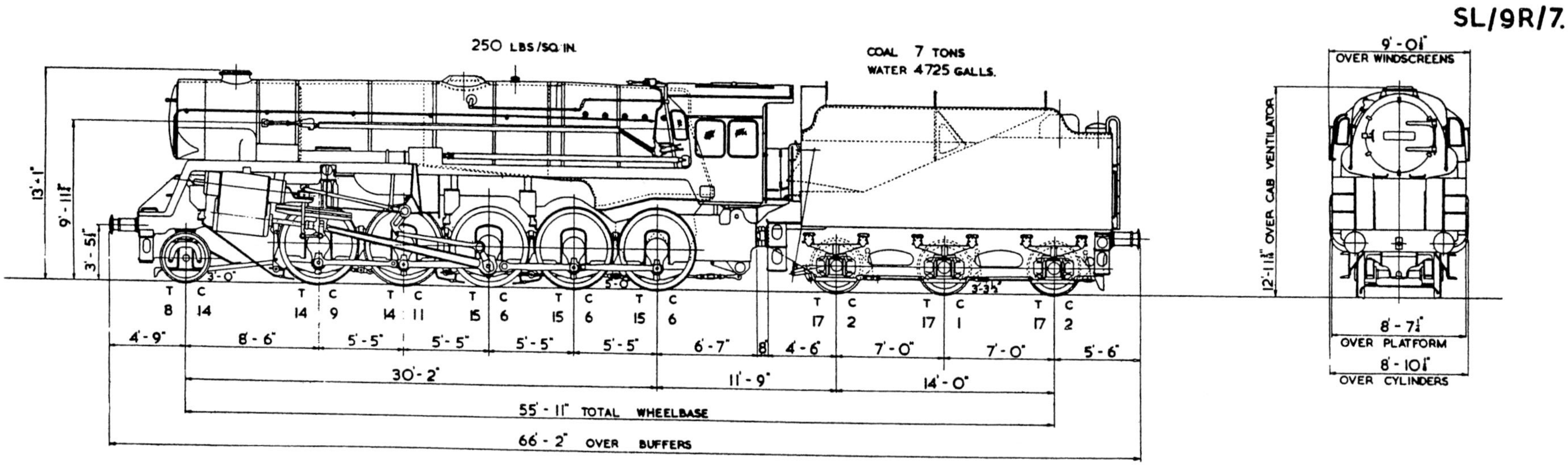

BOILER BARREL DIAMETER (OUTSIDE)	4'-11⅝" INCREASING TO 5'-7½"
FIREBOX (OUTSIDE)	7'-5½" LONG x 7'-0¼" TO 6'-6 7/16" WIDE
TUBES	28 LARGE 5½" O.D. x 7 S.W.G.
	60 SMALL 2⅛" O.D. x 11 S.W.G.
SUPERHEATER ELEMENTS	1¼" O.D. x 9 S.W.G.
LENGTH BETWEEN TUBEPLATES	16'-5"
HEATING SURFACES TUBES	1274 SQ. FT.
FIREBOX	158 SQ. FT.
TOTAL EVAPORATIVE	1432 SQ. FT.
SUPERHEATER	411 SQ FT
FREE FLUE AREA	4·59 SQ FT.
GRATE AREA	40·2 SQ FT

CYLINDERS (TWO)	20" x 28"
TRACTIVE EFFORT	39,667. LBS.
ADHESION FACTOR	4·23
BRAKE % ENGINE & TENDER	72·00%
MINIMUM RADIUS CURVE WITHOUT GAUGE WIDENING	6 CHAINS (OR 4½ CHAINS DEAD SLOW)
BOILER TYPE	B.R.12
TENDER TYPE	B.R.1B.

WEIGHTS	FULL		EMPTY	
	T	C	T	C
ENGINE	83	12	77	3
TENDER	51	5	23	3
TOTAL	134	17	100	6

SCALE
0 2 4 6 8 10 FEET

B.R. CLASS 9. 2-10-0 CROSTI (CONVERSION) ENGINE.

DIAGRAM D

BR 9F 2-10-0 FITTED WITH MECHANICAL STOKER (BR STANDARD DRAWING NO. SL/9R/6)

SL/9R/6

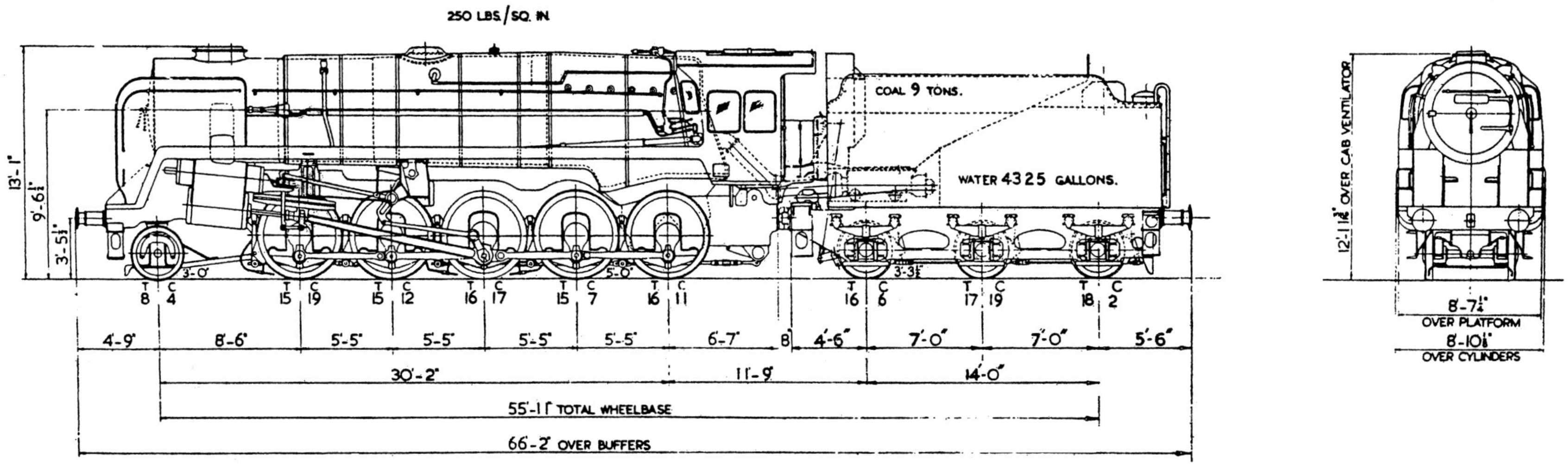

BOILER BARREL DIAMETER (OUTSIDE)	5'-9" INCREASING TO 6'-1"
FIREBOX (OUTSIDE)	7'-5¼" LONG x 7'-0⅛" TO 6'-6¾" WIDE
TUBES	35 LARGE 5¼" O.D. x 7 S.W.G.
	138 SMALL 2" O.D. x 11 S.W.G.
SUPERHEATER ELEMENTS	1⅜" O.D. x 9 S.W.G.
LENGTH BETWEEN TUBEPLATES	15'-3"
HEATING SURFACES. TUBES	1836 SQ. FT.
FIREBOX	179 SQ. FT.
TOTAL EVAPORATIVE	2015 SQ. FT.
SUPERHEATER	535 SQ. FT.
FREE FLUE AREA	5·49 SQ. FT.
GRATE AREA	40·2 SQ. FT.

CYLINDERS (TWO)	20" x 28"
TRACTIVE EFFORT	39,667 LBS.
ADHESION FACTOR	4·56
BRAKE % ENGINE & TENDER	69·5
MINIMUM RADIUS CURVE WITHOUT GAUGE WIDENING	6 CHAINS (OR 4½ CHAINS DEAD SLOW)
BOILER TYPE	B.R.9
TENDER TYPE	B.R.1K.

WEIGHTS	FULL T C	EMPTY T C
ENGINE	88 10	79 16
TENDER	52 7	24 13
TOTAL	140 17	104 9

SCALE 0 2 4 6 8 10 FEET

B.R. STANDARD CLASS 9. 2-10-0 ENGINE
FITTED WITH MECHANICAL STOKER.

DIAGRAM E
BR 8F 2-10-0 PROPOSED 1951 DESIGN (WITH WD 'AUSTERITY-TYPE' CHIMNEY)

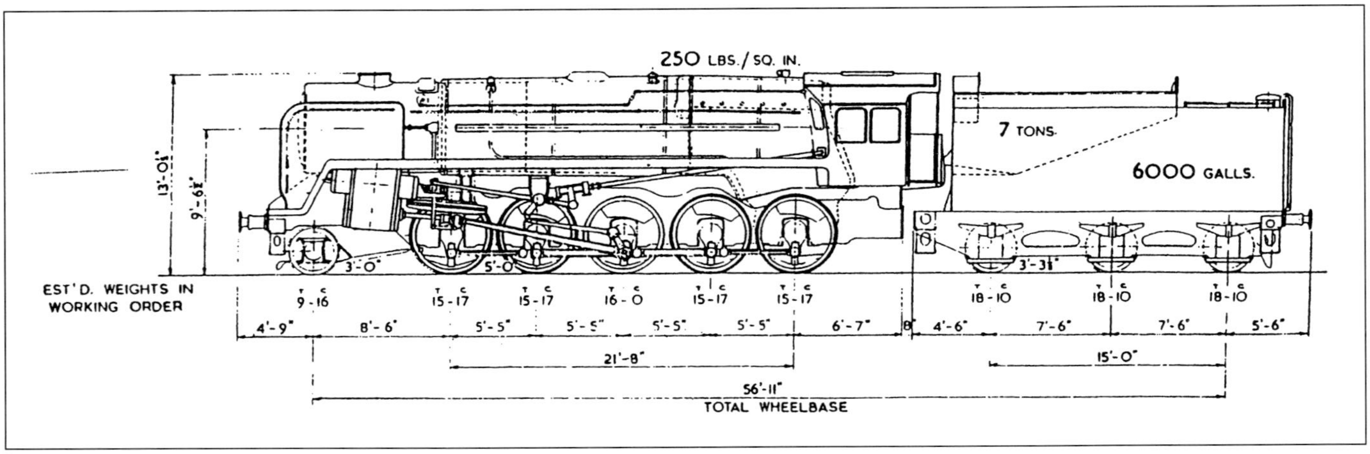

DIAGRAM F
BR 9F 2-10-0 CROSTI BOILER: 1951 DESIGN

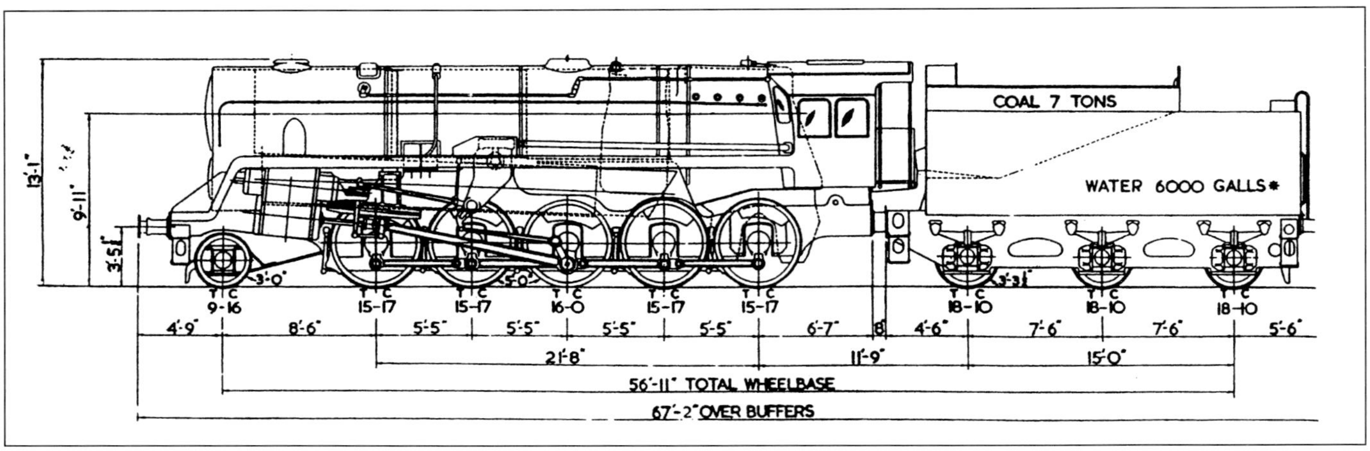

DIAGRAM G
BR 8F 2-8-2: PROPOSED 1948 DESIGN

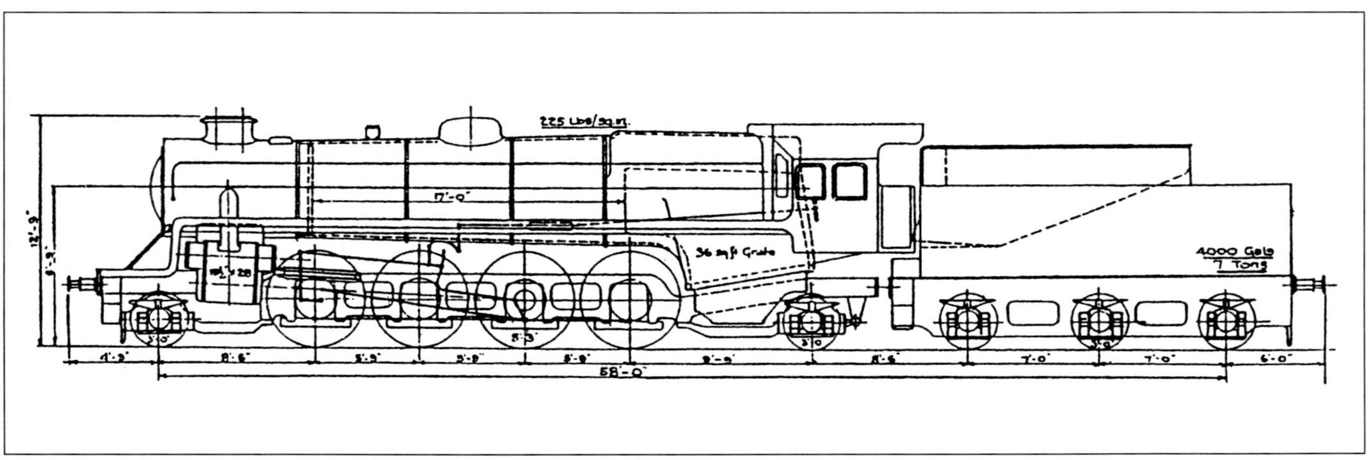

DIAGRAM H
BR 8F 2-8-2 PROPOSED 1951 DESIGN

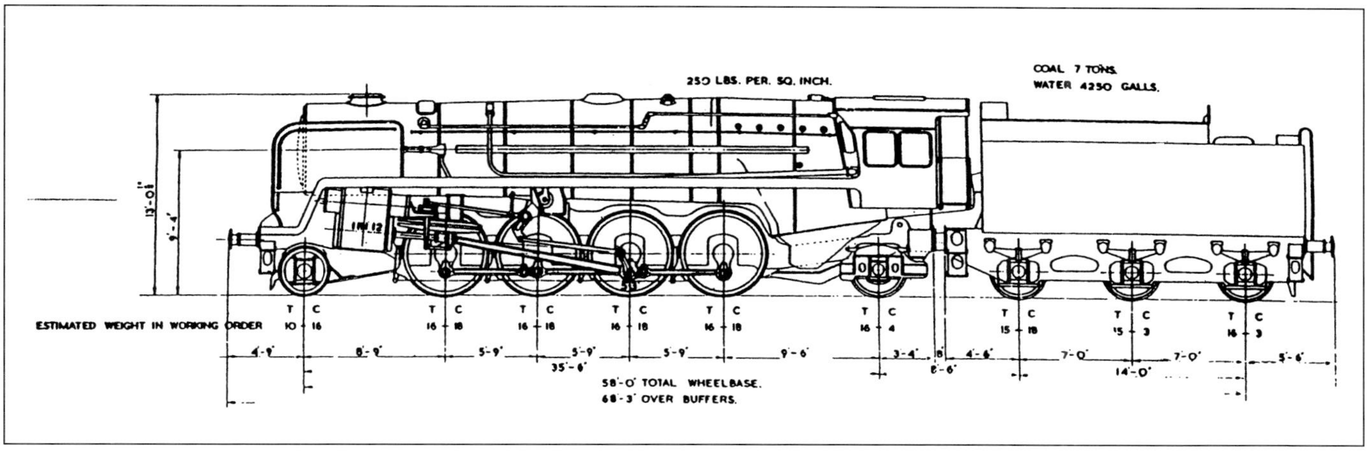

DIAGRAM I
BR 8F 2-8-0: PROPOSED BR HQ 1953 DESIGN

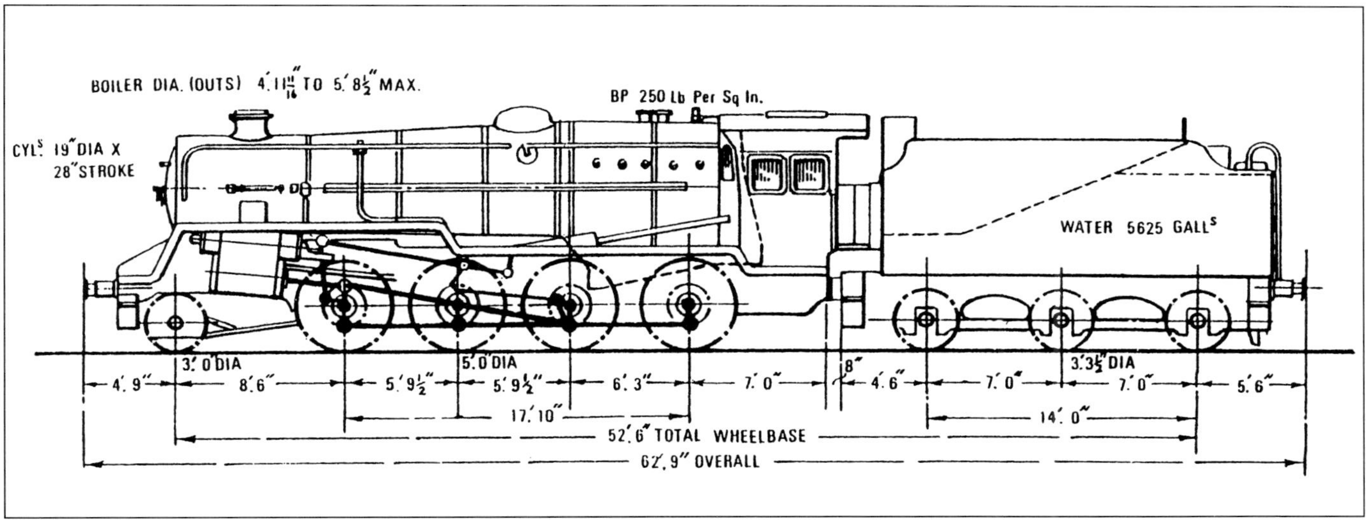

DIAGRAM J
BR 8F 2-8-0: PROPOSED DERBY DEVELOPMENT OFFICE 1953 DESIGN

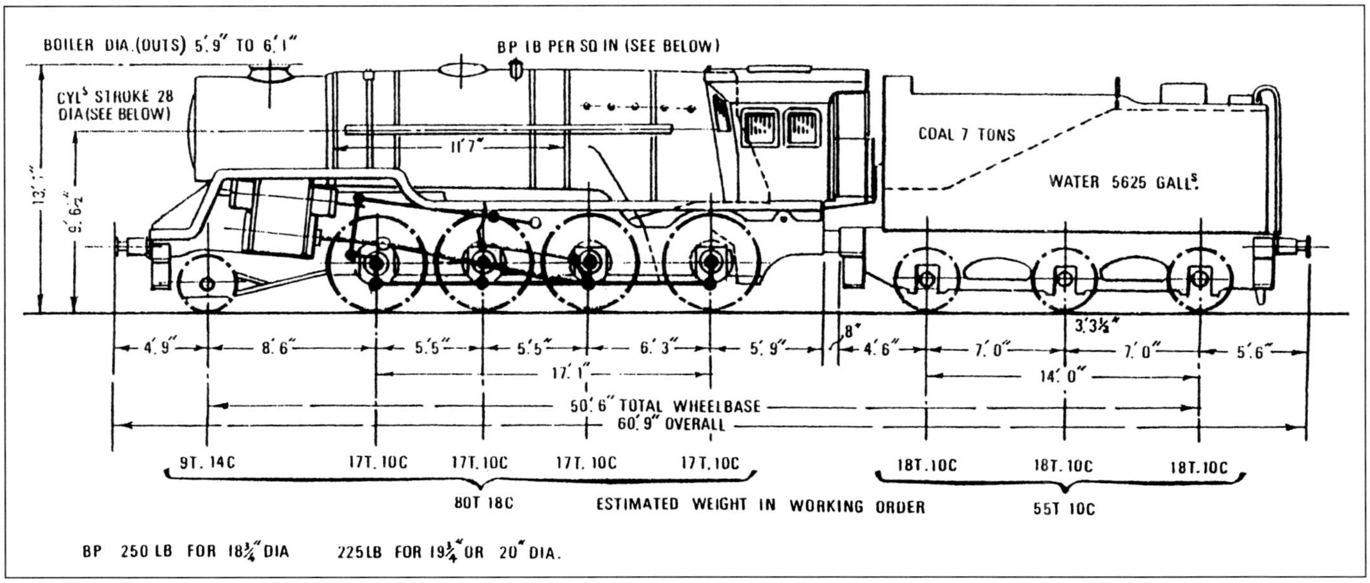

DIAGRAM K
LNER 8F O1 2-8-0 1944 DESIGN

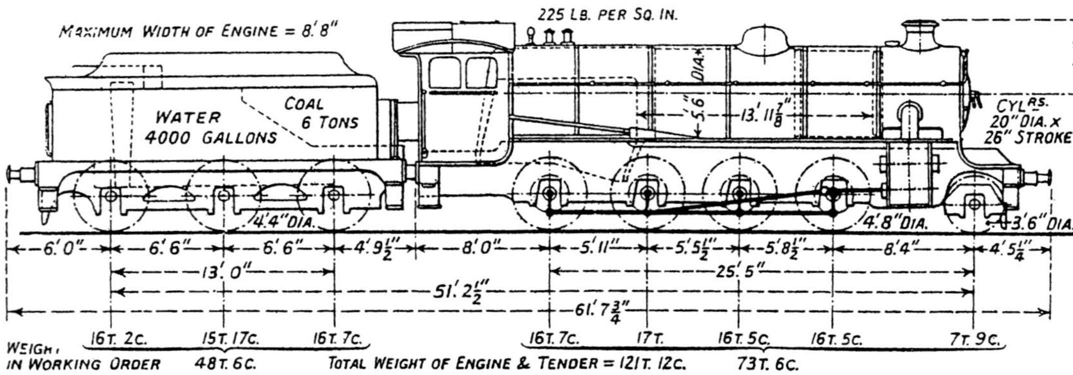

DIAGRAM L
WD 8F 2-10-0 1943 DESIGN

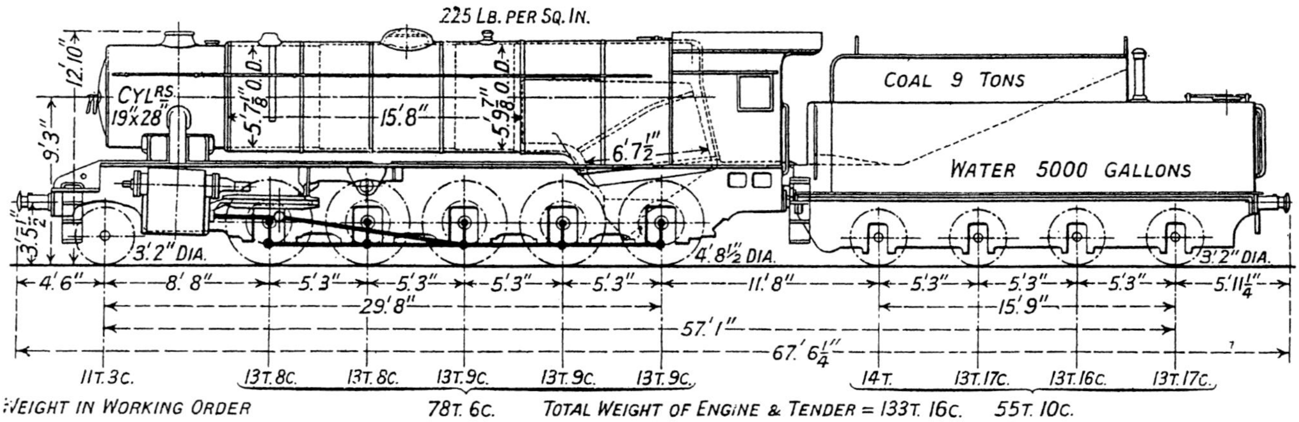

Diagram giving principal dimensions and axle loads

DIAGRAM M
WD 8F 2-8-0 1943 DESIGN

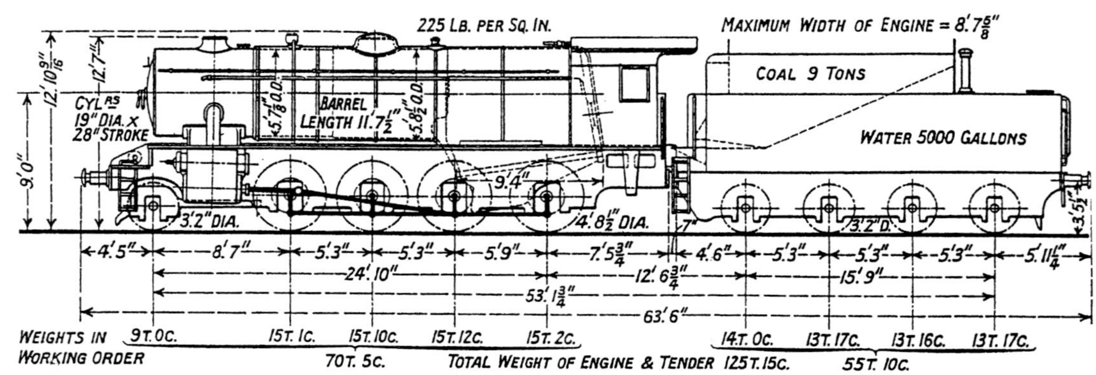

HEATING SURFACE, TUBES—
LARGE AND SMALL... ... ... 1,512 SQ. FT.
FIREBOX ... ... 168 „
TOTAL (EVAPORATIVE) ... ... 1,680 „
SUPERHEATER ... ... 311 „
COMBINED HEATING SURFACES ... ... 1,991 „

SUPERHEATER ELEMENTS ... ... 28—1⅛ IN. DIA. OUTS
LARGE TUBES ... ... 28—5¼ IN. DIA. OUTS. } 12 FT. 0 IN.
SMALL TUBES ... ... 193—1¾ IN. DIA. OUTS. } BET. TUBEPLATE:
GRATE AREA ... ... 28·6 SQ. FT
TRACTIVE EFFORT (AT 85 PER CENT. B.P.) ... ... 34,215 LB

"*Austerity*" *Class*

DIAGRAM N
USA S160 2-8-0 1943 DESIGN

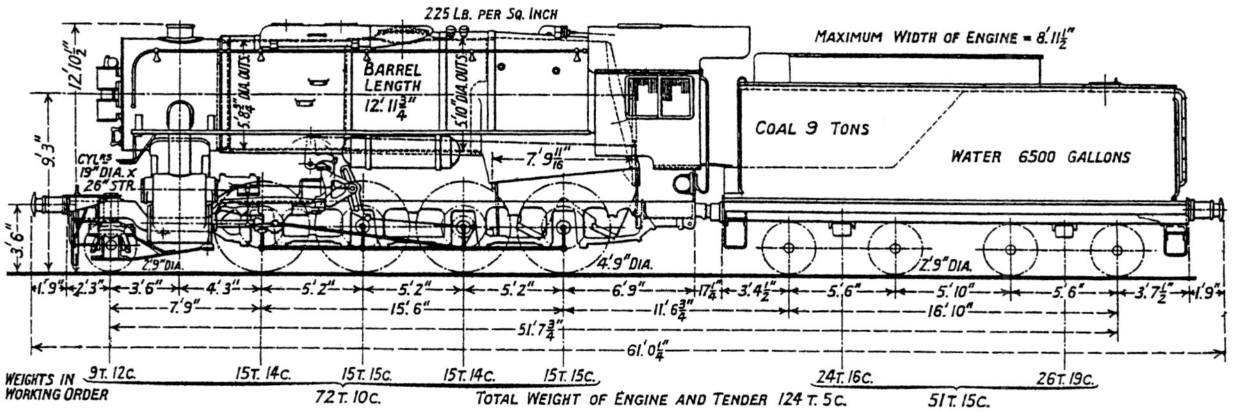

HEATING SURFACE, TUBES—	
LARGE AND SMALL...	1,637 SQ. FT.
FIREBOX	136 „
TOTAL (EVAPORATIVE)	1,773 „
SUPERHEATER	480 „
COMBINED HEATING SURFACES	2,253 „

SUPERHEATER ELEMENTS	30—1½ IN. DIA. OUTS.	
LARGE TUBES	30—5⅜ IN. DIA. OUTS.	13 FT. 4 11/16 IN. BET. TUBEPLATES
SMALL TUBES	150—2 IN. DIA. OUTS.	
GRATE AREA	41 SQ. FT.	
TRACTIVE EFFORT (AT 85 PER CENT. B.P.)	31,490 LB.	

"*S160*" *Class* (*U.S.A.*)

DIAGRAM O
LMS 8F 2-8-0 1935 DESIGN

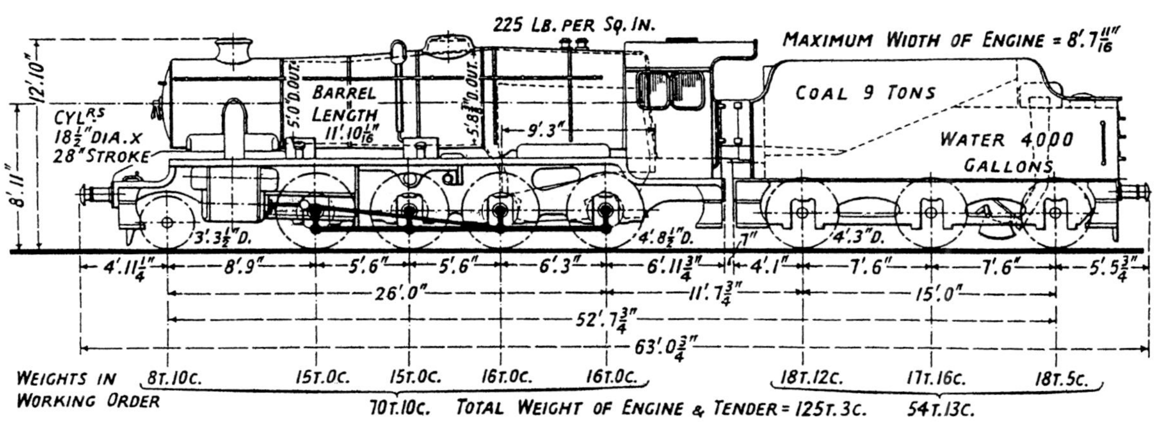

HEATING SURFACE, TUBES—	
LARGE AND SMALL	1,479·0 SQ. FT.
FIREBOX	171·0 „
TOTAL (EVAPORATIVE)	1,650·0 „
SUPERHEATER	215·0 „
COMBINED HEATING SURFACES	1,865·0 „

SUPERHEATER ELEMENTS	21–1⅛ IN. DIA. OUTS.	
LARGE TUBES ...	... 21–5⅛ IN. DIA. OUTS.	12 FT. 3 IN. BET. TUBEPLATES
SMALL TUBES ...	... 202–1¾ IN. DIA. OUTS.	
GRATE AREA	28·65 SQ. FT.	
TRACTIVE EFFORT (AT 85 PER CENT. B.P.)	32,438 LB.	

8F Class (*Taper boiler*)

DIAGRAM P
LMS BEYER GARRATT 2-6-0 + 0-6-2T 1930 DESIGN

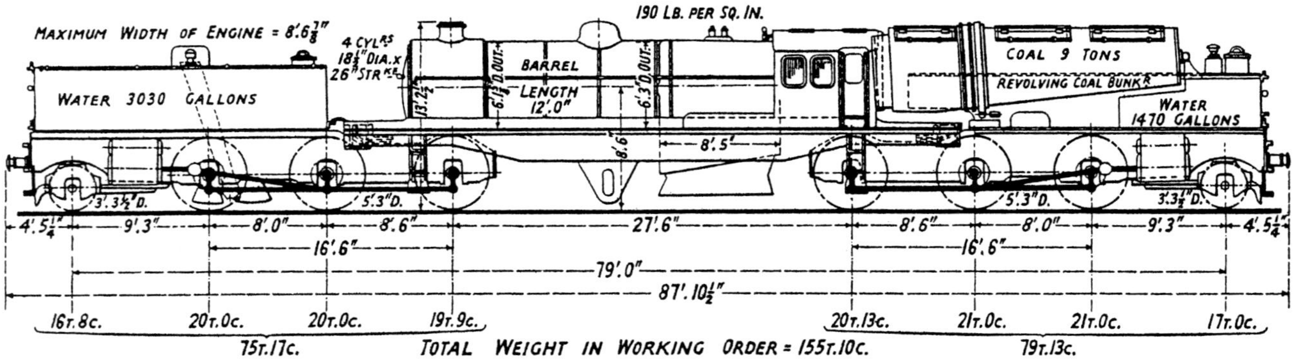

HEATING SURFACE, TUBES—
LARGE AND SMALL ... ... 1,954·0 SQ. FT.
FIREBOX ... ... 183·0 „
TOTAL (EVAPORATIVE) ... ... 2,137·0 „
SUPERHEATER ... ... 500·0 „
COMBINED HEATING SURFACES ... ... 2,637·0 „

SUPERHEATER ELEMENTS ... ... 36–1½ IN. DIA. OUTS.
LARGE TUBES ... ... 36–5¼ IN. DIA. OUTS. } 12 FT. 5 IN.
SMALL TUBES ... ... 209–2 IN. DIA. OUTS. } BET. TUBEPLATES
GRATE AREA ... ... 44·5 SQ. FT.
TRACTIVE EFFORT (AT 85 PER CENT. B.P.) ... ... 45,620 LB.

Beyer-Garratt Locomotive

DIAGRAM Q
LNER P1 2-8-2 1925 DESIGN

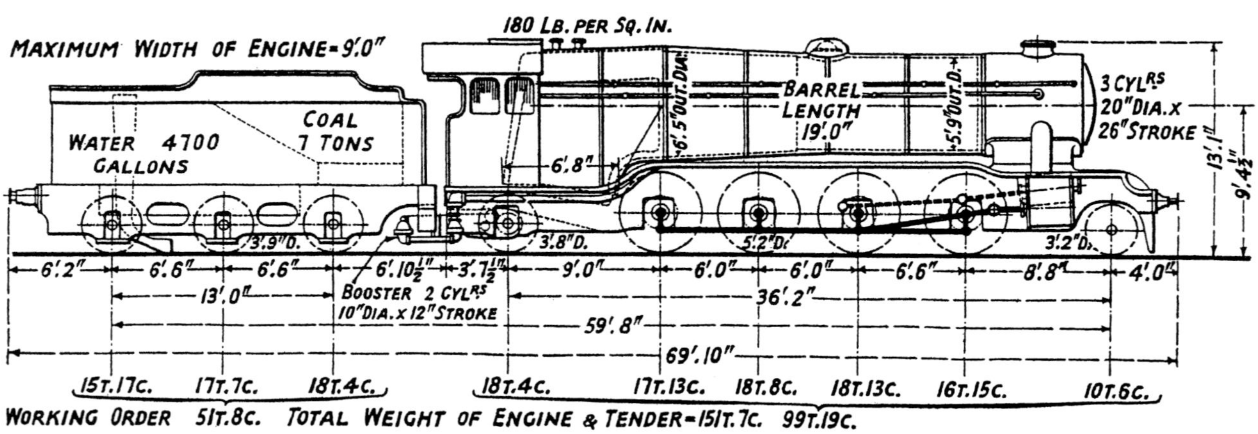

HEATING SURFACE, TUBES—
LARGE AND SMALL ... ... 2,715·0 SQ. FT.
FIREBOX ... ... 215·0 „
TOTAL (EVAPORATIVE) ... ... 2,930·0 „
SUPERHEATER ... ... 525·0 „
COMBINED HEATING SURFACES ... ... 3,455·0 „

SUPERHEATER ELEMENTS ... ... 32–1½ IN. DIA. OUTS.
LARGE TUBES ... ... 32–5¼ IN. DIA. OUTS. } 19 FT.
SMALL TUBES ... ... 168–2¼ IN. DIA. OUTS. } BET. TUBEPLATES
GRATE AREA ... ... 41·25 SQ. FT.
TRACTIVE EFFORT (AT 85 PER CENT. B.P.) ... 38,500 LB.*

* With booster in action tractive effort is increased to 47,000 lb.

P1 Class

DIAGRAM R
GWR 8F 2-8-0 1903 DESIGN AS MODIFIED BY SUPERHEATING

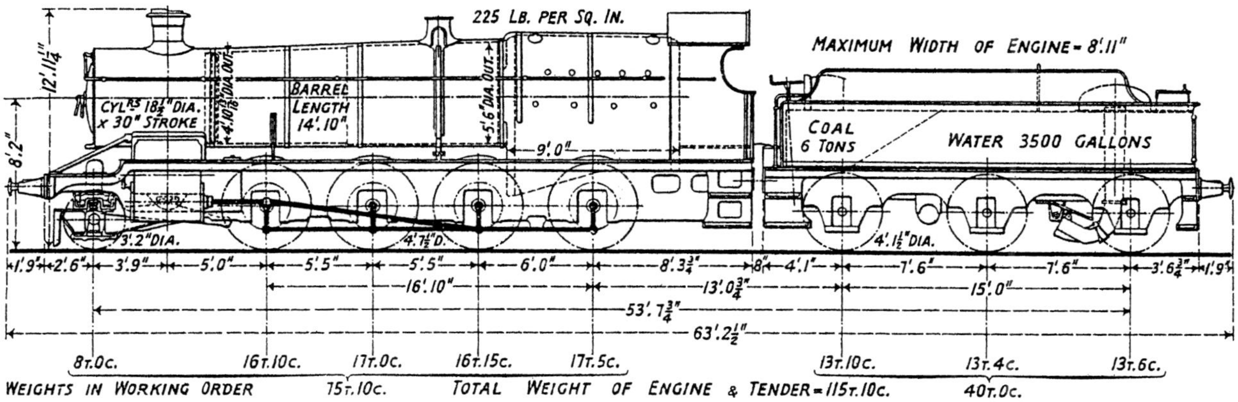

HEATING SURFACE, TUBES—	
LARGE AND SMALL	1,686·60 SQ. FT.
FIREBOX	154·78 ,,
TOTAL (EVAPORATIVE)	1,841·38 ,,
SUPERHEATER	262·62 ,,
COMBINED HEATING SURFACES	2,104·00 ,,

SUPERHEATER TUBES (TRIPLE ELEMENTS) ...		84–1 IN. DIA. OUTS.
LARGE TUBES	14–5⅛ IN. DIA. OUTS.	15 FT. 2$\frac{7}{16}$ IN.
SMALL TUBES	176–2 IN. DIA. OUTS.	BET. TUBEPLATES
GRATE AREA		27·07 SQ. FT.
TRACTIVE EFFORT (AT 85 PER CENT. B.P.) ...		35,380 LB.

"2800" *Class*

DIAGRAM S
GWR COLLETT 2-10-2T: PROPOSED 1937/8 DESIGN

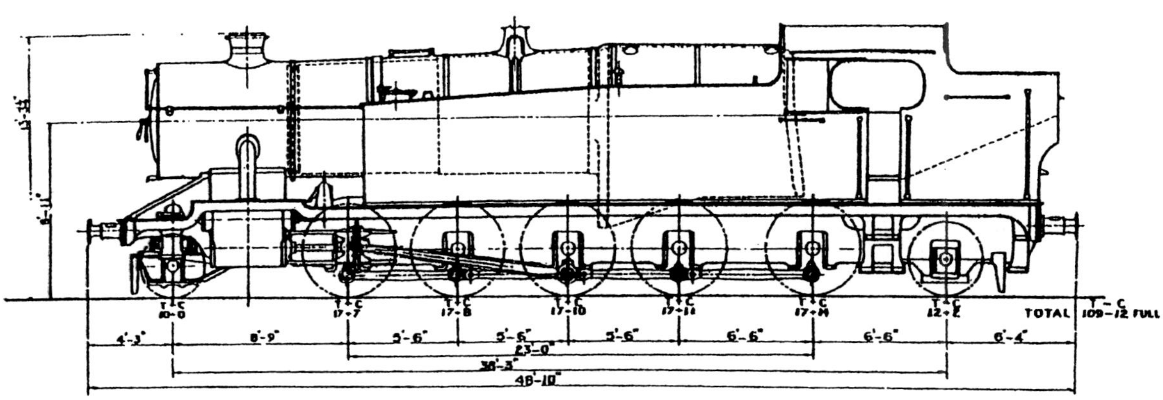

2-10-2T with Standard No. 7 boiler (1937-8)

DIAGRAM T
LMS FOWLER 2-8-2: PROPOSED 1925 DESIGN

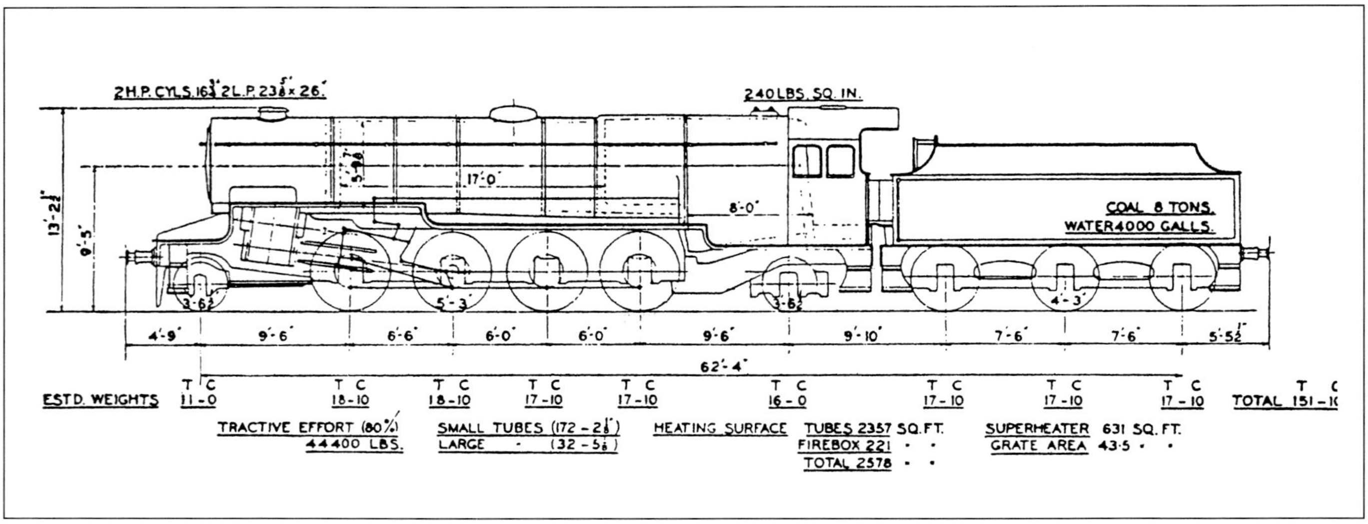

DIAGRAM V
L&YR HUGHES 2-10-0: PROPOSED 1914 DESIGN

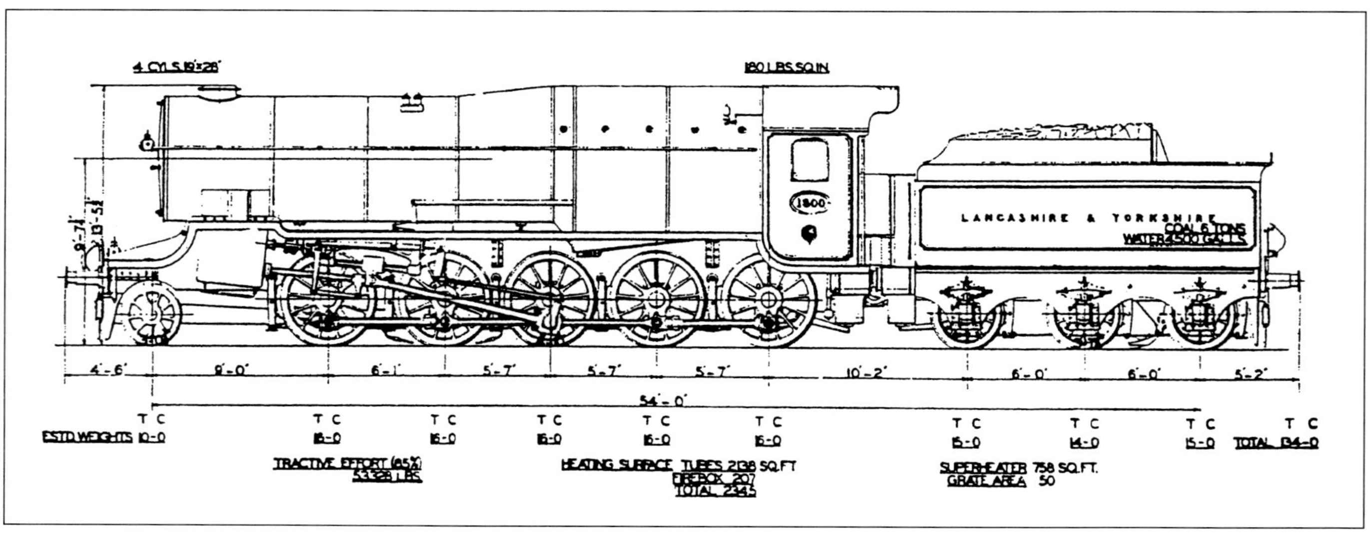

DIAGRAM U
CR PICKERSGILL 2-10-2: PROPOSED 1918 DESIGN

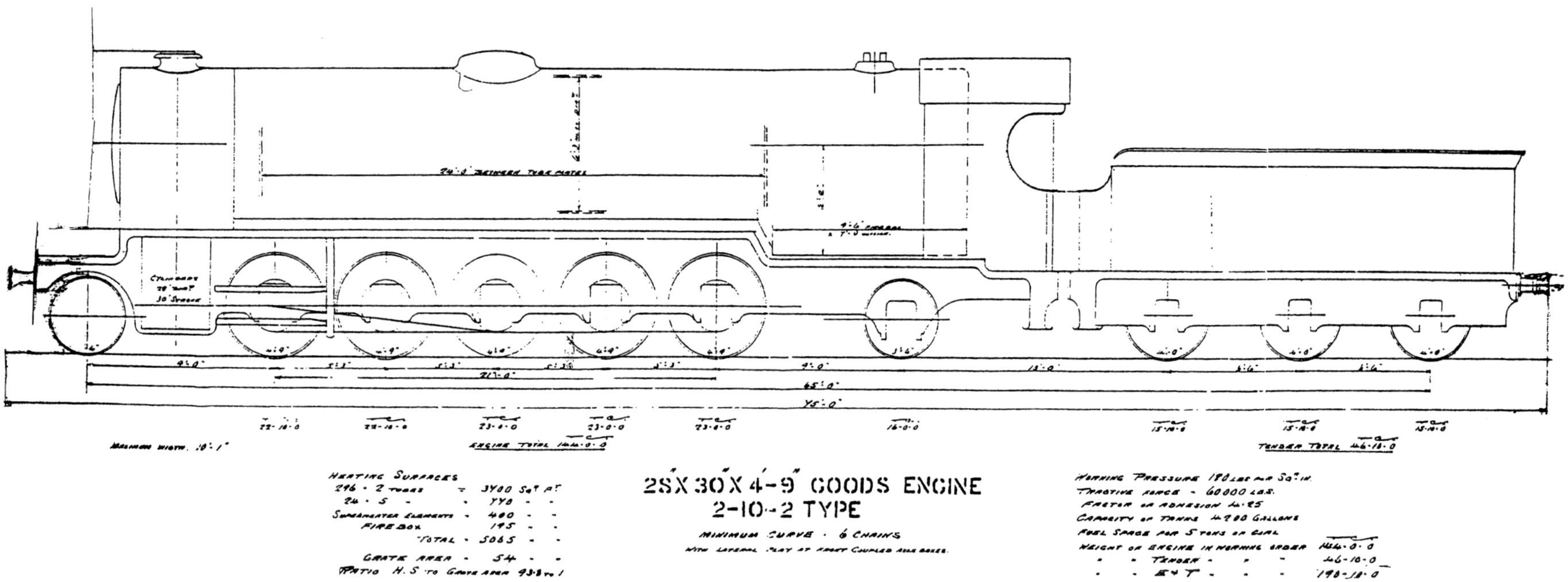

DIAGRAM W
GCR BALDWIN 2-10-2: PROPOSED 1914 DESIGN

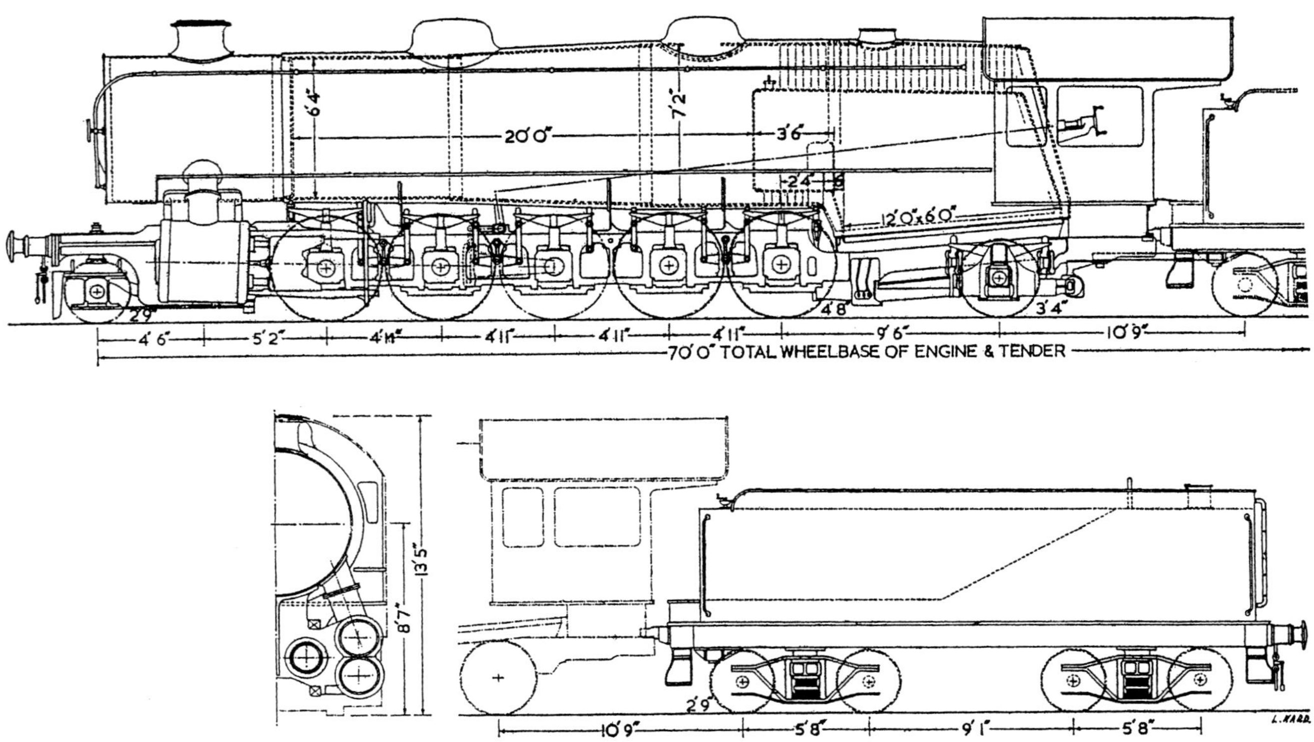

First published in Great Central Volume Three, Fay Sets The Pace 1900-1922, page 322
George Dow, Locomotive Publishing Company, 1965

DIAGRAM X
GCR ROBINSON 2-10-2: PROPOSED 1914 DESIGN

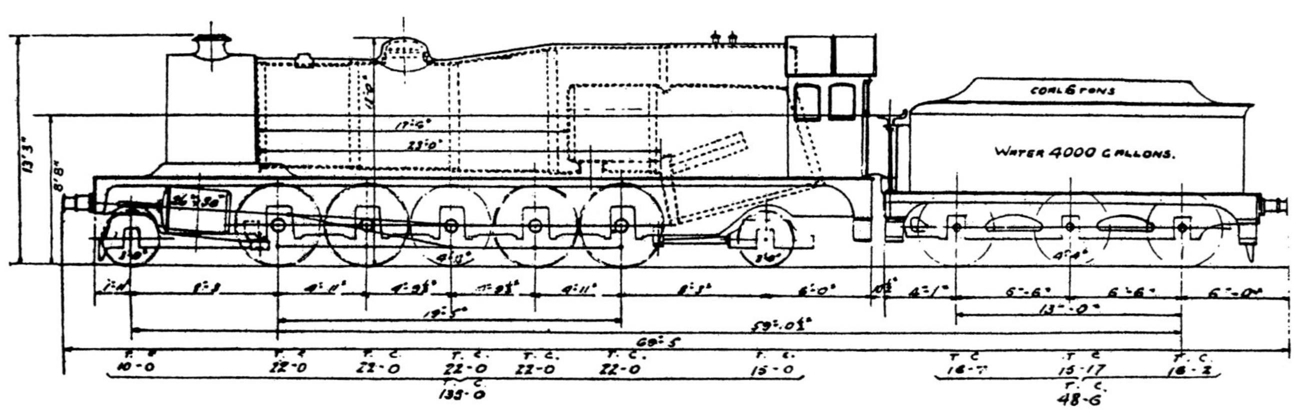

DIAGRAM Y
POWELL 'HEAVY' 2-8-2: PROPOSED CLASS 7P/8F DESIGN

Diagram of proposed Class 7P8F Heavy 2-8-2.

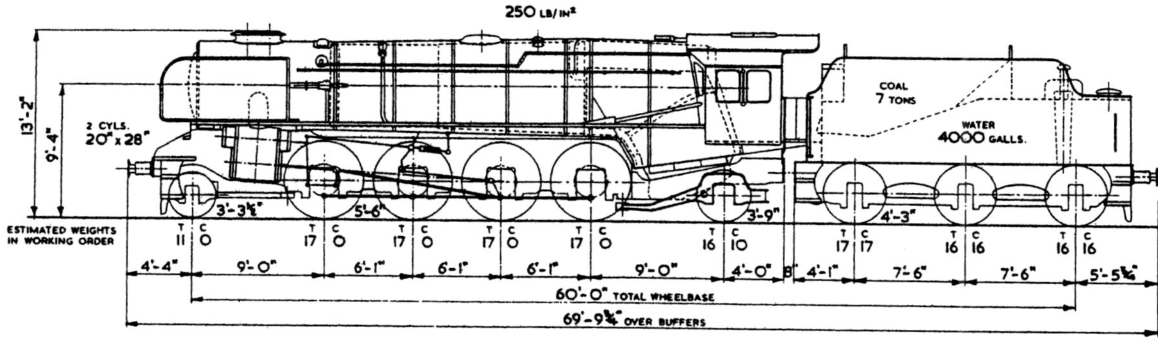

Tube Proportions

Tubes:	
Large	40, 5½in odx 7SWG
Small	136, 2¼in odx 11SWG
Superheater Elements	40 Return Loop, 1⅜in odx 9SWG
Length between Tubeplates	17ft 0in
Free Gas Areas:	
Large Tubes	4.13ft²
Small Tubes	2.66ft²
Total	6.79ft²
A/S Ratios:	
Large Tubes	1/420
Small Tubes	1/435

Heating Surfaces

Tubes	2,264ft²
Firebox	210ft²
Arch Tubes	13ft²
Total Evaporative	2,487ft²
Superheater	677ft²
Total	3,164ft²
Grate Area	42ft²
Free Gas Area as % of Grate Area	16.1%
Tractive Effort	
(85% boiler pressure)	36,106lb
Adhesion Factor	4.22

DIAGRAM Z
POWELL 'LIGHT' 2-8-2: PROPOSED CLASS 6P/7F DESIGN

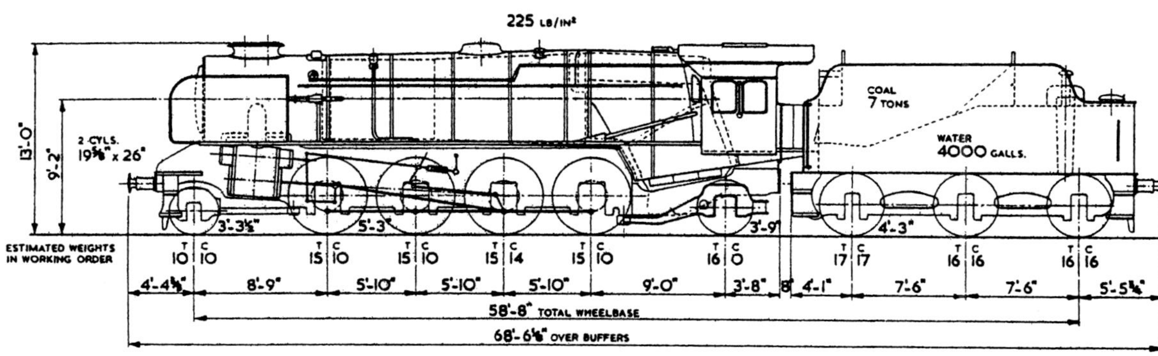

Tube Proportions

Tubes:	
Large	35, 5½in odx 7SWG
Small	108, 2¼in odx 11SWG
Superheater Elements	35 Return Loop, 1⅜in odx 9SWG
Length between Tubeplates	17ft 0in
Free Gas Areas:	
Large Tubes	3.61ft²
Small Tubes	2.12ft²
Total	5.73ft²
A/S Ratios:	
Large Tubes	1/420
Small Tubes	1/435

Heating Surfaces

Tubes	1,878ft²
Firebox	195ft²
Arch Tubes	13ft²
Total Evaporative	2,086ft²
Superheater	592ft²
Total	2,678ft²
Grate Area	36ft²
Free Gas Area as % of Grate Area	15.9%
Tractive Effort	
(85% boiler pressure)	30,398lb
Adhesion Factor	4.58

APPENDIX 1
SOME OBSERVATIONS OF BR STANDARD CLASS 9F 2-10-0s AT SKELTON JUNCTION, TIMPERLEY, JUNE 1966 – MAY 1968

Year	Date	No.	Shed	Track	Train
1966	25.06	92049	BIR	UL	Tanks
	16.07	92102	BIR	UL	Tanks
		92122	BIR	DL	★
	23.07	92025	SPJ	DB	★
	30.07	92101	BIR	DL	★
		92070	BIR	DL	★
	06.08	92059	BIR	UB	Parcels
	27.08	92107	BIR	DL	Coal
		92022	SPJ	UB	Empty minerals
		92024	BIR	UL	Tanks
		92049	BIR	UL	Tanks
		92023	BIR	DB	ICI hopper T-O
	03.09	92103	BIR	UL	Parcels
		92206	YRK	UL	Mixed
		92050	SPJ	DL	Tanks
		92020	BIR	UB/DM	N-Gl Mixed
		92020	BIR	UM/DM	Return LE
		92103	BIR	DL	LE
		92091	SPJ	UL	Tanks
	10.09	92206	YRK	DL	Mixed
		92058	WAR	DB	T-R Covhops
		92023	BIR	UL	Tanks
		92085	BIR	UL	Tanks
	17.09	92047	BIR	DL	Coal
		92073	BIR	DL	Tanks
		92014	BIR	DB	T-R Covhops
		92104	BIR	UL	Tanks
		92089	BIR	UL	Tanks S-NH
	24.09	92104	BIR	UM	LE
		92082	BIR	UB	ICI hopper O-T
		92163	BIR	DB	T-R Covhops
		92134	BIR	DB	Coal
		92050	SPJ	DB	Coal
		92123	BIR	DM	Coal
		92021	BIR	UL	Tanks
		92082	BIR	DB	ICI hopper T-O
		92123	BIR	UM	LE
	08.10	92113	BIR	DM	Coal
		92094	BIR	DB	T-R Covhops
		92119	WAR	DL	Coal
	22.10	92021	BIR	UL	Mixed
		92205	YRK	UL	Empty bogies
		92091	SPJ	DL	Mixed
		92126	WAR	DB	T-R Covhops
		92109	BIR	DL	Mixed
		92107	BIR	UL	Tanks
	29.10	92085	BIR	DL	Mixed
		92131	BIR	UL	Iron ore
		92008	SPJ	UB	Empty minerals
		92206	WAK	UL	Tanks
	15.11	92124	WAR	UL	Mixed
		92205	WAK	DL	Coal
	19.11	92090	BIR	UL	Tanks
		92104	BIR	DL	Mixed
		92021	BIR	UL	Tanks
	24.12	92121	BIR	★	★
		92106	BIR	★	★
		92021	BIR	★	★
	31.12	92094	BIR	★	★
		92162	BIR	★	★
		48119	BIR	★	Tanks (d/h)
		92094	BIR		S-NH
		92077	NEH	★	★
1967	02.01	92001	WAK	★	★
		92069	BIR	★	★
		92020	BIR	★	★
		92131	BIR	★	★
		92139	SPJ	★	★
	07.01	92107	BIR	★	★
		92234	BIR	★	★
1967	07.01	92025	SPJ	DB	T-R Covhops
	14.01	92109	BIR	★	★
		92094	BIR	★	★
		92079	BIR	★	★
		92157	BIR	★	★
		92055	WAR	★	★
		92027	SPJ	★	★
		92234	BIR	DB	T-R Covhops
		92212	CNF	★	★
	04.02	92133	BIR	★	★
		92224	WAR	★	★
		92121	BIR	★	★
		92159	BIR	★	★
		92218	CKR	★	★
		92107	BIR	★	★
		92004	CKR	★	★
		92058	BIR	★	★
		92030	WAK	★	★
		92163	BIR	★	★
	11.02	92094	BIR	★	★
		92047	BIR	★	★
		92154	SPJ	★	★
	18.02	92069	BIR	★	★
		92058	BIR	★	★
		92106	BIR	★	★
		92100	BIR	★	★
		92224	WAR	★	★
	18.03	92153	SPJ	★	★
		92109	BIR	★	Tanks ((d/h)
		92029	BIR		
	01.04	92167	BIR	DL	T-R Covhops
		90397	WAK	UL	Tanks (d/h)
		92211	WAK		
	05.04	92029	BIR	DL	T-R Covhops
		92021	BIR	★	ICI tanks W-I
	08.04	92088	BIR	★	★
		92203	BIR	★	★
		92122	BIR	★	★
		92223	CKR	★	★
	14.04	92159	BIR	UL	Tanks
		92058	BIR	DL	★
		92026	BIR	DL	Tanks
		92069	BIR	UL	Tanks
		92029	BIR	DL	Tanks
	15.04	92218	SPJ	★	★
		92091	SPJ	★	★
		92218	SPJ	★	★
		92026	BIR	DL	Tanks
		92056	WAR	DL	Tanks
		92157	BIR	UL	★
		92154	SPJ	DL	★
		92069	BIR	DL	Tanks
		92117	SPJ	UL	Tanks (d/h)
		92106	BIR		
		92091	SPJ	Dl	Tanks
	21.04	92167	BIR	DL	Tanks
		92122	BIR	UL	Tanks
		92101	BIR	DL	Coal
		48305	SPJ	UL	Tanks (d/h)
		92157	BIR		
		92078	WAR	UL	Mixed
		92166	BIR	UL	Tanks
	22.04	92159	BIR	DL	Tanks
		92022	BIR	UL	Tanks
		92157	BIR	DL	Tanks
	29.04	92054	SPJ	DL	★
		92069	BIR	UL	Tanks
		92022	BIR	UM	Tanks
		92117	SPJ	UL	Tanks
		92165	BIR	DL	★

APPENDIX 1
SOME OBSERVATIONS OF BR STANDARD CLASS 9F 2-10-0s AT SKELTON JUNCTION, TIMPERLEY, JUNE 1966 – MAY 1968

Year	Date	No.	Shed	Track	Train
1967	29.04	92049	BIR	DL	Tanks
		92211	WAK	UB	*
		73158	PAT	UL	Tanks (d/h)
		92156	WAR		
	04.05	44867	STE	DL	Tanks (d/h)
		92121	BIR		
		92113	BIR	UL	Tanks
		92114	CKR	DL	Tanks
		92011	BIR	UL	Tanks
		92048	BIR	DL	Tanks
		92163	BIR	DB	T-R Covhops
	05.05	44913	BIR	UL	Tanks (d/h)
		92022	BIR	UL	
		92048	BIR	DL	SCV
		92126	WAR	UL	A-D mixed
		92223	CKR	DL	Tanks
		92047	BIR	UL	Tanks (d/h)
		92XXX	*		
	06.05	92157	BIR	DL	Coal
		92094	BIR	DB	T-R Covhops
		92046	BIR	UL	Empty minerals
		92022	BIR	DL	Tanks
		92113	BIR	DL	TOB
		44730	BIR	UL	Tanks (d/h)
		92011	BIR		
	08.05	92056	CKR	UL	A-D mixed
		92203	BIR	UL	Tanks
	10.05	92227	SPJ	*	*
		92069	SPJ	UL	Tanks
		92029	BIR	UL	Tanks (d/h)
		92011	BIR		
	13.05	92073	BIR	DM	Coal
		92020	BIR	UL	Tanks
		92088	BIR	DL	Mixed
		45392	HMY	UM	LE (paired)
		92234	BIR		
		45059	HMY	UL	Tanks (d/h)
		92048	BIR		
		92094	BIR	DL	Tanks
	16.05	92163	BIR	DL	Tanks
		92046	BIR	UL	Tanks
		92160	BIR	UL	Tanks
	19.05	92048	BIR	UL	Tanks (d/h)
		92049	BIR		
		92122	BIR	UL	Tanks
		92026	BIR	DL	Tanks
	22.05	92024	BIR	UL	Tanks (d/h)
		92113	BIR		
		92126	WAR	UL	A-D Mixed
		92059	BIR	UL	Tanks (d/h)
		92165	BIR		
	24.05	92058	WAR	UL	A-D Mixed
		92166	BIR	UL	Tanks
		92024	BIR	DL	Tanks
		92050	SPJ	DL	Coal
	25.05	92024	BIR	UL	Tanks
		92154	SPJ	DB	T-R Covhops
		92002	BIR	UL	Tanks
	26.05	92165	BIR	UL	Tanks
		92029	BIR	DL	Tanks
		44897	BIR	UL	Tanks (d/h)
		92234	BIR		S-NH
	01.06	92163	BIR	DL	Tanks
		45232	BIR	UL	Tanks (d/h)
		92127	BIR		
		92049	BIR	UL	Tanks
		92154	SPJ	DM	Mixed
	02.06	92127	BIR	DL	Coal
		44830	BIR	UL	Tanks (d/h)
		92086	BIR		
1967	02.06	92122	BIR	DL	Tanks
		92119	BIR	UL	A-D Mixed
	03.06	92112	BIR	DL	Iron bars
		92022	BIR	DL	Coal
		92166	BIR	UL	Tanks
		92020	BIR	DB	T-S
		92131	BIR	DL	Tanks
		92121	BIR	UL	Tanks
	06.06	92088	BIR	DL	Tanks
		44896	HOL	UL	Tanks (d/h)
		92133	BIR		
		92011	BIR	DL	Coke
		92122	BIR	UL	Tanks
	08.06	92224	WAR	UL	A-D Mixed
		92163	BIR	DL	Tanks
		92056	CKR	DL	Tanks
		92112	BIR	DB	T-R Covhops
		92119	BIR	UL	Tanks
		45130	BIR	DL	Tanks (d/h)
		92088	BIR		
		92224	WAR	DL	Cement
		92132	WAR	UL	Empty Minerals
	09.06	92023	BIR	DB	T-R
		92079	BIR	DL	Tanks
		92056	CKR	DL	Tanks
		92020	BIR	UL	Tanks (d/h)
		92108	BIR		
	12.06	92127	BIR	UL	Tanks
		92224	WAR	DB	Coal
		45089	CRS	UL	Tanks (d/h)
		92121	BIR		
		92218	SPJ	DM	Mixed
		92133	BIR	DB	Mixed
		92026	BIR	UL	Tanks
		92108	BIR	DL	Tanks
		92109	BIR	UB	Tanks
	15.06	92159	BIR	DL	Coal
		92002	BIR	DL	Tanks T-Stan
		44730	BIR	UL	Tanks (d/h)
		92086	BIR		
		92014	BIR	DL	Tanks
		92069	BIR	UL	Tanks
		92082	BIR	UL	Tanks
	16.06	92025	BIR	DB	Coal
		44906	EDG	UL	Tanks (d/h)
		92109	BIR		
		92058	BIR	UL	Tanks
		45130	BIR	UL	Tanks (d/h)
		92023	BIR		
		92048	BIR	DL	Tanks
	17.06	92058	BIR	DB	T-R Covhops
		92029	BIR	DL	Iron ore
		92160	BIR	DL	Tanks
		92021	BIR	UL	Tanks (d/h)
		92123	BIR		
	19.06	45186	CRS	UL	Tanks (d/h)
		92070	BIR		
		92079	BIR	UL	Tanks
		92023	BIR	DL	Tanks
		92088	BIR	UL	Tanks (d/h)
		92014	BIR		
		92139	SPJ	DL	Coal
	20.06	92056	WAR	DL	Tanks
		92002	BIR	UL	Tanks
		44963	BIR	UL	Tanks (d/h)
		92106	BIR		
		92016	CNF	DB	T-R Covhops
	22.06	92113	BIR	DL	Coke
		92025	BIR	UL	Tanks
		92008	SPJ	DB	T-R Covhops

APPENDIX 1
SOME OBSERVATIONS OF BR STANDARD CLASS 9F 2-10-0s AT SKELTON JUNCTION, TIMPERLEY, JUNE 1966 – MAY 1968

Year	Date	No.	Shed	Track	Train
1967	23.06	92002	BIR	UL	Tanks (d/h)
		92106	BIR		
		92091	SPJ	DB	T-R Covhops
		92088	BIR	DB	Coal
	24.06	92102	BIR	*	*
		92127	BIR	DL	LE
		92163	BIR	DB	T-R Covhops
		92008	SPJ	UB	Empty Minerals
		92108	BIR	DB	Mixed
		92152	BIR	UL	Tanks (d/h)
		92088	BIR		S-NH
	03.07	92047	BIR	UL	Tanks (d/h)
		92082	BIR		S-NH
		92048	BIR	DL	Tanks
	04.07	92106	BIR	DL	Tanks
		92022	BIR	DL	Tanks
		92029	BIR	UL	Tanks
	05.07	44823	SPB	UL	Tanks (d/h)
		92101	BIR	UL	
		92165	BIR	DL	Tanks
	07.07	92159	BIR	DL	Tanks
		92073	BIR	DL	Tanks
		92022	BIR	UL	Tanks
		92046	BIR	DL	Mixed
	08.07	92082	BIR	UL	Tanks
		92126	WAR	DB	T-R Covhops
		92079	BIR	DL	LE (paired)
		92025	BIR		
		92157	BIR	DB	G-R Mixed
		92049	BIR	DM	Civ. Eng. Train
		92020	BIR	UL	Tanks
		92110	CKR	UL	Tanks
	10.07	92055	WAR	UL	Mixed
		92025	BIR	UL	Tanks (d/h)
		92167	BIR		
		44897	BIR	UL	Tanks (d/h)
		92029	BIR		
		92101	BIR	DL	Tanks
		92112	BIR	UL	Tanks
	11.07	45130	BIR	UL	Tanks (d/h)
		92123	BIR		S-NH
		92166	BIR	DL	Tanks
		92022	BIR	DL	Tanks T-Stan
		92014	BIR	DB	T-R Covhops
	12.07	45056	SPJ	UL	Tanks (d/h)
		92025	BIR		S-NH
		92167	BIR	DL	Tanks
		92117	SPJ	UB	ICI tanks
		45436	BIR	UL	Tanks (d/h)
		92101	BIR		
		92133	BIR	DL	LE
	14.07	92162	BIR	DL	Tanks
		92224	WAR	UL	A-D Mixed
		44913	BIR	UL	Tanks (d/h)
		92084	BIR		S-NH
		45436	BIR	UL	Tanks (d/h)
		92157	BIR		
	15.07	92046	BIR	*	*
		92109	BIR	*	*
		92027	SPJ	*	*
		92234	BIR	*	*
		92108	BIR	DB	ICI hopper T-O
		92079	BIR	DL	LE
	17.07	92046	BIR	UB	Empty Minerals
		92048	BIR	UL	Tanks
	18.07	92152	BIR	UL	Tanks
		92111	BIR	UL	Tanks
		92234	BIR	DL	LE
	20.07	73131	PAT	UL	Tanks (d/h)
1967	20.07	92131	BIR		S-NH
		92002	BIR	UL	Tanks
		92111	BIR	DB	T-R Covhops
	21.07	45392	HMY	UL	Tanks (d/h)
		92157	BIR		S-NH
	24.07	92026	BIR	UL	Tanks (d/h)
		92020	BIR		
		73000	PAT	UL	Tanks (d/h)
		92082	BIR		
	26.07	92152	BIR	DL	Tanks
		92108	BIR	UL	Tanks (d/h)
		92029	BIR		
		92203	BIR	UL	Tanks (d/h)
		92011	BIR		S-NH
	27.07	92011	BIR	DL	Tanks
		92048	BIR	DL	Tanks
		92046	BIR	DL	T-Stan tanks
		92026	BIR	UL	Tanks (d/h)
		92073	BIR		
	28.07	92111	BIR	UL	Mixed
		92020	BIR	UL	Tanks (d/h)
		92152	BIR		
		92002	BIR	DL	Tanks T-Stan
	02.08	92166	BIR	DL	Tanks
		92165	BIR	DM	Coal
		45280	BIR	UL	Tanks (d/h)
		92101	BIR		
	03.08	92108	BIR	DL	Tanks
		92218	SPJ	DB	T-R Covhops
		92091	SPJ	DM	Mixed
	04.08	92069	BIR	DL	Coal
		92058	BIR	DL	Coal
		92070	BIR	DL	Tanks
	15.08	92117	SPJ	UL	Tanks
		45299	BIR	UL	Tanks (d/h)
		92112	BIR		
		92029	BIR	UL	Tanks (d/h)
		92070	BIR		
		45232	BIR	UL	Tanks (d/h)
		92021	BIR		
		92203	BIR	DL	Tanks T-Stan
	16.08	44859	BIR	UL	Tanks (d/h)
		92113	BIR		S-NH
		92118	CNF	DL	Tanks NH-S
		92014	BIR	UL	Tanks
		92021	BIR	DB	Coal Runcorn
		92167	BIR	UL	Tanks Stan-T
		92069	BIR	DB	Coal
	21.08	92123	BIR	UL	Tanks
		44859	BIR	UL	Tanks (d/h)
		92046	BIR		
		92224	WAR	UL	LE
		92079	BIR	DL	Mixed
	23.08	92029	BIR	UL	A-D Mixed
		45280	BIR	UL	Tanks (d/h)
		92163	BIR		
		92131	BIR	DL	Tanks
		92167	BIR	DB	Mixed
	24.08	92045	BIR	UL	Tanks
		45114	HMY	UL	Tanks (d/h)
		92165	BIR		
		92163	BIR	DL	Tanks
		92024	BIR	UL	Tanks (d/h)
		92160	BIR		
	25.08	92131	BIR	DB	Coke
		92008	WAR	UL	A-D Mixed
		92070	BIR	UL	Tanks
		92047	BIR	DL	Tanks
		45350	WAR	UL	Tanks (d/h)
		92069	BIR		S-NH

APPENDIX 1
SOME OBSERVATIONS OF BR STANDARD CLASS 9F 2-10-0s AT SKELTON JUNCTION, TIMPERLEY, JUNE 1966 – MAY 1968

Year	Date	No.	Shed	Track	Train
1967	25.08	92165	BIR	DL	Tanks
	06.09	92102	BIR	DM	Coal
		92002	BIR	UL	ICI Tanks W-I
		92152	BIR	DL	Tanks
		92054	SPJ	UL	Empty Minerals
		92111	BIR	UL	Tanks
	08.09	92091	SPJ	UL	Empty Minerals
		48182	STE	UL	Tanks (d/h)
		92112	BIR		
		92163	BIR	DL	Tanks
		92049	BIR	UL	Tanks (d/h)
		92152	BIR		
		92160	BIR	UL	Tanks Stan-T
	27.09	45280	BIR	UL	Tanks (d/h)
		92023	BIR		
		44730	BIR	UL	Tanks (d/h)
		92163	UL		
		92108	BIR	UL	Tanks
	29.09	92022	BIR	DL	Mixed
		92024	BIR	DL	Tanks
		92208	CKR	UL	Empty Minerals
	06.10	92108	BIR	DL	Coal Go-G
		92166	BIR	UL	Tanks
		92002	BIR	DL	Coal
		92069	SPJ	DL	Coal
		92165	BIR	UM	LE
		92052	CKR	DL	Tanks T-Stan
	16.10	92084	BIR	DB	Mixed
		92054	SPJ	UB	Empty Minerals
		92029	BIR	*	Gl-B Mix
		92086	BIR	UL	Tanks
	18.10	92102	BIR	*	Gl-B Mix
		92070	BIR	UB	ICI hopper T-O
		92082	BIR	DB	Coal
	21.10	92069	BIR	DL	LE
		92152	BIR	DL	Coal
		92091	SPJ	DL	LE
		92070	BIR	DL	Mixed
	23.10	92029	BIR	UL	Tanks
	24.10	92204	SPJ	UL	Tanks
		92029	BIR	UM	Empty Minerals
		92117	SPJ	DL	Mixed
	30.10	92088	BIR	UM	Empty Minerals
		92152	BIR	DL	Mixed
Most tanks duties now taken over by Type 4 diesels.					
	04.11	92069	(BIR)	DL	Coal to Garston
		92054	(SPJ)	DL	Coal to Garston
	16.12	92054	SPJ	DM	Coal
	17.12	92054	SPJ	DL	Coal
1968	11.02	92218	SPJ	DL	Coal
		44815	TRP	UL	Timber (d/h)
		92054	SPJ		
		92233	CNF	DM	Coal
		92233	CNF	UM	LE
	09.03	92218	SPJ	DB	T-R Covhops
		92160	SPJ	UB	Empty Minerals
		92160	SPJ	DM	LE HM-P
		92218	SPJ	UB	LE R-HM
	16.03	92069	SPJ	UB	Empty Minerals
	11.04	92077	CNF	UL	LE
		92069	SPJ	DL	Mixed
	24.04	92218	SPJ	UB	ICI Tanks R-I
		92069	SPJ	UL	Empty Minerals
Last day of steam at Skelton Junction: 4th May 1968					
	04.05	92160	SPJ	UL	Empty min G-Go
		92118	CNF	UL	Empty min G-Go
		92160	SPJ	DL	Coal Go-G
		92069	SPJ	DL	Coal Go-G

Key * Not recorded

Shed
- BIR Birkenhead
- CKR Carlisle Kingmoor
- CNF Carnforth
- CRS Crewe South
- HMY Heaton Mersey
- HOL Leeds Holbeck
- NEH Newton Heath
- PAT Patricroft
- SPB Springs Branch
- SPJ Speke Junction
- STE Stockport Edgeley
- TRP Trafford Park
- WAK Wakefield
- WAR Warrington
- YRK York

Track
- D Down direction westward from Stockport
- U Up direction eastward towards Stockport
- L Low level line ex-LNWR line to Warrington Arpley
- M Middle line ex-CLC line to Glazebrook and beyond
- B Branch line ex-LMS/CLC line to Northwich & Chester

Train
- A-D Arpley-Dewsnap Sidings (Guide Bridge)
- Covhops Covered hoppers
- d/h double-headed
- Gl-B Glazebrook-Birkenhead
- G-R Godley Junction-Runcorn
- G-Go Garston-Godley Jct. empty minerals
- Go-G Godley Junction-Garston coal
- HM-P Heaton Mersey-Partington
- LE Light engine
- Mix Mixed freight
- N-Gl Northwich-Glazebrook
- NH-S Neville Hill-Stanlow
- O-T Oakleigh Sidings-Winnington-Tunstead limestone empties
- R-HM Runcorn-Heaton Mersey
- R-I Runcorn-Immingham
- S-NH Stanlow-Neville Hill
- SCV Special with Covered Wagons
- Stan Stanlow Oil Refinery
- Stan-T Stanlow-Tuxford
- Tanks Oil tank traffic to and from Stanlow
- T-O Tunstead–Oakleigh sidings Winnington limestone
- T-Stan Tuxford-Stanlow
- T-R Tunstead-Runcorn limestone
- T-S Tunstead-Shotton limestone
- TOB Track lengths on bogies
- W-I Widnes-Immingham

APPENDIX 2

MAXIMUM SPEEDS REPORTED FOR VARIOUS STEAM LOCOMOTIVE CLASSES DRIVING WHEEL REVOLUTIONS PER SECOND AND MEAN PISTON SPEEDS AT QUOTED SPEEDS

No.	Speed	Locomotive Class	Driving Wheels		Cylinder Stroke	Mean Piston Speed
			Diameter	Revolutions per Second		Feet per minute
	mph		inches	at quoted mph	inches	at quoted mph
1	139 ¶	Pennsylvania RR T1 4-4-4-4	80	9.73	26	2530
2	130 ¶	Union Pacific RR Cl. 800 4-8-4	80	9.10	31	2821
3	126	LNER A4 4-6-2 4468 *Mallard*	80	8.82	26	2293
4	125	German State Railway 4-6-4 03.003	90	7.78	26	2022
5	120 ¶	New York Central RR Niagara 4-8-4	79	8.51	32	2723
6	120 ¶	GWR Saint 4-6-0	80½	8.35	30	2505
7	120 ¶	Milwaukee USA 4-6-4	84	8.00	30	2400
8	114	LMS 4-6-2 6220 *Coronation*	81	7.88	28	2207
9	110 • ¶	Norfolk and Western USA Cl. J 4-8-4	68.5	8.99	32	2879
10	108	LNER A3 4-6-2 2750 *Papyrus*	80	7.56	26	1966
11	105	BR Rebuilt Merchant Navy 4-6-2	74	7.95	24	1907
12	102½	GWR King 4-6-0	78	7.36	28	2061
13	102½	GWR Castle 4-6-0 7018 *Drysllwyn Castle*	80½	7.13	26	1854
14	102½	GWR City 4-4-0 3440 *City of Truro*	80	7.18	26	1866
15	102	LNER A2 4-6-2	74	7.72	26	2007
16	101½	LNER V2 2-6-2 (Kylchap double chimney)	74	7.68	26	1997
17	101	BR Cl. 7 4-6-2 70014 *Iron Duke*	74	7.64	28	2140
18	100½	LNER A1 4-6-2	80	7.04	26	1829
19	100	LNER A10 4-6-2 4472 *Flying Scotsman*	80	7.00	26	1820
20	100	LMS Royal Scot 4-6-0	81	6.91	26	1798
21	98	GWR Atbara 4-4-0	80	6.86	26	1784
22	97½	LMS Jubilee 4-6-0 45579 *Punjab*	81	6.74	26	1753
23	97	LMS Rebuilt Patriot 4-6-0 45530 †	81	6.71	26	1744
24	96½★	GWR Castle 4-6-0	80½	6.71	26	1745
25	95	LNER A2/2 4-6-2	74	7.19	26	1869
26	95	LMS Stanier Cl. 5 4-6-0 44966	72	7.39	28	2069
27	95	BR Cl. 5 4-6-0	74	7.19	28	2013
28	94¶	LT&SR 4-6-4T	75	7.02	26	1825
29	93½	LNWR Experiment Cl. 4-6-0	75	6.98	26	1815
30	92½★	LNER A2/2 4-6-2	74	7.00	26	1820
31	91	SR King Arthur 4-6-0	79	6.45	28	1806
32	91	SR West Country 4-6-2	74	6.89	24	1653
33	91	SNCF France Chapelon 4-8-0	71	7.18	25½	1830
34	**90**	**BR Cl. 9F 2-10-0 92184**	**60**	**8.40**	**28**	**2352**
35	90	LMS Fowler 2-6-4T 42387	69	7.30	26	1899
36	90	GWR Hall 4-6-0	72	7.00	30	2100
37	90	LNER B1 4-6-0	74	6.81	26	1771
38	88 ★	GWR Modified Hall 4-6-0	72	6.84	30	2053
39	84 ★	SNCF France Chapelon 4-8-0	71	6.63	25½	1690
40	84	LMS Stanier 2-6-4T	69	6.82	26	1773
41	**80 ø**	**BR Cl. 9F 2-10-0 Crosti 92023**	**60**	**7.47**	**28**	**2091**
42	80	BR Cl. 3 2-6-2T 82025	63	7.11	26	1849
43	77½¶	MR 2P 4-4-0 40551	84.5	5.13	26	1334
44	76	BR Cl. 2 2-6-2T 84008	60	7.09	24	1702
45	75	LMS Fowler Cl. 3 2-6-2T	63	6.67	26	1733
46	74	LNWR DX 0-6-0	60	6.91	24	1658
47	70	LMS Stanier Cl. 8F 2-8-0	56½	6.94	28	1943
48	70	LMS Cl. 4 0-6-0	63	6.22	26	1618
49	68	LNER L1 2-6-4T	62	6.14	26	1597
50	68	LNER K1 2-6-0	62	6.14	26	1597
51	68	LNER N7 0-6-2T	58	6.57	24	1576
52	67	LNWR 'Bill Bailey' 4-6-0	63	5.96	24	1429
53	67	GWR 1400 0-4-2T	62	6.05	24	1452
54	65	SR Q1 0-6-0	61	5.97	26	1552
55	64	LNER K4 2-6-0	62	5.78	26	1503
56	63	LMS Ivatt Cl. 2MT 2-6-0	60	5.88	24	1411
57	58	LNWR G1 0-8-0 'Super D'	53½	6.07	24	1457

Key: ¶ Not authenticated; ★ On level track; • worn tyres (design diameter 70 in); † Named *Sir Frank Ree*; ø On test run

APPENDIX 3
BR STANDARD CL 9F 2-10-0s
LIST OF OFFICIAL BR STANDARD DRAWINGS

Drawing No.	Featuring	Original Allocation	Engine Nos.
SL/9R/1	Standard 9F with BR1G Tender	WR	92000-9, 92203-50
SL/9R/2	Crosti Boiler Engines	LMR	92020-9
SL/9R/3	Standard 9F with BR1F Tender	ER	92010-4, 92030-44, 92067-76 92087-96, 92140-9, 92168-92202
SL/9R/4	Standard 9F with BR1C Tender	LMR	92015-9, 92045-59, 92077-86 92100-39, 92150-64
SL/9R/5	Standard 9F with BR1B Tender	NER	92060-6, 92097-99
SL/9R/6	Mechanical Stoker Engines	LMR	92165-7
SL/9R/7	Converted Crosti Boiler Engines	LMR	92020-9

APPENDIX 4
LOCATION OF SELECTED GOODS YARDS IN GREAT BRITAIN

Yard	Location
Ardsley	4½ miles north of Wakefield Westgate station on the ex-GNR line to Leeds Central
Arpley	½ mile south of Warrington Bank Quay station on the ex-LNWR line to Altrincham
Basford Hall	1 mile south of Crewe station on the WCML
Bordesley Jct.	2 miles south of Birmingham Snow Hill station on the line to London Paddington
Carr	approx. 1 mile south of Doncaster station on the up side of the ECML
Clarence Yard *	south of Finsbury Park station on the down side of the ECML
College	on a terminal spur east of Glasgow St. Enoch station
Decoy	approx. 1 mile south of Doncaster station on the down side of the ECML
Dewsnap	¾ mile east of Guide Bridge on the ex-GCR Woodhead line from Manchester to Sheffield
Dringhouses	1 mile south of York station on the ECML
Durran Hill	east of Petteril Bridge Junction, Carlisle on the ex-MR Settle and Carlisle route to Leeds
Ferme Park *	south of Hornsey station on both sides of the ECML
Forth	junction on south side of Carlisle line approx. ¾ mile west of Newcastle Central station
Gowhole	2½ miles west of Chinley station on the ex-MR Peak Forest route from Derby to Manchester
Gushetfaulds	on a terminal spur off the Caledonian main line out of Glasgow Central
Healey Mills	4 miles west of Wakefield Kirkgate station on the ex-LYR line to Mirfield
Hinksey	½ mile south of Oxford station
Holloway East *	south of Finsbury Park station on the up side of the ECML
Lawley Street	½ mile south of Saltley station on the west side of the line into Birmingham New Street station
Margam	1½ miles south of Port Talbot station on the main line to Cardiff
Millerhill	½ mile north of Millerhill station on the Waverley route from Carlisle to Edinburgh
Mossend	2½ miles north of Motherwell station on the Coatbridge line
Niddrie	1½ miles north of Millerhill station west of the junction of the ECML and Carlisle lines
Park Lane	1 mile north of Felling station on the line to Gateshead
Ripple Lane	1 mile west of Dagenham Dock station on the line to Barking
Skelton Sidings	1½ miles north of York station on west side of ECML to Darlington
Somers Town	adjacent to the west side of St. Pancras station
Stonebridge Park	south of Wembley station on the up side of the WCML
Tees Yard	2 miles west of Middlesbrough station on the line between Newport and Thornaby
Temple Mills	1½ miles north of Stratford station on the Cambridge line
Thornton	½ mile west of Thornton Junction on downside of line from Dunfermline
Tyne Yard	4 miles south of Newcastle-upon-Tyne, on the downside of the ECML at Lamesley
Washwood Heath	north of Saltley station on the east side of the line to Castle Bromwich
Westerleigh	north east of Bristol, south of junction of ex-MR Birmingham line & ex-GWR South Wales line
Whitemoor	1 mile north of March station on the ex-GN/GE joint line to Spalding

* Ferme Park dealt mainly with mineral traffic; Holloway East and Clarence Yard handled express goods, fish and perishables

APPENDIX 5
BR STANDARD Cl. 9F 2-10-0s 92000-92250: TYRE PROFILES

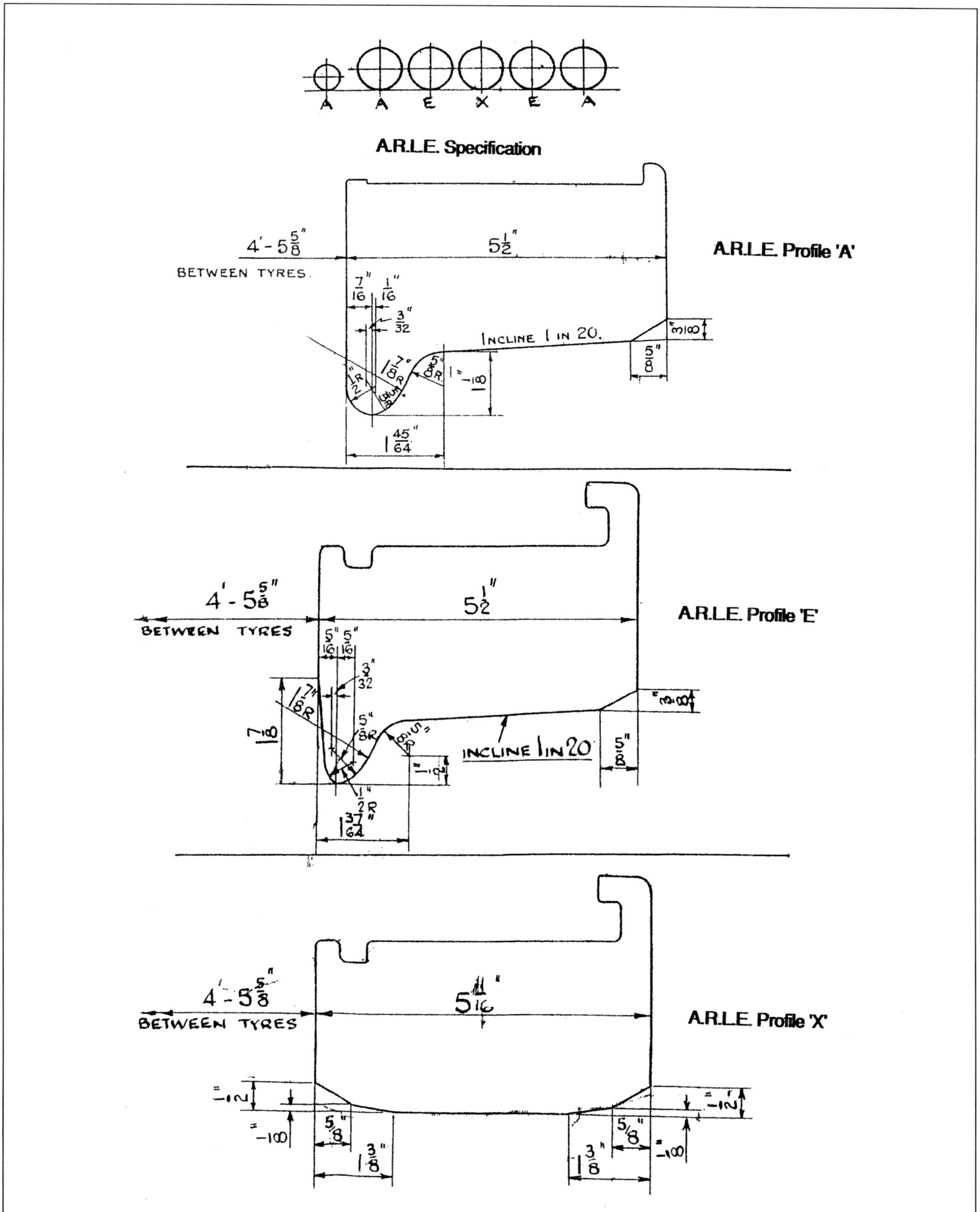

APPENDIX 6
BR STANDARD CLASS 9F 2-10-0s
DYNAMOMETER CAR TESTS

Series Year	Date(s)	Loco	Test Purpose and Route
1. LMR Dynamometer Car No. 3 (BR 1949)			
1954	28.09-22.10	92013	Carlisle-Skipton and return. Performance and Efficiency Tests with Mobile Test Unit.
1955	07.02-10.02	92009	Toton-Brent and return. Class 'C' mineral freight loading trials.
	14.02-17.02	92018	Toton-Brent and return. Class 'C' mineral freight trials. 92018 replaced 92009 following damage to motion during uncontrolled slipping incident at Kettering.
	11.10-10-11	92023	Carlisle-Hurlford and return. Evaluation of Crosti boiler with Mobile Test Unit.
	22.11-09.12	92050	Carlisle-Hurlford and return. Standard 9F comparison v. Crosti 92023 with Mobile Test Unit.
2. WR Dynamometer Car (GWR 1901)			
1954	17.09	92002	Full brake and tender handbrake tests.
1958	28.01-07.02	92178	Steaming performance of engine fitted with double chimney.
3. LMR Dynamometer Car No. 1 (LYR 1913)			
1958/59	12.58-04.59	92094 † 92153 † 92156 †	Toton-Brent and return. Accelerated mineral freight trials using several different 9Fs in tandem.
1959/60	12.59-02.60	92153	Toton-Brent and return. Brake tests for accelerated loose-coupled mineral trains in comparison with BR Sulzer Type 4 2,300 HP Peak diesel electric lcomotive.
4. ER Dynamometer Car (BR 1951)			
1958	09.10-10.10	92196	Doncaster-New England and return. Brake trials for freight load classification.
1961	04.12-17.12	92200	Doncaster-New England and return. Accelerated freight timing trials. A WD 2-8-0, V2 2-6-2 and B1 4-6-0 also took part.

Data Source: NRM York.

† known to have taken part; there may have been others.

APPENDIX 7
BR STANDARD CLASS 9F 2-10-0s
LIST OF OFFICIAL TEST REPORTS

Subject of Test & Report Number	Date	Loco	Test Purpose
Standard Design Single Chimney			
L102	August 1955	92013	Performance and Efficiency Tests with Mobile Test Plant on Carlisle-Skipton route, September 1954. Interim report issued by C.M. & E.E. Department, Derby.
R9	November 1954	92015	Tests on locomotive with reduced Regulator Opening, Issued by Locomotive Testing Station, Rugby.
L104	April 1955	92009/18	Trials with vacuum brake fitted 16 ton mineral wagons on Class 'C' schedules on Toton-Brent route. Issued by C.M. & E.E. Department, Derby.
BR Bulletin No. 13	July 1959	Various	Performance and Efficiency Tests with Exhaust Steam Injector Issued by British Transport Commission.
Crosti Boiler Design			
Test Report (no formal number)	May 1956	92023/50	Comparative Tests of Crosti boiler 92023 with standard boiler 92050. Issued by BR.
L108	Undated	92023/50	Tests to Determine Overall Fuel Consumption including Stand-By Losses for BR Standard and Crosti boiler Locomotives (with LMR Mobile Testing Plant). Issued by C.M. & E.E. Department, Derby.
Giesl Oblong Ejector			
R18	September 1959	92250	BR Standard Class 9F 2-10-0 fitted with Giesl Oblong Ejector, Comparative Tests. Issued by BR Locomotive Testing Station, Rugby.
Mechanical Stoker			
R17	October 1959	92166	Tests on BR Class 9F 2-10-0 Locomotive fitted with Mechanical Stoker. Issued by BR Locomotive Testing Station, Rugby.
Braking Tests			
L138	July 1960	92153	Braking Tests with Loose-Coupled Mineral Trains on the Toton-Brent route in Comparison with Type 4 2,300 HP Diesel Electric Locomotive. Issued by C.M. & E.E. Department, Derby.
Double Chimney November 1957 -February 1958		92178	No formal report issued; experimental data presented in Section 11.1.

Data Source: NRM York

APPENDIX 8
BR STANDARD CLASS 9F 2-10-0s
RUGBY LOCOMOTIVE TESTING STATION
RECORD OF TEST RUNS MAY 1954 TO SEPTEMBER 1959

Run No.	Loco No.	Period of Test	Test Purpose
1118 - 1190	92013	07.05.54 - 20.08.54	Performance & Efficiency: Standard design
1212 - 1228	92015	12.10.54 - 27.10.54	Regulator modifications: pressure drop tests
1352 - 1430	92023	07.06.55 - 28.09.55	Performance & Efficiency: Crosti boiler design
1431 - 1468	92050	07.10.55 - 15.11.55	Standard boiler and Crosti boiler comparison
1765 - 1803	92050	06.03.57 - 26.04.57	Indicator reconciliation for Crosti comparison
2063 - 2141	92166	21.11.58 - 17.03.59	Berkley Mechanical Stoker performance
2142 - 2257 †	92250	09.04.59 - 01.09.59	Giesl Oblong Ejector performance

† Giesl Oblong Ejector fitted from Run No. 2174 (21.05.59) and retained for loco's working life.

Note: 92178 fitted with double blastpipe and chimney was tested on Swindon Plant from 5th November 1957 to 3rd December 1957.

Data Source: NRM York

APPENDIX 9
BR LOCOMOTIVE FLEET: STANDARD LIVERIES, JULY 1949

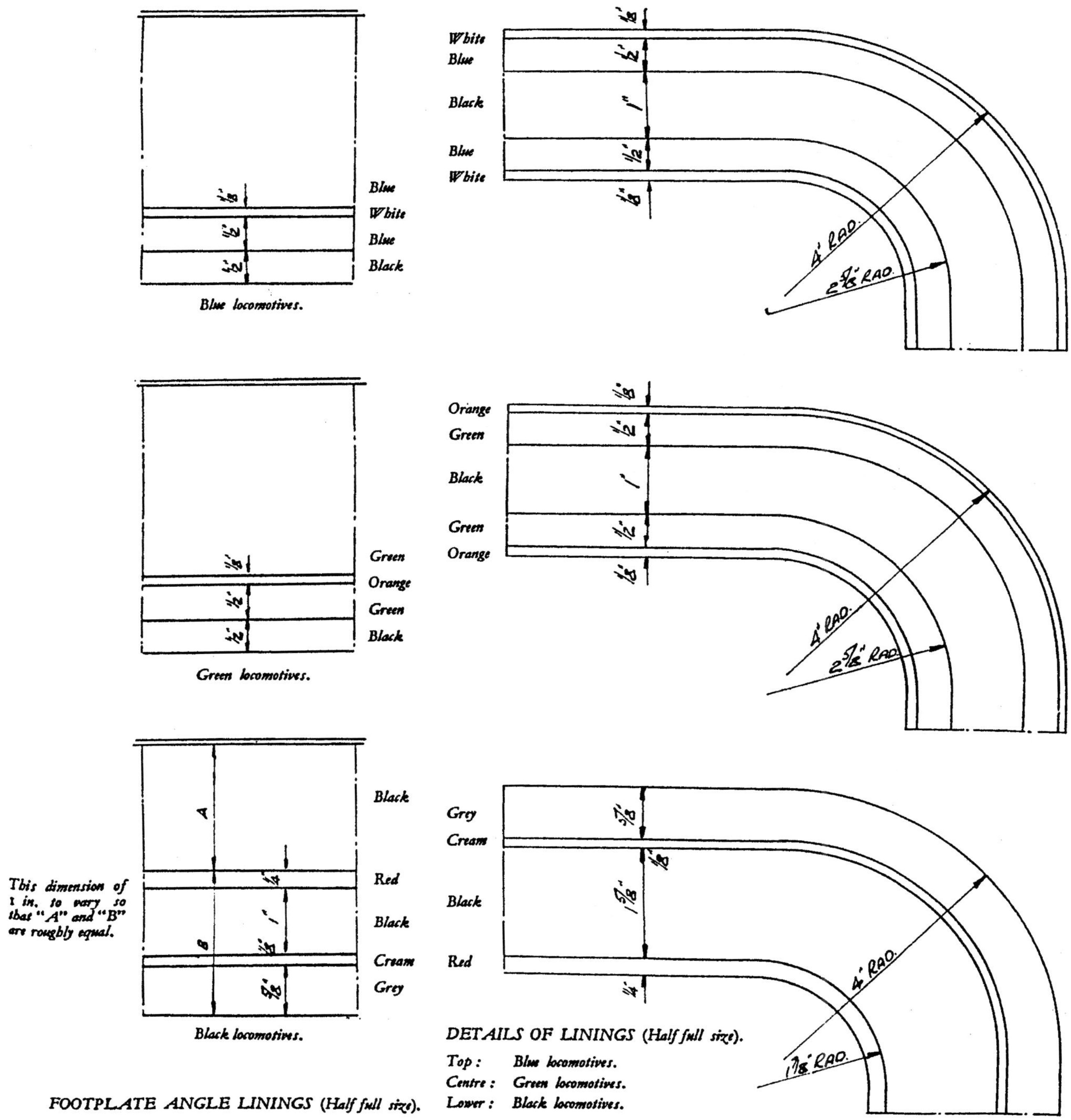

DETAILS OF LININGS (*Half full size*).
Top: *Blue locomotives.*
Centre: *Green locomotives.*
Lower: *Black locomotives.*

FOOTPLATE ANGLE LININGS (*Half full size*).

All parts below the platform angle to be black and unlined; this applies particularly to wheels, axle ends, etc., which may have been previously painted otherwise. The motion to remain bright.

The exposed parts on tender tops to be black. No lining on rear of tender. All parts below the tender panel to be black and unlined. This applies particularly to wheels, frame cut-outs, etc., which may have been previously painted otherwise. The position of the lining on tender sides varies slightly according to the type of tender, but is normally as on cab side panels.

APPENDIX 9
BR LOCOMOTIVE FLEET: STANDARD LIVERIES, JULY 1949

GENERAL DETAILS

STEAM LOCOMOTIVES.

The "British Railways" crest to be placed centrally in the appropriate panels, one left-hand and one right-hand, so that the lion faces forward. Position can be varied slightly if necessary to avoid bolt or rivet heads.

All locomotives to carry the crest.

Cab roofs and all hand-rails to be black.

Buffer beams and casings to be signal red.

Frame extensions, smoke-boxes, saddles, outside steam pipes and cylinder clothing to be black in all cases.

Smoke deflectors to be black and unlined, except in the "Merchant Navy" and "Battle of Britain" classes.

Ex-G.W.R. locomotives and new locomotives built to G.W.R. designs to keep present size and style of cast number plate on cab or bunker sides.

All locomotives to carry cast number plates on the smoke-box door similar in design to that used on former L.M.S.R. locomotives, and in the same position.

Route availability, where applicable, to follow existing practice.

Cast plates for place and date built, tender number and capacity, etc., to remain as on existing locomotives, except that initial of former company to be omitted.

DIESEL AND ELECTRIC LOCOMOTIVES.

Main-line locomotives with cabs at each end; engine numbers to be on each side as near at each end as convenient, with crest in centre.

Main-line and shunting locomotives with single centre or end cabs; engine number on cab side immediately below windows. Crest in centre of bonnet portion.

"Built" plates below engine numbers, but no cast number plate on front or rear.

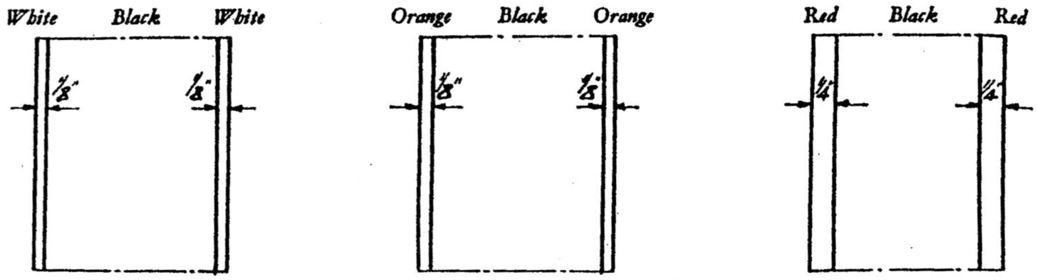

CYLINDER CLOTHING LININGS.
(All half full size.)

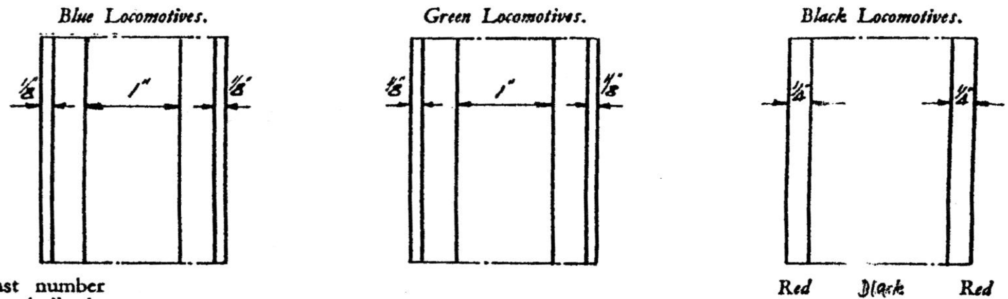

BOILER CASING BANDS.
(Colours of Blue and Green Locomotives as for linings.)

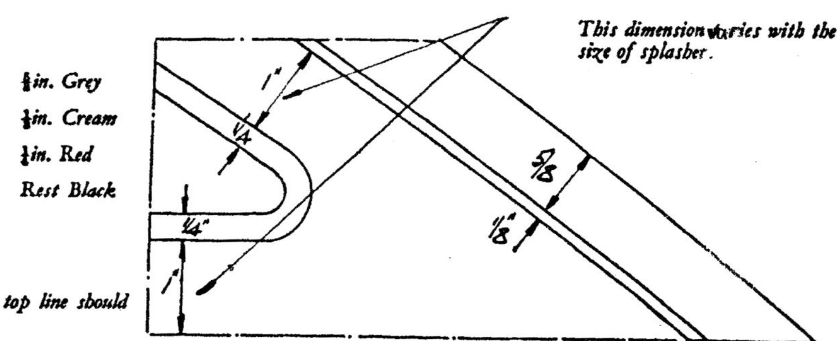

Note.—Where a splasher has a polished brass beading the top line should should be taken from the inside radius of the beading.

Black Locomotives.

LININGS FOR SPLASHERS.
(Half full size.)

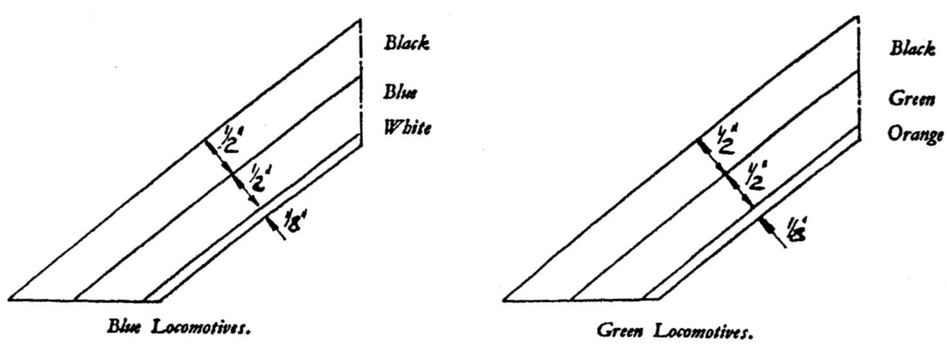

Blue Locomotives. *Green Locomotives.*

Note.—When a splasher is extensively screened by external fittings it will probably not be lined.

APPENDIX 10
UK INLAND COAL CONSUMPTION IN MILLIONS OF TONS 1948-1950

	1948	**1949**	**% Change 1949 v. 1948**	**1950 (provisional)**	**% Change 1950 v. 1949**
Power Stations	28.77	30.09	+ 4.59	32.91	+ 9.37
Gasworks	24.60	25.38	+ 3.17	26.62	+ 3.31
Railways	14.58	14.77	+ 1.30	14.54	- 1.56
Coke Ovens	22.31	22.56	+ 1.12	22.55	-
Iron and Steel Industry	8.67	8.40	- 3.11	8.34	- 0.71
Engineering Industry	3.51	3.57	+ 1.71	3.77	+ 5.60
Other Industry	30.34	31.03	+ 2.27	32.52	+ 4.80
Household Coal (Merchants' Disposals)	31.86	30.90	- 3.01	32.46	+ 5.05
Miners' Concessionary Coal and Colliery Consumption	16.30	15.70	- 3.68	15.75	+ 0.32
Miscellaneous	12.84	13.29	+ 3.50	12.65	- 4.82
Total	193.78	195.69	+ 0.99	201.71	+ 3.08

Data Source: National Coal Board Annual Report and Statement of Accounts
For The Year Ended 31st December 1950
HMSO, London, 5th June 1951.

APPENDIX 11
UK COAL OUTPUT COMPARED WITH CONSUMPTION AND STOCKS IN MILLIONS OF TONS 1949 AND 1950

	1949	1950
Deep-mined Saleable Output	202.68	204.12
Opencast Disposal	12.24	12.62
Stocks at beginning of Year		
Distributed	14.57	14.71
Colliery	1.40	1.53
Grand Total	230.89	232.98
Inland Consumption	195.69	201.71
Exports and Ships' Bunkers	18.96	17.53
Stocks at Year End		
Distributed	14.71	12.43
Colliery	1.53	1.31
Grand Total	230.89	232.98

Data Source: National Coal Board Annual Report and Statement of Accounts For The Year Ended 31st December 1950 HMSO, London, 5th June 1951.

APPENDIX 12
BRITISH RAILWAYS STANDARD HEADCODES

A	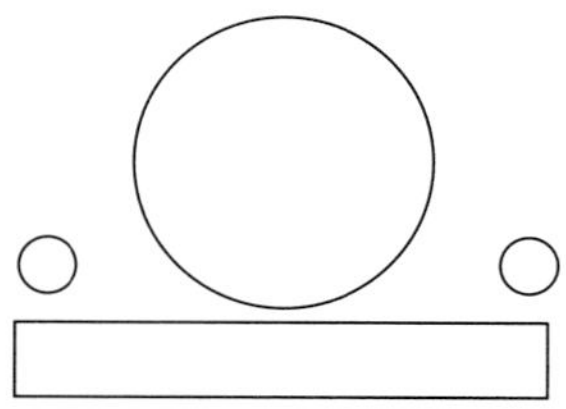	Express passenger or newspaper train; breakdown train or snow plough going to clear the line; light engine proceeding to assist a disabled train.
B	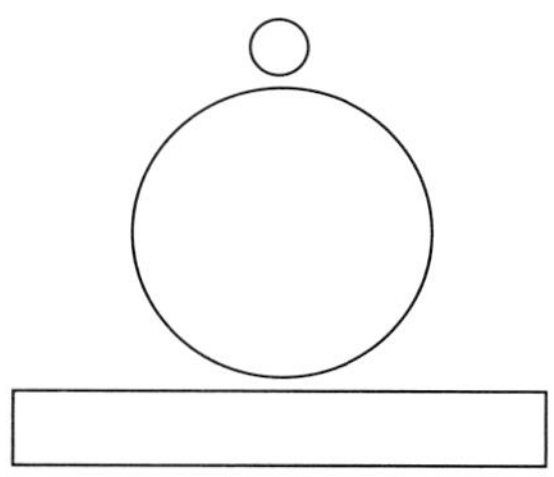	Ordinary passenger, branch passenger or "mixed" train; rail motor; breakdown train not going to clear the line.
C	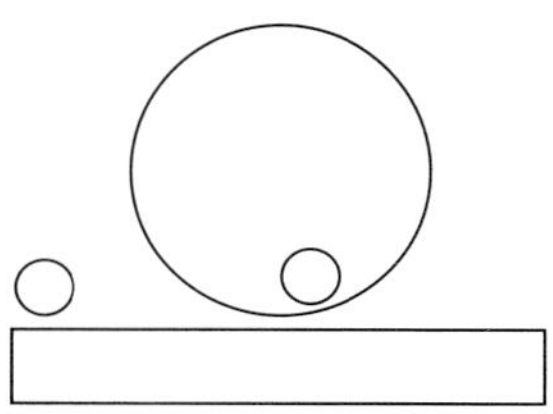	Parcels, fish, fruit, livestock, milk or other perishable train composed entirely of vehicles conforming to coaching stock requirements; express freight, livestock, perishable or ballast train pipe fitted throughout with the automatic vacuum brake operative on not less than half the vehicles; empty coaching stock (not specially authorised to carry "A" code).
D	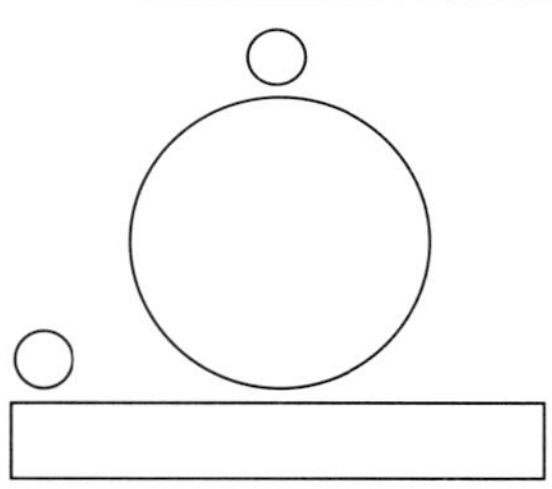	Express freight, livestock, perishable or ballast train with not less than one-third vacuum braked vehicles piped to the engine.
E	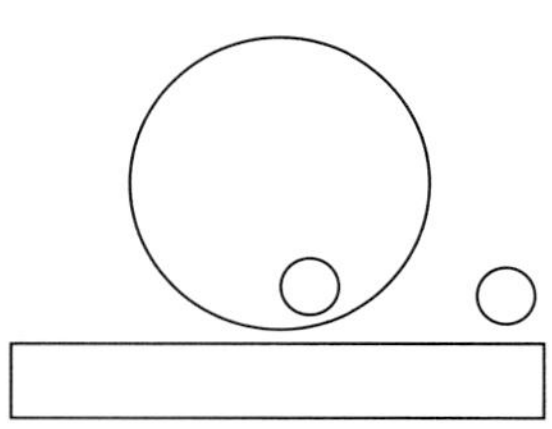	Express freight, livestock, perishable or ballast train with not less than four vacuum braked vehicles piped to the engine OR express freight train of limited load without continuous brake.
F	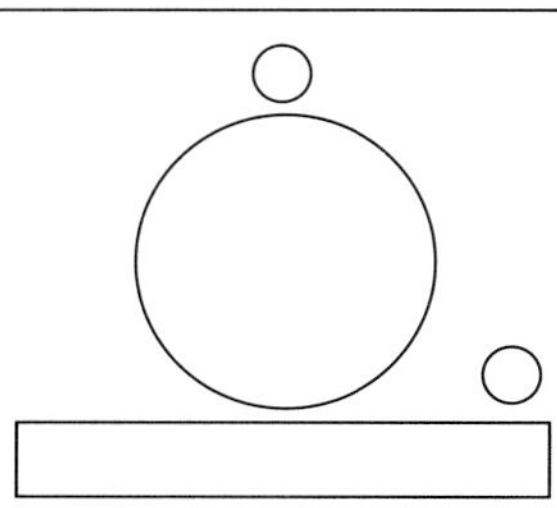	Express freight, livestock or ballast train without continuous brake.

G	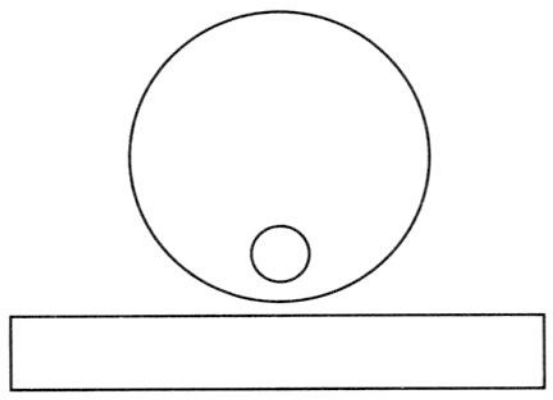	Light engine(s) (LE) or engine with not more than two brakevans (EBV).
H	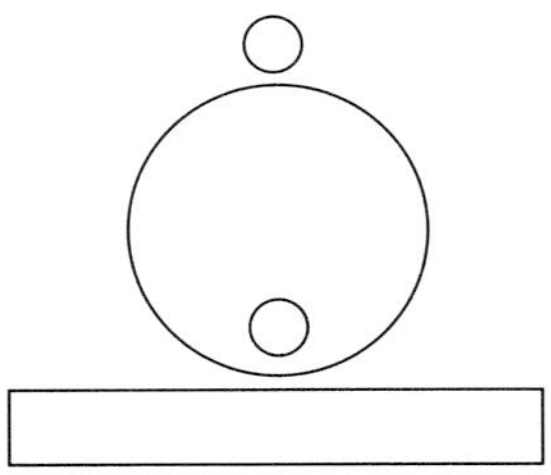	Through freight or ballast train not running under "C", "D", "E" or "F" conditions.
J	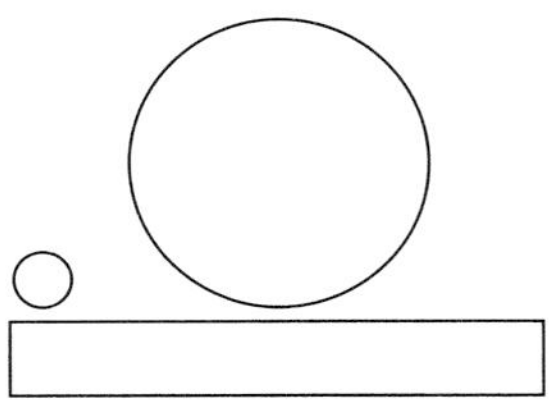	Mineral or empty wagon train.
K	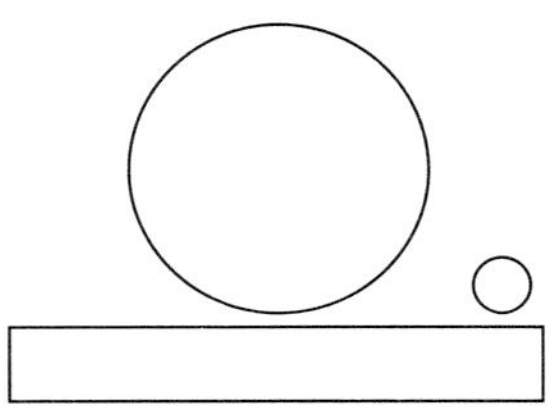	Pick-up or branch goods train.

Notes

1. Not used on the Southern Region where a Route Indicating System was in use.

2. Number of braked wagons specified for a Class 'E' train was later increased to six.

3. The distinctions between the various classes of unfitted trains was not consistently applied. On the MML for example, the coal trains from Toton and Wellingborough to Brent generally ran as Class 'J' while the return empties ran as Class 'F'. Some other unbraked services between these points ran as Class 'H' in both directions.

4. The Annesley to Woodford Halse loaded trains were shown in the Working Timetable in both ER and LMR days as Class 'H' while the return empty wagon services were shown as 'EUB' i.e. 'E' unbraked.

APPENDIX 13
BR STANDARD CLASSES 9F 2-10-0s
DATING OF PHOTOGRAPHS AND OTHER HISTORICAL EVENTS
METHOD FOR CONFIRMING THE DAY OF THE WEEK FOR A GIVEN DATE

Example: 24th May 1963

1. Write down the last two digits of the year: example: 63
2. Divide this number by four and add the quotient, ignoring any remainder: example: 63 + 15 = 78
3. Add the date of the month: example: 78 + 24 = 102
4. Add 1 for January (or 0 if this was a leap year)
   4 for February (or 3 if this was a leap year)
   4 for March
   0 for April
   2 for May: example: 102 + 2 = 104
   5 for June
   0 for July
   3 for August
   6 for September
   1 for October
   4 for November
   6 for December
5. Add 0 if date is in 20th Century: example: 104 + 0 = 104
   2 … 19th Century
   4 … 18th Century
   6 … 21st Century
6. Divide total number by 7. Remainder number gives day of week as follows:
   1 … Sunday
   2 … Monday
   3 … Tuesday
   4 … Wednesday
   5 … Thursday
   6 … Friday: example 104 ÷ 7 = 14, Remainder 6 ie. 24th May 1963 fell on a Friday.
   0 … Saturday

RCTS Publications List – First Edition 2008

Title of Book	*ISBN No.*	**Price*
BR Standard Steam Locomotives:		
Vol 1 Background and the Pacifics	0901115819	£19.95
Vol 2 The 4-6-0 and 2-6-0 Classes	0901115932	£24.95
Vol 3 The Tank Engine Classes	0901115770	£18.95
Locomotives of the LMS:		
The Jubilee 4-6-0s	0901115940	£24.95
LMS Diesels	0901115762	£19.95
Raising Steam on the LMS	0901115851	£24.95
LMS Locomotive Names	0901115797	£18.95
SPECIAL OFFER BUY THIS BOOK FOR £10.00 WHEN BOUGHT WITH L&NWR LOCO NAMES		
L&NWR Locomotive Names	0901115908	£19.95
Locomotives of the LNWR Southern Division – L&BR, LNWR and Wolverton Loco Works	0901115894	£27.95
Highland Railway Locomotives 1855-1895	0901115649	£12.95
Highland Railway Locomotives 1895-1923	090111572X	£16.95
SPECIAL OFFER set of Highland Railway Locomotives		£23.50
Locomotives of the LNER:		
Part 1 Preliminary Survey	0901115118	£12.95
Part 2B Tender Engines Classes B1-B19	0901115738	£13.95
Part 9A Tank Engines Classes L1-N19	0901115401	£10.95
Part 9B Tank Engines Classes Q1-Z5	090111541X	£10.95
Part 10A Deptl Stock, Engine Sheds, etc	0901115657	£10.95
Part 11 Supplementary Information	0901115800	£10.95
The Great Northern Railway in the East Midlands:		
Colwick Yards, Nottingham L Rd-Gedling-Basford	0901115843	£13.95
The Erewash Valley Lines, Pinxton Branch, Awsworth-Ilkeston, Heanor & Stanton Branches	0901115886	£15.95
Nottingham-Grantham, Bottesford-Newark, Melton Mowbray, Leicester line and ironstone branches	090115924	£18.95
A Travellers Guide to the Robin Hood line	0901115835	£2.95
Free if purchased with books from GNinEMids Series		
Special Offer Set of Gt Northern Loco History		£40.95
1: 1847-1866	0901115614	£12.95
2: 1867-1895	0901115746	£19.95
3A: 1896-1911	090111569X	£19.95
3B: 1911-1923	0901115703	£16.95
Plymouth's Railways in the 1930s	0901115916	£12.95
The Railways of Keynsham	0901115827	£9.95
OFFER BUY THIS BOOK FOR £5.00* WHEN BOUGHT WITH PLYMOUTH'S RAILWAYS IN 1930s		
The Birkenhead Railway	0901115878	£14.95

Please consult our website at **rcts.org.uk** for current availability and where orders may be placed on line using our secure server.

UK orders are post free. Overseas postal rates are shown on the website. For non internet overseas orders please add 40% with payment by Sterling cheque or by Visa & Mastercard credit cards.

Please mail orders to The Publications Sales Officer, John Wood, 87 Tiverton Drive, Horeston Grange, Nuneaton CV11 6YJ, England.

SOME OTHER RCTS BOOKS

BRITISH RAILWAYS STANDARD STEAM LOCOMOTIVES

In this major series, the Society presents for the first time the complete story of British locomotive standardisation from the days of the Robinson ROD 2-8-0s to the twelve BR Standard designs totalling 999 locomotives.

Volume 1 Background to Standardisation and the Pacific Classes

Immediately British Railways was formed in January 1948, the Railway Executive instructed Robert Riddles to design a series of standard locomotive designs. The intention was to gain material savings in running and maintenance costs by adopting as standard the best practices of the four independent companies. Paul Chancellor and Peter Gilbert present the Standards' design history and for each of the 66 locomotives in the popular Britannia, Duke and Clan classes its complete construction, modification, allocation and operating history. *Page size 212 x 272mm, Casebound, 184 pages, 151 illustrations including 17 in colour.*

Volume 2 The 4-6-0 and 2-6-0 Classes

Riddles' team produced five 4-6-0 classes totalling 452 engines. Three were based on LMSR designs from Stanier (Cl 5s) and Ivatt (Cl 4 and 2) with the "unfinished" look of the Ivatt 4 pleasingly tidied up. All the new standard classes except the Cl 2 achieved an endearing sense of balance from extending down the high running plate to the front buffer beam and sloping the underside of the cab sheet. These features allowed much pipework to be hidden whilst still achieving improved maintenance access. This book by John Walford presents a fascinating and absorbing review of British railway operations four decades ago. *Size 212 x 272mm, 278 pages, 279 illustrations, 17 in colour.*

Volume 3 The Tank Engine Classes

From Penzance to Wick, the Standard tank classes were designed to modernise secondary route power. Railway enthusiasts throughout the land became familiar with their high running plates which gave the 230 engines of three types their "family" appearance. Author Paul Chancellor presents their full story, from their design origins, construction, modifications, allocation, use and liveries. Whether these engines hauled you reluctantly to school – your reviewer's experience – or you only came across them in preservation, the Class 4's handsome curved tank sides will evoke many a nostalgic memory. With their construction at all six main workshops, local livery variations and national use, there is something for everyone to savour in this book. Diagrams of each design are included. *Page size 212 x 272mm, Casebound, 189 photographs including sixteen in colour.*

THE JUBILEE 4-6-0s

Stanier was lured from the GWR in 1932 to address the LMS problem of heavier trains and small engines requiring much expensive double heading. The Jubilee 4-6-0s were one of his solutions. He had to contend with loading gauge and weight restrictions on the Midland, Caledonian and Highland lines. While two cylinders gave the best acceleration, the hammer blow from 6ft 9in driving wheels would have been unacceptable so three cylinders were used, with a light taper boiler GWR style. 191 were built between 1934 and 1936. In the early days they would not steam though still achieved outstanding mileages of 50,000 – 70,000 annually. Retubing resolved the steaming problems and from 1935 when one was named to commemorate the Silver Jubilee of King George V and Queen Mary they became the Jubilees. With their wide usage, aesthetic looks and romantic names they became very popular. This long awaited book by Ray Townsin presents the complete design, modifications, livery, allocation and use for each engine including much new information. *Size 212 x 272mm, laminated casebound cover, 262 pages, 200 illustrations including 9 in colour.*

LOCOMOTIVES OF THE LNER

Part 11 Supplementary Information

This series of 19 books presents the accredited expert work on the locomotives of the LNER. A reprint of this popular Part 11 first published in 1994 is now available. It presents 85 rare illustrations of LNER traction and information to update the ten earlier books in the series published over the previous 30 years. *Size 145 x 200mm, laminated cover, 98 pages, 86 illustrations.*
Our Publications List show the availability of other books in the Series.

This book is also available in digital format on a CD-Rom. Details on our website at **rcts.org.uk**

RAISING STEAM ON THE LMS

The Evolution of LMS Locomotive Boilers

Readers can almost imagine themselves in the mutual improvement classes at the running shed with this absorbing book! It opens at Grouping with an inherited fleet of poor steaming designs unsuited to the heavy and growing traffic levels. The Board's historic decision to hire Stanier from the rival Great Western and his revolutionary work to equip the LMS with a more suitable locomotive fleet revolved around more effective raising and use of steam. The complete story is presented here, from early LMS practice based on pre-Grouping designs, through Stanier's importation of GWR practices, early results and comprehensive details of his design improvements culminating in the largest British pacifics, the Coronation class. The necessary technical content is presented concisely by author Arthur Cook in useful tables and an Appendix, allowing the text to be presented in an infectious, readable style. *Casebound, page size 180 x 235mm, 233 pages, 138 photographs and drawings, one in colour.*

LMS LOCOMOTIVE NAMES

The Named Locomotives of the LMS and its Constituent Companies

The LNWR had a vigorous naming policy and the Midland Railway an equally determined anti-naming stance. The 1923 grouping set the stage for an absorbing battle within the management teams over naming policy with Derby's early policy success followed by Crewe's ultimate victory. Author John Goodman's absorbing read presents the full story of the LMS and its constituent companies' naming policies and the history of each named engine owned by the LMS, a total of 812. The LNWR contributed 668 of these and a complete presentation of its complex re-naming system is an invaluable inclusion.
Casebound, 211 pages, 124 photographs, 25 drawings.

L&NWR LOCOMOTIVE NAMES

The Named Locomotives of the London & North Western Railway and its Constituent Companies

And

A SEQUEL TO LMS LOCOMOTIVE NAMES

There has never been a collection of locomotive names anything like those on locomotives of the London & North Western Railway. Travellers on the L&NWR must have wondered at their extraordinary variety. Author the Revd John Goodman provides details of the named locomotives owned by the L&NWR and its constituent companies, including the Grand Junction and the Liverpool & Manchester Railways, the Bolton & Leigh and North Union railways, and of the Lancaster & Carlisle and the several companies which were absorbed into it. It covers all the names dating from the times of King William IV to the withdrawal of *Scirocco*, the last L&NWR name to survive in June 1949, and analyses the naming policy through the succession of Chief Mechanical Engineers. The Company policy of re-using engine names over and over again is fully documented and a Glossary of every name is included.

The last section was written as the result of the considerable correspondence following the 1994 publication of *LMS Loco Names* necessitating corrections and providing much entirely new information. The chapters of the Regimental names and a much expanded list of naming ceremonies are particularly welcome.
Casebound, page size 270 x 210mm, 280 pages, 98 illustrations

PLYMOUTH'S RAILWAYS IN THE 1930s

including The GWR's Poor Relation

This book presents railway history with a difference. There are no references to Acts of Parliament, opening ceremonies, and only a few to historical events down the years. Rather, it is a chronicle of memories of the railway in Plymouth covering the decade up to the outbreak of World War II. The memories have been authenticated and an attempt has been made to relate activity back to the very different lifestyles that appertained at the time. The seemingly ridiculously low prices for railway tickets is equated with the then normal cost of living. It all began with a group of schoolboys who met in The Lane overlooking North Road station, at least one member visiting Laira shed every day to obtain a complete picture of what was going on. Author Russell Leitch covers not only the trains of the railway companies, but also the ships on the Atlantic run that made the boat trains famous and the railway air services. Russell draws you back from your armchair an amazing seven decades with his infectious personal memories and detailed notes. An infectious read.
Laminated cover, 112 pages, 60 photographs plus maps, posters and tickets

RCTS

The Railway Correspondence and Travel Society is Britain's leading organisation for people interested in all aspects of railways past, present and future. It is highly regarded by both professional railway people and enthusiasts, a position it has held since its formation 80 years ago. A monthly journal *The Railway Observer*, is sent to each member. In addition, there are indoor meetings at many centres throughout the country and visits to centres of railway interest.

Full details of the Society and how to become a member will gladly be supplied by Vron Cooke, 23 Haig Drive, Slough, SL1 9HA, England, or visit our website www.rcts.org.uk

Correspondence on this book and additional information are welcomed. This, together with ideas for future books and volunteers to help on publications are keenly sought by the Publications Officer, Reg Wood, 70 Heathfields, Downend, Bristol, BS16 6HS, England.